THE WTO IN THE TWENTY-FIRST CENTURY

Three significant issues will determine the future of the WTO: dispute settlement, negotiations, and regional integration. Dispute settlement is widely regarded as one of the major successes of the WTO in its first ten years. Concluding the Doha Round negotiations is one of its main challenges. Regional integration is now at the frontline of debate as regional agreements proliferate and policy-makers and academics come to grips with their impacts on the multilateral trading system. These issues, and the interplay between them, are examined by leading scholars and practitioners in the field of international trade law from the United States, Europe, and Asia-Pacific. In addition, special sections focus on the Asia-Pacific region, its participation in WTO dispute settlement and negotiations, and recent trends towards greater regional integration.

Yasuhei Taniguchi is a Member of the WTO Appellate Body and a Professor of Law at Senshu University Law School, Tokyo.

Alan Yanovich has been Counsellor at the WTO Appellate Body Secretariat since 2001. He was previously a legal advisor at the General Secretariat of the Andean Community.

Jan Bohanes is Associate Attorney at the International Trade and Dispute Resolution Group of Sidley Austin LLP in Geneva. He was previously Legal Officer at the WTO Appellate Body Secretariat.

THE WTO IN THE TWENTY-FIRST CENTURY

Dispute Settlement, Negotiations, and Regionalism in Asia

Edited by

YASUHEI TANIGUCHI, ALAN YANOVICH,
AND JAN BOHANES

CAMBRIDGE
UNIVERSITY PRESS

CAMBRIDGE UNIVERSITY PRESS
Cambridge, New York, Melbourne, Madrid, Cape Town, Singapore, São Paulo

Cambridge University Press
The Edinburgh Building, Cambridge CB2 8RU, UK

Published in the United States of America by Cambridge University Press, New York

www.cambridge.org
Information on this title: www.cambridge.org/9780521875691

First published 2007
Reprinted 2007

A catalogue record for this publication is available from the British Library

ISBN 978-0-521-87569-1 hardback

Transferred to digital printing 2008

CONTENTS

NOTES ON CONTRIBUTORS

Dukgeun Ahn is Assistant Professor of International Trade Law and Policy at the Graduate School of International Studies, Seoul National University. Professor Ahn advises several developing country governments, international organizations as well as various Korean ministries on trade law and policy issues, including WTO disputes, trade negotiation, and trade policy making. He is the author of several books and articles, including the *WTO and East Asia: New Perspectives* (co-edited with Mitsuo Matsushita, London, 2004), and *The WTO Trade Remedy System: East Asian Perspectives* (co-edited with Mitsuo Matsushita and Tain-jy Chen, 2006). He is on the editorial board for the *Journal of International Economic Law* (Oxford). He also teaches at the World Trade Institute in Switzerland. Professor Ahn holds a Ph.D. in both Economics and J.D. from the University of Michigan.

Jan Bohanes is Associate Attorney at the International Trade and Dispute Resolution Group of Sidley Austin LLP in the Geneva office, where he advises businesses, trade associations, and governments on international trade law with a particular focus on WTO law. Previously, he was Legal Affairs Officer at the Appellate Body Secretariat of the WTO. Mr Bohanes has also worked as visiting researcher at the Trade Law Centre for Southern Africa (tralac) in Stellenbosch, South Africa, and as law clerk in the Austrian judiciary system. Mr Bohanes holds a master's law degree as well as a doctorate in law from the University of Vienna, Austria, as well as a Master of Arts in Law and Diplomacy from the Fletcher School of Law and Diplomacy. He has authored publications on international dispute settlement issues, sanitary and phytosanitary matters, and trade and the environment. Recently, he has co-edited a publication with Appellate Body Member Giorgio Sacerdoti and Alan Yanovich, Counsellor at the Appellate Body Secretariat, entitled *The WTO at Ten – The Contribution of the Dispute Settlement System* (Cambridge, 2006).

Chotiras Chavanich has been the President of Eastern Asia University in Thailand since 1994. Prior to that, he held several positions with the Thai government, including in the Royal Project Initiation and Development Board, the National Economic and Social Development Board, and the Secretariat of the Cabinet. He received a Bachelor's degree in Law from Chulalongkorn University, a Masters of Public Policy degree from University of Southern California, and a Ph.D. in Government and Criminal Justice from Claremont University.

William J. Davey holds the Guy Raymond Jones Chair at the University of Illinois College of Law, where he has taught courses in international trade law, European Union law, international business transactions, and corporate/securities law since 1984. From 1995 to 1999, he was Director of the Legal Affairs Division of the WTO. Professor Davey is author of *Legal Problems of International Economic Relations* (with Jackson and Sykes, 4th edn, 2002), *European Community Law* (with Bermann, Goebel, and Fox, 2nd edn, 2002), *Pine & Swine: Canada-United States Trade Dispute Settlement* (1996), and *Handbook of WTO/GATT Dispute Settlement* (with Pescatore and Lowenfeld, 1991–2000), as well as many articles on various international trade law issues. He serves as Associate Editor of the Oxford *Journal of International Economic Law*. After his graduation from the University of Michigan Law School in 1974, he served as a law clerk to Judge J. Edward Lumbard (US Court of Appeals, New York) and Justice Potter Stewart (US Supreme Court), and worked in Brussels and New York for the law firm of Cleary, Gottlieb, Steen & Hamilton. He is a member of the American Law Institute.

James P. Durling is a partner in the International Trade Department of Willkie Farr & Gallagher LLP in Washington, DC. Mr Durling specializes in defending foreign companies and governments in anti-dumping, countervailing duty, and other trade remedy investigations, and providing advice on parties' obligations under the WTO agreements. Additionally, he has significant experience litigating WTO disputes and trade policy disputes between the United States and foreign parties. During his time at Willkie, Mr Durling took a leave of absence to serve as in-house counsel for Yamaha Motor Company and Matsushita Electric Industrial. He has published extensively on international trade topics, particularly trade remedies. Mr Durling holds a B.A. from Haverford College, a J.D. from New York University School of Law, and an M.P.A. from Princeton University.

Henry S. Gao is Assistant Professor at the Faculty of Law of the University of Hong Kong, China. He is also the Deputy Director of the East Asian International Economic Law and Policy Programme. In addition, he is Academic Coordinator for the Asia Pacific Regional Trade Policy Course jointly organized by the WTO and the University of Hong Kong, Legal Expert for the Beijing WTO Affairs Centre, and a member of the Board of Directors of the WTO Law Study Association of the China Law Society. Professor Gao obtained his LLB with the highest distinction from China Youth Politics Institute as the holder of the National Jianhao Scholarship. He pursued his Master of Laws at University College London (UCL), University of London as the first UCL China Scholar. He obtained a J.D degree from Vanderbilt University with the Dean's Scholarship. The focus of his research is WTO, international trade law, corporate law, and law and economics. He is the author of several books and journal articles on these issues.

Mark Halle has been the European Representative and Director for Trade and Investment at the International Institute for Sustainable Development since 1998. From 1994 to 1998, he served as Director of Global Policy and Partnership of the IUCN – The World Conservation Union. He is the author of several articles relating to conservation strategy. Mr Halle received his B.A. in History and French from Tufts University (cum laude), and his Diploma in Historical Studies from the University of Cambridge.

Masayoshi Honma is Professor of Agricultural and Resource Economics at the Graduate School of Agricultural and Life Sciences, University of Tokyo. He has also taught at Seikei University and Otaru University of Commerce. During his academic career, he was a professional staff member at the Food and Agricultural Organization of the United Nations (1995), a visiting research fellow at the International Food Policy Research Institute (1989–1991), and a research associate of economics at Tokyo Metropolitan University (1983–1985). He earned a B.S. in Agricultural Science from Obihiro University of Agriculture and Veterinary Medicine, an M.S. in Agricultural Economics from the University of Tokyo, and a Ph.D. in Economics from Iowa State University. He has published numerous articles on agriculture and the WTO.

Valerie Hughes is a partner in the Ottawa office of Gowling Lafleur Henderson and practices mainly in the area of international law, including international trade law. Ms Hughes was Director of the Appellate Body Secretariat of the WTO in Geneva from August 2001 to December 2005, where she served as chief legal counsel to the WTO Appellate Body. Previously, she spent 19 years with the Government of Canada, during which she held various positions in the public and private international law fields, including Director and General Counsel of the Trade Law Division of the Department of Foreign Affairs and International Trade, Director and General Counsel of the General Legal Services Division of the Department of Finance, and Senior Counsel of the International Law Section of the Department of Justice. Ms Hughes has served as counsel for Canada before numerous international courts and tribunals, including the International Court of Justice, panels established under the NAFTA, WTO panels, and the WTO Appellate Body. She has published widely and is a regular guest lecturer at universities and speaker at international trade law conferences.

John H. Jackson is Professor of Law at Georgetown University Law Center (GULC). He joined the GULC faculty after a distinguished career as Hessel E. Yntema Professor of Law at the University of Michigan. He has been a visiting faculty member at the University of Delhi (India) and the University of Brussels (Belgium), a Consultant on Legal Education to the Ford Foundation, a Research Scholar at the headquarters of the GATT in Geneva, Switzerland, and a Rockefeller Foundation Fellow in Brussels, Belgium. He has served as General Counsel for the Office of the President's Special Representative for Trade in the US Executive Office of the President in Washington, DC (1973–1974), and Associate Vice-President for Academic Affairs at the University of Michigan (1988–1989). He has also advised the US and various foreign governments and international organizations. In 2000 he served as chairperson of a WTO panel for a trade dispute settlement procedure. He has served as a member of the board of editors for the *American Journal of International Law*, and several others. He is the editor-in-chief and a founding editor of the *Journal of International Economic Law* since 1998. Professor Jackson is also Director of the Institute of International Economic Law at GULC. In 1992, he received the Wolfgang Friedman Memorial Award for lifelong contribution to the field of international law, the Columbia University Journal of Transnational Law and the Columbia Society of International Law at Columbia University. He has been an honorary Vice-President of the American Society of International Law. In early 2000 a volume of essays was published in his honour. In November 2002, Professor Jackson delivered the annual Hersch Lauterpacht Memorial Lecture, in Cambridge University, England. The series of three lectures has been extended into a book entitled *Sovereignty, the WTO, and Changing Fundamentals of International Law* (Cambridge, April 2006). In June 2003, he was awarded the honorary degree 'Doctor Iuris Honoris Causa' from Hamburg University Faculty of Law. Also in June 2003, he was appointed by WTO Director-General, Dr Supachai Panitchpadki, to the WTO Consultative Board, chaired by Peter Sutherland. Professor Jackson has published numerous books, articles, and chapters. He holds a B.A. from Princeton, a J.D. from the University of Michigan, and an LL.D. (Hon) from Hamburg University (Germany).

Chulsu Kim is Senior Advisor at Lee International IP and Law Group in Seoul, Korea and Chairman of the Institute for Trade and Investment, a research and consulting organization affiliated with Lee International. Dr Kim previously taught trade policy at Sejong University and served as its President from 2002 to 2006. From 1995 to 1999 he served as Deputy Director-General of the WTO and, prior to this, was Korea's Minister of Trade, Industry and Energy from 1993 to 1994. As Deputy Minister for Trade, he was Korea's chief trade negotiator. From 1987 to 1990, he chaired the Uruguay Round Negotiating Group on MTN agreements in his personal capacity. In 1990, he became the Commissioner of Korea's Intellectual Property Office. In 1991, he was appointed President of Korea Trade and Investment Promotion Corporation, a trade and investment promotion agency of the Korean government. In early 1993, he became Minister of Trade, Industry, and Energy and served until the end of 1994. Shortly after leaving the Cabinet, he was appointed Korea's Ambassador for International Trade. Dr Kim is a graduate of Tufts University (1964) and the University of Massachusetts, where he earned master's and doctorate degrees in political science. He received honorary doctorates in law from the University of Massachusetts (1997) and Franklin Pierce Law Center (2006). Dr Kim advises the Korea International Economic Policy Institute and the Shanghai WTO Consultation Center on international trade matters. In December 2003, he was appointed Visiting Professor at the Institute of Advanced Studies of the United Nations University in Tokyo.

C. L. Lim teaches at the National University of Singapore. He once taught at Queen Mary, University of London and the University of

Wales, Aberystwyth. He is co-author of *The Paradox of Consensualism in International Law* (The Hague/London/Boston, 1998), co-editor of *Renegotiating Westphalia* (The Hague, 1999), the Editor-in-Chief of the *Singapore Year Book of International Law* and the Southeast Asia reporter for the *Oxford Reports on International Law in Domestic Courts*. His writings have appeared in the *Netherlands Year Book of International Law*, the *Nordic Journal of International Law*, the *Austrian Review of International and European Law*, the *Leiden Journal of International Law*, the *Chinese Journal of International Law*, the *Melbourne Journal of International Law* and the *Asian Yearbook of International Law*. Dr Lim was concurrently State Counsel with the Attorney General of Singapore from 2002 to 2003, acting as an international law advisor and counselling the Government on Singapore's free trade agreement negotiations. He also served with the UNCC Governing Council Secretariat in Geneva from 1999 to 2000. He was educated in England at Buckingham, Oxford, and Nottingham, and at the Harvard Law School.

Chang-fa Lo is Professor of Law at the College of Law of the National Taiwan University. He teaches international trade law, competition law, and government procurement law. He served as the Dean from 2003 to 2006. He is also the Director of the Asian Centre for WTO and International Health Law and Policy of the same college. Professor Lo received his SJD from Harvard University School of Law in 1989. He was a short-term visiting professor of Wisconsin University School of Law and Tokyo University Faculty of Law. He served as commissioner of the Fair Trade Commission of Taiwan from 1998 to 2001 and as commissioner of the International Trade Commission which is in charge of investigation of injury of domestic industry under anti-dumping and safeguards laws (1993–2000). He was appointed National Chair Professor of the Ministry of Education of Taiwan, the highest academic recognition in Taiwan. He is the author of ten books, including *New Legal Order Under the WTO: International Economic and Trade Law Studies V* (in Chinese, 1996), *Government Procurement Law and Government Procurement Agreement: International Economic and Trade Law Studies VII* (in Chinese, 1999; 2nd edn, 2004) and *The Legal Culture and System of Taiwan* (New York, 2006). He was appointed as a WTO dispute settlement panelist in 2006.

Gabrielle Marceau is a Canadian lawyer and is currently Counsellor in the Cabinet of WTO Director-General Pascal Lamy. Prior to that, she was with the Legal Affairs Division of the WTO (from 1994). She is also Professor with the Faculty of Law at the University of Geneva, where she teaches WTO law. From 1983 to 1988, and from 1993 to 1994, she worked in Quebec, Canada in private practice, where she specialized in litigation (labour and civil law). She obtained her LL.B. from Sherbrooke University (Quebec) in 1982, her License to Practice Law (Ottawa) in 1983, her LL.M. from the London School of Economics (England) in 1990, and her Ph.D. from the University of London (England) in 1993. Professor Marceau has written widely on matters concerning international trade and dispute settlement in international law.

Mitsuo Matsushita is Professor Emeritus at Tokyo University and Counsel to Nagashima, Ohno & Tsunematsu, a leading international law firm in Tokyo. He served on the Appellate Body from 1995 to 2000. His academic career includes professorships at Sophia University and Tokyo University. He has been a Visiting Professor at Harvard University, Georgetown University, the University of Michigan, Columbia University, and at the College of Europe in Bruges, Belgium. He has written on various aspects of international trade and competition and investment law. In his public career, Professor Matsushita has been attached to the Japanese Ministry of Finance and the Ministry of International Economics and Trade as a member of various councils dealing with telecommunications, customs and tariffs, export and import transactions, and industrial property. He serves as a Member of the Office of the Ombudsman of Trade and Investment, which is part of the Japanese government and deals with market access issues. Professor Matsushita has a Ph.D. from Tulane University and a D.Jur. from Tokyo University.

Manabu Miyagawa is Director of the Economic Security Division of the Japanese Ministry of Foreign Affairs. He previously served as Director of the Ministry's WTO Dispute Settlement Division and represented Japan in the DSU negotiations. Prior to that, he was a Counsellor at the Japanese Mission to the European Union (2001–2004). Mr Miyagawa has also held several other positions within the Ministry of Foreign Affairs, where he has been responsible for European and Asian Affairs. He also worked at the Japanese Embassies in both the United Kingdom (1986–1990) and Thailand (1999–2001). In addition, he has represented Japan in a number of WTO cases and has been involved in negotiations relating to the *Anti-Dumping Agreement* and the *SCM Agreement*.

Hunter Nottage has been Counsel at the Advisory Centre on WTO Law since 2002. In that capacity he has appeared before a number of WTO panels and the Appellate Body, as well as provided legal opinions and training on various issues of WTO law. In 2005, he was counsel for Colombia, Costa Rica, Ecuador, and Guatemala in the banana tariff arbitrations, which are analyzed in his contribution to this book. Previously he was a member of the secretariat of the Organisation for Economic Co-operation and Development, working on trade policy linkages. He has also worked in private litigation and competition law for commercial law firms in Europe, North America, and New Zealand. Mr Nottage holds a first-class Masters in International Law from Cambridge University, and degrees in law and economics from Victoria University, New Zealand. He has authored publications on how to give legal effect to the results of the Doha Round, trade and competition policy interfaces, and regional trade agreements.

Supachai Panitchpakdi is Secretary-General of the UN Conference on Trade and Development. He began his four-year term on 1 September 2005 following his appointment by the UN General Assembly. Dr Supachai previously served as Director-General of the WTO from September 2002 to August 2005. He received his Master's Degree in Econometrics, Development Planning and his Ph.D. in Economic Planning and Development at the Netherlands School of Economics (now known as Erasmus University) in Rotterdam. He completed his doctoral dissertation on Human Resource Planning and Development and conducted research on development models as a visiting Fellow at Cambridge University. He began working at the Bank of Thailand in 1974. In 1986, he relinquished his post as the Director of the Financial Institutions Supervision Department and was appointed Deputy Minister of Finance. After dissolution of Parliament in 1988, he was appointed Director and Advisor, and subsequently President, of the Thai Military Bank. In 1992, Dr Supachai was appointed Senator and led a sub-committee to draw up Thailand's Seventh National Economic and Social Development Plan (1992–1996). Later in 1992, he became Deputy Prime Minister entrusted with overseeing the country's economic and trade policy making and was actively involved in international trade policy. Following the change of government in November 1997 in the wake of Thailand's financial crisis, he was appointed Deputy Prime Minister in charge of economic policies, and Minister of Commerce. In 2001 he was appointed Visiting Professor of the International Institute for Management Development in Lausanne, Switzerland.

Ernst-Ulrich Petersmann is Professor of International and European Law at the European University Institute (EUI) in Florence, Italy, and Joint Chair at the EUI's Robert Schuman Centre for Advanced Studies. He was previously Professor of International and European Law at the University of Geneva, Switzerland, and its Graduate Institute of International Studies. During his 30 years of legal practice, Professor Petersmann represented Germany in various international organizations (the EC, the UN, and the Organisation for Economic Co-operation and Development), acted as legal advisor to the GATT as well as legal consultant for the WTO, and participated in numerous GATT and WTO dispute settlement proceedings as legal advisor, or as a member or chairman of dispute settlement panels. He is Chairman of the International Trade Law Committee of the International Law Association and Associate Editor of several journals on international economic law and international economic relations. Recent publications include: *Constitutionalism, Multilevel Trade Governance and Social Regulation* (co-edited with C. Joerges) (Oxford, 2006); *Developing Countries in the Doha Round* (EUI/RSC, 2005); *Reforming the World Trading System: Legitimacy, Efficiency and Democratic Governance* (Oxford, 2005); *The WTO Dispute Settlement System 1995–2003* (edited with F. Ortino) (Amsterdam, 2004); and *Transatlantic Economic Disputes. The EU, the US and the WTO* (edited with M.A. Polack) (Oxford, 2003).

Frieder Roessler is Executive Director of the Advisory Centre on WTO Law. Mr Roessler was educated in Germany, Switzerland, and the United States. He obtained a Ph.D. in law from the University of Freiburg i.Br. in Germany, and a Master of Arts from the Fletcher School of Law and Diplomacy in the United States. After completing his legal training in Germany, he worked for the World Bank and then for the GATT and the WTO. In 1989 he was appointed WTO Director of Legal Affairs, a post which he held until 1995 when he joined the faculty of law of Georgetown University in Washington, DC. While at the GATT/WTO, he advised dispute settlements panels and prepared drafts of their reports. Mr Roessler was also closely involved in the legal aspects of the Uruguay Round negotiations and participated in the legal drafting process at the end of the Round. After leaving the WTO, he remained actively involved in WTO legal matters; he advised WTO Members involved in WTO dispute settlement proceedings and worked as a consultant on WTO-related matters for governments, professional organizations, and law firms. Mr Roessler was Adjunct Professor at the Jean Moulin University of Lyon and at Paris I. He also taught at the universities of St Gallen

(Switzerland) and Minnesota (United States). Between 1995 and 1998 he gave courses and seminars at Georgetown University on international economic law, the external relations and trade policies of the EC, WTO dispute settlement procedures (with Professor John Jackson), and trade and the environment (with Professor Edith Brown-Weiss). He has published extensively, mainly in the field of international trade law. A collection of his essays was published in 2000 entitled *The Legal Structure, Limits and Functions of the World Trade Order.*

Soichiro Sakuma is General Manager of the Legal Department at Nippon Steel Corporation, where he has worked for more than 20 years on a number of steel trade cases and foreign investment matters. He is a member of the Industrial Structure Council's Sub-committee on Unfair Trade Policies of the Japanese Ministry of Economy, Trade and Industry, and of several other industrial committees. Between 1986 and 1989, he was in the Directorate for Science, Technology and Industry at the Organization for Economic Co-operation and Development. Mr Sakuma obtained his law degree from Tokyo University.

Gregory Shaffer has recently been appointed Wing Tat-Lee Professor of International Law at Loyola University Chicago School of Law. Prior to that, he was Professor of Law at the University of Wisconsin Law School, Director of the UW European Union Centre, and Co-Director and Senior Fellow at the UW Centre on World Affairs and the Global Economy. Prior to teaching, he worked in Paris at the law firms of Coudert Brothers and Bredin Prat. His publications include *Defending Interests: Public-Private Partnerships in WTO Litigation* (Brookings Institution Press, 2003), *Transatlantic Governance in the Global Economy* (with Mark Pollack, Rowman & Littlefield, 2001), and *Regulating Risk in the Global Economy: The United States, Europe and Agricultural Biotechnology* (Oxford, forthcoming 2007). He has also authored over forty articles and book chapters on international trade law, global governance, and globalization's impact on domestic regulation. He has received numerous grants, including two from the National Science Foundation. He received his JD from Stanford Law School and his BA from Dartmouth College.

Andrew L. Stoler is Executive Director of the Institute for International Business, Economics and Law and holds the title of Adjunct Professor of International Trade at the University of Adelaide. Mr Stoler currently serves on the Australian Foreign Minister's Aid Advisory Council and is a member of the Advisory Board of Stanford University's GATT Digital Library. He is a member of the Advisory Committee of the Shanghai WTO Affairs Consultation Centre and Senior Advisor to the Shenzhen WTO Affairs Centre. He also serves on the Board of Directors of the Australian Services Roundtable. Over the course of a long career in international trade, Mr Stoler served as Deputy Director-General of the WTO (1999–2002) and as Deputy Permanent Representative of the United States to the GATT and the WTO (1989–1999). As a senior official of the Office of the US Trade Representative, Executive Office of the President (Washington, DC) he also served as Deputy Assistant US Trade Representative for Europe and the Mediterranean and Director for Canada, Australia, and New Zealand. Mr Stoler holds an MBA in International Business from George Washington University and a BSFS in International Economic Affairs from Georgetown University's School of Foreign Service.

Shigehiro Tanaka is Director for WTO Affairs at the Japanese Ministry of Economy Trade and Industry (METI). He represented Japan in the market access negotiations during the Uruguay Round (1991–1993), and subsequently served as Chief Negotiator on anti-dumping in the Doha Round negotiations (2004–2005). Mr Tanaka has served in various capacities in METI, where he has been responsible for WTO rules, taxation, and corporate affairs for small and medium sized enterprises, and APEC relations. He has been a member of the State of New York Bar since 1990. Mr Tanaka obtained his law degree from the University of Tokyo and holds an LL.M. from Harvard Law School.

Yasuhei Taniguchi has been a member of the WTO Appellate Body since 2000. He is Professor of Law at Senshu University Law School. In addition, he is an attorney at the law firm of Matsuo & Kosugi in Tokyo. Professor Taniguchi obtained a law degree from Kyoto University in 1957 and was fully qualified as a jurist in 1959. His graduate degrees include LL.M., University of California at Berkeley (1963) and J.S.D., Cornell University (1964). He taught at Kyoto University for 39 years and has been Professor Emeritus since 1998. He also has taught at Tokyo Keizai University and as Visiting Professor of Law in the United States (University of Michigan, University of California at Berkeley, Duke University, Stanford University, Georgetown University, Harvard University, New York University, and the University of Richmond), in

Australia (Murdoch University and the University of Melbourne), at the University of Hong Kong and at the University of Paris XII. He is president of the Japanese Association of Arbitrators, Vice-President of the International Association of Procedural Law, and former President of the Japanese Association of Civil Procedure. In addition, Professor Taniguchi is affiliated with various academic societies and arbitral organizations as arbitrator, including the International Council for Commercial Arbitration; the International Chamber of Commerce Institute of World Business Law; the International Law Association; and the American Law Institute. Professor Taniguchi has written numerous books and articles in the fields of civil procedure, arbitration, insolvency, the judicial system and legal profession, as well as comparative and international law related to these fields. His work has been published in Japanese, Chinese, English, French, Italian, German, and Portuguese.

Alan Yanovich is a Counsellor at the WTO Appellate Body Secretariat, where he has worked since 2001. He was a legal adviser at the General Secretariat of the Andean Community from 1997 to 2001. Prior to that, he was a Commercial Secretary at the Colombian Government Trade Bureau in Washington, DC. Mr Yanovich has a J.D. from Georgetown University. He recently co-edited *The WTO at Ten: The Contribution of the Dispute Settlement System* (Cambridge, 2006). Mr Yanovich is Colombian.

Zhang Yuqing is currently Professor of WTO Law at the China University of Political Science and Law. He is also a WTO dispute settlement panelist, arbitrator, attorney at law of Beijing Zhang Yuqing Law Firm, member of the Governing Council of the International Institute for Unification of Private Law (UNIDROIT) and Vice-Chairman of the China International Economic Law Society. He is a former Director-General of the Department of Treaty and Law at the Chinese Ministry of Commerce. Mr Zhang obtained his LL.M. from Georgetown University Law Center in 1986 and his Master of Laws from the University of International Business and Economics, Beijing in 1982. From the 1980s to 2003, Mr Zhang acted as member or head of Chinese government delegations to the UN Commission on International Trade Law, the UNIDROIT, the Hague Conference, as well as the GATT/WTO for preparation of international uniform trade rules and China's accession to the WTO. Mr Zhang is author of several books on contracts, sale of goods, joint ventures, and anti-dumping, and of over 70 articles either in Chinese or English in the fields of WTO, commercial, and economic law.

ACKNOWLEDGEMENTS

We wish to give special thanks to the authors who have contributed to this book. We also wish to acknowledge the contribution made by the organizers of the Tokyo conference celebrating the Tenth Anniversary of the WTO's dispute settlement system and the establishment of the Appellate Body. In particular, we are grateful to Mr Takashi Iwamoto, Executive Director of the Fair Trade Centre, and Mr Takato Ojimi, Vice-President and Managing Director of the Institute of International Studies and Training. Both played a central role in coordinating and funding the Tokyo conference. In addition, we would like to express our appreciation to Valerie Hughes, who was Director of the Appellate Body Secretariat until 2005, and provided invaluable support to the organization of the Tokyo conference and the publication of this book. We are also grateful for the support we have received from Werner Zdouc, current Director of the Appellate Body Secretariat. In addition, we would like to thank those persons who assisted us in preparing this publication, including: Jean-Guy Carrier of the WTO Information and Media Relations Division; Judy Cowell and Pasha Hsieng of the Appellate Body Secretariat; and Finola O'Sullivan, Richard Woodham, and Wendy Gater at Cambridge University Press. Finally, our very special thanks go to Patricia Crawley of the Appellate Body Secretariat for laboriously putting together and reviewing the final manuscript, and for her editorial assistance.

TABLE OF DISPUTE SETTLEMENT CASES AND REPORTS CITED IN THIS BOOK

Short title	**Full title and citation**
Argentina – Ceramic Tiles	Panel Report, *Argentina – Definitive Anti-Dumping Measures on Imports of Ceramic Floor Tiles from Italy*, WT/DS189/R, adopted 5 November 2001, DSR 2001:XII, 6241
Argentina – Clothing and Footwear	*Argentina – Measures Affecting Textiles, Clothing and Footwear*, WT/DS77 *(EC)*
Argentina – Cotton	*Argentina – Transitional Safeguard Measures on Certain Imports of Woven Fabrics of Cotton and Cotton Mixtures Originating in Brazil*, WT/DS190 *(Brazil)*
Argentina – Drill Bits	*Argentina – Definitive Anti-Dumping Measures on Imports of Drill Bits from Italy*, WT/DS157 *(EC)*
Argentina – Footwear (EC)	Appellate Body Report, *Argentina – Safeguard Measures on Imports of Footwear*, WT/DS121/AB/R, adopted 12 January 2000, DSR 2000:I, 515
Argentina – Footwear (EC)	Panel Report, *Argentina – Safeguard Measures on Imports of Footwear*, WT/DS121/R, adopted 12 January 2000, modified by Appellate Body Report, WT/DS121/AB/R, DSR 2000:II, 575
Argentina – Footwear (US)	*Argentina – Measures Affecting Imports of Footwear*, WT/DS164 *(US)*
Argentina – Hides and Leather Affecting	Panel Report, *Argentina – Measures the Export of Bovine Hides and Import of Finished Leather*, WT/DS155/R and Corr.1, adopted 16 February 2001, DSR 2001:V, 1779

Short title	Full title and citation
Argentina – Patent Protection	*Argentina – Patent Protection for Pharmaceuticals and Test Data Protection for Agricultural Chemicals*, WT/DS171 *(US)*; *Argentina – Certain Measures on the Protection of Patents and Test Data*, WT/DS196 *(US)*
Argentina – Pharmaceuticals	*Argentina – Measures Affecting the Import of Pharmaceutical Products*, WT/DS233 *(India)*
Argentina – Poultry Anti-Dumping Duties	Panel Report, *Argentina – Definitive Anti-Dumping Duties on Poultry from Brazil*, WT/DS241/R, adopted 19 May 2003, DSR 2003:V, 1727
Argentina – Preserved Peaches	Panel Report, *Argentina – Definitive Safeguard Measure on Imports of Preserved Peaches*, WT/DS238/R, adopted 15 April 2003, DSR 2003:III, 1037
Argentina – Textiles and Apparel	Appellate Body Report, *Argentina – Measures Affecting Imports of Footwear, Textiles, Apparel and Other Items*, WT/DS56/AB/R and Corr.1, adopted 22 April 1998, DSR 1998:III, 1003
Argentina – Textiles and Apparel	Panel Report, *Argentina – Measures Affecting Imports of Footwear, Textiles, Apparel and Other Items*, WT/DS56/R, adopted 22 April 1998, modified by Appellate Body Report, WT/DS56/AB/R, DSR 1998:III, 1033
Argentina – Wheat Gluten	*Argentina – Countervailing Duties on Imports of Wheat Gluten from the European Communities*, WT/DS145
Australia – Automotive Leather II	Panel Report, *Australia – Subsidies Provided to Producers and Exporters of Automotive Leather*, WT/DS126/R, adopted 16 June 1999, DSR 1999:III, 951
Australia – Automotive Leather II (Article 21.5 – US)	Panel Report, *Australia – Subsidies Provided to Producers and Exporters of Automotive Leather – Recourse to Article 21.5 of the DSU by the United States*, WT/DS126/RW and Corr.1, adopted 11 February 2000, DSR 2000:III, 1189

Short title	Full title and citation
Australia – Clothing and Footwear	*Australia – Textile, Clothing and Footwear Import Credit Scheme*, WT/DS57 *(US)*
Australia – Coated Paper	*Australia – Anti-Dumping Measures on Imports of Coated Woodfree Paper Sheets*, WT/DS119 *(Switzerland)*
Australia – Salmon	Appellate Body Report, *Australia – Measures Affecting Importation of Salmon*, WT/DS18/AB/R, adopted 6 November 1998, DSR 1998:VIII, 3327
Australia – Salmon	Panel Report, *Australia – Measures Affecting Importation of Salmon*, WT/DS18/R and Corr.1, adopted 6 November 1998, modified by Appellate Body Report, WT/DS18/AB/R, DSR 1998:VIII, 3407
Australia – Salmon (Article 21.5 – Canada)	Panel Report, *Australia – Measures Affecting Importation of Salmon – Recourse to Article 21.5 of the DSU by Canada*, WT/DS18/RW, adopted 20 March 2000, DSR 2000:IV, 2031
Australia – Salmonids	*Australia – Measures Affecting the Importation of Salmonids*, WT/DS21 *(US)*
Belgium – Rice	*Belgium – Administration of Measures Establishing Customs Duties for Rice*, WT/DS210 *(US)*
Belgium – Taxes	*Belgium – Certain Income Tax Measures Constituting Subsidies*, WT/DS127 *(US)*
Belgium – Telephone Directory Services	*Belgium – Measures Affecting Commercial Telephone Directory Services*, WT/DS80 *(US)*
Border Tax Adjustments	GATT Working Party Report, *Border Tax Adjustments*, L/3464, adopted 2 December 1970, BISD 18S/97
Brazil – Aircraft	Appellate Body Report, *Brazil – Export Financing Programme for Aircraft*, WT/DS46/AB/R, adopted 20 August 1999, DSR 1999:III, 1161
Brazil – Aircraft	Panel Report, *Brazil – Export Financing Programme for Aircraft*, WT/DS46/R, adopted 20 August 1999, modified by Appellate Body Report, WT/DS46/AB/R, DSR 1999:III, 1221

Short title	Full title and citation
Brazil – Aircraft (Article 21.5 – Canada)	Appellate Body Report, *Brazil – Export Financing Programme for Aircraft – Recourse by Canada to Article 21.5 of the DSU*, WT/DS46/AB/RW, adopted 4 August 2000, DSR 2000:VIII, 4067
Brazil – Aircraft (Article 21.5 – Canada)	Panel Report, *Brazil – Export Financing Programme for Aircraft – Recourse by Canada to Article 21.5 of the DSU*, WT/DS46/RW, adopted 4 August 2000, modified by Appellate Body Report, WT/DS46/AB/RW, DSR 2000:IX, 4093
Brazil – Aircraft (Article 21.5 – Canada II)	Panel Report, *Brazil – Export Financing Programme for Aircraft – Second Recourse by Canada to Article 21.5 of the DSU*, WT/DS46/RW/2, adopted 23 August 2001, DSR 2001:X, 5481
Brazil – Aircraft (Article 22.6 – Brazil)	Decision by the Arbitrators, *Brazil – Export Financing Programme for Aircraft – Recourse to Arbitration by Brazil under Article 22.6 of the DSU and Article 4.11 of the SCM Agreement*, WT/DS46/ARB, 28 August 2000, DSR 2002:I, 19
Brazil – Autos	*Brazil – Certain Automotive Investment Measures*, WT/DS51; *Brazil – Certain Measures Affecting Trade and Investment in the Automotive Sector*, WT/DS52, WT/DS65, WT/DS81
Brazil – Desiccated and Powdered Coconut	*Brazil – Countervailing Duties on Imports of Desiccated Coconut and Coconut Milk Powder from Sri Lanka*, WT/DS30
Brazil – Desiccated Coconut	Appellate Body Report, *Brazil – Measures Affecting Desiccated Coconut*, WT/DS22/AB/R, adopted 20 March 1997, DSR 1997:I, 167
Brazil – Desiccated Coconut	Panel Report, *Brazil – Measures Affecting Desiccated Coconut*, WT/DS22/R, adopted 20 March 1997, upheld by Body Appellate Report, WT/DS22/AB/R, DSR 1997:I, 189
Brazil – Import Licensing	*Brazil – Measures on Import Licensing and Minimum Import Prices*, WT/DS183 *(EC)*

Short title	Full title and citation
Brazil – Jute Bags	*Brazil – Anti-Dumping Duties on Jute Bags from India*, WT/DS229
Brazil – Patent Protection	*Brazil – Measures Affecting Patent Protection*, WT/DS199 *(US)*
Brazil – Payment Terms	*Brazil – Measures Affecting Payment Terms for Imports*, WT/DS116 *(EC)*
Canada – Aircraft	Appellate Body Report, *Canada – Measures Affecting the Export of Civilian Aircraft*, WT/DS70/AB/R, adopted 20 August 1999, DSR 1999:III, 1377
Canada – Aircraft	Panel Report, *Canada – Measures Affecting the Export of Civilian Aircraft*, WT/DS70/R, adopted 20 August 1999, upheld by Appellate Body Report, WT/DS70/AB/R, DSR 1999:IV, 1443
Canada – Aircraft (Article 21.5 – Brazil)	Appellate Body Report, *Canada – Measures Affecting the Export of Civilian Aircraft – Recourse by Brazil to Article 21.5 of the DSU*, WT/DS70/AB/RW, adopted 4 August 2000, DSR 2000:IX, 4299
Canada – Aircraft (Article 21.5 – Brazil)	Panel Report, *Canada – Measures Affecting the Export of Civilian Aircraft – Recourse by Brazil to Article 21.5 of the DSU*, WT/DS70/RW, adopted 4 August 2000, modified by Appellate Body Report, WT/DS70/AB/RW, DSR 2000:IX, 4315
Canada – Aircraft Credits and Guarantees	Panel Report, *Canada – Export Credits and Loan Guarantees for Regional Aircraft*, WT/DS222/R and Corr.1, adopted 19 February 2002, DSR 2002:III, 849
Canada – Aircraft Credits and Guarantees (Article 22.6 – Canada)	Decision by the Arbitrator, *Canada – Export Credits and Loan Guarantees for Regional Aircraft – Recourse to Arbitration by Canada under Article 22.6 of the DSU and Article 4.11 of the SCM Agreement*, WT/DS222/ARB, 17 February 2003, DSR 2003:III, 1187
Canada – Autos	Appellate Body Report, *Canada – Certain Measures Affecting the Automotive Industry*, WT/DS139/AB/R, WT/DS142/AB/R, adopted 19 June 2000, DSR 2000:VI, 2985

Short title	Full title and citation
Canada – Autos	Panel Report, *Canada – Certain Measures Affecting the Automotive Industry*, WT/DS139/R, WT/DS142/R, adopted 19 June 2000, modified by Appellate Body Report, WT/DS139/AB/R, WT/DS142/AB/R, DSR 2000:VII, 3043
Canada – Continued Suspension	*Canada – Continued Suspension of Obligations in the EC – Hormones Dispute*, WT/DS321 *(EC)*
Canada – Dairy	Appellate Body Report, *Canada – Measures Affecting the Importation of Milk and the Exportation of Dairy Products*, WT/DS103/AB/R, WT/DS113/AB/R, and Corr.1, adopted 27 October 1999, DSR 1999:V, 2057
Canada – Dairy	Panel Report, *Canada – Measures Affecting the Importation of Milk and the Exportation of Dairy Products*, WT/DS103/R, WT/DS113/R, adopted 27 October 1999, modified by Appellate Body Report, WT/DS103/AB/R, WT/DS113/AB/R, DSR 1999:VI, 2097
Canada – Dairy (Article 21.5 – New Zealand and US)	Appellate Body Report, *Canada – Measures Affecting the Importation of Milk and the Exportation of Dairy Products – Recourse to Article 21.5 of the DSU by New Zealand and the United States*, WT/DS103/AB/RW, WT/DS113/AB/RW, adopted 18 December 2001, DSR 2001:XIII, 6829
Canada – Dairy (Article 21.5 – New Zealand and US)	Panel Report, *Canada – Measures Affecting the Importation of Milk and the Exportation of Dairy Products – Recourse to Article 21.5 of the DSU by New Zealand and the United States*, WT/DS103/RW, WT/DS113/RW, adopted 18 December 2001, reversed by Appellate Body Report, WT/DS103/AB/RW, WT/DS113/AB/RW, DSR 2001:XIII, 6865

Short title	Full title and citation
Canada – Dairy (Article 21.5 – New Zealand and US II)	Appellate Body Report, *Canada – Measures Affecting the Importation of Milk and the Exportation of Dairy Products – Second Recourse to Article 21.5 of the DSU by New Zealand and the United States*, WT/DS103/AB/RW2, WT/DS113/AB/RW2, adopted 17 January 2003, DSR 2003:I, 213
Canada – Dairy (Article 21.5 – New Zealand and US II)	Panel Report, *Canada – Measures Affecting the Importation of Milk and the Exportation of Dairy Products – Second Recourse to Article 21.5 of the DSU by New Zealand and the United States*, WT/DS103/RW2, WT/DS113/RW2, adopted 17 January 2003, modified by Appellate Body Report, WT/DS103/AB/RW2, WT/DS113/AB/RW2, DSR 2003:I, 255
Canada – Film Distribution	*Canada – Measures Affecting Film Distribution Services*, WT/DS117 *(EC)*
Canada – Herring and Salmon	GATT Panel Report, *Canada – Measures Affecting Exports of Unprocessed Herring and Salmon*, L/6268, adopted 22 March 1988, BISD 35S/98
Canada – Patent Term	Panel Report, *Canada – Term of Patent Protection*, WT/DS170/R, adopted 12 October 2000, upheld by Appellate Body Report, WT/DS170/AB/R, DSR 2000:XI, 5121
Canada – Periodicals	Panel Report, *Canada – Certain Measures Concerning Periodicals*, WT/DS31/R and Corr.1, adopted 30 July 1997, modified by Appellate Body Report, WT/DS31/AB/R, DSR 1997:I, 481
Canada – Pharmaceutical Patents	Panel Report, *Canada – Patent Protection of Pharmaceutical Products*, WT/DS114/R, adopted 7 April 2000, DSR 2000:V, 2289
Canada – Wheat Exports and Grain Imports	Panel Report, *Canada – Measures Relating to Exports of Wheat and Treatment of Imported Grain*, WT/DS276/R, adopted 27 September 2004, upheld by Appellate Body Report, WT/DS276/AB/R, DSR 2004:VI, 2817

Short title	**Full title and citation**
Chile – Alcoholic Beverages	Panel Report, *Chile – Taxes on Alcoholic Beverages*, WT/DS87/R, WT/DS110/R, adopted 12 January 2000, modified by Appellate Body Report, WT/DS87/AB/R, WT/DS110/AB/R, DSR 2000:I, 303
Chile – Edible Oils	*Chile – Provisional Safeguard Measure on Mixtures Of Edible Oils*, WT/DS226 *(Argentina)*
Chile – Price Band System	Appellate Body Report, *Chile – Price Band System and Safeguard Measures Relating to Certain Agricultural Products*, WT/DS207/AB/R, adopted 23 October 2002, DSR 2002:VIII, 3045
Chile – Price Band System	Panel Report, *Chile – Price Band System and Safeguard Measures Relating to Certain Agricultural Products*, WT/DS207/R, adopted 23 October 2002, modified by Appellate Body Report, WT/DS207AB/R, DSR 2002:VIII, 3127
Chile – Sugar	*Chile – Safeguard Measures on Sugar*, WT/DS228 *(Colombia)*; *Chile – Safeguard Measures and Modification of Schedules Regarding Sugar*, WT/DS230 *(Colombia)*
Chile – Swordfish	*Chile – Measures Affecting the Transit and Importation of Swordfish*, WT/DS193 *(EC)*
China – Tax on Circuits	*China – Value-Added Tax on Integrated Circuits*, WT/DS309
Colombia – Polyester Filaments	*Colombia – Safeguard Measure on Imports of Plain Polyester Filaments from Thailand*, WT/DS181 *(Thailand)*
Customs Unions and Free-trade Areas – The Canada-US FTA	GATT Working Party Report, *Customs Unions and Free-Trade Areas, Working Party on the Free-Trade Agreement between Canada and the United States*, L/6927, adopted 12 November 1991, BISD 38S/47
Customs Unions, Free-trade Areas, Regional Agreements – The Czech Republic-Slovak Republic Customs Union	GATT Working Party Report, *Customs Unions and Free-trade Areas, Regional Agreements, Working Party on the Customs Union Between the Czech Republic and the Slovak Republic*, L/7501, adopted 4 October 1994, BISD 41S/112

Short title	Full title and citation
Czech Republic – Wheat Duties	*Czech Republic – Measure Affecting Import Duty on Wheat from Hungary*, WT/DS148
Denmark – IPR Enforcement	*Denmark – Measures Affecting the Enforcement of Intellectual Property Rights*, WT/DS83 *(US)*
EC – Approval and Marketing of Biotech Products	*European Communities – Measures Affecting the Approval and Marketing of Biotech Products*, WT/DS291 *(US)*, WT/DS292 *(Canada)*, WT/DS293 *(Argentina)*
EC – Asbestos	Appellate Body Report, *European Communities – Measures Affecting Asbestos and Asbestos-Containing Products*, WT/DS135/AB/R, adopted 5 April 2001, DSR 2001:VII, 3243
EC – Asbestos	Panel Report, *European Communities – Measures Affecting Asbestos and Asbestos-Containing Products*, WT/DS135/R and Add.1, adopted 5 April 2001, modified by Appellate Body Report, WT/DS135/AB/R, DSR 2001:VIII, 3305
EC – Audio Cassettes	GATT Panel Report, *EC – Anti-Dumping Duties on Audio Tapes in Cassettes Originating in Japan*, ADP/136, 28 April 1995, unadopted
EC – Avionics	*European Communities – Measures Relating to the Development of a Flight Management System*, WT/DS172 *(US)*
EC – Bananas III	Appellate Body Report, *European Communities – Regime for the Importation, Sale and Distribution of Bananas*, WT/DS27/AB/R, adopted 25 September 1997, DSR 1997:II, 591
EC – Bananas III	Panel Reports, *European Communities – Regime for the Importation, Sale and Distribution of Bananas* WT/DS27/R/ECU *(Ecuador)*, WT/DS27/R/GTM, WT/DS27/R/HND *(Guatemala and Honduras)*, WT/DS27/R/MEX *(Mexico)*, and WT/DS27/R/USA *(US)*, adopted 25 September 1997, modified by Appellate Body Report, WT/DS27/AB/R, DSR 1997:II, 695 to DSR 1997:III, 1085

Short title	**Full title and citation**
EC – Bananas III	Award of the Arbitrator, *European Communities – Regime for the Importation, Sale and Distribution of Bananas – Arbitration under Article 21.3(c) of the DSU*, WT/DS27/15, 7 January 1998, DSR 1998:I, 3
EC – Bananas III (Article 21.5 – EC)	Panel Report, *European Communities – Regime for the Importation, Sale and Distribution of Bananas – Recourse to Article 21.5 of the DSU by the European Communities*, WT/DS27/RW/EEC and Corr.1, 12 April 1999, DSR 1999:II, 783
EC – Bananas III (Article 21.5 – Ecuador)	Panel Report, *European Communities – Regime for the Importation, Sale and Distribution of Bananas – Recourse to Article 21.5 of the DSU by Ecuador*, WT/DS27/RW/ECU, adopted 6 May 1999, DSR 1999:II, 803
EC – Bananas III (Ecuador) (Article 22.6 – EC)	Decision by the Arbitrators, *European Communities – Regime for the Importation, Sale and Distribution of Bananas – Recourse to Arbitration by the European Communities under Article 22.6 of the DSU*, WT/DS27/ARB/ECU, 24 March 2000, DSR 2000:V, 2237
EC – Bananas III (US) (Article 22.6 – EC)	Decision by the Arbitrators, *European Communities – Regime for the Importation, Sale and Distribution of Bananas – Recourse to Arbitration by the European Communities under Article 22.6 of the DSU*, WT/DS27/ARB, 9 April 1999, DSR 1999:II, 725
EC – Bed Linen	Appellate Body Report, *European Communities – Anti-Dumping Duties on Imports of Cotton-Type Bed Linen from India*, WT/DS141/AB/R, adopted 12 March 2001, DSR 2001:V, 2049
EC – Bed Linen	Panel Report, *European Communities – Anti-Dumping Duties on Imports of Cotton-Type Bed Linen from India*, WT/DS141/R, adopted 12 March 2001, modified by Appellate Body Report, WT/DS141/AB/R, DSR 2001:VI, 2077

Short title	Full title and citation
EC – Bed Linen (Article 21.5 – India)	Appellate Body Report, *European Communities – Anti-Dumping Duties on Imports of Cotton-Type Bed Linen from India – Recourse to Article 21.5 of the DSU by India*, WT/DS141/AB/RW, adopted 24 April 2003, DSR 2003:III, 965
EC – Bed Linen (Article 21.5 – India)	Panel Report, *European Communities – Anti-Dumping Duties on Imports of Cotton-Type Bed Linen from India – Recourse to Article 21.5 of the DSU by India*, WT/DS141/RW, adopted 24 April 2003, modified by Appellate Body Report, WT/DS141/AB/RW, DSR 2003:IV, 1269
EC – Butter	*European Communities – Measures Affecting Butter Products*, WT/DS72 *(New Zealand)*
EC – Cereals	*European Communities – Duties on Imports of Cereals*, WT/DS9 *(Canada)*
EC – Cheese	*European Communities – Measures Affecting the Exportation of Processed Cheese*, WT/DS104 *(US)*
EC – Chicken Cuts	Appellate Body Report, *European Communities – Customs Classification of Frozen Boneless Chicken Cuts*, WT/DS269/AB/R, WT/DS286/AB/R, and Corr.1, adopted 27 September 2005
EC – Coffee	*European Communities – Measures Affecting Soluble Coffee*, WT/DS209; *European Communities – Measures Affecting Differential and Favourable Treatment of Coffee*, WT/DS154
EC – Computer Equipment	Appellate Body Report, *European Communities – Customs Classification of Certain Computer Equipment*, WT/DS62/AB/R, WT/DS67/AB/R, WT/DS68/AB/R, adopted 22 June 1998, DSR 1998:V, 1851
EC – Computer Equipment	Panel Report, *European Communities – Customs Classification of Certain Computer Equipment*, WT/DS62/R, WT/DS67/R, WT/DS68/R, adopted 22 June 1998, modified by Appellate Body Report, WT/DS62/AB/R, WT/DS67/AB/R, WT/DS68/AB/R, DSR 1998:V, 1891

Short title	Full title and citation
EC – Conifer Wood	*European Communities – Measures Affecting Imports of Wood of Conifers from Canada*, WT/DS137
EC – Copyright	*European Communities – Measures Affecting the Grant of Copyright and Neighbouring Rights*, WT/DS115 *(US)*
EC – Corn Gluten Quotas	*European Communities – Tariff-Rate Quota on Corn Gluten Feed from the United States*, WT/DS223
EC – Cotton Fabrics	*European Communities – Anti-Dumping Investigations Regarding Unbleached Cotton Fabrics from India*, WT/DS140
EC – Export Subsidies on Sugar	Appellate Body Report, *European Communities – Export Subsidies on Sugar*, WT/DS265/AB/R, WT/DS266/AB/R, WT/DS283/AB/R, adopted 19 May 2005
EC – Export Subsidies on Sugar	Panel Reports, *European Communities – Export Subsidies on Sugar, Complaint by Australia*, WT/DS265/R *(Australia)*, WT/DS266/R *(Brazil)*, and WT/DS283/R *(Thailand)*, adopted 19 May 2005, modified by Appellate Body Report, WT/DS265/AB/R, WT/DS266/AB/R, WT/DS283/AB/R
EC – Grains	*European Communities – Duties on Imports of Grains*, WT/DS13 *(US)*
EC – Hormones	Appellate Body Report, *EC Measures Concerning Meat and Meat Products (Hormones)*, WT/DS26/AB/R, WT/DS48/AB/R, adopted 13 February 1998, DSR 1998:I, 135
EC – Hormones	Panel Reports, *EC Measures Concerning Meat and Meat Products (Hormones)*, WT/DS48/R/CAN *(Canada)* and WT/DS26/R/USA *(US)*, adopted 13 February 1998, modified by Appellate Body Report, WT/DS26/AB/R, WT/DS48/AB/R, SR 1998:II, 235 and 699

Short title	Full title and citation
EC – Hormones	Award of the Arbitrator, *EC Measures Concerning Meat and Meat Products (Hormones) – Arbitration under Article 21.3(c) of the DSU*, WT/DS26/15, WT/DS48/13, 29 May 1998, DSR 1998:V, 1833
EC – Motion Pictures	*European Communities – Enforcement of Intellectual Property Rights for Motion Pictures and Television Programs*, WT/DS124 *(US)*
EC – Patent Protection	*European Communities – Patent Protection for Pharmaceutical and Agricultural Chemical Products*, WT/DS153 *(Canada)*
EC – Poultry	Appellate Body Report, *European Communities – Measures Affecting the Importation of Certain Poultry Products*, WT/DS69/AB/R, adopted 23 July 1998, DSR 1998:V, 2031
EC – Poultry	Panel Report, *European Communities – Measures Affecting the Importation of Certain Poultry Products*, WT/DS69/R, adopted 23 July 1998, modified by Appellate Body Report, WT/DS69/AB/R, DSR 1998:V, 2089
EC – Provisional Steel Safeguards	*European Communities – Provisional Safeguard Measures on Imports of Certain Steel Products*, WT/DS260 *(US)*
EC – Rice	*European Communities – Duties On Imports Of Rice*, WT/DS17 *(Thailand)*; *European Communities – Implementation of the Uruguay Round Commitments Concerning Rice*, WT/DS25 *(Uruguay)*
EC – Rice Duties	*European Communities – Restrictions on Certain Import Duties on Rice*, WT/DS134 *(India)*
EC – Sardines	Panel Report, *European Communities – Trade Description of Sardines*, WT/DS231/R and Corr.1, adopted 23 October 2002, modified by Appellate Body Report, WT/DS231/AB/R, DSR 2002:VIII, 3451
EC – Scallops	Panel Reports, *European Communities – Trade Description of Scallops*, WT/DS7/R *(Canada)* and WT/DS12/R, WT/DS14/R *(Peru and Chile)*, 5 August 1996, DSR 1996:I, 89 and 93

Short title	Full title and citation
EC – Steel Anti-Dumping Duties	*European Communities – Anti-Dumping Duties on Certain Flat Rolled Iron or Non-Alloy Steel Products from India*, WT/DS313
EC – Tariff Preferences	Appellate Body Report, *European Communities – Conditions for the Granting of Tariff Preferences to Developing Countries*, WT/DS246/AB/R, adopted 20 April 2004, DSR 2004:III, 925
EC – Tariff Preferences	Panel Report, *European Communities – Conditions for the Granting of Tariff Preferences to Developing Countries*, WT/DS246/R, adopted 20 April 2004, modified by Appellate Body Report, WT/DS/246/AB/R, DSR 2004:III, 1009
EC – The ACP-EC Partnership Agreement	Award of the Arbitrator, *European Communities – The ACP-EC Partnership Agreement – Recourse to Arbitration Pursuant to the Decision of 14 November 2001*, WT/L/616, 1 August 2005
EC – The ACP-EC Partnership Agreement II	Award of the Arbitrator, *European Communities – The ACP-EC Partnership Agreement – Second Recourse to Arbitration Pursuant to the Decision of 14 November 2001*, WT/L/625, 27 October 2005
EC – Trademarks and Geographical Indications	Panel Reports, *European Communities – Protection of Trademarks and Geographical Indications for Agricultural Products and Foodstuffs*, WT/DS290/R *(Australia)* and WT/DS174/R *(US)*, adopted 20 April 2005
EC – Tube or Pipe Fittings	Appellate Body Report, *European Communities – Anti-Dumping Duties on Malleable Cast Iron Tube or Pipe Fittings from Brazil*, WT/DS219/AB/R, adopted 18 August 2003, DSR 2003:VI, 2613
EC – Tube or Pipe Fittings	Panel Report, *European Communities – Anti-Dumping Duties on Malleable Cast Iron Tube or Pipe Fittings from Brazil*, WT/DS219/R, adopted 18 August 2003, modified by Appellate Body Report, WT/DS219/AB/R, DSR 2003:VII, 2701

Short title	Full title and citation
Ecuador – Cement	*Ecuador – Definitive Anti-Dumping Measures on Grey Portland Cement from Mexico*, WT/DS182, WT/DS191
EEC – Oilseeds I	GATT Panel Report, *European Economic Community – Payments and Subsidies Paid to Processors and Producers of Oilseeds and Related Animal-Feed Proteins*, L/6627, adopted 25 January 1990, BISD 37S/86
EEC – Parts and Components	GATT Panel Report, *European Economic Community – Regulation on Imports of Parts and Components*, L/6657, adopted 16 May 1990, BISD 37S/132
Egypt – Canned Tuna	*Egypt – Import Prohibition on Canned Tuna with Soybean Oil*, WT/DS205 *(Thailand)*
Egypt – Matches	*Egypt – Anti-Dumping Duties on Matches from Pakistan*, WT/DS327
Egypt – Steel Rebar	Panel Report, *Egypt – Definitive Anti-Dumping Measures on Steel Rebar from Turkey*, WT/DS211/R, adopted 1 October 2002, DSR 2002:VII, 2667
Egypt – Textiles and Apparel	*Egypt – Measures Affecting Imports of Textile And Apparel Products*, WT/DS305
France – Avionics	*France – Measures Relating to the Development of a Flight Management System*, WT/DS173 *(US)*
France – Taxes	*France – Certain Income Tax Measures Constituting Subsidies*, WT/DS131 *(US)*
Greece – Motion Pictures	*Greece – Enforcement of Intellectual Property Rights for Motion Pictures and Television Programs*, WT/DS125 *(US)*
Greece – Taxes	*Greece – Certain Income Tax Measures Constituting Subsidies*, WT/DS129 *(US)*
Guatemala – Cement I	Panel Report, *Guatemala – Anti-Dumping Investigation Regarding Portland Cement from Mexico*, WT/DS60/R, adopted 25 November 1998, modified by Appellate Body Report, WT/DS60/AB/R, DSR 1998:IX, 3797
Guatemala – Cement II	Panel Report, *Guatemala – Definitive Anti-Dumping Measures on Grey Portland Cement from Mexico*, WT/DS156/R, adopted 17 November 2000, DSR 2000:XI, 5295

Short title	Full title and citation
Hungary – Agricultural Products	*Hungary – Export Subsides in Respect of Agricultural Products*, WT/DS35
Hungary – Steel Safeguard	*Hungary – Safeguard Measure on Imports of Steel Products from the Czech Republic*, WT/DS159
India – Autos	Panel Report, *India – Measures Affecting the Automotive Sector*, WT/DS146/R, WT/DS175/R and Corr.1, adopted 5 April 2002, DSR 2002:V, 1827
India – Customs Duties	*India – Measures Affecting Customs Duties*, WT/DS150 *(EC)*
India – Export Commodities	*India – Measures Affecting Export of Certain Commodities*, WT/DS120 *(EC)*
India – Patents (EC)	Panel Report, *India – Patent Protection for Pharmaceutical and Agricultural Chemical Products, Complaint by the European Communities*, WT/DS79/R, adopted 22 September 1998, DSR 1998:VI, 2661
India – Patents (US)	Appellate Body Report, *India – Patent Protection for Pharmaceutical and Agricultural Chemical Products*, WT/DS50/AB/R, adopted 16 January 1998, DSR 1998:I, 9
India – Patents (US)	Panel Report, *India – Patent Protection for Pharmaceutical and Agricultural Chemical Products, Complaint by the United States*, WT/DS50/R, adopted 16 January 1998, modified by Appellate Body Report, WT/DS50/AB/R, DSR 1998:I, 41
India – Quantitative Restrictions	Appellate Body Report, *India – Quantitative Restrictions on Imports of Agricultural, Textile and Industrial Products*, WT/DS90/AB/R, adopted 22 September 1999, DSR 1999:IV, 1763
India – Quantitative Restrictions	Panel Report, *India – Quantitative Restrictions on Imports of Agricultural, Textile and Industrial Products*, WT/DS90/R, adopted 22 September 1999, upheld by Appellate Body Report, WT/DS90/AB/R, DSR 1999:V, 1799

Short title	Full title and citation
Indonesia – Autos	Panel Report, *Indonesia – Certain Measures Affecting the Automobile Industry*, WT/DS54/R, WT/DS55/R, WT/DS59/R, WT/DS64/R and Corr.1, 2, 3, and 4, adopted 23 July 1998, DSR 1998:VI, 2201
Ireland – Copyright	*Ireland – Measures Affecting the Grant of Copyright and Neighbouring Rights*, WT/DS82 *(US)*
Ireland – Taxes	*Ireland – Certain Income Tax Measures Constituting Subsidies*, WT/DS130 *(US)*
Japan – Agricultural Products II	Appellate Body Report, *Japan – Measures Affecting Agricultural Products*, WT/DS76/AB/R, adopted 19 March 1999, DSR 1999:I, 277
Japan – Agricultural Products II	Panel Report, *Japan – Measures Affecting Agricultural Products*, WT/DS76/R, adopted 19 March 1999, modified by Appellate Body Report, WT/DS76/AB/R, DSR 1999:I, 315
Japan – Alcoholic Beverages II	Appellate Body Report, *Japan – Taxes on Alcoholic Beverages*, WT/DS8/AB/R, WT/DS10/AB/R, WT/DS11/AB/R, adopted 1 November 1996, DSR 1996:I, 97
Japan – Alcoholic Beverages II	Panel Report, *Japan – Taxes on Alcoholic Beverages*, WT/DS8/R, WT/DS10/R, WT/DS11/R, adopted 1 November 1996, modified by Appellate Body Report, WT/DS8/AB/R, WT/DS10/AB/R, WT/DS11/AB/R, DSR 1996:I, 125
Japan – Apples	Appellate Body Report, *Japan – Measures Affecting the Importation of Apples*, WT/DS245/AB/R, adopted 10 December 2003, DSR 2003:IX, 4391
Japan – Apples	Panel Report, *Japan – Measures Affecting the Importation of Apples*, WT/DS245/R, adopted 10 December 2003, upheld by Appellate Body Report, WT/DS245/AB/R, DSR 2003:IX, 4481
Japan – Distribution Services	*Japan – Measures Affecting Distribution Services*, WT/DS45 *(US)*
Japan – Film	Panel Report, *Japan – Measures Affecting Consumer Photographic Film and Paper*, WT/DS44/R, adopted 22 April 1998, DSR 1998:IV, 1179

Short title	Full title and citation
Japan – Leather Quotas	*Japan – Tariff Quotas and Subsidies Affecting Leather*, WT/DS147 *(EC)*
Japan – Pork	*Japan – Measures Affecting Imports of Pork*, WT/DS66 *(EC)*
Japan – Quotas on Laver	*Japan – Import Quotas on Dried Laver and Seasoned Laver*, WT/DS323
Japan – Satellite	*Japan – Procurement of a Navigation Satellite*, WT/DS73 *(EC)*
Japan – Sound Recordings	*Japan – Measures Concerning Sound Recordings*, WT/DS28 *(US)*, WT/DS42 *(EC)*
Japan – Telecommunications Equipment	*Japan – Measures Affecting the Purchase of Telecommunications Equipment*, WT/DS15 *(EC)*
Korea – Alcoholic Beverages	Appellate Body Report, *Korea – Taxes on Alcoholic Beverages*, WT/DS75/AB/R, WT/DS84/AB/R, adopted 17 February 1999, DSR 1999:I, 3
Korea – Alcoholic Beverages	Panel Report, *Korea – Taxes on Alcoholic Beverages*, WT/DS75/R, WT/DS84/R, adopted 17 February 1999, modified by Appellate Body Report, WT/DS75/AB/R, WT/DS84/AB/R, DSR 1999:I, 44
Korea – Bottled Water	*Korea – Measures Concerning Bottled Water*, WT/DS20 *(Canada)*
Korea – Certain Paper	Panel Report, *Korea – Anti-Dumping Duties on Imports of Certain Paper from Indonesia*, WT/DS312/R, adopted 28 November 2005
Korea – Commercial Vessel	Panel Report, *Korea – Measures Affecting Trade in Commercial Vessels*, WT/DS273/R, adopted 11 April 2005
Korea – Dairy	Appellate Body Report, *Korea – Definitive Safeguard Measure on Imports of Certain Dairy Products*, WT/DS98/AB/R, adopted 12 January 2000, DSR 2000:I, 3
Korea – Dairy	Panel Report, *Korea – Definitive Safeguard Measure on Imports of Certain Dairy Products*, WT/DS98/R and Corr.1, adopted 12 January 2000, modified by Appellate Body Report, WT/DS98/AB/R, DSR 2000:I, 49

Short title	Full title and citation
Korea – Inspection	*Korea – Measures Concerning the Testing and Inspection of Agricultural Products*, WT/DS3 *(US)*; *Korea – Measures Concerning Inspection of Agricultural Products*, WT/DS41 *(US)*
Korea – Procurement	Panel Report, *Korea – Measures Affecting Government Procurement*, WT/DS163/R, adopted 19 June 2000, DSR 2000:VIII, 3541
Korea – Resins	GATT Panel Report, *Panel on Korea – Anti-Dumping Duties on Imports of Polyacetal Resins from the United States*, ADP/92 and Corr.1, adopted 27 April 1993, BISD 40S/205
Korea – Shelf Life	*Korea – Measures Concerning the Shelf-Life of Products*, WT/DS5 *(US)*
Korea – Telecommunications	*Korea – Laws, Regulations and Practices in the Telecommunications Procurement Sector*, WT/DS40 *(EC)*
Korea – Various Measures on Beef	Appellate Body Report, *Korea – Measures Affecting Imports of Fresh, Chilled and Frozen Beef*, WT/DS161/AB/R, WT/DS169/AB/R, adopted 10 January 2001, DSR 2001:I, 5
Korea – Various Measures on Beef	Panel Report, *Korea – Measures Affecting Imports of Fresh, Chilled and Frozen Beef*, WT/DS161/R, WT/DS169/R, adopted 10 January 2001, modified by Appellate Body Report, WT/DS161/AB/R, WT/DS169/AB/R, DSR 2001:I, 59
Malaysia – Polyethylene	*Malaysia – Prohibition of Imports of Polyethylene and Polypropylene*, WT/DS1 *(Singapore)*
Mexico – Corn Syrup	Panel Report, *Mexico – Anti-Dumping Investigation of High Fructose Corn Syrup (HFCS) from the United States*, WT/DS132/R and Corr.1, adopted 24 February 2000, DSR 2000:III, 1345

Short title	Full title and citation
Mexico – Corn Syrup (Article 21.5 – US)	Appellate Body Report, *Mexico – Anti-Dumping Investigation of High Fructose Corn Syrup (HFCS) from the United States – Recourse to Article 21.5 of the DSU by the United States*, WT/DS132/AB/RW, adopted 21 November 2001, DSR 2001:XIII, 6675
Mexico – Corn Syrup (Article 21.5 – US)	Panel Report, *Mexico – Anti-Dumping Investigation of High Fructose Corn Syrup (HFCS) from the United States – Recourse to Article 21.5 of the DSU by the United States*, WT/DS132/RW, adopted 21 November 2001, upheld by Appellate Body Report, WT/DS132/AB/RW, DSR 2001:XIII, 6717
Mexico – Customs Valuation	*Mexico – Customs Valuation of Imports*, WT/DS53 *(EC)*
Mexico – Live Swine	*Mexico – Measures Affecting Trade in Live Swine*, WT/DS203 *(US)*
Mexico – Matches	*Mexico – Measures Affecting the Import of Matches*, WT/DS232 *(Chile)*
Mexico – Taxes on Soft Drinks	Appellate Body Report, *Mexico – Tax Measures on Soft Drinks and Other Beverages*, WT/DS308/AB/R, adopted 24 March 2006
Mexico – Taxes on Soft Drinks	Panel Report, *Mexico – Tax Measures on Soft Drinks and Other Beverages*, WT/DS308/R, adopted 24 March 2006, modified by Appellate Body Report, WT/DS308/AB/R
Mexico – Telecoms	Panel Report, *Mexico – Measures Affecting Telecommunications Services*, WT/DS204/R, adopted 1 June 2004, DSR 2004:IV, 1537
Mexico – Transformers	*Mexico – Provisional Anti-Dumping Measure on Electric Transformers*, WT/DS216 *(Brazil)*
Netherlands – Taxes	*Netherlands – Certain Income Tax Measures Constituting Subsidies*, WT/DS128 *(US)*
Nicaragua – Imports from Honduras and Colombia	*Nicaragua – Measures Affecting Imports from Honduras and Colombia*, WT/DS188 *(Colombia)*; WT/DS201
Norway – Trondheim Toll Ring	GATT Panel Report, *Panel on Norwegian Procurement of Toll Collection Equipment for the City of Trondheim*, GPR.DS2/R, adopted 13 May 1992, BISD 40S/319

Short title	Full title and citation
Pakistan – Hides and Skins	*Pakistan – Export Measures Affecting Hides and Skins*, WT/DS107 *(EC)*
Pakistan – Patent Protection	*Pakistan – Patent Protection for Pharmaceutical and Agricultural Chemical Products*, WT/DS36 *(US)*
Panama – Milk	*Panama – Tariff Classification of Certain Milk Products*, WT/DS329
Peru – Buses	*Peru – Countervailing Duty Investigation Against Imports of Buses from Brazil*, WT/DS112
Peru – Import Taxes	*Peru – Tax Treatment on Certain Imported Products*, WT/DS255*(Chile)*
Peru – Taxes on Cigarettes	*Peru – Taxes on Cigarettes*, WT/DS227 *(Chile)*
Philippines – Motor Vehicles	*Philippines – Measures Affecting Trade and Investment in the Motor Vehicle Sector*, WT/DS195 *(US)*
Philippines – Pork and Poultry	*Philippines – Measures Affecting Pork and Poultry*, WTDS74, WT/DS102
Philippines – Resins	*Philippines – Anti-Dumping Measures Regarding Polypropylene Resins from Korea*, WT/DS215
Poland – Autos	*Poland – Import Regime for Automobiles*, WT/DS19 *(India)*
Portugal – Patent Protection	*Portugal – Patent Protection under the Industrial Property Act*, WT/DS37 *(US)*
Romania – Minimum Import Prices	*Romania – Measures on Minimum Import Prices*, WT/DS198 *(US)*
Romania – Wheat	*Romania – Import Prohibition on Wheat and Wheat Flour*, WT/DS240 *(Hungary)*
Slovak Republic – Dairy and Cattle	*Slovak Republic – Measures Concerning the Importation of Dairy Products and the Transit of Cattle*, WT/DS133 *(Switzerland)*
Slovak Republic – Sugar	*Slovakia – Safeguard Measure on Imports of Sugar*, WT/DS235 *(Poland)*
Slovak Republic – Wheat Duties	*Slovak Republic – Measure Affecting Import Duty on Wheat from Hungary*, WT/DS143
South Africa – Pharmaceuticals	*South Africa – Anti-Dumping Duties on Certain Pharmaceutical Products from India*, WT/DS168
Sweden – IPR Enforcement	*Sweden – Measures Affecting the Enforcement of Intellectual Property Rights*, WT/DS86 *(US)*

Short title	Full title and citation
Thailand – H-Beams	Appellate Body Report, *Thailand – Anti-Dumping Duties on Angles, Shapes and Sections of Iron or Non-Alloy Steel and H-Beams from Poland*, WT/DS122/AB/R, adopted 5 April 2001, DSR 2001:VII, 2701
Thailand – H-Beams	Panel Report, *Thailand – Anti-Dumping Duties on Angles, Shapes and Sections of Iron or Non-Alloy Steel and H-Beams from Poland*, WT/DS122/R, adopted 5 April 2001, modified by Appellate Body Report, WT/DS122/AB/R, DSR 2001:VII, 2741
Trinidad & Tobago – Pasta	*Trinidad & Tobago – Certain Measures Affecting Imports of Pasta from Costa Rica*, WT/DS185; *Trinidad & Tobago – Provisional Anti-Dumping Measure on Imports of Macaroni and Spaghetti from Costa Rica*, WT/DS187
Turkey – Fresh Fruit	*Turkey – Certain Import Procedures of Fresh Fruit*, WT/DS237 *(Ecuador)*
Turkey – Pet Food	*Turkey – Import Ban on Pet Food from Hungary*, WT/DS256
Turkey – Pipe Fittings	*Turkey - Anti-Dumping Duty on Steel and Iron Pipe Fittings*, WT/DS208 *(Brazil)*
Turkey – Taxes on Film Revenues	*Turkey – Taxation of Foreign Film Revenues*, WT/DS43 *(US)*
Turkey – Textiles	Appellate Body Report, *Turkey – Restrictions on Imports of Textile and Clothing Products*, WT/DS34/AB/R, adopted 19 November 1999, DSR 1999:VI, 2345
Turkey – Textiles	Panel Report, *Turkey – Restrictions on Imports of Textile and Clothing Products*, WT/DS34/R, adopted 19 November 1999, modified by Appellate Body Report, WT/DS34/AB/R, DSR 1999:VI, 2363
Uruguay – Tax Treatment	*Uruguay – Tax Treatment on Certain Products*, WT/DS261
US – 1916 Act	Appellate Body Report, *United States – Anti-Dumping Act of 1916*, WT/DS136/AB/R, WT/DS162/AB/R, adopted 26 September 2000, DSR 2000:X, 4793

Short title	Full title and citation
US – 1916 Act	Panel Reports, *United States – Anti-Dumping Act of 1916, Complaint by the European Communities*, WT/DS136/R and Corr.1 *(EC)* and WT/DS162/R and Add.1 *(Japan)*, adopted 26 September 2000, upheld by Appellate Body Report, WT/DS136/AB/R, WT/DS162/AB/R, DSR 2000:X, 4593 and 4831
US – Anti-Dumping Measures on Oil Country Tubular Goods	Appellate Body Report, *United States – Anti-Dumping Measures on Oil Country Tubular Goods (OCTG) from Mexico*, WT/DS282/AB/R, adopted 28 November 2005
US – Autos	*United States – Imposition of Import Duties on Automobiles from Japan under Sections 301 and 304 of the Trade act of 1974*, WT/DS6
US – Carbon Steel	Appellate Body Report, *United States – Countervailing Duties on Certain Corrosion-Resistant Carbon Steel Flat Products from Germany*, WT/DS213/AB/R and Corr.1, adopted 19 December 2002, DSR 2002:IX, 3779
US – Carbon Steel	Panel Report, *United States – Countervailing Duties on Certain Corrosion-Resistant Carbon Steel Flat Products from Germany*, WT/DS213/R and Corr.1, adopted 19 December 2002, modified by Appellate Body Report, WT/DS213/AB/R and Corr.1, DSR 2002:IX, 3833
US – Carbon Steel (Brazil)	*United States – Countervailing Duties on Certain Carbon Steel Products from Brazil*, WT/DS218
US – Cattle and Grain Imports	*United States – Certain Measures Affecting the Import of Cattle, Swine and Grain from Canada*, WT/DS144
US – Certain EC Products	Appellate Body Report, *United States – Import Measures on Certain Products from the European Communities*, WT/DS165/AB/R, adopted 10 January 2001, DSR 2001:I, 373

Short title	Full title and citation
US – Certain EC Products	Panel Report, *United States – Import Measures on Certain Products from the European Communities*, WT/DS165/R and Add.1, adopted 10 January 2001, modified by Appellate Body Report, WT/DS165/AB/R, DSR 2001:II, 413
US – Colour TVs	*United States – Imposition of Anti-Dumping Duties on Imports of Colour Television Receivers from Korea*, WT/DS89
US – Continued Suspension	*United States – Continued Suspension of Obligations in the EC – Hormones Dispute*, WT/DS320 *(EC)*
US – Corn Brooms	*United States – Safeguard Measure Against Imports of Broom Corn Brooms*, WT/DS78 *(Colombia)*
US – Corrosion-Resistant Steel Sunset Review	Appellate Body Report, *United States – Sunset Review of Anti-Dumping Duties on Corrosion-Resistant Carbon Steel Flat Products from Japan*, WT/DS244/AB/R, adopted 9 January 2004, DSR 2004:I, 3
US – Corrosion-Resistant Steel Sunset Review	Panel Report, *United States – Sunset Review of Anti-Dumping Duties on Corrosion-Resistant Carbon Steel Flat Products from Japan*, WT/DS244/R, adopted 9 January 2004, modified by Appellate Body Report, WTDS244/AB/R, DSR 2004:I, 85
US – Cotton Yarn	Appellate Body Report, *United States – Transitional Safeguard Measure on Combed Cotton Yarn from Pakistan*, WT/DS192/AB/R, adopted 5 November 2001, DSR 2001:XII, 6027
US – Cotton Yarn	Panel Report, *United States – Transitional Safeguard Measure on Combed Cotton Yarn from Pakistan*, WT/DS192/R, adopted 5 November 2001, modified by Appellate Body Report, WT/DS192/AB/R, DSR 2001:XII, 6067
US – Countervailing Duty Investigation on DRAMS	Appellate Body Report, *United States – Countervailing Duty Investigation on Dynamic Random Access Memory Semiconductors (DRAMS) from Korea*, WT/DS296/AB/R, adopted 20 July 2005

Short title	Full title and citation
US – Countervailing Measures on Certain EC Products	Panel Report, *United States – Countervailing Measures Concerning Certain Products from the European Communities*, WT/DS212/R, adopted 8 January 2003, modified by Appellate Body Report, WT/DS212/AB/R, DSR 2003:I, 73
US – Countervailing Measures on Certain EC Products (Article 21.5 – EC)	Panel Report, *United Measures on Certain EC Products States – Countervailing Measures Concerning Certain Products from the European Communities – Recourse to Article 21.5 of the DSU by the European Communities*, WT/DS212/RW, adopted 27 September 2005
US – DRAMS	Panel Report, *United States – Anti-Dumping Duty on Dynamic Random Access Memory Semiconductors (DRAMS) of One Megabit or Above from Korea*, WT/DS99/R, adopted 19 March 1999, DSR 1999:II, 521
US – DRAMS (Article 21.5 – Korea)	Panel Report, *United States – Anti-Dumping Duty on Dynamic Random Access Memory Semiconductors (DRAMS) of One Megabit or Above from Korea – Recourse to Article 21.5 of the DSU by Korea*, WT/DS99/RW, 7 November 2000
US – Export Restraints	Panel Report, *United States – Measures Treating Exports Restraints as Subsidies*, WT/DS194/R and Corr.2, adopted 23 August 2001, DSR 2001:XI, 5767
US – Florida Excise Tax	*United States – Equalizing Excise Tax Imposed by Florida on Processed Orange and Grapefruit Products*, WT/DS250 *(Brazil)*
US – FSC	Appellate Body Report, *United States – Tax Treatment for 'Foreign Sales Corporations'*, WT/DS108/AB/R, adopted 20 March 2000, DSR 2000:III, 1619
US – FSC	Panel Report, *United States – Tax Treatment for 'Foreign Sales Corporations'*, WT/DS108/R, adopted 20 March 2000, modified by Appellate Body Report, WT/DS108/AB/R, DSR 2000:IV, 1675

Short title	Full title and citation
US – FSC (Article 21.5 – EC)	Appellate Body Report, *United States – Tax Treatment for 'Foreign Sales Corporations' – Recourse to Article 21.5 of the DSU by the European Communities*, WT/DS108/AB/RW, adopted 29 January 2002, DSR 2002:I, 55
US – FSC (Article 21.5 – EC)	Panel Report, *United States – Tax Treatment for 'Foreign Sales Corporations' – Recourse to Article 21.5 of the DSU by the European Communities*, WT/DS108/RW, adopted 29 January 2002, modified by Appellate Body Report, WT/DS108/AB/RW, DSR 2002:I, 119
US – FSC (Article 21.5 – EC II)	Panel Report, *United States – Tax Treatment for 'Foreign Sales Corporations' – Second Recourse to Article 21.5 of the DSU by the European Communities*, WT/DS108/RW2, adopted 14 March 2006, upheld by Appellate Body Report, WT/DS108/AB/RW2
US – FSC (Article 22.6 – US)	Decision by the Arbitrator, *United States – Tax Treatment for 'Foreign Sales Corporations' – Recourse to Arbitration by the United States under Article 22.6 of the DSU and Article 4.11 of the SCM Agreement*, WT/DS108/ARB, 30 August 2002, DSR 2002:VI, 2517
US – Gambling	Appellate Body Report, *United States – Measures Affecting the Cross-Border Supply of Gambling and Betting Services*, WT/DS285/AB/R, adopted 20 April 2005
US – Gambling	Panel Report, *United States – Measures Affecting the Cross-Border Supply of Gambling and Betting Services*, WT/DS285/R, adopted 20 April 2005, modified by Appellate Body Report, WT/DS285/AB/R
US – Gasoline	Appellate Body Report, *United States – Standards for Reformulated and Conventional Gasoline*, WT/DS2/AB/R, adopted 20 May 1996, DSR 1996:I, 3
US – Gasoline	Panel Report, *United States – Standards for Reformulated and Conventional Gasoline*, WT/DS2/R, adopted 20 May 1996, modified by Appellate Body Report, WT/DS2/AB/R, DSR 1996:I, 29

Short title	Full title and citation
US – Groundnut Quotas	*United States – Tariff Rate Quota for Imports of Groundnuts*, WT/DS111
US – Harbour Maintenance Tax	*United States – Harbour Maintenance Tax*, WT/DS118
US – Helms Burton	*United States – The Cuban Liberty and Democratic Solidarity Act*, WT/DS38 *(EC)*
US – Hot-Rolled Steel	Appellate Body Report, *United States – Anti-Dumping Measures on Certain Hot-Rolled Steel Products from Japan*, WT/DS184/AB/R, adopted 23 August 2001, DSR 2001:X, 4697
US – Hot-Rolled Steel	Panel Report, *United States – Anti-Dumping Measures on Certain Hot-Rolled Steel Products from Japan*, WT/DS184/R, adopted 23 August 2001 modified by Appellate Body Report, WT/DS184/AB/R, DSR 2001:X, 4769
US – Lamb	Panel Report, *United States – Safeguard Measures on Imports of Fresh, Chilled or Frozen Lamb Meat from New Zealand and Australia*, WT/DS177/R, WT/DS178/R, adopted 16 May 2001, modified by Appellate Body Report, WT/DS177/AB/R, WT/DS178/AB/R, DSR 2001:IX, 4107
US – Lead and Bismuth II	Panel Report, *United States – Imposition of Countervailing Duties on Certain Hot-Rolled Lead and Bismuth Carbon Steel Products Originating in the United Kingdom*, WT/DS138/R and Corr.2, adopted 7 June 2000, upheld by Appellate Body Report, WT/DS138/AB/R, DSR 2000:VI, 2623
US – Line Pipe	Appellate Body Report, *United States – Definitive Safeguard Measures on Imports of Circular Welded Carbon Quality Line Pipe from Korea*, WT/DS202/AB/R, adopted 8 March 2002, DSR 2002:IV, 1403
US – Line Pipe	Panel Report, *United States – Definitive Safeguard Measures on Imports of Circular Welded Carbon Quality Line Pipe from Korea*, WT/DS202/R, adopted 8 March 2002, modified by Appellate Body Report, WT/DS202/AB/, DSR 2002:IV, 1473

Short title	Full title and citation
US – Live Cattle	*United States – Countervailing Duty Investigation with Respect to Live Cattle from Canada*, WT/DS167
US – Offset Act (Byrd Amendment)	Appellate Body Report, *United States – Continued Dumping and Subsidy Offset Act of 2000*, WT/DS217/AB/R, WT/DS234/AB/R, adopted 27 January 2003, DSR 2003:I, 375
US – Offset Act (Byrd Amendment)	Panel Report, *United States – Continued Dumping and Subsidy Offset Act of 2000*, WT/DS217/R, WT/DS234/R, adopted 27 January 2003, modified by Appellate Body Report, WT/DS217/AB/R, WT/DS234/AB/R, DSR 2003:II, 489
US – Oil Country Tubular Goods Sunset Reviews	Appellate Body Report, *United States – Sunset Reviews of Anti-Dumping Measures on Oil Country Tubular Goods from Argentina*, WT/DS268/AB/R, adopted 17 December 2004
US – Patent Code	*United States – US Patents Code*, WT/DS224
US – Poultry Imports	*United States – Measures Affecting Imports of Poultry Products*, WT/DS100 *(EC)*
US – Procurement	*United States – Measure Affecting Government Procurement*, WT/DS88 *(EC)*, WT/DS95 *(Japan)*
US – Salmon	*United States – Countervailing Duty Investigation of Imports of Salmon from Chile*, WT/DS97
US – Seamless Pipe	*United States – Anti-Dumping Duties on Seamless Pipe from Italy*, WT/DS225 *(EC)*
US – Section 110(5) Copyright Act	Panel Report, *United States – Section 110(5) of the US Copyright Act*, WT/DS160/R, adopted 27 July 2000, DSR 2000:VIII, 3769
US – Section 110(5) Copyright Act (Article 25.3)	Award of the Arbitrators, *United States – Section 110(5) of the US Copyright Act – Recourse to Arbitration under Article 25 of the DSU*, WT/DS160/ARB25/1, 9 November 2001, DSR 2001:II, 667

Short title	Full title and citation
US – Section 129(c)(1) URAA	Panel Report, *United States – Section 129(c)(1) of the Uruguay Round Agreements Act*, WT/DS221/R, adopted 30 August 2002, DSR 2002:VII, 2581
US – Section 211 Appropriations Act	Panel Report, *United States – Section 211 Omnibus Appropriations Act of 1998*, WT/DS176/R, adopted 1 February 2002, modified by Appellate Body Report, WT/DS176/AB/R, DSR 2002:II, 683
US – Section 301 Trade Act	Panel Report, *United States – Sections 301–310 of the Trade Act of 1974*, WT/DS152/R, adopted 27 January 2000, DSR 2000:II, 815
US – Section 337 Tariff Act	GATT Panel Report, *United States Section 337 of the Tariff Act of 1930*, L/6439, adopted 7 November 1989, BISD 36S/345
US – Shrimp	Appellate Body Report, *United States – Import Prohibition of Certain Shrimp and Shrimp Products*, WT/DS58/AB/R, adopted 6 November 1998, DSR 1998:VII, 2755
US – Shrimp	Panel Report, *United States – Import Prohibition of Certain Shrimp and Shrimp Products*, WT/DS58/R and Corr.1, adopted 6 November 1998, modified by Appellate Body Report, WT/DS58/AB/R, DSR 1998:VII, 2821
US – Shrimp (Article 21.5 – Malaysia)	Appellate Body Report, *United States – Import Prohibition of Certain Shrimp and Shrimp Products – Recourse to Article 21.5 of the DSU by Malaysia*, WT/DS58/AB/RW, adopted 21 November 2001, DSR 2001:XIII, 6481
US – Shrimp (Article 21.5 – Malaysia)	Panel Report, *United States – Import Prohibition of Certain Shrimp and Shrimp Products – Recourse to Article 21.5 of the DSU by Malaysia*, WT/DS58/RW, adopted 21 November 2001, upheld by Appellate Body Report, WT/DS58/AB/RW, DSR 2001:XIII, 6529
US – Silicon Metal	*United States – Anti-dumping Duties on Silicon Metal from Brazil*, WT/DS239

Short title	Full title and citation
US – Softwood Lumber III	Panel Report, *United States – Preliminary Determinations with Respect to Certain Softwood Lumber from Canada*, WT/DS236/R, adopted 1 November 2002, DSR 2002:IX, 3597
US – Softwood Lumber IV	Appellate Body Report, *United States – Final Countervailing Duty Determination with Respect to Certain Softwood Lumber from Canada*, WT/DS257/AB/R, adopted 17 February 2004, DSR 2004:II, 571
US – Softwood Lumber IV	Panel Report, *United States – Final Countervailing Duty Determination with Respect to Certain Softwood Lumber from Canada*, WT/DS257/R and Corr.1, adopted 17 February 2004, modified by Appellate Body Report, WT/DS257/AB/R, DSR 2004:II, 641
US – Softwood Lumber IV (Article 21.5 – Canada)	Appellate Body Report, *United States – Final Countervailing Duty Determination with Respect to Certain Softwood Lumber from Canada – Recourse by Canada to Article 21.5 of the DSU*, WT/DS257/AB/RW, adopted 20 December 2005
US – Softwood Lumber IV (Article 21.5 – Canada)	Panel Report, *United States – Final Countervailing Duty Determination with Respect to Certain Softwood Lumber from Canada – Recourse by Canada to Article 21.5 [of the DSU]*, WT/DS257/RW, adopted 20 December 2005 , upheld by Appellate Body Report, WT/DS257/AB/RW
US – Softwood Lumber V	Panel Report, *United States – Final Dumping Determination on Softwood Lumber from Canada*, WT/DS264/R, adopted 31 August 2004, modified by Appellate Body Report, WT/DS264/AB/R, DSR 2004:V, 1937
US – Softwood Lumber V	Report of the Arbitrator, *United States – Final Dumping Determination on Softwood Lumber from Canada – Arbitration under Article 21.3(c) of the DSU*, WT/DS264/13, 13 December 2004

Short title	Full title and citation
US – Softwood Lumber V (Article 21.5 – Canada)	Panel Report, *United States – Final Dumping Determination on Softwood Lumber from Canada – Recourse to Article 21.5 of the DSU by Canada*, WT/DS264/RW, 3 April 2006
US – Softwood Lumber VI	Panel Report, *United States – Investigation of the International Trade Commission in Softwood Lumber from Canada*, WT/DS277/R, adopted 26 April 2004, DSR 2004:VI, 2485
US – Softwood Lumber VI (Article 21.5 – Canada)	Panel Report, *United States – Investigation of the International Trade Commission in Softwood Lumber from Canada – Recourse to Article 21.5 of the DSU by Canada*, WT/DS277/RW, adopted 9 May 2006, modified by Appellate Body Report, WT/DS277/AB/RW
US – Stainless Steel	*United States – Anti-Dumping Measures on Stainless Steel Plate in Coils and Stainless Steel Sheet and Strip from Korea*, WT/DS179 *(Korea)*
US – Steel Plate	Panel Report, *United States – Anti-Dumping and Countervailing Measures on Steel Plate from India*, WT/DS206/R and Corr.1, adopted 29 July 2002, DSR 2002:VI, 2073
US – Steel Safeguards	Appellate Body Report, *United States – Definitive Safeguard Measures on Imports of Certain Steel Products*, WT/DS248/AB/R, WT/DS249/AB/R, WT/DS251/AB/R, WT/DS252/AB/R, WT/DS253/AB/R, WT/DS254/AB/R, WT/DS258/AB/R, WT/DS259/AB/R, adopted 10 December 2003, DSR 2003:VII, 3117

Short title	Full title and citation
US – Steel Safeguards	Panel Reports, *United States – Definitive Safeguard Measures on Imports of Certain Steel Products*, WT/DS248/R, WT/DS249/R, WT/DS251/R, WT/DS252/R, WT/DS253/R, WT/DS254/R, WT/DS258/R, WT/DS259/R, adopted 10 December 2003, modified by Appellate Body Report, WT/DS248/AB/R, WT/DS249/AB/R, WT/DS251/AB/R, WT/DS252/AB/R, WT/DS253/AB/R, WT/DS254/AB/R, WT/DS258/AB/R, WT/DS259/AB/R, DSR 2003:VIII, 3273
US – Sugar Reclassification	*United States – Reclassification of Certain Sugar Syrups*, WT/DS180 *(Canada)*
US – Tariff Increases (Hormone Retaliation)	*United States – Tariff Increases on Products from the European Communities*, WT/DS39 *(EC)*
US – Textiles and Apparel I	*United States – Measures Affecting Textiles and Apparel Products*, WT/DS85 *(EC)*
US – Textiles and Apparel II	*United States – Measures Affecting Textiles and Apparel Products (II)*, WT/DS151 *(EC)*
US – Textiles Rules of Origin	Panel Report, *United States – Rules of Origin for Textiles and Apparel Products*, WT/DS243/R and Corr.1, adopted 23 July 2003, DSR 2003:VI, 2309
US – Tomatoes	*United States – Anti-Dumping Investigation Regarding Imports of Fresh or Chilled Tomatoes from Mexico*, WT/DS49
US – Tuna (EEC)	GATT Panel Report, *United States – Restrictions on Imports of Tuna*, DS29/R, 16 June 1994, unadopted
US – Tuna (Mexico)	GATT Panel Report, *United States – Restrictions on Imports of Tuna*, DS21/R, 3 September 1991, unadopted, BISD 39S/155
US – Underwear	Appellate Body Report, *United States – Restrictions on Imports of Cotton and Man-made Fibre Underwear*, WT/DS24/AB/R, adopted 25 February 1997, DSR 1997:I, 11

Short title	Full title and citation
US – Underwear	Panel Report, *United States – Restrictions on Imports of Cotton and Man-made Fibre Underwear*, WT/DS24/R, adopted 25 February 1997, modified by Appellate Body Report, WT/DS24/AB/R, DSR 1997:I, 31
US – Upland Cotton	Appellate Body Report, *United States – Subsidies on Upland Cotton*, WT/DS267/AB/R, adopted 21 March 2005
US – Upland Cotton	Panel Report, *United States – Subsidies on Upland Cotton*, WT/DS267/R, and Corr.1, adopted 21 March 2005, modified by Appellate Body Report, WT/DS267/AB/R
US – Urea	*United States – Anti-Dumping Measures on Imports of Solid Urea from the Former German Democratic Republic*, WT/DS63 *(EC)*
US – Wheat Gluten	Panel Report, *United States – Definitive Safeguard Measures on Imports of Wheat Gluten from the European Communities*, WT/DS166/R, adopted 19 January 2001, modified by Appellate Body Report, WT/DS166/AB/R, DSR 2001:III, 779
US – Wire Rod and Line Pipe	*United States – Definitive Safeguard Measures on Imports of Steel Wire Rod and Circular Welded Quality Line Pipe*, WT/DS214 *(EC)*
US – Wool Coats	*United States – Measures Affecting Imports of Women's and Girls' Wool Coats*, WT/DS32 *(India)*
US – Wool Shirts and Blouses	Appellate Body Report, *United States – Measure Affecting Imports of Woven Wool Shirts and Blouses from India*, WT/DS33/AB/R and Corr.1, adopted 23 May 1997, DSR 1997:I, 323
US – Wool Shirts and Blouses	Panel Report, *United States – Measure Affecting Imports of Woven Wool Shirts and Blouses from India*, WT/DS33/R, adopted 23 May 1997, upheld by Appellate Body Report, WT/DS33/AB/R, DSR 1997:I, 343

Short title	Full title and citation
US – Zeroing (EC)	Appellate Body Report, *United States – Laws, Regulations and Methodology for Calculating Dumping Margins ('Zeroing')*, WT/DS294/AB/R, adopted 9 May 2006
US – Zeroing (EC)	Panel Report, *United States – Laws, Regulations and Methodology for Calculating Dumping Margins ('Zeroing')*, WT/DS294/R, adopted 9 May 2006, modified by Appellate Body Report, WT/DS294/AB/R
US – Zeroing (Japan)	*United States – Measures Relating to Zeroing and Sunset Reviews*, WT/DS322 *(Japan)*
Venezuela – OCTG Imports	*Venezuela – Anti-Dumping Investigation in Respect of Imports of Certain Oil Country Tubular Goods (OCTG)*, WT/DS23 *(Mexico)*

LIST OF ABBREVIATIONS

ADR	alternative dispute resolution
AFTA	ASEAN Free Trade Area
Anti-Dumping Agreement	*Agreement on Implementation of Article VI of the General Agreement on Tariffs and Trade 1994*
ACP	African–Caribbean–Pacific
APEC	Asia-Pacific Economic Cooperation
ASEAN	Association of Southeast Asian Nations
ATC	*Agreement on Textiles and Clothing*
Biosafety Protocol	2000 UN Cartagena Protocol on Biosafety
BIT	bilateral investment treaty
CAFTA	China–ASEAN Free Trade Agreement
CRTA	Committee on Regional Trade Agreements
CTE	Committee on Trade and Environment
CUSFTA	Canada–United States Free Trade Agreement
DRAMS	dynamic random access memory semiconductors
DSB	Dispute Settlement Body
DSU	*Understanding on Rules and Procedures Governing the Settlement of Disputes*
EC Treaty	Treaty establishing the European Communities
ECHR	European Convention on Human Rights
ECJ	European Court of Justice
ECtHR	European Court of Human Rights
EFTA	European Free Trade Association
EPA	Economic Partnership Agreement
FDI	foreign direct investment
FSC	foreign sales corporation
FTA	free trade agreement
GATS	*General Agreement on Trade in Services*
GATT	*General Agreement on Tariffs and Trade*

GMOs	genetically modified organisms
GPA	*Agreement on Government Procurement*
GSP	General System of Preferences
Harmonized System	Harmonized Commodity Description and Coding System
Harmonized System Convention	*Convention on the Harmonized Commodity Description and Coding System*
ICJ	International Court of Justice
IIPA	International Intellectual Property Association
ILO	International Labour Organization
IMF	International Monetary Fund
LDC	least-developed country
LFN	least-favoured nation
MAS	mutually agreed solution
MEA	multilateral environmental agreement
MERCOSUR	Southern Common Market
METI	Ministry of Economy, Trade and Industry
MFN	most-favoured nation
NAFTA	North American Free Trade Agreement
NCPI	New Commercial Policy Instrument
NGO	non-governmental organization
Paris Convention	*Paris Convention on the Protection of Industrial Property*
PPM	process and production method
PTA	preferential trade agreement
RTA	regional trade agreement
SCM Agreement	*Agreement on Subsidies and Countervailing Measures*
SEOM	Senior Economic Officials Meeting
SPS	sanitary and phytosanitary
SPS Agreement	*Agreement on the Application of Sanitary and Phytosanitary Measures*
SWA	United Kingdom's Scotch Whisky Association
TBR	Trade Barriers Regulation
TBT	technical barriers to trade
TBT Agreement	*Agreement on Technical Barriers to Trade*
TRIPS	trade-related aspects of intellectual property rights
TRIPS Agreement	*Agreement on Trade-Related Aspects of Intellectual Property Rights*

UNCTAD	United Nations Conference on Trade and Development
UNESCO	United Nations Educational, Scientific and Cultural Organization
USDOC	United States Department of Commerce
USITC	United States International Trade Commission
USTR	US Trade Representative
Vienna Convention	*Vienna Convention on the Law of Treaties of 1969*
Working Procedures	*Working Procedures for Appellate Review*
WTO	World Trade Organization
WTO Agreement	*Marrakesh Agreement Establishing the World Trade Organization*

Introduction

This book examines three issues that are central to the future of the World Trade Organization (WTO): dispute settlement; the Doha Development Agenda (DDA) negotiations; and the relationship between regional integration and the multilateral trading system. Dispute settlement is often described as one of the most successful functions of the WTO. Some commentators have expressed concern about the imbalance between the effectiveness of the WTO's dispute settlement mechanism, on the one hand, and the difficulties facing the WTO as a negotiating forum, on the other hand. Some of these concerns may have been put to rest with the successful launch of the DDA in 2001. At the time this book was edited, intense negotiations were taking place in the context of the DDA, but much remained to be negotiated. It has long been recognized that regional integration could support the aims of the multilateral trading system. Today, however, several observers are expressing concern about the proliferation of regional trade agreements (RTAs). These observers fear that, unless the DDA is concluded successfully, there will be greater pressure on WTO Members to pursue bilateral and regional avenues for trade liberalization, which could undermine the multilateral trading system. Thus, these three issues – dispute settlement, multilateral negotiations, and regional trade agreements – are closely inter-related and the future of the WTO in many ways may depend on how these three issues are addressed in the coming years.

This book is unique in providing the reader with a variety of perspectives on each of the three issues examined. It includes essays written by some of the leading academics and practitioners in the field of international trade from Europe, North America, and East Asia.

Part I of this book contains two chapters that reflect on the first ten years of the WTO. The first chapter is authored by Professor Yasuhei Taniguchi, who is a Member of the WTO Appellate Body. The other is written by Dr Supachai Panitchpakdi, Secretary-General of the UN

Conference on Trade and Development (UNCTAD) and former Director-General of the WTO.

The focus of Part II is on the accomplishments and future prospects of the WTO dispute settlement system. Professor John Jackson's chapter looks at challenges to the generally accepted assumptions of international law and international economic law, the perennial question of national sovereignty, as well as the achievements of the dispute settlement system in its first decade. Professor Ernst-Ulrich Petersmann next looks at future challenges for the WTO dispute settlement system. He discusses in particular treaty interpretation, the question of applicable law in WTO dispute settlement and the limited jurisdiction of WTO dispute settlement bodies, as well as the role of the judge in the WTO system. The following chapter by Professor William Davey looks at what results have been achieved through consultations and implementation of panel and Appellate Body reports over the past 11 years, and provides some views on how the dispute settlement system (in particular the available remedies) could be improved so as to facilitate compliance of WTO Members with adverse rulings. Dr Frieder Roessler examines the responsibilities of a Member found to have violated WTO law, and analyzes how this has prevented Members from resorting to that system to assert their rights in many situations. In his chapter, Professor Gregory Shaffer studies the reciprocal relationship of public international law and private actors in litigation and negotiation 'within its shadow' before the WTO, focusing on the mechanisms of public–private interaction within the United States and the European Union. Valerie Hughes discusses the accomplishments of the WTO dispute settlement system. Hunter Nottage and Jan Bohanes look at the issue of arbitration within the WTO dispute settlement system. In particular, they examine the factors that might prompt WTO Members to take recourse to arbitration, rather than standard dispute settlement proceedings, and compare them to the incentives that exist in international commercial or investment arbitration. Alan Yanovich analyzes how the WTO dispute settlement system has evolved in its first ten years thanks to the flexibility inherent in its procedures.

Part III examines the WTO dispute settlement system from an Asian perspective. Dr Chulsu Kim presents a survey of the East Asian participation in the WTO dispute settlement system. Manabu Miyagawa offers a personal assessment of the ongoing DSU reform negotiations based on his own participation in these negotiations. Professor Mitsuo Matsushita examines the interaction between law, policy, and economics by reviewing selected decisions of the Appellate Body. Soichiro Sakuma's chapter looks at the question whether the WTO dispute settlement system is important to business. Shigehiro Tanaka reviews Japan's approach to the use of the WTO and analyzes how a better link could be achieved between business and the WTO.

Part IV discusses the DDA negotiations. Andrew Stoler discusses the central role of market access in the negotiations. Professor Masayoshi Honma looks at agriculture, one of the most difficult issues in the DDA. James Durling studies the use of trade remedies by WTO Members. Professor Henry Gao examines the relationship between the services negotiations and dispute settlement. Dr Chotiras Chavanich focuses on how trade in higher education services can promote sustainable development. Mark Halle argues that, contrary to general opinion, environmental policy has made significant progress in the WTO.

Finally, Part V addresses issues relating to regional integration in East Asia and the relationship between regional integration and the multilateral trading system. In the first chapter, Professor Gabrielle Marceau discusses the best practices for RTAs and free trade agreements (FTAs) adopted by the Asia-Pacific Economic Cooperation (APEC) forum, and suggests that they can contribute to more WTO-consistent RTAs. Professor Dukgeon Ahn looks at trade remedy regimes in some RTAs concluded by East Asian nations, and highlights the different approaches that individual countries in East Asia have taken in this respect, in particular, in connection with safeguard measures. Professor Chin Leng Lim looks at RTAs, the relevant WTO disciplines, and the relationship between the two. Professor Chang-Fa Lo surveys different types of dispute settlement mechanisms in RTAs, their procedural design, as well as their relationship to the WTO dispute settlement system. Professor Zhang Yuqing provides reflections on regionalism in the WTO system and examines the prospects of an East Asian free trade area.

The majority of the essays in this book were presented at a conference that took place in Tokyo, Japan, from 25 to 27 October 2005. This was the third in a series of conferences organized in 2005 and 2006 by several academic institutions, with which some of the Members of the Appellate Body are affiliated, to commemorate the Tenth Anniversary of the WTO's dispute settlement system and the establishment of the Appellate Body. The Tokyo conference was held at the United Nations University. It was organized by the Fair Trade Centre and Tokyo Keizai University, in collaboration with Aoyama Gakuin University, the United Nations University Institute of Advanced Studies, and the Institute for International Studies and Training.

PART I

The WTO at Ten

1

The WTO's tenth anniversary

YASUHEI TANIGUCHI

The year 2005 marked the Tenth Anniversary of the World Trade Organization (WTO). The WTO was built on the multilateral trading system created under the auspices of the *General Agreement on Tariffs and Trade* (GATT), which dated back to 1947.

Japan was first admitted to the GATT in 1955, three years after the end of the allied occupation. I was then a university student living in very poor economic conditions that would be unimaginable for today's Japanese students. Japan has since risen from that lowly state to its present prosperity – thanks, of course, to the extraordinary effort of the Japanese people. However, we must not forget that Japan benefited from liberalized trade under the GATT, particularly after certain restrictions were lifted in the mid-1960s. Since then, Japan has enjoyed all of the benefits provided by the GATT/WTO.

Today, wherever we go in the world, we find many stores flooded with Japanese electronic products and streets filled with Japanese cars; we can easily buy bottles of good Scotch whisky in a neighbourhood liquor store at inexpensive prices. I used to buy Scotch and Cognac at the duty-free stores every time I went abroad. I never do now because I can buy these products in my own town, sometimes even cheaper than in the duty-free stores in foreign airports. This is thanks to the GATT and the WTO.

Decades have passed since Japan joined the GATT, and Japanese people now take its benefits for granted. When we look at Japanese newspapers today, the occasional articles on the WTO are mostly about the pressure applied to Japan by the international community concerning liberalization of trade in various agricultural products, especially rice. I am afraid that the general public in Japan may get the wrong impression that Japan is a victim of the WTO system, rather than one of its main beneficiaries, which is indeed the case.

It goes without saying that the WTO is based on an agreement among sovereign States. What is called WTO law is nothing but an international convention. The whole area belongs to public international law. We often say, 'When there is a society, there is the law.' If the international society is a society, there must be a law, and this is public international law. My own research and teaching always involved the domestic legal system and I had doubts about the extent to which public international law could really be called law. A colleague of mine, who is a professor of public international law, once said in a public lecture that there is no other law that is better observed than public international law. As an example, he mentioned the principle of non-violation of diplomatic premises, which has been painstakingly observed by the international community, even in times of war. I would respond, however, by saying that this example is merely an expression of what we would call a rule of natural law, like 'Thou shall not kill.' Domestic legal systems are equipped with a mechanism for enforcing the law and with the authority to determine whether a law has been violated and, if so, to grant relief. We therefore think that the adage 'Where there is a society, there is the law' also means 'Where there is a society, there is the court.' Indeed, the law and the court are inseparable in any domestic legal system.

Traditionally, in international society, there was no court system. Today, we have the International Court of Justice (ICJ), but, despite its lofty name, it can exercise jurisdiction only when both of the disputing States agree to submit their dispute to it. Otherwise, it cannot give a binding decision. The problem of consent has been overcome in the WTO. In the WTO dispute settlement system, any one of the 149 Members can bring a claim against another Member without requiring the consent of the latter. A WTO panel and the Appellate Body can then give a binding decision on the dispute after having heard both Members according to the rules of procedure, which constitute an integral part of the WTO agreements. Therefore, unlike the ICJ, the WTO dispute settlement is said to have compulsory jurisdiction in the same way as a domestic court.

This has had a remarkable impact on the way that international disputes can be resolved, as long as they come under the jurisdiction of the WTO, namely, trade disputes arising from the WTO agreements. For example, it has become possible, and it has actually happened on several occasions, that a small-country Member's claim against a larger and more powerful Member is upheld and enforced. It is unlikely that such a dispute could have been settled in favour of the small-country Member through diplomatic negotiation. We all know that, in a domestic court system, an individual consumer can win a favourable judgment against a powerful corporation or against the government. The same kind of mechanism has been brought into the international society by virtue of the WTO dispute settlement system. What the WTO adopted ten years ago for its dispute settlement system has brought about a fundamental change in the field of public international law relating to international trade.

The WTO deals, as its name indicates, with international trade. There are currently 149 States and customs territories that are Members of the WTO. It is true that only these Members are bound by the rules of the WTO. Most trading activities are carried out by large and small private entities. Thus, even though the formal subjects of the WTO system are only the Members, millions of private businesses behind them are directly affected by the functioning of the system: if a Member does not behave properly, certain private businesses may be deprived of benefits deriving from the WTO system. This aspect of the WTO raises a question about the relationship between the government and business in a particular country. In Japan, for example, we have seen the development of a political agenda that includes such themes as deregulation, self-responsibility, privatization, and the abolishment of the traditional 'convoy system' in which private businesses were guided and protected by the government. What does this new development have to do with the role of the Japanese government in the WTO, as well as with the possible initiative of the Japanese private industrial sector in relation to it? We can now talk about an internationalization of domestic law and a nationalization of international law in the context of the globalized world of trade. Such a globalization of norms, however, is not limited to the level of government and business. Similar developments may be found in the areas directly affecting an individual's life, for example, in the fields of human rights and the environment.

I hope that this book enhances the understanding of the WTO in general, and its dispute settlement system in particular, and that it makes a contribution, however small, to the further development and improvement of the current multilateral trading system under the WTO.

2

The WTO at ten: its multilateral and regional involvements

SUPACHAI PANITCHPAKDI

Before going into the substance of my remarks about the World Trade Organization (WTO) at ten, and its multilateral and regional involvements, I should like to say something about the work I have done at the WTO and what I am doing in my new role at the United Nations Conference on Trade and Development (UNCTAD).

Whatever the outcome of the Doha Development Agenda, we must never forget the middle name of the Round: development. And development is not the middle name of UNCTAD; it is its first name, middle name and last name. Development – trade and development – is actually the real mandate of UNCTAD, and UNCTAD will always be there to try to complement efforts to promote the understanding and capacity of countries to take part in the negotiations, and also to motivate them to reach an early solution.

When I was at the WTO, I had to contend with a number of lawyers – who happen to constitute the largest group of professionals working there – and I thought it was quite a challenging task, being an economist and having to face meetings with lawyers. But at UNCTAD, you cannot imagine the kind of tasks I have to face with one single group of professionals: not lawyers this time, but economists. Such different professions, but nevertheless, I do think they complement one another. To illustrate this point, I should like to tell a joke, one that has been circulating mainly among economists, but that involves both economists and lawyers.

An experiment was conducted to test the behaviour of three types of human beings: scientists, lawyers, and economists. They put a small mouse in a dark room and sent in the scientist to catch the mouse. The scientist went in and thought about it over and over, trying to devise all possible ways of catching the mouse. He decided he needed to bring some light into the room, and used all the scientific means and contraptions at his disposal, but after a while he gave up; he still couldn't catch the mouse.

Then they sent in the lawyer, and after a while he too came out, saying that while he couldn't catch the mouse, at least he had defined the rules of the game; he had determined how to proceed to corner the mouse and how to behave in catching it. Then they sent in the economist. He came out immediately, saying, 'let's assume we have caught the mouse'.

This is just to provide some perspective on us economists – a bit biased, of course. If you ask your Chinese friend he would say, it is very simple: you send in a cat of any colour and he will catch the mouse anyway. This story shows that there are almost always some practical ways of tackling seemingly intractable situations.

When we started to consider how to celebrate the 10th anniversary of the WTO – in consultation, of course, with the Members, because this is after all a Member-driven organization – I asked whether we would have a budget so that we could tell the world we are now ten years old. This was an occasion worth telling the world about, I thought. 'No, no', they replied; 'you can go and celebrate the tenth anniversary but we won't pay for you to do it'. I said that 'this is, after all, your organization'; but again they said, no budget, no need to celebrate, no need for a reception. So I just cancelled all the receptions that had been planned at the beginning of the year, and instead we planned a series of meetings. We said to ourselves, if you look into the last decade of the history of the *General Agreement on Tariffs and Trade* (GATT) and the WTO, it has been uneven. I say this to be fair to the GATT and the WTO, because some people – or many people – will disagree. There has been a series of failures and crises, and if one reads the newspapers, it sounds even worse. But to be fair to the WTO, sometimes we see successes and sometimes we see failures. When there are successes, a lot of parents come around to claim them. But nobody claims failures – and when there is a failure in our system, the WTO is like an orphan: there are no parents around.

Back to our tenth anniversary celebrations: since there was no cause to celebrate, in the end we decided it would be better to reflect on our recent history through a series of events with universities, research institutions and so forth around the world. We could talk about both our failures and our achievements and assess where we are now. That would be very useful for the organization and fair to all concerned.

We in the secretariat also organized a series of events in Hong Kong, New York, Brussels, and Geneva. In addition, I set up a Consultative Board to produce a report on 'The Future of the WTO'. It is really an outstanding report, from an outstanding group of people, and it was launched in January 2005 as part of the 'celebrations'. Some people ask, whose report is it? It is not my report, but that of my colleagues; I simply sponsored it. The Board members did all their work on a charitable basis, with no honorarium or compensation whatsoever. They put their reputations on the line, and I heartily recommend that everyone read it; it is well written, easy to understand, full of self-criticism of the WTO and perspectives on the future. I would subscribe to a lot of what the report says; although I couldn't say this while I was Director-General of the WTO, I can say so now.

I should now like to move on to the real substance of my contribution to this book, namely, the five or six points by which I think we should be remembered, for better or for worse, and conclude by raising some of the challenges I think lie ahead.

But even before I begin: this decade, 1994–1995 to 2004–2005, has been a memorable one. It has been marked by numerous developments, particularly in the economic field. In Asia, of course, we were confronted in 1998–1999 by one of the most traumatic financial crises in our history. The decade also saw crises emerging in Latin America, Russia and elsewhere. There were also some disasters, like 9/11. We have seen the successful emergence of the information technology industry, towards the end of the 20th century, and also the near meltdown of that industry after Y2K. We have seen the unprecedented proliferation of all kinds of so-called free trade arrangements – because many of them are free trade arrangements in name only. Many so-called free trade agreements (FTAs) are not really FTAs because of their limited coverage: a lot of different names, a lot of Memoranda of Understanding, but as to whether they'll really materialize, whether they'll produce the kind of results we are hoping for – which are to serve as building blocks for multilateral agreements – is hard to say; not many of them are actually producing the kind of results I think the signatories would have liked. So there have been a lot of challenges – challenges against globalization, which the WTO embodies – and a lot of protest marches around the world. For an organization like the WTO, this has been a difficult decade indeed. And one has to look at that background to understand why I think the five or six points I would like to discuss are worth mentioning.

The first point is that despite the problems, the multilateral process has been well maintained. When one looks at Seattle, for example, in 1999, this was one of the events that people would say probably signalled the beginning of the end of multilateralism. People on the street, especially in the United States, were talking about all sorts of things, not only about the WTO but about migrant workers, agriculture, core labour rights, the environment and so forth, and always against the process of globalization. But by that time the WTO was already gaining a sense of direction, a sense that there need to be some rules to this trade game, that we have come together to establish some form of shared sovereignty, of joint sovereign rights, with a predictable future. One leader told me, 'Look, we are living in a very confused and messy world. People are doing things on their own and they have their own problems. But at least we have the World Trade Organization trying to sort things out and bring stability and predictability to the world, or at least to a large part of the global economic system.' So this is one aspect of the WTO I would like the readers to remember and reflect on.

Recent statistics show that world trade expanded an average six-to-seven per cent annually over the past three years, which I would call unprecedented. This expansion took place in areas which had never previously seen any decent expansion, such as sub-Saharan African countries, whose economies grew an average five per cent a year for the first time in decades. Of course, five per cent growth is not enough for Africa to meet the Millennium Development Goals, but at least it is a good start. And if you also look at the way developing countries are participating in the global trading system, you find that South-South trade, which at the start of the decade was something like 20 per cent of the global trading volume, now accounts for at least one third. It is not just that trade has been expanding, but what is even more meaningful is that trade involving poor countries has expanded, which is certainly good news.

My second point concerns the WTO as such. There are 191 member States of the United Nations, whereas the WTO currently has 149 Members; I don't think we can claim to be a world trade organization without full membership of all the world's economies. But at least we have gained 23 new Members in the past decade, having started off with 100 or so founding Members in 1995. It is interesting to see the role of countries that have joined since then to make this institution a more global one.

China, after 13 or 14 years of tortuous negotiations, joined in 2001. So China has come in as a major economy, and you are seeing the results. People used to say that China's joining the WTO was a significant event for the organization, but I think there are other countries whose accession is equally important – the least-developed countries (LDCs). Because in the past ten years a number of middle-income countries joined, as did China, but only two countries – Cambodia and Nepal, both of them LDCs – joined at the Cancun meeting. So it isn't fair to think only of China's joining, since this is an organization that should be seen to belong to the global society. The fact is, some of the world's poorest countries have now joined the WTO, which meant going through the same tortuous procedures. Cham Prasidh, Cambodia's Trade Minister, told me it was like jungle warfare: he had to negotiate with the crocodiles and all the other ferocious animals in the *maison* and around the world. Now, the accession rules are quite harsh but also necessary. But we have tried to simplify and rationalize those rules so that more LDCs can join the organization.

My third point concerns part of the successful undertaking of the WTO, which is that in 2001 we succeeded in launching the so-called 'DDA', the Doha Development Agenda. You will notice two words in this expression: one is 'development', and the other is 'agenda'. The nuance may be slight, but there is a difference between 'round' and 'agenda', and our choice of 'agenda' was deliberate. It refers to an agenda of what we should be discussing and negotiating; it is not just a round. My former colleagues at the WTO are very inventive with what they call 'constructive ambiguity'; and we have been very successful with a lot of ambiguous agreements. So 'round' and 'agenda' are not the same thing; but we are going to move ahead with our agenda.

As to the word 'development': truth be told, the agenda was never conceived as a development agenda. In Seattle, in 1999, it was proposed as a 'millennium agenda'; and then in Doha the name was changed to 'Doha Development Agenda'. The people who were in Doha deserve a lot of credit for that change, given that it was not conceived mainly as a development agenda. I give a lot of credit to the participating countries – and also to my predecessor, Mike Moore – for introducing the word 'development', and for trying to reflect that concept in the content of the Round. It was an event in itself that not only were we successful in launching the Round, but also that we produced a comprehensive and ambitious agenda for it – one that, before the Round is completed, must answer to the mandate of the negotiations, with a lot of emphasis on the development side.

My fourth point – and this is a process that had begun already in Renato Ruggiero's time and continued under Mike Moore and myself – concerns the actual integration of developing countries into the world trading system. Throughout the seven rounds preceding the Uruguay Round, the developing countries did not really participate actively. During the current Doha Round of negotiations, by contrast, we are seeing more active participation by the LDCs, the African–Caribbean–Pacific (ACP) countries, the G-20, the G-33, the Association of Southeast Asian Nations (ASEAN), the African Union, the Caribbean Community, and so forth.

They are now voicing their concerns and defending their interests with great tenacity; take, for example, the discussions on cotton. It was only just before Cancun that there was this proposal on cotton coming from the West African countries – Burkina Faso, Chad, Mali, and Benin. The cotton issue is significant – not because cotton is very significant in the world; it isn't. But it *is* the lifeline of these four countries, where more than ten million people are involved in the industry. Formerly, more than 30 million Africans in more than 20 countries worked in cotton; but because cotton was heavily subsidized by some countries, cotton growers were marginalized and cotton prices have tumbled. So I think that the WTO can be proud of its success in partially, if not fully, integrating developing countries into the world trading system.

The decision made in the areas of trade-related aspects of intellectual property rights (TRIPS) and public health that facilitates access to essential medicines for pandemic diseases suggests just how much developing countries' concerns are being taken into account. People used to criticize TRIPS as a result of the Uruguay Round, saying it was supposed to be only for advanced countries that knew how to invent more intellectual property rights. For the first time, however, TRIPS has been adjusted to take on board an exemption that entitles the poorest of all countries to accede to affordable medicine, which is a great credit to the WTO membership. And again, this would not have been possible without the significant, if not yet full, integration of developing countries into the world trading system.

Here is my fifth point. We talk a lot about working together in order to manage the process of globalization. Books on the subject tell us this process is either endogenous or exogenous – that it can either be manipulated and controlled, or else it just happens autonomously – depending on the author. But mainly we conclude that it's exogenous, driven by technology for development, which happens everyday. You just can't say, like some critics used to, that we can turn back the clock on globalization. A friend of mine said that if you were against globalization, it was like denying the law of gravity. So those of us who work in the international organizations keep saying, look, the way to make globalization work for everyone is not to work on an individual basis. The World Bank, the International Monetary Fund (IMF), and the UN institutions in the economic field cannot *just* work separately; we must also work in tandem, and there must be coherence to our work.

In the last few years, the World Bank, the IMF, the WTO, UNCTAD, the International Trade Centre, and the United Nations Development Programme have been working well together, in a number of areas. One very famous and very practical project is the 'Integrated Framework', in which these six organizations join hands to mainstream trade in the LDCs into the development process. And that process is currently based on the poverty reduction strategy papers drawn up by the World Bank, which mainly address issues of investment in human resources and other social spheres, but which pay very little attention to trade. Whereas what we are seeing at the moment is that while one can give a lot of aid, and forgive a lot of debt, one needs also to directly assist countries in building up supply capacity so that they can make use of trade as a powerful means to support wide-ranging areas of development.

What we are doing with the Integrated Framework, then, is to teach countries how to strategize trade so that it can support sustainable development. In a similar vein, I was delighted to see that at the World Bank and IMF meeting in Washington in 1995, another project was proposed to be carried out jointly by the international organizations: Aid for Trade. This concept used to be called 'aid or trade', or 'trade or aid', but is now 'aid for trade'. The idea is to harness aid to support trade measures, commercial infrastructure and so forth, and this will also help strengthen the IF project.

My sixth point concerns transparency. The WTO has been accused many times of being exclusive, a place where confidentiality is the order of the day. It is accused of being a dark house, where none of the lights are on. Only official government delegations are allowed to participate; members of civil society are not, except in some very specific kinds of meetings. So people question the inclusiveness and transparency of this organization; they accuse it of having a 'democratic deficit'. Now I can say that in the past decade, the WTO may not have been able to eliminate all of these doubts because some forms of the 'green room process' are still needed to gradually build up consensus, starting with a limited number of countries. But certainly improvements have been made, in that there is always a rotation of countries going into the 'green room', and transparency is always guaranteed by the follow-up process of having so-called 'Heads of Delegations' meetings to multilateralize the issues.

Another part of the transparency process – part of the backbone of the WTO – is the process of trade policy review. This is a wonderful mechanism that was conceived as part of the establishment of the WTO, where you sit down and subject one country's trade policy to a review by its fellow Member countries. They can say anything they like about your country, and this is done in rotation; eventually every Member country has to go through the process. But it's a very helpful process; it creates a discussion which I like, because it's not solely about trade negotiations, but concerns trade as part of a whole range of economic policies. It is a process in which countries can explain to the rest of the world what their aspirations are, and what they are intending to do. What is their compliance record with the WTO regulations, and what are the complaints from their fellow WTO Members that they need to address back home? Many, if not most, developing countries have benefited greatly, while others never even thought of having a consistent economic policy paper before they were asked to do this policy review. So the trade policy reviews have not only created transparency within the WTO but have also served as a platform for countries to understand their own economies in a way that helps them devise coordinated economic policy.

The WTO has done 139 such reviews in the past ten years, and we at UNCTAD do similar reviews, on investment, which can boost trade and create jobs. Unfortunately, we do not have the same kind of funding arrangement as the WTO, so we are now working with donors to produce more investment policy reviews, particularly for countries in Africa that have a very dismal record in terms of mobilizing foreign direct investment (FDI).

I now come to my seventh point, which is the work of the WTO Dispute Settlement Body (DSB). Now, if you talk about the backbone of this organization, of course, it is negotiations, market access, rule-setting; and I have also mentioned transparency, and the trade policy reviews. You can set as many rules as you like. Setting rules is important, but to enforce them is another matter. Sometimes we talk about FTAs, regional trade agreements (RTAs), and other kinds of agreements, but most of them are never enforced or keep being postponed, and they don't involve the kind of rule-setting and rule compliance that the WTO has achieved with its DSB. So again, this is a time to be celebrating the successful performance in the past decade of the WTO's dispute settlement mechanism: successful not only because of the 300 cases that have been submitted to it, but also because the organization has maintained its credibility. It is one of the most active international adjudicative bodies in the world, dealing with a complex set of rules. Some would have thought we were dealing only with trade rules; but in fact, the DSB deals also with rules on the environment, and on economic analysis. Adjudications on steel, cotton or sugar, for instance, are not purely about trade issues, but have to consider economic analysis as well.

And I simply cannot pay enough tribute to what my former colleagues in the WTO dispute settlement system have been doing, particularly those in the Appellate Body. You pass a ruling to say that one party is right, and you have hostility from the party that lost the case; you make one party very pleased and you disappoint the other. So the adjudicators never have many friends in the room.

There is a strict impartiality to the system, in that countries can lose some cases and win others, depending on the nature of the cases and not on the strength of the countries. And one very clear advance in the system has been the participation of developing countries. This is a system in which people used to think that only advanced countries with a lot of money could participate and win, because it's really costly. That is why one group of countries has set up a legal affairs advisory centre in Geneva, to advise poor countries at no cost or at concessional costs. These are costly exercises, but nevertheless, developing countries have been participating, with results that are always deemed to be fair.

I said that the system has heard 300 cases in the past ten years alone – the same number as during the first 47 years of the GATT. What does this mean? Two things: first, we must have a lot of problems in the world today – and this is true, because you compete, you intensify your competition, you unintentionally violate the rules, perhaps because you interpret them differently – but, second, it means that people have relied a lot on the DSB because they have confidence in the system. And in spite of the fact that you're seeing a proliferation of RTAs and bilateral FTAs around the world, some of which have dispute settlement mechanisms, not a single one of them can emulate the kind of credibility the WTO is achieving. Many RTA dispute cases are actually referred to the DSB, which I think is a tribute to the DSB, its panellists and the members of the Appellate Body.

I would like to conclude by mentioning some of the challenges for the future. We will need to address how to complete the Doha Round on time with the right level of ambition. I do not doubt that the Round will be completed. I just do not know when. But I do not want the Round to be just 'completed'; it must be completed with the same level of ambition at which it was launched at the Doha meeting in 2001. This is very crucial.

The second challenge is the non-discriminatory basis of the WTO's work. This is, after all, one of the organization's first rules, that it be non-discriminatory. But at the moment, as you can see in the Consultative Group's report on 'The Future of the WTO', we are deluding ourselves if we believe we are working in a world of most-favoured nation (MFN); what we are actually doing is working on the basis of least-favoured nation (LFN). Some five or six countries are still operating on an MFN basis; the rest are on preferential tariff agreements. Look carefully, and you will see this in the report; it is quite alarming. It is not the number that matters; not the signing of agreements, which is merely a political exercise and doesn't bother me very much. What does bother me a lot is that people are distracted from MFN towards LFN, and the cost effectiveness is not there; it's very costly, and the returns are just not justifiable.

The report also refers to the manageability of the system. Now, we have 149 Member countries, and one can see the kind of impasse we have reached. At every turn, people say 'you failed, you are in crisis', which is not true. But because of the magnitude of the problems, unless the WTO Round finishes on time, people will always qualify its undertakings as failures, as major disappointments, as all kinds of terms that point to the system's demise. But in time, the manageability of the system will have to be subject to certain deliberations – not now, because we are involved in the Doha Development Agenda, but at some point we will have to address the timing of the Ministerial Conferences, for example. Is once every two years tenable, or should they be held once a year, as the World Bank and the IMF do? Is it all right to work on this consensus-building basis, which needs to be preserved but can perhaps be modified slightly, so that the process combines efficiency with full democracy? How can we connect between the Geneva process of negotiations and the involvement of the capitals? Too many countries are just totally disconnected, to the detriment of both their own interests and those of the entire membership.

As a former staff member of the WTO, I hope what I have addressed represents a fair and balanced treatment of the organization's past, present and future. The WTO at ten is the right moment to be doing this assessment and to learn the lessons from our past so that the organization can better serve its membership in the future and help create a world trade system that can deliver benefits for everyone.

PART II

Accomplishments and Future Prospects of the WTO Dispute Settlement System

3

The WTO dispute settlement system after ten years: the first decade's promises and challenges

JOHN H. JACKSON[1]

The World Trade Organization (WTO) dispute settlement system is a vast subject, and provides a great opportunity to explore in more detail than I am allowed in this chapter. But I hope that this contribution will provide at least a framework for discussion.

I. Context and landscape: the world of interdependence and its realities[2]

The general question of 'globalization'

It is likely that the last decade of the 20th century, and the first decade of the 21st century, will be remembered as a period during which generally accepted assumptions of international law and international economic law were challenged in fundamental ways. Many of these challenges come from the factors that have lead us to the current period of globalization. Most significantly, these factors are the great reduction in the time and cost of both transport and communications, and the 'refinement' and 'efficiency' of weapons. These factors lead to circumstances that, on the one hand, require international cooperative institutions, but on the other hand, lead some policymakers to conclude that traditional notions of 'sovereignty' and the independence of the nation-state must be reserved

[1] This chapter is partly drawn from a book by the author, *Sovereignty, the WTO, and Changing Fundamentals of International Law* (Cambridge, 2006). That book in turn is partly based on the Lauterpacht Lectures Series, given at Cambridge University in November 2001.

[2] Other works by this author that may interest some readers include: *The Jurisprudence of the GATT and the WTO: Insights on Treaty Law and Economic Relations* (2nd edn, Cambridge, 2000); *The World Trade Organization: Constitution and Jurisprudence* (Chatham House Papers, Royal Institute of International Affairs, 1998); *The World Trading System: Law and Policy of International Economic Relations* (2nd edn, Cambridge, Mass., 1997); *World Trade and the Law of GATT* (Indianapolis, 1969).

for and, in certain circumstances, need to trump international institutions and their norms. One such international institution that cannot escape this landscape of facts 'on the ground', and the policies that relate to them, is the WTO. The natural trade barriers that existed a century ago, with respect to the factors just mentioned (transport and communication changes) have disappeared or have been deeply reduced, and the result is a degree of interdependence which has not, heretofore, been seen. The developments leading to this interdependence, and the circumstances that spin off from it, are producing changes inherently difficult for people and nation-state constituents throughout the world to adjust to and for governments to be able to manage satisfactorily.

Economic policy and the value of markets

Certainly in the last two decades there has been a much stronger recognition of the role and value of markets in enabling institutional economic structures to provide a satisfactory standard of living for constituents, compared to many other structures that have been experimented with during the last hundred years. Nobel Prize winning economists[3] have noted that markets will not work without adequate institutional structures. They indicate that markets without such structure will result in various types of market failures, such as monopoly practices, or asymmetries of information. Consequently, the institutional structure becomes essential for the effectiveness of markets, and this, of course, is a recognition of the need, in some circumstances, for government intervention. For the most part, such intervention simply means rules. This is particularly true at the international level.

Thus, the WTO plays a vital role as a major component of an institutional structure that could be essential (albeit still evolving) for the adequate and effective working of the world market with which we now must cope. A key desideratum of the WTO is its rule structure, and indeed, the WTO treaty language[4] stresses the importance of 'security and predictability'. To achieve these goals, rules must be effective, that is,

[3] Ronald H. Coase, *The Firm, the Market and the Law* (Chicago, 1988), chapter 5 (reprint of 1960 article). See also C.A.E. Goodhart, 'Economics and the Law: Too Much One-Way Traffic?', (1997) 60 *The Modern Law Review*, 1–22; Douglas C. North, *Institutions, Institutional Change and Economic Performance* (Cambridge, 1990); and Joseph E. Stiglitz, *Globalization and its Discontents* (New York, 2002), p. 219.

[4] Article 3.2 of the *Understanding on Rules and Procedures Governing the Settlement of Disputes* (DSU).

must actually be operational and create practicable, 'real world' conditions. This goal, in turn, demands institutional measures that will complement the rules and assist in their effectiveness through adequate compliance, so as to create the conditions of security and predictability. Another way that economists describe this phenomenon is that institutional structures reduce the 'risk premium' of a myriad of economic judgments and decisions by millions of participants in the market.

There are those who quarrel about whether globalization is 'exogenous' or 'endogenous', that is to say, whether globalization is inevitable, or whether it can be stopped or altered by governmental or other human measures. But it seems clear that a certain portion of the factors of globalization have developed through technology which has clearly become a part of day-to-day life, and is not going away. So, no matter what government officials or constituents may think, to a certain extent, globalization is a given, and the key then is for human institutions, national, subnational, or international, to try to shape policies and institutional development in a way that maximizes the beneficial aspects of globalization, while minimizing the detrimental aspects.

General international law: changing fundamentals to cope with globalization and interdependence and conceptual weaknesses of international law

Recently, there has been a great increase in the thinking, scholarship, writing, and speaking about some of the fundamentals of international law and their problems, defects, ambiguities, as well as their strengths. Particularly as to *customary* international law, there is a major literature about the many defects, including a number of very uncertain aspects of how to determine when a customary international norm has come into being, or how it can be changed.

But it is not only customary international law that is criticized. Treaties also have come under greater scrutiny. In particular, the large multilateral worldwide treaties, sometimes known as 'charters' or even 'constitutions', do not well fit some of the traditional treaty law models that seem better suited to explain and govern how bilateral or mini-lateral treaties should operate. In the case of the large treaties, there often develops 'treaty rigidity', because of the extreme difficulty and political impracticability of changing treaties. We see this manifested in connection with the UN Charter, the Bretton Woods institutions, and of course, the WTO (and the *General Agreement on Tariffs and Trade* (GATT) before it). Treaty rigidity leads to notions of how these large multilateral institutional treaties should evolve in their application and interpretation, and these notions, in turn, lead to considerable controversy. Among other things, it can be suggested that the traditional notions about treaty law which have been developed as customary international law (as largely represented by the *Vienna Convention on the Law of Treaties*[5] (*Vienna Convention*)) should be seriously rethought.

In addition to all of this uncertainty, there is a current challenge to the traditional (Westphalian) concept of sovereignty, including commentary that suggests that sovereignty is 'organized hypocrisy'.[6] In fact, sovereignty in its traditional form is no longer accepted in any major way. But part of the dilemma for all international institutions and the users and policymakers dependent on international law is that, when the core concept of sovereignty is so challenged, it can logically lead to the challenge of other core concepts, or corollaries of sovereignty, which are embedded in the accepted structure of international law. These other core concepts include the idea of monopoly of power within the nation-state domestic realm (even when extreme adverse measures are used against the citizenry), the idea of equality of nations (when the differences are so vast, such as China with 1.3 billion people, compared to Grenada, with less than 100,000 citizens), and the theory that a nation-state must always consent before it is obligated to observe an international norm.

International economic law and its most important current embodiment, the WTO, cannot be immune to these various challenges to the legitimacy of international law and traditional international relations. The literature is extensive already, including, among other topics, literature contrasting 'hard power' and 'soft power', and lessons now being demonstrated in a world that is emerging after the enormous impact of the 11 September 2001 events in New York City.

In sum, the importance of international institutions, and the need for better institutional structures, suggest that concepts previously applied only to nation-states (such as good governance and good constitutions) must now be important ingredients in thinking about international institutions.

The WTO, and especially its dispute settlement system, are becoming important models for future international relations. Thus, the tensions surrounding sovereignty (which is often invoked without careful thought,

[5] Done at Vienna, 23 May 1969, in force 27 January 1980, 1155 UNTS 331; 8 International Legal Materials 679, UKTS (1980) 58.

[6] Stephen D. Krasner, *Sovereignty: Organized Hypocrisy* (Princeton, 1999).

and sometimes more as a 'mantra', recited for effect more than to lead to adequate policy analysis) are manifested in the already large body of jurisprudence of the WTO, with its most elaborate and penetrating reflections on some of the issues expressed above.

Building upon this general landscape, section II of this chapter will examine the WTO specifically, and address a bit more of the international context as embodied in the WTO generally, and its political and diplomatic side. Section III will take a careful look at where the WTO dispute settlement system fits into this landscape.

II. The WTO generally

We must now look at the WTO against the backdrop of more than a decade of its existence, and add the context of the previous 47 years of the GATT (recalling that the GATT was made effective only 'provisionally' throughout its history). The GATT was the unfortunate, and birth-defected result of the failure of the once contemplated International Trade Organization (in the Havana Charter of 1948), to come into existence. The result of the 1944 Bretton Woods Conference was to establish the Bretton Woods institutions, particularly the World Bank and the International Monetary Fund (IMF). It was recognized, however, that a trade organization was necessary, and finally, in 1995, some five decades later, when the WTO came into existence, the third leg of the remarkable Bretton Woods 'stool' was put in place.

In the relatively brief period of the WTO's existence thus far, the organization now has 150 Members, with about 30 other nation-states engaging in activities they hope will lead to accession. Already , the Members of the WTO represent 93 per cent of the total trade of the world,[7] and, with the addition of just a few of the applicant countries, including Russia, that percentage will equal nearly all of the world's trade. This is quite a remarkable achievement. Indeed, as the next section of this chapter will later discuss, the unique and extraordinarily powerful dispute settlement system, is part of this development of a WTO that is, as many people have stated, the most important of the international economic institutions that we have in our world today.

In the light of some of the ideas expressed above, the WTO could be seen as a regulatory body, although this would annoy a number of individuals

[7] Statistic of 93 per cent from the United Nations 2002 International Trade Statistics Yearbook, Vol. II (New York, 2004), p. 467.

and other policy observers. There is an argument that has been articulated in a few quarters, that the WTO should 'return to the traditional role' of the GATT and of the WTO Charter, and focus just on 'border measures'. This is a fallacious argument, because it both indulges in a mistaken view about history, and also ignores the needs of the world today. The historical fallacy is borne out by the clauses in the GATT (such as Article III, paragraph 4), and similar trade agreements, which have extraordinarily broad reach into purely domestic economic policy matters, because it was felt important to prevent discrimination against imports, which would undermine the liberal trade measures established for border application. In addition, the world generally recognizes that non-tariff barriers have become, in many ways, much more important than tariffs or quotas, and that there are thousands of different kinds of non-tariff barriers which can be used to essentially stack the deck against imports in the domestic economic playing field.

However, it must be recognized that there are a series of challenges to the WTO, and I will only enumerate some of these challenges, without trying to deal with them in any depth, because I want to spend most of my time on the dispute settlement system.[8] These challenges include:

The question of legitimization and good governance principles, embodying notions of consultation and transparency. This is related to an argument that the WTO represents a 'skewed representation of the world', which, in some people's observation and viewpoint, is too heavily weighted in favour of the rich nations.

The difficulty that the WTO has had in launching a new major round of negotiation is obvious, and has been heavily reported. Ministerials at Seattle in 1999 and Cancun in 2003, are deemed failures, although the intermediate Doha Ministerial of November 2001 seemed encouraging. The difficulties of pursuing the 'Doha Agenda' became all too clear in the run-up to the sixth Ministerial Conference, held in Hong Kong in December 2005.

[8] Some of these matters are carefully discussed in Report by the Consultative Board to the Director-General, 'The Future of the WTO: Addressing Institutional Challenges in the New Millennium' (Geneva, 2005), available at: <www.wto.org/english/thewto_e/10anniv_e/10anniv_e.htm#future> (visited 18 March 2005). The Consultative Board was comprised of: Peter Sutherland (Chairman), Jagdish Bhagwati, Kwesi Botchwey, Niall W. A. FitzGerald, Koichi Hamada, John H. Jackson, Celso Lafer, and Thierry De Montbrial. Brief biological information for each member is available at: <http://www.wto.org/english/news_e/pres03_e/pr345_e.htm> (visited 18 March 2005).

The proliferation of free trade agreements (FTAs) of a whole plethora of styles and modalities has added greatly to the complexity of the 'spaghetti bowl of trade agreements', with which many nations have had to cope. It is also detracting from the WTO and its multilateral system.

There clearly has been a power shift within the WTO, as compared to the older days in the GATT. This, in many ways, is salutary, in the sense that developing countries now have a much larger say in the organization. Although voting is arguably hardly ever used, the fact that two-thirds of the Members are developing countries indicates how large a weight in the organization they potentially have. This weight is being felt.

The relationships of the WTO with non-governmental organizations (NGOs) and civil society generally, have not been easy, nor always constructive. There has been some attempt by the WTO to resolve these issues, but there really must be considerably more careful thought about that. The NGOs are not always entirely transparent themselves (although they argue for transparency in the WTO), and in addition, many NGOs are single-issue bodies that do not face the responsibility of weighing and balancing competing governmental goals.

The organization is much more transparent than was the previous GATT, but there is still a transparency deficit, and there is a feeling that further actions in that regard are needed.

The decision-making has often been characterized as leading to paralysis, most likely because of the consensus rule. This clearly needs more attention.

One of the mantras about the organization has been that it is a 'Member-driven organization', which has led to abuse and misuse by nation-state diplomat representatives against the WTO Secretariat, including even the Director-General.

The relative success, and indeed, the important power of the WTO dispute settlement system has led to certain fears and worries about an imbalance between that system and the non-dispute settlement portion of the WTO organization, namely the diplomatic and political side. This imbalance is arguably not sustainable in the long-run, and there needs to be some serious thought about that.

One could also see some concern about governmental and citizen attitudes towards the WTO, whether expressed in the context of NGOs or otherwise. There has been some harsh criticism in certain parts of the world, including inside the Washington DC beltway. Yet, one could wonder whether this criticism is somehow disconnected from reality, and a product of a certain cadre of 'policy advocates', whether professional or otherwise, who are being compensated for their sometimes unfair criticism. Nevertheless, there have been careful studies that have flagged some worries and criticisms, and there are a number of facets that should be considered.[9]

More on the optimistic side, however, is an extraordinary poll, published in the fall of 2004, by the Chicago Council on Foreign Relations, which is part of a series of such polls, carefully constructed by that organization. It notes quite a remarkable general public support for the WTO and its dispute settlement system.[10]

Another optimistic signal is the fact that in May and June, 2005, the U.S. Congress faced two important actions that were crucial to the further development and activity of the WTO, and in both cases, it has taken actions which support the WTO. The first of these was an action concerning the Trade Promotion Authority, which was the statute enacted by Congress in 2002, granting to the President certain authority necessary for effective US participation in negotiating the new round (the 'Doha Round'). The Statute also provided that if the President asked for a two-year extension of the authority, and if neither house of the Congress voted against it, that the negotiating authority would be extended to 30 June 2007. The President so requested, and in fact, the deadlines passed without any concrete action by Congress, and therefore, the Trade Promotion Authority has been extended.

Similarly, in the Uruguay Round Agreements Act of 1994, a particular clause[11] provided that every five years, after a report by the Administration on US participation in the WTO, any member of Congress could introduce a bill which, if accepted by both houses of Congress, would require withdrawal from the WTO. In June, the House of Representatives voted against such a proposal. The Senate never took up the matter. Thus, the usual ritual of the five-year review of US participation once again

[9] See Consultative Board Report, 'The Future of the WTO'. The World Bank, *Global Economic Prospects 2005: Trade, Regionalism and Development* (Washington, DC, 2004); United Nations Development Programme, *Human Development Report 2005: International Cooperation at a Crossroads* (New York, 2005).

[10] Sixty-nine per cent of the public and 85 per cent of the leaders say that, if the WTO rules against the United States on a complaint filed by another country, the United States should comply with that decision (*Global Views 2004* (Chicago Council on Foreign Relations, 2004), p. 33).

[11] Uruguay Round Agreements Act, Pub. L. No. 103-465, 102, 108 Stat. 4815, 19 USCA, section 3512(a)(1).

endorsed the continued participation by the United States in the WTO. No one thought that withdrawal was likely, although there was attention to the percentages of votes on each side.

III. The first decade of the WTO dispute settlement system

Overview

The WTO dispute settlement system, embodied in the Uruguay Round treaty text, particularly in the *Understanding on Rules and Procedures Governing the Settlement of Disputes* (DSU), is quite remarkable on a number of counts. It is a profound reform of the GATT dispute settlement system. The GATT system was also remarkable, in the sense that it grew over a period of its 47 provisional years, primarily by trial and error and experience, based on very brief treaty texts. The GATT system came to be admired, but it had a series of defects, some related to the fact that the GATT was never intended to be an organization.[12]

A critical problem with the GATT system was the application of the 'consensus rule' for a General Council 'adoption' of a dispute panel report. The consensus rule, in practice, meant that any government could defeat the consensus for adoption of a report, including the government that was found, in that case, to be acting inconsistently with its WTO obligations. This rule was changed during the Uruguay Round; the new system makes adoption of a panel report virtually automatic. But this new system led to concerns (on the part of the negotiators), about relying so heavily upon a panel, and thus, they determined to set up an appeals process, handled by a roster of seven Appellate Body members, who sit in groups of three. This dispute settlement system, in its worldwide application of a wide range of subject matters, and with its two-stage appeals process on all issues of law (not just defects in procedure or exceeding the scope of review or conflicts of interest) is unique today, as a matter of international law juridical activity, and is probably unique in all of world history. It is also remarkable that this system has been operating very effectively, and indeed, very powerfully.

A few statistics suggest some of the trends of the dispute settlement system's success. As of December 6, 2005, there have been 335 complaints

[12] See Jackson, *The World Trading System*; Jackson, *World Trade and the Law of GATT*; and John H. Jackson, William J. Davey, and Alan O. Sykes, *Legal Problems of International Economic Relations: Cases, Materials and Text on the National and International Regulation of Transnational Economic Relations* (4th edn, St Paul, 2002).

brought to the system. In general, it is considered that about half of the complaints brought never move to an actual panel, and thus, seem to be settled one way or another (or withdrawn). This is a good sign, because it suggests that there is a certain amount of predictability and security that allows litigants to face reality and decide not to go further. This seems also reflected in the history of appeals from the first level panels to the Appellate Body, which, on the whole, have been declining as a percentage of the number of First Level Panel reports.

The WTO dispute settlement system has now produced more than 30,000 pages of jurisprudence. This jurisprudence is elaborate, analytical, detailed, and has received high praise, albeit with some specific criticism of some particular cases. A number of intriguing cases have been put forward in this jurisprudence, such as the *US – Shrimp* case, which may be the most profound 'constitutional' case of the system. Other important cases include the *US – Section 301 Trade Act* case, the *US – Offset Act (Byrd Amendment)* case, the *US – Gambling* (Services) case, the *US – Zeroing (EC)* case, and two important cases concerning agricultural subsidies for cotton and sugar, which promise to have considerable influence in the negotiations going forward.

Of course, the record of compliance with the results of the dispute settlement system is of great significance, and the record of compliance is indeed quite good. No system is perfect, but in the WTO dispute settlement system, there is a very large percentage of cases for which there has been satisfactory compliance.[13] There are a number of very prominent and visible cases, however where the record of compliance has not been good, including *EC – Hormones, EC – Bananas III, US – Offset Act (Byrd Amendment)*, and anti-dumping rulings of a number of types. It has been observed that, generally speaking, when the United States can comply with a ruling by administrative action, without going to its Congress for a statutory change, it has done so. It is when the United States has tried to get Congress to change a law which has been held inconsistent with international obligations, that there has been some difficulty.

Policies of dispute settlement and the WTO

Article 3 of the DSU has a number of clauses that relate to underlying fundamental policy objectives of the dispute settlement system, including

[13] William J. Davey, 'The WTO Dispute Settlement System: The First Ten Years' (2005) 8 *Journal of International Economic Law* 1, 17–50.

'predictability and security', and 'prompt and effective settlement of disputes'. It should be noted that those two goals may conflict with each other somewhat, if it is felt that prompt completion of a juridical process might reduce the quality. In addition, Article 3.2 of the DSU admonishes the dispute settlement system not to 'add to or diminish rights or obligations' by a report. Clearly, that language is somewhat oblique and there is some argument that it basically has no meaning, although, in a broad brush, there is a viewpoint that it is deemed to be a precautionary admonition against 'judicial activism'.

In fact, when one analyzes carefully what are a variety of policy objectives and goals for an international dispute settlement system, one can list at least twelve or more goals. Some of those do not apply to the WTO system (for example, the WTO generally is perceived as not providing redress for past harms, thus providing no retroactivity as to damages or other measures). But in addition, various among these dozen or more goals, can either conflict with each other, or at least develop a certain tension, suggesting the need for balancing, or 'proportionality'. But these are subjects to be taken up in other works.[14]

One of the things that emerges quite strongly from a study of the WTO jurisprudence, both at the first level panel and appellate levels, is that it grapples in great depth (perhaps in greater depth than found in any other place), with the 'devilish detail' of the tensions between older concepts of nation-state sovereignty and predominance, compared to newer ideas of the need for international cooperation. Concepts such as the 'standard of review' focus on this, as do various methods of 'interpretation'. Concerning the latter, there is always a tension when interpretation goes so far as to be 'gap-filling' in a way that some would argue is 'legislating' or 'rule-making' instead of interpreting. There is even a doctrine that has been evoked in one case, and attempted as part of advocacy in several other cases in the WTO, which absurdly states that if there is any ambiguity, the acting nation state's actions should be deemed not inconsistent with the agreement. The doctrine is called *in dubio mitius* and it is largely discredited.

The system has now handled so many cases (as of December 2005, 102 First Level Panel reports and 62 Appellate Body Reports have been adopted) that in the last several years a great deal of activity has occurred at the 'post-judgment' phase of compliance. Here, the question becomes

[14] John H. Jackson, 'The Varied Policies of International Juridical Bodies – Reflections on Theory and Practice, Diversity or Cacophony: New Sources of Norms in International Law Symposium' (2004) 25 *Michigan Journal of International Law*, 869–878.

how the system can bring pressures or inducements to encourage nation-states to comply with the obligations as specified in the dispute settlement report concerning them. This is a major question, since some governments have taken the position that international law does not require them to take compliance measures, but may allow them instead to use alternative approaches, such as 'compensatory measures', generally meaning enduring trade barriers brought against them by the winning party. This position has been heavily criticized.[15]

One of the problems with the compliance measures, when they go so far as to result in 'retaliatory counter-measures' is that such counter-measures quite often affect innocent parties within the non-complying state society, who had no causal connection with the problems that gave rise to the judgment of inconsistency. Likewise, these 'retaliatory' measures are generally trade barriers themselves, which means that they go against the whole purpose of the WTO system – to reduce trade barriers.

The dispute settlement power is great enough to have created a considerable tension within the diplomatic and political processes, particularly in decision-making through other than dispute settlement system procedures. Some diplomats have made angry statements about this disparity in power between the activities they engage in, and those which the dispute settlement embraces. This has led to a belief (although not a widely held belief) that the dispute settlement power should be scaled back. The counter-opinion is that the solution is not to reduce the power of the dispute settlement system, but instead to enhance the power of the other processes, including the decision-making, diplomatic and political activities of the organization.

Appraisal

Among the diplomatic community and nation-state governments, there generally seems to be broad satisfaction with the dispute settlement system, such that there is some opinion that the key in relation to thinking about possible reforms of the system is to 'do no harm'. Some proposals, as mentioned above, would weaken the dispute settlement process, and thus, would in fact do harm to the credibility and predictability of the system as it now exists.

[15] See John H. Jackson, 'Editorial Comment: International Law Status of WTO DS Reports: Obligation to Comply or Option to "Buy-Out"?' (2004) 98 *American Journal of International Law*, 109–125; Consultative Board Report, 'The Future of the WTO', p. 54.

But clearly, there are some criticisms and challenges that need to be taken into account in thinking and appraising the dispute settlement system of the WTO. Some of these criticisms have been expressed in exceedingly negative terms, and in most cases, go too far and are not balanced in the sense of trying to weigh some of the goals and objectives of a dispute settlement system which may have some tensions between them. Much of the negative criticism of the dispute settlement system actually occurs in the United States, specifically in the Washington, D.C., area, and almost no place else in the world. This criticism, as noted above, seems to be centred on a small group of persons who are advocates (lawyers and otherwise), and so may not have full credibility. It appears that this negative approach is relatively rare in any place else in the world.

What are some of the problems that do need addressing?

One of those important issues to address is treaty interpretation and, particularly, the interpretation approach of the *Vienna Convention.* It can be argued that this approach sometimes leads to rather extreme textualism towards treaty interpretation and that this textualism is not well suited to the large multilateral and complex treaties, particularly given the problem of treaty rigidity (inability to amend). Instead, it could be argued that the approach that would more likely fulfil the longer term objectives of viability of an international institution by embracing interpretive concepts, including 'evolutionary interpretation', and 'teleological interpretation' would be superior. Maybe those ideas could be read into the ambiguity of the *Vienna Convention.* However, the history of the WTO Appellate Body, at least in its earlier years, has been that that body has manifested a desire for, and actually practiced, a very textual approach. It has been argued that such an approach was wise at the beginning of a new juridical institution, as a way to establish credibility of such institution. Even if that is so, perhaps it is time, and the maturity of the Appellate Body system now warrants, a moderation of that extreme textualism.[16]

Another issue that has been discussed quite a bit is the 'precedent effect' of cases. Clearly, the strict form of precedent known as *stare decisis* does not generally apply to international institutions including the WTO, nevertheless, there exists obvious desire for a certain amount of uniformity in the case decisions. But sometimes it can be difficult to strike the

[16] See Claus-Dieter Ehlermann, 'Reflections on the Appellate Body of the World Trade Organization' (2003) 97 *American Society of International Law, Proceedings*, 77–86.

appropriate balance. There has been considerable criticism even among those in favour of the WTO dispute settlement system, that the Appellate Body and first level panels have somehow gone down the wrong track with respect to the safeguards provisions of the Uruguay Round texts. This is because the Appellate Body and other rulings call for reconciling the new safeguards text of the Uruguay Round Treaty, with the old text of the Article XIX of the GATT 1994 (the so-called 'Escape Clause'), when a conflict rule, as well as the context of negotiating the new safeguards text, would reasonably suggest that the intent of the negotiators was to have the new text trump some parts of the old text. Nevertheless, prior WTO dispute settlement (and GATT) cases are very often cited in later WTO dispute settlement cases. In the *US – Steel Safeguards* dispute,[17] the first level panel report contains 5,800 footnotes, most of which cite to prior WTO cases!

Interpretation is an extraordinarily complex question, and much very thoughtful literature and scholarly opinion, as well as experienced practitioner opinion exists about it. One particularly interesting recent book by a justice of the Supreme Court of Israel, entitled *Purposive Interpretation*,[18] sets forth some powerful policy arguments about interpretive techniques that seem more tuned to long-term goals of certain kinds of legal documents than might be considered to have been the result of some Appellate Body opinions, which seem to focus more than necessary on the text itself as opposed to accommodating strongly understood basic goals of an institution.

Some of this focus on the text could be attributed to an idea of 'original intent' of the draft persons (although international law tends to downplay 'preparatory work' as a source for interpretation).

IV. Conclusion

There is very little doubt in this author's mind that the first eleven years (and hopefully beyond) of the new dispute settlement system of the WTO, which prominently features a very elaborate appellate process, is deserving of very high praise. One can say that, without being willing to endorse every single decision that has come out of that system, but in broad brush, there is very much of the 30,000 plus pages of jurisprudence to admire. It is a remarkable juridical procedure. The Appellate Body and dispute

[17] Appellate Body Report, *US – Steel Safeguards*; Panel Report, *US – Steel Safeguards*.

[18] Aharon Barak, *Purposive Interpretation in Law* (Princeton, 2005).

settlement jurisprudence is all the more deserving of praise in the light of the landscape and context set forth in the sections I and II of this chapter, which certainly have elements that make the role of the juridical body more difficult. It is certainly fitting to pay tribute to the dispute settlement system of the WTO as such, but of course, especially to the participants in that system, including all of those persons who have served with great diligence and responsibility, as Appellate Body members. Often that service was given in the context of substantial detriment to the particular Appellate Body members, not only in terms of economic compensation, but in terms of family life and the aggravation of travel, as well as very long hours of deliberation and drafting. They deserve much credit.

4

WTO dispute settlement practice 1995–2005: lessons from the past and future challenges

ERNST-ULRICH PETERSMANN

I. Lessons from the past

Most dispute settlement procedures of the *General Agreement on Tariffs and Trade* (GATT) and of the World Trade Organization (WTO) resulted from previous dispute settlement practices and were progressively codified (for instance, in 1966, 1979, 1982, 1989, and in 1994) in response to particular GATT and WTO legal problems.[1] The frequent use of 'constructive ambiguity' as a diplomatic method for facilitating political consensus on the conclusion of broadly framed GATT and WTO agreements, as well as the compulsory jurisdiction provided for in the WTO *Understanding on Rules and Procedures Governing the Settlement of Disputes* (DSU) as a means to 'clarify the existing provisions of those agreements in accordance with customary rules of interpretation of public international law' (Article 3.2 of the DSU), entail a far-reaching delegation of (quasi-)judicial powers to WTO dispute settlement bodies. Negotiating incomplete agreements and delegating the future clarification of contested treaty interpretations to an interdependent system of WTO dispute settlement bodies reduced bargaining costs and enhanced the effectiveness of collective bargaining. Yet, many WTO governments remain reluctant to admit the systemic consequences of this 'judicialization' of WTO rules for the future evolution of the 'member-driven' WTO system. Past WTO case-law confirms that the WTO jurisprudence of independent international judges may differ from the views of national trade officials.

Most trade diplomats continue to perceive the WTO as a separate trade regime that must remain focused on *national* interests, trade liberalization,

[1] See Ernst-Ulrich Petersmann, *The GATT/WTO Dispute Settlement System. International Law, International Organizations and Dispute Settlement* (The Hague, 1997).

and promotion of economic development through trade. WTO jurisprudence, by contrast, focuses on an 'objective assessment' of the *common* intentions of all 149 WTO Members and interprets WTO law as part of a broader international legal system that requires WTO Members to comply with all their international legal obligations in good faith. Both the *diplomatic national perspective* as well as the *quasi-judicial international perspective* differ from the *cosmopolitan* '*civil society perspective*' that is increasingly voiced by non-governmental organizations (NGOs), (inter)parliamentary meetings (for instance, during WTO Ministerial Conferences) and in *amicus curiae* submissions to WTO dispute settlement bodies. This is the case, for instance, when NGOs question the legitimacy of power-oriented, producer-driven economic regulation in the WTO (such as trade-distorting restrictions and export subsidies for cotton and sugar), the lack of constitutional safeguards for transparent, democratic rule-making in the WTO, or the one-sided focus in WTO negotiations on producer welfare rather than on general consumer welfare.[2] Transparent 'governance by discussion' with civil society, and independent judicial review of compliance with WTO rules, may not only enhance the democratic support and effectiveness of WTO rules by limiting power-oriented trade policies. Public discussion of some of the legal controversies that are bound to arise in future WTO jurisprudence may also assist the political and (quasi-)judicial WTO bodies in the future clarification of the often contested meaning of WTO rights and obligations, and may help parliaments and civil society to better understand WTO rules and policies.

1. *Lacunae in WTO law and lack of legal guidance by WTO Members*

The more than 340 disputes filed under the WTO DSU since 1995, and the so far more than 200 WTO dispute settlement findings (in more than 110 panel reports, 70 appellate reports, 20 arbitration awards, 15 compliance panel reports, and other dispute settlement findings), have revealed a number of shortcomings of the WTO dispute settlement system.[3] In some instances, WTO dispute settlement bodies felt compelled to fill

[2] See the contributions by members of the European Parliament and the United States Congress in Ernst-Ulrich Petersmann (ed.), *Reforming the World Trading System. Legitimacy, Efficiency, Democratic Governance* (Oxford, 2005).

[3] For systematic analyses of GATT and WTO jurisprudence, see Ernst-Ulrich Petersmann (ed.), *International Trade Law and the GATT/WTO Dispute Settlement System* (London, The Hague, 1997); and Federico Ortino and Ernst-Ulrich Petersmann (eds), *The WTO Dispute Settlement System 1995–2003* (The Hague, 2004).

'gaps' in WTO dispute settlement procedures (for instance, regarding burden of proof, preliminary rulings, due process of law) by resorting to general principles of national or international law. Some shortcomings – such as the 'sequencing problem' resulting from certain inconsistencies between Articles 21 to 23 of the DSU[4] – have been dealt with in the WTO negotiations, since 1997, on the review of, and further improvements to, the WTO dispute settlement procedures as well as by ad hoc arrangements among WTO Members. Even though WTO Members have (so far) submitted more than sixty proposals for additional reforms of the WTO dispute settlement system, it appears likely that WTO Members will continue to develop the DSU only very prudently and without radical reforms.[5] Other shortcomings have been dealt with in the increasing number of regional trade agreements (RTAs) and regional dispute settlement mechanisms among WTO Members,[6] as well as in the 1999 Agreement among WTO Members establishing the Advisory Centre on WTO Law, which aims at assisting less-developed countries (LDCs) in using WTO dispute settlement procedures more effectively.[7] The WTO Dispute Settlement Body (DSB) has so far never decided *not* to adopt a panel or Appellate Body report (under Articles 16 and 17 of the DSU), notwithstanding the widespread criticism by WTO Members of certain dispute settlement findings.[8] Nor have the WTO Ministerial Conference

[4] The 'sequencing problem' results from the fact that the time periods prescribed in Articles 22.2 and 22.6 of the DSU for the authorization of countermeasures (namely, thirty to sixty days after the expiry of the reasonable period of time) are not sufficient to complete the compliance review procedure under Article 21.5 (namely, 90 days for the panel plus possible appeal). The requirement in Article 23 of the DSU (namely, that WTO Members follow the procedures of both Articles 21 and 22 without unilateral determination of a violation of WTO obligations and of nullification of benefits under WTO law) could not be complied with in WTO practice without an additional agreement as to how to make these time-periods mutually coherent.

[5] The numerous reform proposals are analyzed in Ortino and Petersmann, *WTO Dispute Settlement System*, chapters 1–12.

[6] See for instance, Ernst-Ulrich Petersmann and Mark Pollack (eds), *Transatlantic Economic Disputes. The EU, the United States and the WTO* (Oxford, 2003); Julio Lacarte and Jaime Granados (eds), *Inter-Governmental Dispute Settlement: Multilateral and Regional Approaches* (London, 2004); Locknie Hsu, 'Dispute Settlement Systems in Recent Free Trade Agreements of Singapore' (2003) 4 *Journal of World Investment*, 277–314.

[7] See Frieder Roessler, 'Special and Differential Treatment of Developing Countries under the WTO Dispute Settlement System', in Ortino and Petersmann, *WTO Dispute Settlement System*, pp. 87–90.

[8] For example, when the Appellate Body Reports in *Canada – Dairy (Article 21.5 – New Zealand and US)* and *Canada – Dairy (Article 21.5 – New Zealand and US II)* were discussed in the WTO DSB, many WTO Members criticized 'the new test that the Appellate

or the General Council adopted authoritative interpretations of WTO rules (under Article IX of the *Marrakesh Agreement Establishing the World Trade Organization* (*WTO Agreement*), for instance, in order to correct certain controversial legal interpretations (for instance, concerning the admissibility of *amicus curiae* briefs) by WTO dispute settlement bodies.[9] It also appears unlikely that WTO Members will reach consensus on overruling legal interpretations developed by WTO dispute settlement bodies (for instance, with respect to the 'zeroing methodology' for the calculation of dumping margins) as part of future Doha Round agreements. Since the entry into force of the *WTO Agreement* in 1995, WTO Members have accepted a dynamic, progressive development of WTO rules through WTO jurisprudence. There has been little guidance by the political bodies of the WTO as to what lessons could be drawn from this jurisprudence as well as from the frequent criticism by WTO Members of that jurisprudence, for instance criticism voiced in the DSB.

2. *Strengths and weaknesses of the WTO dispute settlement system*

The fact that most requests for consultations under the DSU are *not* submitted to third party adjudication by panels, and that requests for the establishment of a dispute settlement panel have been regularly granted

Body has read into the Agreement on Agriculture for the purpose of determining whether a 'payment' existed under Article 9.1(c) . . . . Cost of production appeared nowhere in the text of the Agreement on Agriculture, nor was it clear why 'proper value', which itself was a term that did not appear in the Agreement on Agriculture, equated to cost of production . . . . It was odd that the WTO would not consider the market as being a good indicator of the value of goods' (WT/DSB/M/116, p. 70 (statement by the representative of the United States)). The panel finding, which had used both domestic market prices as well as world market prices as benchmarks for determining 'payments in kind', had been reversed by the Appellate Body without convincing arguments. 'The finding of the Appellate Body clearly went beyond the ordinary meaning of the words in the Agreement on Agriculture . . . The Appellate Body had failed a fundamental obligation of the treaty interpreter . . . The Appellate Body had clearly gone beyond what WTO Members agreed in the Uruguay Round negotiations' (WT/DSB/M/141, p. 4 (statement by the representative of Canada)).

[9] For example, when the WTO Appellate Body construed Articles 13 and 17 of the DSU as permitting unsolicited *amicus curiae* briefs by non-governmental organizations (NGOs), a special meeting of the WTO's General Council was convened and expressed strong criticism: 'The Appellate Body had unfortunately ignored the overwhelming sentiment of Members against acceptance of unsolicited *amicus curiae* briefs. By introducing this additional procedure, which amounted to soliciting *amicus curiae* briefs from NGOs, the Appellate Body had indicated that it wanted to go one step further in total disregard of the views of the overwhelming majority of the WTO Membership' (see WT/GC/M/60, statement by the representative of India).

by the DSB without undue delay, are signs of a functioning dispute settlement system. The increasing involvement of LDCs in WTO dispute settlement proceedings, the decreasing number of appeals from panel cases, and the relatively high record of implementation of WTO dispute settlement rulings within a 'reasonable period of time' (see Article 21 of the DSU) offer further evidence that the WTO dispute settlement system functions reasonably well. Most WTO Members share the view that the five phases of the WTO dispute settlement system – that is:

(i) consultations and political settlements of the complaint;
(ii) (quasi-)judicial panel proceedings aimed at resolving legal disputes;
(iii) appellate review of 'issues of law covered in the panel report and legal interpretations developed by the panel' (Article 17.6 of the DSU);
(iv) adoption of dispute settlement rulings and their implementation under the surveillance of the DSB; and
(v) the exceptional authorization of countermeasures in case of non-compliance with WTO dispute settlement findings –

do not require urgent reforms in view of the pragmatic improvements adopted in WTO dispute settlement practices (for instance ad hoc agreements on additional working procedures of panels, on transparency of panel proceedings, additional third party rights, the 'sequencing' of compliance panel procedures and authorization of countermeasures, resort to cross-retaliation by LDCs, financial compensation in case of non-compliance and continued violations of copyrights). The lack of agreement on an 'early harvest' in the Doha Round negotiations on DSU reforms (similar to the 1989 dispute settlement reforms during the Uruguay Round negotiations), and the 'member-driven bottom up approach' favoured by the current chairman (in 2005) of the Doha Round negotiations on further improvements to the DSU (in contrast to the much more assertive leadership by the chairman of the Uruguay Round negotiations on dispute settlement reforms), bear witness to this widely positive evaluation of the WTO dispute settlement system.

There is also broad agreement that the WTO dispute settlement procedures remain confronted with many weaknesses that may not be remedied in the Doha Round negotiations, for example because WTO Members are not ready to transform the WTO dispute settlement procedures into a more effective judicial system with more effective legal remedies (such as reparation of injury pursuant to the general international law rules on state responsibility for violations of international law). For instance:

Even though – due to their ad hoc selection for only one or a few dispute settlement panels and their inadequate remuneration – most WTO panelists are less and less familiar with the more than two hundred WTO dispute settlement reports, and their 'legal autonomy' and independence from the WTO Secretariat are no longer effectively secured,[10] WTO Members appear unwilling to replace the ad hoc dispute settlement panels (mainly composed of WTO diplomats) by a WTO Court of First Instance with more independent legal experts.

As WTO dispute settlement procedures may last more than 3 years – even in case of obviously illegal trade measures (like the European Communities' import restrictions on bananas and the United States' safeguard measures on steel) – until they actually lead to the termination of illegal trade measures or to sanctions following the expiry of the reasonable period of time, the dispute prevention function of the WTO dispute settlement procedures remains weak.

There is no provisional relief during WTO dispute settlement procedures.

Nor does the DSU provide for compensation for past harm suffered, or for reimbursement of the legal expenses of the winning party to the dispute.

LDCs often remain disadvantaged in WTO dispute settlement proceedings, for instance, due to the lack of legal and financial resources, the absence of specific legal rights (for instance, under the Generalized System of Preferences (GSP)) and of effective 'sanctioning potential'.

Although many intergovernmental WTO disputes (for instance, over private intellectual property rights and administrative trade restrictions) could be avoided by more effective domestic legal and judicial remedies, most WTO governments continue to prevent their respective domestic courts from applying WTO rules, from enforcing WTO dispute settlement findings, and from exercising more effective judicial control over trade policy-making.

[10] For example, at a WTO conference at Singapore's National University on 2 September 2005, Singapore's Ambassador Tommy Koh (who chaired several WTO dispute settlement panels) criticized the WTO practice of *not* paying a per diem to government officials serving as WTO panellists as 'ridiculous'.

3. Future challenges for WTO jurisprudence

These and other deficiencies of WTO dispute settlement procedures are among the many challenges confronting the future WTO dispute settlement practices. Only a few of them are likely to be addressed by WTO Members through agreements on further improvements to the WTO dispute settlement rules and procedures. Notwithstanding the separate track of the DSU reform negotiations in the Doha Round, there is a clear lack of leadership and of ambition in these 'member-driven negotiations'. Hence, the ultimate outcome may only be a pragmatic compromise on a few core proposals for reforms (for instance, on panel-composition, transparency, special and differential treatment of LDCs, enhanced third-party rights, accelerated time-frames for dispute settlement procedures involving safeguard measures, provision for remand procedures, clarification of the 'sequencing' issue, as well as new procedures for termination of retaliation authority).

Even if such improvements should prove possible in the Doha Round negotiations, WTO dispute settlement bodies will remain confronted with requests to clarify the often contested meaning of numerous other WTO rules. For example, as every international agreement remains incomplete, the 'judicial function' may require the clarification of 'gaps' in WTO dispute settlement procedures if that should prove necessary 'to preserve the rights and obligations of Members under the covered agreements', without 'add(ing) to or diminish(ing) the rights and obligations provided in the covered agreements' (Article 3.2 of the DSU). Section II of this chapter focuses on the following challenges for future WTO judges:

(i) The increasing importance of contextual and functional methods of international treaty interpretation and the controversies about the relevance of non-WTO rules of international law for interpreting WTO rules (see section II.1 below).
(ii) The legal obligation of all WTO Members to comply with all their international legal obligations in good faith; the limited jurisdiction of WTO dispute settlement bodies; the limited scope of applicable rules of international law in WTO dispute settlement proceedings; and the increasing judicial clarification of 'the basic principles . . . underlying this multilateral trading system' (Preamble to the *WTO Agreement*) as a potentially open-ended source of WTO law to be clarified through WTO practice, notably so as to ensure 'procedural due process of law', 'security and predictability to the multilateral trading system' (Article 3 of the DSU) (see section II.2 below).

(iii) The legitimate role of WTO judges in diverse areas of the WTO legal system (for instance regarding trade in goods, trade in services, and intellectual property rights), questions of 'judicial policy' and of 'judicial restraint' vis-à-vis other WTO bodies and WTO Members, judicial independence, judicial 'balancing' of market access rights with WTO provisions protecting non-economic policies, and cooperation among international judges and courts (see section II.3).

Like in any other system of separation of powers and 'checks and balances' among legislative, administrative, and judicial governance institutions, it is important for the future evolution of the WTO dispute settlement system that the WTO's rule-making bodies (in particular the WTO Ministerial Conference and the WTO General Council), administrative bodies (for instance the WTO Secretariat) and also 'civil society' continue to scrutinize – and, if necessary, criticize – future legal findings of WTO panels, the Appellate Body and WTO arbitrators. Such 'deliberative politics' and 'governance by discussion' offer democratic methods of gradually improving WTO rules, and may also strengthen political support by 'cosmopolitan constituencies' (to use a term by Pascal Lamy) for the rules-based world trading system.

4. *WTO jurisprudence as an essential part of world trade governance: cui bono?*

In constitutional democracies as well as in the citizen-driven world trading system, legislative, administrative and judicial functions of governance should be conceived and designed as mutually complementary safeguards for the protection of rule of law, the rights of domestic citizens, and their general interests (for instance with respect to consumer welfare).[11] Such a citizen-oriented conception of the WTO objective of 'sustainable development' is, however, not shared by many trade diplomats and WTO governments which often perceive the WTO as a power-oriented instrument of advancing macro-economic growth and 'national interests' as defined by the respective rulers. As rule-making by consensus among 149 WTO Members is inevitably more difficult than agreement

[11] For an explanation of such a citizen-oriented 'constitutional approach' to international trade law see Ernst-Ulrich Petersmann, 'Multilevel Trade Governance in the WTO Requires Multilevel Constitutionalism', in Christian Joerges and Ernst-Ulrich Petersmann (eds), *Constitutionalism, Multilevel Trade Governance and Social Regulation* (Oxford, 2006), chapter 1.

among three panel or Appellate Body members on legal interpretations of WTO rules, it is misleading to lament that 'the (quasi-)judicial arm has proven already to be much stronger than the political arm of the WTO'.[12] The large number of international agreements concluded in the context of the WTO since 1995 – for instance, on the accession of more than 25 new WTO Members, liberalization and regulation of services, harmonization of accounting standards, 'waivers' from WTO obligations in order to promote public access to medicines, preferential treatment of LDCs, control of trade in 'conflict diamonds' – and the enormous administrative work in the WTO's numerous negotiating and administrative bodies (like the Trade Policy Review Mechanism), bear witness to the multiple activities of the WTO's political, administrative, and rule-making bodies.

Both 'member-driven rule-making' and case-specific WTO jurisprudence are subject to constitutional limits in the *WTO Agreement* which confers only limited powers on the legislative, administrative, and (quasi)-judicial WTO bodies and asserts legal primacy over the multilateral agreements incorporated into the Annexes of the *WTO Agreement*, as well as over the domestic laws and regulations of WTO Members (see Article XVI of the *WTO Agreement*).[13] It appears legitimate that several recent WTO disputes (such as *US – Upland Cotton*, *EC – Export Subsidies on Sugar*, *EC – Approval and Marketing of Biotech Products*, and *EC – Geographical Indications*) pursued not only the settlement of bilateral disputes, but also the clarification of WTO obligations in order to improve bargaining positions (for instance those of cotton and sugar-exporting countries) in the Doha Round of multilateral trade negotiations.[14] The more trade negotiators perceive WTO negotiations and WTO dispute

[12] Claus-Dieter Ehlermann, 'Six Years on the Bench of the "World Trade Court": Some Personal Experiences as Member of the Appellate Body of the WTO', in Ortino and Petersmann, *WTO Dispute Settlement System*, pp. 499 and 527.

[13] On the different constitutional, legislative, administrative and (quasi-)judicial functions of the WTO see Ernst-Ulrich Petersmann, 'From "member-driven governance" to constitutionally limited "multilevel trade governance" in the WTO', in Giorgio Sacerdoti, Alan Yanovich, and Jan Bohanes (eds), *The WTO at Ten: The Contribution of the Dispute Settlement System* (Cambridge, 2006), chapter 7.

[14] For detailed empirical evidence that many of the more than 45 WTO dispute settlement panels involving agricultural, fishery, or forestry products have been established over the preceding years with a view to improving the bargaining power of the complaining countries in WTO negotiations and progressively developing WTO rules through agreed WTO dispute settlement rulings, see Ernst-Ulrich Petersmann, 'Strategic Use of WTO Dispute Settlement Proceedings for Advancing WTO Negotiations on Agriculture', in Petersmann, *Reforming the World Trading System*, pp. 127–144.

settlement proceedings as complementary tools for the progressive development of WTO rules, the more WTO dispute settlement bodies should limit their case-specific legal interpretations with caution and circumspection, and the stronger the need for clearer guidance by WTO Members as well as by public discussions on the many 'principled problems' that will continue to challenge WTO jurisprudence and its political acceptability by governments and civil society.

II. Some 'principled challenges' for future WTO jurisprudence

1. *Treaty interpretation as a 'holistic task'*

According to Article 3.2 of the DSU, the 'dispute settlement system of the WTO . . . serves to preserve the rights and obligations of Members under the covered agreements, and to clarify the existing provisions of those agreements in accordance with customary rules of interpretation of public international law.' The Appellate Body used its first two reports to clarify that the rules of interpretation of public international law laid down in Articles 31 and 32 of the *Vienna Convention on the Law of Treaties*[15] (*Vienna Convention*) have 'attained the status of a rule of customary or general international law.'[16] Throughout its jurisprudence, the Appellate Body has increasingly acknowledged that the requirement in Article 31 of the *Vienna Convention* – that is, that 'a Treaty shall be interpreted in good faith in accordance with the ordinary meaning to be given to the terms of the treaty in their context and in the light of its object and purpose' – constitutes 'one holistic rule',[17] whose different elements (text, context, object and purpose) may be difficult to separate:

> Interpretation pursuant to the customary rules codified in Article 31 of the *Vienna Convention* is ultimately a holistic exercise that should not be mechanically subdivided into rigid components.[18]

(a) Limits of textual interpretation

The Appellate Body reads Article 31 of the *Vienna Convention* as requiring a certain sequence in the interpretative process and a legal

[15] Done at Vienna, 23 May 1969, in force 27 January 1980, 1155 UNTS 331; 8 International Legal Materials 679, UKTS (1980) 58.

[16] Appellate Body Report, *US – Gasoline*, p. 17, DSR 1996:I, 3, 16; Appellate Body Report, *Japan – Alcoholic Beverages II*, p. 10, DSR 1996:I, 97, 104.

[17] Panel Report, *US – Section 301 Trade Act*, para. 7.22.

[18] Appellate Body Report, *EC – Chicken Cuts*, para. 176.

hierarchy to be given to the text of the particular provision to be interpreted:

> A treaty interpreter must begin with, and focus upon, the text of the particular provision to be interpreted. It is in the words constituting that provision, read in their context, that the object and purpose of the states parties to the treaty must first be sought. Where the meaning imparted by the text itself is equivocal or inconclusive, or where confirmation of the correctness of the reading of the text itself is desired, light from the object and purpose of the treaty as a whole may usefully be sought.[19]

The frequent recourse to dictionaries in the Appellate Body's reports has prompted some observers to criticize that the *Shorter Oxford Dictionary* has become one of the 'covered agreements', and that the greater weight attached to 'the ordinary meaning of the terms of the treaty' than to the 'context' and 'purpose' of the treaty reflects an unwillingness by the Appellate Body 'to situate its legal analyses within a framework which firmly articulates both the normative and policy considerations and consequences of its decisions.'[20] Other commentators have welcomed the Appellate Body's rigorous textual interpretation as 'providing security and predictability to the multilateral trading system' (Article 3.2 of the DSU, first sentence) and as protecting WTO jurisprudence from criticism that dispute settlement findings 'add to or diminish the rights and obligations provided in the covered agreements' (Article 3.2, third sentence). WTO jurisprudence seems to confirm that the results of literal interpretation have been more easily acceptable for WTO Members than other legal interpretations based on functional arguments (such as the need to 'complete the analysis') or contextual arguments (such as multilateral environmental agreements accepted by *some* WTO Members only). Yet, in *US – Gambling*, the Appellate Body itself acknowledged that 'dictionaries alone are not necessarily capable of resolving complex questions of interpretation, as they typically aim to catalogue *all*

[19] Appellate Body Report, *US – Shrimp*, para. 114.

[20] See Henrik Horn and Joseph Weiler, 'European Communities – Trade Description of Sardines: Textualism and its Discontent', in Henrik Horn and Petros C. Mavroidis (eds), *The WTO Case Law of 2002* (Washington, 2005), pp. 248–275. For example, from a systematic and functional perspective, the Appellate Body's literal and 'evolutionary' interpretation of 'exhaustible natural resources' (Article XX(g) of the GATT 1994) as including animals (Appellate Body Report, *US – Shrimp*, para.128) may undermine the system of Article XX of the GATT 1994 (for instance , the 'necessity test' prescribed in Article XX(b) for the protection of 'animal or plant life or health').

meanings of words – be those meanings common or rare, universal or specialized.'[21]

According to the Appellate Body, 'the task of ascertaining the meaning of a treaty provision with respect to a specific requirement does not end once it has been determined that the text is silent on that requirement. Such silence does not exclude the possibility that the requirement was intended to be included by implication.'[22] An important corollary of the interpretative 'principle of effectiveness' is, according to the Appellate Body, 'that a treaty should be read as a whole, and, in particular, its sections and parts should be read as a whole.'[23]

(b) Increasing importance of contextual interpretation

The limits of textual interpretation became particularly evident in WTO disputes over the interpretation of tariff bindings under the GATT 1994 and of specific commitments under the *General Agreement on Trade in Services* (GATS). GATT tariff bindings and GATS commitments tend to be drafted unilaterally by the WTO Member concerned, on the basis of internationally agreed classification systems (like the *Convention on the Harmonized Commodity Description and Coding System* (*Harmonized System Convention*)), entered into force in 1988), before being incorporated into WTO law as an integral part of the multilateral WTO rules. The Appellate Body has clarified that

> the task of ascertaining the meaning of a concession in a Schedule, like the task of interpreting any other treaty text, involves identifying the *common intention* of Members, and is to be achieved by following the customary rules of interpretation of public international law, codified in Articles 31 and 32 of the *Vienna Convention*.[24]

Yet, GATT and WTO jurisprudence has recognized long since that GATT schedules on tariff bindings may have to be construed with due regard to the Harmonized Commodity Description and Coding System (Harmonized System) and its Explanatory Notes.[25] As the *Harmonized System Convention* itself has not been ratified by all WTO Members, this Convention does not qualify as an 'agreement' and 'context' in the

[21] Appellate Body Report, *US – Gambling*, para. 164.
[22] Appellate Body Report, *US – Carbon Steel*, para. 65.
[23] Appellate Body Report, *Korea – Dairy*, para. 81.
[24] Appellate Body Report, *US – Gambling*, para. 159.
[25] See Appellate Body Report, *EC – Computer Equipment*, and Appellate Body Report, *EC – Chicken Cuts*.

sense of Article 31.2(a). The Appellate Body acknowledged, however, that the broad consensus among GATT Contracting Parties to use the Harmonized System as the basis for their WTO Schedules of Tariff Commitments constitutes an 'agreement' and 'context' (within the meaning of Article 31.2(a) of the *Vienna Convention*) for the purpose of interpreting tariff commitments in the WTO Members' Schedules.[26] In *Mexico – Telecoms* and *US – Gambling*, the WTO panels also referred to the 'Services Sector Classification List' and the 1993 'Scheduling Guidelines' as interpretative tools, even though these documents had been prepared by the GATT Secretariat rather than by the parties to the negotiations. Regarding the interpretation of GATS Schedules of Specific Commitments, the Appellate Body reversed the panel's findings in *US – Gambling* that the 'Services Sectoral Classification List' (GATT document W/120) and the '1993 Scheduling Guidelines' were 'context' for the interpretation of GATS Schedules of commitments: 'We do not accept, as the Panel appears to have done, that, simply by requesting the preparation and circulation of these documents and using them in preparing their offers, the parties in the negotiations have accepted them as agreements or instruments related to the treaty.'[27]

(c) Interpretative guidance by subsequent practice and 'relevant rules of international law applicable in the relations between the parties' (Article 31.3 of the *Vienna Convention*)

Just as future WTO jurisprudence will have to define more precisely the scope of 'context' (for instance, the delimitation between paragraphs (a) and (b) of Article 31.2 of the *Vienna Convention*), so has the interpretative relevance of subsequent agreements and other 'relevant rules of international law applicable in the relations between the parties' (Article 31.3 of the *Vienna Convention*) assumed increasing importance in WTO dispute settlement proceedings. Whereas most WTO Members perceive WTO law as a separate trade regime with limited trade policy competences, WTO dispute settlement bodies are increasingly confronted with legal claims and arguments that WTO law must be interpreted and applied as part of a broader international legal system. In *US – Shrimp*, the legal interpretations by the Appellate Body were influenced by its finding that the 'contemporary concerns of the community of nations

[26] Appellate Body Report, *EC – Chicken Cuts*, para. 199.
[27] Appellate Body Report, *US – Gambling*, para. 176.

about the protection and conservation of the environment' needed to be taken into account.[28] In the pending WTO dispute settlement proceedings regarding the European Communities' import restrictions for genetically modified organisms (GMOs), the European Communities referred to this interpretative principle in support of the European Communities' claim that WTO rules (for instance, on 'like products' and labelling requirements) must be construed with due regard to the United Nations Convention on Biodiversity, the UN Cartagena Protocol on Living Modified Organisms, and the right under general international law to take precautionary measures.[29] Yet, can the interpretation of WTO rules be guided by international law rules that have not been accepted by all WTO Members? Does the limited dispute settlement function permit WTO dispute settlement panels taking into account rules of international law that, even though not accepted by all WTO Members, have been accepted by all the parties to the dispute concerned?[30]

Already in its first report in *US – Gasoline*, the Appellate Body noted that the DSU requirement to interpret the covered agreements 'in accordance with customary rules of interpretation of public international law' (Article 3.2 of the DSU) 'reflects a measure of recognition that the General Agreement is not to be read in clinical isolation from public international law.'[31] Notably the WTO's *Agreement on Technical Barriers to Trade* (*TBT Agreement*), *Agreement on the Application of Sanitary and Phytosanitary Measures* (*SPS Agreement*), GATS, GATS schedules of 'specific commitments' (Articles XV-XX of the GATS), and the *Agreement on Trade-Related Aspects of Intellectual Property Rights* (*TRIPS Agreement*) include numerous references to international agreements concluded outside the WTO, such as rules adopted by international standardizing bodies (Article 5 of the *TBT Agreement*), 'international systems for conformity assessment' (Article 9 of the *TBT Agreement*), international agreements related to technical regulations (Article 10 of the *TBT Agreement*), the International

[28] Appellate Body Report, *US – Shrimp*, para.129.

[29] See Ernst-Ulrich Petersmann, 'The WTO Dispute over Genetically Modified Organisms: Interface Problems of International Trade Law, Environmental and Biotechnology Law', in Francesco Francioni and Tullio Scovazzi (eds), *Biotechnology and International Law* (Oxford, 2006), pp. 173–200.

[30] The *Vienna Convention* uses the term 'party' in the sense of contracting party rather than 'party to a dispute'. Yet, as Article 31.2(a) of the *Vienna Convention* speaks of 'all parties', and Article 31.2(b) of 'one or more parties', the mere reference to 'parties' in Article 31.3(c) could be construed as referring to several, but not necessarily all the parties of the agreement concerned.

[31] Appellate Body Report, *US – Gasoline*, p. 17, DSR 1996:I, 3, 16.

Plant Protection Convention and other international (phyto)sanitary standards (Article 3 of the *SPS Agreement*), international air transport, telecommunications and other agreements regulating international services, and intellectual property agreements negotiated in the context of the World Intellectual Property Organization. The number of WTO dispute settlement reports referring to public international law rules and principles, including general principles of law (for instance, on burden of proof, good faith, due process of law, and *jura novit curia*), continues to increase steadily, both with regard to questions of procedural law as well as regarding substantive rights and obligations of WTO Members.

WTO jurisprudence distinguishes between 'factual references' to international agreements as part of the 'objective assessment of the facts of the case' (Article 11 of the DSU), and use of international agreements as applicable law. In *US – Shrimp (Article 21.5 – Malaysia)*, for example, the Appellate Body found that,

> to avoid 'arbitrary or unjustifiable discrimination', the United States had to provide all exporting countries 'similar opportunities to negotiate' an international agreement. Given ... the decided preference for multilateral approaches voiced by WTO Members and others in the international community in various international agreements for the protection and conservation of endangered sea turtles . . ., the United States, in our view, would be expected to make good faith efforts to reach international agreements that are comparable from one forum of negotiation to the other .... The Panel rightly used the Inter-American Convention as a factual reference in this exercise of comparison . . . The mere use by the Panel of the Inter-American Convention as a basis for a comparison did not transform the Inter-American Convention into a 'legal standard'. Furthermore, although the Panel could have chosen a more appropriate word than 'benchmark' to express its view, Malaysia is mistaken in equating the mere use of the word 'benchmark', as it was used by the Panel, with the establishment of a legal standard.[32]

Similarly, in the interpretation of the term 'conservation of exhaustible natural resources' in Article XX(g) of the GATT 1994, the Appellate Body referred to other international agreements as evidence of facts rather than as applicable legal standards:

> From the perspective embodied in the preamble of the WTO Agreement, we note that the generic term 'natural resources' in Article XX(g) is not

[32] Appellate Body Report, *US – Shrimp (Article 21.5 – Malaysia)*, paras. 122 and 130. This quotation appears to use the term 'legal standard' as a description for the legal result which the United States should have achieved by negotiations, rather than as a description of the 'applicable law' in this dispute.

> 'static' in its content or reference but is rather 'by definition, evolutionary.' It is, therefore, pertinent to note that modern international conventions and declarations make frequent references to natural resources as embracing both living and non-living resources . . .[33]

This 'evolutionary interpretation' of Article XX(g) of the GATT 1994 as being applicable also to 'living resources' (such as sea turtles) implied that the stricter 'necessity requirement' (in Article XX(b) of the GATT 1994) for measures protecting 'animal or plant life or health' was effectively replaced by the looser 'relating to' requirement (in Article XX(g) of the GATT 1994) – without any convincing explanation or need in view of the increasingly flexible, judicial interpretation of the term 'necessary' as referring to 'a range of degrees of necessity.'[34] This example of 'judicial rule-making' illustrates the potential dangers of 'creative jurisprudence' (ab)using the potential universe of contextual, interpretative arguments in an 'eclectic' manner. In *EC – Chicken Cuts*, the relationship between the variety of contextual interpretative arguments likewise remained unclear: even though the Appellate Body could not classify the *Harmonized System Convention* as 'relevant rules of international law applicable in the relations between the parties' (in the sense of Article 31.3(c) of the *Vienna Convention*) because several WTO Members never ratified this Convention, it interpreted the European Communities' tariff commitments in the context of the *Harmonized System Convention* and, arguably, reached the same interpretative results. Similarly, in *US – Gambling*, the Appellate Body reversed the panel's finding that the 'Services Sectoral Classification List' (document W/120) and the '1993 Scheduling Guidelines' could be used as context (in the sense of Article 31.2 of the *Vienna Convention*), but used the same documents as 'supplementary means of interpretation' (pursuant to Article 32(a) of the *Vienna Convention*) with essentially the same interpretative results.[35]

[33] Appellate Body Report, *US – Shrimp*, para. 130.

[34] See Appellate Body Report, *Korea – Various Measures on Beef*, para. 161: 'We believe that, as used in the context of Article XX(d), the reach of the word "necessary" is not limited to that which is "indispensable" or "of absolute necessity" or "inevitable" . . . . The term "necessary" refers, in our view, to a range of degrees of necessity. At one end of this continuum lies "necessary" taken to mean as "making a contribution to." We consider that a "necessary" measure is, in this continuum, located significantly closer to the pole of "indispensable" than to the opposite pole of simply "making a contribution to".'

[35] See Appellate Body Report, *US – Gambling*, para. 176 and footnote 210. The panel in *Mexico – Telecoms* had deliberately left open the legal question of whether the 1993 Scheduling Guidelines qualified as 'context' or as a 'supplementary means' of interpreting Mexico's GATS commitments: 'In any case, we consider that the source, content and use of

The factual and legal determination of 'relevant subsequent practice' for purposes of treaty interpretation pursuant to Article 31.3 of the *Vienna Convention* entails similar uncertainties. The Appellate Body found, in *Japan – Alcoholic Beverages II*, that 'subsequent practice' within the meaning of Article 31.3(b) requires a

> 'concordant, common and consistent' sequence of acts or pronouncements which is sufficient to establish a discernible pattern implying the agreement of the parties (to a treaty) regarding its interpretation.[36]

In *US – Gambling*, the Appellate Body clarified that establishing 'subsequent practice' within the meaning of Article 31.3(b) involves two elements:

> (i) there must be a common, consistent, discernible pattern of acts or pronouncements; and (ii) those acts or pronouncements must imply agreement on the interpretation of the relevant provision.[37]

In *EC – Chicken Cuts*, the Appellate Body shared

> the Panel's view that not each and every party must have engaged in a particular practice for it to qualify as a 'common' and 'concordant' practice. Nevertheless, practice by some but not all parties is obviously not of the same order as practice by only one, or very few parties. To our mind, it would be difficult to establish a 'concordant, common and discernible pattern' on the basis of acts or pronouncements of one, or very few parties to a multilateral treaty, such as the WTO Agreement. We acknowledge, however, that, if only some WTO Members have actually traded or classified products under a given heading, this circumstance may reduce the availability of such 'acts or pronouncements' for purposes of determining the existence of 'subsequent practice' within the meaning of Article 31(3)(b).[38]

Yet, in establishing agreement of parties that have not engaged in a particular trade practice,

> lack of reaction should not lightly, without further inquiry into attendant circumstances of a case, be read to imply agreement with an interpretation

Footnote 35 *(cont.)*
the Explanatory Note make it part of the "circumstances" of the conclusion of the GATS, within the meaning of Article 32 of the *Vienna Convention*. We may therefore properly have recourse to the Explanatory Note to confirm our understanding of the ordinary meaning of Article I:2(a) of the GATS' (Panel Report, *Mexico – Telecoms*, para. 7.44).

[36] Appellate Body Report, *Japan – Alcoholic Beverages II*, p. 13, DSR 1996:I, 97, 106.

[37] Appellate Body Report, *US – Gambling*, para. 192.

[38] Appellate Body Report, *EC – Chicken Cuts*, para. 259.

> by treaty parties that have not themselves engaged in a particular practice followed by other parties in the application of the treaty. This is all the more so because the interpretation of a treaty provision on the basis of subsequent practice is binding on all parties to the treaties, including those that have not actually engaged in such practice.[39]

In conclusion, contextual interpretation and judicial recourse to 'supplementary means of interpretation' – which, according to the Appellate Body, are not exhaustively defined in Article 32 of the *Vienna Convention*[40] – are neither mathematical nor mechanical methods of clarifying the contested meaning of WTO rules, but inevitably involve normative and functional considerations that call for strict 'constitutional checks and balances' in order to remain politically legitimate and acceptable. The less legislative guidance WTO Members give regarding the textual meaning and objectives of WTO rules, the broader remains the 'judicial margin of appreciation' of WTO dispute settlement bodies in the 'objective assessment of the matter before it' (Article 11 of the DSU), including the contested meaning and clarification of applicable WTO rules.

(d) The impact of 'object and purpose' on the 'ordinary meaning to be given to the terms of the treaty' and on the 'balancing' of rights and obligations

WTO jurisprudence increasingly attaches importance to the 'object and purpose' not only of specific WTO provisions, but also of the WTO agreements as a whole. In its first report on *US – Gasoline*, the Appellate Body underscored that 'the purpose and object of the introductory clauses of Article XX [of the GATT 1994] is generally the prevention of "abuse of the exceptions . . .". If those exceptions are not to be abused or misused, . . . the measures falling within the particular exceptions must be applied reasonably, with due regard both to the legal duties of the party claiming the exception and the legal rights of the other parties concerned.'[41] In *US – Shrimp*, the Appellate Body further clarified that the 'standards of the chapeau, in our view, project both substantive and procedural requirements'; 'the task of interpreting and applying the chapeau is . . . essentially the delicate one of locating and marking out a line of equilibrium between the right of a Member to invoke an exception under Article XX and the rights of the other Members under varying

[39] Ibid., para. 273. [40] Ibid., para. 283.

[41] Appellate Body Report, *US – Gasoline*, p. 22, DSR 1996: I, 3, 21.

substantive provisions (for example, Article XI) of the GATT 1994, so that neither of the competing rights will cancel out the other and thereby distort and nullify or impair the balance of rights and obligations constructed by the Members themselves in that Agreement.'[42] Similar to the longstanding GATT jurisprudence on 'non-violation complaints' protecting the balance of reciprocal GATT market access commitments, so the chapeau of Article XX 'embodies the recognition on the part of WTO Members of the need to maintain a balance of rights and obligations between the right of a Member to invoke one or another of the exceptions of Article XX, specified in paragraphs (a) to (j), on the one hand, and the substantive rights of the other Members under the GATT 1994, on the other hand.'[43]

A 'balancing test' is also applied in determining the 'necessity' of trade restrictions:

> [D]etermination of whether a measure, which is not 'indispensable', may nevertheless be 'necessary' within the contemplation of Article XX(d), involves in every case a process of weighing and balancing a series of factors which prominently include the contribution made by the compliance measure to the enforcement of the law or regulation at issue, the importance of the common interests or values protected by that law or regulation, and the accompanying impact of the law or regulation on imports or exports.[44]

In *EC – Asbestos*, the Appellate Body emphasized that

> [i]n this case, the objective pursued by the measure is the preservation of human life and health through the elimination, or reduction, of the well-known, and life-threatening, health risks posed by asbestos fibres. The value pursued is both vital and important in the highest degree. The remaining question, then, is whether there is an alternative measure that would achieve the same end and that is less restrictive of trade than a prohibition.[45]

In *US – Gambling*, the Appellate Body agreed with the panel that the WTO jurisprudence relating to Article XX of the GATT 1994 was relevant also for interpreting the general exceptions in Article XIV of the GATS, notably regarding the need for a 'two-tier analysis' of a measure that a

[42] Appellate Body Report, *US – Shrimp*, paras. 159–160.

[43] Ibid., paras. 156–157.

[44] Appellate Body Report, *Korea – Various Measures on Beef*, para. 164.

[45] Appellate Body Report, *EC – Asbestos*, para. 172.

Member seeks to justify under Article XIV of the GATS,[46] as well as the need for 'a process of weighing and balancing a series of factors' in the determination of the 'necessity' of restrictions for the protection of 'public morals' and 'public order.' The Appellate Body used, in *US – Gambling*, the following seven balancing factors, that is:

(i) the 'relative importance' of the interests or values furthered by the challenged measure;
(ii) the contribution of the measure to the realization of the ends pursued by it;
(iii) the restrictive impact of the measure on international commerce;
(iv) a comparison between the challenged measure and possible alternatives in the light of the importance of the interests at issue;
(v) the absence of another 'reasonably available', WTO-consistent alternative;
(vi) respect for the right of each WTO Member 'to achieve its desired level of protection with respect to the objective pursued under paragraph (a) of Article XIV'; and
(vii) a differentiated distribution of the burden of proof between the responding party invoking an affirmative defence (for instance, the respondent needs to establish a *prima facie* case that its measure is 'necessary' for the protection of public morals or public order) and the complaining country (which may have to prove the availability of a WTO-consistent alternative measure in 'the universe of less trade-restrictive alternative measures').[47]

This ever more complex 'process of weighing and balancing a series of factors' and of policy objectives in the judicial interpretation of WTO rules illustrates the increasing sophistication of the judicial standards for the review of trade restrictions. In *EC – Computer Equipment*, the Appellate Body clarified that 'the security and predictability of "the reciprocal and mutually advantageous arrangements directed to the substantial reduction of tariffs and other barriers to trade" is an object and

[46] Appellate Body Report, US – Gambling, para. 292, states:

> A panel should first determine whether the challenged measure falls within the scope of one of the paragraphs of Article XIV . . . . Where the challenged measure has been found to fall within one of the paragraphs of Article XIV, a panel should then consider whether that measure satisfies the requirements of the chapeau of Article XIV.

[47] On this 'process of weighing and balancing a series of factors' see Appellate Body Report, *US – Gambling*, paras. 305–311.

purpose of the *WTO Agreement*, generally, as well as of the GATT 1994.'[48] In *US – Gambling*, the Appellate Body agreed with the panel's findings that 'the importance of the security and predictability of Members' specific commitments . . . is equally an object and purpose of the GATS.'[49] In *EC – Chicken Cuts*, the Appellate Body further clarified that it

> is well accepted that the use of the singular word 'its' preceding the term 'object and purpose' in Article 31(1) of the *Vienna Convention* indicates that the term refers to the treaty as a whole . . . Thus, the term 'its object and purpose' makes it clear that the starting point for ascertaining 'object and purpose' is the treaty itself, in its entirety. At the same time, we do not believe that Article 31(1) excludes taking into account the object and purpose of particular treaty terms, if doing so assists the interpreter in determining the treaty's object and purpose on the whole. We do not see why it would be necessary to divorce a treaty's object and purpose from the object and purpose of specific treaty provisions, or *vice versa*. To the extent that one can speak of the 'object and purpose of a treaty provision', it will be informed by, and will be in consonance with, the object and purpose of the entire treaty of which it is but a component.[50]

The numerous difficulties of balancing the 'object and purpose of a treaty provision' with the 'object and purpose of the entire treaty' were illustrated by the Appellate Body's reversal – in *EC – Tariff Preferences* – of the panel's legal interpretations of the non-discrimination requirements under the 'Enabling Clause'. In response to India's challenge of the European Communities' GSP, the panel held that the term 'non-discriminatory' in the WTO's 'Enabling Clause' required 'that identical tariff preferences under GSP schemes be provided to all developing countries without differentiation, except for the implementation of *a priori* limitations' and preferential treatment for the least-developed among the LDCs.[51] On appeal, the Appellate Body recognized that 'Members' respective needs and concerns at different level of economic development may vary according to the different stages of development of different Members', hence:

'the term "non-discriminatory" . . . does not prohibit developed-country Members from granting different tariffs to products originating in different GSP beneficiaries, provided that . . . identical treatment is available to all similarly-situated GSP beneficiaries that have the

[48] Appellate Body Report, *EC – Computer Equipment*, para. 82.
[49] Appellate Body Report, *US – Gambling*, paras. 188–189.
[50] Appellate Body Report, *EC – Chicken Cuts*, para. 238.
[51] Panel Report, *EC – Tariff Preferences*, paras. 7.161 and 7.176.

"development, financial and trade needs" to which the treatment in question is intended to respond';[52]

the existence of a 'development, financial (or) trade must be assessed according to an objective standard';[53] and

'the particular need at issue must, by its nature, be such that it can be effectively addressed through tariff preferences', without imposing 'unjustifiable burdens on other Members'.[54]

In response to this important clarification of the development and non-discrimination objectives of the Enabling Clause, the European Communities adopted a new GSP system aimed at promoting 'sustainable development' by differentiating tariff preferences depending on whether LDCs have ratified and effectively implemented the major UN human rights conventions, International Labour Organization (ILO) conventions, UN environmental conventions, UN conventions on drugs, and the UN Convention Against Corruption.[55] If such 'objective standards' and development objectives should be challenged by LDCs, future WTO jurisprudence may have to clarify whether WTO rules and objectives (such as 'sustainable development', non-discriminatory treatment of LDCs) can justify differential tariff treatment depending on the compliance of LDCs with UN and ILO conventions. As the jurisdiction of WTO panels is limited to examining legal claims under the WTO covered agreements, WTO dispute settlement bodies should leave it to the WTO Members concerned to prove the existence of alleged violations of UN and ILO conventions (for instance, by invoking special dispute settlement procedures available under such conventions).

In *EC – Chicken Cuts*, the Appellate Body rightly cautioned 'against interpreting WTO law in the light of the purported 'object and purpose' of specific provisions, paragraphs or subparagraphs of the WTO agreements, or tariff headings in Schedules, in isolation from the object and purpose of the treaty as a whole.'[56] Yet, the various WTO objectives (such as 'the objective of sustainable development' proclaimed in the Preamble to the *WTO Agreement*) are so broad that divergent claims over their

[52] Appellate Body Report, *EC – Tariff Preferences*, paras. 173 and 190.

[53] Ibid., paras. 161–163. [54] Ibid., paras. 164–167.

[55] Council Regulation (EC) No. 980/2005 of June 2005 (OJ 2005 I 169/1). The European Communities' new GSP scheme for 2006–2015 was explicitly designed to reflect 'the integral nature of the concept of sustainable development' as defined by the Appellate Body, compare James Harrison, 'Incentives for Development: The EC's Generalized System of Preferences, India's WTO Challenge and Reform' (2005) 42 *Common Market Law Review*, 1663–1689.

[56] Appellate Body Report, *EC – Chicken Cuts*, para. 239.

interpretation appear inevitable. For example, is the judicial admission of *amicus curiae* briefs consistent with the intergovernmental structures of WTO rules? Should the 'sustainable development' objective be construed in accordance with the UN Declarations on the 'human right to development'?[57] Or should it be construed in accordance with the long tradition in economic thought (from Adam Smith via Friedrich Hayek up to Nobel Prize-winning economist Amartya Sen) that trade and economic development are only *instruments* for promoting individual freedom as the ultimate goal of economic life and the most efficient means of enhancing economic development?[58] Does the explicit recognition – for instance, in the *TRIPS Agreement* and in the 2001 Protocol on the Accession of China – of WTO obligations to protect private procedural rights, property rights and 'rights to trade', including 'the right to import and export goods',[59] confirm that WTO rules protect not only rights and obligations among WTO Members, but also legal 'security and predictability' for the benefit of private traders and other market participants? Or do the 'sovereignty' of WTO Members and the intergovernmental structures of WTO law exclude such citizen-oriented legal interpretations, unless explicitly accepted (for instance, by China in its accession protocol), as it seems to be implied in the Appellate Body's reversal of the panel's finding in *India – Patents (US)* 'that the legitimate expectations of Members and private rights holders concerning conditions of competition must always be taken into account in interpreting the *TRIPS Agreement*'?[60]

2. *Applicable law and limited jurisdiction of WTO dispute settlement bodies*

Many WTO Members appear to construe the limited terms of reference of WTO panels (see Article 7 of the DSU), and the specific prohibition of

[57] This has been argued by Robert Howse, 'Mainstreaming the Right to Development into International Trade Law and Policy at the WTO', UN Economic and Social Council (ECOSOC), E/CN.4/Sub.2/2004/17 (2004).

[58] On defining economic development not only in macroeconomic terms, but also in terms of individual decisional autonomy, individual 'immunity from encroachment', and substantive 'opportunity to achieve', see Amartya Sen, *Rationality and Freedom* (Cambridge, Mass., 2002), for instance, chapter 17 on 'markets and freedoms'; Friedrich A. Hayek, *The Constitution of Liberty* (London, 1960), p. 35: 'Economic considerations are merely those by which we reconcile and adjust our different purposes, none of which, in the last resort, are economic (except those of the miser or the man for whom making money has become an end in itself).

[59] This right is explicitly recognized in China's Accession Protocol, WT/L/432, Part I.5, p. 4.

[60] Appellate Body Report, *India – Patents (US)*, para. 45.

adding to or diminishing 'the rights and obligations provided in the covered agreements' (Articles 3.2 and 19.2 of the DSU), as implying that both legal claims as well as legal defences in WTO dispute settlement proceedings must be based on the WTO agreements, unless otherwise agreed. In case of such 'standard terms of reference', WTO dispute settlement bodies have no mandate to directly apply non-WTO rules of international law if such *direct application* (in contrast to the *interpretation* of WTO rules in conformity with 'any relevant rules of international law applicable in the relations between the parties' pursuant to Article 31.3(c) of the *Vienna Convention*) could result in 'add(ing) or diminish(ing) the rights and obligations provided in the covered agreements.'

The Appellate Body has, so far, not pronounced on the controversial legal question of whether non-WTO rules of international law may constitute not only relevant legal context for interpreting WTO rules (section II.2(a) below), but may also be *directly applicable* in WTO dispute settlement proceedings (sections II.2(b) and II.2(c) below). Professor Pauwelyn,[61] for instance, has claimed that:

notwithstanding the limited jurisdiction of WTO dispute settlement bodies for hearing only claims based on WTO law, general international law and non-WTO agreements may be directly applicable law in WTO dispute settlement proceedings;

non-WTO rules (such as human rights, environmental, and labour law) may therefore be used as legal defences in WTO dispute settlement proceedings; and

in view of their 'integral' compliance obligations vis-à-vis the community as a whole, such human rights, environmental, and labour law obligations of WTO Members may justify departures from reciprocal WTO obligations that may be modified bilaterally without permission of third WTO Members.

While it is undisputed that general international law applies to the conduct of states unless they have effectively 'contracted out of it', the consistency of Pauwelyn's broad interpretation of the jurisdiction and applicable law in WTO dispute settlement proceedings with the explicit limitation (for instance, in Articles 3, 7, 11, and 19 of the DSU) of the jurisdiction of WTO dispute settlement bodies to the 'covered agreements' remains contested in both WTO practice as well as in legal

[61] See Joost Pauwelyn, *Conflict of Norms in Public International Law. How WTO Rules Relate to Other Rules of International Law* (Cambridge, 2003).

literature.[62] Likewise, Pauwelyn's related views of WTO obligations as bilateral in nature and subject to mutually agreed *inter se* modifications, and of the higher legal rank of 'integral' *erga omnes* obligations under human rights law and environmental law, remain controversial (for instance, in view of the amendment procedures in Articles IX and X of the *WTO Agreement*, and the inconsistency of bilaterally agreed trade restrictions with the multilateral WTO objectives of non-discriminatory conditions of competition and trade).[63] Neither GATT and WTO practice nor UN practice have so far identified any concrete examples of conflicts between GATT/WTO rules, on the one hand and general international law, on the other hand (for instance, the universal human rights obligations of all WTO Members). Just as human rights guarantee not only individual rights but also general legal principles that must be mutually balanced in order to reconcile and optimize the diversity of constitutional rights, so may WTO rights and obligations also include general legal principles, as explicitly acknowledged in the Preamble and in other provisions of the *WTO Agreement*,[64] that may help WTO dispute settlement bodies in mutually reconciling and balancing WTO rights and obligations by resorting to 'general principles of WTO law', without pronouncing on the politically controversial question of 'direct applicability' of non-WTO law in WTO dispute settlement proceedings.

[62] See for instance the review and criticism of Pauwelyn's book by Joel Trachtman (2004) 98 *American Journal of International Law*, 855–861, and Gabrielle Marceau, 'WTO Dispute Settlement and Human Rights' (2002) 13 *European Journal of International Law*, 753–814.

[63] International law (see Article 41.1(b) of the *Vienna Convention*) permits *inter se* agreements among some of the parties to an international agreement only if they are consistent with the object and purpose of the agreement concerned. In GATT and WTO jurisprudence, bilaterally agreed departures from GATT and WTO rules protecting non-discriminatory conditions of competition are traditionally presumed to 'nullify or impair' competitive benefits to the detriment of third WTO Members. Human rights may have a higher constitutional rank in domestic laws and as part of international *ius cogens*. It is doubtful, however, whether UN human rights treaties can claim such a higher legal rank in international law with regard to other international treaties (like the *WTO Agreement*) that protect freedom, non-discrimination, rule of law and consumer welfare vis-à-vis discriminatory, welfare-reducing national restrictions. For, such 'human rights values' underlying WTO rules may be no less important than other human rights values that are invoked as justifying trade restrictions. WTO jurisprudence rightly insists on balancing the rights and obligations concerned with due respect for the diversity of national value systems (for instance 'public order' conceptions).

[64] On the today general recognition that every legal system consists not only of rules but also of more general principles, see Richard Dworkin, *Taking Rights Seriously* (Cambridge, Mass., 1978). On the recognition of almost 40 different 'principles' in WTO law and WTO jurisprudence see Götz J. Göttsche, *Die Anwendung von Rechtsprinzipien in der Spruchpraxis der WTO-Rechtsmittelinstanz* (Berlin, 2005). On the dual functions of human rights and other constitutional rights as rules, as well as principles for optimizing

The *WTO Agreement* sets out specific 'secondary rules' (for instance, about amendments of the 'primary' WTO rights and obligations, legal responsibility for breaches of WTO obligations) that claim priority over the secondary rules provided by general international law. Yet, no international treaty can function as a 'self-contained regime' (*lex specialis*) completely separated from general international law (for instance, from *pacta sunt servanda*, good faith interpretation of treaty rules, respect for 'sovereign equality', non-use of force, and other *ius cogens* rules of international law). For instance, in case of dissolution of a WTO Member party to a WTO dispute, the general international law rules on state succession and legal responsibility may be applicable to the claims made by or against the dissolved state. In numerous provisions of the *WTO Agreement*, all WTO Members have recognized that WTO law consists not only of specific treaty rights and obligations, but also of 'basic principles and . . . objectives underlying this multilateral trading system' (Preamble to the *WTO Agreement*).[65] Under the GATT 1947, these objectives and principles tended to be defined by economists and politicians without regard to international law. WTO jurisprudence, by contrast, has begun to identify the general international *legal principles* underlying:

the *procedural* WTO rules (like good faith interpretation, due process of law, transparency, prohibition of abuse of rights, and 'judicial economy');
the *substantive* WTO rules (like rule of law, legal security, most-favoured nation (MFN) treatment, and national treatment); and
the other 'relevant rules of international law applicable in the relations between the parties' to the *WTO Agreement* (like 'sovereign equality' of states, the duty to cooperate).

Legal 'principles' have proven to be increasingly important not only for promoting 'procedural justice' and due process of law in WTO dispute

rules depending on what is factually and legally possible in the particular circumstances, see Robert Alexy, *A Theory of Constitutional Rights* (Oxford, 2002), chapter 3.

65 Apart from the Preamble to the *WTO Agreement*, the term 'principle' is explicitly mentioned in numerous GATT provisions (for instance, Articles III, VII, X, XIII, XX, XXIX, and XXXVI of the GATT 1994) as well as other WTO provisions (for instance Article X of the GATS and Articles 7, 8, and 62 of the *TRIPS Agreement*) and WTO Ministerial Declarations. Whereas rules apply only to specific situations based on a clearly defined 'if-then-structure', principles are more open norms, applicable to many more factual situations and requiring the 'balancing' of diverse principles in order to concretise their legal relevance for the interpretation or supplementation of rules.

settlement proceedings (see section II.2(d) below); they may also legitimize and facilitate the mutual balancing of substantive WTO rules in order to maintain 'substantive justice' in WTO legal practices, notably regarding the scope of market access rights of WTO Members and the broad WTO exceptions protecting their sovereign rights to pursue non-economic objectives and policies (see section II.2(e) below). Recourse to such principles may help to adapt incomplete treaty rules to the dynamically changing trading practices and to avoid the dogmatic controversies about the limited scope of jurisdiction and direct applicability of non-WTO law in WTO dispute settlement proceedings.

(a) Interpretation and application of WTO law in conformity with other rules of international law

WTO law, like any other comprehensive rule-of-law system with compulsory jurisdiction for the peaceful settlement of disputes over the reciprocal rights and obligations and the contested interpretation of general rules, cannot accomplish many of its objectives (like 'providing security and predictability to the multilateral trading system', as set out in Article 3 of the DSU) without recourse to general legal principles, as explicitly recognized in numerous WTO provisions. Given that every WTO Member has to comply with all its international legal obligations in good faith, the application of certain WTO rules – such as the determination of a violation of a WTO obligation, or the task of the DSB to make dispute settlement 'recommendations and rulings . . . aimed at achieving a satisfactory settlement of the matter in accordance with the rights and obligations under this Understanding and under the covered agreements' (Article 3.4 of the DSU) – may require not only the *interpretation* of WTO rules taking into account 'any relevant rules of international law applicable in the relations between the parties' (Article 31.3(c) of the *Vienna Convention*) as well as 'common concerns' of WTO Members reflected in non-WTO legal instruments. Many WTO provisions (for instance, Article XXI of the GATT 1994 and Article XIV *bis* of the GATS regarding UN Charter obligations) also recognize the need for the *application* (for instance, by the political WTO bodies and the DSB) of non-WTO rules in order to enable WTO Members to comply with UN law and with their other international legal obligations. The numerous explicit requirements – in many areas of WTO law regulating trade in goods, services, and intellectual property rights – to respect multilateral international agreements concluded outside the WTO, and to 'monitor the process of international harmonization and coordinate efforts in this regard with the relevant international organizations (Article 3.5 of the *SPS Agreement*), confirm that WTO Members did not intend to apply WTO rules as a 'self-contained regime' without regard to their other obligations under international law. As every WTO Member has ratified the UN Charter, UN human rights conventions and other worldwide agreements (such as ILO conventions, the constitutive agreements of other worldwide organizations), the interpretation and application of WTO rules may be influenced by non-WTO rules and legal obligations under general international law. The WTO jurisprudence filling the numerous 'gaps' in WTO dispute settlement procedures often relies not only on the ordinary meaning of specific WTO provisions (for instance, Articles 11 and 17 of the DSU as a textual basis for the admissibility of *amicus curiae* submissions), but also on their declared objectives as a justification of the inherent powers of WTO dispute settlement bodies (for instance, inherent powers to adopt preliminary rulings, to open panel proceedings to the public with the consent of the parties to the dispute, as well as to extend third party rights at the request of the parties).

(b) Limited jurisdiction of WTO dispute settlement bodies

The question of interpreting WTO rules in conformity with non-WTO rules (section II.2(a) above) must be distinguished from questions concerning the limited coverage of the DSU (Article 1 of the DSU), the limited terms of references of WTO panels (Articles 7 and 19 of the DSU), of the Appellate Body (Articles 17 and 19 of the DSU) and of 'arbitration within the WTO' (Articles 21 to 25 of the DSU). It remains to be clarified to what extent this limited jurisdiction also limits the power of WTO dispute settlement bodies to directly apply non-WTO rules if one party, or all parties to a WTO dispute, require(s) such application of non-WTO rules. For example, can the limited power to adopt agreed 'special terms of reference' (for instance, under Articles 7.3 and 25.2 of the DSU) justify dispute settlement findings based on non-WTO rules? Would such dispute settlement findings 'add to or diminish the rights and obligations provided in the covered agreements' (which include rights under the DSU)? Would it run counter to the explicit task of WTO dispute settlement proceedings (for instance, to provide 'security and predictability to the multilateral trading system' and 'preserve the rights and obligations of Members under the covered agreements', as set out in Article 3.2 of the DSU) if the parties to the dispute requested a WTO panel to apply *inter se* agreements that supersede general WTO provisions among the parties to the dispute? Do the standard terms of reference (Article 7.1 of the DSU) prevent a WTO panel from applying non-WTO rules invoked unilaterally by the defendant as a justification of departures from WTO rules? Could it undermine the WTO dispute settlement system if WTO dispute settlement findings were inconsistent with general international law (for instance, universal human rights) or subsequent international agreements concluded outside the WTO? Should such conflicts between WTO rules and non-WTO rules be settled outside the WTO, for instance, in the special dispute settlement procedures of multilateral environmental agreements like the 2000 UN Cartagena Protocol on Biosafety (Biosafety Protocol), which – according to its Preamble – shall neither 'be interpreted as implying a change in the rights and obligations of a Party under any existing international agreements' nor be 'subordinate to other international agreements'? Unless these questions are clarified by WTO Members (for instance, in the context of their negotiations on further improvements of the DSU), WTO dispute settlement bodies may find it difficult to avoid requests for clarifying such controversial legal issues. In the pending dispute over the European Communities' approval procedures for GMOs, the panel was requested to examine the legal relationship between various WTO agreements and other global agreements (such as the Convention on Biodiversity and the Biosafety Protocol) and regional agreements (like European Community law) on the basis of conflict clauses in WTO law, as well as in the Biosafety Protocol and in general international law (such as freedom of contract and other legal principles such as *lex specialis, pacta sunt servanda, pacta tertiis non nocent non prosunt*).

The limited scope of jurisdiction of the political and (quasi-)judicial WTO dispute settlement bodies must be distinguished from the question of applicable law (section II.2(c) below). For instance, WTO panels have no jurisdiction to judicially enforce compliance with non-WTO rules. Yet, 'arbitration within the WTO . . . subject to mutual agreement of the parties' (Article 25 of the DSU) might extend the scope of applicable law beyond WTO law, for example by extending the legal and judicial remedies to cover reparation of injury and financial compensation. WTO law nowhere specifically excludes the right of WTO Members to extend the jurisdiction of WTO dispute settlement bodies so as to interpret and apply WTO rules in conformity with other international legal obligations of WTO Members. The task of the DSB suggests that 'a satisfactory settlement of the matter in accordance with the rights and obligations under this Understanding and under the covered agreements' (Article 3.4 of the DSU) cannot be achieved by dispute settlement recommendations that violate other legal obligations of all WTO Members. There is no empirical evidence in GATT and WTO dispute settlement practice since 1948 that GATT and WTO Members have ever adopted any such dispute settlement rulings in violation of other international legal obligations of all GATT and WTO Members. For instance, even though WTO law includes no specific references to human rights obligations of WTO Members, the various reports by the UN High Commissioner for Human Rights on the human rights dimensions of WTO rules have nowhere identified a clear conflict between WTO rules, WTO dispute settlement findings, and the universal human rights obligations of WTO Members, notwithstanding the possibility of such conflicts in the domestic implementation and application of WTO rules in individual WTO Members.[66] This empirical evidence seems to confirm the view that WTO rules, and the limited jurisdiction of WTO dispute settlement bodies, are flexible enough to be interpreted and applied in conformity with the human rights obligations of all WTO Members.[67]

(c) Applicable law in WTO panel proceedings

In WTO dispute settlement practice, panels and the Appellate Body have explicitly rejected interpreting WTO rules 'in clinical isolation' from other fields of international law. The WTO adjudicatory organs increasingly resort to multilateral environmental agreements (MEAs) and general rules of international law for purposes of *interpreting* WTO rules; they have also examined the legal consistency of RTAs with WTO law.[68] There is broad agreement that the DSU requires the complainant to base its legal claims on the 'covered WTO agreements' (Article 7 of the DSU). WTO lawyers disagree on whether the DSU implicitly authorizes WTO dispute settlement panels to apply non-WTO law as a defence against WTO complaints and in order to 'fill gaps' in WTO rules and dispute

[66] For a discussion of the various UN reports see Ernst-Ulrich Petersmann, 'The Human Rights Approach Advocated by the UN High Commissioner for Human Rights and by the ILO: Is It Relevant for WTO Law and Policy?' (2004) 7 *Journal of International Economic Law*, 605–627.

[67] See, for instance, Ernst-Ulrich Petersmann, 'Trade and Human Rights I', and Sheldon Leader, 'Trade and Human Rights II', in Patrick F. Macrory, Arthur E. Appleton, and Michael G. Plummer (eds), *The WTO: Legal, Economic and Political Analysis* (Berlin, 2005), Vol. I, pp. 623–696.

[68] See Pauwelyn, *Conflict of Norms*, pp. 244–272. On WTO jurisprudence relating to free trade agreements see Lorand Bartels, 'WTO Dispute Settlement Practice on Article XXIV GATT', in Ortino and Petersmann (eds), *The WTO Dispute Settlement System*, pp. 263–273. The recent WTO panel and Appellate Body reports in *Mexico – Taxes on Soft Drinks* rejected Mexico's claim that its discriminatory taxes in violation of GATT Article III were justified as a counter-measure in response to previous violations of the North

settlement procedures;[69] or whether the DSU limits the mandate of WTO dispute settlement bodies to the application of the 'covered WTO agreements', not only regarding legal claims but also legal defences and 'gap-filling.'[70] Both views recognize that many WTO rules explicitly refer to international treaties negotiated outside the WTO, and that the requirement to clarify WTO rules 'in accordance with customary rules of interpretation of public international law' (Article 3 of the DSU) calls for taking into account 'any relevant rules of international law applicable in the relations between the parties' (in the sense of Article 31.3(c) of the *Vienna Convention*). The controversy over the scope of the applicable law in WTO dispute settlement proceedings is thus closely related to the previously mentioned questions of jurisdiction and methods of treaty interpretation:

Does the correct interpretation of the limited jurisdiction of WTO dispute settlement panels exclude direct application of non-WTO international law in WTO dispute settlement proceedings? Or does the DSU implicitly authorize application of non-WTO international law not only for interpreting WTO rules, but also as directly applicable law?

Do the customary rules of international treaty interpretation (as codified in Article 31.3(c) of the *Vienna Convention*) allow taking into account only international law rules accepted by *all* the parties to the treaty concerned? Or does the dispute settlement function of WTO dispute settlement bodies justify taking into account international rules accepted by all the parties to the dispute, even if some third WTO Members that are not legally affected by the dispute settlement rulings at issue have not accepted the non-WTO rules concerned?

So far, WTO dispute settlement panels and the Appellate Body have been reluctant to apply directly bilateral or multilateral agreements[71] or

Footenote 68 (*cont.*)

American Free Trade Agreement (NAFTA) by the United States. On WTO jurisprudence relating to MEAs see Emanuel Opuku Awuku, 'WTO Dispute Settlement Practice and Trade-Related Environmental Measures', in Ortino and Petersmann, *WTO Dispute Settlement System*, pp. 341–352.

[69] This is the view of, for instance Pauwelyn, *Conflict of Norms*, pp. 459–461.

[70] This is the view of, for instance, Joel P. Trachtman, 'The Domain of WTO Dispute Resolution' (1999) 40 *Harvard International Law Journal*, 333, 342. See also Trachtman's critical review of the above-mentioned book by Pauwelyn in (2004) 98 *American Journal of International Law*, 855–861.

[71] See the Appellate Body's refusal to apply the bilateral Oilseeds Agreement in the *EC – Poultry* dispute: 'The Oilseeds Agreement . . . is a bilateral agreement negotiated by the

legal defences directly based on general international law.[72] They have wisely avoided dispute settlement findings on the controversy whether non-WTO international law is applicable directly, and whether non-WTO law can waive or amend WTO rules outside the formal WTO procedures for waivers and amendments (Articles IX and X of the *WTO Agreement*).[73] In most WTO disputes, interpreting WTO rules – as well as the 'principles underlying this multilateral trading system' – in conformity with general international law to the extent necessary for accomplishing the dispute settlement functions (such as allocating the burden of proof among the parties to a WTO dispute, determining a 'violation' of WTO obligations, providing 'security and predictability' within the meaning of Article 3 of the DSU) is likely to lead to the same legal findings as in the case of the controversial, 'direct' application of general international law.[74]

European Communities and Brazil under Article XXVIII of the GATT 1947, as part of the resolution of the dispute in *EEC – Oilseeds*. As such, the Oilseeds Agreement is not a 'covered agreement' within the meaning of Articles 1 and 2 of the DSU' (Appellate Body Report, *EC – Poultry*, para. 79, referring to GATT Panel Report, *EEC – Oilseeds I*). In *Mexico – Taxes on Soft Drinks*, the Appellate Body stated: 'We see no basis in the DSU for panels and the Appellate Body to adjudicate non-WTO disputes . . . . Accepting Mexico's interpretation would imply that the WTO dispute settlement system could be used to determine rights and obligations outside the covered agreements' (Appellate Body Report, *Mexico – Taxes on Soft Drinks*, para. 56).

[72] See the Appellate Body's refusal to determine whether the precautionary principle was applicable as a rule of customary international law in the *EC – Hormones* case: 'We consider . . . that it is unnecessary, and probably imprudent, for the Appellate Body in this appeal to take a position on this important, but abstract, question. We note that the panel itself did not make any definitive finding with regard to the status of the precautionary principle in international law and that the precautionary principle, at least outside the field of international environmental law, still awaits authoritative formulation. It appears to us important, nevertheless, to note some aspects of the relationship of the precautionary principle to the *SPS Agreement*. . . The precautionary principle indeed finds reflection in Article 5.7 of the *SPS Agreement*. . . It is reflected also in the sixth paragraph of the preamble and in Article 3.3' (Appellate Body Report, *EC – Hormones*, paras. 123–124).

[73] In *Korea – Procurement*, the panel noted as *obiter dictum*: 'Customary international law applies generally to the economic relations between the WTO Members. Such international law applies to the extent that the WTO agreements do not 'contract out' from it. To put it another way, to the extent there is no conflict or inconsistency, or an expression in a covered WTO agreement that implies differently, we are of the view that the customary rules of international law apply to the WTO treaties and to the process of treaty formation under the WTO' (Panel Report, *Korea – Procurement*, para. 7.96). The findings do not specify to what extent the *WTO Agreement* should be interpreted as implicitly authorizing panels to apply general international law rules for fulfilling their dispute settlement functions.

[74] See Joost Pauwelyn, 'How to Win a World Trade Organization Dispute Based on Non-WTO Law?' (2003) 37 *Journal of World Trade*, 997–1030, 1004: 'This author considers it more appropriate to draw a line between interpretation with reference to other norms and

(d) Judicial clarification of 'the basic principles . . . underlying this multilateral trading system': the example of procedural 'due process of law'

The *WTO Agreement* does not explicitly address numerous procedural legal issues that may be raised in WTO dispute settlement proceedings. For instance, how should the DSB and WTO dispute settlement panels have reacted if – in the dispute over the European Communities' import restrictions on bananas – Germany had intervened in support of the WTO complaints against the European Communities? Could Germany have requested the establishment of a WTO panel to examine its legal claim that the European Communities restrictions (adopted by a majority decision of the EC Council against the opposition of Germany) had violated Germany's rights and obligations under WTO law? How should WTO panels respond to legal claims that the 'matter' (Article 7 of the DSU) referred to the panel falls within the exclusive jurisdiction of a regional dispute settlement system (for instance the North American Free Trade Agreement (NAFTA) or the Southern Common Market (MERCOSUR)) and has already been decided by a regional dispute settlement ruling (*res adjudicata*)?[75]

In *EC – Hormones*, the Appellate Body held that

> the DSU, and in particular its appendix 3, leave panels a margin of discretion to deal, always in accordance with due process, with specific situations that may arise in a particular case and that are not explicitly regulated.[76]

Regarding the jurisdiction of panels, the Appellate Body clarified, in *Mexico – Corn Syrup (Article 21.5 – US)*, that

Footnote 74 (*cont.*)
application of other norms. Others end up with the same result – that is, a panel can refer to non-WTO rules binding only on the disputing parties – based solely on a wider notion of treaty interpretation under Articles 31 and 32 of the *Vienna Convention*.'

75 This legal issue was raised in Brazil's complaint against Argentina's anti-dumping duties on poultry. The numerous NAFTA Chapter 19 disputes on United States measures on imports of lumber from Canada, and the various WTO dispute settlement proceedings relating to the same United States restrictions and countervailing duties, concerned different 'matters' (that is, the legal claims in NAFTA Chapter 19 disputes over the inconsistency of the United States measures with United States law differ from the legal claims in WTO dispute settlement proceedings relating to the alleged WTO-inconsistency of the United States measures). The Appellate Body in *Mexico – Taxes on Soft Drinks* explicitly noted 'that Mexico has expressly stated that the so-called 'exclusion clause' of Article 2005.6 of the NAFTA had not been 'exercised' (Appellate Body Report, *Mexico – Taxes on Soft Drinks*, para. 54).

76 Appellate Body Report, *EC – Hormones*, footnote 138 to para. 152.

> panels have to address and dispose of certain issues of a fundamental nature, even if the parties to the dispute remain silent on those issues. In this regard, we have previously observed that 'the vesting of jurisdiction in a panel is a fundamental prerequisite for lawful panel proceedings.' For this reason, panels cannot simply ignore issues which go to the root of their jurisdiction – that is, to their authority to deal with and dispose of matters. Rather, panels must deal with such issues – if necessary, on their own motion – in order to satisfy themselves that they have authority to proceed.[77]

Hence, as WTO panels must check their own jurisdiction at their own initiative, interpreting the jurisdiction of WTO dispute settlement bodies might require taking into account agreements among the parties to the dispute that limit or exclude WTO jurisdiction (for instance, Article 292 of the Treaty establishing the European Communities (EC Treaty) concerning the exclusive jurisdiction of the European Court of Justice (ECJ) or Article 2005 of the NAFTA on the exclusive jurisdiction of NAFTA panels). Other procedural issues, such as the increasing WTO jurisprudence on the legitimate scope of 'judicial economy', may fall within the discretionary authority of panels. Regarding third party rights, for example, the Appellate Body in *US – 1916 Act* concluded that

> a Panel's decision whether to grant 'enhanced' participatory rights to third parties is thus a matter that falls within the discretionary authority of that panel. Such discretionary authority is, of course, not unlimited and is circumscribed, for example, by the requirements of due process.[78]

WTO panels and the Appellate Body do not always specify whether they refer to general principles of national law or of international law in the interpretation and application of WTO dispute settlement rules and procedures,[79] for example, if they refer to 'requirements of good faith, due process and orderly procedure',[80] or to the 'widely accepted rule that an international tribunal is entitled to consider the issue of its own jurisdiction

[77] Appellate Body Report, *Mexico – Corn Syrup (Article 21.5 – US)*, para. 36 (footnote omitted). Many WTO panel reports explain the scope of jurisdiction of the panel, see Panel Reports, *US – 1916 Act (EC)* and *US – 1916 Act (Japan)*, para. 5.19: 'we consider that it is justifiable to explain why, in our view, the competence of the Panel to address a violation of Article VI and the Anti-Dumping Agreement is not affected . . .'

[78] Appellate Body Report, *US – 1916 Act*, para. 150.

[79] This is criticized by Corinna Sandrock, *Allgemeine Rechtsgrundsätze im Verfahrensrecht der WTO*, 2004. On the four different categories of 'general principles of law' see, for instance, Pauwelyn, *Conflict of Norms*, pp. 125–126.

[80] Appellate Body Report, *Mexico – Corn Syrup (Article 21–5 – US)*, para. 47.

on its own initiative, and to satisfy itself that it has jurisdiction in any case that comes before it'.[81] Nor do they always specify whether such principles are recognized in WTO law, such as 'the demands of due process that are implicit in the DSU'.[82] As 'the procedural rules of WTO dispute settlement are designed to promote . . . the fair, prompt and effective resolution of trade disputes',[83] many general principles of law (for instance, concerning the distribution of burden of proof, *iura novit curia*, etc.) and of international law (for instance, the interpretative principle of *in dubio mitius* as a corollary of respect for state sovereignty[84]) may be classifiable as 'basic principles underlying this multilateral trading system' that are implicit in, or required by, the WTO dispute settlement rules and procedures, in order to realize their respective objectives (such as 'providing security and predictability to the multilateral trading system', pursuant to Article 3.2 of the DSU). The clarification of these 'basic principles' of WTO law, and their occasional departures from other general principles of international law (for instance, regarding the legal interest to initiate dispute settlement proceedings and *locus standi*),[85] remains a challenge for future WTO jurisprudence, and may avoid the need to take position on the controversy of whether non-WTO rules may be 'directly applicable' by WTO dispute settlement bodies.

(e) Judicial review of trade measures based on general international law rules? The example of human rights

GATT and WTO jurisprudence have contributed to the progressive clarification of many substantive GATT and WTO rules (for instance, concerning the prohibition of subsidies and the calculation of anti-dumping duties). Many substantive WTO rules are based on centuries-old legal principles (like MFN treatment and national treatment) or refer to international agreements concluded outside the WTO (like the intellectual property conventions referred to in the *TRIPS Agreement*). In all countries, judicial review of government regulation of markets is faced

[81] This rule was applied by the Appellate Body in footnote 30 of its report in *US – 1916 Act*.

[82] Appellate Body Report, *India – Patents (US)*, para. 94.

[83] Appellate Body Report, *US – FSC*, para. 166.

[84] This interpretative principle was applied by the Appellate Body in *EC – Hormones* as being 'widely recognized in international law' (Appellate Body Report, *EC – Hormones*, para. 165).

[85] In the WTO dispute over the European Communities import restrictions on bananas, the European Communities claimed that the United States had no 'legal right or interest' as it did not export any bananas (Panel Reports, *EC – Bananas III*, para. 2.21). The Appellate Body confirmed the finding by the panel that the DSU did not require a 'legal interest to sue' (Appellate Body Report, *EC – Bananas III*, para. 132).

with fundamental problems of legitimacy. These legitimacy problems increase if, as in the WTO:

the market access commitments assert legal primacy over domestic laws (see Article XVI:4 of the *WTO Agreement*);
the dispute settlement procedures prescribe judicial deference vis-à-vis protectionist producer regulations (see Article 17.6 of the *Agreement on Implementation of Article VI of the General Agreement on Tariffs and Trade 1994* (*Anti-Dumping Agreement*)) and are dominated by trade bureaucrats, without adequate guarantees of judicial independence (for instance, of WTO panellists); and
the applicable law and 'balancing principles' include no reference to human rights, democratic procedures, constitutional protection of general citizen interests (such as consumer welfare), or to other sources of democratic legitimacy and social justice.[86]

All WTO Members have committed themselves to respect for human rights in international law (for instance, in UN human rights instruments and the UN Charter), as well as in their domestic laws. Even though the diversity of human rights traditions is reflected in the diversity of national, regional, and worldwide human rights rules and practices, every WTO Member has human rights obligations. The increasing number of human rights arguments in economic disputes in the ECJ and in the European Court of Human Rights (ECtHR) suggests that it may only be a matter of time until human rights arguments will also be invoked by WTO Members in WTO dispute settlement proceedings. This could be the case, for instance, in order to justify trade measures for the protection of 'public morals' (Article XX(a) of the GATT 1994) or 'public order' (Article XIV of the GATS) or human rights-consistent interpretations of other WTO rules. Past GATT and WTO practice suggests that:

the 'public interest clauses' in WTO law (for instance, in Article 7 of the *TRIPS Agreement* on 'objectives' and Article 8 of the *TRIPS Agreement* on 'principles');
the WTO 'exceptions' (for instance, in Article XX of the GATT 1994, Article XIV of the GATS, and Article 30 of the *TRIPS Agreement*);
the broad mandate of panels (for instance, to 'make such findings as will assist the DSB in making the recommendations or in giving the rulings

[86] See Ernst-Ulrich Petersmann, 'Theories of Justice, Human Rights and the Constitution of International Markets' (2003) 37 *Loyola of Los Angeles Law Review*, 407–460.

provided for in that/those agreement(s)', as set out in Article 7 of the DSU);

the admissibility of *inter se* agreements among WTO Members (for instance, on the 'human rights conditionality' of preferential trade agreements (PTAs) concluded by the European Communities and the United States with LDCs); and

offer enough flexibility for WTO dispute settlement bodies to interpret WTO rules in conformity with the human rights obligations of the WTO Members concerned. Arguably, even though the WTO agreements nowhere refer specifically to human rights, the numerous WTO provisions on the sovereign rights of WTO Members to protect 'public morals' and 'public order' already include 'social clauses' and 'human rights clauses' enabling WTO Members to comply with their respective national and international human rights obligations. Yet, it remains an important challenge for future WTO jurisprudence to develop appropriate methodologies for interpreting and applying WTO rules in conformity with human rights. Human rights law and WTO jurisprudence suggest that, in examining the potential impact of human rights on the interpretation of WTO rules, the following four different kinds of trade regulations should be distinguished and might require different 'balancing principles'.

International trade sanctions for the promotion of human rights abroad

In past GATT and WTO practice concerning international trade sanctions, the respondent countries often refrained from requesting the establishment of a GATT panel (for instance, in the case of trade sanctions against Argentina and Cuba). In the few cases where a GATT Working Party (for instance, in the case of United States trade sanctions against Czechoslovakia) or a GATT panel (for instance, in the case of trade sanctions against Nicaragua and South Africa) examined the trade embargoes, human rights arguments were not addressed in the relevant findings. Where a WTO dispute settlement body has to examine the influence of human rights law on the interpretation of WTO rules, it has to respect the 'sovereign equality' between the two WTO Members concerned (for instance, as regards ratification of international human rights conventions) and the 'margin of appreciation' of each WTO Member in designing its domestic human rights legislation and in prioritizing scarce resources for the realization of human rights and social needs.

The sovereign freedom of WTO Members might, however, be limited, as reflected in the UN resolutions 'that sanctions and negative conditionalities which directly or indirectly affect trade are not appropriate ways of promoting the integration of human rights in international economic policy and practice.'[87] Given that Article XXI of the GATT 1994 explicitly provides that 'nothing in this Agreement shall be construed . . . (c) to prevent any contracting party from taking any action in pursuance of its obligations under the United Nations Charter for the maintenance of international peace and security', UN Security Council resolutions prescribing economic sanctions can justify departures from WTO rules (see Article 103 of the UN Charter). The legal relevance of other UN resolutions on the interpretation of WTO rules needs to be examined on a case-by-case basis. For instance, the resolution adopted in 2000 by the ILO on action against Myanmar in response to grave breaches of the ILO's Forced Labour Convention only *recommended* ILO members to 'review, in the light of the conclusions of the Commission of Inquiry, the relations that they may have with the member State concerned and take appropriate measures to ensure that the said member cannot take advantage of such relations to perpetuate or extend the system of forced or compulsory labour referred to by the Commission of Inquiry, and to contribute as far as possible to the implementation of its recommendations made.' While this ILO recommendation may influence the interpretation of WTO rules (for instance, the interpretation of Article XX of the GATT 1994), it neither envisages trade sanctions nor waives (pursuant to the specific WTO rules for amendments and waivers) the various WTO obligations limiting recourse to discriminatory trade restrictions.[88] Examination of the WTO-consistency of trade restrictions in response to alleged violations

[87] Resolution 1999/30 of 26 August 1999 on 'Trade Liberalization and its Impact on Human Rights', adopted by the Subcommission (of the UN Commission on Human Rights) on the Promotion and Protection of Human Rights.

[88] Myanmar, a WTO Member, refrained from invoking WTO dispute settlement procedures against the trade sanctions imposed by various WTO Members (for instance, under the Burmese Freedom and Democracy Act 2003 adopted by the United States Congress). The claim by some WTO lawyers that – in the event of a conflict between WTO rules (prohibiting discriminatory trade embargos) and the ILO recommendation – 'the later and more specific norm, the ILO recommendation should then prevail over the WTO prohibition' (Pauwelyn, 'How to Win a WTO Dispute', 1023), appears to differentiate too little among the various legal safeguards in WTO rules which may justify well-targeted sanctions (for instance, with respect to products produced in violation of ILO standards), but may legally limit recourse to sanctions if they should aggravate the human rights situation in the target country (in this specific case Myanmar).

of human rights in international relations among WTO Members may also have to take into account whether the WTO Members concerned have specifically committed themselves to respect for human rights in their trade relations (for instance, in the human rights clauses included in the Cotonou Agreement and in other trade agreements between the European Communities and least-developed WTO Members). Multilateral agreements on the collective promotion of human health (for instance, through the Framework Convention on Tobacco Control adopted by the World Health Organization in 2003) and of other human rights values (for instance, the 2003 Kimberley Process Certification Scheme for limiting illicit trade in 'conflict diamonds') may support recourse to human rights arguments as relevant context for interpreting WTO rules (such as Article XX(b) of the GATT 1994 on the protection of human health against the risks of smoking). As WTO Members are often likely to invoke their higher *national* or *regional* human rights obligations rather than lower minimum standards in UN human rights law, WTO dispute settlement bodies might also have to examine whether – in reconciling the sovereign rights and obligations of importing and exporting WTO Members under human rights law and international trade law – human rights arguments have to be based on universally accepted UN standards or whether they can also be justified by higher national or regional standards.

International trade preferences for the promotion of human rights abroad

In response to India's challenge of the discriminatory effects of certain preferences granted under the European Communities' GSP, the WTO Appellate Body clarified that

> the term 'non-discriminatory' . . . does not prohibit developed-country Members from granting different tariffs to products originating in different GSP beneficiaries, provided that . . . identical treatment is available to all similarly-situated GSP beneficiaries that have the 'development, financial and trade needs' to which the treatment in question is intended to respond;[89]

> the existence of a 'development, financial (or) trade must be assessed according to an objective standard';[90] and

[89] Appellate Body Report, *EC – Tariff Preferences*, paras. 173 and 190.
[90] Ibid., paras. 161–163.

> the particular need at issue must, by its nature, be such that it can be effectively addressed through tariff preferences, without imposing 'unjustifiable burdens on other Members'.[91]

In order to comply with the dispute settlement findings, the European Communities has adopted a new GSP system aimed at promoting 'sustainable development' by differentiating tariff preferences depending on whether LDCs have ratified and effectively implemented major UN human rights conventions, ILO conventions, UN environmental convention, UN conventions on drugs and the UN Convention against corruption.[92] This use of UN human rights law as an 'objective standard' for differentiating trade preferences among LDCs may give rise to future WTO disputes on whether preference-granting WTO Members have correctly interpreted and applied UN human rights standards as justifying trade preferences for, and differentiation among, LDCs. As the jurisdiction of WTO panels is limited to examining legal claims under the covered WTO agreements, WTO dispute settlement bodies should leave it to the WTO Members concerned to prove the existence of alleged violations of human rights (for instance, by invoking special dispute settlement procedures available under human rights conventions or under RTAs) and the 'particular need . . . addressed through tariff preferences.' WTO dispute settlement procedures seem to offer adequate flexibility for avoiding the 'direct application' of international human rights law by WTO dispute settlement bodies.

International trade restrictions for the protection of human rights inside the domestic jurisdiction

WTO disputes over the European Communities' import restrictions on hormone-fed beef[93] and asbestos[94] illustrate that WTO rules grant importing countries broad regulatory discretion regarding restrictions of imported goods with proven health risks (like asbestos) as well as for precautionary measures for goods with potential health risks (like beef produced by using certain growth hormones). As UN human rights conventions prescribe minimum standards that do not prevent WTO Members from accepting higher human rights standards in regional

[91] Ibid., paras. 164–167. [92] See note 55 above.

[93] Appellate Body Report, *EC – Hormones*; Panel Reports, *EC – Hormones (Canada)* and *EC – Hormones (US)*.

[94] Appellate Body Report, *EC – Asbestos*; Panel Report, *EC – Asbestos*.

human rights conventions (such as the European Convention on Human Rights (ECHR) and the EU Charter of Fundamental Rights) and in national human rights laws, the WTO-consistency of import restrictions designed to protect the human rights of *domestic* citizens (for instance, health protection measures pursuant to Article XX(b) of the GATT 1994, Articles 30 and 31 of the *TRIPS Agreement*) may be influenced by *national* or *regional* human rights law as a legitimate concretization of the minimum standards in UN human rights conventions and the broad 'public order' provisions in WTO law. The two following examples illustrate that many human rights arguments in trade disputes before the ECJ and in the ECtHR could be similarly raised in WTO dispute settlement proceedings.

The Omega case in the ECJ

In the *Omega* case,[95] the ECJ held that a prohibition of imported foreign services was legally justified on the ground that it was necessary for protecting public policy by prohibiting a commercial activity affronting human dignity (laser games simulating acts of homicide). The respondent government (the municipality of the German city of Bonn) justified the prohibition by the constitutional protection of human dignity as a human right in Article 1 of the German Basic Law as well as in Article 1 of the EU Charter of Fundamental Rights. UN human rights conventions, by contrast, recognize respect for human dignity only as a legal principle and source of inalienable human rights, but not as a human right in itself.[96] If the same import restrictions on the supply of international services (laser games simulating acts of homicide) had been challenged in a WTO dispute settlement proceeding, the importing country (Germany) and the European Communities could have invoked the same human rights arguments in support of the legal justification of the import restrictions as being 'necessary to protect public morals' or 'to maintain

[95] See Case C-36/2002, *Omega*, Judgment of 14 October 2004, in (2005) *Common Market Law Reports*, 91–130.

[96] In the Preambles of the 1966 UN Covenants on Civil and Political Human Rights and on Economic, Social and Cultural Human Rights, the more than 150 signatory states of these human rights covenants recognized 'that, in accordance with the principles proclaimed in the Charter of the United Nations, recognition of the inherent dignity and of the equal and inalienable rights of all members of the human family is the foundation of freedom, justice and peace in the world', and 'that these rights derive from the inherent dignity of the human person' (See Klaus Dicke, 'The Founding Function of Human Dignity in the Universal Declaration of Human Rights', in David Kretzmer and Eckhardt Klein (eds), *The Concept of Human Dignity* (The Hague, 2002), pp. 111–120).

public order' in terms of Article XIV(a) of the GATS. These WTO concepts recognize that 'public morality' and 'public order' may legitimately vary from one community to the other.[97] WTO dispute settlement bodies have already recognized the legitimate discretion of the national authorities concerned to define 'public morality' and 'public order' in conformity with their respective national values.[98]

Among international lawyers, it remains controversial whether the customary methods of international treaty interpretation (as codified in Article 31.3(c) of the *Vienna Convention*) permit the *worldwide* WTO dispute settlement bodies to take into account *regional* human rights guarantees (like the legal guarantee of respect for human dignity in Article 1 of the EU Charter of Fundamental Rights[99]) as a 'relevant rule of international law applicable in the relations between the parties' to a WTO dispute settlement proceeding. Even if Article 31.3(c) of the *Vienna Convention* were construed as referring to international law rules accepted by *all* parties to the treaty concerned (that is, all WTO Members), WTO dispute settlement bodies may have to acknowledge that the right to protect 'public order' inside the domestic jurisdiction may imply the right of the importing country to apply higher national human rights standards than in the exporting country, or bilateral 'human rights clauses' incorporated into *inter se* agreements between the importing and exporting WTO Members concerned in conformity with WTO law (for instance, the human rights clauses in the trade and development agreements between the European Communities and more than 120 other countries).

The Schmidberger case in the ECJ

In the *Schmidberger* case,[100] the ECJ had to examine the extent of an European Communities member State's obligation to ensure the free movement of goods and freedom of transit in situations where a

[97] See, for instance, footnote to Article XIV(a) of the GATS, which states: 'The public order exception may be invoked only where a genuine and sufficiently serious threat is posed to one of the fundamental interests of society.'

[98] See, for instance, Panel Report, *US – Gambling*, para. 6.461: 'Members should be given some scope to define and apply for themselves the concepts of "public morals" and "public order" in their respective territories, according to their own systems and scales of values . . . [T]he Appellate Body has stated on several occasions that Members, in applying similar societal concepts, have the right to determine the level of protection that they consider appropriate.'

[99] The text is published in OJ 2000 C 364/1–22, 18 December 2000, and is also included in the 2004 Treaty establishing a Constitution for Europe.

[100] See Case C-112/00, *Schmidberger v Austria* (2003) *Common Market Law Reports*, 1043–1092, 1069.

demonstration permitted by the Austrian authorities on the most important Alpine transit route between Austria and Italy had the effect of blocking this motorway for nearly 30 hours. If the transported goods had come from a third WTO Member, or if the private transport company – which claimed that the failure of the Austrian authorities to ban the demonstration amounted to a trade restriction inconsistent with the EC Treaty (Article 28) – had been registered in another WTO Member (for instance, the United States), the other WTO Member could have initiated a WTO dispute settlement proceeding on a similar legal complaint (that is, the inconsistency of the authorization of the political demonstration with GATT and GATS obligations to protect the freedom of transit). This could have confronted the WTO dispute settlement bodies with the same methodological question of how to reconcile the trade obligations of the WTO Member concerned (Austria) with its human rights obligations to protect the freedom of expression and freedom of assembly of the demonstrators (as guaranteed in Articles 10 and 11 of the ECHR and in the national constitution of Austria).

In its judgment of 12 June 2003, the ECJ confirmed its settled case-law that the prohibition of trade restrictions in Article 28 of the EC Treaty also applies where a member State abstains from adopting measures that are required to remove obstacles erected by *private* individuals, rather than by the action of the *state*, to the free movement of goods: 'a demonstration which resulted in the complete closure of a major transit route . . . for almost 30 hours . . . must, therefore, be regarded as constituting a measure of equivalent effect to a quantitative restriction which is, in principle, incompatible with the Community law obligations arising from Articles 30 [now Article 28] and 34 [now Article 29] of the Treaty, read together with Article 5 [now Article 10] thereof, unless that failure to ban [the demonstration] can be objectively justified.'[101] The ECJ recalled its longstanding jurisprudence that both the European Communities and its member States are required to respect fundamental rights, and that measures incompatible with human rights are not acceptable in the European Communities. The Court then examined how to reconcile the EC Treaty guarantees of free movement of goods with the protection of freedom of expression and freedom of assembly, as guaranteed in the ECHR (Articles 10 and 11). The Court concluded from the express wording of Articles 10 and 11 that 'the exercise of those rights may be restricted, provided that the restrictions in fact correspond

[101] Ibid., p. 1086, para. 64.

to objectives of general interest and do not, taking account of the aim of the restrictions, constitute disproportionate and unacceptable interference, impairing the very substance of the rights guaranteed . . . In those circumstances, the interests involved must be weighed having regard to all the circumstances of the case in order to determine whether a fair balance was struck between those interests.'[102]

The Court then emphasized the following two 'balancing principles': First, the competent national government authorities 'enjoy a wide margin of discretion in that regard. Nevertheless, it is necessary to determine whether the restrictions placed upon intra-Community trade are proportionate in the light of the legitimate objective pursued, namely, in the present case, the protection of fundamental rights.'[103] In this respect, the Court concluded that 'the national authorities were reasonably entitled . . . to consider that the legitimate aim of that demonstration could not be achieved in the present case by measures less restrictive of intra-Community trade.'[104] In a subsequent case relating to an alleged interference of Austrian consumer protection regulations with freedom of expression, the ECJ clarified that the 'discretion enjoyed by the national authorities in determining the balance to be struck between freedom of expression and . . . (consumer protection and fair trading) varied for each of the goals justifying restrictions on that freedom and depended on the nature of the activities in question. When the exercise of the freedom did not contribute to a discussion of public interest and, in addition, arose in a context in which the Member States had a certain amount of discretion, review by the Court was limited to an examination of the reasonableness and proportionality of the interference.'[105]

Second, rather than examining the human rights concerned under the *rule-of-reason* exception to Article 28, or as a justification under Article 30 of the EC Treaty, the Court ruled that '(t)he fact that the authorities of a Member State did not ban a demonstration in circumstances such as those of the main case is not incompatible with Articles 30 and 34 of the EC Treaty [now, after amendment, Articles 28 and 29], read together with Article 5 of the EC Treaty [now Article 10].'[106] Such a judicial method of deliberately avoiding to 'pigeonhole a justification based on the need to respect for human rights into one of the justificatory categories'[107] of the

[102] Ibid., p. 1089, paras. 80–81. [103] Ibid., para. 82. [104] Ibid., p. 1091, para. 93.

[105] Case C-71/02, *Karner Industrie-Auktionen*, CMLR 2004, 75, para. 51.

[106] *Schmidberger*, p. 1092, para. 1.

[107] Christopher Brown, 'Annotation of the *Schmidberger* case' (2003) *Common Market Law Review*, 1499–1512, 1504.

EC Treaty might be more difficult to follow by WTO dispute settlement bodies. This is because WTO law and WTO jurisprudence neither recognize human rights nor a 'rule of reason' as 'basic principles' of WTO law that inherently limit the 'reasonable scope' of WTO rights and obligations. Contrary to the methodology used by the ECJ for reconciling the trade and human rights obligations of European Communities member States inside the European Communities, WTO dispute settlement bodies are likely to take into account human rights justifications of discriminatory trade restrictions only in the context of 'affirmative defences' (such as Article XX of the GATT 1994, Article XIV of the GATS) invoked by the WTO Member concerned.

Human rights-related non-discriminatory international trade regulation

The non-discrimination principles in both international trade law as well as human rights law rest on the legal and economic insight that general human welfare can be promoted best by non-discriminatory government regulation. Non-discriminatory government measures for the promotion of human rights either need no legal justification under WTO law (for instance, under Article III of the GATT 1994) or are easily justifiable under the numerous WTO exceptions for non-economic policy measures (such as Article XX of the GATT 1994). The proposals for further harmonization of domestic laws in the context of the WTO – for instance, by elaborating additional WTO rules on intellectual property rights, liberalization and regulation of public services (for instance, educational, health and telecommunications services, supply of water, electricity), trade facilitation, competition, environmental and investment rules – have prompted many NGOs to raise human rights concerns.[108] For example, future WTO rules on private rights (such as the private 'rights to trade' protected in the WTO Protocol on the accession of China), anti-competitive private practices, legal protection of confidential private data, private access to financial assistance in the context of trade-facilitation, limitations on private intellectual property rights, and the administration of a WTO Register for private geographical indications may give rise to legal claims in WTO dispute settlement proceedings that the administration of such WTO obligations, and related domestic implementing regulations, may be

[108] See Tomas Cottier, Joost Pauwelyn, and Lisa Bürgi (eds), *Human Rights and International Trade* (Oxford, 2005); and Practical Guide to the WTO for Human Rights Advocates (Geneva: 3D-Trade, Human Rights, Equitable Economy, 2004).

inconsistent with human rights law. For instance, how should WTO dispute settlement bodies respond to legal claims that the denial of patents of genetic material on grounds of respect for human rights (for instance, as codified in the 1997 Council of Europe Convention on Human Rights and Biomedicine), or respect for the Convention on Biodiversity (for instance, in case of genetic material illegally exported from the state of origin without the prior informed consent of that state as required under the Convention on Biodiversity), entails a violation of the *TRIPS Agreement*?[109] The following examples from the jurisprudence in European courts on the balancing of market freedoms and fundamental rights illustrate the potential complexity and diversity of balancing principles used inside WTO Members regarding non-discriminatory, trade-related regulations.

ECJ jurisprudence on trade-related biotechnology rights

In a judgment on an application by the Netherlands for annulment of European Communities Directive 98/44 (EC Directive) on the legal protection of biotechnological inventions, the ECJ had to decide, *inter alia*, on the plea that the patentability of isolated parts of the human body provided for by Article 5(2) of the Directive reduced living human matter to a means to an end and thereby undermined human dignity. It was also claimed that the absence of a provision requiring verification of the consent of the donor or recipient of products obtained by biotechnological means undermined the right to self-determination. The Court affirmed, without further explanation, that 'it is for the Court of Justice, in its review of the compatibility of acts of the institutions with the general principles of Community law, to ensure that the fundamental right to human dignity and integrity is observed.'[110] If a similar complaint were brought by another WTO Member challenging the consistency of the EC Directive with the European Communities' obligations under WTO law, the limited WTO jurisdiction of dispute settlement panels – and the more limited scope of the applicable law in WTO dispute settlement proceedings – would have prevented a WTO dispute settlement body from arriving at similar conclusions. For example, the universal commitments in

[109] See Sabrina Safrin, 'Hyperownership in a Time of Biotechnological Promise: The International Conflict to Control the Building Blocks of Life' (2004) 98 *American Journal of International Law*, 641–685.

[110] Case C-377/98, *Netherlands v European Parliament and EU Council* [ECR] 2001, I-7079, para. 70.

UN human rights conventions to respect human dignity would *not* justify a conclusion that WTO Members must respect human dignity as a human right in the interpretation and application of WTO rules.[111] In contrast to the legal admissibility of direct actions against European Communities legal acts in the ECJ, the DSU does not provide for direct complaints by WTO Members against acts of WTO bodies (for instance a 'waiver decision' by the WTO Ministerial Conference). WTO dispute settlement bodies may be confronted only indirectly with legal complaints that obligations under the *WTO Agreement* (for instance Article XVI:4) and DSU rules (for instance, on jurisdiction and applicable law) must be construed in conformity with the human rights obligations of WTO Members.[112] Both WTO as well as ECJ jurisprudence seem to apply stricter standards of judicial review to *discriminatory* trade measures than to *non-discriminatory* regulations based, for example, on the *TBT Agreement* and *SPS Agreement*.[113]

The ECJ has noted that – in interpreting fundamental rights – the European Communities jurisprudence 'must take into account' the case-law of the ECtHR.[114] Yet, the ECJ balances economic freedoms with other 'fundamental rights' case-by-case without explicit recognition of human rights as hierarchically superior to 'fundamental economic rights'. The ECtHR, by contrast, imposes a higher burden of proof for claims that *economic* freedoms should prevail over fundamental *political* rights; the Court tends to apply a 'strict interpretation' to the scope of exception clauses in the ECHR, but recognizes a 'margin of appreciation' of national authorities regarding the 'necessity' of non-discriminatory, domestic restrictions (for instance, economic regulation) balancing different human rights values.[115]

[111] See notes 96 and 110 above, as well as Roger Brownsword (ed.), *Global Governance and the Quest for Justice*, Vol. 4: Human Rights (Oxford, 2004), notably, chapters 12 and 13.

[112] Article 1 of the DSU acknowledges that 'the rules and procedures of this Understanding shall also apply to consultations and the settlement of disputes between Members concerning the rights and obligations under the provisions of the Agreement Establishing the World Trade Organization . . . and of this Understanding'.

[113] See Veiko Heiskanen, 'The Regulatory Philosophy of International Trade Law' (2004) 38 *Journal of World Trade*, 1–36, 25–29 and 33.

[114] For a discussion of these cases see Allan Rosas, 'The Legal Sources of EU Fundamental Rights: A Systemic Overview', in Nicolas Colneric et al. (eds), *Une Communauté de Droit. Festschrift für G.C.R. Iglesias* (Berlin, 2003).

[115] On these two principles, and their inherent tensions, in the jurisprudence of the ECtHR, see, for instance, Donna Gomien, David Harris, and Leo Zwaak, *Law and Practice of the European Convention on Human Rights and the European Social Charter* (Strasbourg, 1996), pp. 211–219.

Human rights and unfair competition rules: the Hertel case in the European Court of Human Rights

In *Hertel v Switzerland*, the ECtHR had to review the consistency of Swiss court judgments on 'unfair competition' and freedom of commercial speech with the guarantees of freedom of expression in Article 10 of the ECHR. The different 'balancing approaches' applied by the Swiss courts and by the ECtHR illustrate that – even inside Europe – views on the proper balancing of economic and non-economic freedoms differ considerably. WTO dispute settlement bodies, if confronted with similar problems in the interpretation of trade and unfair competition rules (for instance, in the *TRIPS Agreement* and Article 10*bis* of the *Paris Convention on the Protection of Industrial Property* (*Paris Convention*)), may need to exercise even more deference vis-à-vis divergent national legal and constitutional traditions.

The commercial court in the Canton of Berne, on the basis of the 'principle that there is no hierarchy of fundamental rights', had considered it necessary to weigh against the constitutional rights invoked by Dr Hertel (such as freedom of expression and freedom to carry out scientific research) the right to freedom of trade and industry as guaranteed by the Swiss Constitution.[116] Based on the Swiss Unfair Competition Act, the court prohibited Dr Hertel 'from stating that food prepared in microwave ovens is a danger to health and leads to changes in blood of those who consume it that indicate a pathological disorder and present a pattern that could be seen as the beginning of a carcinogenic process.' The Swiss Federal Court dismissed the appeal by Dr Hertel, *inter alia*, on the ground that the 'smooth operation of competition and economic freedom, freedom of expression, scientific freedom and freedom of the press must be guaranteed as well as possible, but at the same time limited so that the various constitutional objectives may be reconciled in practice.'

The ECtHR proceeded from the premise that exceptions to freedom of expression (Article 10) must be construed strictly, and that the margin of appreciation of the Swiss authorities in matters of commercial speech was reduced by the fact that the statements by Dr Hertel had been part of 'a debate affecting the general interest, for example over public health.' The majority of the judges considered the Swiss court injunction limiting the freedom of expression of Dr Hertel as not 'necessary in a democratic society', and therefore a violation of Article 10 of the ECHR. The three

[116] The following quotations and facts are taken from the Judgment of the ECtHR of 25 August 1998, *Hertel v Switzerland* (59/1997/843/1049), published in Reports 1998-VI.

dissenting judges argued that the ECtHR should respect the considerable margin of appreciation of national authorities in unfair competition cases rather than 'substitute its own evaluation for that of the national courts, where those courts considered, on reasonable grounds, the restrictions to be necessary.' By way of implementing the ECtHR judgment, the Federal Court revised the previous court injunction and acknowledged the freedom of Dr Hertel to make public statements on the dangerous effects of the use of microwave ovens; but the Federal Court subjected the freedom of expression of Dr Hertel to the condition that such statements must also refer 'to current differences of opinion' so as to avoid unfair distortions of competition.[117] In response to another application by Dr Hertel, the ECtHR dismissed the second complaint since the applicant was no longer limited to expressing his views, albeit subject to limitations.[118]

Article 2 of the *TRIPS Agreement* incorporates the rules relating to unfair competition of the *Paris Convention* (Article 10*bis*) into the *TRIPS Agreement.* WTO law also includes other prohibitions of 'anti-competitive practices', false or misleading information that can be enforced through national and WTO dispute settlement proceedings so as to limit market failures (such as information asymmetries) and protect the proper functioning of markets (for instance, in their role as information mechanisms and dialogues about values).[119] WTO dispute settlement bodies may, therefore, be required to interpret national and international competition and intellectual property regulations in conformity with the human rights obligations of WTO Members. As freedom of information and expression, including freedom of speech and of the press, are of constitutional importance for the proper functioning of *economic* markets no less than of *political* markets (that is, democracy), the European jurisprudence and 'balancing principles' on reconciling economic and non-economic 'fundamental freedoms' may offer lessons for future WTO jurisprudence.

Even though the *WTO Agreement* has been drafted in terms of rights and obligations of WTO Members, many WTO rules recognize obligations to protect the private rights of market participants, such as the 'rights to trade' of private individuals (as explicitly protected in the 2001

[117] *Bundesgerichtsentscheidungen* 125 III 185.

[118] Decision of the ECtHR of 17 January 2002, Application No. 53440/99.

[119] See, for instance, the comprehensive competition rules included into the 1997 GATS Protocol on Telecommunications that were recently applied by the panel in *Mexico – Telecoms.*

WTO Protocol on the Accession of China), procedural rights (for instance, in customs valuation, anti-dumping, countervailing duty, safeguards, government procurement procedures, and preshipment inspection procedures), property rights and judicial remedies. Some WTO agreements (such as the *Agreement on Government Procurement* (*GPA*) in Article XX, and the *Agreement on Preshipment Inspection* in Article 4), as well as the domestic trade laws in many WTO Members (such as Article 300(7) of the EC Treaty), require WTO Members and domestic courts to interpret domestic trade regulations in conformity with WTO obligations for the benefit of individual citizens. The UN High Commissioner for Human Rights has also rightly pointed out that – what are referred to as rights of WTO Members in the numerous 'public interest clauses' and 'general exceptions' in WTO law – may be obligations under UN human rights law.[120] Future WTO jurisprudence is likely to be increasingly confronted with legal claims that – in the review of the WTO-consistency of national legislative, administrative or judicial trade measures – international and domestic trade rules must be construed with due regard to the obligations of all WTO Members to comply with all their international law obligations in good faith, including their human rights obligations.

3. *The role of the judge in the WTO legal system*

WTO panels and the Appellate Body issue only *advisory* reports with recommendations addressed to WTO Members, rather than legally binding judgments. Hence, they exercise only 'quasi-judicial' functions, different from those of truly independent courts. Even though WTO panels and the Appellate Body have claimed for themselves certain inherent powers (for instance, the power to examine their jurisdiction *proprio motu*, to adopt *interim* rulings, to admit *amicus curiae* briefs, and to 'complete the legal analysis' at the appellate level), analogies with the inherent powers of national and international courts may be misleading.[121] WTO jurisprudence remains characterized by deference vis-à-vis WTO Members and the WTO political bodies (section II.3(a) below), the scope of which may differ depending on the particular context of WTO rules (section II.3(b) below). Moreover, the independence of WTO dispute settlement bodies remains legally and institutionally limited (section II.3(c) below); it could be reinforced by international cooperation among judges (section II.3(d) below).

[120] See note 65 above.

[121] See Friedl Weiss, 'Inherent Powers of National and International Courts', in Ortino and Petersmann, *WTO Dispute Settlement System*, pp. 177–190.

(a) Judicial deference vis-à-vis WTO Members and political WTO bodies

In *India – Quantitative Restrictions*, the Appellate Body rejected the argument that the absence of a determination by the WTO Committee on Balance-of-Payments Restrictions whether import restrictions maintained by India were or were not consistent with Article XVIII of the GATT 1994 should prompt a panel or the Appellate Body to refrain from making legal findings on this controversial legal issue, so as to respect the 'institutional balance' between the political and the (quasi-)judicial WTO bodies:

> if the exercise of judicial restraint were to lead in practice . . . to panels refraining from considering disputes regarding the justification of balance-of-payments restrictions, such exercise of judicial restraint would . . . be inconsistent with Article XXIII of the GATT 1994, as elaborated and applied by the DSU.[122]

Likewise, in *Turkey – Textiles*, the Appellate Body recognized the right of panels to examine the consistency of RTAs with Article XXIV of the GATT 1994, although the WTO Committee on Regional Trade Agreements had refrained from making such a determination. As the GATT 1994 *Understandings on the Interpretation of Articles XVIII and XXIV of the General Agreement on Tariffs and Trade 1994* clearly confirm the applicability of Article XXIII of the GATT 1994 to matters arising from the application of Articles XVIII and XXIV of the GATT 1994, the Appellate Body rightly acknowledged that the political review procedures in the political WTO Committees did not exclude the jurisdiction of WTO dispute settlement panels. The unambiguous WTO rules could not be disregarded in order to safeguard an alleged 'institutional balance' that is not provided for in WTO law.[123]

[122] Appellate Body Report, *Turkey – Textiles*, para. 108.

[123] For a criticism of this WTO jurisprudence as undue 'judicial activism' see Frieder Roessler, 'The Institutional Balance between the Judicial and the Political Organs of the WTO', in Marco Bronckers and Reinhard Quick (eds), *New Directions in International Economic Law. Essays in Honour of Professor John H. Jackson* (The Hague, 2000), pp. 325–346. See also Lorand Bartels, 'The Separation of Powers in the WTO: How to Avoid Judicial Activism' (2004) 53 *International and Comparative Law Quarterly*, 861–890; Richard H. Steinberg, 'Judicial Lawmaking at the WTO: Discursive, Constitutional and Political Constraints' (2004) 98 *American Journal of International Law*, 247–265; and John P. Kelly, 'Judicial Activism in the WTO: Developing Principles of Self-Restraint' (2002) 22 *Northwestern Journal of International Law and Business*, 353–380.

The respective powers of WTO dispute settlement bodies depend not only on the explicit rules in the DSU, but also on the broader legal and institutional context of WTO law. For instance, the Appellate Body stated:

> It is not the task of either panels or the Appellate Body to amend the DSU or to adopt interpretations within the meaning of Article IX:2 of the WTO Agreement. Only WTO Members have the authority to amend the covered agreements or to adopt such interpretations. Determining what the rights and obligations under the covered agreements ought to be is not the responsibility of panels and the Appellate Body; it is clearly the responsibility solely of the Members of the WTO.[124]

The proposals by Chile and the United States, in the Doha Round negotiations on improvements and clarifications of the DSU, for 'providing some form of additional guidance to WTO adjudication bodies concerning (i) the nature and scope of the task presented to them (for example when the exercise of judicial economy is most useful), and (ii) rules of interpretation of the WTO agreements'[125] illustrate the dynamic interactions between WTO Members and WTO dispute settlement bodies. This was also reflected in the strong criticism by the WTO's General Council of the Appellate Body's acceptance of unsolicited *amicus curiae* briefs;[126] it is further illustrated by the limited power of the Appellate Body to draw up its own working procedures 'in consultation with the chairman of the DSB and the Director-General', and to communicate these working procedures to the Members for their information (Article 17.9 of the DSU). The various communications in which the Appellate Body notified and explained its successive amendments (in 1997, 2002, 2003, and 2005, respectively) of its 1996 *Working Procedures for Appellate Review* (*Working Procedures*), explicitly took account of Members' comments and, for instance, 'urge[d] members to take action themselves to deal with the numerous problems that arise in appeals that run over WTO holiday periods.'[127]

The DSB, panels, and the Appellate Body 'cannot add to or diminish the rights and obligations provided in the covered agreements' (Articles 3.2 and 19.2 of the DSU). However, acquiescence by WTO Members and WTO bodies in controversial dispute settlement practices – such as the 'completing of the legal analysis' by the Appellate Body in order to promote the 'prompt settlement' of disputes (see Article 3.3 of the DSU),

[124] Appellate Body Report, *US – Certain EC Products*, para. 92.
[125] See TN/DS/W/28 and the 25 February 2005 communication by the United States (JOB(05)/23). [126] See note 9 above. [127] WT/AB/WP/W/9, 7 October 2004.

even if the legal claims had not been examined in the panel report – may evolve into 'subsequent practice' confirming the judicial interpretations of WTO law. Yet, dispute settlement practices may also be discontinued or modified by WTO Members through new Doha Round agreements (for instance, by limiting *amicus curiae* briefs or authorizing the Appellate Body to remand certain issues of fact and of law to first-level panels).

The legal and institutional restraints on WTO jurisprudence are also acknowledged in the interpretative methods applied by WTO dispute settlement bodies. The Appellate Body has held, for example:

> The legitimate expectations of the WTO Members are reflected in the language of the WTO Agreement itself. The duty of a treaty interpreter is to examine the words of the treaty to determine the intentions of the parties. This should be done in accordance with the principles of treaty interpretation set out in Articles 31 and 32 of the *Vienna Convention*. But these principles of interpretation neither require nor condone the imputation into a treaty of words that are not there, or the importation into a treaty of concepts that were not intended.[128]

Thus, some WTO dispute settlement panels have exercised 'judicial economy' by refraining from making findings on controversial legal interpretations where such legal findings were not necessary for 'achieving a satisfactory settlement of the matter in accordance with the rights and obligations' of WTO Members (see Article 3.4 of the DSU) and the same legal issues were under consideration in political WTO negotiations on additional WTO rules.[129] For instance, contrary to the legal findings of a few GATT 1947 dispute settlement panels that illegal anti-dumping duties had to be reimbursed in line with the general international law rules on state responsibility, such dispute settlement findings have not been repeated under the WTO in view of Article 19 of the DSU as well as the controversial proposal, in the Doha Round negotiations, on explicitly introducing such a new WTO obligation.[130] Arbitrations under Article 21.3(c) of the DSU have rather emphasized 'the well-established principle that "choosing the means of implemen-

[128] Appellate Body Report, *India – Patents (US)*, para. 45.

[129] The panel in *Mexico – Telecoms*, emphasized at para. 7.3 of its report:

> The limited legal task of dispute settlement findings: Our legal findings are thus limited to the disputed meaning and scope of certain GATS obligations and commitments of Mexico in the very particular context of this bilateral dispute, and do not go beyond what we consider indispensable for deciding on the legal claims submitted to this Panel.

[130] See the 30 June 2005 proposal by Canada in TN/RL/GEN/48.

tation is, and should be, the prerogative of the implementing Member".'[131] WTO dispute settlement bodies have also emphasized the need to respect the sovereign decision of WTO Members on their respective *level of protection* of human, animal and plant life or health, the environment, national security or 'public morals'. For instance, in the *Australia – Salmon* case, the Appellate Body emphasized that the establishment of an appropriate level of protection 'is a prerogative of the Member concerned and not of a panel or of the Appellate Body'; however, 'in cases where a Member does not determine its appropriate level of protection, or does so with insufficient precision, the appropriate level of protection may be established by panels on the basis of the level of protection reflected in the SPS measure actually applied.'[132] WTO dispute settlement panels cannot one-sidedly rely on declarations of the defending party concerning the alleged purpose of the contested measure without making an 'objective assessment of the facts' (Article 11 of the DSU) and of the claims of the complaining party regarding the regulatory purpose of a contested measure by another WTO Member. In this respect, WTO law may require stricter standards of review than the judicial deference warranted under some domestic constitutional systems for review by national judges and European Communities judges of legislative measures.[133]

(b) The scope of judicial deference depends on the particular context of WTO law

WTO jurisprudence has so far tended to define its standards of judicial deference depending on the particular text, context, objective and purpose of the WTO rules concerned (for instance, the specific rules in the *SPS Agreement* and the *TBT Agreement*, respectively), without resorting to general standards of judicial deference, such as those applied by the ECJ.[134] Even if the respondent WTO Member bears the burden of

[131] Appellate Body Report, *US – Offset Act (Byrd Amendment)*, para. 52.

[132] Appellate Body Report, *Australia – Salmon*, paras. 199 and 207.

[133] In *EC – Hormones*, the Appellate Body found that 'the applicable standard is neither *de novo* review as such nor 'total deference', but rather the 'objective assessment of the facts' (Appellate Body Report, *EC – Hormones*, para. 165). In *Japan – Apples*, the Appellate Body confirmed that favouring 'Japan's approach to risk and scientific evidence over the views of the experts conflicts with the Appellate Body's articulation of the standard of "objective assessment of the facts"' (Appellate Body Report, *Japan – Apples*, para. 165). Drawing the line between permissible 'objective assessment' and prohibited '*de novo* review' raises many other problems (see Appellate Body Report, *US – Cotton Yarn*, para. 78).

invoking and proving 'affirmative defences' (for instance, the general exceptions in Article XX of the GATT 1994, Article XIV of the GATS, as well as the security exceptions in Article XXI of the GATT 1994), WTO jurisprudence tends to respect non-economic measures based on such 'public interest clauses' with considerable deference vis-à-vis non-economic policy goals. The role of the judge in disputes over the interpretation, application or enforcement of WTO rules may differ, depending on whether the legal claims relate to (non-)discriminatory regulations of trade in goods, services or private intellectual property rights at the intergovernmental level among WTO Members or involving private economic operators. For instance, in contrast to GATT rules and TBT rules, many SPS provisions ascribe a special role to science in the assessment and prevention of the risks, as well as in the determination of the WTO-consistency of SPS measures:

'Members shall ensure that any sanitary or phytosanitary measure . . . is based on scientific principles and is not maintained without sufficient scientific evidence, except as provided for in paragraph 7 of Article 5' (Article 2.2 of the *SPS Agreement*).

'Members may introduce or maintain sanitary or phytosanitary measures which result in a higher level of sanitary or phytosanitary protection than would be achieved by measures based on the relevant international standards, guidelines or recommendations, if there is a scientific justification' (Article 3.3 of the *SPS Agreement*).

SPS measures must be 'based on an assessment . . . of the risks' (Article 5.1 of the *SPS Agreement*) which 'shall take into account available scientific evidence' (Article 5.2 of the *SPS Agreement*).

'In cases where relevant scientific evidence is insufficient, a Member may provisionally adopt sanitary or phytosanitary measures on the basis of available pertinent information' (Article 5.7 of the *SPS Agreement*).

[134] See, for instance, Case C-127/95, *Norbrook* [ECR] 1998, I-1531, para. 90: 'In a sphere in which the Community legislature is called on to undertake complex assessments based on technical and scientific information which is liable to change rapidly, judicial review of the exercise of its powers must be limited to examining whether it has been vitiated by a manifest error of assessment or a misuse of powers or whether the legislature has manifestly exceeded the limits of its discretion'. European Communities jurisprudence defines 'misuse of powers . . . as the adoption by a community institution of a measure with the exclusive or main purpose of achieving an end other than that stated or evading a procedure specifically prescribed by the Treaty for dealing with the circumstances of the case' (Case C-180/96, *UK v Commission* [ECR] 1996 I-3903, para. 64).

Hence, even non-discriminatory environmental measures consistent with GATT rules and TBT rules may violate the *SPS Agreement* in the absence of 'sufficient scientific evidence.' Where WTO panellists have lacked adequate scientific expertise,[135] WTO dispute settlement panels have repeatedly made use of their right to 'seek information from any relevant source and . . . consult experts to obtain their opinion on certain aspects of the matter', including with respect to 'a factual issue concerning a scientific or other technical matter raised by a party to the dispute' (Article 13.2 of the DSU), in order to objectively assess whether there is 'sufficient scientific evidence' (Article 2.2 of the *SPS Agreement*) and a 'scientific justification' (Article 3.3 of the *SPS Agreement*). The more important the social value protected by WTO rules is, the more it may influence the legal interpretation of the WTO rules concerned and the exercise of judicial deference:

> It seems to us that a treaty interpreter assessing a measure claimed to be necessary to secure compliance of a WTO-consistent law or regulation may, in appropriate cases, take into account the relative importance of the common interests or values that the law or regulation to be enforced is intended to protect. The more vital or important those common interests or values are, the easier it would be to accept as 'necessary' a measure designed as an enforcement instrument.[136]

In view of the limited number of general legal obligations under the GATS (compared with the more comprehensive GATT obligations for trade in goods), the methods applied by WTO dispute settlement bodies in interpreting national schedules of sectoral services commitments may differ from the methods applied in the interpretation of general GATT rules and of GATS services commitments in sectors subject to more stringent international regulation.[137] Likewise, WTO disputes involving commitments under the *TRIPS Agreement* to protect private intellectual property rights of 'nationals of other Members' (see Article 1.3 of the

[135] WTO Members have so far not made use of the possibility of nominating five (rather than only three) members of a dispute settlement panel, including technical experts.

[136] Appellate Body Report, *Korea – Various Measures on Beef*, para. 162.

[137] See Panel Report, *Mexico – Telecoms*, para. 7.3:

> Our focus on telecommunications may mean that certain elements of our findings in this particular services sector may not be relevant for other services sectors with different legal, economic and technical contexts. Our findings also do not adversely affect the large degree of regulatory autonomy which WTO Members, individually and collectively, retain under the GATS.

TRIPS Agreement), or the 'independent review procedures' pursuant to Article 4 of the *Agreement on Preshipment Inspection* providing for arbitration within the WTO regarding disputes among private 'preshipment inspection entities and exporters' (Article 4), may require particular legal and judicial balancing principles, different from principles applied in other contexts, given that *private* rights, rather than state rights, are involved.

(c) Should the 'diplomatic panel jurisprudence' be further legalized?

The *Rules of Conduct for the Understanding on Rules and Procedures Governing the Settlement of Disputes*, adopted by the DSB on 3 December 1996, prescribe the following 'governing principle':

> Each person covered by these Rules . . . shall be independent and impartial, shall avoid direct or indirect conflicts of interest and shall respect the confidentiality of proceedings of bodies pursuant to the dispute settlement mechanism, so that through the observance of such standards of conduct the integrity and impartiality of that mechanism are preserved (section II).[138]

Since the entry into force of the *WTO Agreement*, no violation of the 'proper performance of [the] . . . dispute settlement duties' of panelists, Appellate Body members, arbitrators, experts and Secretariat members appears to have been formally established, notwithstanding rare cases of self-disclosure of potential conflicts of interests or matters that could 'give rise to justifiable doubts as to that person's independence or impartiality'. As provided for in Article 17.7 of the DSU, the Appellate Body is legally assisted and administratively supported by an Appellate Body Secretariat composed of highly qualified legal experts; this Secretariat is linked to the WTO Secretariat only administratively, but is otherwise separate so as to ensure the independence of the Appellate Body. Even though the appointment of Appellate Body members provides only for a part-time occupation, their legal status (in particular, a four-year term renewable once), expertise, financial compensation and support by the Appellate Body Secretariat offer strong incentives for their judicial independence. This is confirmed by the fact that, similarly to the practice of national and international tribunals claiming 'inherent powers' necessary for the proper functioning of courts, the Appellate Body has likewise defended its inherent powers. Examples for such inherent powers are the

[138] See World Trade Organization, *A Handbook on the WTO Dispute Settlement System* (Geneva, 2004), pp. 170–178.

authority to 'complete the legal analysis' of legal claims not addressed in the panel findings as well as the authority to admit *amicus curiae* briefs, even against the will of the majority of WTO Members.

Unlike the permanent Appellate Body, WTO panels are ad hoc bodies composed by experts who, in practice, are often paid only a modest per diem (600 Swiss francs) for the limited number of days of their work at Geneva. Their other full-time professional commitments are frequently so demanding that panelists may have only limited time to devote to panel proceedings. Most panelists are nominated only once or a few times to serve on a WTO dispute settlement panel, and have neither comprehensive knowledge of GATT/WTO jurisprudence nor time and incentives for reading regularly the numerous GATT and WTO dispute settlement reports. Hence, the ever more comprehensive factual and legal findings in WTO panel reports are drafted by the WTO Secretariat staff assisting the panel, often with very little input by individual panellists, who may have expertise in certain areas (for instance, anti-dumping practices or telecommunications), without, at the same time, being familiar with other areas of WTO rules and WTO jurisprudence. In certain phases of WTO panel proceedings (including hearings with the parties), some panellists have occasionally been available only on telephone due to other conflicting professional commitments. Furthermore, notably in WTO disputes (for instance, on trade remedies, anti-dumping, and countervailing duties) where the secretariat staff assisting panels comes from a WTO division involved in political WTO negotiations on reforms of the applicable WTO rules, the Secretariat's *legal* advice may be influenced by its *political* advice given in the context of WTO negotiations. From a legal perspective, it would appear desirable to remedy these deficiencies of current WTO panel proceedings by establishing – as proposed by the European Communities in the Doha Development negotiations on improvements to the DSU – a permanent WTO panel body or, alternatively, a 'roster of dedicated and experienced panelists' that should be available at all times to serve on a panel upon request and shall remain abreast of WTO dispute settlement activities and other relevant WTO developments. Yet, due to the preference of WTO diplomats for nominating trade diplomats as panelists and due to the strong influence of the WTO Secretariat, WTO panel proceedings are likely to continue operating as a 'diplomatic jurisprudence', which – thanks to the quasi-judicial supervision by the WTO Appellate Body and the political supervision by the intergovernmental DSB – may offer a unique mix of economic, political and legal dispute settlement perspectives.

(d) International cooperation among judges and courts?

Due to the mercantilist biases and reciprocity principles that are characteristic of international trade law, national and regional courts in most WTO Members do not apply WTO rules and accord higher standards of judicial deference to domestic trade restrictions than WTO panels and the Appellate Body may be entitled to exercise under the DSU.[139] So far, the reality of multilevel trade governance by national, regional and WTO bodies lacks effective support by multilevel judicial cooperation among national and international courts. The only two ECJ judgments on intergovernmental trade disputes among EC member States since the entry into force of the EC Treaty in 1958 demonstrate that, also in the WTO, most intergovernmental disputes over national trade restrictions and private rights (for instance, intellectual property rights) could be avoided if domestic courts were authorized to apply and enforce WTO rules. Yet, as long as WTO Members (including the European Communities and the United States) explicitly enjoin their domestic courts *not* to apply WTO rules unless exceptionally permitted,[140] the intergovernmental WTO dispute settlement procedures offer a 'second best remedy' that continues to operate more effectively than the international dispute settlement procedures in all other worldwide organizations.

The judgments by the International Court of Justice (ICJ) refer only rarely to the jurisprudence of other international courts, except for judgments by the ICJ's predecessor, the Permanent Court of International Justice. The WTO Appellate Body, by contrast, frequently refers to judgments of the ICJ and of other international courts, just as the International Tribunal for the Law of the Sea, arbitral tribunals set up by the International Centre for Settlement of Investment Disputes, the ECJ, and the ECtHR increasingly refer to the jurisprudence of other international courts. Respect for the judgments of other international courts and international cooperation among international judges may strengthen the rule of international law and the overall coherence of the international legal system, for instance in the increasing number of trade disputes that are also under review in regional dispute settlement

[139] See Thomas Cottier and Petros C. Mavroidis (eds), *The Role of the Judge in International Trade Regulation* (Ann Arbor, 2003).

[140] See John H. Jackson and Alan Sykes (eds), *Implementing the Uruguay Round* (The Hague, 1997); Ernst-Ulrich Petersmann, 'On Reinforcing WTO Rules in Domestic Laws', in John J. Barcelo III and Hugh Corbett (eds), *Rethinking the World Trading System* (Lexington, 2006), chapter 11.

mechanisms (such as NAFTA panels, the EC, the European Free Trade Association (EFTA), and MERCOSUR courts). It may further help WTO dispute settlement bodies in finding the proper balance between the market access commitments of WTO Members and the WTO provisions protecting non-economic concerns of national governments. In the context of European integration, the legitimacy and effectiveness of the ECJ were greatly enhanced by cooperation among national and EC judges, by private access to the ECJ, and by the use of national legal and judicial systems as effective enforcement mechanisms.[141] Similarly, the WTO legal and dispute settlement system could be rendered more effective if national, regional and WTO trade rules and judicial safeguards were integrated into a mutually complementary, interlocking 'constitutional system' for the protection not only of the rights of governments, but also of the rights of private traders, producers, investors and consumers interested in the decentralized protection of rule of law and open markets. The contractual and reciprocal nature of international trade agreements renders the hope for a customary 'common law' of international trade illusory.[142] Yet, the compulsory jurisdiction of WTO dispute settlement bodies and of regional trade courts sets incentives for a progressive 'constitutionalization' of international trade rules and policies for the benefit of welfare-increasing cooperation among free citizens across frontiers.

[141] See Miguel P. Maduro, *We the Court – the European Court of Justice and the European Economic Constitution* (Oxford, 1998); and Renaud Dehousse, *The European Court of Justice. The Politics of Judicial Integration* (London, 1998).

[142] For a different view, see Joseph H.H. Weiler (ed.), *The EU, the WTO and NAFTA. Towards a Common Law of International Trade* (Oxford, 2000).

5

Evaluating WTO dispute settlement: what results have been achieved through consultations and implementation of panel reports?

WILLIAM J. DAVEY[1]

This chapter examines the operation and accomplishments of two under-studied aspects of the World Trade Organization (WTO) dispute settlement system – the consultation process and the implementation results. After a brief summary of the operation of the WTO dispute settlement system – focusing on consultations and the implementation process – it examines in detail the results of consultations and the record on implementation. As part of that examination, it looks at proposals on consultations and implementation that have been made over the years in the ongoing dispute settlement reform negotiations.[2]

I. Brief overview of the WTO dispute settlement process[3]

An effective dispute settlement system is critical to the operation of the WTO. In the words of the *Understanding on the Rules and Procedures Governing the Settlement of Disputes* (DSU), it 'is a central element in providing security and predictability to the multilateral trading system'.[4] There are essentially four phases in the WTO dispute settlement process: consultations, the panel process, the appellate process and surveillance of implementation.

The first step in the process is consultations. A WTO Member may ask for consultations with another Member if the complaining Member

[1] Edwin M. Adams Professor of Law, University of Illinois College of Law.

[2] The conclusions drawn are somewhat tentative, as additional information about some disputes is needed in order to analyze them.

[3] A more detailed description of the WTO dispute settlement system, from which this section is taken, can be found in William J. Davey, 'The WTO Dispute Settlement Mechanism', Illinois Public Law Research Paper No. 03–08, 25 June 2003, available at: <http://ssrn.com/abstract=419943>.

[4] Article 3.2 of the DSU.

believes that the other Member has violated a WTO agreement or otherwise nullified or impaired benefits accruing to it. The goal of the consultation stage is to enable the disputing parties to understand better the factual situation and the legal claims in respect of the dispute and to resolve the matter without further proceedings. The DSU provides that '[t]he aim of the dispute settlement mechanism is to secure a positive solution to a dispute. A solution mutually acceptable to the parties to a dispute and consistent with the [WTO] agreements is clearly to be preferred.'[5]

If consultations are requested under Article XXII of the *General Agreement on Tariffs and Trade* (GATT) *1994* or the equivalent provision of another WTO agreement,[6] WTO Members with a substantial trade interest may request to be joined in the consultations as third parties.[7] If the Member asked to consult agrees that the claim of substantial interest is well-founded, the request to join will be honoured. If, however, consultations are requested under Article XXIII (or its equivalent), there is no provision for third parties to join in the consultations.

The manner in which the consultations are conducted is up to the parties. The DSU has no rules on consultations beyond that they are to be entered into in good faith and are to be held with 30 days of a request. Typically, they are held in Geneva and involve capital-based officials, as well as the local WTO delegates of the parties. During the consultations, both parties are likely to try and learn more about the facts and the legal arguments of the other party. Written questions may be exchanged and written answers requested. Despite the fact that the structure of consultations is undefined and there are no rules for conducting them, as explained below, consultations lead to settlements (or at least the apparent abandonment of a case) in respect of a significant number of consultation requests.

If consultations fail to resolve the dispute within 60 days of the request for consultations, the complaining WTO Member may request the Dispute Settlement Body (DSB) to establish a panel to rule on the dispute.[8] Pursuant to the DSU, if requested, the DSB is required to establish a panel no later than the second meeting at which the request for a panel appears on the agenda, unless there is a consensus in the DSB to the

[5] Article 3.7 of the DSU. At this stage, as well as at later stages in the process, there is a possibility of utilizing the good offices of the WTO Director-General or mediation to settle a dispute (Article 5 of the DSU). This is seldom done, however.

[6] The equivalent provisions are listed in a footnote to Article 4.11 of the DSU.

[7] Article 4.11 of the DSU.

[8] Article 4.7 of the DSU.

contrary.[9] Thus, unless the Member requesting the establishment of a panel consents to delay, a panel will be established within approximately 90 days of the initial request for consultations. After the panel is established by the DSB, three individuals are selected – by agreement of the parties or by the Director-General – as panelists.[10] A panel normally meets with the parties shortly after its selection to set its working procedures and time schedule. The standard proposed timetable for panels makes provision for two meetings between the panel and the parties to discuss the substantive issues in the case. Each meeting is preceded by the filing of written submissions and often followed by panel questions addressed to the parties. After completing the fact-gathering and argument phase, the panel issues a draft of the 'descriptive part' of its report, which summarizes the arguments of the parties and on which the parties may submit comments. Following receipt of comments, the panel issues its 'interim report', which contains the descriptive part as revised, as well as the panel's findings and recommendations. In light of comments received from the parties on the interim report, the panel then issues its final report. After its circulation to WTO Members, the final report is referred to the DSB for formal adoption, which is to take place within 60 days unless there is a consensus not to adopt the report or an appeal of the report to the WTO Appellate Body.

The Appellate Body consists of seven individuals, appointed by the DSB for four-year terms. The Appellate Body hears appeals of panel reports in divisions of three, although its rules provide for the division hearing a case to exchange views with the other four Appellate Body members before the division finalizes its report.[11] The members of the division that hears a particular appeal are selected by a secret procedure that is based on randomness, unpredictability and the opportunity for all members to serve without regard to national origin.[12] The Appellate Body is required to issue its report within 60 (at most 90) days from the date of the appeal,[13] and its report is to be adopted automatically by the DSB within 30 days, absent consensus to the contrary.

The final phase of the WTO dispute settlement process is the surveillance stage. The purpose of this stage is to ensure that DSB recommendations (based on adopted panel and Appellate Body reports) are implemented. If a

[9] Article 6.1 of the DSU. [10] Article 8 of the DSU.

[11] Rule 4(3) of the *Working Procedures for Appellate Review*, WT/AB/WP/5, 5 January 2005.

[12] Ibid., Rule 6(2).

[13] Article 17.5 of the DSU. Except for the first few cases, 90 days has been the standard.

panel and/or the Appellate Body find that an agreement has been violated, it typically recommends that the Member concerned bring the offending measure into conformity with its WTO obligations.[14] While a panel may suggest ways of implementation, it is ultimately left to that Member to determine how to implement.[15] Under the surveillance function, the offending Member is required to state its intentions with respect to implementation within 30 days of the adoption of the applicable report(s) by the DSB. If immediate implementation is impractical, a Member is to be afforded a reasonable period of time for implementation.[16] Absent agreement, that period of time may be set by arbitration. The DSU provides that, as a guideline for the arbitrator, the reasonable period of time should not exceed 15 months.[17]

If a party fails to implement the report within the reasonable period of time, the prevailing party may request compensation.[18] If that is not forthcoming, it may request the DSB to authorize it to suspend concessions (that is, take retaliatory action) owed to the non-implementing party.[19] DSB authorization is automatic, absent consensus to the contrary, subject to arbitration of the level of suspension if requested by the non-implementing Member.[20] The rules on suspension of concessions work without problem when it is agreed that there has been no implementation. However, if there is a disagreement over whether there has been satisfactory implementation, the provisions of the DSU do not work harmoniously. On the one hand, Article 21.5 of the DSU provides that such a disagreement shall be referred to the original panel, where available, which shall issue its report in 90 days. At the same time, Article 22.2 of the DSU provides that if a Member fails to bring its nonconforming measure into compliance, the DSB must authorize (if requested and absent consensus to the contrary) the suspension of concessions within 30 days of the expiration of the reasonable period of time. An Article 21.5 proceeding would normally not be completed within 30 days of the expiration of the reasonable period of time. As a consequence, a number of questions arise. Can the procedures be followed simultaneously or must the Article 21.5 procedure precede the Article 22 procedure? Can the deadline for DSB authorization of suspension pursuant to the negative consensus rule be suspended until completion of an Article 21.5 proceeding? While these questions have yet to be formally resolved, the current practice is to start both procedures and suspend the

[14] As a consequence, WTO remedies are typically viewed as prospective in nature. There is no reparation of past damage awarded. [15] Article 19.1 of the DSU.
[16] Article 21.3 of the DSU. [17] Article 21.3 of the DSU. [18] Article 22.2 of the DSU.
[19] Articles 22.2 and 22.6 of the DSU. [20] Articles 22.6 and 22.7 of the DSU

Article 22 proceeding pending the outcome of the Article 21.5 proceeding and to agree that the negative consensus rule will apply at the end of the Article 22 proceedings.

In light of this general outline of the WTO dispute settlement procedures, I now turn to a more detailed examination of the results of consultations and the implementation of panel reports.

II. Results of consultations

1. Overview[21]

Of the 181 disputes[22] started with a consultation request prior to 1 July 2002, there are 107 disputes that either did not result in an adopted panel report or are not now pending before an active panel.[23] It appears that they were resolved as follows:

Settled or dropped, after panel established	18[24]
Settled, with notification to DSB	26[25]

[21] This section is taken from Davey, 'WTO: The First Ten Years'.

[22] I categorize related consultations requests as involving one dispute. The categorization and the reasons therefor are explained in more detail in Davey, 'WTO: The First Ten Years', 45–46. The footnotes herein indicate the groupings I have made.

[23] The 1 July 2002 cut-off date allows consideration of over 80 per cent of the 324 consultation requests made in the first 10 years of the operation of the WTO system. Many of the requests after the cut-off involve pending cases.

[24] *EC – Scallops (Canada)* (DS7); *US – Wool Coats* (DS32); *Hungary – Agricultural Products* (DS35); *US – Helms Burton* (DS38); *Turkey – Taxes on Film Revenues* (DS43); *EC – Butter* (DS72); *US – Procurement* (DS88, DS95); *Nicaragua – Imports from Honduras and Colombia* (DS188 and DS201); *Argentina – Cotton* (DS190); *Chile – Swordfish* (DS193); *Philippines – Motor Vehicles* (DS195); *Brazil – Patent Protection* (DS199); *Belgium – Rice* (DS210); *Peru – Taxes on Cigarettes* (DS227); *Turkey – Fresh Fruit* (DS237); *US – Florida Excise Tax* (DS250); *EC – Provisional Steel Safeguards* (DS260); *Uruguay – Tax Treatment* (DS261).

[25] *Malaysia – Polyethylene* (DS1); *Korea – Shelf Life* (DS5); *EC – Grains* (DS13); *Poland – Autos* (DS19); *Korea – Bottled Water* (DS20); *Venezuela – OCTG Imports* (DS23); *Japan – Sound Recordings (US)* (DS28) and *(EC)* (DS42); *Pakistan – Patent Protection* (DS36); *Portugal – Patent Protection* (DS37); *Korea – Telecommunications* (DS40); *Japan – Satellite* (DS73); *Philippines – Pork and Poultry* (DS74, DS102); *Ireland – Copyright* (DS82); *Denmark – IPR Enforcement* (DS83); *US – Textiles and Apparel I and II* (DS85, DS151); *Sweden – IPR Enforcement* (DS86); *EC – Copyright* (DS115); *Australia – Coated Paper* (DS119); *EC – Motion Pictures* (DS124); *Greece – Motion Pictures* (DS125); *Argentina – Patent Protection* (DS171, DS196); *Romania – Minimum Import Prices* (DS198); *Philippines – Resins* (DS215); *US – Patent Code* (DS224); *Mexico – Matches* (DS232); *Slovak Republic – Sugar* (DS235); *Romania – Wheat* (DS240); *Peru – Import Taxes* (DS255). Note that *Argentina – Patent Protection* has only been partially settled.

Settled, without notification	20 [26]
Dropped (for legal, political, commercial reasons)	24 [27]
Dropped (trade remedy measure not imposed/removed/expired)	15 [28]
Pending?	4 [29]

Overall, this suggests that the consultation process has worked rather effectively. Almost all of the cases examined were disposed of. However, it is useful to try to analyze the results in some more detail, particularly in respect of the cases where there was no formal announcement of settlement.

[26] *Korea – Inspection* (DS3 and DS41); *US – Autos* (DS6); *Japan – Telecommunications Equipment* (DS15); *Brazil – Autos* (DS51, DS52, DS65, DS81); *Mexico – Customs Valuation* (DS53); *US – Poultry Imports* (DS100); *Brazil – Payment Terms* (DS116); *US – Harbour Maintenance Tax* (DS118); *Slovak Republic – Dairy and Cattle* (DS133); *EC – Conifer Wood* (DS137); *Slovak Republic – Wheat Duties* (DS143); *US – Cattle and Grain Imports* (DS144); *Czech Republic – Wheat Duties* (DS148); *India – Customs Duties* (DS150); *EC – Coffee* (DS154, DS209); *Hungary – Steel Safeguard* (DS159); *Brazil – Import Licensing* (DS183); *Mexico – Live Swine* (DS203); *Egypt – Canned Tuna* (DS205); *Turkey – Pet Food* (DS256). Note that *Korea – Inspection, US – Harbour Maintenance Tax*, and *EC – Conifer Wood* have only been partially settled.

[27] *US – Tariff Increases (Hormones Retaliation)* (DS39); *Japan – Distribution Services* (DS45); *Japan – Pork* (DS66); *Belgium – Telephone Directory Services* (DS80); *EC – Cheese* (DS104); *Pakistan – Hides and Skins* (DS107); *US – Groundnut Quotas* (DS111); *Canada – Film Distribution* (DS117); *India – Export Commodities* (DS120); *Belgium – Taxes* (DS127) (also *Netherlands – Taxes* (DS128), *Greece – Taxes* (DS129), *Ireland – Taxes* (DS130), and *France – Taxes* (DS131)); *EC – Rice Duties* (DS134); *Argentina – Wheat Gluten* (DS145); *Japan – Leather Quotas* (DS147); *EC – Patent Protection* (DS153); *Argentina – Drill Bits* (DS157); *South Africa – Pharmaceuticals* (DS168); *EC – Avionics* (DS172); *France – Avionics* (DS173); *US – Sugar Reclassification* (DS180); *Turkey – Pipe Fittings* (DS208); *US – Carbon Steel (Brazil)* (DS218); *EC – Corn Gluten Quotas* (DS223); *Brazil – Jute Bags* (DS229); *Argentina – Pharmaceuticals* (DS233); *US – Silicon Metal* (DS239). In a few of these cases, the relevant authorities may view these cases as pending or being monitored, but I think that they can legitimately be considered as dropped.

[28] *US – Tomatoes* (DS49); *US – Urea* (DS63); *US – Corn Brooms* (DS78); *US – Colour TVs* (DS89); *US – Salmon* (DS97); *Peru – Buses* (DS112); *EC – Cotton Fabrics* (DS140); *US – Live Cattle* (DS167); *Colombia – Polyester Filaments* (DS181); *Ecuador – Cement* (DS182, DS191); *Trinidad & Tobago – Pasta* (DS185, DS187); *Mexico – Transformers* (DS216); *US – Seamless Pipe* (DS225); *Chile – Edible Oils* (DS226); *Chile – Sugar* (DS228, DS230).

[29] *India – Import Restrictions* (DS149, DS279); *US – Section 337 Tariff Act Amendments* (DS186); *Brazil – Minimum Import Prices* (DS197); *US – Section 306 Trade Act* (DS200). These cases should probably be viewed as dropped. Although the relevant authorities consider them to be open, there have been no reported consultations in the latter three cases for over five years. It is clear, however, that if the United States were to take certain actions under Section 337 or Section 306 (the carousel provision), the European Communities would restart these cases or start new cases. The US case against Brazil and the EC case against India are in the nature of perennial complaints about the practices of those two countries. If a specific problem arises, it is likely that a new consultation request would be filed.

2. *Types of results*

There are various ways that the results of consultations can be categorized. For the WTO Member who initiates the consultations, the clearest favourable result is achieved when the measure at issue is withdrawn and not replaced, even though the measure may have had some negative impact on its trade while it was in force. Potentially less favourable is the situation where the measure is withdrawn, but is replaced with another measure, which may have WTO-consistency problems of its own. A favourable settlement may also be achieved when the consultations lead to a favourable change or clarification in the way that the measure at issue is to be applied. It is difficult to assess these differences in the case of consultations where the complaining party has generally accepted a settlement of the case. The act of settlement indicates that the complainant is satisfied with result, regardless of whether the settlement is effected by a withdrawal, modification or clarification of the measure. Thus, for purposes of this analysis, whether the measure was withdrawn, modified, or clarified would not seem to much matter. Accordingly, I count the results of settlements as having appropriately resolved the dispute, although it should be noted that in four cases, the settlement was considered to be only a partial resolution of the dispute.

In contrast, with respect to the dropped cases, there was, of course, no agreed settlement. In such cases, it is useful to consider whether the contested measure was removed or not, and if not, what action, if any, by the respondent led to the dropping of the case. In this regard, I have noted two types of dropped cases – (i) those where a challenged trade remedy measure was either not imposed or was terminated within 18 months and (ii) others. Given the time taken to process a dispute in the WTO system, the non-appearance or disappearance of the measure within 18 months is probably the best result that the dispute settlement system can guarantee through formal proceedings. Thus, the former type of case would seem to provide a satisfactory result for the complainant, except, of course, for the trade disruptive effect while the measure was threatened or in force.

As to the other dropped cases, it appears that they were resolved as follows:

Non-trade remedy measure removed	4 [30]
Abandoned (probably no significant violation provable)	7 [31]

[30] *US – Tariff Increases (Hormones Retaliation)* (DS39); *Japan – Pork* (DS66); *India – Export Commodities* (DS120); *EC – Corn Gluten Quotas* (DS223).

[31] *Japan – Distribution Services* (DS45) – the law that was the main target of the request was significantly changed within about two years; the negative result in *Japan – Film* (DS44)

No continuing commercial interest	3 [32]
Issue referred to courts or to general WTO negotiations	4 [33]
Other	6 [34]

The first category – removed non-trade remedies – gives a completely satisfactory result to the complainant.[35] In the next three types of cases, there appears that there was nothing in the way of useful results

suggested that this case might not have succeeded if pursued in panel proceedings); *EC – Cheese* (DS104) (The European Communities apparently demonstrated compliance with WTO rules); *US – Groundnut Quotas* (DS111) (the Argentine complaint about the United States' tariff rate quota did not seem to have a clear legal basis); *Argentina – Wheat Gluten* (DS145) (involved missing deadlines under the *Agreement on Subsidies and Countervailing Measures* (*SCM Agreement*), no remedy likely if pursued); *Argentina – Drill Bits* (DS157) (involved missing deadlines under the *Agreement on Implementation of Article VI of the General Agreement on Tariffs and Trade 1994* (*Anti-Dumping Agreement*), no remedy likely if pursued). I include in this category two tit for tat cases that were never seriously pursued, even following losses in the main case: *Belgium – Taxes* (DS127) (also *Netherlands – Taxes* (DS128), *Greece – Taxes* (DS129), *Ireland – Taxes* (DS130), and *France – Taxes* (DS131)) – this was a 'tit for tat' case for the *US – FSC* dispute, cases seemed mostly to involve insignificant measures; and *EC – Patent Protection* (DS153) – this was a 'tit for tat' case for the *Canada – Patent Protection* dispute.

32 *Belgium – Telephone Directory Services* (DS80) (initiation apparently helped commercial interest negotiate an acceptable outcome with Belgian government); *Canada – Film Distribution* (DS117) (merger of commercial interests on opposing sides of dispute); *EC – Avionics* (DS172) and *France – Avionics* (DS173) (The US company behind the request was concerned with business relations in the European Communities).

33 *Japan – Leather Quotas* (DS147) (referred to Doha negotiations where satisfactory result thought to be more likely obtained); *Nicaragua – Imports from Honduras and Colombia* (DS188, DS201) (WTO issues arose out of territorial dispute referred to International Court of Justice (ICJ)); *US – Carbon Steel (Brazil)* (DS218) (concerned US privatization methodology in countervailing duty cases, referred to US courts); *US – Silicon Metal* (DS239) (an anti-dumping case where favourable result was obtained in court proceedings a few months after consultations requested).

34 *US – Sugar Reclassification* (DS180) (Canadian objection to US reclassification that had initially been enjoined by US court, but reversed on appeal; not pursued by Canada and not listed in 2005 Canadian market access agenda; strength of legal claim not clear); *Turkey – Pipe Fittings* (DS208) (duty has remained in force (now under sunset review), not pursued following initial consultations by Brazil, which has otherwise been an active complainant in panel proceedings – suggesting that the strength or significance of the case may not have been that great); *EC – Rice Duties* (DS134); *South Africa – Pharmaceuticals* (DS168); *Brazil – Jute Bags* (DS229); *Argentina – Pharmaceuticals* (DS233). The four latter cases all involved India as a complainant. Although the strength of the legal claims is not apparent to me, it may be that the cases were not pursued to the extent that they could have because of resource constraints. It may also be possible that the latter three were not pursued because of political reasons arising out of India's overall relationships with the respondents.

35 In one instance, the resolution may not have been all that timely – *India – Export Commodities* (DS120).

obtainable from pursuing WTO dispute settlement. The same may be true of the 'other' category, as the legal basis for the claims is not clear.

Overall, complainants seem to have done well in achieving results through WTO consultations, although it sometimes takes considerable time, as discussed in section III below. There does not seem to be any particular pattern as to the type of settlement obtained as between developed and developing countries, whether as complainants or respondents.[36]

3. *Timing of results*

One major complaint about WTO dispute settlement that is often made by businesses is that it takes too long to get results. In examining the cases where settlements were achieved in consultations, the following indicates how long it took to achieve those settlements. This exercise is by its very nature rather imprecise, but some useful general indications can be established. The imprecision arises from the difficulty in fixing the starting and end points to be used. While the underlying problem typically arises prior to the request for consultations, I have used the date of the request for consultations for the starting point of the timing measurement. I have used the date that the settlement was (or was agreed to be) implemented where available and the date of the settlement where that is not known to me. Both of these choices tend to understate the period during which trade was adversely affected by the challenged measure, but they do tend to focus on the time that the dispute was 'in' the WTO dispute settlement system.

Within 6 months	30	40% [37]
Within 6 to 12 months	13	17% [38]

[36] More work needs to be done to be satisfied with this conclusion, but such differences are not immediately apparent.

[37] *Malaysia – Polyethylene* (DS1); *US – Autos* (DS6); *Japan – Telecommunications Equipment* (DS15); *Venezuela – OCTG Imports* (DS23); *US – Wool Coats* (DS32); *Portugal – Patent Protection* (DS37); *US – Tariff Increases (Hormones Retaliation)* (DS39); *Korea – Telecommunications* (DS40); *US – Tomatoes* (DS49); *Japan – Pork* (DS66); *Japan – Satellite* (DS73); *US – Salmon* (DS97); *US – Poultry Imports* (DS100); *Australia – Coated Paper* (DS119); *EC – Cotton Fabrics* (DS140); *Slovak Republic – Wheat Duties* (DS143); *US – Cattle and Grain Imports* (DS144); *Czech Republic – Wheat Duties* (DS148); *Colombia – Polyester Filaments* (DS181); *Ecuador – Cement* (DS182, DS191); *Argentina – Cotton* (DS190); *Mexico – Transformers* (DS216); *EC – Corn Gluten Quotas* (DS223); *US – Patent Code* (DS224); *US – Seamless Pipe* (DS225); *Chile – Edible Oils* (DS226); *Peru – Taxes on Cigarettes* (DS227); *US – Silicon Metal* (DS239); *Romania – Wheat* (DS240); *Peru – Import Taxes* (DS255).

[38] *Poland – Autos* (DS19); *Pakistan – Patent Protection* (DS36); *US – Helms Burton* (DS38); *Philippines – Pork and Poultry* (DS74, DS102); *Pakistan – Hides and Skins* (DS107);

Within 12 to 18 months	16	21% [39]
Within 18 to 24 months	3	4% [40]
More than 2 years	13	17% [41]
Unclear	[28]	n.a. [42]

These numbers underscore that the consultations process serves a very valuable function. It provides a mechanism that resolves most cases much more promptly than the formal panel/Appellate Body process.

4. Summary

Overall, the consultations process seems to work quite well for cases that do not go on to the formal panel/Appellate Body process.

Brazil – Payment Terms (DS116); *EC – Motion Pictures* (DS124); *Greece – Motion Pictures* (DS125); *US – Live Cattle* (DS167); *Trinidad & Tobago – Pasta* (DS185, DS187); *Chile – Swordfish* (DS193); *Philippines – Resins* (DS215); *Chile – Sugar* (DS228, DS230); *Slovak Republic – Sugar* (DS235).

[39] *Korea – Shelf Life* (DS5); *EC – Scallops (Canada)* (DS7) and *(Peru and Chile)* (DS12, DS14); *Korea – Bottled Water* (DS20); *Japan – Sound Recordings (US)* (DS28) and *(EC)* (DS42); *Turkey – Taxes on Film Revenues* (DS43); *US – Urea* (DS63); *US – Corn Brooms* (DS78); *US – Procurement* (DS88, DS95); *US – Colour TVs* (DS89); *Peru – Buses* (DS112); *Romania – Minimum Import Prices* (DS198); *Brazil – Patent Protection* (DS199); *Belgium – Rice* (DS210); *Turkey – Fresh Fruit* (DS237); *EC – Provisional Steel Safeguards* (DS260); *Uruguay – Tax Treatment* (DS261).

[40] *EC – Grains* (DS13) (grouped with *EC – Cereals* (DS9) and *EC – Rice* (DS17, DS25)); *Sweden – IPR Enforcement* (DS86); *India – Export Commodities* (DS120).

[41] *Korea – Inspection* (DS3, DS41); *Hungary – Agricultural Products* (DS35); *Brazil – Autos* (DS51, DS52, DS65, DS81); *Mexico – Customs Valuation* (DS53); *EC – Butter* (DS72); *Ireland – Copyright* (DS82) and *EC – Copyright* (DS115); *Denmark – IPR Enforcement* (DS83); *US – Textiles and Apparel I and II* (DS85 and DS151); *EC – Conifer Wood* (DS137); *Argentina – Patent Protection* (DS171, DS196); *Nicaragua – Imports from Honduras and Colombia* (DS188, DS201); *Philippines – Motor Vehicles* (DS195); *Mexico – Matches* (DS232).

[42] I have not counted those cases where the date of the resolution was unclear in calculating the percentages. Those cases involved some of the 'settled, not notified' cases, but were mostly 'dropped – other' cases, where no date could probably ever be firmly fixed. *Japan – Distribution Services* (DS45); *Belgium – Telephone Directory Services* (DS80); *EC – Cheese* (DS104); *US – Groundnut Quotas* (DS111); *Canada – Film Distribution* (DS117); *US – Harbour Maintenance Tax* (DS118); *Belgium – Taxes* (DS127) (also *Netherlands – Taxes* (DS128), *Greece – Taxes* (DS129), *Ireland – Taxes* (DS130), *France – Taxes* (DS131)); *Slovak Republic – Dairy and Cattle* (DS133); *EC – Rice Duties* (DS134); *Argentina – Wheat Gluten* (DS145); *Japan – Leather Quotas* (DS147); *India – Customs Duties* (DS150); *EC – Patent Protection* (DS153); *EC – Coffee* (DS154, DS209); *Argentina – Drill Bits* (DS157); *Hungary – Steel Safeguard* (DS159); *South Africa – Pharmaceuticals* (DS168); *EC – Avionics* (DS172) and *France – Avionics* (DS173); *US – Sugar Reclassification* (DS180); *Brazil – Import Licensing* (DS183); *Mexico – Live Swine* (DS203); *Egypt – Canned Tuna* (DS205); *Turkey – Pipe Fittings* (DS208); *US – Carbon Steel (Brazil)* (DS218); *Brazil – Jute Bags* (DS229); *Argentina – Pharmaceuticals* (DS233); *US – Florida Excise Tax* (DS250); *Turkey – Pet Food* (DS256).

III. Implementation of panel/Appellate Body reports

1. Overview

Of the 181 disputes started with a consultation request prior to 1 July 2002, there were 74 disputes where panels had issued reports as of September 2005. As of that date, one of those disputes involved a pending case, in the sense that the reasonable period of time for implementation had not expired.[43] Of the remaining 73 disputes where reports had been adopted,[44] the complainant lost in ten of them, such that no implementation was required.[45] Of the 63 other disputes, there had been implementation in 53.[46] That leaves ten disputes where there had been no

[43] *EC – Trademarks and Geographical Indications (US)* (DS174) and *(Australia)* (DS290).

[44] The WTO on its website lists more reports as having been adopted as of this date. The difference is explained by the fact that this study counts a number of cases, where multiple reports were issued, as involving one dispute.

[45] *Brazil – Desiccated Coconut* (DS22) (also *Brazil – Desiccated and Powdered Coconut* (DS30)); *Japan – Film* (DS44); *EC – Computer Equipment* (DS62, DS67, DS68); *EC – Asbestos* (DS135); *US – Section 301 Trade Act* (DS152); *Korea – Procurement* (DS163); *US – Export Restraints* (DS194); *US – Section 129(c)(1) URAA* (DS221); *US – Textiles Rules of Origin* (DS243); *US – Corrosion-Resistant Steel Sunset Review* (DS244). There was also no violation found in the *Guatemala – Cement I* case (DS60), but I have grouped that case with *Guatemala – Cement II* (DS156), where a violation was found.

[46] *US – Gasoline* (DS2, DS4); *Japan – Alcoholic Beverages II* (DS8, DS10, DS11); *Australia – Salmon* (DS18) (also *Australia – Salmonids* (DS21)); *US – Underwear* (DS24); *EC – Bananas III* (DS27) (also DS16, DS105, DS158); *Canada – Periodicals* (DS31); *US – Wool Shirts and Blouses* (DS33); *Turkey – Textiles* (DS34) (grouped with DS29 and DS47); *India – Patents (US)* (DS50) and *(EC)* (DS79); *Indonesia – Autos* (DS54, DS55, DS59, DS64); *Argentina – Textiles and Apparel* (DS56) (also *Argentina – Clothing and Footwear* (DS77)); *US – Shrimp* (DS58) (also DS61); *EC – Poultry* (DS69); *Korea – Alcoholic Beverages* (DS75, DS84); *Japan – Agricultural Products II* (DS76); *Chile – Alcoholic Beverages* (DS87, DS110) (also DS109); *India – Quantitative Restrictions* (DS90) (also DS91, DS92, DS93, DS94, DS96); *Korea – Dairy* (DS98); *US – DRAMS* (DS99); *Canada – Dairy* (DS103, DS113); *Canada – Pharmaceutical Patents* (DS114); *Argentina – Footwear (EC)* (DS121) (also DS123 and DS164); *Thailand – H-Beams* (DS122); *Australia – Automotive Leather* (DS126) (also DS106 and *Australia – Clothing and Footwear*, DS57); *Mexico – Corn Syrup* (DS132) (also DS101); *US – 1916 Act (EC)* (DS136) and *(Japan)* (DS162); *US – Lead and Bismuth II* (DS138); *Canada – Autos* (DS139, DS142); *EC – Bed Linen* (DS141); *India – Autos* (DS146, DS175); *Argentina – Hides and Leather* (DS155); *Guatemala – Cement I and II* (DS60 and DS156); *Korea – Various Measures on Beef* (DS161, DS169); *US – Certain EC Products* (DS165); *US – Wheat Gluten* (DS166); *Canada – Patent Term* (DS170); *US – Lamb* (DS177, DS178); *US – Stainless Steel* (DS179); *Argentina – Ceramic Tiles* (DS189); *US – Cotton Yarn* (DS192); *US – Line Pipe* (DS202) (also *US – Wire Rod and Line Pipe*, DS214); *Mexico – Telecoms* (DS204); *US – Steel Plate* (DS206); *Chile – Price Band System* (DS207) (also DS220); *Egypt – Steel Rebar* (DS211); *US – Carbon Steel* (DS213); *EC – Tube or Pipe Fittings* (DS219); *EC – Sardines* (DS231); *Argentina – Preserved Peaches* (DS238); *Argentina – Poultry Anti-Dumping Duties* (DS241); *Japan – Apples* (DS245); *EC – Tariff*

implementation or a disagreement between the parties over implementation.[47] That suggests a successful implementation rate of 83 per cent,[48] which is fairly successful for state-to-state dispute settlement.[49]

To get a truer picture of the results of WTO dispute settlement, however, it is necessary to look at the form of implementation – was the problem measure removed or modified or essentially maintained? How long did it take to achieve the results?

2. *Forms of implementation*

As in the case of consultations, there are various possibilities that may be utilized in implementing a panel report. Since there is often no

Preferences (DS246) (grouped with *EC – GSP* (DS242)); *US – Steel Safeguards* (DS248, DS249, DS251, DS252, DS253, DS254, DS258, DS259) (also DS274). In some of these cases, the complaining party has protested the WTO-consistency of implementation, but has decided to accept it, tacitly or otherwise, by not pursing the matter further.

47 The ten cases include *EC – Hormones* (DS26, DS48) (the European Communities claims it has implemented and has commenced cases (*US – Continued Suspension* (DS320), *Canada – Continued Suspension* (DS321)) against the United States and Canada alleging that their continued imposition of suspension of concession is not permitted under WTO rules); *Brazil – Aircraft* (DS46); *Canada – Aircraft* (DS70) and *Canada – Aircraft Credits and Guarantees* (DS222) (also DS71); *US – FSC* (DS108) (the United States has replaced the basic tax legislation at issue with a measure acceptable to the European Communities, but the European Communities has successfully challenged, at the panel level, certain transitional provisions under which the old legislation continues in force); *US – Section 110(5) Copyright Act* (DS160); *US – Section 211 Appropriations Act* (DS176); *US – Hot-Rolled Steel* (DS184); *US – Countervailing Measures on Certain EC Products* (DS212) (The United States has implemented with respect to most, but not all, of the individual countervailing duty cases challenged); *US – Offset Act (Byrd Amendment)* (DS217, DS234) and *US – Softwood Lumber* (*Lumber IV* (DS257) on appeal of the Article 21.5 panel report, with *Lumber V* (DS264) and *Lumber VI* (DS277) pending before Article 21.5 panels, also grouped with *Lumber III* (DS236; DS247). Concessions are currently suspended in the *EC – Hormones* and *US – Offset Act (Byrd Amendment)* cases.

48 To focus on the rate of implementation at any given point of time may give a misleading impression of the operation of the WTO dispute settlement system. Typically, the results of panel/Appellate Body reports are eventually implemented.

49 The WTO success rate is comparable to the rate achieved by the GATT dispute settlement system through 1989 (See Robert E. Hudec, *Enforcing International Trade Law* (Salem, 1993), chapter 11). It is probably true, however, that some difficult cases were never brought to the GATT system because of the right of the losing party to 'block' any adverse consequences of a decision against it. Moreover, the success rate of the GATT system declined considerably in the 1990s. In this regard, it is interesting to compare the success rate of the ICJ. Tom Ginsburg and Richard H. McAdams, 'Adjudicating in Anarchy: An Expressive Theory of International Dispute Resolution' (2004) 45 *William & Mary Law Review*, 1229, 1308–1312 (finding a 68 per cent compliance rate, as defined by the authors, for a sample of cases before the ICJ).

agreement on implementation, it is useful to break down the cases along the following lines. The clearest favourable result is achieved when the measure at issue is withdrawn and not replaced. Potentially less favourable is the situation where the measure is either (i) modified – a not uncommon result in anti-dumping and countervailing duty cases or (ii) withdrawn, but replaced with another measure. In either situation, the modified or new measure may have WTO-consistency problems of its own. In fact, for a period of time (roughly 1999–2002), there seemed to be fairly frequent resort to DSU Article 21.5 proceedings, which provide a mechanism for testing whether an implementation measure is WTO consistent. The frequent invocation of these proceedings underlines the problem of modified or replacement measures.[50]

In examining how various Members have implemented adverse dispute settlement findings, it is instructive to consider how the form of implementation has often followed some clear patterns by agreement. To be more specific, it appears that dispute settlement proceedings involving safeguard cases under the *Agreement on Safeguards* or the *Agreement on Textiles and Clothing* (*ATC*) typically lead to a withdrawal of the measure.[51] Of course, the time taken by the dispute settlement proceedings means that the defaulting country in effect achieves its protection goals for a considerable period of time. Nonetheless, the cases tend to be definitively resolved by the expiration of the reasonable period of time. The same appears to be true of violations of the *Agreement on Trade-Related Aspects of Intellectual Property Rights* (*TRIPS Agreement*). Essentially, the defaulting country to date has removed the TRIPS-inconsistency, if it has attempted to implement at all.[52]

In contrast, in anti-dumping and countervailing duty cases, the typical result has been a modification of the challenged measure, which in many cases has not resulted in a significant reduction in the trade impact of the measure. For example, of the 17 disputes involving successful challenges to individual anti-dumping/countervailing duty measures,[53] the

[50] This section will be based in part on a paper presented at the Chung Hua Institute for Economic Research, Taipei, 30 August 2005, William J. Davey, 'Implementation of the Results of WTO Trade Remedy Cases', Illinois Public Law Research Paper No. 05–20, available at: <http://ssrn.com/abstract=863905> (visited 19 April 2006).

[51] Ibid.

[52] *India – Patents (US)* (DS50); *India – Patents (EC)* (DS79); *Canada – Pharmaceutical Patents* (DS114); *Canada – Patent Term* (DS170).

[53] These cases are described and analyzed in more detail in Davey, 'Implementation of WTO Trade Remedy Cases'. For purposes of this analysis, I have counted the *US – Softwood Lumber V* (anti-dumping) and *US – Softwood Lumber IV* (countervailing duty) cases separately.

challenged measure was revoked in four cases;[54] was revoked in three other cases, but only after an Article 21.5 proceeding challenging implementation had been commenced;[55] was significantly reduced in three cases;[56] and was not significantly reduced in seven cases.[57] Cases involving sanitary and phytosanitary (SPS) measures have also presented implementation problems because measures have been only modified. Thus, most SPS cases have been resolved, if at all, only after a considerable period of time and in two of the four cases, after an Article 21.5 proceeding.[58] There have been a number of straight subsidy cases under the *Agreement on Subsidies and Countervailing Measures* (*SCM Agreement*). The implementation problems with those cases typically have involved a refusal to stop providing subsidies immediately or not to pay those already granted. Cases arising under the *Agreement on Agriculture* also seem to have often involved modified measures that raised problems.[59] Indeed, almost all of the Article 21.5 cases have involved the *Agreement on Agriculture*, the *Agreement on Implementation of Article VI of the General Agreement on Tariffs and Trade 1994* (*Anti-Dumping Agreement*), the *SCM Agreement* as well as the *Agreement on the Application of Sanitary and Phytosanitary Measures* (*SPS Agreement*).[60]

[54] *Argentina – Ceramic Tiles*; *Argentina – Poultry Anti-Dumping Duties*; *Guatemala – Cement I* and *Guatemala – Cement II* (because Mexico's first attempt to challenge the measure in the WTO was rejected on procedural grounds, the measure was ultimately in force for over four years); *US – Lead and Bismuth II*.

[55] *US – DRAMS*; *EC – Bed Linen*; *Mexico – Corn Syrup* (the challenged anti-dumping measure was in a sense 'replaced' by a tax that has since been found to discriminate against imports in a WTO-inconsistent manner).

[56] *US – Stainless Steel*; *US – Countervailing Measures on Certain EC Products* (some measures were revoked; others saw a significant reduction in duties; others were involved in an Article 21.5 proceeding; the reductions were a result of a combination of US court decisions and WTO implementation).

[57] *US – Hot-Rolled Steel*; *US – Steel Plate* (significant reduction, but remained at 42 per cent); *US – Softwood Lumber V* (anti-dumping) (increase, which was challenged in pending Article 21.5 proceedings); *US – Softwood Lumber IV* (countervailing duty) (NAFTA panel rulings seem to have led to significant reductions); *EC – Tube or Pipe Fittings*; *Egypt – Rebar*; *Thailand – H-Beams*.

[58] *EC – Hormones* (implementation in dispute); *Australia – Salmon* (implementation only after Article 21.5 proceedings); *Japan – Agricultural Products II* (implementation after long delay); *Japan – Apples* (implementation after Article 21.5 proceedings).

[59] *Canada – Dairy* (two Article 21.5 proceedings); *EC – Poultry* (complaint of non-compliance not pursued); *Chile – Price Band System* (complaint of non-compliance not pursued).

[60] The exceptions are *EC – Bananas III* and *US – Shrimp*. The other 14 Article 21.5 cases involved: (on subsidies) *Australia – Automotive Leather II*; *Brazil – Aircraft* (two Article 21.5 proceedings); *Canada – Aircraft*; *Canada – Dairy* (two Article 21.5 proceedings); and *US – FSC* (two Article 21.5 proceedings); (on SPS issues) *Australia – Salmon* and

With the exception of cases arising under the GATT 1994, it is difficult to draw any conclusions as to the type of implementation and potential problems in respect of the other WTO agreements because there have been an insufficient number of cases. As to the many GATT cases, in most instances, the cases have involved specific legal provisions applicable to specific products – often ones that violate antidiscrimination rules. For the most part, these cases have resulted in the discriminatory or other WTO-inconsistent measure being repealed.[61] In some cases, measures have been modified, with some elements of discrimination possibly being maintained.[62]

Developing countries seem to have fared as well as developed countries in obtaining results in respect of implementation of panel/Appellate Body reports. As noted, they are more responsible in implementing adverse decisions overall. As to having to deal with foot-dragging by respondents, that seems to be a matter of principal concern in developed country vs. developed country disputes.[63]

3. *Timing of implementation*

While implementation typically occurs, as discussed above, it is often delayed, particularly when the challenged measure is replaced or modified, as opposed to being withdrawn. Thus, a considerable period of time elapses between the commencement of a case by consultation request and final implementing action.[64]

(a) Implementation overall

As of December 2004, roughly 60 per cent of panel reports requiring implementation had been implemented promptly – either within the

Footnote 60 (*cont.*)
Japan – Apples; (on anti-dumping or countervailing duty issues) *US – DRAMS*; *Mexico – Corn Syrup*; *EC – Bed Linen;* and *US – Countervailing Measures on Certain EC Products.*

[61] *US – Gasoline* (one discriminatory element expired; the other was modified and not subsequently challenged, although questions were raised); *Argentina – Hides and Leather*; *Canada – Autos*; *Canada – Periodicals*; *Canada – Wheat Exports and Grain Imports*; *Chile – Alcoholic Beverages*; *EC – Tariff Preferences*; *India – Autos*; *India – Quantitative Restrictions*; *Indonesia – Autos*; *Japan – Alcohol Beverages II*; *Korea – Alcoholic Beverages*; *Korea – Various Measures on Beef*; *Turkey – Textiles*; *US – Countervailing Measures on Certain EC Products.* Note that the European Communities does not accept that full implementation has occurred.

[62] *EC – Bananas III* (Article 21.5 proceedings, followed by a waiver and arbitration proceedings aimed at a 2006 settlement); *US – Gasoline* (see preceding note).

[63] See Table 5.2.

[64] This section is based on William J. Davey, 'Implementation in WTO Dispute Settlement: An Introduction to the Problems and Possible Solutions', RIETI Discussion Paper, Series 05-E-00X, available at: <http://www.rieti.go.jp/en/publicatoins/summary/05030017.html> (visited 19 April 2006).

original reasonable period of time for implementation or shortly thereafter. In addition, another 20 sper cent had been implemented, albeit with significant delay (the average delay after the time set for implementation was 13 months, as indicated in Table 5.3). Of the remaining cases, six of them (10 per cent) involved situations where there was a dispute over implementation. In three of them, there would have been prompt implementation if the respondent prevailed in an Article 21.5 proceeding, but they did not;[65] while the other three cases will in any event involve significantly delayed implementation even if the most recent measure is found to be WTO consistent.[66] As to the remaining six cases (10 per cent), where non-implementation was admitted, it was unclear when they will be implemented.

As indicated in Table 5.3, non-implementation is primarily a problem of the United States (four of six cases) and delayed implementation is primarily a problem of the Quad (the United States, the European Communities, Japan, and Canada) plus Australia (12 of 15 cases).[67] Developing countries have usually implemented within the original reasonable period of time (81 per cent) or within five months thereafter (9 per cent). Only twice has a developing country been the subject of an Article 21.5 proceeding – *Mexico – Corn Syrup (Article 21.5 – US)* and *Brazil – Aircraft (Article 21.5 – Canada)* – and only in one case is non-implementation by a developing country a long-standing problem – *Brazil – Aircraft (Article 21.5 – Canada)*. This means that any solution attempting to address the problems of non-implementation and delayed implementation must deal effectively with foot-dragging by the Quad countries.

(b) Implementation record by WTO agreement

It appears that the implementation record varies significantly depending on the WTO agreement at issue. As Table 5.4 indicates, there

[65] The three cases are *Japan – Apples*, *US – Countervailing Measures on Certain EC Products*, and *US – Softwood Lumber IV*. The United States lost in respect of two of the three measures challenged in the *US – Countervailing Measures on Certain EC Products* case, and Japan lost in the *Japan – Apples* case, and neither appealed. The United States lost in the *US – Softwood Lumber IV* case and has appealed.

[66] The three cases are *EC – Hormones* (53 months); *US – FSC* (49 months); *US – 1916 Act* (39 months). I would note that implementation may have been tacitly accepted in the *US – 1916 Act* case, although there are transitional issues that may become relevant depending on the results of pending cases.

[67] I have included the three cases (*EC – Hormones*, *US – FSC*, and *US – 1916 Act*) where implementation is now disputed, but where it is clear that implementation occurred only long after the expiration of the reasonable period of time.

are no implementation problems with safeguard cases, of which there have been 10. Of course, the time taken to attack a safeguard in the WTO allows it to exist long enough so that it probably serves its purpose before its removal is required. Nonetheless, safeguards have been promptly removed when found to be in violation of WTO rules. It is also interesting that GATT cases, of which there have been 18, have also generally not presented implementation problems. As indicated in Table 5.4, 12 of the 16 cases arising under the GATT 1994 were promptly implemented and of the four that were not, only *EC – Bananas III* was significantly delayed, as the other three cases were implemented within five months of the expiration of the reasonable period of time.

In terms of the implementation record under the various WTO agreements, there have been three particular problem areas. Probably the most difficult area has involved subsidies. Of the four cases, two have not been implemented at all (the regional aircraft subsidies dispute between Brazil and Canada[68]), one has been implemented prospectively after long delay (*US – FSC*: 49 months after the expiration of the original reasonable period of time) and one was implemented after 10 months delay (*Australia –Automotive Leather*). The one subsidies case under the *Agreement on Agriculture* (*Canada – Dairy*) also took a long time to implement (28 months after expiration of the reasonable period of time).[69] Thus, of the five subsidies cases, two remain unimplemented and the other three took years, on average, to be implemented.

SPS cases have also proved to be difficult in respect of implementation. As of the end of 2004, two cases were in subsequent panel proceedings – *EC – Hormones* and *Japan – Apples.* Even if found to be WTO-consistent now, implementation by the European Communities in *EC – Hormones* occurred some 59 months after expiration of the reasonable period of time – a period explained in part by the need for it to undertake new scientific studies and in part by the its complex legislative procedures. The two cases where implementation has been accepted took a long time to implement following expiration of the set reasonable period of time – *Australia – Salmon* (23 months) and *Japan – Agricultural Products II* (20 months).

There have also been problems with implementation in the trade remedies area, although to a large extent, the implementation problems in this area mainly concern the United States. In three of the seven cases

[68] *Brazil – Aircraft* and *Canada – Aircraft.*

[69] The other two cases under the *Agreement on Agriculture* were implemented within the reasonable period of time.

involving the United States, the problem is or was the need for congressional action (*US – 1916 Act*, *US – Offset Act (Byrd Amendment)*, *US – Hot-Rolled Steel*); and in two of the cases, implementation is only contested and may still be upheld or accepted (*US – Countervailing Measures on Certain EC Products* and *US – Softwood Lumber IV*). In the other two cases involving the United States, the delay was not all that great (*US – DRAMS* and *US – Countervailing Measures on Certain EC Products*).[70] It should be underlined, of course, that the total time taken to challenge a national trade remedy measure in WTO dispute settlement – from consultation request to implementation deadline, combined with the fact that implementation may often be accomplished by a revision (as opposed to the elimination) of the challenged measure – means that the WTO dispute settlement system may not provide a particularly effective means of mitigating the trade impact of trade remedy measures.

Finally, it should be mentioned that the three cases under the *TRIPS Agreement* brought against WTO Members other than the United States have been implemented promptly,[71] but the two cases involving the United States, which require congressional action to revise statutory provisions, have not been implemented.[72]

Based on the foregoing, it would appear that the problem WTO agreements for implementation of dispute settlement results are the *SCM Agreement* and the *SPS Agreement*. In the case of subsidies, the problem may be that an industry that is able to obtain governmental subsidies in the first place (whether through political power or by convincing the government that the national interest justify the subsidies) is likely to be able to delay implementation. In the case of the *SPS Agreement*, it would appear that public concerns over food safety and the impact of those concerns on politicians has been a significant problem that has delayed implementation in SPS cases. In addition, the fact that one of the subsidy cases and all of the SPS cases involve agricultural products – an area that is new to international oversight – may be an additional complicating factor in slowing implementation. In any event, any attempt to improve the implementation record at the WTO must take account of these apparent problem areas. In addition, it is worth mentioning that the overall time taken for safeguards and trade remedy cases may mean that even prompt implementation, typically by removal or revision of the

[70] The only other case in this category is *EC – Bed Linen*.

[71] *Canada – Patent Term*; *Canada – Pharmaceutical Patents*; *India – Patents*.

[72] *US – Section 110(5) Copyright Act*; *US – Section 211 Appropriations Act*. As noted above, the dispute in *US – Section 110(5) Copyright Act* was temporarily settled (until 31

contested measure, will not control improper use of safeguard and trade remedy measures. Thus, other remedies may need to be considered.

IV. Where are reforms needed?

Although the record suggests that the consultation and implementation phases of WTO dispute settlement work reasonably well, it is appropriate to consider whether additional reforms would be useful, especially in respect of implementation. The following sections discuss reforms that have been proposed in the ongoing dispute settlement reform negotiations. In one sense, these discussions started in the 1998 DSU Review process and have continued to this day.[73] During these discussions, WTO Members have usually expressed general satisfaction with the operation of the DSU, but they have also proposed myriad changes. This section will discuss some of the more important reforms proposed by WTO Members or others in respect of improving the consultation and implementation phases of dispute settlement. Particular attention is given to the reforms that the chairman of the negotiating group on dispute settlement proposed in an attempt to conclude the negotiations in May 2003, since at that time he apparently thought that they had a chance of being accepted, although no agreement was in fact reached.[74]

1. Consultations

The preliminary conclusions reached in section II above suggest that the consultation procedure works relatively well in promoting mutually agreed solutions despite its informality. Indeed, given the brevity of the minimally required consultation period (71 days[75]), the significant

Footnote 72 (*cont.*)

December 2004) by US payment of compensation and the reasonable period of time in *US – Section 211 Appropriations Act* has been extended by two years to 31 December 2004.

73 For a history of the discussions, see William J. Davey, 'Reforming WTO Dispute Settlement', in Dukgeun Ahn and Mitsuo Matsushita (eds), *WTO and East Asia New Perspectives* (London, 2004), chapter 5.

74 The proposals were contained in the so-called Chairman's Text, TN/DS/9.

75 Although the DSU specifies a minimum period of 60 days for consultations, there is an accepted practice that a request for the establishment of a panel should not be made before expiration of the formally required 60-day period. Given the advance notice required for meetings of the DSB, there is in fact a period of 71 days at a minimum between the request for consultations and the establishment of a panel. It has been proposed to cut the 60-day period to 30 days, but this may be impractical as arranging the necessary meetings may take more time.

filtering effect of the consultation process is a small price to pay in time for that benefit. What sorts of reforms have been proposed to the consultation process?[76]

(a) Transparency

As the discussion of the results of consultations makes clear, it is often not possible to ascertain precisely what happens in consultations, particularly when that is the only stage in a dispute. The Chairman's Text would modify the existing requirement to notify settlements contained in Article 3.6 of the DSU so as to specify when they should be notified (within 60 days) and that they should contain sufficient information so that they may be evaluated by other WTO Members. I would, in addition, argue that the Member requesting consultations should be required to indicate the status of the consultations on an annual basis. While this would impose a minor administrative burden, it is in the interests of the WTO, its Members, and others to know what happens to matters brought into the WTO dispute settlement system.

(b) The problem of good faith in consultations

There are complaints by some WTO Members that the consultation process is not useful, or at least not as useful as it could or should be. Some of these complaints are based on experiences where the consultations were not particularly helpful in resolving the dispute, but were rather treated as an annoying procedural step to be overcome as soon as possible. It is undoubtedly true that there are such cases. But that does not demonstrate that the consultation requirement is undesirable. Rather, it highlights that some serious disputes require resolution in the panel/Appellate Body process and that is obvious from the beginning. For example, the European Communities argued in the *EC – Bananas III* case that the consultations in that case did not serve the purpose for which they were intended, that is, there was no mutually agreed solution reached.[77] Given the history of the case, it is scarcely surprising that the consultations did not succeed. It seemed clear that the European Communities' system was discriminatory in a number of ways

[76] This section is based in part on William J. Davey, 'WTO Dispute Settlement: Segregating the Useful Political Aspects and Avoiding "Over-legalization"', in Marko Bronckers and Reinhard Quick (eds), *New Directions in International Economic Law: Essays in Honour of john H. Jackson* (The Hague, 2000), pp. 291–317.

[77] Panel Reports, *EC – Bananas III*, paras. 7.17–7.21. The panel rejected the European Communities' argument and it was one of the few issues not appealed.

detrimental to the complaining parties and beneficial to European Communities' operators. The prospect that the European Communities would change its system to the detriment of its operators was scarcely likely. The case was inevitably going to be resolved only after a panel ruled whether the discriminatory aspects were WTO-consistent or not. Other cases like that will occur from time to time. The advantage of the filtering provided by the consultation requirement remains, however, as long as some panels are avoided.

(c) Consultations as a 'discovery' mechanism

There are also complaints that the consultation process should be made more useful in preparing cases for the panel stage. For example, it has been proposed that a consulting party should be required to respond in writing to questions propounded by the other party so as to clarify the issues for the panel process. In my view, the imposition of such a requirement would present a risk of inappropriately mixing the political aspects with the legal aspects of dispute settlement. While the clarification of issues in consultations is certainly not to be discouraged, it is the panel process that should ultimately perform that function.[78] The basic function of consultations is to force the parties to talk to each other in a meaningful way before they initiate the formal panel process. To add a discovery function to the consultation process would transform it from a political one into a legal one. To the extent that that occurs, it is less likely that the parties will settle their differences. Instead, the focus will be on tactics designed to improve, or at least to avoid harming, one's position before a panel. As such, the consultation process would involve lawyers to a greater extent and would need to be under third-party supervision, a virtual impossibility without the creation of a permanent panel body. Moreover, the formalization of the consultation procedure would probably work to the disadvantage of developing countries, since it would raise the stakes early in the dispute settlement process before they may have arranged for legal assistance.

Of course, if a 'discovery' function in consultations were to fill a pressing need in the WTO dispute settlement system, it would have to be considered even if there were negative consequences for the settlement of

[78] In *India – Patents (US)*, the Appellate Body wrote: 'All parties engaged in dispute settlement under the DSU must be fully forthcoming from the very beginning both as to the claims involved in a disputes and as to the facts relating to those claims. Claims must be clearly stated. Facts must be disclosed freely. This must be so in consultations as well as in the more formal setting of panel proceedings' (Appellate Body Report, *India – Patents (US)*, para. 94).

cases. However, it would seem that need can be as effectively (indeed, probably more effectively) met by continuing to allow parties to request panels to ask questions of the other party in the panel process.[79]

(d) Improving the prospects of settlement in consultations

Given the political nature of the consultation process and its goal of promoting mutually agreed solutions, if there is a change to be made to the consultation process, it should be one that makes such solutions more, not less, likely. One possibility that could be usefully explored is a greater use of mediation or conciliation. While this possibility is specifically provided for in Article 5 of the DSU and is said to be available at any time, in fact it is virtually never used. Part of the reason for that may be that the role of mediator is assigned to the Director-General and it is probably the case that most Directors-General would prefer not to insert themselves into disputes. Indeed, in most cases it is probably better if they do not do so, since by doing so they could compromise their position as an impartial party in other contexts, such as negotiations.

This suggests that an expansion of the mediation/conciliation role will probably have to be implemented through use of non-Secretariat persons, or, if technically in the Secretariat, at least persons having no other function besides mediation/conciliation. One can imagine this role being played by retired officials, whether from the Secretariat, the Appellate Body or diplomats with panel experience. If supported by a small legal staff, such individuals might well be able to give the parties a clearer idea of the likely outcome of a case, such that the outlines of a settlement might be easier to achieve. Given that this role would only be a limited, part-time one, there would not be great expense involved.

Thus, if it is desired to improve the consultation process, the focus should not be on making it more legalistic or in giving what happens in consultations special meaning in subsequent panel and Appellate Body proceedings, but rather through the introduction of procedures that make settlements more likely. When one distinguishes the political and legal aspects of WTO dispute settlement, this approach seems obvious and compelling.

[79] Placing the questioning process under the control of panels would be necessary if the WTO dispute settlement system develops a concept that a respondent is not obligated to reply to allegations until a prima facie case is established. So far, this argument seems to have been rejected by the Appellate Body (See Appellate Body Report, *Canada – Aircraft*, paras. 181–194).

2. *Implementation*

Section III of this chapter suggests that the major problem with implementation is that it sometimes does not occur, and often occurs only after considerable delay. This suggests that serious consideration should be given (i) to speeding up the formal dispute settlement process and (ii) to improving the surveillance monitoring process[80] and, most importantly, improving the remedies that are available in the event of non-compliance.

(a) Speeding up the formal dispute settlement process

While the issue of timing has been raised in the DSU reform negotiations, in my view there has not been a serious discussion of the issue. The May 2003 Chairman's Text does not address significantly the issue of shortening time-frames. Indeed, it is likely that the sequencing and remand proposals contained in the Text would greatly increase the time taken for some cases to be processed in the dispute settlement system. The additional 30 days provided for the Appellate Body could potentially add 30 days to every appeal.[81] Moreover, the additional special and differential treatment provisions and third-party rights may lead to more time being taken for briefing in some cases. The only time saving in the proposal is the elimination of the second meeting requirements for establishment of panels – which will save only a few weeks.

One can ask if it really matters if the time frames are extended. I think it does for two reasons. First, as noted above, one of the major complaints about the WTO dispute settlement system is that it takes too much time.[82] Even if a Member adopts a clearly WTO-inconsistent measure, the complainant may have to wait for years before there is final decision of inconsistency. If the measure is eventually removed within the reasonable period of time, the complaining Member will receive no compensation for the period that the measure was in effect. This fact may create a

[80] The proposed Chairman's Text contains a number of useful proposals in this regard, which I will not explore in this paper.

[81] The proposal on an interim appellate report does not specify any time limit for that step, but if it were to be adopted, it would undoubtedly add some time to the overall appellate process, although I believe that it could be accomplished without difficulty in the extra 30 days provided to the Appellate Body in the Chairman's Text.

[82] 'Mexican Study Cites Non-compliance as Top Problem in WTO Dispute System', *BNA International Trade Reporter*, Vol. 20, 14 November 2003, p. 1902. A number of proposals in the negotiations aim at speeding-up aspects of the surveillance/implementation phase (See the Korean proposal for a fast-track option for determining reasonable period of time, TN/DS/W/35.)

cynicism on the part of Members and encourage measures (such as safeguards, to take one example) that cause trade damage but lead to no sanction of any kind so long as they are removed when the dispute settlement process finally runs its course. If anything, this problem of delay is serious overall and seems not to be improving. In the first approximately four years of the system's operation (through April 1999), I calculated that the overall average time from panel establishment to report adoption was a bit over 15 months, as opposed to the 12 months' goal in the DSU for appealed cases (9 months for non-appealed cases). Recent statistics compiled by Mexico suggest that the 15–16 month average remains true today, even though the rate of non-appealed cases has doubled.[83] To this time must be added the reasonable time for implementation, which I calculate as having averaged around 9 months. Second, since 1998, the United States has consistently (although not always with much emphasis) taken the position that DSU reforms should not add to the overall time to process cases. To the extent that it is serious and intends to insist on its position,[84] and given that certain reforms such as sequencing and remand are badly needed, any agreement on DSU reform will have to take a serious look at reducing some of the current time frames.

Even if an agreement on sequencing and remand did not require time savings elsewhere, it is arguable that the integrity and reputation of the system require them. If that is the case, what can be done to reduce time frames? A serious consideration of this issue requires a step-by-step examination of how savings might be achieved at each step of the panel, appellate and implementation process.

Panel composition

Once a panel has been established, the first major source of delay is in the composition of panel. Although this is foreseen to take 20–30 days in the DSU,[85] it typically takes much longer. For example, the average time for

[83] 'Noncompliance Top Problem in WTO', *BNA Reporter*, p. 1902.

[84] It was commonly said immediately after the Uruguay Round that the time limits in the DSU were driven by a US desire to fit the DSU process into the timing requirements of Section 301 of the Trade Act of 1974. Even though the DSU time limits are often not met, it appears that the DSU procedures and Section 301 are not inherently incompatible. (See *US – Sections 301 Trade Act.*) Nonetheless, the United States has long stressed the need for speedy dispute settlement.

[85] The 20-to-30-day target is not explicitly stated in the DSU, but after 20 days of unsuccessful attempts at panel composition, a party may ask the Director-General to compose the panel within 10 days (Article 8.7 of the DSU).

composition of the nine panels working in mid-January 2004 was 68 days (the median was 48 days), and all but one of them had been composed by the Director-General (that is, not by agreement of the parties). A permanent panel system would save one and one-half to two months, on average, since panelists could be assigned immediately after establishment. Without such a system, it is difficult to imagine much improvement unless parties resort to the Director-General as soon as possible. Such resort seems unlikely.

Panel briefing

At the moment, guidelines contained in Annex 3 to the DSU provide for up to six weeks for the filing of the complainant's first written submission and up to three weeks thereafter for the respondent's submission. Although in my experience most complainants have insisted on the six-week period, there is no justification for it. They should know what their case is about and they largely control the timing of the proceeding through establishment and composition. Allowing them six weeks to prepare their initial submission is totally unnecessary. Beyond that, it is unfair to the respondent, which should have relatively more time to prepare a response since it does not know exactly what the arguments will be. Complainants should be required to file their briefs within, at most, two weeks of panel composition and respondents should be given three or four weeks to respond.[86] This would save several weeks compared to the current practice. The opposition to this proposal seems to be based on a desire by complainants not to forego the strategic advantage they now have. But since that advantage is unfair, this change is clearly a very easy and fair way to save several weeks.

Panel meetings

Traditionally, panels have held two substantive meetings with parties. There have long been complaints that the first meeting is not all that useful since it is mainly a rehash of the contents of the first submissions, plus a bit of rebuttal by the complainant. In fact, it is not unusual for the key issues in a case not to be thoroughly developed until the second

[86] Australia has proposed that complainants be required to file their first submissions even earlier (TN/DS/W/49, p. 8) (within five days of composition). It had initially proposed setting an even earlier date (TN/DS/W/8, p. 5) (on filing a request for establishment of a panel).

meeting, especially where a respondent is relying on an exception. As currently structured and understood, there would seem to be little time to be saved in the panel meetings. To do so, would essentially require the adoption of a one-meeting-only structure. This would save a month or so, but it would fundamentally alter the way disputes unfold. In a one-meeting system, if the complainant failed to present a prima facie case in its first submission, the matter could simply be dismissed. Now, the expectation is that the panel will make enquiries to clarify arguments, which may result in an inadequate case becoming adequate. Moreover, the Appellate Body has ruled that a panel may not refuse to consider claims within its terms of reference even if they are not raised as of the time of the first meeting.[87] Thus, the final scope of the complainant's case is not now known until the end of the second meeting (or even later, if the panel asks for more information and/or argument subsequent to the second meeting).

In the long run, I think that it will be appropriate to move to a one-meeting system. This will require greater preparation by complainants in making their initial submission and presenting their case. It will also permit greater efficiency in resolving cases since inadequately presented cases will simply be dismissed. This would be more judicial-like and would probably lead to more court-like proceedings, including with respect to assessment of written and oral evidence. The increased burden that this sort of change would put on complainants, especially developing-country complainants, makes it unpalatable. For the moment, the active role of the panel in defining and clarifying issues over the course of two meetings seems indispensable.

Panel report preparation

There are four aspects of report preparation that should be mentioned – preparation of the descriptive part, preparation of the substantive report, the interim review stage and translation. The preparation of the descriptive part and the substantive part of the report occur simultaneously, so

[87] I appreciate that, in speaking of the burden of proof, the Appellate Body has suggested that there is a requirement that the complainant present a prima facie case before the respondent is required to respond (See Appellate Body Report, *EC – Hormones*, para. 98). In practice, that requirement is difficult to implement as would be done in a court because of the expectation, if not duty, of inquiry and clarification that panels bear and the mere existence of two required meetings with the parties. The consequence is that cases change and develop between the two meetings.

that saving time with respect to the descriptive part will not necessarily result in the earlier issuance of the final report. However, the Secretariat's resources for panel support are generally overtaxed. Thus, reducing input on the descriptive part will free resources that in some instances can be used to support the earlier completion of the substantive report. The current efforts to have parties supply executive summaries of their arguments, which then effectively become the descriptive part of the report, should be made obligatory.

As to the drafting of the substantive report, there are two changes that could save time. The first is the adoption of the permanent panel system. Now, the ad hoc panels must reassemble to discuss the drafting of the report. The difficulty of scheduling such meetings (most panelists have other jobs) inevitably adds to the time it takes to produce a report. Permanent panelists would be expected to spend more time in Geneva and be available on short notice. They would also be used to working with one another and with report preparation in general. Second, a serious attempt should be made to reduce the length of the reports. Not infrequently it seems to me that they could be pruned significantly and usefully in a serious edit. That takes time, of course, and ad hoc panelists are unlikely to be in a position to do that – it is more important for them to make sure they all agree on what has been written than to figure out how to make reports shorter. Somehow, the drafting ethos needs to change.

The interim report requirement adds five weeks to the process. I think that it has some useful features, but its elimination would be an easy way to save five weeks. It may be necessary to forego the limited benefits of interim reports if all of the changes prolonging the process are made. Moreover, those benefits could be maintained by allowing parties to file motions with the panel to correct or clarify the report while it is being translated.

The question of translation is a matter of resources. Generally, dispute settlement reports are given priority (with the Appellate Reports given the highest priority). With greater resources, a couple of weeks could probably be saved in most cases, although there will always be times when negotiations or important meetings will result in a backlog of translation work.

Panel report adoption

Perhaps the best example of unnecessary time in the DSU process is the 60 days provided for adoption of the panel report or appeal in lieu thereof. That time could easily be reduced to 30 days. While governments that have lost a case claim that they need all of the time to decide whether to appeal because of the need to consult with interested parties and deal with complex inter-agency decision-making, the reality is that they know the result of the case when they receive the interim report and could (indeed, they should) start any necessary decision-making at that time. Even if the interim report phase is eliminated, the 60-day period should be reduced by at least two to three weeks.[88]

Appeal and adoption of report

It would seem difficult to reduce the time taken for appeals significantly, although I see no reason to expand the time (unless an interim review procedure is added). Indeed, at the moment, even though the Appellate Body regularly takes 90 days from the notice of appeal to circulate its report, the date on the signature page is often earlier, suggesting that but for translation fewer than 90 days are actually required in many cases. It would, however, be possible to save two weeks by providing for faster adoption of Appellate Body reports. It has typically taken 25 days or so for adoption, which is required to occur within 30 days by DSU Article 14. If a DSB meeting is automatically scheduled on issuance, the average could become 11 days.

Reasonable period for implementation

It was always unfortunate that the major WTO players in the early WTO cases insisted on 15 months for implementation (*US – Gasoline, Japan – Alcoholic Beverages II, Canada – Periodicals*, and *EC – Bananas III*). While the average has fallen to nine months or so, and it is now clearly accepted that the 15 months referred to as a guide for arbitration is not to be viewed as a minimum or standard time,[89] these periods are still too long. Under the standard approach to setting the period, the focus is on the length of the legislative process, which rewards complex systems. It seems to me that having a complex legislative system is fine and perhaps even admirable, but it should not give a violator a reward by lengthening the penalty-free period during which it is able to inflict damage on others.

[88] One could argue that the process of DSB adoption could simply be eliminated. I tend to favour its continuance because I think that it is useful and important to the system to focus Members' attention on the results of specific cases and invite them to comment (See Davey, 'WTO: Segregating the Aspects and Avoiding "Over-legalization" ', pp. 291–317.

[89] Award of the Arbitrator, *EC – Hormones*, para. 25.

The reasonable period of time should be capped at a level lower than 15 months, if necessary with some leeway for developing countries in special circumstances. A period of six or nine months should be sufficient. That means that some Members will have great difficulty complying on time, but the fact that they will become subject to suspension of concessions or other remedy should have a salutary effect in focusing their efforts on implementation.

Sequencing

The Chairman's Text contained a proposal on sequencing and there seems to be general agreement that this or a similar change is needed and important in that it clarifies ambiguities in the DSU text. However, if improving time frames is an important consideration, then certain changes would be desirable. First, the 90-day period for having the compliance panel report is probably unrealistic, unless it is provided that normally the panel will meet only once with the parties and will not issue an interim report. That was the procedure followed by the only panel to date that met the 90-day deadline (*EC – Bananas III*). In some cases, this expedited schedule may not be appropriate (for example, if experts must be consulted), but every effort needs to be made to keep this process a relatively quick one.[90] Second, the *EC – Bananas III* case also demonstrated that the level of nullification of impairment, which is the difficult issue in deciding on the level of suspension, can be done at the same time as determining the consistency of the new measure. Indeed, if it is so done, then the reasoning on that issue would be subject to appeal, which would be desirable in any event. While care must be taken to ensure that these proceedings are not so expedited as to compromise the quality of the panel and appellate reports (after all, some of these cases have been as complex as the original proceedings), this is a stage of the proceedings that can add a great deal of time to the overall amount of time required to process a case. Thus, care must be taken to see that compliance proceedings do not drag out unnecessarily.

Conclusion

Making all of the suggested changes could save a lot of time, especially if a permanent panel system is adopted. To recapitulate the changes in the

[90] Interestingly, the provision on remand in the Chairman's Text provides for a possible extension from 90 days to six months, even though a remanded case is the same case, whereas a compliance panel case is usually different.

basic panel/appellate stage [gains from permanent panel body in brackets]:

[Panel composition	6 weeks]
Panel briefing	3 weeks
Panel report preparation	
[Scheduling	2 weeks]
Interim report	5 weeks
Panel report adoption	4 weeks
Appellate Body report adoption	2 weeks
Total	14 weeks
	[22 weeks with panel body]

Thus, the current 15–16 month period from establishment to adoption could be reduced by three or four months – to 12 months (or to less than ten months with a permanent panel body). This would reduce concerns about possible time additions proposed in the sequencing and remand provisions.[91]

(b) Improving remedies for non-compliance

General considerations

In considering how to improve the implementation record of the WTO dispute settlement system, it is necessary first to consider the current remedies for non-implementation and how they are structured. It is probably the case that the overall positive record of implementation in the WTO is due to the good faith desire of its Members to see the dispute settlement system work effectively. The more active users of the system are repeat players, and they appear as both complainants and respondents. Accordingly, it is in their overall interests that the system function effectively. However, there will be cases where such good faith cannot be relied upon. When a WTO Member faces difficulty in implementation, the issue quickly becomes one of assessing the consequences of non-implementation. That, in turn, requires a consideration of the nature and structure of the WTO's remedies for non-compliance with DSB rulings and recommendations.

In the event of non-implementation within the reasonable period of time provided, the DSU provides two potential remedies, both of which

[91] I suspect that adoption of a permanent panel system could result in further time savings, but also that over time, such a system would become a bit more bureaucratic, and hence a bit slower. Accordingly, I have not assumed in this discussion that such efficiencies would occur.

are said to be temporary ones pending implementation.[92] Those remedies are compensation and the suspension of concessions (often simply called 'retaliation'). To date, with one exception, compensation has not often been used, except to excuse compliance for a limited period of time.[93] The exception was *US – Section 110(5) Copyright Act*, where the United States made a cash payment to the European Communities to excuse three years or so of non-compliance. The period covered by the compensation ended as of 31 December 2004, and no extension has been announced as of this writing. I will not give further consideration to compensation as a remedy in this introduction. Except for minor matters, the political problems that preclude implementation will probably also prevent reasonable compensation. While the idea of 'forced' compensation has been raised,[94] there are obvious implementation problems in dealing with a Member that is already not in compliance with its WTO obligations.

The suspension of concessions is typically thought of as the basic remedy for non-implementation of WTO dispute settlement results. In fact, however, it has not often been used. The GATT Contracting Parties authorized it only once[95] and it was supposedly never actually implemented. In the WTO to date, suspension of concessions has been authorized and used in only four cases: by the United States in *EC – Bananas III*; by the United States and Canada in *EC – Hormones*; by the European Communities in *US – FSC*; and by the European Communities, Japan, Canada, and Mexico in *US – Offset Act (Byrd Amendment)*. It has been authorized, but not used by Ecuador in *EC – Bananas III*, by Canada in *Brazil – Aircraft*, by Brazil in *Canada – Aircraft*, and by several Members in *US – Offset Act (Byrd Amendment)*. The level of suspension was arbitrated in *US – 1916 Act*, but the European Communities never sought authority to suspend concessions.

To understand the impact of an authorization to suspend concessions, it is important to recall that WTO remedies are prospective. The level of suspension is calculated from the end of the reasonable period of time. In addition, it is important to consider the two principal aims of suspension – to restore the balance of concessions that was upset when

[92] Article 3.7 of the DSU.

[93] For example, this was the case in *Japan – Alcohol Beverages II*, *Turkey – Textiles*, and *US – Line Pipe*.

[94] Joost Pauwelyn, 'Enforcement and Countermeasures in the WTO' (2000) 94 *American Journal of International Law*, 335–347, 335.

[95] William J. Davey, 'Dispute Settlement in GATT' (1987) 11 *Fordham International Law Journal*, 51–109, 99.

one Member violated its obligations (a temporary aim since compliance is the preferred result); and to give that Member an incentive to comply.[96] The current problem with achieving the first aim – rebalancing – is that if retaliation is authorized, rebalancing takes place at a lower level of trade liberalization that had previously been agreed to. It would be desirable if a remedy could be devised that would not lead to less liberalization overall. Moreover, retaliation harms the Member imposing the higher tariffs as well as the target of the retaliation.

In respect of the second aim – incentive to comply – there are two issues – timing and level of compensation or retaliation. At present, because remedies are prospective, there is an incentive initially to delay the time at which point they might be implemented, such as by seeking a long reasonable period of time for compliance and then forcing the complainant to go through an Article 21.5 panel (and Appellate Body) proceeding. Moreover, if the threat of retaliation does not work, it is possible that the actual existence of retaliation will become viewed as the status quo and a long-term solution, even though the WTO rules in theory require compliance. This is a real possibility given that under the DSU the level of retaliation is to be equivalent to (that is, is not to exceed) the level of nullification or impairment.[97] In other words, the offending Member is not to be penalized for its non-implementation.

There is a more general problem with suspension of concessions. While it seems to work when threatened by a large country against a smaller one, and has worked when implemented by one major power against another, it may not be an effective remedy for a small country (even if it can target sensitive large country sectors such as copyright holders). Moreover, the *EC – Bananas III* and *EC – Hormones* cases show that it is not always effective, at least not immediately, between major powers. It should be noted, however, that retaliation by the European Communities against the United States seemed to have a political effect in the *US – FSC* case that led to implementation by the United States, even if the significance of the economic impact of the retaliation was not clear. In addition, the European Communities' and others' threat of retaliation seemed to work in the *US – Steel Safeguards* case.[98] Nonetheless,

[96] Article 22.1 of the DSU; Award of the Arbitrator, *EC – Bananas III*, para. 6.3.

[97] Article 22.4 of the DSU.

[98] In safeguards cases, if the safeguard is found to be WTO-inconsistent, the country applying the safeguard will owe compensation to other WTO Members, who may 'take' the compensation if there is no agreement. Thus, in a safeguard case, there is usually a retaliation-like remedy available without reliance on the DSU.

occasional inefficacy of suspension of concessions and the unfavourable position in which it leaves developing countries may soon combine to create a serious credibility problem for the system that must be confronted.[99]

These considerations lead to the obvious question of whether there are other remedies beyond compensation and retaliation that might be more effective in the WTO context. One obvious possibility would be the payment of fines or damages. One obvious problem would be the disparity in fine-paying ability among WTO Members. The system would have to be designed to avoid the possibility that rich Members could effectively buy their way out of obligations in a way not available to the poor Members. That might be accomplished by tying the amount of fines to the size of the Member's economy, or otherwise providing for a sliding scale that would minimize 'discrimination' against poor Members. While a system of fines or damages has not been discussed in much detail in the past, such provisions have been included in free trade agreements (FTAs) recently negotiated by the United States.[100] For example, under their provisions, after the level of suspension of concessions had been set, the non-complying country would have the option of paying an amount equal to one-half level of suspension in lieu of having the concessions suspended. These provisions may suggest that the traditional government unwillingness to submit to the possibility of fines may be changing.

Specific proposals

In the light of the above-described general considerations, what practical improvements might be suggested to improve implementation of WTO dispute settlement decisions? I believe that several changes should be given serious consideration. In particular, I think that the WTO remedies for non-implementation should incorporate (i) the possibility of substituting fines or damages as a remedy in lieu of suspension of concessions;

[99] See Davey, 'Dispute Settlement in GATT', 99–103. For a general analysis of the effectiveness of economic sanctions, see Gary Clyde Hufbauer, Jeffrey J. Schott, and Kimberly Ann Elliot, *Economic Sanctions Reconsidered* (2nd edn, Washington, DC, 1990).

[100] See, for example, Article 22.15(5) of the FTA between Chile and the United States, available at: <http://www.ustr.gov/assets/Trade_Agreements/Bilateral/Chile_FTA/Final_Texts/asset_upload_file783_4015.pdf>, p. 9; and Article 20–6(5) of the FTA between Singapore and the United States, available at <http://www.ustr.gov/assets/ Trade_Agreements/Bilateral/Singapore_FTA/Final_Texts/asset_upload_file708_4036.pdf>, p. 227 (visited 19 April 2006).

(ii) some degree of retroactivity, so as to encourage compliance within the reasonable period of time; and (iii) some adjustment mechanism to increase the sanctions over time, so as to preclude non-compliance from becoming an acceptable status quo position. I discuss each in turn.

Money payments

Because suspension of concessions has been used generally only by members of the Quad, I think it is evident that another remedy more meaningful to the typical WTO Member is needed. The obvious possibility is to allow a prevailing party to choose between suspension of concessions and receipt of a periodic monetary payment. While there may be enforcement problems in that it may difficult to ensure the payment is made, the right to receive a payment will still be more valuable than the never-used and probably unusable right to suspend concessions. There are some signs that payments of fines or damages may be gaining in acceptability, as demonstrated by their inclusion in US FTAs. Moreover, the US Congress recently authorized around US $50 million for the United States to use to pay 'damages' in trade cases. However, to date, it has only appropriated about US $3 million for this purpose (for use in the *US – Section 110(5) Copyright Act* case).

Perhaps the greatest downside of relying on money payments is enforceability. One way to solve the enforceability problem would be to require WTO Members to create funds from which damages could be paid without specific legislative approval. This should not be all that controversial as it is the way I believe that monetary awards arising from civil judgments against governments are typically paid. In any event, if a payment is not made when due, there would always be the fallback of suspension of concessions.

Retrospective assessment

The prospective nature of WTO remedies currently gives countries no incentive to comply promptly and may even encourage foot-dragging. To minimize this problem and to create incentives for prompt compliance, it should be provided that any remedy (whether retaliation or money payment) will be calculated from a date prior to the date set for implementation (for example, date of adoption of the relevant report or date of panel establishment or even earlier). Since no remedy would be imposed if implementation occurs within the reasonable period of time, there would be an incentive to meet that deadline for implementation.

Increasing sanctions over time

Increasing sanctions over time would also seem to offer some real possibilities for improving implementation. Such a procedure would help to avoid the perception that the payment of fines or damages is simply an alternative to compliance. In a sense, this concept has been used by the European Communities in the *US – FSC* case, where the duty it imposed on a long list of United States' products started at 5 per cent and was increased at a rate of 1 per cent each month. The monthly change focused attention on the case each month and the impending increase, even if small, created an incentive to act so as to forestall it. In United States' congressional debates on the foreign sales corporation (FSC) implementation legislation, at least some members of Congress have made this point. Because of the huge size of the FSC sanctions – US $4 billion – a phase-in made practical sense in any event. But the same concept could be used in other cases, so long as it is agreed to allow sanctions to increase over time from the initial amount.

Concluding thoughts on improving implementation

In the previous section of this chapter, the point was made that any solution attempting to address the WTO's implementation problems must deal effectively with (i) the recent United States' failures to implement and to the occasional foot-dragging by the Quad countries (and Australia), and (ii) with the particular implementation problems in the areas of subsidies, SPS and trade remedies.

In terms of United States' failures to implement, it is, of course, a hopeful sign that the United States Congress in late 2004 enacted legislation to implement the *US – FSC* and *US – 1916 Act* decisions (subject to transitional issues). In the latter case, implementation was due to the inclusion by the leadership of a provision to repeal the 1916 Act in a conference report where neither the House nor Senate versions of the bill at issue contained such a provision. This suggests some concern on the part of the United States, including Congress, not to be seen as ignoring WTO obligations. In any event, to the extent that pressure can be effectively put on the United States to implement WTO rulings, it would seem to me that the above changes would increase such pressures. The same is true in the case of the other Quad members. In particular, the adoption of questionable implementation measures would be much less likely if a system of retrospective remedies was put in place. Moreover, the provision of increased sanctions that would increase the cost over time of non-implementation would clearly provide an incentive not to delay implementation. In the end, of course, WTO remedies may be insufficient to influence the behaviour of major powers, but the proposed changes in the remedy system would seem to be a positive step in the right direction.

The use of retrospective remedies and increased sanctions over time would likely help solve the particular implementation problems that are seen in the subsidy and SPS areas. In each case, the cost of non-compliance would increase and that would help offset the political opposition to implementation. That would not necessarily be the case in respect of safeguards and trade remedies. As outlined above, the assumption of the current system (and the proposed changes thereto) is that compliance within the set reasonable period of time would absolve a country from suffering the application of any remedy. Yet in the area of safeguards and trade remedies that would still allow a country to impose the safeguard or trade remedy, enjoy its effect and only be compelled to remove it after the WTO dispute settlement procedure had run its course. Thus, questionable safeguards and trade remedies might continue to be imposed and then removed after a couple of years of disrupting trade. It would seem to me that the only way to solve this problem would be to require payment of reparations if the imposition of such measures is found to be WTO-inconsistent. I think that these cases are often too complex to expect that a system of preliminary (pre-judgment) remedies or accelerated time-frames could make much difference. Since these measures often stop trade and may not result in the collection of duties in any event, a rule on refund of duties would also not address the problem in general. Providing for reparations (by way of damages for impediments to trade flows) might work. However, while reparations are the standard remedy in international law for violations of a state's obligations, importing such a concept into the WTO would probably be viewed by WTO Members as a more drastic and less acceptable change than the adjustments to the current remedies proposed above.

V. Conclusions

The consultations process under the DSU has worked effectively and only minor improvements need be made to that process. While the implementation record of the WTO dispute settlement system is fairly good, the problem of a few longstanding problem cases of non-implementation suggest that proposals for improvements in the area of remedies for non-compliance should be considered seriously.

Table 5.1 *Overall time frames – country by country (as of December 2004)*

Case		*Elapsed time (as of December 2004 for unimplemented cases)*	*Country medians (+ = continuing to increase)*	
DS2	*US – Gasoline*	35 months	**US Overall**	**32 months**
DS24	*US – Underwear*	15 months		
DS33	*US – Wool Shirts and Blouses*	9 months	**US General**	**36.5 months**
DS58	*US – Shrimp*	38 months	**US Trade Remedies**	**34+ months**
DS99	*US – DRAMS*	32 months	**US Safeguards**	**21 months**
DS108	*US – FSC*	85 (contested)	**US TRIPS**	**66.5+ months**
DS136	*US – 1916 Act*	78 (contested)		
DS138	*US – Lead and Bismuth II*	21 months		
DS160	*US – Section 110(5) Copyright Act*	72 months (continuing)		
DS165	*US – Certain EC Products*	2 months		
DS166	*US – Wheat Gluten*	27 months		
DS176	*US – Section 211 Appropriations Act*	66 months (continuing)		
DS177	*US – Lamb*	28 months		
DS179	*US – Stainless Steel*	26 months		
DS184	*US – Hot-Rolled Steel*	62 months (continuing)		
DS192	*US – Cotton Yarn*	20 months		
DS202	*US – Line Pipe*	27 months		
DS206	*US – Steel Plate*	28 months		
DS212	*US – Countervailing Measures on Certain EC Products*	36 months (contested)		
DS213	*US – Carbon Steel*	41 months		
DS217	*US – Offset Act (Byrd Amendment)*	49 months (continuing)		
DS248	*US – Steel Safeguards*	21 months		
DS257	*US – Softwood Lumber IV*	32 months (contested)		
DS56	*Argentina – Textiles and Apparel*	32 months	**Argentina**	**27.5 months**
DS121	*Argentina – Footwear (EC)*	23 months		

Table 5.1 *(continued)*

Case		*Elapsed time (as of December 2004 for unimplemented cases)*	*Country medians (+ = continuing to increase)*	
DS155	*Argentina – Hides and Leather*	38 months		
DS189	*Argentina – Ceramic Tiles*	27 months		
DS238	*Argentina – Preserved Peaches*	28 months		
DS241	*Argentina – Poultry Anti-Dumping Duties*	17 months		
DS31	*Canada – Periodicals*	31 months	**Canada**	**33 months**
DS70	*Canada – Aircraft*	94 months		
DS222	*Canada – Aircraft Credits and Guarantees*	(continuing)		
DS103	*Canada – Dairy*	68 months		
DS114	*Canada – Pharmaceutical Patents*	34 months		
DS139	*Canada – Autos*	32 months		
DS170	*Canada – Patent Term*	26 months		
DS26	*EC – Hormones*	93 months (contested)	**EC**	**46 months**
DS27	*EC – Bananas III*	108 months (settled at 63 months)		
DS69	*EC – Poultry*	25 months		
DS141	*EC – Bed Linen*	53 months		
DS219	*EC – Tube or Pipe Fittings*	39 months		
DS231	*EC – Sardines*	27 months		
DS50	*India – Patents*	34 months	**India**	**44 months**
DS90	*India – Quantitative Restrictions*	44 months		
DS146	*India – Autos*	46 months		
DS8	*Japan – Alcoholic Beverages II*	30 months	**Japan**	**30 months**
DS76	*Japan – Agricultural Products II*	52 months		

Table 5.1 *(continued)*

Case		*Elapsed time (as of December 2004 for unimplemented cases)*	*Country medians (+ = continuing to increase)*	
DS245	*Japan – Apples*	28 months (contested)		
DS75	*Korea – Alcoholic Beverages*	32 months	**Korea**	**32 months**
DS98	*Korea – Dairy*	33 months		
DS161	*Korea – Various Measures on Beef*	31 months		
DS18	*Australia – Salmon*	55 months	**Australia**	**50.5 months**
DS126	*Australia – Automotive Leather II*	46 months		
DS110	*Chile – Alcoholic Beverages*	39 months	**Chile**	**39 months**
DS207	*Chile – Price Band System*	39 months		
DS46	*Brazil – Aircraft*	103 months (continuing)		
DS211	*Egypt – Steel Rebar*	34 months		
DS60	*Guatemala – Cement I*			
DS156	*Guatemala – Cement II*	49 months		
DS54	*Indonesia – Autos*	33 months		
DS132	*Mexico – Corn Syrup*	57 months		
DS122	*Thailand – H-Beams*	43 months		
DS34	*Turkey – Textiles*	64 months		
			OVERALL	34 months

Table 5.2 *Country-by-country implementation (as of December 2004)*

Country	*Implemented without significant delay*	*Implemented with significant delay (over 4 months)*	*Pending dispute*	*Not implemented*	*Total*
United States	*Underwear*	*Gasoline*	*Countervailing Measures on Certain EC Products*	*Offset Act (Byrd Amendment)*	23
	Wool Shirts and Blouses	*DRAMS*	*FSC*	*Section 110(5) Copyright Act*	
	Shrimp	*Carbon Steel*	*1916 Act*	*Hot-Rolled Steel*	
	Lead and Bismuth II		*Softwood Lumber IV*	*Section 211 Appropriations Act*	
	Certain EC Products				
	Wheat Gluten				
	Stainless Steel				
	Lamb				
	Cotton Yarn				
	Line Pipe				
	Steel Plate				
	Steel Safeguards				
Argentina	*Footwear (EC)*	*Textiles and Apparel*			6
	Hides and Leather				
	Ceramic Tiles				
	Preserved Peaches				
	Poultry Anti-Dumping Duties				
Canada	*Periodicals*	*Dairy*		*Aircraft*	6
	Pharmaceutical Patents				
	Autos				
	Patent Term				
EC	*Poultry*	*Bananas III*	*Hormones*		6
	Sardines	*Bed Linen*			
	Tube or Pipe Fittings				
India	*Patents*				3
	Quantitative Restrictions				
	Autos				
Japan	*Alcoholic Beverages II*	*Agricultural Products II*	*Apples*		3
Korea	*Alcoholic Beverages*				3
	Dairy				
	Various Measures on Beef				

Table 5.2 *(continued)*

Country	*Implemented without significant delay*	*Implemented with significant delay (over 4 months)*	*Pending dispute*	*Not implemented*	*Total*
Australia		*Salmon* *Automotive Leather II*			2
Chile	*Alcoholic Beverages* *Price Band System*				2
Brazil				*Aircraft*	1
Egypt	*Steel Rebar*				1
Guatemala	*Cement*				1
Indonesia	*Autos*				1
Mexico		*Corn Syrup*			1
Thailand	*H-Beams*				1
Turkey		*Textiles*			1

Table 5.3 *Summary of implementation record by country (as of December 2004)*

Country	*Implemented without significant dealy*	*Implemented with significant delay (average delay)*	*Pending dispute over implement-ation*	*Not implemented*	*Total*
The Quad and Australia					
United States	12	3 (7 months)	4	4	23
Canada	4	1 (28 months)	-	1	6
EC	3	2 (28 months)	1	-	6
Japan	1	1 (20 months)	1	-	3
Australia	-	2 (16 months)	-	-	2
	20 (50%)	**9 (14.3 months)**	**6**	**5**	**40**
Developing countries					
Argentina	5	1 (5 months)	-	-	6
India	3	-	-	-	3
Korea	3	-	-	-	3
Chile	2	-	-	-	2
Brazil	-	-	-	1	1
Egypt	1	-	-	-	1
Guatemala	1	-	-	-	1
Indonesia	1	-	-	-	1
Mexico	-	1 (20 months)	-	-	1
Thailand	1	-	-	-	1
Turkey	-	1 (5 months)	-	-	1
	17 (81%)	**3 (10 months)**	**0**	**1**	**21**
	37 (61%)	**12 (13.3 months)**	**6**	**6**	**61**

Table 5.4 *Agreement-by-agreement implementation (as of December 2004)*

Agreement (Total cases)	*Implemented without significant delay*	*Implemented with significant delay (over 4 months*	*Pending dispute when implemented, will be significant delay)*	*Not implemented*
GATT (16)	*US – Shrimp* *US – Certain EC Products*	*US – Gasoline* *Argentina – Textiles and Apparel*		
	Argentina – Hides and Leather	*EC – Bananas III*		
	Canada – Periodicals	*Turkey – Textiles*		
	Canada – Autos *Chile – Alcoholic Beverages* *India – Quantitative Restrictions* *India – Autos* *Indonesia – Autos* *Japan – Alcoholic Beverages II* *Korea – Alcoholic Beverages* *Korea – Various Measures on Beef*			
Agriculture (3)	*EC – Poultry* *Chile - Price Band System*	*Canada – Dairy*		
Subsidies (4)		*Australia – Hides and Leather*	*US – FSC*	*Brazil – Aircraft* *Canada – Aircraft*
SPS (4)		*Australia – Salmon*	*EC – Hormones*	
		Japan – Agricultural Products II	*Japan – Apples*	
TBT (1)	*EC – Sardines*			
Trade Remedy (18)	*US – Stainless Steel*	*US – DRAMS*	*US – Counter-vailing Measures on Certain EC Products*	*US – Offset Act (Byrd Amendment)*
	US – Lead and Bismuth II	*US – Carbon Steel*	*US – 1916 Act*	*US – Hot-Rolled Steel*

Table 5.4 *(continued)*

Agreement (Total cases)	*Implemented without significant delay*	*Implemented with significant delay (over 4 months*	*Pending dispute when implemented, will be significant delay)*	*Not implemented*
	US – Steel Plate	*EC – Bed Linen*	*US – Softwood Lumber IV*	
	Argentina – Ceramic Tiles			
	Argentina – Poultry Anti-Dumping Duties			
	EC – Tube or Pipe Fittings			
	Egypt – Steel Rebar			
	Guatemala – Cement			
	Mexico – Corn Syrup			
	Thailand – H-Beams			
Safeguard (10)	*US – Underwear*			
	US – Wool Shirts and Blouses			
	US – Wheat Gluten			
	US – Lamb			
	US – Line Pipe			
	US – Cotton Yarn			
	US – Steel Safeguards			
	Argentina – Footwear (EC)			
	Argentina – Preserved Peaches			
	Korea – Dairy			
TRIPS (5)	*Canada – Pharmaceutical Patents*			*US – Section 110(5) Copyright Act*
	Canada – Patent Term			*US – Section 211 Appropriations Act*
	India – Patents			

6

The responsibilities of a WTO Member found to have violated WTO law

FRIEDER ROESSLER

I admire the achievements of panels and the Appellate Body, and of the unsung heroes who assist them behind the scenes. Over the past decade, they have succeeded in developing a coherent jurisprudence and in maintaining the support of the membership of the World Trade Organization (WTO) for the dispute settlement system. However, when evaluating the performance of the WTO dispute settlement system, one should not only examine how panels and the Appellate Body handled the complaints that were actually submitted to them. An evaluation of that system is only complete if it comprises also an analysis of the complaints that Members did not bring. The focus of this chapter is on one feature of the WTO dispute settlement system that has prevented Members from resorting to that system to assert their rights in many situations.

The statutes of international tribunals generally do not contain rules limiting the tribunal's right to determine the responsibilities of a State found to have committed a wrongful act. Thus, the Statute of the International Court of Justice (ICJ) does not impose any such limitation; nor did the procedures followed by the panels established under the *General Agreement on Tariffs and Trade* (GATT) *1947*. The *Understanding on Rules and Procedures Governing the Settlement of Disputes* (DSU) of the WTO is an exception. Article 19.1 of the DSU provides:

> Where a panel or the Appellate Body concludes that a measure is inconsistent with a covered agreement, it shall recommend that the Member concerned bring the measure into conformity with that agreement. (Footnotes omitted)

Most Members of the WTO and most panels have concluded from this provision that a Member of the WTO found to have adopted a measure violating WTO law incurs only one responsibility: to bring that measure into conformity with WTO law; no other compensatory or corrective action is due. The United States expressed this position before a panel as follows:

> [R]etroactive remedies are inconsistent with the established practice of panels of refraining from recommending remedies that attempt somehow to restore the *status quo ante* or otherwise compensate the prevailing party for WTO-inconsistent actions taken by the defending party.[1]

If panels cannot recommend retroactive remedies to the WTO Dispute Settlement Body (DSB), Members found to have violated WTO law do not incur any responsibilities under WTO law with respect to situations that have ceased to exist or acts that are of such a nature that they cannot be withdrawn. The European Communities has described this as an 'established and accepted' feature of WTO law:

> The absence of remedy for past and consummated violations has always been a well-known feature of the GATT/WTO system. It is established and accepted that it can lead in some cases to there being no remedy at all for the complaining party.[2]

With the exception of the panel in *Australia – Automotive Leather II (Article 21.5 – US)*,[3] all WTO panels have limited themselves to recommending that the measures found to be inconsistent be brought into conformity with the relevant WTO agreement. That panel, based on Article 4.7 of the *Agreement on Subsidies and Countervailing Measures (SCM Agreement)*, recommended that the subsidies it had found to be inconsistent with that Agreement be repaid to the Australian government.[4]
Article 4.7 of the *SCM Agreement* provides:

> If the measure in question is found to be a prohibited subsidy, the panel shall recommend that the subsidizing Member withdraw the subsidy without delay.

The wording of this provision suggests that the subsidizing Member must do more than just cease to maintain the prohibited subsidy; it must 'withdraw' it without delay. For instance, if an export subsidy has been disbursed to an enterprise but not yet used by that enterprise, the

[1] Panel Report, *Guatemala – Cement I*, para. 5.63.

[2] European Communities' oral statement, para. 32, Panel Report, *Canada – Aircraft (Article 21.5 – Brazil)*, Annex 3-3.

[3] Panel Report, *Australia – Automotive Leather II (Article 21.5 – US)*[0], para. 6.48. On this case generally, see Gavin Goh and Andreas Ziegler, 'Retrospective Remedies in the WTO after *Automotive Leather*' (2003) 6 *Journal of International Economic Law*, 545–564.

[4] Panel Report, *Australia – Automotive Leather II*, para. 10.3.

requirement to 'withdraw' the subsidy could be interpreted to imply a requirement to ensure the repayment of the subsidy so that it can no longer be used for future exports. Nevertheless, most of the Members that spoke at the DSB meeting at which the report in *Australia – Automotive Leather II (Article 21.5 – US)* was adopted were highly critical of the panel's recommendation and strongly defended the view that panels are not entitled to recommend that Members be requested to remove the consequences of illegal acts.[5]

The consultations required under the DSU, the examination of the case by a panel, the review of the panel report by the Appellate Body, and the determination of the implementation period available to the respondent all take a considerable amount of time. While these complex, four-stage procedures all take their course, the complainant must bear the adverse economic consequences of the measure at issue. The ICJ has the power 'to indicate, if it considers that circumstances so require, any provisional measures which ought to be taken to preserve the respective rights of either party'.[6] There is no corresponding provision in the DSU. The complainant has therefore effectively no procedural remedy before the end of the implementation period. Only at that point in time, and only if the defendant does not implement the DSB's rulings and recommendations, may the complainant request compensation or, in the absence of an agreement on compensation, an authorization to suspend concessions.

The lack of retroactive remedies, combined with the lack of interim relief, has the following consequences:

It is possible to violate – effectively unsanctioned – obligations under the WTO agreements for considerable periods of time simply by refusing to engage in constructive consultations, unnecessarily complicating the panel proceedings, appealing the panel report on whatever grounds and forcing the complainant to request an arbitrator to determine the length of the implementation period. The procedures intended to ensure the enforcement of WTO law can therefore be turned into a mechanism to escape WTO law.

It is meaningless to bring a case against acts that cannot by their nature be withdrawn, such as the late registration of a patent, the discriminatory allocation of a government procurement contract or the failure to grant

[5] See WT/DSB/M/75, pp. 5–9. For a review of GATT and WTO jurisprudence on this matter, see Patricio Grané, 'Remedies under WTO Law' (2001) 4 *Journal of International Economic Law*, 755–772.

[6] Article 41 of the Statute of the ICJ.

an import license promptly. The panel report in *Norway – Trondheim Toll Ring*, a case that arose in 1992 under the Tokyo Round *Agreement on Government Procurement*, illustrates the consequences of this limitation.[7] The panel was asked by the United States to rule on the procurement of toll collection equipment that had already been installed at the time of its proceedings. The panel's recommendation to bring the measure into conformity with the Agreement was therefore meaningless. The United States 'won' the case but was left empty-handed because the panel refused to recommend any form of reparation.[8]

It is also pointless to seek the remedy provided by Article 19.1 if the relevant WTO law is applicable only for a limited period of time. Pakistan's complaint against a safeguard measure imposed by the United States under the *Agreement on Textiles and Clothing* (*ATC*) provides an illustration. About three years passed between the imposition of the measure and the end of the implementation period.[9] Under the *ATC*, a safeguard measure could be imposed only for a period of three years.[10] The Article 19.1 remedy was thus accorded to Pakistan at a point in time when the WTO law invoked by the United States no longer applied. No developing-country Member brought a case under the *ATC* during the three years preceding its termination, presumably because the limitations of Article 19.1 of the DSU made the Agreement in those final years unenforceable.

Article 19.1 was included in the DSU at the insistence of the United States, which was concerned about four adopted GATT panel reports that had recommended that an inconsistently levied anti-dumping or countervailing duty be repaid.[11] The United States proposed this provision to prevent a repetition of such recommendations. The problem that arose in *Norway – Trondheim Toll Ring* was addressed by including in the Uruguay Round *Agreement on Government Procurement* (*GPA*) an obligation to provide in *domestic law* for a challenge procedure, under which a supplier, faced with a procurement decision inconsistent with the Agreement, can obtain rapid relief, including interim measures . . . to preserve commercial opportunities.[12] However, none of the other WTO

[7] GATT Panel Report , *Norway – Trondheim Toll Ring.*

[8] For a detailed discussion of this case, see Petros C. Mavroidis, 'Government Procurement Agreement – The Trondheim case: the remedies issue' (1993) 48 *Aussenwirtschaft*, 77–94.

[9] See Minutes of the Meeting of the Dispute Settlement Body held on 5 November 2001, WT/DSB/M/112, paras. 21–22.

[10] Article 6.12 of the *ATC.*

[11] See Committee on Anti-Dumping Practices, Minutes of the Meeting held on 21 October 1991, GATT document ADP/M/35.

[12] Article XX of the *GPA.*

agreements contains a similar provision even though the need to obtain rapid relief is not unique to government procurement. For instance, the requirement under the *Agreement on Import Licensing Procedures* that import licenses must be issued within 10 days[13] could be enforced much more effectively through interim measures imposed by domestic courts than through the DSU procedures.

In *India – Patents (US)*, the United States had to bear the consequences of the limitations imposed on panels and the Appellate Body by Article 19.1 of the DSU. In that case, the United States requested the panel to find that Article 70.8 of the *Agreement on Trade-Related Aspects of Intellectual Property Rights* (*TRIPS Agreement*) required India to ensure that persons, who had filed or would have filed patent applications, receive the filing date they would have received if India had established procedures for the registration of patents consistent with that provision. The United States thus effectively requested a finding that Article 70.8 obliged India to correct the consequences of its failure to register patents. India promptly argued that the United States, in the guise of an interpretation of Article 70.8, was asking for a remedy not provided for under Article 19.1 of the DSU. The panel accepted India's argument and refrained from making the finding requested by the United States.[14]

The responsibilities of a WTO Member that has violated its WTO obligations are much more limited than the responsibilities incurred under general international law by a State that has committed a wrongful act. The International Law Commission of the United Nations has adopted draft articles on State responsibility.[15] They provide that

> [t]he State responsible for the internationally wrongful act is under an obligation: (a) To cease that act, if it is continuing; (b) To offer appropriate assurances and guarantees of non-repetition, if circumstances so require.[16]

The draft articles further provide:

> 1. The responsible State is under an obligation to make full reparation for the injury caused by the internationally wrongful act.
> 2. Injury includes any damage, whether material or moral, caused by the internationally wrongful act of a State.[17]

[13] Article 2.2(a)(iii) of the *Agreement on Import Licensing Procedures.*

[14] Panel Report, *India – Patents (US)*, paras. 3.1(a), 4.14, and 7.65.

[15] International Law Commission's Draft Articles on Responsibility of States for International Wrongful Acts, *Official Records of the General Assembly, Fifty-sixth session*, Supplement No. 10 (A/56/10), chapter IV.E.2.

[16] Ibid., Article 30.

[17] Ibid., Article 31.

Responsibilities as broadly defined in the draft articles of the International Law Commission may not be appropriate in the world trade order. The responsibility to pay compensation in the form of an amount of money would in most circumstances be unworkable because it is rarely possible to calculate accurately the damage caused by a violation of WTO law and to identify the individuals that have effectively borne the adverse impact. In GATT and WTO practice, compensation has therefore normally been accorded in the form of the grant of alternative market access opportunities. However, I see no reason why a duty to re-establish the situation that would have existed in the absence of the illegal act would not be reasonable and appropriate in certain situations. For instance, if a country has failed to establish a system for granting patents, why should it not be asked to give inventors *ex post* the rights that they would have had under a properly established patent registration system, as the United States requested in *India – Patents (US)*? Why should an illegal anti-dumping order not be revoked *ex tunc* in certain circumstances? Why should a Member that refused to permit the establishment of a bank in violation of its commitments under the *General Agreement on Trade in Services* (GATS) not be required to give that particular bank the permission rather than to merely change its practices in future cases? Those who argue against such responsibilities need to explain why large areas of WTO law should remain unenforceable through the DSU.

The position of the United States on the question of the scope of the recommendations by panels was dominated by its internal political constraints in the field of anti-dumping and countervailing duties. Its interests in other areas, in particular intellectual property rights, services, and government procurement were therefore not taken into account in the drafting of WTO law. Under the North American Free Trade Agreement (NAFTA), the United States agreed to refund, with interest, anti-dumping duties and countervailing duties, if a panel so rules.[18] The United States conducts its trade policies on the basis of detailed laws leaving relatively little discretion to the executive branch. Many of the United States' trading partners accord their executive branch broad discretionary powers in the conduct of trade policies. In a dispute settlement system in which laws can be challenged more easily than individual measures under discretionary legislation, the United States is therefore at a disadvantage. In the long run, the United States may for these reasons

[18] Article 1904.15(a) of the NAFTA.

arrive at a national position on this issue that balances the interests of import-competing industries against those of its export industries, service providers and holders of intellectual property rights.

The question of the responsibilities of a State that has violated its international obligations is too complex to be resolved through simple rules of the kind that a legislator can formulate. This may explain why the international law on this matter has been developed by tribunals, not the drafters of treaties. The question would also be best resolved in the WTO on a case-by-case basis by prudent judges guided by principles of law. I therefore believe that panels and the Appellate Body should be freed from the limitations of Article 19.1 of the DSU and be given the possibility to develop jurisprudence providing for remedies that go beyond the cessation of the illegal act.

7

'Public–private partnerships' in WTO dispute settlement: the US and EU experience

GREGORY SHAFFER[1]

I. The blurring of the public and the private in international trade law

Law's rising prominence in international economic relations is nowhere seen more clearly than in the realm of international trade law following the creation of the World Trade Organization (WTO) on 1 January 1995. WTO law consists of rules that a centralized institution, the WTO Dispute Settlement Body (DSB), enforces through adopting judicial judgments that, if not complied with, trigger sanctions. While the WTO lacks police power, WTO judicial bodies have the power to authorize a winning party to withdraw trade concessions against a losing party who does not comply with the judgment. All states, even the most powerful states, have responded to WTO judgments by modifying domestic regulations and practices, or, in the few cases where domestic politics blocked modification, accepted any resulting sanctions. In the first eleven years following the WTO's formation, 335 formal complaints were filed, resulting in 95 adopted panel and Appellate Body reports and numerous settlements, with 20 panels pending.[2] International trading relations have been governed increasingly through law – or better stated, through power mediated by law – with the great powers and developing countries increasingly initiating legal complaints between and among each other.

[1] This chapter condenses and updates the information in the author's book *Defending Interests: Public–Private Partnerships in WTO Litigation* (Washington, DC, 2003). A version of this chapter translated into Japanese can be found in the journal *Kokusai-Shoji-Homu (International Business Law and Practice)* (Japanese Institute of International Business Law, Fall 2005).

[2] WTO Secretariat, 'Update of WTO Dispute Settlement Cases', WT/DS/OV/25, 12 December 2005.

The blurring of the public and the private spurs the growth of international economic law. WTO law, while formally a domain of *public* international law, profits and prejudices *private* parties. As international economic relations become legalized, lawyers listen and market their wares. Private parties, in particular well-connected, wealthier and better-organized ones, attempt to use the WTO legal system to advance their commercial ambitions. A more effective WTO public law incites US and European private legal strategies, which in turn yield further WTO public law. WTO law thereby becomes more credible and private actors are better able to exercise influence in its shadow. No doubt WTO law represents a significantly enhanced legal framework as compared to the *General Agreement on Tariffs and Trade* (GATT), even though the dispute settlement system of the GATT, the WTO's predecessor organization existing from 1948 to 1995, was legalized over time, and even though political and social forces still constrain WTO law's deployment. The WTO system is broader in scope and membership, more precise in application, more binding in effect, and more actively used. The reaction of private parties throughout the world in opposition or support of the WTO system and its stream of legal complaints and verdicts is just one indication of WTO law's relevance to states and their constituents.

The growing interaction between private enterprises, their lawyers, and US and EU public officials in the bringing of most trade claims reflects a trend from predominantly intergovernmental decision-making toward private litigation strategies involving direct public–private exchange at the national and international levels. Given the trade-liberalizing rules of the WTO, this trend has an outward-looking, export-promoting orientation, comprised of more systematic challenges, often by larger and well-organized commercial interests, to foreign barriers to trade. International trade disputes are, in consequence, not purely public or intergovernmental. Nor, however, do they reflect a simple cooptation by businesses, particularly large and well-organized ones, of government officials. Rather, they involve the formation of public–private networks to pursue varying, but complementary goals.

This chapter presents in condensed form a larger study of the reciprocal relationship of international public law and private actors in litigation and negotiation within its shadow before an international institution – the WTO – that has become the most legalized of all international institutions. The study builds on over one hundred interviews with former and current officials at the Office of the US Trade Representative (USTR), other US agencies, the European Commission, member States of the

European Union, representatives of US and EU business trade associations, and private lawyers based in Washington and Brussels. Since the United States and the European Union have been by far the dominant players in this system, the study focuses on mechanisms of public–private interaction within them, which now appear to be spreading to other WTO Members, such as Brazil, in ways adapted to their governance contexts.

II. Public–private networks in perspective: new forms of governance

This chapter addresses a form of governance as a complement to public-governmental hierarchies and private markets, that of governance through *public–private networks*. These networks bring together public and private actors to address discrete policy issues, thereby blurring the public–private distinction. In a world of growing complexity, governments increasingly have delegated traditionally 'public' functions to the private sector. Governments then attempt to 'steer' outcomes through overseeing these private actors' activities. According to R. A. W. Rhodes, a theorist of comparative politics, governance increasingly takes place through 'self-organizing, inter-organizational networks' composed of public and private actors that intentionally pursue shared goals.[3] Non-governmental actors do not merely influence public representatives (as in Dahl's notion of polyarchy) or respond to them (as in Weber's concept of hierarchy). Rather, mixed networks of public and private actors co-ordinate in policy formation and implementation.

These mixed networks of government officials and private groups are brought together by *resource interdependencies*. As Rhodes points out, it is the diffusion of resources among various actors that explains the need for networked forms of governance in a world of growing complexity, since neither central governments nor any other single actor possesses the resources necessary to govern without the cooperation of others. Governments need informational resources that private actors provide. While Weber focused on a 'bureaucratic organization's' use of 'knowledge' to exercise control, scholars such as Rhodes show how state agencies increasingly depend on private entities to obtain knowledge and effectively deploy it in implementing policy. As Walter Powell writes, 'A

[3] Roderick A. W. Rhodes, 'The New Governance: Governing without Government' (1996) 44 *Political Studies*, 660; R. A. W. Rhodes, *Understanding Governance: Policy Networks, Governance, Reflexivity and Accountability* (Philadelphia, 1997).

basic assumption of network relationships is that one party is dependent on resources controlled by another, and that there are gains to be had by the pooling of resources.'[4]

Not all public and private actors, however, enjoy equal opportunities to participate in these networks. Th*e relative power and influence of actors within these networks is determined by the diffusion of resources and actors' per capita stakes in outcomes.* First, actors may hold constitutional, legal, organizational, financial, political, informational, or other resources. For example, public actors hold constitutional and legal powers that endow them with authority. In the WTO context, only states may bring claims before the WTO DSB. Private actors thus depend on them to represent their interests. Private actors, however, also have organizational, financial, political and informational resources that can benefit public authorities. In the context of WTO dispute settlement, private associations have the financial means to hire legal experts to help develop legal arguments; hold essential information about the marketplace needed to develop a factual basis for legal claims; and deploy political resources through lobbying, campaign financial support, and public informational campaigns. Public authorities rely on these various resources. In short, public and private actors reciprocally depend on each other's resources to accomplish their respective goals.

Resources alone, however, are not sufficient to explain actors' participation in mixed networks. Resources are limited and their deployment costly. Participation also depends on actors' relative stakes in outcomes, and, in particular, on the per capita *benefits* from participating, compared to the informational and organizational *costs* of doing so. Groups with high per capita stakes are more likely to obtain and provide information to the policy-making process. In contrast, those with low per capita stakes are less likely to engage in policy strategizing where the per capita benefits of fully understanding the issues and organizing themselves are too low to justify the costs. Even where they each could benefit by collectively contributing to an association representing their interests, they may hope to free ride on others.

High per capita stakes, resource interdependencies, and the reciprocal interests of public officials and private firms thus together spur public–private collaborations. Since governmental representatives retain

[4] Walter Powell, 'Neither Market nor Hierarchy: Network Forms of Organization', in Grahame Thompson, Jennifer Frances, Rosalind Lovacic, and Jeremy Mitchell (eds), *Markets, Hierarchies and Networks: The Coordination of Social Life* (London, 1991), p. 272.

significant constitutional, legal, and other resources, they thereby typically remain the most important players in public–private networks at the international level. Private actors, however, also play central roles in cross-border networks, just as they do in domestic regulatory contexts. As enterprises engage in cross-border exchange, their per capita stakes in international economic governance mechanisms rise. They press for greater legal certainty in export markets. Through their encounters with foreign regulatory barriers, they obtain valuable information which they have the incentive to package and forcefully present to domestic and transnational policy-makers. As firms and trade associations become repeat players in the challenge of foreign trade barriers, they develop a knowledge of how to strategically use the WTO legal process when needed. This chapter assesses the strategies used within the United States and the European Union, the two most powerful WTO Members.

III. Public–private partnerships in the United States for opening foreign markets: the United States' leading edge

The United States was the first country under the GATT trading system to create a legalistic procedure whereby private firms could petition their government to challenge foreign trade barriers – Section 301 of the 1974 Trade Act. In contrast to most legal scholarship that examines the formal legal attributes of Section 301, this chapter views Section 301 as part of a broader informal process of public–private exchange behind the curtains of US challenges to foreign trade barriers.

Because the United States aggressively challenges foreign market barriers, some commentators criticize US trade policy as a tool for powerful business interests. Sylvia Ostry, former Canadian ambassador during the Uruguay Round trade negotiations, was widely quoted for maintaining, 'America does not have a trade policy. It has clients.'[5] Ostry implied that US interests are up for sale, in particular to those funding presidential and congressional campaigns. She writes, 'High policy is seen as a responsibility as much of the senior levels of the business community as of the government.'[6]

The United States' support for Chiquita's opposition to the European Union's banana licensing regime provides a clear example. The controlling

[5] See, for example, 'At Daggers Drawn: First Bananas, Now Beef, Soon Genetically Modified Foods', *The Economist*, 8 May 1999, p. 17.

[6] Sylvia Ostry, *Governments and Corporations in a Shrinking World: Trade and Innovation Policies in the United States, Europe and Japan* (New York, 1990), p. 19.

shareholder of the Chiquita banana company was among the top three contributors to the Democratic and Republican Parties in 1998. The Centre for Responsive Politics, a non-partisan and non-profit organization, reports that Carl Lindner, Chiquita's president and primary shareholder, contributed over US $2.4 million over the 1996 and 1998 election cycles.[7] One former USTR official confirms that it certainly appeared that Lindner hoped 'to buy' the WTO case from the USTR.[8]

With congressional and executive support, the USTR dedicated tens of thousands of personnel hours to challenging EU barriers to Chiquita banana imports. The litigation involved four WTO panels, a total of over one thousand pages of written briefs, buttressed by thousands of pages of annexes, and an eventual settlement in Chiquita's interest. Just as the USTR fended for Chiquita's bananas, so it battled for Kodak's film, Cattlemen's beef, and Pfizer's patents, bringing WTO claims on their behalf. Under this conception of privatized trade policy, if business is the USTR's client, then campaign funds and related forms of consideration must constitute the USTR's legal fees.

In bringing a case under WTO rules, however, the USTR does not assume the traditional role of private counsel toward its business client because the USTR cannot focus solely on winning a case through employing the strongest arguments. Rather, the USTR almost always has a conflict-of-interest with its 'client' industry or firm. The USTR, unlike a private law firm representing a 'client', must consider potential cases in which WTO Members challenge US government policies and other US interests that may need to be defended. Cases involving food and drug standards, subsidies and anti-dumping claims, to give just a few examples, inherently raise these conflicts. In any individual WTO claim brought by the United States, the USTR also must be concerned about setting precedents for later cases in which the United States could be on the defensive.

Under the current international system, the relation of US private interests and public authorities is neither as Ostry suggests, that of lawyer-client, nor, as some trade liberals desire, that of firms acting independently of government. Rather, as a result of the intergovernmental structure of the WTO system, firms must work with the USTR as a partner if they wish to successfully challenge foreign trade barriers under WTO rules. The separate,

[7] Contribution information is available at: <www.opensecrets.org/index.asp> (visited March 2003).

[8] This was related to me in an interview with a former USTR official in Washington, DC (18 October 2001).

reciprocal, overlapping interests of the USTR and the private sector give rise to ad hoc, hybrid public–private networks. The USTR depends on private sector lobbying in order to obtain support in Congress and the administration for adopting USTR policy goals and supporting USTR practical needs, from the granting or extension of 'fast-track' negotiating authority, or the ratification of new trade agreements, to approving the WTO accession of China or Russia, or the allocation of budgetary funds.

Countervailing forces, however, may intervene in a public–private trade network. Other commercial interests may counter-lobby. Activists promoting non-commercial causes, such as the provision of low-cost drugs to African AIDS victims, may undermine business-government strategies. Despite what some commentators suggest, firms are not 'clients' that can dictate USTR actions, and the USTR is not simply a gun for hire. Firms rather must negotiate ad hoc partnerships with the USTR, collaborating with the USTR where their interests coincide and domestic politics permits.

Over time, this interaction of public and private actors has intensified on account of structural changes from above (the relative legalization of the international trading system) and pressure from below (firms more aggressively demanding the removal of foreign trade barriers as they become more dependent on cross-border trade and investment in a globalizing economy). Section 301 constitutes a specific legal provision for private solicitation of public assistance on trade matters. It also represents much more. It forms part of a larger informal process of national public and private actors, holding interdependent resources, working through networks to advance their reciprocal interests in a globalizing economy. They do so by deploying and operating in the shadow of public international trade law.

US private firms' strategic use of the WTO dispute settlement process

Successfully working a public–private collaboration to liberalize foreign trade barriers requires inter-firm coordination, an intensive exchange of information between public authorities and private firms, strategic use of leverage points against foreign governments, and the harnessing of political clout. This section addresses how US private firms network and deploy the WTO dispute settlement process.

Coordinating through trade associations

Unless one or two firms dominate an industry, such as Boeing for airplanes or Chiquita and Dole for bananas, firms enhance their chances of successfully challenging foreign trade restrictions when they coordinate their activities through a trade association. Even where a single firm dominates an industry, it may act under the gloss of an industry association. For example, a former USTR official notes that Arthur Daniel Midlands is the dominant member of the Corn Refiners Association, and Seagrams is the dominant member of the distilled spirits association, but still they handled trade dispute through the associations.[9] Through a trade association, a large firm can present a united industrial front, maintaining that it represents a broader national interest. Through a trade association, it hopes to more effectively rally political support in Congress when needed.

The trade association's representative is a middleman playing a diplomat's role, explaining positions, receiving pressure, and exerting pressure. As a former USTR official confirms, the association representative often acts similarly to 'guys in our foreign embassies', having to explain how Washington works to its membership and explain to Washington what its membership wants. Moreover, dominant firms 'can make it tough' for trade association representatives, just as US political representatives can make a US diplomat's life tough in an international organization, or the United States can make life tough for a representative of an international organization when the representative tries to balance the views of the United States against those of other members.

There are trade associations for just about everything in Washington. There were more than 23,000 national associations and 64,000 regional, state and local associations by the mid-1990s. These figures compare to merely 5,000 national associations in 1955 and 13,000 in 1975.[10] Just to cover the capital's daily special of pork, milk and corn, there are the National Pork Producers Counsel, the National Milk Producers Foundation and the Corn Refiners Association. For firms relying on intellectual property protection, the Pharmaceutical Research and Manufacturers of America represents the pharmaceutical industry, and the International Intellectual Property Association (IIPA) represents the publishing, film, recording and software industries.[11] These industries also are represented by sector-specific associations, which, in turn, are

[9] Interview in Washington, DC (18 October 2001).

[10] Ronald G. Shaiko, 'Lobbying in Washington: A Contemporary Perspective', in Paul S. Herrnson, Ronald G. Shaiko, and Clyde Wilcox (eds), *The Interest Group Connection: Electioneering, Lobbying And Policymaking In Washington* (Washington, DC, 1999), p. 7.

[11] Regarding, the IIPA coalition, see 'International Intellectual Property Alliance', available at: <www.iipa.com> (visited January 2002).

members of IIPA, including the Association of American Publishers, the American Film Marketing Association, the Business Software Alliance, the Interactive Digital Software Alliance, the Motion Picture Association of America, the National Music Publishers Association, and the Recording Industry Association of America. Firms also form ad hoc associations targeting specific foreign measures: witness the Coalition against Australian Leather Subsidies. The Coalition was formed to bring a Section 301 petition in August 1996, challenging Australia's grant of subsidies to its leather industry. Since the Coalition remained unsatisfied with an Australian undertaking to terminate its leather subsidies, it pressed the USTR to bring a WTO case in May 1998 against Australian subsidies for 'automotive leather', which Australia agreed to remove in 1999 and eventually settled in 2000.

WTO cases increasingly demand significant time, expense and effort. The USTR is unlikely to expend scarce resources and limited political capital within the US interagency process when a claim against a foreign government is not backed by broad sectoral support. Where the USTR agrees to form an ad hoc public–private network on a specific trade matter, it wants a strong partner. Smaller claimants may pursue successful public–private collaborations if well-organized and if presenting a strong case. Large firms, in fact, are not always successful, especially when there is a large countervailing interest that may constrain the United States. Large and well-organized commercial interests, however, generally are more successful in working the process.

Public–private exchange of information

Firms do not simply 'buy' USTR assistance by collectively garnering congressional backing. To convince the USTR to take a case to the WTO, a firm normally must present the USTR with a strong legal case supported by a detailed factual record. The USTR wants a strong partner not only in terms of ensuring broad industry support; it wants a winning case. The USTR does not want to waste its resources, impair its international credibility, and tarnish its reputation before Congress by bringing and then losing a weak legal case before the WTO. As former USTR official Judith Bello writes, administrative officials 'tend to be institutionally risk-averse', and thus 'are likely to feel substantial pressure to win any challenge they elect to make of another government's practice.'[12]

[12] Judith Bello, 'Some Practical Observations About WTO Settlement of Intellectual Property Disputes' (1997) 37 *Virginia Journal of International Law*, 357–367, 359–360.

Building a strong legal case requires an intensive exchange of information between the relevant public authority (the USTR) and private firms. The process begins with the identification of foreign trade barriers and culminates in a negotiated settlement or the bringing of a WTO complaint, and, if successful, the monitoring of compliance. The USTR has limited resources, in particular to compile and organize the factual basis for a successful WTO claim. It thus relies on industry assistance. Since US industries, in turn, rely on the USTR to defend their interests under WTO law, they are pleased to oblige. If the USTR is unsatisfied with the factual dossier provided, it asks for more information. Firms are, in many ways, the USTR's eyes. Although US embassies may help compile information, firms know best the impact of a trade restriction on the market in which they operate or wish to enter.

Large and well-organized firms are often repeat players who, over time, learn to work the system. As firms become experienced with the process, they increasingly anticipate what the USTR needs. The process becomes routinized. In particular in the area of intellectual property protection, industry associations gather and compile information well in advance of the USTR's annual notice in the Federal Register requesting assistance in identifying and prioritizing foreign trade barriers.[13] The IIPA, for example, works with its members to gather information from around the world throughout the year. On the basis of the information gathered, the IIPA prepares a detailed submission to the USTR in early February of each year focusing on copyright 'piracy' and inadequate copyright enforcement around the world. In its report, the IIPA stresses the loss of high-wage US jobs and billions of dollars of revenue to the US economy (and implicitly, to the Association's members).[14] Over the years, the Association submitted 600-page reports each February that specify how the USTR should prioritize countries in its final Special 301 report – categorizing countries for the 'priority' list, the 'priority watch' list, and the 'watch' list. According to an IIPA representative, the Association's success in influencing US governmental priorities is demonstrated by the

[13] See, for example, 'Request for Public Comment With Respect To the Annual National Trade Estimate Report on Foreign Trade Barriers', *US Federal Register* (2005), Vol. 70, 55204–55205.

[14] See, for example, Corbett Daly, 'International Intellectual Property Alliance Urges USTR to Step Up Pressure on Ukraine', *BNA International Trade Reporter*, Vol. 18, 22 February 2001, p. 301. See also International Intellectual Property Alliance (2005), *Special 301 Report on Global Copyright Protection and Enforcement*, available at <http://www.iipa.com/special301_TOCs/2005_SPEC301_TOC.html>.

similarity between the IIPA's initial submissions and the government's ultimate findings in the Special 301 reports.[15]

Since not every country can be a priority foreign country, the Association targets those countries of greatest economic value (in terms of lost revenue) and precedential value (in terms of the global impact of winning a case). As one trade lawyer noted, 'You do not bring *Brown v Board of Education* until you successfully establish a supportive case law.'[16] To enhance pressure on other countries to enact and implement more protective copyright laws, the IIPA wants the USTR to choose cases that it clearly can win under the *Agreement on Trade-Related Aspects of Intellectual Property Rights* (*TRIPS Agreement*).

The USTR uses the submissions of private firms to pressure foreign governments to change their practices prior to the USTR publishing its annual reports. The process is constructed to stimulate negotiations. This construction often results in a fight over the facts before the USTR initiates a Section 301 investigation or files a complaint at the WTO.[17] The battle over the facts involves not only US and foreign governmental representatives, but also US (and sometimes foreign) firms and their legal representatives. If the foreign government does not undertake to change its practices or otherwise convince the USTR that the US industry has misrepresented the facts, it is listed in the relevant report, which can trigger the filing of a WTO complaint.

Working the interagency process

Once the trade association compiles the relevant information, it attempts to 'educate' the members of the US Interagency 301 Committee about the facts. Other than for agricultural matters (where the United States Department of Agriculture plays the lead role), associations typically start with the USTR since it leads the interagency process and is viewed as their ally and primary partner in the process. Associations, sometimes in co-ordination with their member firms, pay periodic visits to every agency representative on the Section 301 committee, as well as their superiors within these agencies. Since there are divisions within, as well as between government agencies, an industry needs to create strong working relationships with key contacts in each agency in order to teach them

[15] Telephone interview with IIPA representative (17 May 1999).

[16] Telephone interview with member of Washington trade bar (20 May 1999). For foreign readers unfamiliar with US constitutional jurisprudence, Brown is the seminal school desegregation case decided by the United States Supreme Court in 1954.

[17] Telephone interview with IIPA representative (17 May 1999).

to appreciate – and support – industry's concerns. Firms deploy their informational resources to persuade public authorities to work on their behalf. Firms find the United States Department of Commerce (USDOC) to be a particularly friendly agency, sometimes referred to as a 'clientele' agency.[18]

Firms most frequently cite the Departments of State, Treasury, and Defense as 'problem agencies'. The Treasury Department may oppose challenging a foreign trade barrier because an aggressive trade action could interfere with its efforts to shore up a country's financial system. The Defense Department will not want to compromise its use of air bases in Turkey over complaints about 'pirated' Disney videos or Madonna compact discs, no matter how valuable they may be to a US industry or firm. Trade associations generally are concerned most with the Department of State. There is an old saying among Washington lobbyists that, 'In the Department of State, you can find a desk for every country in the world except for the America desk.'[19] Ambassadors are promoted because they are 'diplomatic' and maintain friendly relations with officials of the countries where they are based. Associations report that they often must work to counter (what they term) 'misinformation' provided by a foreign country desk in the Department of State, forwarded from a US foreign embassy, which in turn was obtained from foreign government sources.[20]

The dialogue over trade barriers, in other words, becomes more than an intergovernmental one. It involves private firms debating factual and legal issues with representatives of multiple US agencies and foreign government officials. Foreign firms often hire Washington lawyers to present their version of events, further complicating the process. In the *Japan – Film* case, for example, Fuji hired a US law firm to respond to Kodak's Section 301 petition at the US national level, and, ultimately, to assist it (and Japan) in the WTO intergovernmental procedure. The combined legal fees of Dewey Ballantine (for Kodak) and Willkie Farr & Gallagher (for Fuji) were estimated to exceed US $12,000,000 in that case.[21] The fight over the facts, occurring throughout the Section 301 and WTO

[18] Confirmed in interviews with trade association representatives and Washington trade lawyers (17–20 May 1999).

[19] Telephone interview with Gary Horlick (May 1999). See also Paula Stern, 'Commentary', in Jagdish Bhagwati and Hugh Patrick (eds), *Aggressive Unilateralism: America's 301 Trade Policy and the World Trading System* (New York, 1990), pp. 193–194 (citing Congressional concerns with the State Department).

[20] Telephone interview with a representative from an intellectual property trade organization (17 May 1999).

[21] Confirmed in interview with member of the Washington trade bar (20 May 1999).

processes, can be an expensive one, favouring large or well-organized commercial interests.

Inciting congressional pressure

Industry does not rely solely on persuasion of agency representatives about the facts. Firms work the political process as well, contacting congressional representatives directly and in coordination with industry associations, whether through their 'government affairs' divisions or through hiring outside lobbyists. Many of the leading lobbyists in Washington are law firms with major international trade practices. For example, in terms of first semester 1999 lobbying receipts, Patton Boggs was rated number two, Akin, Gump, Strauss, Hauer & Feld, number five, and Hogan & Hartson, number seven among lobbying firms in Washington.[22]

Firms press their case to local congressional representatives and those on the international trade subcommittees of the Senate Finance Committee and the Ways and Means Committee of the House of Representatives. Local congressional representatives, in turn, contact their colleagues on these committees. Whenever a USTR official visits Congress, congressional representatives raise specific trade matters – whether about meat, steel or leather – however unrelated to the meeting's agenda. In the WTO bananas case, for example, the republican congressional representative from Cincinnati, Ohio (the headquarters of Chiquita), helped rally key members of the trade subcommittee of the Ways and Means Committee to demand that the USTR bring the WTO case.[23] When the European Union did not comply with the WTO Appellate Body's ruling, congressional representatives drafted legislation that would have compelled the USTR to retaliate had the President not responded by committing to retaliate on his own. To assure a doubting Congress, President Clinton, politically vulnerable from the Monica Lewinsky scandal and House impeachment hearings, was compelled to confirm the undertaking to retaliate against the European Union by letter to the Senate Majority Leader and the Speaker of the House of Representatives.[24] At one point, Senate Majority Leader Trent Lott even

[22] See N. Lewis, 'Spheres of Influence Grow in Washington', *New York Times*, 16 November 1999, pp. C1 and C27. See also J.H. Birnbaum, 'Officials Fail to Track Lobbying, Report Says', *Washington Post*, 8 April 2005, p. E1 (noting that Akin Gump and Patton Boggs remain among top lobbying firms).

[23] Telephone interview with a House staff member to House subcommittees (20 May 1999).

[24] See Marc Selinger, 'Clinton Averts Vote on EU Trade', *Washington Times*, 13 October 1998, p. B9.

attached a legislative rider that would 'require industry approval of any trade deal the US negotiates to reduce sanctions against the European Union for the Commission's beef and banana policies.'[25]

In the *EC – Hormones* case, the beef industry likewise pressed the USTR to take its case to the WTO and to retaliate against the European Union for failing to comply with the WTO Appellate Body's ruling. The beef industry's trade organizations – the American Meat Institute, the National Cattlemen's Association and the US Meat Export Association – orchestrated a country-wide press on the USTR.[26] With members throughout the country, the beef industry could request large numbers of congressional representatives to demand action. As one USTR representative stated, 'We know the intensity of the issue by how we are approached. A phone call from a congressman means a lot more than a letter.'[27] Phone calls from congressmen throughout the country mean even more. The threat of draft legislation forcing the USTR to act is most persuasive. Industries with significant operations in politically important states – such as California, New York, Texas, and Florida – can, in particular, effectively work the political process.

The use of leverage points: publishing reports and initiating investigations

The US public–private process is designed to establish a series of leverage points for public officials to pressure foreign governments to change their trade policies and practices. These leverage points include the following: (i) the deadline for private submissions of information to the USTR concerning foreign trade barriers, which the USTR will use in preparing its annual trade reports to Congress; (ii) the deadline for the publication of USTR reports which, in turn, prioritize countries and their practices; (iii) the deadline for initiating and concluding Section 301 investigations; and (iv) the many deadlines in the WTO dispute settlement system. This list is not exclusive. Imaginative firms and their legal counsel devise multiple pressure-inducing tools. To name just one, trade lawyer Richard Cunningham notes how firms have lobbied the United States International Trade Commission (USITC) to conduct sectoral studies of foreign barriers in order to establish facts and political momentum for a United States case before the WTO.[28] The USTR, as public authority

[25] See 'Lott Rider Faces Fierce Opposition from Lawmakers, Others', *Inside US Trade*, Vol. 18, 27 October 2000, 1.

[26] Telephone interview with representatives from the cattlemen's trade association (20 May 1999). [27] Telephone interview with USTR official (14 May 1999).

[28] Interview in Washington, DC (18 October 2001).

acting on behalf of US commercial interests, deploys multiple strategies and successive deadlines and leverage points to steadily ratchet up pressure on foreign governments.

The USTR gathers information from public and private sources and attempts to rank trade matters by their relative importance. Where USTR officials are overburdened, which is often the case, the US governmental reports restate the formulations submitted by private industry. The USTR prepares numerous reports that identify trade barriers, such as the annual National Trade Estimates Report, Trade Policy Agenda and Annual Report, Special 301 report, and annual reports on foreign government procurement practices and barriers in the telecommunications sector. A report's publication can represent a 'plateau in an ongoing dialogue' with foreign authorities.[29] As a USTR official confirms, 'What is valuable is the deadline. It does not matter what the date is.'[30] The USTR may even provide 'draft' reports to foreign officials in a last ditch effort to persuade them to change a regulatory policy or practice. If pre-publication negotiations are unsuccessful, the practice is listed, forming the basis for initiating a WTO complaint.

These trade reports have served as shadow WTO complaints, manoeuvred to induce concessionary settlements. Sometimes, the United States raises industry concerns before the relevant WTO committees responsible for overseeing WTO agreements, while it negotiates a bilateral settlement. In 2000, the Slovak Republic, Romania, Pakistan, and Bangladesh each announced before the WTO Committee on Balance of Payments Restrictions their respective reductions and phase outs of import controls on balance-of-payments grounds, to US exporters' benefit. They did so in the shadow of an earlier US case against India's import restrictions on balance of payments grounds, which India lost.[31] The USTR similarly announced that 'US pressure on Hungary regarding restrictive import policies for beef products resulted in Hungary's decision to open a special quota for high-quality North American beef', and that US pressure on Korea resulted in a favourable modification of its administration of rice quotas. In each case, the United States did not need to file a formal WTO complaint.

Litigating before the WTO

If the USTR, in consultation with industry, decides to file a complaint before the WTO Dispute Settlement Body (DSB), the exchange of information

[29] Telephone interview with former USTR member (14 May 1999). [30] Ibid.

[31] Appellate Body Report, *India – Quantitative Restrictions.*

and general coordination between public trade officials and the affected industry intensifies. Demand for public–private collaboration has heightened since the WTO's formation in 1995 because the WTO dispute settlement system offers greater legal certainty. No longer may a defendant government block the formation of a judicial panel, the adoption of a panel ruling, or the authorization of sanctions, as under the former GATT regime. Given the number of complicated cases that USTR counsel now must litigate, the need for sophisticated factual development and legal argument, the tight deadlines imposed by the WTO's *Understanding on Rules and Procedures Governing the Settlement of Disputes* (DSU), and the political stakes of winning or losing WTO cases, the USTR often requires industry to submit convincing factual and legal memoranda as a prerequisite to its filing of a WTO complaint. In the *Korea – Alcoholic Beverages* case, for example, the USTR asked industry representatives to take pictures of bars, check web sites and advertisements and prepare a detailed market analysis for the USTR before it filed the suit.[32] As a USTR official confirms, the USTR wants a commitment from firms to respond to 'time-sensitive demands for materials from [WTO] panels'. As encapsulated in the remarks of one USTR lawyer, 'We at USTR rely on industry.'[33]

Private industry's role in WTO disputes has grown as WTO cases have become more factually and legally complex. As WTO panels increasingly employ a highly contextualized, case-specific approach, as opposed to an application of generic rules, the demands on WTO complainants and defendants in presenting and explicating the facts accumulate. Private industry representatives have become fundamental for the establishment of the factual record. The *EC – Bananas III*, *Japan – Film*, and *Argentina – Textiles and Apparel* cases are three examples among many of cases involving facts provided to public authorities by private parties. The *EC – Bananas III* case, for example, involved over a dozen claims under four WTO agreements. The initial panel decision alone was over four hundred and seventy pages, much of it setting forth the case's factual background involving a detailed description of the European Union's byzantine banana quota and licensing regime. US attorneys involved in the case maintain that a mark of the United States' success is that the factual description in the WTO panel report was largely taken from the US

[32] Telephone interview with USTR representative (19 May 1999); telephone interview with representative of distilled spirits association (19 May 1999).

[33] Telephone interview with USTR official in Washington, DC (19 May 1999); confirmed in interview with USTR official (18 October 2001). See also Bello, 'Some Practical Observations', 359–360.

brief.[34] Much of that US factual description had, in turn, been prepared by Chiquita and its lawyers.[35] Similarly, in the *Japan – Film* case, 'twenty thousand pages of original Japanese-source documents were placed in evidence', which was provided by the affected companies and their lawyers.[36] In a case challenging Argentina's customs treatment of US footwear and textiles, the USTR provided data on the customs treatment of 118 separate tariff categories.[37] Nike 'worked the hill' to incite scores of congressmen to press the USTR to litigate the case. Nike then provided the USTR with the required back-up support.[38]

Because of the demands of the WTO process, industries typically hire Washington trade lawyers to assist them. In many cases, private counsel has entirely written the first draft of the brief's factual section. For the legal analysis, counsel attempts to meet with USTR lawyers throughout the process to develop legal arguments and apply the facts. Counsel provides sample briefs or memoranda from which representatives at the USTR can cut and paste, as well as mark-ups of the USTR's drafts. The USTR does not necessarily take all or even part of what outside private counsel offers, but the USTR often makes use of outside counsel's offerings whether because the USTR finds the briefs helpful, because the USTR is overwhelmed, or because of political pressure. Sometimes lower-level USTR legal counsel receive mixed messages, as political winds shift, being told to 'take responsibility for drafting everything', and then to 'stop doing it yourself and start farming out to private firms.'[39]

IV. Public–private partnerships in the European Union: moving toward a US model?

Just as the USTR has advanced US private interests, the European Commission has advanced the interests of European enterprises before the WTO's dispute settlement system and in its shadow. As with the USTR, the Commission's success in international trade litigation and

[34] Telephone interview with USTR official (19 May 1999); confirmed in interview in Brussels with former member of the Legal Service of the European Commission (22 June 1999).

[35] Telephone interview with USTR official (19 May 1999).

[36] Alan Wm. Wolff, 'Reflections on WTO Dispute Settlement' (1998) 32 *International Lawyer*, 951–958.

[37] Appellate Body Report, *Argentina – Textiles and Apparel*, para. 61.

[38] Telephone interview with a former member of USTR (24 April 2003).

[39] Interviews with USTR officials in Washington, DC (19 August and 18 October 2001). See also Rossella Brevetti, 'Lawyer Sees Growing Role for Private Counsel in WTO Cases', *BNA International Trade Reporter*, Vol. 18, 3 May 2001, p. 720.

settlement negotiations also depends on information provided to it by affected firms and industries. Mutually advantageous European public–private partnerships have resulted. Organized commercial interests have benefited through potential expansion into foreign markets and enhanced access to, and influence over, the EU institution responsible for negotiating with foreign governments on trade matters. The European Commission has benefited through bolstering its effectiveness in negotiating and litigating European trade claims. The Commission thereby has enhanced its stature among member States and powerful commercial constituents within the European Union, and among foreign governments, including the United States, internationally. In international trade negotiations, bilaterally and within the WTO, the European Commission has assumed a more dynamic leadership role.

EU public–private partnerships, however, operate quite differently than those in the United States. The European Union's more fragmented market, less litigious business culture, and more distant Brussels-based policy-making process have slowed the development of EU public–private trade networks. Directly or indirectly, the European Commission must seek approval of its trade policy initiatives by the EU member States, often by consensus. Individual member States can impede the Commission's endeavours. In addition, many European firms remain predominantly nation-based, even though European market integration has progressed significantly. European firms thus have had fewer contacts with the Commission in Brussels than US firms with officials in Washington. As a result, the Commission at times has proactively sought contact with private firms. At times, the Commission has had to lobby firms to lobby it.

Because of the Commission's dominant role in forging EU public–private partnerships, this section focuses on the Commission's strategies more than the previous one focused on the USTR's. Although Commission-dominated public–private partnerships differ from those in the United States, they too have been quite successful in making use of the WTO system, in particular since 1997 when the Commission's new 'Market Access Strategy' began to bear fruit. Although US and EU political structures diverge, US and EU trade litigation strategies have achieved comparable results.

The European Union's shift from a defensive to a market access strategy

From the European Union's creation in 1958 through to the WTO's in 1995, EU trade policy was relatively defensive in posture, reacting to foreign imports and domestic demands for protection on the one hand, and to new trade liberalization proposals advanced by the United States, often to dismantle those EU barriers, on the other hand. The original proposal for establishing a liberal trade regime under the GATT was driven by the United States, not war-torn Europe. The United States pressed for the development of a more liberal trade regime immediately following the Second World War based on negotiations of reciprocally reduced tariffs. US leaders such as Secretary of State Cordell Hull maintained that a liberal international regime was needed to avoid repetition of the protectionist policies of the 1930s that they believed contributed to economic retrenchment and nationalist tensions that, in turn, facilitated the rise of the Nazi party, leading to the century's Second World War.[40] American leaders believed that liberal economic policies would help rejuvenate Europe and thereby stem communist expansion from the Soviet east.

The United States continued to play a leading role in the negotiation of seven rounds of multilateral trade negotiations, culminating in the completion of the Uruguay Round and the creation of the WTO. During the Uruguay Round negotiations, EU negotiators often were forced to respond to US proposals as opposed to taking the initiative. Although there was broad member State support for EU positions in the services and intellectual property negotiations, differences among member States concerning agricultural and textile policies, in particular, divided more liberal-oriented northern European states from more protectionist-oriented members from the south. The result could be delay and caution, anathema to productive initiatives. As Hugo Paemen, the European Commission's lead negotiator during the Uruguay Round writes, 'Tensions between the Commission and Council over how the latter should exercise this control function created problems at important stages in the negotiations, inhibiting the Commission's ability to be flexible and proactive.'[41] At one point, French Prime Minister Alain Juppe attempted to undercut the Commission's authority by publicly lashing

[40] Kenneth Dam, *The GATT: Law and International Economic Organization* (Chicago, 1970); I. Mac Destler, *American Trade Politics* (3rd edn, Washington, DC, 1995), pp. 5–6. See also Judith Goldstein, *Ideas, Interests, and American Trade Policy* (New York, 1993), pp. 137–163.

[41] Hugo Paemen and Alexandra Bensch, *From the GATT to the WTO: The European Community in the Uruguay Round* (Leuven, 1995); Stephen Woolcock and Michael Hodges, 'EU Policy in the Uruguay Round', in Helen Wallace and William Wallace (eds), *Policy-Making in the European Union* (4th edn, New York, 1996), p. 321.

out at EU Trade Commissioner Sir Leon Brittan, 'We do not trust you, Monsieur Brittan, and we will never trust you.'[42]

Following the WTO's establishment in January 1995, the United States was quick to employ the WTO's more legalized dispute settlement system, while the European Union was initially on the defensive. The United States, working in conjunction with private enterprises and trade associations, initiated a series of high profile cases against the European Union, challenging long-standing, politically-sensitive EU barriers to the importation of bananas and beef. The United States brought eight of the first fifteen WTO complaints resulting in panel decisions. The European Union, on the other hand, was a complainant only twice (and those were cases also brought by the United States against Japan's alcohol taxes and Indonesia's national car regime).

The European Union's role was soon to change, as the European Commission felt pressured to take the initiative. In February 1996, the European Commission did so, announcing a new 'Market Access Strategy' whose aim was to make the European Union's trade policy more proactively focused on opening foreign markets for EU firms, rather than on defending the European Union's domestic market from foreign goods. The Commission began to target more resources toward opening export markets. The strategy's essence has been to comprehensively identify foreign barriers to EU imports, prioritize them, and press foreign governments to eliminate them. Commissioner Britton officially announced the Market Access Strategy not before an audience of member State bureaucrats, but at a business symposium to which executives from major EU exporting companies were invited. At the Directorate-General I Press Conference, he declared a 'D-Day for European Trade Policy', promising 'We are going onto the offensive, using our trade powers forcefully but legitimately to open new markets around the world.'[43] These highly publicized remarks marked a sea change from the European Union's more prudent, inward-looking, reactive trade policy of the past.

The process of bringing a trade claim begins with the awareness of an injury, which is then linked to a third party violation of a right. To develop this awareness, Commissioner Brittan established within the Trade Directorate-General a new 'Market Access Unit' whose primary role was to interact with EU business interests concerning the trade problems that

[42] See Lionel Barber et al., 'US Stands Ground on Farm Pact: Statement as France Renews Threats to Veto GATT Deal', *Financial Times*, 23 September 1993, p. 26; and 'Except us', *The Economist*, 16 October 1999, p. 53.

[43] See 'EU Launches Market Strategy', *Eurocom Monthly Bulletin* (December 1996).

they faced. The unit created an immense database listing foreign trade barriers by sector and country. Businesses could notify barriers through direct contact with the Market Access Unit or indirectly through a sector-specific or country desk within the Commission, a member State official, a member State foreign embassy, or one of the European Union's foreign missions, of which there are well over 130.[44]

From a cynic's perspective, organizing a database is a perfect project for bureaucrats – or, in this case, that multilingual breed, 'Eurocrats'. It is not policy; it is not a solution to business problems; but it is lots of paper – over 400,000 pages if you printed out the database.[45] The USDOC similarly created a database, but many US firms disparaged it, as did many interviewed in the USTR and the USDOC itself.

Interviewed EU business representatives, on the contrary, have spoken favourably of the Commission's database.[46] The database has served a collateral purpose in Europe not required in the United States. By publicizing its export-oriented strategy through the database, the Commission hoped to forge new links between the private sector and the Trade Directorate-General that otherwise were underdeveloped or did not exist. In the United States, businesses already came to the USTR when they faced trade barriers. The Commission lacked this luxury. While the USTR responded to onslaughts of private sector lobbying reinforced by congressional phone calls and committee grilling, the Commission had to contact firms to contact it. The Commission had to rally European enterprises to create the public–private networks necessary for trade law's successful application. The Commission hired consultants to provide detailed sectoral reports on trade barriers, hosted well-publicized informational fora on trade policy which it urged business executives to attend, distributed glossy brochures and otherwise solicited European businesses to work with it on EU trade matters.

Given the USTR's unilateral use of Section 301 – in particular in the heyday of the 1980s – to muscle foreign countries to import US products, US firms knew that the USTR fought for their export interests. European firms had no such faith. In fact, the more trade liberal-oriented countries in Europe, such as Germany, the Netherlands, and the UK, opposed the European Union's early version of Section 301, the New Commercial

[44] See 'European Commission External Relations Directory', available at <http:// europa.eu.int/comm/external_relations/repdel/index_rep_en.cfm> (visited November 2005).

[45] Interview with Dorian Prince (1999). Dorian Prince is the former head of the European Commission's Market Access Unit.

[46] Interviews with multiple trade associations in Brussels (June 1999).

Policy Instrument (NCPI), and worked to impede its effective implementation. In the early NCPI case brought by the Dutch company AKZO against a US law barring imports on intellectual property grounds (Section 337 of the Tariff Act of 1930), the Dutch government opposed and tried to obstruct the European Union's bringing of the GATT case.[47] The Dutch and other export-oriented EU member States feared that permitting private firms to bring NCPI cases could trigger a mercantilist unravelling of the liberal trade regime, rather than contribute to its enforcement.

Brittan's Directorate-General Trade, however, significantly altered the European Union's outlook on the offensive use of the WTO dispute settlement system. The Market Access Unit has provided a primary contact and voice within the Commission to defend and work on behalf of EC exporting interests. As of November 2005, the Market Access Unit consisted of 18 professionals, specialized geographically and sectorally so that they build knowledge and relationships with their client sector.[48] The unit compiles, investigates and coordinates interdepartmental investigations of barriers to EC trading interests.[49] In these investigations, the Commission determines whether the trade barrier exists, what information is needed, whether the barrier constitutes a violation of a WTO, bilateral or other agreement, the extent of its economic impact, whether the European Communities can effectively address it diplomatically or legally, and, if so, how best to proceed.[50] In 2005, the Unit was receiving about five to ten contacts per month that would trigger new interdepartmental discussions as to how to the assignment and allocation of responsibility for the matter's investigation and potential resolution.[51]

[47] Interviews with members of the Brussels trade bar and a former member of the Commission's Legal Service in Brussels (22 June 1999). For the NCPI case, see OJ 1986 No. C25/20. For the GATT Section 337 case, see GATT Panel Report, *US – Section 337 Tariff Act.*

[48] Telephone interview with Mathew Baldwin, head of the Market Access Unit (11 November 2005).

[49] For a time, an EC inter-agency group, the Market Access Action Group, consisting of representatives from different directorates-general, directorates, units and desks within the Commission, periodically met to assign responsibility for investigating trade barriers and to prioritize them. Although the group was discontinued because participants found that the meetings were an inefficient use of time, inter-service collaboration continues. Telephone interview with member of the Market Access Unit, November 2005. See also Crowell & Moring, 'Interim Evaluation of the European Union's Trade Barriers Regulation' (2005), p. 29, a report prepared for and funded by the European Commission, available at <http://trade-info.cec.eu.int/doclib/docs/2005/october/tradoc_125451.pdf> (visited December 2005).

[50] Telephone interview with member of the Market Access Unit (11 November 2005).

[51] Ibid.

The Market Access Unit can obtain preliminary analysis from the European Communities' WTO Dispute Settlement Unit as to whether the European Communities would have a viable complaint under WTO rules. This unit, which was created in 1998, consisted of 15 lawyers as of November 2005.[52] Its primary role is to investigate and prepare potential WTO complaints on behalf of the European Communities, including pursuant to the Trade Barriers Regulation (TBR) examined below. It also provides ad hoc advice on WTO legal matters to other units within the Commission, and, in particular, the Market Access Unit. Although some interviewed officials felt that the two units could work together more effectively at an earlier stage,[53] the units aim to have a relatively 'seamless collaboration'.[54]

When the Market Access Unit identifies a trade barrier, the Commission can deploy a number of tools to press for its removal. The Commission will likely first see how the issue may be settled through bilateral or multilateral negotiations. Most frequently, it will raise concerns bilaterally, perhaps using existing bilateral trade agreements or negotiations as leverage. The European Communities have entered into 28 bilateral trade agreements, more than any other WTO Member.[55] In some cases, it could include the issue as part of a package in the Doha round of trade negotiations or resolve it as part of a WTO accession, as with China, Chinese Taipei, and Russia.

Unlike the United States, the European Union has yet to systematically publish barriers in an annual trade report and attempt to use this publication as a means of leverage.[56] The Commission has rather hired consultants to conduct periodic studies of trade barriers faced by a particular

[52] Telephone interview with Jean-Francois Brakeland, head of the Dispute Settlement Unit (11 November 2005).

[53] Telephone interviews in November 2005. See also Crowell & Moring, 'Interim Evaluation', pp. 29–31.

[54] Telephone interview with member of the Market Access Unit (11 November 2005).

[55] See 'EC Regional Trade Agreements', available at <http://europa.eu.int/comm/trade/issues/bilateral/countries/docs/ecrtagr.pdf> (visited November 2005). In comparison, the United States lists 15 on its website. See 'USTR Bilateral Agreements', available at <http://www.ustr.gov/Trade_Agreements/Bilateral/Section_Index.html> (visited November 2005) and 'USTR Regional Trade Agreements', available at <http://www.ustr.gov/Trade_Agreements/Regional/Section_Index.html> (visited November 2005) or 'US Trade Related Agreements', available at <http://www. ustr.gov/assets/Document_Library/Reports_Publications/2005/2005_Trade_Policy_Agenda/asset_upload_file202_7310.pdf> (visited November 2005).

[56] Compare US trade practice described in Shaffer, *Defending Interests*, pp. 40–44.

sector, and prepared country reports on an ad hoc basis.[57] Although it has published an annual report that lists US trade barriers, it has done so primarily as a parry to the US report, subjecting the United States to its own tactics. The unit could conceivably adopt a broader annual report in the future, perhaps focusing on EC exporters' major markets, borrowing and tailoring from US practice.[58]

To prepare for the launching of a potential WTO complaint, the Trade Directorate-General will assign officials to build a dossier. Most frequently, a member of the Dispute Settlement Unit will take the lead as *chef de file*, although someone from a specialized unit for subsidies or anti-dumping claims may do so for claims in those areas. If the case cannot be settled, then the Commission can either bring it directly to the WTO, after first notifying and receiving informal member State approval, or commence an internal investigative legal procedure pursuant to the European Union's TBR, as described below. The Commission and private parties typically commence legal procedures only if they have exhausted local and diplomatic alternatives or if they feel that further diplomacy and lobbying efforts are either fruitless or can be enhanced through taking legal action.[59]

Alternative EU tracks for challenging foreign trade barriers

The Commission may initiate a WTO complaint against a foreign trade barrier on behalf of a European commercial interest through one of two EU procedures. Under the traditional Article 133 procedure, EU member State representatives meet with Commission trade officials on a weekly basis to monitor the Commission's implementation of EU trade policy. Before the Commission launches a WTO case, it obtains informal member State approval through a committee of member State representatives. Alternatively, under the EU TBR, European private enterprises may petition the Commission to investigate foreign trade barriers and represent their interests before the WTO in a manner analogous to US Section 301. As part of its Market Access Strategy, the European Commission has promoted business use of the TBR.

[57] See Crowell & Moring, 'Interim Evaluation', p. 18 (noting 'Reports have been prepared for around ninety of the European Union's trading partners, both WTO Members and non-members', and that the reports are available on the Internet).

[58] Telephone interview with member of the Market Access Unit (11 November 2005).

[59] Telephone interviews with Commission officials and private counsel for EC businesses (November 2005). See also Crowell & Moring, 'Interim Evaluation', p. 39.

The Article 133 process

The European Union's system for implementing trade policy can be more convoluted than the United States' because of the European Union's quasi-federal, quasi-intergovernmental political structure. EC member States attempt to enhance their leverage over global trade policy by pooling their resources and speaking with a single voice through the European Commission. At the same time, the member States are wary of granting too much authority to the Commission, which, in advancing some member State interests, could harm their own. The Commission's legal stance in any WTO complaint can implicate not only multiple European export interests, but also EU and member State internal regulations.

The traditional means for the European Union to initiate trade complaints in the GATT (and now the WTO) is through what is known as the Article 133 process in reference to the Treaty establishing the European Communities (EC Treaty) article governing EU trade policy. Whereas much has been written on the relative roles and competencies of the member States and Commission under Article 133 in the negotiation and approval of trade agreements, this section shows how the Commission and European businesses deploy the Article 133 process to advance their interests through public–private networks operating in the shadow of WTO law.

The Article 133 Committee, which consists of one representative from each member State, originally was created to 'consult' with the European Commission in an advisory capacity about the Commission's implementation of Council decisions.[60] The Committee, however, exercises authority informally. The Committee almost never takes a vote in its meetings. Votes are usually not necessary, since decisions typically are made by consensus.

When issues proliferate, a bureaucracy's grasp of the underlying facts and specialized understanding of law augment its authority. The Commission predominates in the deployment of trade law, whether through initiating trade complaints or conducting settlement negotiations in the law's shadow. The Commission prevails because the Commission has acquired greater expertise in handling the technicalities and increasing demands of WTO law. Only the Commission investigates,

[60] For an overview of the Article 133 Committee, see Fiona Hayes-Renshaw and Helen Wallace, *The Council of Ministers* (New York, 1996), pp. 86–90. There are informal 'sub-groups' of the Article 133 Committee involving services, automobiles, steel and mutual recognition agreements (Interview with Commission Official in Directorate-General Trade (16 June 2001).)

defends and challenges trade barriers before the WTO's DSB, and thus member State representatives lack the Commission's acquired knowledge. In the words of one member State representative to the Article 133 Committee, national representatives typically defer to the Commission as 'the professor'.[61] Another member State representative confirms that Commission officials 'are specialists because they argue WTO cases;' member States 'no longer have these types of specialists', resulting in 'greater deference'.[62] The member States therefore delegate *de facto* decision-making power to the Commission. With enlargement of the European Union to 25 member States in 2004, the Commission's relative expertise and authority on trade matters compared to that of member State authorities should increase.[63]

Where necessary, the Commission works behind-the-scenes with member State representatives to forge consensus on a matter before formally presenting it to the Article 133 Committee. Failing consensus, the Commission attempts to ensure that its recommendation is supported by at least a 'qualified majority' of member States. As one Commission official boasted, 'Eventually, we get them.'[64] Although differences between member States can arise over the treatment of WTO disputes, Commission officials rarely have to act as promotional brokers to bridge these differences.

Because the Commission's *de facto* powers have increased, European businesses can work more effectively with a central contact in Brussels on international trade matters, either bypassing national authorities or (more typically) working in coordination with them. Businesses thereby may play more active roles, despite the reputation of the Article 133 process as a state-centric procedure, and despite the fact that Article 133 meetings take place behind closed doors without private parties present. Guided by a Commission representative, sophisticated businesses can ensure sufficient support within the Article 133 Committee prior to the Commission's submission of a proposal. Where needed, they can coordinate positions with businesses in other member States so that each respectively contacts its representative for endorsement. If a matter is raised at an Article 133 Committee meeting, the meeting merely may

[61] Interview in Brussels (25 June 1999). [62] Interview in Brussels (23 June 1999).

[63] The Commission, however, is facing the challenge of managing such an increased number of member State representatives (Telephone interview, member of Directorate-General Trade (11 November 2005).)

[64] Interview with Commission official in Directorate-General Trade in Brussels (21 June 1999).

ratify a decision that has already been made. For example, although the United Kingdom's Scotch Whisky Association (SWA) played the leading role in the Japan, Korea and Chile alcohol cases, it also worked with the Confederation of European Producers of Spirits and its constituent members. These included French cognac producers who contacted French representatives.

Commission officials maintain that it is a mistake to think that, just because the TBR route is not used, the Commission does the entire investigation without the requirement of industry input. For example, the three successful EC challenges against allegedly discriminatory alcohol taxes in Japan, Korea, and Chile all required intensive input from the affected EC trade association, the SWA. As Tim Jackson of the SWA states:

> We must . . . be ready to assist the Commission (which sadly does not have unlimited resources to pursue such matters) often at very short notice when a WTO case is under way. For example, during the Japan case we had to commission market research to help the Commission refute some of Japan's initial submission . . . . It is a 'partnership' exercise with other industry colleagues, respective Governments and the Commission.[65]

The association also assisted 'the Commission by gathering market information/research for their Korea and Chile cases', which again resulted in successful outcomes for the Commission and the spirits industry.[66] According to SWA's outside legal counsel, it arranged for the econometric studies of the cross-elasticity of demand of the foreign and domestic products that played a crucial role in these cases.[67]

[65] Remarks of Tim Jackson, head of the SWA, at a conference in Geneva (May 1997), distributed at conference (on file with author). Confirmed in interview with USTR official (19 May 1999) and a member of the Legal Service of the European Commission (22 June 1999) (noting how the trade association provided statistics, pictures of bars, advertisements). See also 'U.S., Europe, Canada Protest Delays In Amending Japan's Liquor Tax Structure', *BNA International Trade Reporter*, 27 November 1996, p. 1814 (citing the SWA's direct negotiations with Japanese politicians and government officials).

[66] Remarks of Tim Jackson. The three alcohol cases are *Japan – Alcoholic Beverages II, Korea – Alcoholic Beverages,* and *Chile – Alcoholic Beverages.*

[67] Telephone interview (18 November 2005). The WTO panel in the Korean case, for example, found that the industry study 'provided useful information' and was 'helpful' in its determination of the key issue as to whether the spirits were 'competitive' or 'substitutable' products (Panel Report, *Korea – Alcoholic Beverages*, paras. 10.91–10.92). A product's 'cross-price elasticity of demand' or 'elasticity of substitution' refers to the impact of one product's price differential (including an account of discriminatory internal taxes) on another product's consumption (ibid., para. 10.44).

The TBR: Europe's reply to US Section 301

European businesses have a more direct track to solicit Commission representation of their interests – the TBR, enacted in December 1994 in anticipation of the WTO's formation.[68] The TBR grants individual private enterprises legal rights to petition the European Commission to investigate trade matters and bring trade claims on their behalf. Although the TBR grants a business the right to force the Commission to act, in practice, just as under US Section 301, businesses ultimately depend on public officials to represent their interests before foreign governments and WTO panels. Private firms typically realize that antagonism is self-defeating.

Businesses thus collaborate with the Commission in applying the TBR, forming ad hoc public–private networks, as in the United States. Businesses choose which mechanism to use – TBR or the Article 133 route – in consultation with, and in response to, the Commission's advice. When Volkswagen, for example, complained to the Commission about a problem that it encountered with a Colombian sales tax on automobiles, the Commission advised it to file a TBR complaint. Volkswagen's attorneys twice came to the Commission with drafts on which Commission officials made suggestions for improvement, before Volkswagen finalized its submission.[69] Similarly, in the TBR complaint against Brazilian tyres, the Directorate-General Trade advised the European trade association, BIPAVER, regarding how to make use of the TBR process.[70]

In early years, businesses sometimes deferred almost entirely to the Commission as to whether to proceed under the TBR or Article 133 process. For example, while the Italian silk federation, Federtessile, formally filed an early TBR complaint against the United States' application of rules of origin to Italian silk products, Federtessile had not even heard of the TBR until the Commission, in search of successful test cases, suggested it.[71] The United States was requiring that the silk products be

[68] The TBR's formal name is Council Regulation (EC) No. 3286/94 of 22 December 1994.

[69] Interview with Commission official in the TBR unit in Brussels (13 June 2001). See also Notice of initiation of an examination procedure concerning an obstacle to trade, within the meaning of Council Regulation (EC) No 3286/94, consisting of trade practices maintained by Colombia in relation to the imports of motor vehicles, OJ 2000 No. C236/05.

[70] Telephone interview with private legal counsel (18 November 2005). BIPAVER is the trade association for the retread tyre industry.

[71] Telephone interview with Tettamanti (19 February 1998). Tettamanti is a representative of Federtessile, based outside of Milan, Italy.

labelled as 'made in China', where the fabrics were woven, and not Italy, where they were dyed and finished.[72] The 'China' label undermined the fabrics' quality claims and subjected them to quantitative quotas applied to Chinese textiles. Such a labelling did not bode well for selling Italian silk products at luxury goods prices in the US market.

In the TBR complaint procedure, Federtessile was represented by no outside or in-house counsel. Rather, the Italian silk federation was entirely dependent on the Commission to prepare its complaint and lead it through the TBR procedure. The federation supplied the Commission with all relevant factual information for purposes of the Commission's investigation, the WTO filing, consultations and ultimate settlement with the United States. The public–private partnership, formed at the Commission's instigation, was a success for both parties. US rules of origin eventually were modified to the Italian silk industry's satisfaction. The Italian silk industry sang the Commission's praises. The Commission, in turn, touted the silk case as a great success. The Commission now could better promote business use of the TBR.

The Commission has played a guiding role in other TBR cases as well. For example, COTANCE, which represents hundreds of small leather tanners, brought TBR complaints against Argentine and Japanese market access barriers. It did so following a Commission-financed consultant's report concerning foreign trade barriers facing the leather industry.[73] Again, the leather industry was dependent on the Commission's entrepreneurship. The steel trade association Eurofer also initiated TBR complaints against the United States' 1916 Antidumping Act and against Brazil's import licensing system. However, Eurofer was founded in 1976 under the Commission's initiative, and still remains close to the Commission.[74]

TBR cases, nonetheless, require producer input since they are often factually intensive, and producer input has grown over time. Cases involving foreign administrative measures require ongoing EU public–private monitoring to attempt to check foreign abuses. The TBR case concerning Argentine import practices for textiles involved

[72] See Commission Decision of 18 February 1997 on the initiation of international consultation and dispute settlement procedures concerning changes to US rules of origin for textile products resulting in the non-conferral of Community origin on certain products processed in the European Community, OJ 1997, No. L62/43. In legal terms, the US test should be whether the products underwent a 'substantial transformation' in Italy, with the United States initially ruling that they had not.

[73] Interview with the representative of leather trade association COTANCE in Brussels (22 June 1999); confirmed in Dorian Prince interview.

[74] Eurofer is the European Confederation of Iron and Steel Industries.

Argentine customs valuations of a broad array of products.[75] The TBR procedure facilitated the needed public–private collaboration.

The TBR procedure also has sparked the interest of private legal counsel in Brussels. The legalistic nature and greater transparency of TBR procedures, compared to the Article 133 process, explains why lawyers have written extensively about it, even though the Article 133 procedure is used more frequently. Private lawyers help promote the TBR's use through promotional brochures and articles that they circulate to clients. These lawyers often work for Brussels affiliates of US law firms, such as Wilmer Cutler & Pickering, Sidley Austin LLP, Steptoe & Johnson, Hogan & Hartson, and Cleary Gottlieb.[76] They too have business incentives to publicize the TBR instrument, and have had some success. Businesses appear to work more frequently today with outside legal counsel on TBR complaints.[77]

TBR is much more than a legal procedure. It is a conduit that helps link the public and the private. Members of the TBR unit refer to businesses as their 'customers', which, as any good entrepreneur, they seek.[78] The TBR facilitates the forging of ongoing relationships between business and the Directorate-General Trade to assess and challenge foreign trade practices in light of WTO rules and negotiate settlements in the shadow of those rules.

Use of the Article 133 and TBR tracks to date

Although the TBR has gained acceptance, the Article 133 process has been used in over 80 per cent of all WTO complaints that the European Union has initiated. Use of the TBR, however, increased in the late

[75] Interview with Commission official in TBR unit in Brussels (13 June 2001).

[76] See, for example, Marco Bronckers, 'Private Response to Foreign Unfair Trade Practices – United States and EC Complaint Procedures' (1984) 6 *Northwestern Journal of International Law and Business*, 651 (now working for Wilmer, Cutler & Pickering); Paulette Vander Schueren and Davide Luff, 'The Trade Barriers Regulation and the Community's Market Access Policy' (1996) 2 *European Foreign Affairs Review*, 2 (Vander Schueren was a partner at Coudert Brothers, and has switched to Mayer Brown Rowe & Maw, Brussels); Cleary Gottlieb, *EC Trade Report* (Brussels, October–December 2004); and Geert Zonnekeyen, 'The EC "Trade Barriers Regulation": More Opportunities for Community Industries?' (1995) 1 *International Trade Law and Regulation*, 143 (who has worked for a number of Brussels law firms, including Baker & McKenzie).

[77] Telephone interviews with Commission officials, November 2005, confirming earlier interview with Petros Sourmelis, official in the TBR unit in Brussels (13 June 2001).

[78] For example, when the author called a Commission official in the TBR unit and mentioned that he had set up an interview with a representative from COTANCE, the leather trade association in Brussels that had filed two TBR complaints, the Commission official replied, 'Oh, so you are talking to one of our customers' (Brussels, 21 June 1999). The term was also used by Commission officials in telephone interviews conducted in November 2005.

1990s, signalling a shift toward enhanced public–private coordination in Europe, since firms began to play a more integral role in the process. This shift, in turn, has shaped the use of the less transparent Article 133 procedure, as private enterprises increasingly work with the Commission and member States behind-the-scenes to rally support for their claims.

The Directorate-General Trade's Dispute Settlement Unit would prefer for the TBR to be used more frequently, so that the unit receives better cooperation from the affected private sector, which must respond to its questionnaires if an investigation is to proceed.[79] Moreover, the TBR can facilitate coordination within the affected sector so that the Directorate-General Trade receives information in a more structured manner.[80]

Firms may prefer certain aspects of the TBR procedure to the Article 133 process. First, the technical nature of TBR work provides the Commission and firms with somewhat greater autonomy, so long as issues do not become politicized. Even though the Article 133 process typically works fluidly, the more Commission-friendly rules and technical nature of TBR procedures can influence a firm's expectations and behaviour. For example, the different voting rules under the TBR can enhance somewhat the leverage of Commission-business partnerships against reticent EU member States. Under the TBR, the Commission's decision to file a WTO complaint can be overturned only by a qualified majority vote of the Council, whereas a Commission proposal under Article 133 requires qualified majority approval. Firms thus may bring a TBR complaint where they feel that a member State could block an Article 133 decision. For example, the German company Dornier Luftfahrt had been unsuccessful in obtaining the Article 133 Committee's authorization for the Commission to initiate a WTO complaint against Brazilian subsidies to one of its competitors, Embraer. EU suppliers to the Brazilian company located in other member States indirectly benefited from these subsidies and lobbied their member States to oppose any EU action. These member States, however, were unable to stop the initiation of a TBR investigation, which ultimately led to the European Union's filing of a third-party submission in support of Canada's WTO complaint against these Brazilian subsidies, to Dornier Luftfahrt's benefit.[81]

[79] Telephone interview with member of the Dispute Settlement Unit (11 November 2005).

[80] Ibid.

[81] Jean Charles Van Eeckhaute, 'Private Complaints against Foreign Unfair Trade Practices: The EC's Trade Barriers Regulation' (1999) 33 *Journal of World Trade Law*, 199–213, 211; Marco Bronckers and Natalie McNelis, 'The EU Trade Barriers Regulation Comes of Age' (2001) 35 *Journal of World Trade*, 427–482, 457.

Second, the TBR may offer some advantages to smaller enterprises or large firms with relatively less important commercial claims. One of the goals of the European Union's Market Access Strategy is to provide smaller businesses that lack established Brussels contacts with better access to Commission officials. The Commission's Market Access Unit developed its database, in part, so that it could be in better contact with small and medium-sized businesses through the Internet.[82] The Commission reports some success, claiming that companies employing less than 400 people are the most frequent users of its market access database.[83]

The TBR grants these enterprises the legal right to have the European Commission investigate an issue on their behalf, provide them with all non-confidential information available, conduct a hearing at which arguments may be presented, and publish the relevant decision in the *Official Journal of the European Communities.* Although businesses work with the Commission as a partner, not as an adversary, the law forms a framework for business-Commission relations that can strengthen businesses' leverage.

The Commission's TBR unit maintains that its technical, law-oriented procedures reduce the pressure on it to balance a member State's political interests against a small enterprise's trade problems. Claims can proceed under the TBR when they otherwise might lack member State support before the Article 133 Committee. Leather tanners, silk fabric finishers, and producers of Parma ham, for example, are not politically powerful industries. Moreover, they are predominantly small family-owned enterprises located in northern Italy, where they lack close contacts with Italian officials in Rome.[84] The TBR increases the likelihood that EU officials will address their trading problems, and they have correspondingly benefited. For example, in the Italian silk case, the silk producers were not supported by EURATEX, the Europe-wide textile trade association, because some of EURATEX's members would benefit from more stringent US rules of origin. In particular, European weavers benefited from US labelling rules that required more production processes to be completed in Europe for a product to receive a European label. Yet, the Italian silk producers prevailed through use of the TBR mechanism.[85]

82 Interview with Dorian Prince (1998).
83 Interviews with Dorian Prince (1998, 1999). In the interviews, Prince claimed that over 55 per cent of daily queries concerning the data base come from such companies.
84 Interview with Dorian Prince (1999).
85 Telephone interview with a member of the TBR unit (February 1998).

Similarly, the TBR complaint of the Irish Music Rights Organization (IMRO) against provisions of US copyright law involved only a relatively minor amount of royalties for a trade association from a smaller EU member. Yet the European Union successfully defended IMRO's interests before the WTO, leading to the United States' agreement to pay financial compensation that the European Union can channel back to IMRO's members. Some business associations maintain that the TBR unit is more responsive to their trade concerns than members of the Article 133 Committee and other divisions within the Commission.[86]

Third, similar to the United States' use of Section 301, Commission-business partnerships may use the more transparent TBR procedure as a tool to increase pressure on foreign governments without commencing a formal WTO complaint. As the TBR scores initial successes and becomes better known, the Commission believes that the bringing of a TBR complaint can pressure foreign governments, especially less powerful ones, to negotiate and modify practices. Over time, the Commission and private firms have learned to use the TBR more tactically to pressure certain foreign governments.[87] The Commission can use the TBR procedure to notify foreign governments more forcefully that if they do not implement WTO requirements, a WTO complaint will follow. The TBR report can serve as a shadow WTO complaint and an incentive for settlement without invoking formal WTO legal procedures.

The Commission, working with private industry, deploys the TBR more as a 'problem-solving device' than a means to litigate outcomes. As Bronckers and McNelis write, 'European industry is advised, first and foremost, to use the TBR as a means to persuade the European Union's trading partners to settle disputes quickly and amicably.'[88] A Commission official in the TBR unit calls the TBR 'an instrument of suasion', referring to changes made in Korean and Brazilian customs administration practices in response to TBR investigations and negotiations in their shadow.[89] Volkswagen, for example, brought a TBR complaint concerning alleged discriminatory tax practices in Colombia in the

[86] Telephone interview with Tettamanti (19 February 1998).

[87] Interview with Petros Sourmelis (13 June 2001).

[88] Bronckers and McNelis, 'EU Trade Barriers Regulation', 453. Confirmed in interview with Commission official in the TBR unit in Brussels (13 June 2001).

[89] Interview with TBR unit official (13 June 2001). The European Union filed a WTO complaint against Brazil on 14 October, 1999, and then reached an agreement with Brazil that Brazil would not apply its non-automatic import licensing system to the European Union's exports. The Commission continues to monitor Brazil's practices (See WT/DS183/1).

hope of exercising more 'leverage' in negotiating a tax reduction.[90] The 2004 complaint against Uruguay involving taxes on spirits and the 2003 complaint against Turkey involving intellectual property protection have allegedly already resulted in favourable concessions without the need for a time-consuming, unpredictable and less diplomatic WTO complaint.

The Commission also may commence a TBR investigation to put the third country on notice that it is monitoring the country's regulatory behaviour. IFPI, an association of sound recording companies, for years monitored Thailand's enforcement of copyrights in conjunction with the TBR unit's administration of a complaint originally filed in 1991 and not concluded until 2005.[91] Although endless TBR monitoring could weaken the TBR as an instrument, the process can be used as leverage to retain pressure on countries to crack down on intellectual property infringers, under threat that a WTO complaint could follow. Monitoring is viewed as a 'containment strategy' to 'forestall negative developments'.[92]

Overall, large multinational businesses and those that are members of national or EU trade associations with offices in Brussels are best positioned to work the system, whether under Article 133 or the TBR. The SWA, whose members comprise a major UK export sector, is renowned for successfully working with the Commission to pry open foreign markets. The industry's initial success in the 1996 *Japan – Alcoholic Beverages II* case, concerning alleged tax discrimination in favour of Japanese producers, spurred it to work with the Commission in the European Union's successful WTO complaints against Korean and Chilean tax practices that favoured their local beverages *soju* and *pisco*. When Chile modified its internal tax regime in light of the *Japan – Alcoholic Beverages II* decision, the European Union brought a new complaint, alleging that the modified law still violated the anti-discrimination rules of GATT Article III. After the Appellate Body found against it, Chile lowered its taxes on all distilled spirits to the same level applied to *pisco*.[93] A sophisticated repeat player, the SWA likewise has worked with the Commission on the WTO terms of accession of China, Chinese Taipei, and Russia, among others.[94] Other members of the Confederation of

[90] Interview with Commission official in the TBR unit in Brussels (13 June 2001) (See note 69 above.)

[91] Telephone interview with member of the Dispute Settlement Unit (14 November 2005).

[92] Telephone interview with member of the Dispute Settlement Unit (14 November 2005).

[93] Rossella Brevetti, 'Chile Modifies Distilled Spirits Taxes to Comply with Adverse WTO Ruling', *BNA International Trade Reporter*, Vol. 18, 1 February 2001, pp. 204–205.

[94] Remarks of Tim Jackson, head of the SWA, at a conference in Geneva (May 1997).

European Producers of Spirits also have deployed the European Union's trade instruments. French associations of cognac producers and Bordeaux winemakers each brought TBR complaints, one against Brazil's non-recognition of the 'cognac' geographical indication, and the other against Canada's failure to protect the 'Bordeaux' and 'Médoc' geographical indications.[95]

The European Communities in WTO litigation

Once the Commission decides to proceed to WTO litigation, the EC's Legal Service takes the lead on the file. As of November 2005, the Legal Service had about thirteen lawyers working on WTO matters, an increase of about three/four since early 2003.[96] The Legal Service will, however, continue to work closely with those assigned to the file in the D-G Trade, and, when needed, with the private sector and its counsel, which may have helped the D-G Trade build the factual and legal case. Although private lawyers state that the Legal Service tends to keep a greater distance from them than do officials in the D-G Trade, the Legal Service too will often work with private counsel to help build the case, including if new issues arise at the hearings or in legal submissions. Though private lawyers may wish that the Legal Service focused more closely on their client's commercial interests, private legal counsel find that the lawyers in the Legal Service are highly competent professionals.

During the first two years of the WTO, the United States was far more active in WTO dispute settlement than the European Union, filing 23 WTO complaints (resulting in eight panel reports), while the Commission filed only nine (resulting in only two panel reports, both of which included the United States as co-complainant). In 1997, the situation began to change and the European Union became much more active between 1997 and 2000. Commission investigations and public–private collaborations have resulted in the European Union requesting more consultations before the WTO DSB than any other WTO Member, including the United States. The European Union has requested 45 WTO consultations, while the United States has requested

[95] See also web site concerning the TBR maintained by the Commission, available at <www.europa.eu.int/comm/trade/policy/traderegul/index_en.htm>.

[96] E-mail from Eric White, head of WTO dispute settlement in the Legal Service (17 November 2005).

40, and the European Union was complainant in 24 cases resulting in adopted panel or Appellate Body reports, compared to 23 for the United States.[97]

V. Conclusion

The development of public–private partnerships in the United States and Europe to address international trade claims is a rational response to a more legalized international trading system. WTO legal rights affect company and industry-specific interests. Details concerning market share and legal arguments are the province of business executives and legal advocates, not State – or European Union – bureaucrats. The more legalized international trading system creates stronger incentives for well-placed private actors to engage public legal processes before international legal fora. To litigate effectively in the WTO system, government officials need the specific information that businesses and their legal representatives can provide. Officials therefore strive to establish better working relations with industry on trade matters. The engagement of private firms, in turn, helps public officials render public international law more effective. Hence, the reciprocal relationship between WTO law as public international law and private interest.

Overall, the legalization of the international trade system has induced greater convergence of US and EU trade policies in regards to the challenging of trade barriers. The binding nature of the WTO dispute settlement system has somewhat constrained unilateralism in US trade policy, even while US unilateralism has intensified in most other policy areas.[98] Simultaneously, the European Union has adapted to a legalized WTO system – that was initially promoted by the United States – through adopting analogues to US-style public–private trade litigation strategies.

With the creation of the WTO, an area of international law has become more like law as we commonly perceive it. Yet, as this chapter shows, WTO law is not the neutral technocratic process some of its proponents idealize it to be. Even the richest WTO Members have become dependent on the assistance of private parties. If the United States and the European Union are dependent on assistance from private firms and

[97] See WTO website, 'Disputes by country', at <http://www.wto.org/english/tratop_e/dispu_e/dispu_by_country_e.htm> (visited November 2005).

[98] See, for example, Bill Emmott, 'Our Law, Your Law', *The Economist*, 29 June 2002, p. 20 (survey).

trade associations, what does this bode for other countries' participation in the system? Those who support the creation of international trading rights need be cognizant of how they will be used. Although countries other than the United States and the European Union may be at a disadvantage before the WTO's current dispute settlement system, forsaking such law will not rid the world of systemic biases. Rather, WTO Members will need to develop mechanisms to offset disadvantages that they face in light of the way in which the WTO's legalized system operates. The choice is among imperfect alternatives. It is likely that many other Members will attempt to adapt mechanisms of public–private coordination to their varying contexts and to attempt to steer them to advance their respective interests.

8

Accomplishments of the WTO dispute settlement mechanism

VALERIE HUGHES

The Members of the World Trade Organization (WTO) had remarkably ambitious goals for their newly minted dispute settlement system. In the *Marrakesh Declaration of 15 April 1994*, Ministers 'salute[d] the historic achievement' represented by the conclusion of the Uruguay Round, stating that it would 'strengthen the world economy and lead to more trade, investment, employment and income growth throughout the world.' Notably, in that same document, Ministers 'welcomed' 'in particular' the new dispute settlement system. Ministers underlined 'the stronger and clearer legal framework they [had] adopted for the conduct of international trade, *including a more effective and reliable dispute settlement mechanism*.'[1]

This pride-of-place enjoyed by dispute settlement in the WTO system stands in marked contrast to the role that dispute settlement considerations played at the Havana Conference in 1947, when the *General Agreement on Tariffs and Trade* (GATT) came into being. Ambassador Julio Lacarte-Muró, the first Chairman of the Appellate Body, who was present at the Havana Conference, has said that dispute settlement was a minor consideration in 1947 that did not receive much attention.[2] Not surprisingly, therefore, dispute settlement was treated in just two Articles (XXII and XXIII) of the GATT 1947. It could hardly have been more different at the conclusion of the Uruguay Round in 1994. Dispute settlement had clearly become a pivotal element of the Uruguay Round agreements.

[1] *Marrakesh Declaration of 15 April 1994* (emphasis added).

[2] Julio A. Lacarte-Muró, 'El mecanismo de solución de diferencias del GATT y la OMC: Enseñanzas del pasado', paper presented in Mexico City on 10 November 2005 at a seminar on 'Dispute Settlement Understanding and the WTO: Past, Present and Future', organized by the Secretaría de economía and the Universidad nacional autónoma de México, Facultad de derecho y division de estudios de posgrado (paper on file with the author).

That WTO Members had ambitious aspirations for the new dispute settlement system is also evident in the opening provisions of the *Understanding on Rules and Procedures Governing the Settlement of Disputes* – the agreement setting out the procedures for dispute settlement, generally referred to as the DSU. Article 3.2 of the DSU describes the dispute settlement system as a 'central element' in providing 'security and predictability' to the multilateral trading system. The same article states that the dispute settlement system serves to 'preserve the rights and obligations' of Members under the WTO agreements.

Clearly, the WTO dispute settlement system had a lot to live up to. The good news is that it has even surpassed Members' expectations. The WTO dispute settlement system is THE success story of the WTO. It has contributed to the credibility of the WTO as an institution. It has also demonstrated that the WTO is more than simply a forum for negotiating rules. Finally, it has provided a reliable means to enforce those rules.

The successes of the WTO dispute settlement system have been detailed in numerous articles and by numerous experts. One such tribute is found in a report entitled 'The Future of the WTO: Addressing institutional challenges in the new millennium',[3] prepared in 2004 at the request of former WTO Director-General Dr Supachai Panitchpakdi. Dr Supachai commissioned eight leading experts from around the globe to prepare a report on the future of the WTO.[4] The chapter dedicated to the dispute settlement system describes the system as a 'very significant and positive step forward in the general system of rules-based international trade diplomacy.'[5] It also concludes that 'there exists much satisfaction with its practices and performance.'[6]

Just how do we measure the success of the WTO dispute settlement system? I would suggest three indicators in particular. First, the WTO system represents a vast improvement over the GATT dispute settlement system. Secondly, the new system has produced a rich body of ever-expanding jurisprudence, both with respect to procedural rules and the substantive obligations under the various WTO agreements. Thirdly, there is broad-based confidence in the system on the part of

[3] Report by the Consultative Board to the Director-General Supachai Panitchpakdi, 'The Future of the WTO: Addressing institutional challenges in the new millennium' (Geneva, 2004), available at <www.wto.org/english/thewti_e/10anniv_e/future_wto_e/pdf>.

[4] The eight experts are: Peter Sutherland (Chairman), Jagdish Bhagwati, Kwesi Botchwey, Niall FitzGerald, Koichi Hamada, John H. Jackson, Celso Lafer, and Thierry de Montbrial.

[5] Report by the Consultative Board, p. 49. [6] Ibid.

WTO Members, as evidenced by its frequent use by developed and developing-country Members.

In this chapter, I will look at each of these indicators with a view to demonstrating that the accomplishments of the WTO dispute settlement system are numerous and varied and deserve to be celebrated.

I. Improvements over the GATT dispute settlement system

The GATT dispute settlement system enjoyed a considerable degree of success, but most GATT scholars would agree with the general assessment that the quality of the legal decisions was, at best, uneven. Moreover, the system could be very slow and permitted Contracting Parties[7] to delay, even for years, bringing matters to dispute settlement and, once there, to drag out the process of reaching some sort of conclusion. Another of the perceived weaknesses of the GATT dispute settlement system was that it permitted Contracting Parties to block the establishment of panels as well as the adoption of panel reports, because these had to be achieved through positive consensus. Not surprisingly, the party being complained against or the party that had lost a case would have a strong incentive to block establishment of a panel or the adoption of a panel report, thus preventing consensus. It must be said, in fairness, that this happened less often than one might have thought. Nevertheless, there were some problems in this respect. A third flaw of the GATT system was that it was considered to be 'more responsive to the interests of the strong than the interests of the weak.'[8]

It was with these deficiencies in mind that the drafters of the DSU sought to make improvements over the GATT system. It is widely recognized that they have succeeded. Under the WTO system, it is no longer possible to block the establishment of panels or the adoption of reports, unless there is a positive consensus to do so. In other words, whereas under the GATT one needed a consensus *in order to* establish a panel or to adopt a report, under the WTO, one needs a consensus *against* doing so. This is referred to as the reverse consensus rule. As a result, the establishment of panels and adoption of reports has become virtually

[7] Countries that were party to the GATT were referred to as Contracting Parties. The WTO has Member countries as well as certain other non-country Members.

[8] Robert E. Hudec, *Enforcing International Trade Law: The Evolution of the Modern GATT Legal System* (Salem, NH, 1993), p. 353.

automatic, which adds significantly to the credibility and efficiency of the system.

The WTO dispute settlement system comprises many more procedural rules than did the GATT system. The two GATT Articles (XXII and XXIII) have been expanded to 27 provisions governing dispute settlement in general, which are found in the DSU, plus several special rules found in other WTO agreements,[9] as well as 32 rules governing appellate procedure, which are set out in the *Working Procedures for Appellate Review*[10] (Working Procedures). The new system thus was intended to be more rules-based than power-based, and most WTO scholars would agree that this objective has indeed been realized. Under the circumstances, the new system is considered to be more legalistic than diplomacy-oriented, and dispute settlement under the WTO tends to involve specialist lawyers more often than it does diplomats skilled in diplomacy. This was not the case under the GATT and, admittedly, is one feature of the new system that not everyone would consider an improvement! It is believed, however, that the shift to a rules-based system has contributed to the greater participation by developing country Members than was the case under the GATT.

Perhaps the most significant enhancement to the dispute settlement system was the establishment of the Appellate Body, creating the automatic right, without leave, to appellate review. It was a rather bold step at the time, for appellate review in international dispute settlement was quite uncommon in 1994.[11] Although the right of appeal was, at least for some WTO Members, a critical feature of the new system, the DSU negotiators anticipated that there would be few appeals. This has not turned out to be the case, as close to 70 per cent of panel reports were appealed during the first decade of the new system.[12] In my view, this is a positive sign, demonstrating Members' confidence in the Appellate Body. Moreover, it has led to the development of a very rich and varied body of jurisprudence, a subject that I will address next.

[9] See Appendix 2 to the DSU, which lists these special rules.

[10] WT/AB/WP/5, 4 January 2005.

[11] Indeed, this is true even today. There is no appellate review at the International Court of Justice (ICJ), the International Tribunal for the Law of the Sea, or under the North American Free Trade Agreement (NAFTA), for example.

[12] The rate of appeal fluctuates from year to year. Initially, the appeal rate was 100 per cent. In 2002, it was at its lowest, at 50 per cent (See WTO, *Appellate Body Annual Report for 2005*, WT/AB/5, p. 22).

II. Jurisprudence: treaty interpretation and rules of procedure in the DSU

Customary rules of interpretation

During its first ten years, the Appellate Body was called upon to interpret various provisions of the DSU. Perhaps its most important of such rulings came, not surprisingly, in the very first appeal, in connection with a case brought by Brazil and Venezuela against the United States about a gasoline regulation (*US – Gasoline*).[13] Article 3.2 of the DSU states that the dispute settlement system serves to clarify – that is, interpret[14] – the provisions of the WTO agreements in accordance with 'customary rules of interpretation of public international law.' The Appellate Body determined in *US – Gasoline* that the general rule of interpretation codified in Article 31 of the *Vienna Convention on the Law of Treaties*[15] (*Vienna Convention*) had 'attained the status of a rule of customary or general international law'[16] and that, as such, it 'form[ed] part of the 'customary rules of interpretation of public international law' which the Appellate Body has been directed, by Article 3.2 of the DSU, to apply in seeking to clarify the provisions of'[17] the *Marrakesh Agreement Establishing the World Trade Organization* (*WTO Agreement*). This ruling set the stage for all of the appellate jurisprudence that followed; the Appellate Body has systematically applied this rule of interpretation in every decision to date. Article 31(1) of the Vienna Convention requires that a treaty be interpreted 'in good faith in accordance with the ordinary meaning to be given to the terms of the treaty in their context and in the light of its object and

[13] Appellate Body Report, *US – Gasoline*, p. 3, DSR 1996:I, 3, 3–4.

[14] Article 3.2 refers to the process of 'clarifying' the provisions of WTO agreements in dispute settlement proceedings, rather than 'interpreting' those provisions. The reason is that Article IX of the *WTO Agreement*, the umbrella WTO agreement, provides that the 'Ministerial Conference and the General Council shall have the *exclusive authority to adopt interpretations* of this Agreement and of the Multilateral Trade Agreements' and that the 'decision to adopt an interpretation shall be taken by a three-fourths majority of the Members.' The Article IX procedure has never been used and, for all practical purposes, when a panel or the Appellate Body 'clarifies' a provision of one of the WTO agreements, it is in effect interpreting it. However, I note that the foremost authority on the law of treaties, Lord McNair, has written that '[s]trictly speaking, when the meaning of the treaty is clear, it is "applied", not "interpreted". Interpretation is a secondary process which only comes into play when it is impossible to make sense of the plain terms of the treaty, or when they are susceptible of different meanings.' (See Lord McNair, *The Law of Treaties* (Oxford, 1961), p. 365, footnote 1.)

[15] Done at Vienna, 23 May 1969, in force 27 January 1980, 1155 UNTS 331; 8 International Legal Materials 679, UKTS (1980) 58.

[16] Appellate Body Report, *US – Gasoline*, p. 17, DSR 1996:I, 3, 16.

[17] Ibid.

purpose.' Applying this rule, the Appellate Body has focused on treaty terms – that is, the text of provisions at issue in an appeal. As the Appellate Body has explained, 'Article 31 of the Vienna Convention provides that the words of the treaty form the foundation for the interpretive process'[18] and, quoting the International Court of Justice (ICJ), observed that 'interpretation must be based above all upon the text of the treaty.'[19] The Appellate Body also made clear that the 'duty of a treaty interpreter is to examine the words of the treaty to determine the intentions of the parties.'[20] The Appellate Body's systematic approach of putting emphasis on the text has proved highly beneficial to the system, as it has fostered a degree of 'predictability' in dispute settlement, one of the goals of the system found in Article 3.2 of the DSU.

The Appellate Body and the parties that have argued before it have relied on all three elements set forth in Article 31(1) of the *Vienna Convention*, namely: 'ordinary meaning,' 'context,' and 'object and purpose'. In analyzing the 'ordinary meaning' of a treaty term, the Appellate Body has often turned to dictionaries – at least as a first step – to ascertain the import of a particular provision at issue.[21] The Appellate Body will often look to English, French, and Spanish definitions of terms – the three official languages of the WTO[22] – to ascertain the common usage of a particular term.[23] Sometimes, however, dictionary definitions do not provide a definitive resolution to an interpretation issue, with the result that further inquiry is necessary.[24]

Reference to the 'context' of a provision, be it in the provision at issue itself or elsewhere in the *WTO Agreement* or agreements, for the purposes of determining the meaning of a treaty term, is also frequent.[25] Context

[18] Appellate Body Report, *Japan – Alcoholic Beverages II*, p. 11, DSR 1996:I, 97, 105.

[19] Ibid. The Appellate Body was quoting from the ICJ decisions in *Territorial Dispute (Libyan Arab Jamahiriya/Chad), Judgment*, (1994) ICJ Reports, p. 20, and *Maritime Delimitation and Territorial Questions between Qatar and Bahrain, Jurisdiction and Admissibility, Judgment*, (1995) ICJ Reports, p. 18.

[20] Appellate Body Report, *India – Patents (US)*, para. 45.

[21] See, for example, Appellate Body Report, *Canada – Dairy*, para. 108; Appellate Body Report, *US – Offset Act (Byrd Amendment)*, para. 248; Appellate Body Report, *US – Softwood Lumber IV*, paras. 58–59; and Appellate Body Report, *EC – Chicken Cuts*, paras. 174–175.

[22] See, for example, Appellate Body Report, *EC – Bed Linen (Article 21.5 – India)*, footnote 153; and Appellate Body Report, *US – Upland Cotton*, para. 424 and footnote 510.

[23] See also Article 33 of the *Vienna Convention*, which provides that the terms of a treaty are presumed to have the same meaning in each authentic text.

[24] See, for example, Appellate Body Report, *US – Gambling*, paras. 163–167.

[25] See, for example, Appellate Body Report, *US – Carbon Steel*, paras. 69–72; and Appellate Body Report, *EC – Chicken Cuts*, paras. 175, 188–189, and 193.

may also comprise documents outside the treaty itself, as provided for in Article 31(2)(a) and (b) of the *Vienna Convention.* Article 31(2)(a) refers to 'any agreement relating to the treaty which was made between all the parties in connexion with the conclusion of the treaty' and Article 31(2)(b) to 'any instrument which was made by one or more parties in connexion with the conclusion of the treaty and accepted by the other parties as an instrument related to the treaty.' In a recent appeal, the Appellate Body determined that a consensus by WTO Members to use the Harmonized Commodity Description and Coding System (Harmonized System) as the basis for preparing their WTO schedules was an agreement relating to the *WTO Agreement* made in connection with the conclusion of the *WTO Agreement.* Hence that consensus was determined to fall within the meaning of Article 31(2)(a) of the *Vienna Convention*, and, therefore, constituted context for the purpose of interpreting a Member's schedule to the *WTO Agreement.*[26] In another appeal, the Appellate Body did not agree with a panel's finding that certain scheduling guidelines drafted by the GATT Secretariat constituted context under Article 31(2)(b) of the *Vienna Convention.* The Appellate Body observed that authorship by a delegated body would not necessarily preclude an instrument from falling within Article 31(2)(b), but it did not consider that there was sufficient evidence that the guidelines in question constituted an agreement related to the *WTO Agreement*, or that they had been accepted by the WTO parties as an instrument related to the WTO treaty. Thus, the guidelines could not be used as context in interpreting the Member's schedule in that case.[27]

The Appellate Body has also looked to the 'object and purpose' of the treaty to assist with interpretation of WTO provisions, relying on the preambles of the WTO agreements, the titles of articles, and the content of the provisions themselves, to ascertain a particular object and purpose.[28] Object and purpose is not confined to the overall object and purpose of a treaty; according to the Appellate Body, regard may be had to the object and purpose of a treaty provision.[29]

[26] Appellate Body Report, *EC – Chicken Cuts*, paras. 192–199.

[27] Appellate Body Report, *US – Gambling*, paras. 175–178.

[28] See, for example, Appellate Body Report, *Korea – Alcoholic Beverages*, paras. 120 and 127; Appellate Body Report, *Canada – Autos*, para. 84, Appellate Body Report, *US – Carbon Steel*, paras. 70–74; Appellate Body Report, *EC – Tariff Preferences*, para. 169; Appellate Body Report, *US – Softwood Lumber IV*, para. 64; and Appellate Body Report, *EC – Chicken Cuts*, paras. 238–243.

[29] See, for example, Appellate Body Report, *Argentina – Footwear (EC)*, para. 91.

The Appellate Body has often inquired into Members' actions to ascertain whether they amount to 'subsequent practice in the application of the treaty which establishes the agreement of the parties regarding its interpretation,' within the meaning of Article 31(3)(b) of the *Vienna Convention.*[30] According to an early decision by the Appellate Body, which quoted treaty law experts Sinclair and Yasseen, the practice must be 'a "concordant, common and consistent" sequence of acts or pronouncements which is sufficient to establish a discernible pattern implying the agreement of the parties regarding its interpretation.'[31] More recently, the Appellate Body clarified the two aspects to establishing 'subsequent practice' under Article 31(3)(b): first, there must be a common, consistent, and concordant pattern of acts or pronouncements, and, secondly, those acts or pronouncements must imply agreement on the interpretation of the relevant provision.[32] The Appellate Body has yet to rule that a Member's actions meet the Article 31(3)(b) standard, with the result that that provision has not yet been relied upon in interpreting a WTO provision.

The Appellate Body has also referred to treaty interpretation tools not specifically referred to in Article 31, albeit less frequently, including the principle of effectiveness, which provides that all treaty terms must be given effect.[33] The Appellate Body has described this principle as a 'fundamental tenet of treaty interpretation flowing from the general rule of interpretation set out in Article 31'[34] and as '[o]ne of the corollaries' of that rule.[35] In overturning a panel's decision that Article XIX of the GATT

[30] See, for example, Appellate Body Report, *Japan – Alcoholic Beverages II*, p. 13, DSR 1996:I, 97, 106; Appellate Body Report, *US – Gambling*, para. 192; and Appellate Body Report, *EC – Chicken Cuts*, paras. 255–276.

[31] Appellate Body Report, *Japan – Alcoholic Beverages II*, pp. 12–13, DSR 1996:I, 97, 106 (quoting Ian Sinclair, *The Vienna Convention on the Law of Treaties* (2nd edn, Manchester, 1984), p. 137; Mustafa Kamil Yasseen, 'L'interprétation des traités d'après la Convention de Vienne sur le Droit des Traités' (1976-III) 151 *Recueil des Cours*, 48–49, 48).

[32] Appellate Body Report, *US – Gambling*, para. 192.

[33] See, for example, Appellate Body Report, *US – Gasoline*, p. 23, DSR 1996:I, 3, 21; Appellate Body Report, *Japan – Alcoholic Beverages II*, p. 12, DSR 1996:I, 97, 106; Appellate Body Report, *US – Underwear*, p. 16, DSR 1997:I, 11, 24; Appellate Body Report, *Canada – Dairy*, para. 133; Appellate Body Report, *Korea – Dairy*, para. 81; Appellate Body Report, *Argentina – Footwear (EC)*, para. 81; and Appellate Body Report, *US – Offset Act (Byrd Amendment)*, para. 271.

[34] Appellate Body Report, *Japan – Alcoholic Beverages II*, p. 12, DSR 1996:I, 97, 106.

[35] Appellate Body Report, *US – Gasoline*, p. 23, DSR 1996:I, 3, 21. The International Law Commission considered this principle to be embodied in Article 31(1) of the *Vienna Convention*. (See Robert Jennings and Arthur Watts (eds), *Oppenheim's International Law* (9th edn, London, 1992), Vol. I, p. 1280, footnote 25.)

1994 had been subsumed within the *Agreement on Safeguards* and determining instead that all safeguard measures must conform to both Article XIX and the *Agreement on Safeguards*, the Appellate Body explained that 'a treaty interpreter must read all applicable provisions of a treaty in a way that gives meaning to *all* of them, harmoniously.'[36]

The Appellate Body has also relied, on one occasion explicitly,[37] on the principle of *in dubio mitius*, which provides that if the meaning of a term is ambiguous, the meaning that is less onerous to the party assuming an obligation is to be preferred. In *EC – Hormones*, the Appellate Body disagreed with a panel's equating the meanings of 'based on' and 'conform to', and said that it 'cannot lightly assume that sovereign states intended to impose upon themselves the more onerous, rather than less burdensome, obligation by mandating *conformity* or *compliance with*' [38] international sanitary and phytosanitary (SPS) standards, rather than simply having to base its measures on such standards.

Another significant decision regarding treaty interpretation generally, and the meaning of the phrase 'customary rules of interpretation of public international law' in Article 3.2 of the DSU specifically, came in the Appellate Body's second report, *Japan – Alcoholic Beverages II*. There, the Appellate Body said that '[t]here can be no doubt that Article 32 of the *Vienna Convention*, dealing with the role of supplementary means of interpretation, has also attained [the] status'[39] of a customary rule of interpretation of public international law. Article 32 provides that:

> Recourse may be had to supplementary means of interpretation, including the preparatory work of the treaty and the circumstances of its conclusion, in order to confirm the meaning resulting from the application of article 31, or to determine the meaning when the interpretation according to article 31:
> (a) leaves the meaning ambiguous or obscure; or
> (b) leads to a result that is manifestly absurd or unreasonable.

The Appellate Body has relied on the phrases 'preparatory work of the treaty'[40] and 'circumstances of [a treaty's] conclusion',[41] found in Article

36 Appellate Body Report, *Argentina – Footwear (EC)*, para. 81 (original emphasis).
37 Appellate Body Report, *EC – Hormones*, para. 165 and footnote 154.
38 Ibid., para. 165 (original emphasis).
39 Appellate Body Report, *Japan – Alcoholic Beverages II*, p. 10, DSR 1996:I, 97, 104.
40 See, for example, Appellate Body Report, *EC – Poultry*, para. 83; and Appellate Body Report, *US – Carbon Steel*, paras. 77–78 and footnote 76.
41 See, for example, Appellate Body Report, *EC – Computer Equipment*, paras. 86 and 92; and Appellate Body Report, *EC – Chicken Cuts*, paras. 282–309.

32, to assist with its interpretation task in some cases. Generally, however, it has relied less frequently on Article 32 than on Article 31 of the *Vienna Convention.* This is not especially surprising, given that there are no official *travaux préparatoires* of the WTO agreements. The limited reliance on Article 32 may also suggest that the Appellate Body gives prominence to the interpretation tools codified in Article 31 that focus on the text of the treaty, and that it views Article 32 as setting out a 'supplementary' – but not always necessary – tool of interpretation.

This brief survey of some of the decisions on treaty interpretation reveals that the Appellate Body has developed a considerable body of law on the rules of interpretation codified in the *Vienna Convention* and has applied those rules in a variety of situations addressing a number of complex problems. The recent Appellate Body Report in *EC – Chicken Cuts*, for example, includes a highly informative analysis of Articles 31 and 32 of the *Vienna Convention.* One interpretation tool that the Appellate Body has yet to use, however, is found in Article 31(3)(c) of the *Vienna Convention*, referring to 'relevant rules of international law applicable in the relations between the parties,' which an interpreter may take into account together with context. This approach to treaty interpretation remains controversial in WTO dispute settlement and is linked to the ongoing vigorous debate in international trade law circles about the relevance of public international law generally to WTO dispute settlement. It is only a matter of time before the Appellate Body will have to deal with this issue head on.[42] In the meantime, however, WTO Members' frequent resort to the WTO dispute settlement mechanism has resulted in the creation of a genuine treasure trove of law on treaty interpretation that is unrivalled in the jurisprudence of other international adjudicative bodies.

Burden of proof

The DSU makes no reference to burden of proof, with the result that the Appellate Body had to address this lacunae early on. In *US – Wool Shirts and Blouses*, the Appellate Body said:

> It is . . . hardly surprising that various international tribunals, including the International Court of Justice, have generally and consistently accepted and applied the rule that the party who asserts a fact, whether the claimant or the respondent, is responsible for providing proof thereof. Also, it is a

[42] A question under this provision arose in the *EC – Approval and Marketing of Biotech Products* ('GMO') dispute, which was still at the panel phase at the time of this writing (May 2006).

> generally accepted canon of evidence in civil law, common law and, in fact, most jurisdictions, that the burden of proof rests upon the party, whether complaining or defending, who asserts the affirmative of a particular claim or defence.[43] (Footnotes omitted)

This early decision proved to be highly significant, for virtually every WTO panel, as well as every participant in WTO dispute settlement, refers back to this early decision when addressing the burden of proof. Also important are a number of subsequent decisions that refine the burden of proof rules, such as those addressing the establishment of a *prima facie* case[44] and the proof of affirmative defences.[45] The Appellate Body developed its approach despite there being no direction on burden of proof in the rules of procedure drawn up by WTO Members. There has been no movement by the Members to develop their own code on burden of proof or rules of evidence, suggesting that they are content with the status quo.

Due process

As with rules of evidence and burden of proof, there is no DSU provision referring to the concept of due process. Nevertheless, in *India – Patents (US)*, the Appellate Body said 'the demands of due process that are implicit in the DSU make [the need to be fully forthcoming from the very beginning] especially necessary during consultations.'[46] The Appellate Body has also referred to the requirement of due process in a number of other decisions, including *US – FSC (Article 21.5 – EC)*,[47] and *Australia – Salmon*.[48] Although there is no provision in the DSU referring to due process, this requirement has become embedded in the system by virtue of the jurisprudence, and there is no question now that it forms part of the WTO dispute settlement procedure. This is further credit to the Appellate Body.

Objective assessment by panels

Article 11 of the DSU has come up time and again in WTO jurisprudence. It provides that panels are to

[43] Appellate Body Report, *US – Wool Shirts and Blouses*, p. 14, DSR 1997:I, 323, 335.

[44] See, for example, Appellate Body Report, *EC – Hormones*, para. 104.

[45] See, for example, Appellate Body Report, *Brazil – Aircraft (Article 21.5 – Canada)*, para. 66; and Appellate Body Report, *EC – Tariff Preferences*, paras. 104–105.

[46] Appellate Body Report, *India – Patents (US)*, para. 94.

[47] Appellate Body Report, *US – FSC (Article 21.5 – EC)*, para. 243.

[48] Appellate Body Report, *Australia – Salmon*, paras. 272–278.

> make an objective assessment of the matter before it, including an objective assessment of the facts of the case and the applicability of and conformity with the relevant covered agreements, and make such other findings as will assist the DSB in making the recommendations or in giving the rulings provided for in the covered agreements.

The interpretation and application of Article 11 have developed considerably from the early years of WTO dispute settlement. The first time this requirement was examined in detail was in the *EC – Hormones* case. There, the Appellate Body explained that 'not every error in the appreciation of the evidence . . . may be characterized as a failure to make an objective assessment of the facts.'[49] The Appellate Body went on to explain that an 'error of judgment in the appreciation of evidence' does not rise to a failure to meet the Article 11 requirement, and that it was necessary that a panel make an 'egregious error that calls into question the good faith of a panel.'[50] The Appellate Body also said that the 'deliberate disregard' of evidence or the 'wilful distortion' of evidence would also put a panel offside its Article 11 obligations.[51]

After the *EC – Hormones* decision was circulated, it was 'understood' that a claim under Article 11 of the DSU should be very rare, and that an allegation that a panel had failed to meet its obligations under Article 11 would be tantamount to an accusation of bad faith on the part of panel members. This approach was reinforced in several subsequent decisions, such as *EC – Poultry*,[52] *Korea – Alcoholic Beverages*,[53] and *US – Carbon Steel*.[54] More recently, however, panels are regularly challenged in appellate proceedings by WTO Members for failing to meet the obligations set out in Article 11, and such challenges often succeed. It would appear that the threshold for an Article 11 violation is not as high as it was in earlier days of the WTO, and that an allegation of such failure does not carry the highly negative stigma that it once did.

The adjustment in approach perhaps started to appear in *Chile – Price Band System*. There, the Appellate Body noted that Article 11 goes beyond a panel's appreciation of the evidence before it, as Article 11 obliges panels not only to make 'an objective assessment of the facts of the case', but also to make 'an objective assessment of the matter before it'. In that dispute, the panel made a finding on a claim that had not been advanced by the

[49] Appellate Body Report, *EC – Hormones*, para. 133. [50] Ibid. [51] Ibid.

[52] Appellate Body Report, *EC – Poultry*, para. 133.

[53] Appellate Body Report, *Korea – Alcoholic Beverages*, para. 164.

[54] Appellate Body Report, *US – Carbon Steel*, para. 142.

claimant. Therefore, according to the Appellate Body, the panel had failed to make an objective assessment of the *matter before it*, essentially because it had made a finding on a *matter that was not before it.*[55]

The jurisprudence on Article 11 was subject to further fine-tuning in *US – Oil Country Tubular Goods Sunset Reviews.* The Appellate Body faulted the panel in that case for basing its conclusions solely on aggregate statistics listed in an exhibit, without conducting a qualitative analysis of even some of the specific cases reflected in the aggregate statistics.[56] In *US – Countervailing Duty Investigation on DRAMS*, the Appellate Body disapproved of a panel's approach in assessing evidence on several grounds, including that it failed to examine evidence in its totality and assessed only individual pieces of evidence to determine if each one was sufficient to prove certain conclusions, that the panel erred in assessing whether certain evidence could support the drawing of certain inferences, and in refusing to admit certain evidence.[57] In *EC – Export Subsidies on Sugar*, the Appellate Body said that, in declining to rule on the complaining parties' claims under Article 3 of the *Agreement on Subsidies and Countervailing Measures* (*SCM Agreement*), the panel precluded the possibility of a remedy being made available to the complaining parties pursuant to Article 4.7 of the *SCM Agreement.* The Appellate Body thought this ran afoul of the panel's obligations under Article 11 of the DSU 'to make such other findings as will assist the [Dispute Settlement Body] in making the recommendations or in giving the rulings provided for in the covered agreements.'[58]

Other rules of procedure

The Appellate Body has examined various other procedural matters addressed in the DSU, including standing, or the right to bring claims under Article 3,[59] consultations as a prerequisite to the panel process under Article 4,[60] the proper content of requests for the establishment of a panel under Article 6,[61] a panel's terms of reference under Article 7,[62]

[55] Appellate Body Report, *Chile – Price Band System*, para. 173.

[56] Appellate Body Report, *US – Oil Country Tubular Goods Sunset Reviews*, paras. 209–215.

[57] Appellate Body Report, *US – Countervailing Duty Investigation on DRAMS*, paras. 188–190.

[58] Appellate Body Report, *EC – Export Subsidies on Sugar*, para. 335.

[59] See, for example, Appellate Body Report, *EC – Bananas III*, para. 134.

[60] See, for example, Appellate Body Report, *Mexico – Corn Syrup (Article 21.5 – US)*, para. 58.

[61] See, for example, Appellate Body Report, *US – Carbon Steel*, paras. 124–127.

[62] See, for example, Appellate Body Report, *Brazil – Desiccated Coconut*, pp. 21–22, DSR 1997:I, 167, 186–187.

multiple complainant cases and separate panel reports under Article 9,[63] third party rights under Article 10,[64] the 'basic rationale' of panel findings under Article 12,[65] the right of panels to seek information under Article 13 (which includes the controversial issue of admissibility of *amicus curiae* briefs),[66] the scope of appellate review (issues of law versus findings of fact) under Article 17,[67] and implementation of Dispute Settlement Body (DSB) rulings under Article 21.[68]

In sum, the Appellate Body jurisprudence on treaty interpretation and rules of procedure represents one of the most significant accomplishments of the WTO dispute settlement system. It has contributed importantly to the development of the law from two dimensions. First, the Appellate Body's approach to treaty interpretation through a systematic approach giving primacy to the text has led to the security and predictability in the multilateral trading system that Members called for in the opening provisions of the DSU. Secondly, the Appellate Body's approach to procedural matters, including burden of proof, due process, and standard of review under Article 11 of the DSU, may be credited with contributing significantly to the great confidence that WTO Members have in the WTO dispute settlement system.

I turn now to consider the accomplishments of the Appellate Body in terms of its jurisprudence regarding substantive WTO obligations.

III. Jurisprudence: substantive obligations

The subject-matter of WTO obligations is quite varied; it concerns market access for goods and services, trade in agriculture, SPS measures, technical barriers to trade, trade remedies, and trade-related aspects of intellectual property, to name a few. Trade disputes concern many of these obligations and are about various products, commodities and other things, including bananas, beef, underwear, cigarettes, memory chips, and aircraft. Many disputes have been about steel products; several have dealt with trade in softwood lumber; still others have dealt with online

[63] See, for example, Appellate Body Report, *US – Offset Act (Byrd Amendment)*, paras. 306–317.

[64] See, for example, Appellate Body Report, *US – FSC (Article 21.5 – EC)*, paras. 232–252.

[65] See, for example, Appellate Body Report, *Mexico – Corn Syrup (Article 21.5 – US)*, paras. 103–110.

[66] See, for example, Appellate Body Report, *US – Shrimp*, paras. 79–81.

[67] See, for example, Appellate Body Report, *EC – Hormones*, para. 132.

[68] See, for example, Appellate Body Report, *Canada – Aircraft (Article 21.5 – Brazil)*, paras. 38–52.

gambling services, or patents and trademarks. The practical consequences of these trade disputes are often staggering. For example, in the *US – FSC (Article 22.6 – US)* arbitration, the trade effects were valued at over US$ 4 billion per year.[69] In the case of trade in genetically modified organisms, the subject of an ongoing dispute, the world market was valued at US$ 17 billion.[70]

In the early days of WTO dispute settlement, disputes generally involved only two or three parties. More recently, however, disputes are being brought by several complaining parties and several WTO Members are participating in a non-party capacity as 'third parties' or 'third participants.'[71] For example, in *US – Steel Safeguards*, there were nine complaining parties, and in *US – Offset Act (Byrd Amendment)*, there were 11 complaining parties. In *US – Upland Cotton*, ten WTO Members participated in the appeal as third participants and in *EC – Export Subsidies on Sugar*, there were 18 third participants. This is clear evidence that the subject-matter of WTO disputes today is often relevant to numerous WTO participants simultaneously.

The WTO agreements that are most frequently litigated at the panel level are the GATT 1994, the *SCM Agreement*, the *Agreement on Implementation of Article VI of the General Agreement on Tariffs and Trade 1994* (*Anti-Dumping Agreement*), and the *Agreement on Agriculture*. At the appellate level, the most frequently litigated agreements are the DSU, the GATT 1994, the *SCM Agreement*, and the *Anti-Dumping Agreement*.

Most-favoured nation treatment

Although panels and the Appellate Body have been called upon to interpret numerous provisions in numerous WTO agreements, surprisingly, the most fundamental of principles, most-favoured nation (MFN), has been treated rarely. *Canada – Autos* is one example. In that case, the Appellate Body struck down a Canadian measure (which originated in the Canada–United States Auto Pact) that was origin-neutral on its face, but operated to give an advantage to products from some Members that

[69] Decision by the Arbitrator, *US – FSC (Article 22.6 – US)*, section VI.B.

[70] Thomas Bernauer, *Genes, Trade and Regulation* (Princeton, 2003), p. 6.

[71] Article 10 of the DSU permits WTO Members to participate as third parties if they have a 'substantial interest' in the matter before the panel. Third parties receive copies of some of the written submissions and are permitted to attend some hearings. Third parties may also participate in appellate proceedings and are referred to as third participants.

was not accorded immediately and unconditionally to like products from all Members.[72]

National treatment

The concept of national treatment, by contrast, found in Article III of the GATT 1994, has come up in numerous cases. Article III provides, in part:

> *National Treatment on Internal Taxation and Regulation*
>
> 1. The contracting parties recognize that internal taxes and other internal charges, and laws, regulations and requirements affecting the internal sale, offering for sale, purchase, transportation, distribution or use of products, and internal quantitative regulations requiring the mixture, processing or use of products in specified amounts or proportions, should not be applied to imported or domestic products so as to afford protection to domestic production.
> 2. The products of the territory of any contracting party imported into the territory of any other contracting party shall not be subject, directly or indirectly, to internal taxes or other internal charges of any kind in excess of those applied, directly or indirectly, to like domestic products. Moreover, no contracting party shall otherwise apply internal taxes or other internal charges to imported or domestic products in a manner contrary to the principles set forth in paragraph 1.
>
> ...
>
> 4. The products of the territory of any contracting party imported into the territory of any other contracting party shall be accorded treatment no less favourable than that accorded to like products of national origin in respect of all laws, regulations and requirements affecting their internal sale, offering for sale, purchase, transportation, distribution or use. The provisions of this paragraph shall not prevent the application of differential internal transportation charges which are based exclusively on the economic operation of the means of transport and not on the nationality of the product.
>
> ...

The Appellate Body had occasion to interpret Article III early on, in *Japan – Alcoholic Beverages II*, and many times since then. The Appellate Body said in that early case that the fundamental purpose of Article III is to avoid protectionism, and explained that the national treatment obligation requires Members to provide equality of competitive conditions for

[72] Appellate Body Report, *Canada – Autos*, paras. 78–79.

imported products in relation to domestic products.[73] The Appellate Body said further that the concept of 'likeness' (referring to 'like products' under Article III:2) is 'a relative one that evokes the image of an accordion.'[74] The famous phrase, '[t]he accordion of 'likeness' stretches and squeezes in different places as different provisions of the *WTO Agreement* are applied',[75] is one of the oft-cited gems of WTO jurisprudence. The Appellate Body also explained in *Japan – Alcoholic Beverages II* that the phrase 'so as to afford protection' in Article III:1 is not about intent; it is an issue of how the measure in question is applied.[76]

The Appellate Body generally has followed established GATT practice in interpreting the term 'like products' as used in Article III, although its ruling in *EC – Asbestos* arguably introduced a further dimension. The 1970 *Border Tax Adjustments* case under the GATT established the following criteria for determining 'likeness':

(i) the product's end uses in a given market;
(ii) consumers' tastes and habits, which change from country to country; and
(iii) the product's properties, nature and quality.[77]

The Appellate Body has followed this approach on a number of occasions, including in *Japan – Alcoholic Beverages II.* In *EC – Asbestos*, however, which concerned a challenge under Article III:4 brought by Canada regarding a European ban on asbestos-containing products, the Appellate Body indicated that evidence relating to health risks associated with a product may be pertinent to determining likeness, although it considered that this would not be a separate criterion, as it would fall under physical properties and consumers' tastes and habits.[78]

General exceptions

The Appellate Body's early interpretation of Article XX of the GATT 1994, entitled 'General Exceptions', raised eyebrows at the time, but is

[73] Appellate Body Report, *Japan – Alcoholic Beverages II*, pp. 16–17, DSR 1996:I, 97, 108–110. [74] Ibid., p. 21, DSR 1996:I, 97, 114. [75] Ibid.

[76] Ibid., pp. 27–28, DSR 1996:I, 97, 119–120.

[77] Report of the Working Party, *Border Tax Adjustments*, BISD 18S/97, para. 18. A fourth criterion – tariff classification – was added by subsequent GATT panels. (See Appellate Body Report, *EC – Asbestos*, para. 101 and footnote 74.)

[78] Appellate Body Report, *EC – Asbestos*, para. 113. See also the Concurrent Opinion of one member of the Division in that appeal (paras. 149–154), which was along the same lines but expressed in stronger terms.

now followed without question. Article XX provides, in part:

> *General Exceptions*
>
> Subject to the requirement that such measures are not applied in a manner which would constitute a means of arbitrary or unjustifiable discrimination between countries where the same conditions prevail, or a disguised restriction on international trade, nothing in this Agreement shall be construed to prevent the adoption or enforcement by any contracting party of measures:
>
> (a) necessary to protect public morals;
>
> (b) necessary to protect human, animal or plant life or health;
>
> . . .
>
> (d) necessary to secure compliance with laws or regulations which are not inconsistent with the provisions of this Agreement, including those relating to customs enforcement, the enforcement of monopolies operated under paragraph 4 of Article II and Article XVII, the protection of patents, trade marks and copyrights, and the prevention of deceptive practices;
>
> . . .
>
> (g) relating to the conservation of exhaustible natural resources if such measures are made effective in conjunction with restrictions on domestic production or consumption;
>
> . . .

In *US – Gasoline*, as confirmed in *US – Shrimp*, the Appellate Body explained that Article XX requires a two-tier analysis: first, there must be provisional justification under the specific exemptions in paragraphs (a) through (j), followed by further appraisal under the introductory clause or 'chapeau.'[79] According to the Appellate Body, reversing this sequence of analysis constitutes legal error.[80] The rich jurisprudence under Article XX of the GATT 1994 examines various terms found in that provision, such as 'necessary',[81] which the Appellate Body has interpreted as involving a process of weighing and balancing a series of factors, 'exhaustible natural resources',[82] which the Appellate Body said includes renewable resources, 'arbitrary and unjustifiable discrimination',[83] and 'disguised restriction on international trade'.[84] This jurisprudence has informed the

[79] Appellate Body Report, *US – Gasoline*, p. 22, DSR 1996:I, 3, 20–21; Appellate Body Report, *US – Shrimp*, paras. 117–121.

[80] Appellate Body Report, *US – Shrimp*, para. 122.

[81] Appellate Body Report, *Korea – Various Measures on Beef*, paras. 161–164.

[82] Appellate Body Report, *US – Shrimp*, paras. 128–130.

[83] Ibid., para. 150; Appellate Body Report, *US – Shrimp (Article 21.5 – Malaysia)*, paras. 122–123.

[84] Appellate Body Report, *US – Gasoline*, p. 25, DSR 1996:I, 3, 23.

inquiry into the meaning of Article XIV under the *General Agreement on Trade in Services* (GATS), which deals with services and follows much of the language found in Article XX dealing with goods.[85]

SCM Agreement

The Appellate Body is called upon regularly to interpret provisions of the *SCM Agreement.* For example, it is often requested to decide whether certain measures fit within the definition of a subsidy found in Article 1 of that Agreement. In so doing, the Appellate Body has had to consider the meaning of various definitional terms including 'financial contribution,' which it said includes a wide range of transactions through which something of economic value is transferred by a government but does not capture all government measures capable of conferring a benefit,[86] 'entrusts,' which it concluded connotes giving a private body responsibility to carry out a task but is not limited to acts of delegation,[87] and 'benefit,' which it explained presupposes that there is a recipient and implies some kind of comparison such that the recipient is better off as a consequence of having received the financial contribution.[88]

Also significant were the Appellate Body's decisions with respect to the meaning of Article 3 of the *SCM Agreement*, specifically whether certain measures were prohibited because they constituted subsidies contingent in fact or in law upon export performance,[89] or subsidies contingent upon the use of domestic over imported goods.[90] For example, the Appellate Body observed in one case that in determining whether a measure is *contingent* on export performance, it is not sufficient to demonstrate solely that a government *anticipated* that exports would result; it must establish that export was conditional upon the granting of the subsidy.[91]

Recently, the Appellate Body examined for the first time the meaning of 'serious prejudice' to the interests of another WTO Member through the use of a subsidy, under Article 6 of the *SCM Agreement.*[92] Its inquiry included consideration of what factors may be examined to determine if

85 See Appellate Body Report, *US – Gambling*, paras. 291–292.
86 Appellate Body Report, *US – Softwood Lumber IV*, para. 52.
87 Appellate Body Report, *US – Countervailing Duty Investigation on DRAMS*, para. 109.
88 Appellate Body Report, *Canada – Aircraft*, paras. 154 and 157.
89 Ibid., paras. 166–167. See also Appellate Body Report, *Canada – Autos*, para. 100.
90 Appellate Body Report, *Canada – Autos*, paras. 139–143.
91 Appellate Body Report, *Canada – Aircraft*, paras. 166 and 171.
92 Appellate Body Report, *US – Upland Cotton*, paras. 407–408, 416–417, 431–433, 434–436, 461, and 465–466.

'significant price suppression' has occurred. It observed that in the absence of explicit guidance on assessing significant price suppression in Article 6 itself, it saw no reason to exclude factors examined by the panel such as general price trends and magnitude of production and exports by the respondent.[93] It also considered which market is relevant for a serious price suppression analysis and concluded that it could be the world market if there is a world market for the product in question.[94]

Other important decisions respecting the *SCM Agreement* have concerned the temporal limit of countervailing duties and their review under Article 21; the Appellate Body has pointed out that termination of countervailing duties that have been in place for five years is the rule and continuation is the exception, and that continuation must be founded on persuasive evidence that revocation of the duty would lead to injury to the domestic industry.[95] The Appellate Body has also inquired into what constitutes 'specific action against a subsidy' under Article 32 of the *SCM Agreement*, finding that a measure must be specific and must dissuade subsidization in order to be governed by Article 32, although it is not necessary that the measure come into direct contact with the imported product or foreign producer.[96]

Anti-Dumping Agreement

The *Anti-Dumping Agreement* has been the subject of numerous disputes that have come before the Appellate Body in recent years, most if not all of which involve highly technical inquiries. For example, issues relating to the proper calculation of dumping margins under Article 2 have come up time and again. One such issue is the calculation methodology used by the United States referred to in WTO parlance as 'zeroing', where negative dumping margins are given a value of zero with the result that the dumping margin, and therefore the duty, is greater. The zeroing methodology has been challenged by the European Communities and Japan, as well as by Canada in connection with the long-standing dispute over softwood lumber. It has been struck down in part by the Appellate Body and upheld in part at the panel level, and is sure to be considered again by the Appellate Body.[97]

[93] Ibid., para. 434. [94] Ibid., para. 408.

[95] Appellate Body Report, *US – Carbon Steel*, para. 88.

[96] Appellate Body Report, *US – Offset Act (Byrd Amendment)*, paras. 236 and 253–254.

[97] See Panel Report, *US – Softwood Lumber V (Article 21.5 – Canada)*, which was under appeal at the time of this writing (May 2006). See also the challenge brought by the European Communities in *US – Zeroing (EC)*, as well as the challenge brought by Japan in *US – Zeroing (Japan)*.

The inquiry under Article 3 of the *Anti-Dumping Agreement* into the causal relationship between dumped imports and injury to the domestic industry has proved to be especially complex, as has the requirement not to attribute to dumped imports injury caused by other factors.[98] The nature and methodology of reviews of dumping orders under Article 11 (that is, reviews five years after imposition) have also been the subject of a number of Appellate Body reports.[99] Finally, the standard of review in anti-dumping cases, as set forth in Article 17.6 of the *Anti-Dumping Agreement*, has drawn considerable attention in WTO dispute settlement; Appellate Body jurisprudence provides that panels must not engage in independent fact-finding exercises when assessing the establishment of facts by domestic investigating authorities.[100]

Agreement on Agriculture

Given the importance and sensitivity of trade in agricultural products, it is not surprising that the *Agreement on Agriculture* has been the subject of frequent dispute settlement activity. The Appellate Body has had to examine the WTO consistency of various agricultural export subsidies,[101] as well as the meaning of several terms and phrases found in the Agreement. For example, under Article 9 governing export subsidy commitments, terms such as 'payments',[102] 'financed',[103] 'by virtue of',[104]

[98] See, for example, Appellate Body Report, *US – Hot-Rolled Steel*, paras. 223–228; and Appellate Body Report, *EC – Tube or Pipe Fittings*, para. 156.

[99] Appellate Body Report, *US – Corrosion-Resistant Steel Sunset Review*; Appellate Body Report, *US – Oil Country Tubular Goods Sunset Review*; and Appellate Body Report, *US – Anti-Dumping Measures on Oil Country Tubular Goods*.

[100] See, for example, Appellate Body Report, *Thailand – H-Beams*, paras. 116, 118, and 137; Appellate Body Report, *US – Hot-Rolled Steel*, paras. 55, 57, 59–60, and 62; Appellate Body Report, *EC – Bed Linen*, para. 65; Appellate Body Report, *EC – Bed Linen (Article 21.5 – India)*, paras. 108, 118, and 167–169; Appellate Body Report, *Mexico – Corn Syrup (Article 21.5 – US)*, paras. 84 and 90; and Appellate Body Report, *EC – Tube or Pipe Fittings*, para. 128.

[101] See, for example, Appellate Body Report, *US – FSC*; Appellate Body Report, *US – Upland Cotton*; and Appellate Body Report, *EC – Export Subsidies on Sugar*.

[102] Appellate Body Report, *Canada – Dairy*, paras. 107–108; Appellate Body Report, *Canada – Dairy (Article 21.5 – New Zealand and US)*, paras. 76 and 96–97; Appellate Body Report, *Canada – Dairy (Article 21.5 – New Zealand and US II)*, paras. 96–97; and Appellate Body Report, *EC – Export Subsidies on Sugar*, paras. 262–265 and 267.

[103] Appellate Body Report, *Canada – Dairy (Article 21.5 – New Zealand and US)*, para. 114; Appellate Body Report, *Canada – Dairy (Article 21.5 – New Zealand and US II)*, paras. 132–133 and 140; Appellate Body Report, *EC – Export Subsidies on Sugar*, para. 236.

[104] Appellate Body Report, *EC – Export Subsidies on Sugar*, para. 237.

and 'governmental action'[105] have been the subject of detailed analysis; in the light of this jurisprudence, it is necessary to scrutinize very carefully the facts and circumstances of a disputed measure to determine whether it falls within the list of export subsidies subject to reduction commitments under Article 9. Article 10 on circumvention and threat thereof has also been the subject of disputes,[106] including with respect to the reversal of the burden of proof under paragraph 10(3)[107] and the finding that export credit guarantees are not exempt from export subsidies disciplines by virtue of paragraph 10(2), referring to Members' undertaking to work toward the development of disciplines to govern them.[108]

The recent appeal in *US – Upland Cotton* raised numerous novel issues under the *Agreement on Agriculture.* Several United States measures were challenged by Brazil under multiple provisions; the challenge resulted in an Appellate Body Report of over 300 pages, the longest and perhaps one of the most complicated to date. The 'Peace Clause' (Article 13, entitled Due Restraint) regarding time-based[109] exemptions from certain actions under the *SCM Agreement* for certain domestic support measures was subject to detailed analysis by the Appellate Body for the first time in that appeal.[110] Article 6 as it relates to direct payments exempted from domestic support reduction commitments and Annex 2 setting out criteria for types of direct payments that constitute non-distorting or minimally distorting support payments were also scrutinized in that case.[111] The Appellate Body Report in *EC – Export Subsidies on Sugar* is instructive with respect to the interpretation of terms in Article 3 of the *Agreement on Agriculture,* such as 'commitments limiting subsidization'[112] and

[105] Appellate Body Report, *Canada – Dairy (Article 21.5 – New Zealand and US)*, paras. 112–113; Appellate Body Report, *Canada – Dairy (Article 21.5 – New Zealand and US II)*, para. 128.

[106] See Appellate Body Report, *US – FSC*, paras. 148–152; and Appellate Body Report, *US – Upland Cotton*, paras. 704–710.

[107] Appellate Body Report, *Canada – Dairy (Article 21.5 – New Zealand and US II)*, para. 71.

[108] Appellate Body Report, *US – Upland Cotton*, paras. 607–609, 615–619, and 623–626. Although the majority determined that export credit guarantees were subject to the disciplines, one Member of the Division disagreed and included a separate opinion with respect to this issue in paras. 631–641.

[109] The Peace Clause was applicable during 'the implementation period,' which was nine years. See the chapeau to Article 13 of the *Agreement on Agriculture.*

[110] See, for example, Appellate Body Report, *US – Upland Cotton*, paras. 347, 361–372, and 381–382.

[111] See, for example, ibid., paras. 321–329, 333–334, and 340.

[112] See Appellate Body Report, *EC – Export Subsidies on Sugar*, para. 209.

'budgetary outlay and quantity commitment levels'[113] that must be specified in Members' schedules. Finally, a number of appeals have addressed the question of the relationship between the *Agreement on Agriculture* and other WTO agreements.[114]

GATS

The GATS has received relatively limited attention in dispute settlement at the appellate level. Although scope of application and definitional issues related to measures 'affecting trade in services' under Article I were addressed in *EC – Bananas III*[115] and *Canada – Autos*,[116] it was only in the recent *US – Gambling* appeal that substantive services obligations were dealt with in any detail. The analyses by the Appellate Body in that case of the types of limitations that may not be maintained by virtue of Article XVI where market access commitments are undertaken,[117] the approach it followed in the interpretation of the United States' GATS schedule of commitments,[118] and its discussion of the chapeau and one of the general exceptions under Article XIV (necessity to protect public morals or to maintain public order)[119] contribute significantly to the nascent law on trade in services.

Summary

This brief survey of some of the Appellate Body pronouncements on substantive WTO obligations does little more than scratch the surface of the extensive body of jurisprudence found in the more than 70 Appellate Body Reports circulated in the first ten years and it fails utterly to convey the profound insight and the many nuances found in those rulings. Nevertheless, it does demonstrate that, remarkably, in just ten years, the Appellate Body has ruled on a vast array of issues – covering both procedural and substantive law – and developed a highly significant body of

[113] See ibid., paras. 193–200.

[114] See, for example, Appellate Body Report, *EC – Bananas III*, paras. 155 and 157; Appellate Body Report, *Canada – Dairy (Article 21.5 New Zealand and US)*, paras. 123–124; Appellate Body Report, *US – Upland Cotton*, paras. 532–533, 546–549, 571, and 647; and Appellate Body Report, *EC – Export Subsidies on Sugar*, paras. 221–223 and 338–339.

[115] Appellate Body Report, *EC – Bananas III*, paras. 220–221.

[116] Appellate Body Report, *Canada – Autos*, paras. 151–152, 155, 165, and 167.

[117] See Appellate Body Report, *US – Gambling*, paras. 214 and 221–252.

[118] See ibid., paras. 160 and 175–208.

[119] See ibid., paras 291–327, 348–357, and 367–372.

law. No other international adjudicative body has come close to matching this achievement.[120]

IV. Broad-based confidence of WTO Members

The third indicator of the success of the WTO dispute settlement system identified at the beginning of this chapter is the broad confidence that Members of the WTO have in the system. Statistics tell a compelling story. In the 47 years of GATT dispute settlement, about 300 disputes were brought before the dispute settlement mechanism (including adopted and unadopted reports). In the first ten years of WTO dispute settlement, 95 panel reports and 64 Appellate Body reports were adopted,[121] to say nothing of the disputes that were still in the system or that had been commenced but were resolved without the need to proceed through each stage of the dispute settlement mechanism.[122]

About 40 per cent of WTO Members participated as complainant or respondent before panels during the period 1995 through 2005, and about 20 per cent as appellant or appellee before the Appellate Body. If one were to include third party participation in the count, the numbers would rise to more than 50 per cent before panels and about 45 per cent before the Appellate Body.[123] This is a very strong testament to the broad-based confidence enjoyed by the WTO dispute settlement system.

Significantly, it is not only the developed country Members of the WTO that have been active in WTO dispute settlement. Developing-country Members are also regular participants, a stark contrast to the situation under the GATT. In fact, between January 1995 and October 2005,[124] developing-country Members had brought 51 requests for consultations against other developing-country Members, and 74 such requests against developed-country Members. Developed-country Members are not that much further ahead; during the same period, they

[120] Compare, for example, the ICJ experience during its first 50 years. It was not utilized regularly and when it was, the disputes were not as varied in subject matter as those before the Appellate Body.

[121] As of 31 December 2004. In addition, there were 17 arbitration awards and one mediation. At the end of the eleventh year (2005), the number of adopted panel reports had risen to 115, and Appellate Body reports to 73.

[122] There were 324 requests for consultations in the first ten years; 127 panels were established covering 158 disputes.

[123] These data are taken from the WTO website, available at <www.wto.org>.

[124] The October 2005 cut-off date was chosen originally to coincide with the timing of the Tokyo conference.

brought 75 consultation requests against developing-country Members and 127 requests against other developed-country Members. It is true that developed-country Members tended to be less active than developed-country Members in the first few years of the WTO. However, after the year 1999, developing-country Members began taking a more active role, often outpacing developed-country Member activity as claimant.[125]

Interestingly, the most frequent players in appeals include several developing-country Members. Although the United States and the European Communities are way ahead of most other Members in terms of appearances before the Appellate Body, countries such as Argentina, Brazil, China, India, Korea, Mexico, and Thailand are included in the 'top ten' list, with Argentina, China, and Thailand sharing the tenth spot.[126]

As this book arises from the conference hosted in Tokyo, it is appropriate to focus on Japan's participation. As of the end of 2005, Japan had been involved in 26 disputes, including 12 as complainant and 14 as respondent (although some involved multiple complaints and were considered by a single panel, such as in *Japan – Alcoholic Beverages II*, brought by the European Communities, Canada and the United States). Of the 12 disputes as complainant, Japan was successful in seven: two complaints against Indonesia dealing with automotive investment measures, which were considered by a single panel;[127] one complaint against Canada with respect to measures dealing with automobiles,[128] and four trade remedies complaints against the United States.[129] Japan was unsuccessful in one complaint against the United States involving anti-dumping measures.[130]

[125] This happened in 2000, 2001, 2003, and 2005. This is based on information obtained from the Legal Affairs Division of the WTO.

[126] At the end of 2005, the United States had appeared before the Appellate Body 23 times as appellant, eight times as other appellant, 41 times as appellee, and 23 times as third participant, making a total of 95 appearances. The European Communities' history is 10 times as appellant, 11 times as other appellant, 26 times as appellee, and 33 times as third participant, totalling 80 appearances. Brazil's numbers are 8, 3, 10, 9, and 30; India's numbers are 5, 1, 5, 13, and 24; Korea's numbers are 4, 2, 5, 6, and 17; Mexico's numbers are 3, 1, 4 , 13, and 21; Argentina's numbers are 2, 1, 3, 4, and 10; China's numbers are 0, 1, 1, 8, and 10; and Thailand's numbers are 3, 0, 4, 3, and 10 (See *Appellate Body Annual Report for 2005*, pp. 23–25).

[127] *Indonesia – Autos* (the European Communities and the United States were also complainants).

[128] *Canada – Autos* (the European Communities was also a complainant).

[129] *US – 1916 Act*; *US – Hot-Rolled Steel*; *US – Offset Act (Byrd Amendment)* (Australia, Brazil, Canada, Chile, the European Communities, India, Korea, Mexico, and Thailand were also complainants); and *US – Steel Safeguards* (Brazil, China, the European Communities, Korea, New Zealand, Norway, and Switzerland were also complainants).

[130] *US – Carbon Steel.*

Of the remaining complaints filed by Japan, one against the United States on automotive measures was resolved,[131] one each against Brazil (automotive measures) and the United States (government procurement) are inactive,[132] and one involving trade remedies against the United States is ongoing.[133] In the 14 disputes as respondent, Japan has won one (about measures affecting photographic film brought by the United States,[134]) lost five (three about taxes on alcoholic beverages brought by the United States, the European Communities and Canada that were dealt with by a single panel,[135] and two about SPS measures on agricultural products brought by the United States[136]) and reached mutually agreed solutions in four (one each brought by the United States and the European Communities about sound recordings,[137] one brought by the European Communities about procurement of a navigation satellite,[138] and one brought by Korea about import quotas on laver[139]). The remaining four complaints against Japan (three of which were brought by the European Communities and concern telecommunications, pork imports and leather quotas, and one brought by the United States about distribution services) are inactive.[140]

Japan has been an active participant at the appellate level. It has appeared a total of 35 times before the Appellate Body – as appellant four times,[141] as other appellant four times,[142] as appellee eight times,[143] and as third participant 19 times.[144]

In sum, Japan generally has been successful in challenging various automotive regimes and trade remedies laws. As respondent, Japan has lost disputes concerning taxation and SPS measures. Japan has a good record for resolving disputes, having notified mutually agreed solutions in about 20 per cent of its disputes.

131 *US – Autos.* 132 *Brazil – Autos; US – Procurement.* 133 *US – Zeroing (Japan).*
134 *Japan – Film.* 135 *Japan – Alcoholic Beverages II.*
136 *Japan – Agricultural Products II; Japan – Apples.*
137 *Japan – Sound Recordings* (United States; European Communities).
138 *Japan – Satellite* (European Communities).
139 *Japan – Quotas on Laver* (European Communities).
140 *Japan – Telecommunications Equipment* (European Communities); *Japan – Distribution Services* (United States); *Japan – Pork* (European Communities); *Japan – Leather Quotas* (European Communities).
141 *Japan – Alcoholic Beverages II; Japan – Agricultural Products II.*
142 *Canada – Autos; US – 1916 Act; US – Hot-Rolled Steel.*
143 *Japan – Alcoholic Beverages II; Japan – Agricultural Products II; Canada – Autos; US – 1916 Act; US – Hot-Rolled Steel.*
144 For the names of the 19 disputes see *Appellate Body Annual Report for 2005*, pp. 24 and 26–33.

V. Conclusion

The accomplishments of the WTO dispute settlement system are many and varied; it is possible to describe only some of them in this brief chapter. The success of the system is due, no doubt, to many factors, not the least of which is the dedication of the Appellate Body Members.

Although many are quick to pounce on the perceived failures of the WTO, the institution does not always receive the praise it deserves for its many and significant successes. The WTO dispute settlement system, by contrast, is generally lauded as the greatest achievement of the WTO. This is because it is widely regarded as being fair, effective and efficient. It enjoys the confidence of WTO Members, both developed and developing, and is credited with contributing importantly to the development of international law. It would be a challenge, if not an impossibility, to name another international adjudicative body that can claim comparable success, especially in its first ten years of operation.

9

Arbitration as an alternative to litigation in the WTO: observations in the light of the 2005 Banana Tariff Arbitrations

HUNTER NOTTAGE AND JAN BOHANES

> *This [Arbitral] Chamber is to have all the virtues which the law lacks. It is to be expeditious where the law is slow, cheap where the law is costly, simple where the law is technical, a peace-maker instead of a stirrer up of strife.*
>
> At the inauguration of the London Court of Arbitration in 1892[1]

> *Commercial arbitration is . . . uncommonly well adapted to developing new rules and practices better suited to the conditions of the modern world.*
>
> Sir Robert Jennings[2]

The 2005 Banana Tariff Arbitrations[3] were arguably the most important arbitrations to have been conducted under the auspices of the World Trade Organization (WTO). These arbitrations examined issues of economic and political significance for the multiple complainants and third parties involved. They raised questions of substantive complexity entailing a workload comparable to litigation in WTO panel and Appellate Body proceedings.[4] The Banana Tariff Arbitrations were however unique compared to previous cases litigated in the WTO. They were held outside the scope of normal WTO dispute settlement procedures set out in the *Understanding on Rules and Procedures Governing the Settlement of Disputes* (DSU) and, as such, were the first *sui generis* arbitrations held

The authors would like to thank Todd Friedbacher and Luke Nottage for helpful comments and discussions. Responsibility remains entirely with the authors.

1 Manson (1893) IX L.Q.R. 86.

2 Taken from the forward to Alan Redfern and Martin Hunter, *The Law and Practice of International Commercial Arbitration* (1st edn, London, 1986).

3 Award of the Arbitrator, *EC – The ACP–EC Partnership Agreement*, 1 August 2005 (the 'First Banana Tariff Arbitration') and Award of the Arbitrator, *EC – The ACP–EC Partnership Agreement II*, 27 October 2005 (the 'Second Banana Tariff Arbitration'). (Collectively, the 'Banana Tariff Arbitrations'.)

4 See section II.2(a) of this chapter.

under the auspices of the WTO. Furthermore, they involved procedures and time-frames that differed significantly from cases previously litigated in the WTO and were completed extremely expeditiously in comparison. Arguably, as an alternative to litigation in the WTO, the Banana Tariff Arbitrations were a resounding success.

Despite their effectiveness, beyond the mandatory use of arbitration as a step in the implementation stage of WTO dispute settlement proceedings,[5] the Banana Tariff Arbitrations were only the second time that WTO Members had consented to arbitration as means to resolve a dispute in the WTO. The first occasion, the arbitration in *US – Section 110(5) Copyright Act (Article 25)*[6] (herein, the 'Copyright Arbitration'), also successfully resolved the dispute.

In contrast to the limited use of voluntary arbitration in the WTO, in private international commercial disputes arbitration has superseded litigation as the preferred means of dispute settlement.[7] In the context of private international commercial disputes it has been noted that, while there used to be a debate on the advantages and disadvantages of arbitration as opposed to litigation, 'opinion has shifted strongly in favour of international arbitration for the resolution of disputes involving international commerce', and that, where disputes arise from 'an international business transaction, the balance comes down very firmly in favour of arbitration.'[8]

In the light of the recent successful arbitrations in the WTO, and the prominence of arbitration in international commercial dispute

[5] Articles 21.3(c) and 22.6 of the DSU envisage arbitration for resolving discrete questions relating to the implementation of recommendations and rulings of the Dispute Settlement Body (DSB). They are not the focus of this chapter as they cannot operate as an alternative to litigation for resolving more general disputes in the WTO (See the last paragraph of section II.1 of this chapter).

[6] Award of the Arbitrators, *US – Section 110(5) Copyright Act (Article 25)* (See section II.2(b) of this chapter).

[7] Alan Redfern and Martin Hunter with Nigel Blackaby and Constantine Partasides, *The Law and Practice of International Commercial Arbitration* (4th edn, London, 2004), para. 1–01. By way of illustration, in 2005 the International Chamber of Commerce received 521 requests for arbitration of which the amount in dispute exceeded US$1,000,000 in over 50 per cent of cases. In 1986, the International Chamber of Commerce received 344 requests. (See <http://www.iccwbo.org/court/english/right_topics/stat_2005.asp>.) Other arbitral institutions also report an increasing number of cases (for example, see the statistics collected at: <http://www.hkiac.org/HKIAC/HKIAC_English/main.html>, and this does not tell the whole story as many (perhaps most) arbitrations are conducted without the involvement of an arbitral institution.

[8] Redfern and Hunter et al., *International Commercial Arbitration*, paras. 1–50 and 1–51.

settlement outside the WTO, this chapter analyzes the potential of arbitration as an alternative to litigation in the WTO. In doing so, this chapter outlines the reasons why arbitration has been preferred in private international commercial disputes and examines whether similar conditions occur in the WTO context. The conclusion is that the same conditions do not fully apply in the WTO and, therefore, the potential of arbitration as an alternative to litigation in the WTO is limited to certain specific situations. These situations include disputes where both parties want an expeditious and binding determination or to ensure strict confidentiality, as well as where the dispute relates to an area that is not directly enforceable under the DSU, such as the conditions of a waiver or a mutually agreed solution (MAS). The chapter concludes with certain considerations when structuring arbitration as an alternative to litigation in the WTO.

I. Arbitration compared to litigation and 'alternative dispute resolution'

In dispute settlement theory, a distinction is typically made between *legal* means of dispute resolution and *diplomatic* means of dispute resolution. Legal means of dispute resolution include arbitration and litigation and are characterized by a binding decision based on the law. Diplomatic means of dispute resolution include the so-called 'alternative dispute resolution' (ADR) mechanisms such as good offices, conciliation, mediation, and inquiry, and are characterized by non-binding recommendations based on the parties' underlying interests.[9]

Distinguishing arbitration from litigation is not as straightforward as both involve an independent third party making a binding decision on the basis of predetermined rules. There are, however, some important structural differences between arbitration and litigation.

In contrast to litigation where the dispute is referred to a standing court with pre-established procedures, arbitration requires the parties to set up the machinery to handle the dispute themselves. In this regard, parties to an arbitration are 'masters of the arbitral process to an extent impossible in proceedings in a court of law.'[10] For example, arbitration typically permits the parties to decide the number and method of appointment of the arbitral tribunal, the powers the tribunal should

[9] John Graham Merrills, *International Dispute Settlement* (3rd edn, Cambridge, 2000), p. 89.
[10] Redfern and Hunter et al., *International Commercial Arbitration*, paras. 1–13.

possess, and how the proceedings are to be conducted (for example, the number and nature of submissions and oral hearings, the time-limit for the issuance of the award, whether the award can be appealed, etc.). Importantly, arbitration also grants the parties control over the jurisdiction of the arbitral tribunal and the basis for its decision. In this manner, the parties can instruct the arbitral tribunal to decide the matter exclusively in accordance with municipal law, international law, equity, a combination of those rules, or some other rules.[11] It has been said that this characteristic of arbitration 'is a key element in encouraging inter-state arbitration as it enables the parties to exercise close control over the process'.[12] Notably, if it turns out that the framework prescribed by the parties has been deviated from by the arbitral tribunal this may be grounds for setting aside the decision.[13] However, this does not usually extend to review of errors of law or fact, which tends to make arbitration faster than litigation.

Arbitration very often differs significantly from ADR mechanisms such as good offices, conciliation, mediation and inquiry. Linguistically, ADR should encompass all forms of dispute resolution that are 'alternatives' to litigation. Generally, however, arbitration has been distinguished from ADR mechanisms which do not result in binding decisions but rather non-binding recommendations to the parties. This characteristic of ADR is consistent with its purpose, which is not to determine who is legally correct and who is legally wrong, but rather to facilitate a mutually agreeable solution by reconciling both parties' interests.[14]

This chapter does not analyze the potential of ADR (in the narrower sense) as an alternative to litigation in the WTO. Nonetheless, it ought to be noted that various provisions in the DSU provide WTO Members with the possibility to resort to the ADR mechanisms of good offices, conciliation and mediation as alternatives or supplements to litigation if they so agree.[15] While these procedures have been seldom used in

[11] Merrills, *International Dispute Settlement*, pp. 95–105. See also, Redfern and Hunter et al., *International Commercial Arbitration*, pp. 1–13.

[12] Merrills, *International Dispute Settlement*, p. 112. See also Klaus Peter Berger, 'Understanding International Commercial Arbitration', in Centre for Transnational Law (CENTRAL) (ed.) *Understanding International Commercial Arbitration* (Muenster, 2000), p. 5.

[13] Merrills, *International Dispute Settlement*, p. 105.

[14] However, at times there may be considerable overlap between arbitration and other ADR mechanisms. For example, some forms of ADR can involve considerable direction from the third-party facilitator, such as 'evaluative' mediation by a retired judge.

[15] Article 5 of the DSU, and also Articles 3.12 and 24.2 of the DSO if the dispute involves at least one developing-country Member or least-developed-country Member.

practice,[16] there have been calls to further promote their use in the future[17] and one recent successful mediation by the WTO Director-General. These circumstances suggest that these mechanisms may also warrant further analysis.[18] In addition, some commentators have noted that ADR may play a useful role as an alternative to the compulsory consultations required under Article 4.11 of the DSU prior to panel and Appellate Body proceedings.[19] It may also be feasible to incorporate mediation into the WTO arbitration processes discussed in this chapter, mirroring the increased interest and experience in 'arb-med' (arbitration-mediation) in international commercial arbitration involving private parties.[20]

II. Arbitration in the WTO

1. *The current provisions providing for arbitration in the WTO agreements*

Article 25 of the DSU relates exclusively to arbitration recognizing that

> [e]xpeditious arbitration within the WTO as an alternative means of dispute settlement can facilitate the solution of certain disputes that concern issues that are clearly defined by both parties.

[16] Article 5 of the DSU has never been utilized. Article 3.12 of the DSU also has never been utilized, however, the provisions of the Decision of 5 April 1966 on Procedures Under Article XXIII to which it refers have been resorted to by developing countries on six occasions between 1978 and 1993. (See WTO, *Analytical Index: Guide to GATT Law and Practice* (Geneva, 1995), Vol. 2, pp. 765–766.)

[17] See, for example, Article 5 of the Dispute Settlement Understanding, Communication from the Director-General, WT/DSB/25, 17 July 2001.

[18] See Request for Mediation by the Philippines, Thailand and the European Communities, Joint Communication from the European Communities, Thailand and the Philippines, WT/GC/71, 1 August 2003; as well as, Request for Mediation by the Philippines, Thailand and the European Communities, Communication from the Director-General, WT/GC/66 and WT/GC/66/Add.1. See also Donald McRae, 'What is the Future of WTO Dispute Settlement?' (2004) 7(1) *Journal of International Economic Law* 3–17, 9–10.

[19] McRae has noted that 'the utility of those consultations is questionable' and points to proposals to 'turn them into a facilitated process' (See McRae, 'Future of the WTO Dispute Settlement?, 10.) Davey has also noted that in improving the prospects of settlement in consultations, 'one possibility that could be usefully explored is a greater use of mediation or conciliation' (See William J. Davey, 'WTO Dispute Settlement: Segregating the Useful Political Aspects and Avoiding "Over-legalisation"', in Marko Bronkers and Reinhard Quick (eds), *New Directions in International Economic Law: Essays in Honour of John H. Jackson* (The Hague, 2000), 291–307, at 295.

[20] See generally Michael Schneider, 'Combining Arbitration with Mediation', in Albert Jan Van den Berg (ed.), *International dispute resolution: towards an international arbitration culture* (The Hague, 1998), p. 57.

Typical of arbitration more generally, arbitration under Article 25 of the DSU is subject to the 'mutual agreement of the parties', who are also required to 'agree on the procedures to be followed'.[21] Thus, it is for WTO Members to decide on the number and method of appointment of the arbitrator, the manner in which the proceedings are to be conducted, the issues to be decided and, for *sui generis* arbitrations, the applicable law.[22]

There are few constraints on Article 25 arbitrations. These constraints are that the parties notify their agreement to resort to arbitration to all WTO Members sufficiently in advance of commencing arbitration; that they notify the award to the Dispute Settlement Body (DSB) and any relevant committees; and that they 'agree to abide by the arbitration award' to which Articles 21 and 22 of the DSU relating to implementation apply.[23] Another possible constraint is the requirement in Article 3.5 of the DSU stipulating that arbitration awards shall be consistent with the WTO agreements and shall not impede the objectives of, or nullify or impair benefits under, those agreements. Other WTO Members have no rights to participate in an Article 25 arbitration unless there is agreement by the parties to the arbitration allowing for their participation.[24] While an arbitration award must be notified to the DSB, it becomes binding on the parties immediately and is not conditional on DSB approval.

The DSU also envisages mandatory arbitration under Articles 21.3(c) and 22.6 of the DSU as steps in the implementation stage of a dispute. Article 21.3(c) provides that the 'reasonable period of time' for implementation of recommendations and rulings of the DSB shall be determined 'through binding arbitration' where the parties to the dispute cannot reach mutual agreement on the time period; and Article 22.6 provides that where a Member objects to the 'level of suspension' of concessions or obligations authorized by the DSB in retaliation for non-implementation of its recommendations and rulings it can refer that question to arbitration. These arbitrations will not be the focus of this chapter, as they are only capable of resolving discrete questions relating to the implementation of recommendations and rulings of the DSB. As such, these mandatory arbitrations do not operate as an alternative to litigation for resolving more general disputes in the WTO, in contrast to the

[21] Article 25.3 of the DSU.

[22] Arbitrations under Article 25 of the DSU would appear limited to examinations of issues under the 'covered agreements', as provided for under Article 1 of the DSU. *Sui generis* arbitrations do not have the same limitation, allowing the applicable law to be broader. (See discussion in section IV.2(c) of this chapter.)

[23] Articles 25.2, 25.3, and 25.4 of the DSU.

[24] Article 25.3 of the DSU.

procedures envisaged under Article 25 of the DSU or those of *sui generis* arbitrations.[25] For this same reason, the arbitration procedures envisaged under both the *Agreement on Subsidies and Countervailing Measures* (*SCM Agreement*) and the *General Agreement on Trade in Services* (*GATS*) are also not the focus of this chapter.[26]

2. *The practice of arbitration in the WTO*

(a) The 2005 Banana Tariff Arbitrations

On 1 August 2005 the arbitral tribunal issued its award in the First Banana Tariff Arbitration, and on 27 October 2005 the arbitral tribunal issued its award in the Second Banana Tariff Arbitration. These arbitrations were not held pursuant to Article 25 of the DSU and outside the scope of normal WTO dispute settlement procedures in the DSU. Rather, they were based on procedures outlined in a waiver of the European Communities' obligation under Article I:1 of the *General Agreement on Tariffs and Trade* (GATT) *1994*, contained in the document 'European Communities – The ACP-EC Partnership Agreement, Decision of 14 November 2001' (the so-called 'Doha Waiver').[27] As such, they were the first *sui generis* arbitrations to be held under the auspices of the WTO.

The Doha Waiver granted the European Communities a waiver from the most-favoured-nation (MFN) obligation under Article I:1 of the GATT 1994 until 31 December 2007 to the extent necessary to permit the European Communities to provide preferential tariff treatment for imports of products originating in African, Caribbean, and Pacific (ACP) States as required by the ACP-EC Partnership Agreement in Article 36.3, Annex V, and its Protocols.[28]

[25] Moreover, recourse to Article 21.3(c) and 22.6 arbitrations does not depend on mutual consent of the parties, but is mandatory; where the parties to a dispute do not agree on the relevant legal issues, one party can compel the other party to engage in the arbitral proceedings.

[26] These provisions envisage arbitration to determine whether a programme constitutes a non-actionable subsidy (Article 8.5 of the *SCM Agreement*), whether the conditions of non-actionability of a notified programme have been violated (Article 8.5 of the *SCM Agreement*), whether counter-measures taken in response to actionable and prohibited subsidies are appropriate (Articles 4.11 and 7.10 of the *SCM Agreement*), and whether compensatory adjustments following the modification or withdrawal of commitments in a GATS schedule are adequate (Article XXI of the GATS).

[27] Ministerial Conference Decision, European Communities – The ACP-EC Partnership Agreement, WT/MIN(01)/15, 14 November 2001.

[28] Ibid., para. 1.

With respect to bananas, the application of the Doha Waiver beyond 31 December 2005 was made subject to compliance with certain terms and conditions. These terms and conditions required that by 1 January 2006, in the context of the European Communities' commitment to shift from a tariff quota system to a tariff only system for MFN banana imports,[29] the European Communities would rebind its MFN import tariff on bananas at a level that 'would result in at least maintaining total market access for MFN banana suppliers'.[30] It further provided for 'multilateral control on the implementation of this commitment'[31] through the two-stage arbitration procedure that resulted in the 2005 Banana Tariff Arbitrations.

The First Banana Tariff Arbitration was initiated on 30 March 2005 by nine Latin-American banana-exporting countries[32] (the 'Interested Parties') in response to an EC communication that it planned to rebind its import tariff for MFN bananas at the level of € 230/tonne.[33] The Interested Parties argued that a tariff of € 230/tonne would not 'result in at least maintaining total market access for MFN banana suppliers' as required by the Doha Waiver. This claim was upheld by the arbitral tribunal in its award.[34]

The Doha Waiver provided that, in the event that the European Communities lost the First Banana Tariff Arbitration, it would be granted an opportunity to 'rectify the matter'.[35] Consequently, on 13 September

[29] This commitment was made in the context of understandings of the European Communities reached with Ecuador and the United States as part of the resolution of the *EC – Bananas III* dispute, whereby the European Communities was to 'introduce a Tariff Only regime for imports of bananas no later than 1 January 2006'. (See European Communities – Regime for the Importation, Sale and Distribution of Bananas, Understanding on Bananas between Ecuador and the EC, WT/DS27/60, G/C/W/274, 9 July 2001, p. 2, para. B; and European Communities – Regime for the Importation, Sale and Distribution of Bananas, Communication from the United States, WT/DS27/59, G/C/W/270, 2 July 2001, p. 2, para. B.)

[30] Doha Waiver, 11th preambular paragraph.

[31] Ibid.

[32] Colombia, Costa Rica, Ecuador, Guatemala, Honduras, and Panama followed by Brazil, Nicaragua, and Venezuela in the ensuing days. (See European Communities – The ACP-EC Partnership Agreement – Recourse to Arbitration Pursuant to the Annex to the Decision of 14 November 2001, WT/L/607/Add.1 to Add.9.)

[33] Article XXVIII:5 Negotiations, Schedule CXL – European Communities, Addendum, G/SECRET/22/Add.1, 1 February 2005.

[34] The arbitrator determined that the European Communities' 'envisaged rebinding [of € 230/tonne] would not result in at least maintaining total market access for MFN banana suppliers, taking into account all EC WTO market-access commitments relating to bananas' (See Award of the Arbitrator, *EC – The ACP-EC Partnership Agreement*, para. 94.)

[35] Annex to the Article I Doha Waiver, 5th tiret.

2005, the European Communities notified the Interested Parties that it intended to rectify the matter by setting its import tariff for MFN bananas at the level of € 187/tonne and establishing a zero duty tariff-rate quota of 775,000 tonnes per year for ACP bananas. The European Communities then initiated the Second Banana Tariff Arbitration pursuant to the Doha Waiver to determine whether its Second proposal 'would result in at least maintaining total market access for MFN banana suppliers'. Once again, the (identically constituted) arbitral tribunal determined that the EC proposal failed that standard and that, consequently, the European Communities had 'failed to rectify the matter, in accordance with the fifth tiret of the Annex to the Doha Waiver.'[36]

The 2005 Banana Tariff Arbitrations involved a workload comparable to those of many panel and Appellate Body proceedings. Reflecting the economic importance of banana exports into the European Communities for many WTO Members, the arbitrations involved ten parties (nine Latin-American countries and the European Communities), and the fourteen third parties (made up of relevant ACP banana-exporting countries).[37] In terms of workload, the First Banana Tariff Arbitration required the arbitral tribunal to examine the parties' various first submissions and rebuttal submissions, written responses to questions, and comments on the other parties' written responses to questions. The Second Banana Tariff Arbitration required examination of an equivalent number of submissions. In addition, in both arbitrations, the relevant ACP banana exporting countries submitted collective submissions to the arbitral tribunal. In total, these submissions and their annexes resulted in over a thousand pages of written argument. Substantively, beyond their legal argumentation, the submissions included factual material contained in annexes, as well as detailed economic argumentation, data and modelling. The oral hearings of the arbitrations extended over five days, typical of hearings in panel and Appellate Body proceedings.

The 2005 Banana Tariff Arbitrations required an arbitrator able to adjudicate a dispute of very considerable economic and political significance. As there was no agreement between the parties on a sole arbitrator, the Director-General of the WTO decided to appoint an arbitral tribunal

[36] Award of the Arbitrator, *EC – The ACP-EC Partnership Agreement II*, para. 127.

[37] Belize, Cameroon, Côte d'Ivoire, Dominica, Dominican Republic, Ghana, Grenada, Jamaica, Kenya, Madagascar, Saint Lucia, Saint Vincent & the Grenadines, Suriname, and Tanzania.

of three individuals to undertake that task.[38] It was chaired by John Weekes, a former Canadian Ambassador to the WTO and Chair of the WTO General Council, and included two Appellate Body members, Judge John Lockhart and Professor Yasuhei Taniguchi.[39] To support the arbitral tribunal, WTO staff were made available from an unprecedented four Divisions: Legal Affairs, the Appellate Body Secretariat, Agriculture, and Economic Research and Statistics. This can be contrasted with Appellate Body proceedings, where the Appellate Body members are exclusively serviced with staff from the Appellate Body Secretariat, and panel proceedings where panelists are serviced with staff from the Legal Affairs Division or Rules Division and, on occasion, staff from one other division. The breadth of WTO Secretariat support provided to the arbitral tribunal reflected the substantive scope and complexity of the dispute.

One of the most noteworthy aspects of the 2005 Banana Tariff Arbitrations was the speed with which the entire proceedings were completed. The First Banana Tariff Arbitration was requested on 30 March 2005, and the award of the arbitral tribunal issued four months later on 1 August 2005. This period of time included 30 days for the selection of the arbitrators, and 90 days to then render an award. The Second Banana Tariff Arbitration was even quicker, as it was requested on 26 September 2005[40] and the award issued a mere 30 days later on 27 October 2005. Both Banana Tariff Arbitrations resulted in written awards of the arbitral tribunal, which were notified to the General Council of the WTO and made available to all WTO Members as well as to the public through the WTO website.

(b) The Copyright Arbitration

The Copyright Arbitration was the first and only time since the establishment of the WTO that Members have had recourse to arbitration pursuant to Article 25 of the DSU. The Copyright Arbitration was intended to address a specific issue arising in the context of the implementation of the panel report in *US – Section 110(5) Copyright Act.* That panel report upheld the European Communities' argument that Section 110(5)(B) of

[38] Annex to the Doha Waiver, 4th tiret, providing that if there was a failure of the parties to agree on the arbitrator within ten days, then 'the arbitrator shall be appointed by the Director-General of the WTO, following consultations with the parties, within 30 days of the arbitration request'.

[39] European Communities – The ACP-EC Partnership Agreement – Recourse to Arbitration pursuant to the Annex to the Decision of 14 November 2001, Appointment of the Arbitrator – Communication by the Director-General, WT/L/607/Add.12, 12 May 2005.

[40] Award of the Arbitrator, *EC – The ACP-EC Partnership Agreement II*, para. 9.

the US Copyright Act was inconsistent with certain provisions of the *Agreement on Trade-Related Aspects of Intellectual Property Rights* (*TRIPS Agreement*),[41] and the copyright arbitration was intended to determine the consequent 'level of nullification and impairment of benefits to the European Communities as a result of Section 110(5)(B) of the US Copyright Act'.[42] This request was made to assist both parties in agreeing to 'mutually acceptable compensation', in accordance with Article 22.2 of the DSU, for the violation of the *TRIPS Agreement*.[43]

On 23 July 2001, the European Communities and the United States notified the DSB of their mutual agreement to resort to arbitration pursuant to Article 25 of the DSU.[44] In accordance with the requirements of Article 25.2 of the DSU, the European Communities and the United States included in that notification 'agreed procedures' for the conduct of the Article 25 arbitration.[45] Those procedures provided a mechanism for the selection of the arbitrators whereby the original panelists would be selected if available, and where not alternate arbitrators would be chosen by the WTO Director-General.[46] As only one of the original panelists was available, in accordance with the procedures, the WTO Director-General selected two alternate arbitrators.[47]

The procedures also outlined the steps of the arbitration, which were to include concurrent written submissions, concurrent rebuttal submissions, an oral hearing, written replies to questions from the arbitrators, and the opportunity to comment in writing on the other parties' written replies.[48]

A principal motivation behind the parties resorting to Article 25 of the DSU in the Copyright Arbitration was a desire to obtain a rapid decision prior to the adjournment of the US Congress by the end of the year.[49] As

[41] The panel held that Section 110(5)(B) of the US Copyright Act of 1976, as amended by the Fairness in Music Licensing Act of 1998, 'does not meet the requirements of Article 13 of the *TRIPS Agreement*' and therefore '*recommends* that the Dispute Settlement Body request the United States to bring subparagraph (B) of Section 110(5) into conformity with its obligations under the *TRIPS Agreement*'. (See Panel Report, *US – Section 110(5) Copyright Act*, paras. 7.1–7.2.)

[42] Joint communication of 23 July 2001 from the Permanent Mission of the United States and the Permanent Delegation of the European Commission to the Chairman of the Dispute Settlement Body, United States – Section 110(5) of the US Copyright Act – Recourse to Article 25 of the DSU, WT/DS160/15.

[43] Award of the Arbitrators, *US – Section 110(5) Copyright Act (Article 25)*, paras. 2.3–2.5.

[44] Joint communication of the United States and the European Commission, note 43 above.

[45] Ibid. [46] Ibid, p. 2, para. 1 of the agreed procedures.

[47] Margaret Liang and David Vivas-Eugui joined Ian Sheppard as arbitrators (Award of the Arbitrators, *US – Section 110(5) Copyright Act (Article 25)*, paras. 1.3–1.4).

[48] Ibid, para. 1.7. [49] Ibid, para. 1.12.

the arbitrators noted, 'one of the main concerns expressed by the parties when this matter was referred to arbitration was that we proceed expeditiously'.[50] In response to this desire, the request for arbitration was made on 23 July 2001, the arbitrators selected by 13 August 2001, and the award issued to the parties two months later, on 12 October 2001.[51] The entire proceeding, from the request for arbitration to notification of the award to the DSB and TRIPS Council on 9 November 2001, was completed in less than four months. As with the Banana Tariff Arbitrations, the Copyright Arbitration resulted in a written award of the arbitrators, which was notified to the DSB and the TRIPS Council and made available to all WTO Members as well as to the public through the WTO website.

III. Arbitration in private international commercial disputes

As noted at the outset of this chapter, arbitration has superseded litigation as the preferred means of dispute settlement in private international commercial disputes. There are four principal reasons why this preference has developed.[52]

1. The advantages of arbitration over litigation in private international commercial disputes

(a) The decision is internationally enforceable against the losing party

Probably the main reason why parties now use arbitration rather than national courts in private international commercial disputes is that the judgment of a national court is generally only enforceable domestically. In contrast, thanks to a network of regional and international treaties, particularly the 1958 UN Convention on the Recognition and Enforcement of Foreign Arbitral Awards (New York Convention),[53] arbitration leads to an award which tends to be legally enforceable in many jurisdictions.[54] As of June 2006, there were 137 signatories to the New

[50] Ibid, para. 1.13. [51] Ibid, para. 1.8.

[52] See also Margaret Wang, 'Are Alternative Dispute Resolution Mechanisms Superior to Litigation in Resolving Disputes in International Commerce?' (2000) 16 *Arbitration International*, 189.

[53] See <http://www.uncitral.org/uncitral/en/uncitral_texts/arbitration/NYConvention_status.html>.

[54] See generally, Redfern and Hunter et al., *International Commercial Arbitration*, paras. 1–18 and 1–19.

York Convention, including most major trading nations, developing countries, and least-developed countries (LDCs), making it one of the world's most widely ratified multilateral treaties.

Inspired by this success, on 30 June 2005, The Hague Conference on Private International Law concluded a Convention on Choice of Court Agreements. That convention provides that, in principle, a chosen domestic court's judgment would be enforceable in other states that had ratified the convention.[55] However, as of June 2006, no states have ratified the convention.[56] Even if it gains a similar number of adherents as the New York Convention, commercial parties will still need to be persuaded that courts are more suited to resolving private international commercial disputes than arbitrators chosen by the parties.

(b) The lack of an international court

Unless disputes are between states, and therefore the states concerned could submit the case to the WTO dispute settlement system or the International Court of Justice (ICJ), 'there is no [international] court to deal with international commercial disputes'.[57] Consequently, parties wishing to enforce private legal rights through the courts need to rely on domestic courts. In an international context, however, these domestic courts have the disadvantage that they are often foreign to the claimant, may be in a jurisdiction that is relatively inexperienced in dealing with international commercial transactions, may use a language different to that of the essential documents and evidence, and may require the claimant to rely on the services of foreign lawyers. For these reasons, Redfern and Hunter conclude that for business people, 'the prospect of bringing a claim arising out of an international business transaction before a foreign court is unattractive'.[58]

In contrast, arbitration allows the parties to argue their differences using their own lawyers, in an increasingly familiar forum combining elements of common and civil law traditions, in front of arbitrators who are

[55] The convention also provides that a court chosen (usually as the exclusive forum) by the parties would have to take jurisdiction, and that no other court could seize jurisdiction.

[56] See <http://www.hcch.net/index_en.php?act=conventions.text&cid=98>. See also Thalia Kruger, 'The 20th Session of the Hague Conference: A New Choice of Court Convention and the Issue of E.C. Membership' (2006) 55 *International and Comparative Law Quarterly*, 447.

[57] Redfern and Hunter et al., *International Commercial Arbitration*, paras. 1–51.

[58] Ibid.

usually selected because of their familiarity with the international commercial transactions being examined. Arbitration thus offers a 'neutral forum',[59] as opposed to the other party's domestic courts.

(c) Flexible, faster, and cheaper proceedings

The flexibility of arbitral proceedings, derived from party autonomy to develop the arbitration's procedures, provides the potential for arbitration to be a faster and cheaper alternative to litigation. As we have seen, unlike litigation where disputes are referred to a standing court with pre-established procedures, arbitration allows parties the freedom to work out for themselves the procedures best suited to the particular circumstances of the particular dispute.[60] This flexibility, extending to the number and nature of submissions and hearings, the time-limit for issuance of the award, and whether the award can be appealed, can have important implications on the time and costs of the proceedings.[61]

At a time when litigation is becoming increasingly lengthy and costly in many jurisdictions (due to, amongst others, overcrowding of court lists, an over-legalization of the process, extended procedural delaying tactics, and long appeal processes), these advantages of arbitration have proved attractive.

That said, as confirmed in a survey published in 1996, by around 1990 many practitioners had become concerned that international commercial arbitration had become only slightly faster and no cheaper than litigation.[62] Blame for this tended to be attributed to the involvement of large Anglo-American law firms extending sophisticated litigation management techniques developed in domestic common law contexts; and, more broadly, to a new generation of specialists in international commercial arbitration.[63]

Nonetheless, by the late 1990s there were signs that arbitration practitioners, institutions, and law-makers were responding to such

[59] See Christian Bühring-Uhle, *Arbitration and mediation in international business: designing procedures for effective conflict management* (Boston/The Hague, 1996).

[60] See section I of this chapter.

[61] See Catherine Li, 'Evaluating the Various Non-Litigation Processes for Resolving Disputes: The Cost-Effectiveness Approach' (2001) 18 *Journal of International Arbitration*, 435.

[62] See Christian Bühring-Uhle, *Arbitration and mediation in international business: designing procedures for effective conflict management* (Boston/The Hague, 1996); and Yves Dezalay and Bryant G. Garth, *Dealing in virtue: international commercial arbitration and the construction of a transnational legal order* (Chicago, 1996).

[63] Ibid.

concerns.[64] While it seems that the main improvements have come in more expeditious proceedings as opposed to savings in costs, the flexibility of arbitration proceedings continues to be a reason for its preference over litigation in private international commercial disputes.

(d) Confidentiality

Confidentiality is another major reason that arbitration is preferred over litigation. Unlike proceedings in many domestic courts, where the press and public have access to the proceedings or the record of the proceedings, international commercial arbitration tends not to be open to the public. As a former Secretary-General of the International Chamber of Commerce put it:

> The users of international commercial arbitration, *i.e.* the companies, governments and individuals who are parties in such cases, place the highest value on confidentiality as a fundamental characteristic of international commercial arbitration. When enquiring as to the features of international commercial arbitration which attracted parties to it as opposed to litigation, confidentiality of the proceedings and the fact that these proceedings and the resulting award would not enter into the public domain was almost invariably mentioned.[65]

However, there remains considerable variation among national legal systems about the applicability and scope of confidentiality obligations in arbitrations.[66]

IV. Observations on the applicability of arbitration as an alternative to litigation in the WTO

1. The advantages of arbitration over litigation in private international commercial disputes do not fully apply in the WTO context

Having outlined the main reasons why arbitration has been preferred over litigation in private international commercial disputes, this section examines whether similar conditions occur in the WTO context.

64 Luke Nottage, 'The vicissitudes of transnational commercial arbitration and the lex mercatoria: a view from the periphery' (2000) 16 *Arbitration International*, 53.

65 Expert report of Stephen Bond, 'Esso/BHP v Plowman' (1995) 11 *Arbitration International* 8, 273.

66 See, for example, Alexis Brown, 'Presumption Meets Reality: An Exploration of the Confidentiality Obligation in International Commercial Arbitration' (2001) 16 *American University International Law Review*, 969.

The motivation for preferring arbitration over litigation in private international commercial disputes due to the lack of an international court to resolve private international commercial disputes does not exist in the WTO context as the WTO panels and the Appellate Body provide an international 'court' able to resolve WTO law disputes. As the WTO dispute settlement system also contains enforcement mechanisms, the motivation of ensuring the enforcement of the decision that exists in the private international commercial context also does not apply in the WTO context. For these reasons, it would appear that the conditions motivating the use of private international commercial arbitration do not fully apply in the WTO context.

Nonetheless, a preference for arbitration over litigation in a WTO context might occur in certain specific situations, such as where both parties want an expeditious yet binding solution, and/or to ensure stricter confidentiality. It might also occur in situations where the dispute would not otherwise be directly enforceable under the DSU, such as disputes over compliance with the conditions to waivers or MAS. These specific situations are examined below.

2. *Arbitration may serve as an alternative to litigation in specific circumstances*

(a) Disputes where both parties want an expeditious determination

Article 3.3 of the DSU emphasizes that 'prompt settlement of [disputes] is essential to the effective functioning of the WTO and a proper balance between the rights and obligations of WTO Members'. Despite this goal of prompt settlement of disputes, delay is one of the major criticisms of litigation undertaken in the WTO dispute settlement system. William Davey, former Director of the Legal Affairs Division, concludes an analysis of the first ten years of the WTO dispute settlement system with the observation that 'experience to date suggests that one problem with the WTO dispute settlement system is that in too many cases, it takes too long to resolve disputes'.[67] Davey notes that the consequences of these delays could be considerable as 'the delays do make the system less attractive to businesses and could in the long run lead to less and less use of the system.'[68]

[67] William J. Davey, 'The WTO Dispute Settlement System: The First Ten Years' (2005) 8(1) *Journal of International Economic Law*, 17–50, 50.

[68] William J. Davey, 'The WTO: Looking Forwards' (2006) 9(1) *Journal of International Economic Law*, 3–29, 12.

By way of illustration of the time periods typical for litigation in the WTO, normal panel proceedings have taken an average of 14 months from the date of establishment of the panel to the date the DSB considers the panel report for adoption.[69] This period of time surpasses the general rule in Article 20 of the DSU to 'not exceed nine months' for this stage of the litigation. Furthermore, panel proceedings are not the sole stage in litigation in the WTO, as they must be preceded by formal consultations which in general require a minimum two-month period.[70] Members also have the right to appeal the panel report to the Appellate Body, an appeal process which may add a further three months to the litigation process. Thus, on average, panel proceedings have taken at least 16 months for completion, a period that can be three months longer if appealed.

In contrast to these lengthy time periods for the completion of litigation in the WTO, the time periods for completion of the 2005 Banana Tariff Arbitrations and the Copyright Arbitration were extremely expeditious. The period between the request for the First Banana Tariff Arbitration and the issuance of the award was four months, a time period that was reduced to a mere one month for the Second Banana Tariff Arbitration. The Copyright Arbitration responded to the concerns of the European Communities and the United States for a rapid decision by rendering its award within four months of the request for arbitration.

The significance of the speed with which these arbitrations have been completed, when compared to the considerable delays of litigation in the WTO, may provide the primary motivation for Members selecting arbitration as an alternative to litigation to resolve future disputes in the WTO. Trade disputes in the WTO are typically motivated by commercial opportunities for private businesses in foreign or domestic markets through the removal of protectionist measures.[71] Where those businesses are confronted with the choice between the numerous delays the litiga-

[69] As of 6 March 2006, the average number of days between the establishment of the panel by the DSB and the date the DSB considers the panel report for adoption for all disputes adopted by the DSB that were not appealed was 441 days. (See <http://www.worldtradelaw.net/dsc/database/adoptiontiming1.asp>.)

[70] Pursuant to Article 4.7 of the DSU, the period between the request for consultations and the establishment of the panel is normally 60 days (Article 4.7 of the DSU). Pursuant to Articles 4.3 and 4.6 of the DSU, this period may be shorter, between ten and 60 days, in the exceptional circumstances that the Member being consulted does not respond within ten days of receipt of the request, does not consult within 30 days of the receipt of the request, or agrees that consultations have failed to settle the dispute.

[71] WTO disputes are on occasion initiated also for systemic reasons, or to achieve clarity of the law.

tion approach entails, and the extremely expeditious option of arbitration, one would often expect a clear preference for arbitration. This is particularly so in the WTO system, where there are no retrospective remedies for businesses affected by illegal protectionist measures. Unfortunately, this advantage of arbitration for a claimant may be perceived as a disadvantage for any respondent wishing to maintain illegal measures for as long as possible. In such situations it may be difficult to achieve the mutual agreement of the parties required for arbitration. However, this difficulty may not arise as often as expected, as even private businesses of a respondent Member may value certainty with respect to their commercial landscape, rather than being in 'limbo' during potentially years of litigation, which may have a chilling effect on investments, long-term contracts, and hinder the ability to undertake desired adjustments. Even governments who think they may lose WTO law disputes may prefer to have a clear result sooner rather than later, for example, to force reform on recalcitrant vested interests at home.

It should however be noted that, while the time period for arbitration has, so far, been considerably quicker than that for litigation, Article 25 arbitration envisages an additional time period relating to the implementation of the arbitrator's award akin to that relating to the implementation of recommendations and rulings of the DSB following panel or Appellate Body litigation. Article 25 of the DSU provides that 'Articles 21 and 22 of [the DSU] apply *mutatis mutandis* to arbitration awards'. Consequently, if a Member cannot comply immediately with the award, it is granted a reasonable period to do so, which as a guide should not exceed fifteen months from adoption.[72] In addition, there is the potential for panel proceedings under Article 21.5 of the DSU to determine whether a Member has complied with the award, as well as arbitration under Article 22.6 of the DSU where there is disagreement on the level of suspension of concessions that may be applied where there is a lack of implementation. While these time periods could cause further delays in the implementation of Article 25 arbitration awards, they are necessary for WTO litigation processes as well. They are not, however, required following *sui generis* arbitration.[73]

[72] Article 21.3(c) of the DSU.

[73] See discussion in section IV.3(a) of this chapter. In private international commercial arbitration, as well, extra time must be factored in for cross-border enforcement and execution of awards. However, in the shadow of the law (particularly the New York Convention), awards are generally voluntarily complied with, probably quite quickly in most cases.

(b) Disputes where both parties want stricter confidentiality

(i) Confidentiality in standard dispute settlement proceedings

In contrast to the practice before a number of international tribunals,[74] WTO dispute settlement proceedings are not open to the public, and also entail additional confidentiality obligations. Confidentiality is applicable through all stages of a dispute (from consultations to retaliation) and covers written submissions to the panel or the Appellate Body,[75] oral hearings, the case record, the deliberations of the panel or the Appellate Body, and any communications with secretariat officials assigned to the case.[76] The duty to maintain confidentiality extends to all panelists or Appellate Body members,[77] WTO Secretariat officials,[78] as well as to all governments that are parties to a dispute including delegation members and external advisors.[79]

Beyond such 'standard' confidentiality, WTO dispute settlement provisions refer to information specifically designated as 'confidential' by the Member submitting such information. The DSU enjoins WTO Members and panels to treat such information as 'confidential'.[80] A panel has clarified this to mean that parties and third parties have the responsibility to ensure that no member of their delegation (which would presumably also include legal advisors) shall disclose to any person outside the delegation any information designated as 'confidential'.[81]

In contrast, the DSU does not provide specific procedures for protecting business-confidential information (BCI).[82] As a result, WTO dispute

[74] For instance, the ICJ, the International Tribunal for the Law of the Sea, or the European Court of Human Rights (ECHR).

[75] See Article 18.2 of the DSU and paragraph 3 of the Working Procedures in Appendix 3 of the DSU.

[76] Confidentiality requirements are contained in the text of the DSU, the Working Procedures in Appendix 3 of the DSU, as well as in the *Rules of Conduct for the Understanding on Rules and Procedures Governing the Settlement of Disputes*, WT/DSB/RC/1, 11 December 1996 (Rules of Conduct). Even if not mentioned expressly in the DSU, confidentiality requirements also necessarily extend also to arbitration proceedings under Articles 21.3(c) and 22.6. [77] See Section IV.1 of the Rules of Conduct. [78] Ibid.

[79] Panel Report, *Korea – Alcoholic Beverages*, para. 10.31.

[80] Article 18.2, third sentence, of the DSU; paragraph 3, third sentence, of Appendix 3 to the DSU. Moreover, Article 13 of the DSU on a panel's right to seek information provides that '[c]onfidential information which is provided [to the panel by any individual, body, or a Member's authority] shall not be revealed without formal authorization from the individual, body, or authorities of the Member providing the information' (Article 13.1, last sentence). [81] Panel Reports, *EC – Export Subsidies on Sugar*, para. 2.15.

[82] According to Prost, this is because DSU provisions were drafted at a time when the experience with the dispute settlement system related mainly to disputes that did not involve the

settlement practice has over the past ten years repeatedly seen individual parties request panels to make use of their discretion to adopt ad hoc case-specific special procedures for protecting BCI. In response, panels have on some occasions made use of their discretion under Article 12 of the DSU to adopt such special procedures.[83] The special procedures so adopted have included, for instance, the requirement that only 'approved persons may have access to BCI submitted',[84] that the panel not disclose BCI in its report, that electronic copies be avoided, that BCI be stored in separate designated locations and be returned or destroyed after panel proceedings.[85] Procedures for protecting BCI have been adopted not only in panel proceedings, but also in arbitration proceedings pursuant to Article 22.6 of the DSU.[86] For its part, the Appellate Body has to date refused to adopt case-specific special rules governing the treatment of BCI on the grounds that the existing confidentiality requirements provide sufficient guarantees to safeguard the integrity of such information.[87]

(ii) Shortcomings and gaps in confidentiality in standard dispute settlement proceedings

Despite its seemingly comprehensive nature, confidentiality in WTO dispute settlement suffers from a number of significant limitations. 'Standard' confidentiality is limited in that, for example, panel or

use of proprietary information, but rather centred on 'relatively simple and clear breaches of international obligations'. (Olivier Prost, 'Confidentiality Under The DSU', in Bruce Wilson and Rufus Yerxa (eds), *Key Issues in WTO Dispute Settlement – The First Ten Years* (Cambridge, 2005), p. 194.)

83 The panels in *Korea – Commercial Vessels* (Panel Report, para. 1.15), *Australia – Automotive Leather II (Article 21.5 – US)* (Panel Report, paras. 3.2–3.6), *Australia – Automotive Leather II* (Panel Report, para. 4.1), *Canada – Aircraft* (Panel Report, para. 9.54–9.69) *Egypt – Rebar*, *US Wheat Gluten*, and *Brazil – Aircraft* (Panel Report, para. 1.10) adopted such special procedures.

84 These approved or designated persons may also have to sign specific Declarations of Non-Disclosure.

85 See, for instance, the Procedures for the Protection of Business Confidential Information adopted by the panel in *Korea – Commercial Vessels* (Panel Report, Attachment 2, pp. 167 ff).

86 Decision by the Arbitrators, *EC – Bananas III (US) (Article 22.6 – EC)*, paras. 2.1 ff. In some Article 22.6 arbitrations, two versions of the award were prepared, one issued to the parties and containing confidential data, another not containing such data and circulated to the entire membership as well as the public. (See Decision of the Arbitrators, *Canada – Aircraft Credits and Guarantees (Article 22.6 – Canada)*; Decision of the Arbitrators, *Brazil – Aircraft (Article 22.6 – Brazil)*; and Award of the Arbitrators, *US – Section 110(5) Copyright Act (Article 25)*, paras. 1.22–1.24.)

87 See Appellate Body Report, *Canada – Aircraft*, paras. 125–147; and Appellate Body Report, *Brazil – Aircraft*, paras. 103–125.

Appellate Body reports are eventually circulated to all WTO Members and the public.[88] As a result, the protection of information and arguments made by parties in written and oral submissions is only temporary, as the reports provide a summary of the parties' arguments and sometimes even the full text of the written submissions (at the panel stage).[89] Often this information is made available to WTO Members and the public, even before the reports have been finalized, through 'leaks' by Member governments of interim panel reports or confidential advance copies of the final report.[90] The disregard for the confidentiality rule with respect to interim reports has escalated in recent years. In one case, government officials of the 'winning' party organized a press conference to publicly discuss the findings in an interim panel report, and in another a NGO released on the internet the full copy of the interim panel report in the still-ongoing 'GMO' (genetically modified organisms) dispute a few weeks after its release to the parties.[91] Other more limited examples of breaches of 'standard' confidentiality have occurred in practice, but they do not appear to be as widespread or systematic.[92] While the authors are not aware that there have been breaches of confidentiality with respect to information designated as confidential pursuant to Article 18.2 of the DSU, similar risks no doubt exist.

With respect to BCI, the text of the DSU as well as practice of the past ten years does not offer parties security that their BCI will be protected. As noted above, beyond generic references to 'confidential' information,

[88] In panel proceedings, parties to the dispute receive an advance confidential copy of the report several weeks before the circulation of the report; in proceedings before the Appellate Body, parties are sometimes given an advance copy, too, but only a few hours before the official circulation of the report.

[89] Where submissions contain information specifically designated as 'confidential', Article 18.2 obliges parties to a dispute to provide, upon request of a Member, a non-confidential summary of the information contained in its written submission that could be disclosed to the public.

[90] See, for instance, the *US – Gambling* dispute, in which the panel stated that the conduct of both Antigua & Barbuda and the United States was inappropriate and violated the confidentiality requirement (Panel Report, *US – Gambling*, paras. 5.3–5.13).

[91] Typically, the leaking government will be the winning party and the key factor motivating such practice is most likely the desire to announce victory to the domestic constituencies as soon as possible. The effect of the practice is arguably to put pressure on the defending party to terminate its measure sooner rather than later; in addition, a somewhat more nefarious effect from the judicial perspective is to put pressure on the panelists so as to raise the barrier for modifying their report in the course of the interim review process.

[92] See Appellate Body Report, *Thailand – H-Beams*, paras. 62–78. See also Panel Reports, *EC – Export Subsidies on Sugar*, paras. 7.86–7.99, with respect to certain proprietary information on cost of production of sugar.

the DSU does not contain any specific provisions or particular procedures to effectively safeguard BCI. Consequently, it has been for the parties in disputes to request the panels to use their discretion under Article 12 of the DSU to adopt special procedures for BCI protection. The problem that these parties have confronted, however, is that while a number of panels have accepted requests by parties for special procedures for the protection of BCI,[93] other panels have rejected such requests[94] or instead adopted special procedures that were less far-reaching than those requested by the parties.[95]

While panels have been more inclined to adopt such special procedures for protecting BCI where both parties to the dispute agreed on special procedures, case law indicates that agreement between parties is not dispositive in this respect. At least some panels have felt entitled to modify special procedures for BCI protection even when they were agreed upon and proposed by both parties. At times, panels have modified such proposed procedures out of concern for third-party rights or against one party's objections.[96] At other times, express objections by third parties did not deter panels from adopting the parties' proposed special procedures for the protection of BCI.[97] Such case law underlines the discretionary nature of the adoption of special procedures for the protection of BCI. Even admitting that the specific facts of each case may compel different results, practice with respect to protecting BCI does not always appear to reflect a transparent, coherent, coordinated, and predictable approach by panels.[98]

[93] See, for instance, Panel Report, *Canada – Aircraft*, para 4.171; Panel Report, *Australia – Leather II*, para. 4.1; and Panel Report, *Australia – Leather II (Article 21.5 – US)*, para. 3.2.

[94] See, for instance, Panel Report, *Canada – Dairy*, para. 2.15.

[95] For instance, in *Canada – Wheat Exports and Grain Imports*, where the panel did not adopt the procedures proposed by Canada and not objected to by the United States. The panel was concerned that the proposed procedures did not sufficiently take into account third-party interests and, therefore, adopted a modified version of the proposed procedures (Panel Report, *Canada – Wheat Exports and Grain Imports*, para. 6.8, sub-paras. 11–14).

[96] Panel Report, *Canada – Wheat Exports and Grain Imports*, para. 6.8, sub-paras. 11–14. See also Decision of the Arbitrators, *EC – Bananas III (Article 22.6 – EC)*, paras. 2.1 ff; and Prost, 'Confidentiality Under the DSU', p. 197.

[97] Panel Report, *Australia – Leather II (Article 21.5 – US)*, paras. 3.4–3.6.

[98] See also Prost, 'Confidentiality Issues Under the DSU', p. 197. In addition to concerns about safeguarding the confidentiality of data, a party may face an additional problem; under the existing case law, even if a panel cannot oblige a party to provide confidential information, confidentiality concerns do not provide a justification for the refusal by a party to provide panels with requested information and panels have the discretion to draw adverse factual inferences from such a refusal. (Panel Report, *Indonesia – Autos*, para. 14.235; Appellate Body Report, *Canada – Aircraft*, para. 198.)

As a final important weakness, the WTO system offers virtually no mechanism to ensure that breaches of confidentiality are effectively sanctioned. WTO practice shows that breaches of confidentiality bear few consequences besides occasional (indirect) reprimanding statements by a panel. More tangible and credible sanctions, such as might be available in a domestic legal system, simply do not exist.[99]

In the light of the above discussion, it is obvious that confidentiality under standard dispute settlement procedures in the WTO is not particularly well guaranteed and that businesses have only limited certainty as to how WTO adjudicatory bodies may treat BCI in a particular dispute. The protection of confidential information may, however, be of considerable practical importance as it may directly affect the willingness of private enterprises to participate in WTO dispute settlement proceedings.

For these reasons, WTO Members may be interested in ensuring a greater degree of confidentiality. For instance, parties might wish to avoid leaks that currently occur under standard WTO procedures. Moreover, parties might wish to engage in proceedings in which they have greater latitude in designing rules for the protection of BCI and ensuring those rules are applied. Finally, parties might also, in exceptional cases, wish to keep the contents of a report itself confidential.

(iii) Does arbitration offer a solution?

Arbitration under Article 25 of the DSU or *sui generis* arbitration could make it easier for parties to have predictable and higher levels for protection of BCI. By having recourse to arbitration rather than to standard dispute settlement procedures, WTO Members would gain complete control over the formulation of the rules governing the protection of BCI thereby eliminating the uncertainty of how precisely a panel would treat

[99] Thus, for instance, legal action by a private company that supplied confidential information (initially to its government that in turn provided that information to the panel) against another government that allegedly 'leaked' that information to a competitor would have to occur before a municipal court and would most likely have only very limited chances of success. (See also Prost, 'Confidentiality Issues Under the DSU', p. 199.) Moreover, sometimes the competitor may be sitting on the opposing WTO government's delegation. For instance, the delegation of Indonesia in the *Korea – Certain Paper* dispute included individuals from the Indonesian paper industry. Despite Korea's misgivings, the panel did not find the participation of those individuals in the Indonesian delegation to be objectionable, in particular since Korea had not requested the adoption of special procedures to protect any potentially business-confidential information (Panel Report, *Korea – Certain Paper*, paras. 7.10–7.18).

BCI in a given case. Furthermore, recourse to arbitration and the concomitant greater procedural autonomy would enable the parties to exclude the participation of third parties, thereby eliminating an element that has in the past swayed at least some panels away from special BCI procedures. Of course, it may still be necessary for an arbitrator to decide a disagreement relating to confidentiality issues that may arise in the course of the proceedings. However, it is unlikely that parties would not have a firm agreement on confidentiality issues prior to the initiation of arbitral proceeding, in particular if confidentiality were a motivating factor to have recourse to arbitration in the first place.

Regarding breaches of 'standard' confidentiality, Article 25 or *sui generis* arbitration may not resolve all the current problems in standard dispute settlement proceedings. So far, 'standard' confidentiality breaches have occurred on the side of governments and the observance of 'standard' confidentiality in arbitrations would also largely depend on the good will of governments. That said, the freedom for parties to an arbitration to craft precise procedural rules makes it possible to exclude some of those elements of standard dispute settlement procedures that arguably encourage leaking – for instance, the issuance of interim reports or providing advance copies of the final report to parties.[100]

A question arises regarding the extent to which arbitration proceedings might permit parties to keep confidential an entire arbitral award. Arguably Article 25 arbitration would not allow for this as the award itself has to be 'notified' to the DSB and to the council or committee of any relevant agreement. As other WTO Members may raise any point relating to the award, this implies that the contents of the award must be made known to them. In contrast, in *sui generis* arbitration proceedings, the parties would appear to have the freedom to keep the entire arbitral award secret – or, alternatively, to only announce the result to WTO Members, but not the entire text of the award.

The extent to which WTO Members would desire to keep confidential entire awards is of course debatable. A number of Members are advocates of greater transparency in standard WTO dispute settlement procedures,

[100] The flexibility of arbitration proceedings may permit the creation of *sui generis* confidentiality safeguards. For instance, it is conceivable that members of a delegation be made subject to civil liability rules of a particular legal order (for instance, that of Switzerland as the WTO's host country) for purposes of specific arbitration proceedings. Alternatively, a form of security could be envisaged (for instance, in the form of a bond posted by the parties to the arbitration) that would be forfeited in case of a breach of confidentiality. (The authors are indebted to Todd Friedbacher for this thought.)

thus keeping an entire award confidential would be incongruent with their stated policies. Even transparency-averse WTO Members may not wish to keep entire arbitration awards confidential, given that victory in an inter-governmental dispute is useful not only as a legal 'judgment' in and of itself, but also because it generates political pressure on the losing party, in particular in a multilateral forum. Such a judgment will provide significant political incentives for the losing government to bring itself into compliance so as to maintain its international credentials as a law-abiding member of the legal community, and/or to overcome problematic vested interests at home. Keeping the contents of a judgment or award confidential undoubtedly detracts from these effects. In addition, secrecy about the contents of an arbitral award may raise public suspicion about the legitimacy of the complaining government's claims and further detract from the political and diplomatic usefulness of the award.

(c) Disputes for which the DSU does not have jurisdiction

It is possible that *sui generis* arbitration could be used to resolve disputes that are otherwise not directly enforceable under the DSU, such as disputes over compliance with the terms and conditions to waivers or MAS. The precedent for such an approach is the experience with the Banana Tariff Arbitrations, which resolved a dispute regarding compliance with conditions to a waiver.

Article 1.1 of the DSU provides that DSU procedures can only be used to resolve disputes brought pursuant to the *Marrakesh Agreement Establishing the World Trade Organization* (*WTO Agreement*), the DSU, as well as the multilateral and plurilateral trade agreements listed in Appendix 1 to the DSU (collectively, the 'covered agreements'). Article 7.1 of the DSU further limits a panel's terms of reference to the examination of a matter referred to it in the light of the provisions of the 'covered agreements' cited by the parties.

Waivers and MAS are not defined as 'covered agreements' in Appendix 1 to the DSU and therefore any dispute over compliance with their terms and conditions cannot be the source of a claim in a proceeding under the DSU. Consequently, where a Member has granted a waiver or MAS on certain terms and conditions and considers that they have not been satisfied by the other Member, it cannot seek an answer on that question *directly* under the DSU. Members could do so *indirectly* by re-litigating the issue from the beginning, arguing violation of a provision of the covered agreements that cannot be justified by the waiver or MAS (because its conditions have not been met). This indirect approach, however, would result in considerable delays before Members would have a ruling on the question of whether the conditions have, or have not, been met.

This next section briefly analyzes some of the advantages and disadvantages of *sui generis* arbitration as an alternative to litigation under the DSU as a means to resolving disputes over the compliance with conditions to agreements that are not 'covered agreements'.

(i) *Conditions to waivers*

Article IX of the *WTO Agreement* confers on the Ministerial Conference the right to accord waivers releasing Members from their legal obligations under the *WTO Agreement* and the multilateral trade agreements annexed to it. Waivers provide a legal defence to claims of violation of those covered agreements.

Waivers often specify terms and conditions that the Member to whom the waiver is granted must fulfil. If a Member acts inconsistently with those terms and conditions, it can no longer invoke the waiver as a defence. The problem that arises is that occasionally there may be a genuine disagreement as to whether a Member has met the terms and conditions of a waiver, and therefore whether the Member can continue to invoke it as a defence or not.

In these situations, *sui generis* arbitration could be used as means of resolving the dispute. It offers the advantage that it can provide a legal decision on the issue in a short period of time. The Banana Tariff Arbitrations were completed in four months and one month, respectively. The alternative, re-litigating the entire issue under the DSU by claiming violation of a provision of the covered agreements that cannot be justified by the waiver (as its conditions have not been met), would require consultations, panel, and potentially Appellate Body proceedings, before Members would have a ruling. This process would entail delays of approximately 16 months, more if appealed.

The advantage of the speed of an arbitral ruling on such a dispute will largely depend on whether the Member found to be acting inconsistently with the conditions of a waiver is willing to alter its behaviour. If not, as *sui generis* arbitration cannot be enforced using existing DSU enforcement mechanisms,[101] the only way a Member could enforce the failure of a Member to comply with the conditions of a waiver would be to re-litigate the entire proceeding. Therefore, in situations where the other

[101] See section IV.3(a) of this chapter.

Member is not willing to alter its behaviour, *sui generis* arbitration could have the disadvantage of delaying the commencement of the re-litigation of the issue in the DSU.

The Banana Tariff Arbitrations, both of which were included in the Doha Waiver as a mechanism to determine whether the conditions of the waiver were fulfilled, provides an illustration of the advantage of a rapid decision, and the potential disadvantage of the lack of an immediate remedy were the European Communities to fail to alter its behaviour to comply with the conditions of the waiver.[102]

(ii) Mutually agreed solutions

MAS are case-specific agreements concluded when parties settle a dispute without a formal panel and/or Appellate Body ruling. Settlement occurs rather frequently in WTO dispute settlement, no doubt reflecting the complex inter-state and economic interests involved and, perhaps, still its origins in less 'legalized' dispute resolution processes. It would appear that about one third of all cases are settled, typically at the consultation stage and, occasionally, after a panel has been established.[103] A portion of those settlements result in MAS that are officially notified to the DSB.[104] By the authors' count, as of April 2006, 34 MAS – comprising 51 formally distinct disputes (that is, 15 per cent of all WTO disputes since 1995) – have been formally notified to the DSB.[105] This number renders MAS an important part of dispute settlement practice.

[102] Accordingly, some of the Interested Parties in the Banana Tariff Arbitrations have initiated proceedings under the normal dispute settlement procedures of the DSU in order to gain an enforceable ruling from the DSB.

[103] Davey, 'WTO: The First Ten Years', 48. It may be noted that not all non-settled cases result in a panel or Appellate Body ruling; it appears that some 25 per cent of the cases are simply dropped by the complainant or remain pending for extended periods of time until the panel lapses pursuant to Article 12.12 of the DSU (45–46).

[104] There is concern about terms of settlements that have not been officially notified a circumstance which has given rise to some concern in the DSU review and has prompted calls for better disciplines in this respect. The underlying concern is that the precise conditions of settlement may be WTO-inconsistent in that they ignore rights of WTO Members not parties to the dispute and/or that, without the benefit of transparency, stronger WTO Members could force inequitable terms of settlement on smaller and less powerful parties.

[105] *Egypt – Matches* (DS327/3); *Japan – Quotas on Laver* (DS323/5); *Panama – Milk* (DS329/2); *China – Tax on Circuits* (DS309/8); *Japan – Apples* (DS245/21); *Egypt – Textiles and Apparel* (DS305/4); *EC – Steel Anti-Dumping Duties* (DS313/2); *US – Florida Excise Tax* (DS250/3); *Uruguay – Tax Treatment* (DS261/7); *EC – Sardines* (DS231/18); *Canada – Dairy* (DS103/33, 113/33); *Turkey – Fresh Fruit* (DS237/4); *Ireland – Copyright* (DS82/3), *EC – Copyright* (DS115/3); *Argentina – Patent Protection* (DS 171/3, 196/4);

MAS notified to the DSB illustrate, in varying degrees of detail, that parties often include terms and conditions as part of their settlement agreement. For instance, MAS may contain a precise description of the action to be taken by the defendant country,[106] a reference to the national regulatory or legislative measure that has already been promulgated and that brings about or reflects the MAS,[107] the text of a memorandum of understanding,[108] or simply an announcement, without further details, of the type of action that will be or has been taken.[109]

Despite the DSU's express preference for settling disputes through mutual agreement rather than litigation,[110] the DSU sets forth only rudimentary procedures dealing with MAS. With Article 3.6 of the DSU providing that MAS to matters formally raised under the DSU shall be notified to the DSB and the relevant councils and committees, where any Member may raise any point relating thereto. Critically, the DSU does not provide for a procedural avenue for the complaining party to argue, at a later stage, that the terms and conditions of the MAS are not being respected by the responding party, and to obtain a ruling by a WTO adjudicatory body on that issue.[111]

Compounding the absence of a clearly designated procedure for resolving disputes over compliance with the terms and conditions of MAS, very little has been said to date by the panels or the Appellate Body about the precise legal nature and import of MAS. The only existing authoritative statement on MAS is found in the panel report in *India – Autos*, which opined that an MAS is not a 'covered agreement' within the meaning of Article 1.1 of the DSU.[112] As is the case for waivers, therefore,

Slovak Republic – Sugar (DS235/2); *Belgium – Rice* (DS210/6); *Romania – Minimum Import Prices* (DS198/2); *Brazil – Patent Protection* (DS199/4); *EC – Bananas III* (DS27/58); *Denmark – IPR Enforcement* (DS83/2); *EC – Motion Pictures* (DS124/2); *Greece – Motion Pictures* (DS 125/2); *Australia – Salmonids* (DS21/10); *US – Textiles and Apparel II* (DS151/10); *Australia – Automotive Leather II* (DS126/11); *Argentina – Cotton* (DS190/2); *EC – Butter* (DS72/7); *India – Quantitative Restrictions* (DS93/8 and DS90/2, DS91/2, DS92/2, DS93/2, DS94/2, DS96/2); *Sweden – IPR Enforcement* (DS86/2); *Philippines – Pork and Poultry* (DS74/5, DS102/6); *Japan – Satellite* (DS73/5); *US – Textiles and Apparel I* (DS85/9); *Turkey – Taxes on Film Revenues* (DS43/3); *Japan – Sound Recordings* (DS28/4); *Poland – Autos* (DS19/2); *EC – Scallops* (DS7/12) *(Canada)* (DS12/12, DS14/11) *(Peru and Chile)*.

[106] *Japan – Quotas on Laver*, WT/DS323/5.

[107] *Japan – Apples*, WT/DS245/21.

[108] *China – Tax on Circuits*, WT/DS309/8.

[109] *Egypt – Matches*, WT/DS327/3, stating that price undertakings will be concluded.

[110] Article 3.7 of the DSU.

[111] See Panel Report, *India – Autos*, para. 7.114.

[112] Ibid., para. 7.118. The only possible argument to the contrary is that MAS are provided for in the text of the DSU and that, therefore, MAS emanate from the DSU, which is, of course, itself a covered agreement. This argument, however, appears rather strained and is highly unlikely to be accepted by a WTO panel or the Appellate Body.

the problem that Members are confronted with is that a claim alleging non-compliance with the terms and conditions of an MAS does not fall within the scope of disputes that can be brought under the DSU.

Hence, there is a gap in the DSU when a WTO Member wishes to obtain a ruling that another Member is not complying with the terms and conditions of a MAS. Filling this gap would require an amendment to the text of the DSU, such as that proposed by the European Communities, according to which proceedings under Article 21.5 of the DSU would be 'opened up' for claims based on MAS.[113]

As an alternative, one can also envisage *sui generis* arbitration as a possible option for resolving disputes over compliance with the terms and conditions of a MAS.[114] Such an approach would mirror the use of *sui generis* arbitration to resolve disputes regarding conditions to waivers. The advantage would be decisions in a short period of time. The disadvantage would, however, remain that the awards could not be enforced using the DSU enforcement mechanisms where a Member nonetheless fails to alter its behaviour following the arbitration award.

Nevertheless, in practice, Members may not always wish to resolve disagreements over MAS through recourse to arbitration or other legalistic means. Members have arguably so far perceived MAS as more political, rather than legal, instruments – a view that is arguably also supported by the observation that not all MAS are notified to the DSB. Where this is the case, Members may not wish to have recourse to third-party binding adjudication in resolving disputes over MAS.

Even assuming that WTO Members will, in the future, litigate more over questions relating to MAS, *sui generis* arbitration will not always suit situations where the complaining party wishes to challenge another Member's implementation measure. This is because the Member may not

[113] Contribution of the European Communities and its Member States to the Improvement of the WTO Dispute Settlement Understanding, Communication from the European Communities, TN/DS/W/1, 13 March 2002, p. 7. In this context, it should of course be avoided that a DSU procedure be used to verify compliance with an MAS that is inconsistent with WTO agreements. At least some MAS notified to the DSB do not appear to be consistent with some WTO provisions, for instance provisions relating to the prohibition of quotas or the MFN principle (for example, in cases where the parties agreed that exports from the complaining party would enter the market of the defending party on the basis of a preferential quota, opened exclusively for suppliers from the complaining party).

[114] The use of an MAS in a WTO adjudicatory process will more likely arise along the lines of the dispute in *India – Autos* – namely, that a defending party will rely on the MAS as a procedural bar to claims raised by the complaining party or, at least, as part of the applicable law in assessing those claims.

want to limit its arguments exclusively with reference to the MAS. Rather, the complaining party may want to challenge the implementing measure under any provision of any of the covered agreements.[115] Of course, Members may stipulate, in the terms of reference of a *sui generis* arbitration, that the implementing measure be examined not only under the terms of the MAS, but also under any cited provision of WTO law.[116]

(d) Political dimensions of WTO litigation

Among factors that may constitute incentives or disincentives for using arbitration proceedings in the WTO context, it is important to keep in mind the political dimension and the concomitant idiosyncrasies of WTO dispute settlement. As is well known, international trade disputes often reflect internal conflicts between interest groups in the defending state. The trade restrictive measures at issue may have been initially adopted by a government unable to resist protectionist pressures from powerful constituencies. A judgment from the WTO that such measures are WTO-inconsistent will strengthen the hand of the defendant government, as well as that of domestic constituencies with opposing commercial interests, in the domestic conflict in the defendant state. Where the relevant protectionist domestic interests are well-entrenched, a settlement at the consultations stage may simply be unacceptable within the domestic political context and will not generate sufficient pressure to overcome the resistance of the interest group at issue. What is 'needed' is a full-blown loss in a WTO dispute settlement proceeding.

How could circumstances such as these affect the potential of arbitration as an alternative to litigation in the WTO context? Some might argue that pursuing a WTO dispute, not through the 'standard' DSU litigation procedures, but rather through arbitration, may lead to a perception that the resulting decision is somehow of lesser value than a panel and Appellate Body report. A losing defendant government may be concerned about being accused domestically as not having exhausted all possible lines of defence available under the DSU and that by agreeing to expedited, more flexible procedures, it 'sold out' the relevant domestic

[115] For instance, this could occur when a measure allegedly taken pursuant to an MAS goes beyond the scope of the MAS and/or extends into areas that go beyond the original dispute. For instance, the defending party could remove a sanitary and phytosanitary (SPS) market-access barrier on a specific product by implementing a new wholesale quarantine procedure applicable to a wide range of products.

[116] However, if that is the case, then that part of the dispute could also be decided under normal panel or Appellate Body proceedings under the DSU.

interest group. As a result, in cases where a domestic protectionist interest group is particularly powerful, an arbitral award may not have the same useful political effect as a 'standard' panel and Appellate Body report in forcing the protectionist interest group to back down.

On the other hand, experience with the *sui generis* Banana Tariff Arbitrations has been positive. There has been no suggestion by either the European Communities or the specific interest groups at issue in that dispute, that the two unfavourable arbitral awards were not taken seriously by virtue of their *sui generis* character as they didn't result from 'standard' DSU litigation proceedings. Hence, the political dimension of the decision whether to have recourse to arbitration procedures will most likely have to be assessed on a case-by-case basis. Some disputes will, by virtue of their domestic political contentiousness, lend themselves to arbitration better than others. Who is selected as arbitrator for such WTO arbitrations should also be of relevance. Less concerns are likely to arise, especially at this initial phase when all concerned are getting used to these processes, if arbitrators are experienced panelists or indeed (as in the Banana Tariff Arbitrations) members of the Appellate Body itself.

3. *Considerations when structuring arbitrations in the WTO*

(a) Ensure that the decision is enforceable

Parties deciding to have recourse to arbitration in the WTO should consider whether they wish to make the resulting arbitral award enforceable through the existing DSU enforcement mechanisms. Arbitral awards pursuant to Article 25 of the DSU are expressly enforceable through those mechanisms, with Article 25.4 explicitly providing that Articles 21 and 22 of the DSU apply *mutatis mutandis* to Article 25 arbitration awards. *Sui generis* arbitration awards, in contrast, are unlikely to be enforceable through Articles 21 and 22 of the DSU.[117]

Enforceability would typically be a key concern in private commercial or investor-State arbitration, but need not necessarily be so in the WTO context. It is true that an attractive element of WTO dispute settlement is its enforcement mechanism. At the same time, however, WTO dispute

[117] While it is conceivable that a *sui generis* arbitration agreement might contain a clause reserving the right for the complaining party to have recourse to Articles 21 and 22 of the DSU, it is far from clear to what extent WTO Members would accept and allow for such practice.

settlement, whether in the 'standard' panel and Appellate Body procedures or arbitration procedures, remains a mixed politico-legal exercise. Compliance with an adverse ruling is often a decision heavily influenced by political considerations and not necessarily exclusively determined by the existence of a formal sanctioning mechanism (suspension of concessions). As a result, where political pressure for compliance (both international and domestic) resulting from an adverse arbitral award is strong, a *sui generis* arbitration award may stand as good a chance of being complied with as any panel or Appellate Body report, even in the absence of a formal enforcement mechanism.

(b) Ensure qualified arbitrators and secretariat support

Qualified arbitrators are essential for successful arbitration proceedings. In the private commercial arbitration context, it has been said that

> [t]he choice of the persons who compose the arbitral tribunal is vital and often the most decisive step in the arbitration. It has rightly been said that arbitration is only as good as the arbitrators.[118]

The success of arbitration in the WTO will also largely depend upon the arbitrators selected and the support they are offered. In selecting arbitrators in the WTO context, parties may therefore wish to appoint individuals well versed in the substance of WTO law, such as previous panelists, Appellate Body members or government officials and academics with demonstrated expertise. Certainly the experience in the Copyright Arbitration (where the arbitrators were chaired by the chair of the panel in the original dispute) and the Banana Tariff Arbitration (where the arbitrators were two sitting Appellate Body members as well as a former Canadian Ambassador to the WTO), illustrates that arbitrators experienced in WTO law can be effective.

At the same time, given that parties will often have recourse to arbitration proceedings precisely in order to avoid inconveniences or pitfalls associated with standard WTO dispute settlement procedures, they might also consider appointing arbitration specialists who are not necessarily experts in WTO law. These individuals would have the skills to conduct expedited proceedings that make full use of the advantages arbitration offers over standard litigation procedures, without being burdened by preconceived notions of WTO dispute settlement practice.

[118] Jean-Flavien Lalive, 'Mélanges en l'honneur de Nicolas Valticos', in René-Jean Dupuy, *Droit et Justice* (Paris, 1989), p. 289.

With respect to legal and administrative support for arbitrators, experience in WTO dispute settlement litigation suggests that qualified secretariat support from WTO staff is essential for the functioning of panel and Appellate Body proceedings. The arbitrators in the Banana Tariff Arbitrations were also assisted by a team of WTO Secretariat staff from an unprecedented four WTO divisions, which assisted them to complete their tasks within the tight timeframes of those arbitrations.

Members considering arbitration in the WTO context therefore ought to take into account the need to ensure qualified legal and administrative support. As mentioned, there may be benefits in this support being provided by the WTO Secretariat. Nonetheless, support could also be provided by individuals not affiliated with the WTO Secretariat. While the DSU requires support by the WTO Secretariat to panels (Article 27.1 of the DSU) and the Appellate Body (Article 17.7 of the DSU), it does not do so with respect to arbitration under Article 25 of the DSU. This is all the more true for *sui generis* arbitration. Of course, more often than not, parties may be interested in providing arbitrators with the support of the WTO Secretariat in the light of its expertise and reputation for impartiality. However, should parties to the arbitration wish to provide for 'outside' secretariat support, they would be free to do so. In addition, arguably, the Director-General of the WTO is under no legal obligation to provide WTO Secretariat support for arbitration (certainly not for *sui generis* arbitration), or to give such arbitration proceedings the same priority as that given to standard dispute settlement procedures (even if the political reality may dictate otherwise). As a consequence, in times of high standard dispute settlement activity and low availability of WTO Secretariat resources, parties to the arbitration may be pushed towards using at least partially outside secretariat support for the arbitrators in order not to delay the proceedings.

(c) Ensure certainty with respect to the involvement of third parties

Article 25.3 of the DSU provides that arbitration pursuant to Article 25 will not include third parties unless there is explicit agreement by the main parties to the arbitration permitting their participation. *Sui generis* arbitration has no pre-determined procedures regarding third-party participation and, therefore, Members resorting to *sui generis* arbitration should develop those procedures in advance if they want to ensure certainty with respect to third-party involvement in the proceedings.

In the absence of procedures developed in advance, the involvement of third parties may be left to the discretion of the arbitrators. This occurred in the Banana Tariff Arbitrations where the arbitral tribunal accepted the request of 14 ACP countries to participate, in a limited manner, in the arbitration. In a letter explaining its decision, the arbitral tribunal noted that the Doha Waiver Annex provides 'no rule precluding participation by such Members', and therefore that the Doha Waiver Annex 'leaves it to the Arbitrator's discretion to organize and manage the conduct of the proceedings'.[119] Nonetheless, the arbitral tribunal limited the participation of the relevant ACP countries to making one collective written submission and a single brief statement at the hearing so that their participation affected neither the timetable of the proceedings nor the time-frame for the conclusion of the arbitration as foreseen in the Doha Waiver.

(d) Develop procedures in advance

The experience in the bananas tariff arbitration with respect to third-party involvement illustrates that, unless parties develop procedures for the arbitration in advance, they will be vulnerable to the arbitrator's discretionary decisions regarding the procedures governing the arbitration.

A similar situation occurred in the Copyright Arbitration where the parties had not agreed to procedures in advance concerning the treatment of BCI. Consequently, the arbitrators decided that they would use their discretion and 'rely on the practice of the Appellate Body' which included permitting the arbitrators to make their own determination as to which information would be kept confidential in the final award, according to the criteria 'that confidentiality for business reasons was sufficiently warranted'.[120] This can be contrasted with the arbitrators' approach to the allocation of the burden of proof in that proceeding where the arbitrators followed the procedures agreed to in advance by the parties, noting that those procedures 'expressly instruct us to follow the allocation of burden of proof rules applied in proceedings under Article 22.6' of the DSU.[121]

The difficulty with developing procedures in advance of arbitration, however, is the time involved and willingness of the parties to negotiate and agree to those procedures. In private international commercial arbitration, this difficulty is often averted by referring to default rules of arbitration that would be applicable in the absence of prior agreement such

[119] Letter from the arbitrator to the parties, dated 18 May 2005.

[120] Award of the Arbitrators, *US – Section 110(5) Copyright Act (Article 25)*, para. 1.24.

[121] Ibid., para. 4.4.

as the UN Commission on International Trade Law (UNCITRAL) Arbitration Rules. The other common method used in private international commercial arbitration to avoid giving arbitrators too much discretion to determine the procedures governing arbitration is to use 'institutional' arbitration, such as those administered by the International Chamber of Commerce or the International Centre for the Settlement of Investment Disputes, which have predetermined procedural rules for the arbitration.

Members wishing to utilize arbitration as an alternative to litigation in the WTO may therefore benefit from developing in advance certain model default rules on arbitration, serving a similar function as UNCITRAL Arbitration Rules. These would operate in the absence of agreement by the parties on the applicable procedures. They would avoid the time and costs of parties negotiating in advance every procedural rule for WTO arbitration, as well as the risk of granting too much discretion to the arbitrators to determine the procedures to be followed where agreement is not possible. At the same time, parties would be free to deviate from those default rules thus retaining the flexibility to adjust arbitration procedures to achieve specific objectives.

V. Conclusion

A curiosity of WTO dispute settlement practice is the almost exclusive reliance on litigation at a time when domestic legal systems, and private parties in international commercial disputes, are increasingly questioning the litigation model. The length of time to resolve disputes through litigation, the costs involved, and the lack of flexibility has resulted in a trend towards using alternatives to litigation, including arbitration. This trend is particularly clear in the context of private international commercial disputes where arbitration has superseded litigation as the preferred means of dispute settlement.

In contrast, WTO Members have demonstrated a clear preference to litigate their disputes. In the first ten years of the WTO dispute settlement system, litigation has been initiated on over 300 occasions resulting in over 200 panel and Appellate Body reports. This caseload rivals over 80 years of litigation in the ICJ (and its predecessor the Permanent Court of International Justice (PCIJ)) and is greater than that of 50 years of dispute resolution in the GATT.[122] At the same time, litigation in the

[122] McRae, 'The Future of the WTO Dispute Settlement', 9.

WTO suffers from many of the same limitations as litigation in domestic legal systems – including the time it takes to gain a final determination, the associated legal costs, and the lack of flexibility to develop procedures adapted to the specific circumstances of each dispute.

This chapter analyzes the potential of arbitration as an alternative to litigation in the WTO. It does so in the light of the recent successful Banana Tariff Arbitrations, the first *sui generis* arbitrations to be held under the auspices of the WTO. These arbitrations examined issues of a substantive scope and complexity typical of panel and Appellate Body proceedings, and demonstrated that arbitration could operate as an effective alternative to litigation in a WTO context. A similar positive outcome was achieved in the Copyright Arbitration, the only other occasion that WTO Members consented to voluntary arbitration as a means to resolve a dispute in the WTO.

Professor Donald McRae has noted that in the WTO context, 'domestic law experience in forms of dispute resolution developed as an alternative or supplement to litigation needs careful consideration'.[123] To that end, this chapter has examined the extent to which the conditions motivating the preference for arbitration over litigation in private international commercial disputes occur in the WTO context. Overall, the chapter concludes that the same conditions do not fully apply in the WTO context and therefore the potential of arbitration is likely to be limited to certain specific situations. Nonetheless, in those specific situations, arbitration could be of considerable value.

If arbitration were to be used more regularly as an alternative to litigation in the WTO it will be important to avoid it becoming overformalized, slow, and just as expensive as regular litigation. For a period in the 1990s, this had occurred in private international commercial arbitration, and an awareness of those risks would be of value when developing procedures for future WTO arbitrations.

[123] Ibid., 10.

10

The evolving WTO dispute settlement system

ALAN YANOVICH

The dispute settlement system of the World Trade Organization (WTO) is generally regarded as a big success. Most commentators agree that the system has worked remarkably well in its first ten years.[1] Many factors explain the system's success. In this chapter, I focus on one factor that, in my view, helps explain this success: the WTO dispute settlement system's ability to evolve. Indeed, the WTO dispute settlement system has not remained static. Rather, the system has been evolving as each case raises new issues and poses new challenges.

Negotiations to reform the *Understanding on Rules and Procedures Governing the Settlement of Disputes* (DSU) have been ongoing for several years.[2] Some of the proposals that have been tabled seek to address perceived deficiencies in the system. Other proposals are more ambitious and would change the nature of the system. While the negotiations have not advanced as rapidly as initially hoped,[3] this does not seem to pose a threat to the functioning of the system. The system has been able to overcome, in practice, some of the deficiencies that have been identified. At the same time, the system continues to evolve in such a way that new solutions could be found for issues that may arise in the future.

The WTO dispute settlement system has been able to evolve because DSU rules provide a degree of flexibility to WTO Members. The ability to evolve is also linked to the fact that the DSU leaves the WTO adjudicative

The views expressed in this chapter are personal and do not reflect the views of the Appellate Body, the Appellate Body Secretariat, or the WTO.

1 See, for example, Consultative Board Report, 'The Future of the WTO', chapter 6.

2 For an overview of the DSU review negotiations and of the main proposals, see Valerie Hughes, 'The WTO dispute settlement system – from initiating proceedings to ensuring implementation: What needs improvement?', in Sacerdoti, Yanovich, and Bohanes, *The WTO at Ten*, pp. 193–234.

3 The Doha Ministerial Declaration called for the DSU reform negotiations to conclude in May 2003. The mandate of the negotiations has been extended and there is no longer a defined deadline for their conclusion.

bodies – that is, panels and the Appellate Body – some discretion in adopting their own working procedures. This chapter provides examples of how the WTO dispute settlement system has evolved in its first ten years of operation. It examines evolution linked to both the practice of WTO Members and the procedures of panels and the Appellate Body.

* * *

In some respects, the evolution of the WTO dispute settlement system is similar to that of its predecessor. Dispute settlement under the *General Agreement on Tariffs and Trade* (GATT) *1947* evolved over almost 50 years. The GATT 1947 contained essentially two provisions on dispute settlement, namely Articles XXII and XXIII. It began as a system of conciliation and gradually moved closer to adjudication.[4] The procedures developed under the GATT were codified in an understanding adopted in 1979 during the Tokyo Round.[5] Subsequently, much of what developed under the GATT as practice became the basis for the dispute settlement procedures agreed in the Uruguay Round in the form of the DSU, although with some significant changes.[6]

To an extent, it could be said that the potential for evolution of the WTO dispute settlement system is higher than that of the GATT. This is because dispute settlement activity is more intense in the WTO than it was under the GATT. In the first ten years of the WTO (1995–2004), there were 324 disputes formally initiated, 129 panels established, and 89 panel reports circulated.[7] In addition, the WTO dispute settlement system includes new forms of proceedings that did not exist in the GATT, such as appeals, arbitrations to determine the reasonable period of time under Article 21.3(c), arbitrations to examine the level of suspension of concessions under Article 22.6, and compliance proceedings under Article 21.5. These proceedings also saw intense activity in the first ten years of the WTO, during which time there were 59 Appellate Body reports

4 Georges Abi-Saab, 'The WTO dispute settlement system and general international law', in Rufus Yerxa and Bruce Wilson (eds), *Key Issues in WTO Dispute Settlement: The first ten years* (Cambridge, 2005), pp. 7–11.

5 Understanding Regarding Notification, Consultation, Dispute Settlement and Surveillance, BISD 26/210. Jackson refers to this as a 'restatement of procedures' (See John Jackson, *The World Trading System: The law and policy of international economic relations* (2nd edn, Cambridge, MA, 1997), p. 116).

6 For a discussion of some of the most important changes, see Jackson, *The World Trading System*, pp. 124–127.

7 Bruce Wilson, 'The WTO Dispute Settlement System and its Operation: A brief overview of the first ten years', in Yerxa and Wilson, *WTO: The first ten years*, pp. 20–21.

circulated, 19 arbitrations under Article 21.3(c), 9 arbitrations under Article 22.6, and 14 (out of the 89 total panel reports mentioned above) compliance panel reports circulated under Article 21.5.[8] Despite this intense activity, the evolution of dispute settlement procedures under the WTO has been gradual; the nature of the system has not changed.

* * *

In many instances, the evolution of the WTO dispute settlement system results from the initiative of WTO Members. Often this involves agreement between the parties to the dispute. At other times, it may result from initiatives by an individual WTO Member or a group of Members.

The obvious example of a practice involving agreement between the parties to the dispute relates to the issue of sequencing.[9] The issue first came up in the *EC – Bananas III* dispute and it has become one of the first issues to be identified as requiring changes to the DSU. In general terms, the sequencing issue relates to the question of how to coordinate requests for authorization to suspend concessions or other obligations under Article 22 of the DSU and examination of the WTO-consistency of a measure taken to comply with the rulings and recommendations of the Dispute Settlement Body (DSB) pursuant to Article 21.5 of the DSU.[10] Proposals have been made to resolve the sequencing issue since DSU reform was first discussed, but so far no change has been made to the DSU. In practice, however, WTO Members have been able to overcome the issue by mutual agreement whereby the requests for suspension of concessions and referral to an Article 21.5 panel are made simultaneously, but the retaliation procedures are suspended until the Article 21.5 procedures are concluded.[11] There is a second type of agreement whereby the parties agree to preserve a Member's right to request authorization to suspend concessions until after the Article 21.5 process is completed, even if this is after the expiry of the deadline foreseen in Article 22 of the DSU.[12]

Another example, which is more recent, relates to transparency. Panel meetings with the parties are closed to other WTO Members[13]

[8] Ibid, p. 21.

[9] For further information about sequencing and the proposals that have been made on this issue, see the contribution by Manabu Miyagawa, chapter 12 of this book.

[10] See WTO Secretariat, *A Handbook on WTO Dispute Settlement* (Cambridge, 2004), p. 85.

[11] See *WTO Handbook*, pp. 85–86. For an example of such an arrangement, see WT/DS245/10.

[12] Ibid., p. 86.

[13] As explained below, WTO Members that have reserved their rights as third parties are given an opportunity to present their views at a special session reserved for that purpose during the panel's first substantive meeting with the parties.

and to the public. Several WTO Members and non-governmental organizations have been calling for more openness in the WTO's dispute settlement procedures. This would include making the parties' submissions publicly available and opening the hearings to the general public. There are several proposals relating to transparency under consideration in the DSU negotiations.[14] In the meantime, however, the European Communities, Canada and the United States jointly requested that the panel hearing with the parties in an ongoing dispute be open to the public. The panel agreed and the first substantive meeting with the parties was transmitted live on closed circuit television to another room in the WTO building where the public could watch.[15] The panel hearing with the third parties remained closed because not all of the third parties agreed to open it. The panel recently announced that its second meeting would similarly be transmitted via closed circuit television.[16]

Transparency also serves as an example of how the procedures can evolve at the initiative of individual Members. Article 18.2 of the DSU states that, even though written submission to the panel or the Appellate Body are confidential, '[n]othing . . . shall preclude a party to the dispute from disclosing statements of its own positions to the public.' Several WTO Members, such as the United States,[17] make their submissions public and post them on internet. Some WTO Members who have been assisted by the Advisory Centre on WTO Law have also allowed their submissions to be posted on the Advisory Centre's website.[18] At the same time, this example illustrates the limits to what WTO Members can achieve acting individually. Some WTO Members have sought to promote transparency by requesting, pursuant to Article 18.2 of the DSU, that the other parties to the dispute provide a non-confidential summary of the information contained in their written submission. According to one experienced

[14] See, for example, the Further Contribution of the United States to the Improvement of the Dispute Settlement Understanding of the WTO Related to Transparency – Revised Legal Drafting, T/DS/W/86; and Contribution of Canada to the Improvement of the WTO Dispute Settlement Understanding – Communication from Canada, TN/DS/W/41.

[15] See WT/DS320/8 and WT/DS321/8.

[16] The announcement was posted on the WTO website: <http://www.wto.org/english/tratop_e/dispu_e/public_hearing_sep06_e.htm>.

[17] The United States' briefs are available at <http://www.ustr.gov/Trade_Agreements/Monitoring_Enforcement/Dispute_Settlement/WTO/Section_Index.html>.

[18] The Advisory Centre's website is <http://www.acwl.ch>.

practitioner, 'Members' responses to those requests have not always been satisfactory.'[19]

Remedies is an area where there has been interesting developments arising from the complaining parties acting individually or as a group. The most traditional form of suspension of concessions or other obligations in the WTO is to increase tariffs on imports of certain goods from the respondent WTO Member.[20] However, WTO Members have requested authorization to suspend concessions or other obligations in other ways. In *US – 1916 Act*, the European Communities sought authorization 'to suspend the application of the obligations under the GATT 1994 and the *Anti-Dumping Agreement* in order to adopt an equivalent regulation to the 1916 Act against imports from the United States.'[21] Not everyone agreed with this approach. Chile noted with concern that 'two wrongs don't make a right' and cautioned that this approach 'would give rise to an arms race, the outcome of which would be difficult to determine.'[22] In *US – Offset Act (Byrd Amendment)*, some of the complaining parties requested authorization to suspend obligations in an amount that would vary each year according to the amounts distributed under the Byrd Amendment.[23] The arbitrator accepted, and the DSB approved, suspension in the amount of 72 cents for each US dollar disbursed. Canada also requested authorization to suspend the requirement to make an injury determination in the context of anti-dumping investigation on United States imports.[24] In *US – FSC*, the European Communities opted for an incremental approach. After having received authorization to suspend concessions amounting to US$ 4 billion, the European Communities initially imposed an additional tariff of 5 per cent on a list of United States products, but indicated that the additional tariff would automatically increase by 1 per cent each month until it reached a ceiling of 17 per cent.[25]

[19] Daniel Brinza, 'DSU reform: If it is not broken – improve it?', in Sacerdoti, Yanovich, and Bohanes, *The WTO at Ten*, p. 249. Some WTO Members have proposed imposing a deadline for parties to provide non-confidential summaries of their written submissions. (See, for example the proposals of the European Communities and Japan, TN/DS/W/1 and TN/DS/W/32, respectively.)

[20] Under certain circumstances, a WTO Member may seek authorization to suspend concessions on services or intellectual property. (See Article 22.3 of the DSU.)

[21] WT/DS136/15, p. 2. Japan made a similar request.

[22] WT/DSB/M/117, para. 15.

[23] WT/DS234/25.

[24] Ibid.

[25] Council Regulation (EC) No. 2193/2003 of 8 December 2003 establishing additional customs duties on imports of certain products originating in the United States of America, OJ L 328/3.

One of the proposals that has been made in the context of DSU reform is the possibility for the collective enforcement of WTO obligations by all WTO Members *vis-à-vis* the defaulting Member.[26] To some extent, it could be said that WTO Members are already acting collectively in dispute settlement. Several disputes have been initiated by multiple WTO Members, which at times are acting in a coordinated manner.[27] Sometimes this coordination seems to extend to the implementation stage, with several WTO Members requesting authorization to suspend concessions simultaneously against the same respondent.[28]

An issue that has emerged recently relates to the lifting of countermeasures. The DSU contains no express rules on this issue, but provides that the suspension shall be temporary and only be applied until such time as the WTO-inconsistent measure has been removed. There is currently disagreement between the European Communities, on the one hand, and the United States and Canada, on the other, on whether the measures taken by the European Communities to comply with the recommendations and rulings of the DSB in the original *EC – Hormones* dispute are WTO-consistent. The United States and Canada refuse to lift their countermeasures because, in their view, the European Communities' measures are not fully consistent with the WTO agreements. Some considered that, in this situation, the European Communities should have sought an Article 21.5 panel.[29] The European Communities opted to request a new panel that will examine the WTO-consistency of the countermeasures being applied by Canada and the United States.[30]

It is beyond the scope of this chapter to examine whether joint complaints and enforcement by groups of WTO Members and these non-traditional examples of suspension of concessions may contribute to the efficient functioning of the dispute settlement system. These

[26] See Text for LDC Proposal on Dispute Settlement Understanding Negotiations, TN/DS/W/37, 22 January 2003; and Text for the African Group Proposals on Dispute Settlement Understanding Negotiations, TN/DS/W/42, 24 January 2003.

[27] Examples of recent disputes with multiple complainants include *US – Offset Act (Byrd Amendment)*, *EC – Export Subsidies on Sugar*, and *US – Steel Safeguards*.

[28] 'Five complainants seek retaliation against U.S. over Byrd law', *Inside U.S. Trade*, 16 January 2004, available at <http://www.insidetrade.com>.

[29] See Miyagawa, chapter 12 of this book.

[30] See Canada – Continued Suspension Of Obligations in the *EC – Hormones* Dispute, Request for the Establishment of a Panel by the European Communities, WT/DS321/6, 14 January 2005; and United States – Continued Suspension of Obligations in the EC – Hormones Dispute, Request for the Establishment of a Panel by the European Communities, WT/DS320/6, 14 January 2005.

developments, however, illustrate that the area of WTO remedies is still evolving.

The DSU allows WTO Members in certain instances to depart from the standard dispute settlement procedures.[31] WTO Members may opt for arbitration under Article 25 of the DSU as an alternative to the adjudication before dispute settlement panels and the Appellate Body. In addition, WTO Member may pursue other forms of alternative dispute resolution, such as mediation, good offices, and conciliation under Article 5 of the DSU. This flexibility has seldom been used by WTO Members, which continue to rely predominantly on panel and Appellate Body adjudication to resolve their disputes.[32]

Nevertheless, there is an instance where WTO Members chose to depart completely from the procedures available in the DSU and agreed to a *sui generis* form of arbitration pursuant to an annex to the Waiver Decision on the ACP-EC Partnership Agreement approved by the WTO Ministerial Conference at Doha.[33] According to that Waiver Decision, the European Communities, the ACP States, and a group of WTO Members who export bananas, followed a special form of arbitration to examine whether the envisaged rebinding of the EC tariff on bananas would result in at least maintaining total market access for most-favoured nation (MFN) banana suppliers. The special arbitration procedure provided a two-stage process, and it was undertaken by two Appellate Body Members acting in their individual capacity and by a former Canadian Ambassador to the WTO.[34]

* * *

The DSU leaves a degree of discretion to panels or the Appellate Body in drawing up their working procedures. These rules too have evolved as both panels and the Appellate Body have gained experience with their application.

As regards the Appellate Body, Article 17.9 of the DSU provides that 'Working procedures shall be drawn up by the Appellate Body in

[31] For a detailed discussion of the possibility of resorting to arbitration, see the contribution by Jan Bohanes and Hunter Nottage, chapter 9 of this book.

[32] According to Wilson, during the first ten years of the WTO, Members resorted to the good offices, mediation or arbitration provision of the DSU in only two instances (Wilson, 'The WTO and its Operation', p. 21).

[33] European Communities – The ACP-EC Partnership Agreement, Decision of 14 November 2001, WT/MIN(01)/15.

[34] Award of the Arbitrator, *EC – The ACP-EC Partnership Agreement*; Award of the Arbitrator, *EC – The ACP-EC Partnership Agreement II.*

consultation with the Chairman of the DSB and the Director-General, and communicated to the Members for their information.' The Appellate Body adopted the *Working Procedures for Appellate Review* (*Working Procedures*) in 1996. When the *Working Procedures* were circulated to Members of the WTO, the Chairman explained that the Appellate Body 'intend[ed] to keep [its] Working Procedures under constant review', and that it would not hesitate to amend them where it felt that 'a particular procedure could be improved in the light of [its] practical experience.'[35] The *Working Procedures* were last amended in January 2005.[36]

One of the most significant changes made to the *Working Procedures* relates to the participation of third parties.[37] Under the original version of the *Working Procedures*, third parties before a panel that wished to participate in the appeal were required to file a written submission. Some third parties sought permission to attend the oral hearing even though they had not filed a written submission. In response to these requests, the Appellate Body developed a practice of allowing such third participants to attend the oral hearing as 'passive observers'. Subsequently, the Appellate Body modified Rule 24 of the *Working Procedures* to facilitate third-party participation in appellate proceedings. Under the new version of Rule 24, third participants may choose not to file a written submission and, instead, may appear at the oral hearing and make an oral statement by simply notifying the Appellate Body Secretariat of their intention to do so. Although it may be too early to draw conclusions, it does appear that the change has led to an increase in participation of third parties in appellate proceedings.[38]

WTO panels do not have uniform working procedures. The DSU provides model working procedures for panels in Appendix 3, but panels may depart from them 'after consulting the parties to the dispute'.[39] The working procedures that are now routinely adopted by panels go beyond those provided in Appendix 3, and address issues that are not dealt with in Appendix 3. For instance, a panel's working procedures may establish deadlines for the parties to request preliminary rulings and for

[35] WT/AB/WP/W/1, 7 February 1996, p. 3. [36] WT/AB/WP/5, 4 January 2005.

[37] For a detailed discussion of the evolution of the *Working Procedures* since they were initially adopted in 1996, see Victoria J. Donaldson and Alan Yanovich, 'The Appellate Body's *Working Procedures for Appellate Review*', in Sacerdoti, Yanovich, and Bohanes, *The WTO at Ten*, pp. 386–423. [38] See *Appellate Body Annual Report for 2005*, p. 6.

[39] Article 12.1 of the DSU.

submitting factual evidence.[40] Another example is where parties submit only written comments on the interim report and do not request a further meeting of the panel with the parties. Each party is given an opportunity to comment in writing on the other party's comments on the interim report.

Some panels have also granted enhanced rights to third parties. Under the DSU, third parties are given the right to participate in a special session held at the time the panel has its first substantive meeting with the parties. In addition, the DSU provides that third parties will receive copies of the first written submission of the parties. In several cases (for example, *EC – Bananas III*), however, third parties have requested and have been granted the opportunity to attend also the second substantive meeting with the panel, and to receive copies of the parties' rebuttal submissions.

Panels and the Appellate Body have also confronted the absence of specific rules of evidence in the DSU. Gradually, panels and the Appellate Body have developed rules on the burden of proof and on various matters relating to the submission of evidence, including the treatment of business confidential information, a panel's right to seek information from any source, drawing adverse inferences from a party's refusal to submit evidence and the treatment of circumstantial evidence. Another issue that arose early on was whether WTO Members could be represented by private counsel. Since the Appellate Body responded affirmatively to this issue in *EC – Bananas III*, private counsel now appear regularly on behalf of WTO Members or form part of their delegations.

As Professor Georges Abi-Saab of the WTO Appellate Body has described it: 'Once established, institutions evolve according to their inner dynamics; international experience reveals that an entity, however ambiguous or lacunary its institutional makeup, once it perceives itself as entrusted with the exercise of the judicial function, evolves according to a legal genetic code towards greater judicialization.'[41] One would expect this evolution will continue as panels and the Appellate Body carry on performing the functions that they have been entrusted with under the DSU.

* * *

[40] See, for example, the working procedures for the panel in *US – Gambling*, which are attached as Annex A to the panel report. These provide that requests for a preliminary ruling must be filed by no later than the party's first written submission and that factual evidence should be submitted by no later than the first substantive meeting of the panel, except when the evidence is necessary for rebuttal or in order to answer questions.

[41] Georges Abi-Saab, 'The Appellate Body and Treaty Interpretation', in Sacerdoti, Yanovich, and Bohanes, *The WTO at Ten*, chapter 25, p. 456.

These examples illustrate that the WTO dispute settlement system has not remained static, but rather is constantly evolving. Change is not sudden and dramatic, it is a gradual evolution in response to problems as they arise. Even though change may be gradual, it is no less effective. Thanks to this evolution, the WTO dispute settlement system has been able to overcome some of the deficiencies that have been identified and to adapt to situations as they arise.

It is likely that the system will continue to adjust and evolve gradually. New issues will arise and the system should be able to deal with some of these on a case-by-case basis. Issues for which practical solutions have been found may no longer requires formal changes to the text of the DSU. When formal change is desirable, then the solutions found in practice should serve as a useful basis for reform as was the case under the GATT. When introducing formal changes to the DSU, however, it will be important to maintain sufficient flexibility for the system to adjust and evolve as new issues arise.

PART III

Asian Perspectives on WTO Dispute Settlement

11

East Asia in the WTO dispute settlement mechanism

CHULSU KIM

In Part II of this book, the authors discuss the accomplishments and future challenges facing the World Trade Organization (WTO) and its dispute settlement mechanism. In this chapter, I present my observations on the subject of East Asian participation in the dispute settlement mechanism of the WTO. By East Asia, I mean the region encompassing the five WTO Members of Northeast Asia (that is, Japan, China, Korea, Chinese Taipei, and Hong Kong, China) and the ten countries of the Association of Southeast Asian Nations (ASEAN) (namely, Brunei Darussalam, Cambodia, Indonesia, Laos, Malaysia, Myanmar, the Philippines, Singapore, Thailand, and Viet Nam).[1] As most countries in this region were latecomers to the multilateral trading system, their participation in the *General Agreement on Tariffs and Trade* (GATT) and its dispute settlement system was marginal. Their role in the WTO has increased considerably in all aspects of its work, including in its strengthened dispute settlement system. As most of the countries in East Asia are now WTO Members, their participation in the dispute settlement mechanism is likely to expand in the future.

In the GATT, East Asian Contracting Parties, except Japan, had limited participation in the dispute settlement system. They were involved more as respondents than as complainants. Only two East Asian countries other than Japan were involved in GATT dispute cases. Thailand had two disputes with the United States concerning tobacco, one in which Thailand was a complainant and the other in which it was a respondent. Korea, which joined the GATT in 1967, was challenged twice by the United States, on beef and polyacetal resins, and it brought a complaint against the European Communities on television sets.

[1] As of 31 December 2005, Laos and Viet Nam were not Members of the WTO. Both were in the process of negotiating their accessions.

Japan, on the other hand, brought 12 complaints mostly against anti-dumping measures by the United States and the European Communities, and it was challenged in 28 cases by the United States and the European Communities, most of which involved agriculture, textile, and leather import restrictions maintained by Japan. Whereas many cases were filed against Japan since it joined the GATT in 1955, Japan seldom brought a dispute to the GATT until the late 1980s. In the GATT, Japan seemed to have preferred to resolve the disputes through negotiation and compromise rather than adjudication, both as complainant and respondent. Further, even when the panels had been established, this practical and less legalistic approach appeared to have been favoured for resolving disptues. Thus, only 2 out of the 12 cases brought by Japan concluded with panel decisions. Similarly, among the 28 cases brought against Japan, only 6 cases ended with a substantive report by the panel.

In the GATT, East Asian Contracting Parties were hesitant litigators who preferred to resolve trade disputes through quiet and informal means. As respondents, they often had no choice but to follow legal procedures initiated by their trading partners; they initiated only a few cases on their own. This may reflect East Asian cultural aversion to open conflicts and legal settlements.

During the past ten years under the WTO system, however, East Asian Members have been much more active participants in the dispute settlement mechanism as in all other aspects of the WTO's work. Japan and Korea have been the most frequent complainants and respondents, but there has been an increased level of participation of developing countries in the region. In fact, the first WTO dispute case was brought in early 1995 by an East Asian country, Singapore, against Malaysia concerning an import prohibition on polyethylene and polypropylene.

As of 1 May 2006,[2] a total of 50 WTO complaints had been filed by East Asian Members and they had been challenged in 42 cases. Unlike in the GATT, East Asian WTO Members have been much more active as complainants than as respondents. Korea, Japan and Thailand were the most active complainants, with 13 cases for Korea, and 12 cases each for Japan and Thailand. In terms of number of cases filed as complainants, Korea ranks seventh, and Japan and Thailand both rank eighth, after the United States, the European Communities, Canada, Brazil, India, and Mexico. As

[2] The statistics that follow about East Asian participation in WTO dispute settlement are also current to 1 May 2006.

respondents, Japan was challenged most often with 15 cases, closely followed by Korea with 13 cases. In terms of the number of cases filed against them, Japan ranks fifth, and Korea ranks eighth after the United States, the European Communities, India, Argentina, Japan, Canada, and Mexico. While Japan and Korea participated in more than half of the cases involving East Asian countries, both as complainants and respondents, the other East Asian Members are becoming much more active in recent years.

Little less than half of all disputes brought by East Asian Members were against the United States with 24 cases, followed by the European Communities in a distant second with 7 cases. The disputes among the East Asian Members themselves were relatively few with seven cases. The subject matter of the East Asian complaints was principally the violation of the GATT 1994 and trade remedy measures taken by trading partners on steel, semi-conductors, textiles, and electronic products. More than half of the cases brought by East Asian Members were resolved through consultations. The East Asian Members won all but 2 of the 23 cases in which the panel report or the Appellate Body report was adopted.

The United States and the European Communities were also the preponderant complainants against East Asian Members with 20 and 12 cases, respectively. The complaints filed against East Asian Members targeted much more diverse areas, such as agriculture, sanitary and phytosanitary (SPS) measures, subsidies and countervailing measures, import licensing, trade-related investment measures, trade-related aspects of intellectual property rights, and anti-dumping measures, to name a few. Again, more than half of the completed cases brought against East Asian Members were resolved through consultations. As respondents, East Asian countries lost all but 3 out of the 18 cases in which the panel report or the Appellate Body report were adopted. Compared with other WTO Members, East Asian Members have good records of implementing panel or Appellate Body recommendations.

In the case of Japan, most of the cases it filed were directed at US anti-dumping measures, and the complaint was often jointly pursued with the European Communities. It also challenged successfully the automotive policies of the United States, Brazil, Indonesia, and Canada. As respondent, Japan was challenged most frequently by the United States and the European Communities, on issues related to domestic taxes, distribution services, and SPS measures for agricultural products. In December 2004, Korea challenged Japan's import quotas on laver.

As complainant, Korea has also successfully challenged US anti-dumping measures. Meanwhile, Korea was challenged in diverse areas, ranging from SPS, technical barriers to trade, government procurement, safeguards, domestic taxes, and retailing distribution systems. In the early years of the WTO, Korea tried to settle these complaints without resorting to legal procedures. However, as it gained more experience and won more cases, Korea has become determined to take a more legalistic approach to resolving trade disputes.

Thailand is one of the most active developing-country complainants in the WTO dispute settlement mechanism. While it has been challenged only once, it lodged 12 complaints mostly against the European Communities, but also against other developing countries on issues relating to market access for agricultural and textile products. The Philippines has filed four complaints against both developed and developing countries on import restrictions on agricultural products, and it has been challenged four times on import restrictions on automobiles, polypropylene, pork, and poultry. Other Members in the region, such as Indonesia, Malaysia, China, Chinese Taipei, and Singapore, have also participated in the WTO dispute settlement mechanism in a limited number of cases as complainants and respondents.

While East Asian countries have been involved in a substantial number of disputes in the WTO, it may be argued that they still cling to their non-litigious tradition of the past. This is evidenced by the increasing tendency to participate as co-complainants or third parties and the substantial number of disputes being resolved through consultations. In addition, the lack of expertise in WTO law, as well as the substantial legal costs of litigating in the WTO dispute settlement system, appear to be major obstacles for East Asian Members to bring their cases to the WTO, particularly for developing-country Members.

The East Asian Members have also actively participated in the negotiations on the reform of the *Understanding on Rules and Procedures Governing the Settlement of Disputes* (DSU) taking place since the late 1990s. They have so far made useful and constructive proposals, aimed at enhancing the efficiency and transparency of the WTO dispute settlement mechanism, particularly concerning the implementation phase of the current procedures. More specifically, Japan and Korea have submitted extensive proposals concerning Articles 21 and 22 of the DSU: China has made proposals with the aim of increasing the scope of third-party participation in panel proceedings; Malaysia's proposal relates to the litigation costs for developing countries.

The limited participation to date of China in the WTO dispute settlement system is surprising, to say the least. Since it joined the WTO in

December 2001, China has participated as a complainant in one case and has been named a respondent in four cases. Many had expected China to become embroiled in numerous WTO disputes, not only because China is likely to face many obstacles abroad in its exports, but also because it would not be easy for China to fully abide by the obligations it had undertaken at the time of accession. Some even feared that the Dispute Settlement Body (DSB) would be inundated with cases involving China. Almost four years later, these concerns have failed to materialize.

It appears that China still prefers to settle disputes in a quiet, practical, and informal way through bilateral consultations. In addition to financial constraints and lack of experience in WTO litigation, China's reluctance to use the WTO dispute settlement system seems to be deeply rooted in its culture as in other East Asian countries. Nevertheless, China's trading partners seem to recognize the fact that as a new Member of the WTO, China requires more time to adjust to the complex WTO rules. The restraint exercised by China's trading partners in terms of bringing WTO cases against China appears also to be motivated by the perception that bringing such cases would not be commercially advantageous.

It is not certain whether this situation will continue for long. While China's trading partners, especially powerful ones, will continue to accommodate China's wishes to approach trade disputes in a quiet, bilateral manner, where possible, they are likely to explore alternative methods of resolving disputes, such as through the WTO dispute settlement mechanism, when these bilateral contacts do not produce results. The level of discontent appears to be quite high among China's trading partners, for example, in the area of intellectual property rights protection. Therefore, it appears that pressure within China's trading partners to use the WTO mechanism for resolving disputes with China is likely to increase after China implements most of its accession terms in the next few years.

Given the explosive growth of China's economy and trade and the evolving nature of its economic system, more trade disputes with its trading partners seem inevitable. While China and its trading partners seem to prefer not to deal with trade disputes in a multilateral context at the moment, it is possible that disputes could move to the WTO dispute settlement system in the future. In fact, China seems to be preparing for this eventuality by participating in nearly all disputes as a third party, thereby gaining more experience in this field. As has been found by Japan and Korea in the last decade, the multilateral approach to dispute resolution under the WTO may even help China resolve trade issues in a more stable and less confrontational manner.

Another interesting aspect of the East Asian participation in the WTO dispute settlement system has been the relatively small number of disputes between countries within the region itself. There have been so far only six such cases. Given the economic dynamism of the region and the rapid *de facto* economic integration taking place in East Asia, a substantial increase in the number of trade disputes among the regional countries can be expected in the future, particularly among the three larger countries in Northeast Asia, namely, Japan, China, and Korea. As the relations among the three countries are also often aggravated by historical and political factors, the use of the WTO dispute settlement mechanism, through its more transparent and less confrontational process, may be particularly important in reducing tension and stabilizing trade relations among the three countries. The absence or the lack of effective dispute settlement procedures at the regional level also increases the importance of the WTO dispute settlement system.

The East Asian countries, except Japan, were relatively minor players in the GATT and its dispute settlement system. As their economic profiles have grown, they have become active participants in the WTO dispute settlement system. The importance of the WTO dispute settlement system is likely to be enhanced as China implements its WTO obligations and the region becomes more integrated economically. The WTO dispute settlement system, which has contributed to the stability of the world trading system and has helped make it more predictable, may play a similar role in the East Asian regional context as well.

12

Japan's perspectives on the present Dispute Settlement Understanding negotiations

MANABU MIYAGAWA

In this chapter, I offer my personal assessment of the ongoing negotiations to reform the *Understanding on Rules and Procedures Governing the Settlement of Disputes* (DSU), based on my participation in the negotiations from January 2004 to September 2005.

I. The dispute settlement system in the past ten years

More than 300 cases have been referred to the dispute settlement system of the World Trade Organization (WTO) in the past ten years. Japan has been a party in more than twenty cases; in half of the cases as a complaining party and in the other half as a responding party. I have had the privilege to participate in some of these cases, and have been involved in the different phases of dispute settlement, including: consultations, the panel, the Appellate Body, the compliance panel, the arbitration, and most recently, the decision to suspend concessions and other obligations, which was the first time Japan took retaliatory measures in ten years. I have come to firmly believe that the present dispute settlement system, as a whole, is a masterpiece created with great wisdom by the original negotiators and cared for with much dedication and enthusiasm by WTO Members, panelists, members of the Appellate Body, and the WTO Secretariat.

The many benefits that WTO Members have received from the system include several significant institutional advantages. First, expansion of policy alternatives and faster solution of disputes. Secondly, accumulation of jurisprudence. Finally, increasing collaboration between diplomats, lawyers and law professors.

1. The dispute settlement system has expanded policy alternatives for WTO Members and accelerated the process of solving trade problems

First, the dispute settlement system has strengthened the multilateral approach to solving specific bilateral trade issues, which in the past had tended to be resolved through negotiations between the disputing countries only. I think that, thanks to the dispute settlement system, some bilateral trade problems have been solved without a prolonged bilateral negotiation, which is usually complicated by non-trade interests, such as domestic politics, legacies from the bilateral history, or sometimes even by military and security considerations. Trade disputes under the WTO dispute settlement system may not be totally free from those non-trade concerns, but, in comparison, the disputes can be dealt with from an almost purely factual and legal perspective. There are some recent examples of effective solution of bilateral trade issues through the WTO dispute settlement mechanism, such as in *Japan – Apples*. In that case, following the panel's and the Appellate Body's rulings and recommendations about the Japanese phytosanitary measures for imported apples from the United States, the governments of both countries reached a mutually satisfactory solution eliminating the excessive measures, which were not supported by scientific evidence and deemed to be inconsistent with the relevant WTO agreements. Also, in another recent dispute between Japan and the United States, the United States decided to abolish the 1916 Antidumping Act, which was ruled to be inconsistent with the corresponding WTO agreement.

Without the WTO's effective dispute settlement system, there would be more futile bilateral negotiations that would not bring about solutions for the disputing parties. From the viewpoint of a WTO Member, this has certainly provided an expanded list of policy alternatives to address trade disputes, that is, whether to go for the WTO dispute settlement procedures and/or to continue bilateral negotiations. Actually, in some cases, a WTO Member can calculate what would be the possible combined effects of the WTO dispute settlement procedure and of simultaneous bilateral negotiations at each of the different stages of the dispute settlement mechanism, such as consultations, panel proceedings (before and after the issuance of an interim report), the appellate stage, and so on. Accordingly, a WTO Member can craft the most suitable litigation and negotiation strategy based on the most appropriate allocation of diplomatic and human resources.

2. *Abundant jurisprudence accumulated in the past ten years*

Secondly, the dispute settlement system has accumulated significant jurisprudence, which can be relied upon not only during the panel and Appellate Body process, but also before having recourse to the dispute settlement procedures. For example, this jurisprudence can be relied on in domestic decision-making because the relevant jurisprudence can indicate the likelihood of success of a potential case. Thus, the existence of such jurisprudence has improved the security and predictability of the multilateral trading system. In particular, the rulings made by the Appellate Body have been repeatedly cited in the written submissions of the disputing parties and in the reports of both panels and the Appellate Body, thus greatly contributing to accumulation of WTO jurisprudence. After ten years, thanks to this case-law, it has become more predictable, in some cases, to see if one can win the case before initiation of the dispute settlement process.

Having said that, the possibility of predicting the outcome, even if the prediction were to be correct at the end of the day, does not prevent a WTO Member from choosing to defend a measure in the context of dispute settlement procedures when there are strong interests supported by some domestic constituencies. It can happen both at the panel and appellate stages, for example, by appealing after complete defeat before the panel. There is also an extreme recent case in which a measure of a defending party was ruled to be inconsistent with the WTO agreements both by the panel and Appellate Body. However, the party was compelled, because of strong pressure from the domestic constituencies, to seek an extension of the reasonable period of time for implementation, and even to claim that the covered agreement should be amended in the WTO rules negotiations so that the inconsistent measure should become consistent. This is problematic.

3. *Collaboration between diplomats, lawyers, and law professors*

Thirdly, the WTO dispute settlement system has promoted collaboration between trade diplomats, lawyers and law professors. The operation of the system is carried out by a balanced coordination among those three players. Having said that, at the conceptual level, there has always been tension between different schools of thought; on the one hand, those who believe in a more rapid 'legalization' of the system (hereinafter, the 'legalization school'), and on the other hand, those who are convinced of the advantages of retaining the elements of bilateral negotiation through the exercise of the 'sovereignty' of the respective member States, or in other words, through Member control (hereinafter, the 'sovereignty school'). At a glance, such different views might seem theoretical, but, in reality, this is an important point for any DSU negotiator. I think that many negotiators spend some time contemplating this basic question before starting to draft specific proposals or responses to the issues on the table.

All in all, the dispute settlement system has evolved in a positive manner, largely driven by this good coordination among the three players despite the conceptual tension dividing the different schools of thought. Hence, it seems appropriate to view how the present negotiations on improvement and clarification of the DSU would proceed in the context of such unique evolution, driven both by interactions among the major players and the conceptual tension between the 'legalization' and 'sovereignty' schools.

II. Overall assessment of the current DSU negotiations[1]

Given the remarkable overall record of the dispute settlement system in the past ten years, one might still wonder why the WTO Members need negotiations to improve and clarify the present text of the DSU. In fact, the negotiations, in which Japan has actively participated since 1998, have not led to a single change in the DSU. As someone said, 'if it ain't broke, don't fix it'. That is the sentiment which I have noticed is widely shared among many fellow negotiators of the DSU.

At the same time, another sentiment of the DSU negotiators, if I may try to describe it, is that 'even if it is not broken, let's try to improve it, where possible'. This sentiment arises from the fact that there have been certain procedural deficiencies in the DSU that each Member has had to cope with while utilizing the system in the past ten years. When a WTO Member points to some problems in the DSU, such an assertion is often based not only a systemic concern, but also on the actual experiences from specific cases as a disputing or third party. Views based on both systemic concerns and direct experiences often have the most persuasive power.

[1] For a comprehensive overview of the DSU negotiations, see Valerie Hughes, 'The WTO dispute settlement system – From initiating proceedings to ensuring implementation: What needs improvement?', in Sacerdoti, Yanovich, and Bohanes, *The WTO at Ten*, chapter 12.

1. *Focused approach*

Now let me turn to the ongoing negotiations. In 2005, there were seven meetings of the Special Session of the Dispute Settlement Body (DSB), in most of which I participated, and momentum was gained in terms of the contents of the proposals and WTO Members' commitment to the negotiation. As of the end of 2005, there were about eight specific topics and related proposals on the negotiation table: remand, sequencing, post-retaliation, third-party rights, additional guidance to WTO adjudicative bodies, panel composition, time-savings, and transparency.[2]

This is a realistic number of proposals which allows WTO Members to engage in the negotiation with a view to starting a text-based discussion. There should not be a deadline that is too strict and beyond which the Members will not be allowed to submit new proposals. However, in order to conclude the negotiation at an appropriate time, it is necessary and practical to have a focused agenda that can be translated into a draft text of amendments.

2. *Constructive discussion – broader participation?*

There seem to be several reasons why the current negotiations have been revitalized gradually. First, there is the continued commitment and good will of participating WTO Members, the Chairman and the Secretariat. Constructive exchange of views on the aforesaid eight topics has taken place both in formal and informal modes. Secondly, movement in the overall Doha Development Agenda negotiations has affected the DSU negotiations indirectly, but positively, notwithstanding that the DSU negotiations are independent from the single undertaking.

However, it is difficult to evaluate the degree of participation in the negotiations by a broader circle of WTO Members. The negotiations have been open and transparent to all the Members of the WTO, and many countries have participated in the negotiations actively. Nevertheless, some Members, particularly some developing-country Members, have not participated in the meetings. It is very important to assess correctly and objectively what the absence of some Members from the negotiations would mean and entail for future stages of the negotiation involving discussion of a draft text of amendments tabled by the Chairman. As of the end of September 2005, this was hard to predict. It is worth mentioning that conscious efforts to resume dialogue with some developing-country

[2] Report by the Chairman to the Trade Negotiations Committee, TN/DS/12, 21 July 2005.

Members have been made. I will touch upon this point in section IV below.

III. Some major issues and priorities for Japan

As I mentioned earlier, there should not be too strict a deadline beyond which Members will not be allowed to submit new proposals. Against such background, among the eight topics mentioned in the Chairman's report to the Trade Negotiations Committee, there are a couple of important issues for Japan.

1. Sequencing and post-retaliation

Among the eight topics, there are two proposals with respect to which Japan is a joint proponent together with another WTO Member.

Sequencing

The proposal on 'sequencing' seeks to clarify the sequence between a compliance panel's determination under Article 21.5 of the DSU and the authorization to suspend concessions by the DSB. Currently, ad hoc arrangements between the disputing parties are made to resolve this matter. For example, in the summer of 2004, Japan and the United States agreed in writing to procedures relating to sequencing in *Japan – Apples*, following adoption of the reports of the panel and Appellate Body in that case.[3] There are other examples where similar procedures were agreed by the parties and applied successfully. Our proposal would be to codify such practice, thereby improving the predictability and transparency of the dispute settlement procedures.

The present proposal on 'sequencing' is not new. 'Sequencing' has been discussed by WTO Members for a long time. For example, Japan, Canada, Costa Rica, the Czech Republic, Ecuador, the European Communities and its member States, Hungary, Korea, New Zealand, Norway, Peru, Slovenia, Switzerland, Thailand, and Venezuela made a joint proposal in 1999 before the Seattle Ministerial Meeting.[4] The present proposal has basically built on this and other past discussions and proposals. Therefore, it can be assumed that very strong support exists for the idea of codifying 'sequencing'. Reflecting such systemic interest shared by many

[3] See WT/DS245/10. [4] WT/MIN(99)/8.

Members, there have been other proposals submitted on 'sequencing', and both formal and informal discussions are under way among the proponents in search of an agreed view on the specific points in each proposal. For example, we believe that in light of the provisions of the DSU that set out the types of requests that can be made, and the jurisprudence of the past ten years, the right to request the establishment of a compliance panel should be given to the complaining party only, whereas there is a different view that such right can be given to either the complaining or responding party.

Post-retaliation

The proposal on 'post-retaliation' seeks to create a procedure to cease the suspension of concessions after it has been authorized. There is no established mechanism through which a WTO Member that has been subject to suspension of concessions can challenge and remove a previously granted DSB authorization to suspend obligations once that Member has achieved compliance. There seems to be growing support for the need to add such procedure to the DSU.

2. Transparency

The panel process is conducted on a confidential basis. Proposals on transparency have been made that seek to open this process to the public. Japan believes that this issue is quite important. There are, roughly speaking, two forms of transparency under discussion; one is transparency with respect to parties' written submissions and the other involves opening the hearings. Transparency for the panel hearing is particularly contentious, and some Members have expressed strong opposition to this proposal arguing that the government-to-government nature of the WTO dispute settlement mechanism must be preserved.

On 12–15 September 2005, the very first open hearing took place in the *US – Continued Suspension* and *Canada – Continued Suspension* disputes. The hearing was opened to the public in response to a joint request by the disputing parties and about 200 people watched the panel proceedings through a closed circuit system. I have heard mostly positive accounts of this first trial, not only from the disputing parties, but also from those who watched the proceedings. It is reasonable to predict that the number of open panels will gradually increase driven by similar requests by the disputing parties and that this will happen even while the

DSU negotiations are ongoing. In addition, there are WTO Members that already publish their written submissions on the internet. In 2005, Japan published, for the first time, the briefs it had submitted in a WTO dispute. These briefs had been submitted before the WTO panel in the *US – Zeroing (Japan)* dispute.[5]

Given its sensitivity, debate on this issue will be one of the crucial factors that will affect the eventual outcome of the negotiation.

3. *Panel composition*

Selection of panelists under the present DSU sometimes has been problematic. The selection takes, on average, much longer than the 20 days stipulated by the DSU. This is because the disputing parties are entitled to express preferences on the candidates suggested by the Secretariat. In the past, Japan has participated in disputes that have involved such a prolonged selection process. Many WTO Members seem to admit that this is problematic and some proposals have been made such as, for example, the establishment of a permanent roster of panelists.[6]

An opinion by the former Chairman of the Appellate Body, Professor Claus-Dieter Ehlermann, is a useful reference on this point. He has stated:

> It is my view therefore highly desirable to modify the actual panel system and to guarantee structurally the stability of panels and, thus, the independence of their members. Two avenues should be actively explored. One is the establishment of a standing panel with members appointed for a certain number of years, following the example of the Appellate Body. In order to allow for a certain specialization, the standing panel could be composed of different sections (divisions) with expert panelists. Another, less ambitious reform would be to establish a limited list of potential panel members, which should however not be too large. Panelists would have to be chosen from that limited list.[7]

The issue of panel composition will remain an important one in the DSU negotiations. If a meaningful reform could be agreed, it would represent substantial progress for the system.

[5] See <http://www.mofa.go.jp/policy/economy/wto/ds/index.html> and <http://www.meti.go.jp/english/policy/index_externaleconomicpolicy.html>.

[6] See, for example, the proposal of the European Communities, TN/DS/W/38.

[7] Claus-Dieter Ehlermann, 'Six Years on the Bench of the "World Trade Court", Some Personal Experiences as a Member of the Appellate Body of the World Trade Organization' (2002) 36 *Journal of World Trade*, 605–639, 628.

IV. What will be the key elements for the successful conclusion of the present negotiations?

Since 1998, many proposals have been tabled, and most of the major proposals were included in the draft text prepared, in May 2003, by the former Chairman of the DSB Special Session. The draft text in itself was a comprehensive list of what could be amended in the present DSU. However, the draft text contained too many points and brackets, and failed to create sufficient momentum to conclude the negotiations.

Based on the recognition of the shortcomings of such an overly comprehensive approach, and taking into account the stock of previous discussions and proposals, the present negotiations, which resumed in a meaningful way in 2004, are taking a more self-restrained and focused approach. Members who have made proposals have examined their drafts carefully before submission and have had informal exchanges of views with other Members. Therefore, the current proposals on the eight topics mentioned earlier are more focused in terms of the number of topics covered, but also in terms of their quality. This is a positive aspect of the negotiation process, which might lead to a successful conclusion of the negotiation in the not so distant future.

However, certain other issues may cause difficulties. First, development issues will be a crucial element toward the end of the negotiations. This issue has the potential to bring the overall negotiation to a stalemate or to lead to complete failure, if it is not treated appropriately. Secondly, two different schools of thought, that is, the 'legalization' and 'sovereignty' schools have different views on some specific issues, such as transparency and panel composition among others. As I mentioned at the outset of the chapter, this is a fundamental issue which affects the overall direction and the objectives of the negotiation. Thirdly, there are different degrees of ambition with regard to the problem of compliance with DSB rulings and recommendations. The compliance issue is important, but, unlike the first two issues, this element would not jeopardize the overall negotiation.

1. Development issues – improved access to the dispute settlement system

The DSU already includes a number of provisions addressing the special needs of developing and least-developed countries (LDCs). However, there are some proposals from developing countries that address their difficulties in using the system because of a lack or shortage of human and financial resources.

In the recent negotiations, the Chairman perceived that '[i]n respect of the special and differential treatment proposals referred to the DSB Special Session in May 2003, it has been agreed that, in reporting to the General Council, I would propose that the Special Session report further at a later stage when our work is more advanced.'[8]

2. 'Legalization' or 'sovereignty (Member control)'?

The DSU has already led to a considerable advancement in terms of the 'legalization' of the system that existed under the period of the *General Agreement on Tariffs and Trade* (GATT). As pointed out by many experts in this area, such legalization includes introduction of the negative consensus principle, establishment of the Appellate Body, rules on the suspension of concessions and other obligations, that is, retaliatory measures, and so on. As for the desirability of further legalizing the present system, there seem to be differing views among the negotiators of WTO Members.

Some relevant issues that arise in connection with the different perspectives of the 'legalization' and 'sovereignty' schools are discussed below. There is no overall single answer to this 'legalization' or 'sovereignty' question from the viewpoint of the users of the system.

Consultations

Consultations have been effective under the DSU. In the past ten years, more than half of the cases were solved or at least terminated in the course of the consultations. That means that some consultations achieve substantive results, while others are merely formalistic. Japan has been a party to both kinds of consultations. One of the reasons why the disputing parties sometimes prefer to engage in substantive discussion at this stage is that they consider that it offers a better chance of reaching a mutually satisfactory agreement than the stages that follow where the parties have already submitted specific factual and legal claims before the panel. The decision whether to proceed to the establishment of the panel primarily depends on the nature of each dispute. But there may also be different cultural values between WTO Members from different regions

[8] Report by the Chairman to the Trade Negotiations Committee, TN/DS/12, 21 July 2005, para. 4.

of the world. In some regions, one might tend to attach more importance to reaching solutions through consultations, and in other regions it may be considered that it is better to proceed faster to the panel stage because it offers a better opportunity to solve the problem. Japan has recently become a responding party in a case brought by Korea. As of the end of 2005, there were only two cases in which Japan was a disputing party against other Asian countries, out of more than twenty cases brought by Japan. It is premature to make general observations, but, I would suggest that there seems to be an inherent cultural value among Asian countries attaching greater importance to the function of consultations. It seems to imply that Asians are culturally more cautious in terms of avoiding the possibility of undermining the function and usefulness of the WTO consultations.

There is another relevant question that may be viewed from the perspective of the debate between the 'legalization' and 'sovereignty' schools of thought. The DSU gives discretion to a responding party to accept whether other WTO Members who have so requested can participate in the consultations. One question on the table is whether the DSU should be amended so that a responding party must either accept the requests of all of the WTO Members wishing to join the consultations or reject all of them, rather than having discretion to accept some, but not others. An automatic admission of all parties to the consultation seems to be a more 'legalized' approach, while allowing the responding party to pick and choose, as stipulated in the present DSU, seems to respect WTO Member control of the process. On this particular point, Japan has expressed its preference for the latter approach, that is, the status quo under the DSU.

Panel

There are some proposals that seem to imply further 'legalization' of the DSU. One of the most relevant questions is whether the present ad hoc selection process of panelists should be amended in favour of the establishment of a permanent roster of panelists. As mentioned in section III.3 above, those who favour a permanent roster of panelists are driven by the delays in the selection of panelists under the present procedures, and they hope that a panel roster will improve the quality of panel reports. Creation of a panel roster would be another step in the process of 'legalization' of the system. However, if effective control is maintained through the DSB, one can also argue that a standing panel would imply 'legalization' under the appropriate 'sovereign' control of WTO Members.

Appellate Body

As of the end of 2005, the Appellate Body had circulated 73 reports. It is the 'highest court' in the WTO dispute settlement system, and the jurisprudence developed in the reports of the Appellate Body has strengthened the dispute settlement system. There is the 90-day deadline for circulation of Appellate Body reports, which is shorter than the time given to panels. In most cases, this deadline has been strictly observed. It is widely perceived that the Appellate Body has been the most successful part of the dispute settlement system. One of the institutional elements, which has been conducive to success, is said to be 'collegiality'; all seven Appellate Body members discuss every appeal, even though only three Appellate Body members hear and decide an appeal. 'Collegiality' has ensured 'consistency and coherence in decision-making', and has allowed the Appellate Body 'to draw on the individual and collective expertise of the Members', in accordance with Rule 4(1) of the *Working Procedures for Appellate Review*[9] (*Working Procedures*).

Maybe due to such an excellent record, there are few proposals in the context of the DSU negotiations that attempt to reform the Appellate Body. There are, however, a couple of relevant issues related to the appellate process, which can also be analyzed from the perspective of the debate between the 'legalization' and 'sovereignty' schools of thought.

First, there are proposals to introduce a remand procedure. Article 17.6 of the DSU stipulates that appeals 'shall be limited to issues of law covered in the panel report and legal interpretations developed by the panel'. When factual findings by the panel and undisputed facts are insufficient, the Appellate Body cannot complete its legal analysis. The proposals under negotiations aim to address this deficiency.[10] Japan is not a proponent of any proposal on remand procedure. We are aware of the merits of the proposals, but have some concern about possible delays in the process that may be caused by a remand procedure. Introduction of a remand procedure could further 'legalize' the dispute settlement system, but it would also largely depend on how the procedure is utilized on day- to-day basis.[11]

[9] WT/AB/WP/5. [10] See TN/DS/W/38 and TN/DS/W/56.

[11] There are other proposals relating to the Appellate Body such as judicial recess and participation by third parties.

V. Beyond the conclusion of the present negotiations

1. Prospects of the present DSU negotiations

If all the aforementioned elements are addressed and there is the political will to conclude the DSU negotiations, it would be perhaps late 2006 or early 2007 when we would finally see the completion of the negotiation. Nobody can predict the exact scope of the agreed amendments, but I hope that the final package is substantial, without necessarily having to be too broad or comprehensive. In case there is no agreement despite the efforts made by WTO Members, I personally think that there should be some reference document that compiles all the formal and informal proposals made by WTO Members, as well as uncompleted draft Chairman's texts, and an annex with the transcripts of the negotiation meetings. Some present and past proposals are well thought out, and if they are not reflected in the final amendments resulting from the present negotiations, they deserve to be kept as they may be useful to future users of the dispute settlement system. Moreover, in another ten years' time, there might be a new demand for reviewing the DSU, and then future negotiators will be able to build on what has been achieved in the present negotiations.

2. What will happen in the coming ten years?

Thus, the dispute settlement system seems to be evolving all of the time. What will happen in the coming decade?

First of all, in Asia, as its economies expand and the economic relations between countries in the region become stronger and more mature, it is likely for Asian WTO Members to have more frequent recourse to the WTO dispute settlement system to solve their disputes. We have already seen such a tendency or correlation between the maturity of economic relations and the frequency of having recourse to the dispute settlement system. This is, for example, evident in the number of cases between the European Communities and the United States, and between Japan and the United States. Maybe some Asian WTO Members will try to utilize the consultations stage more fully than before, partly because of a culture that favours negotiation in this region and partly because of geographical proximity. If the number of frequent users of the system increases, this will have implications for the future review of the DSU in another ten years' time. Naturally, the more frequently one uses the dispute settlement system, the more expertise one will accumulate, but one will require more human resources. I believe that Asian countries, including Japan, will continue their efforts to strengthen such human resources not only in the governmental sectors, but also in the educational and business sectors, in order to accommodate increasing demand for solving trade issues through the WTO dispute settlement system.

Secondly, it should be noted that there are different avenues for addressing trade disputes between governments. These avenues include the WTO dispute settlement system, but also bilateral and regional fora. For example, in Asia, more bilateral free trade agreements (FTAs) are being negotiated and these often incorporate certain dispute settlement mechanisms. Japan has recently negotiated FTAs with Singapore, the Philippines, Thailand, Korea, and Indonesia, and the list of possible partners seems to be expanding. In ten years' time, we will have a better understanding of the achievements and deficiencies of such bilateral dispute settlement mechanisms and of the relationship between the WTO dispute settlement system and those FTA dispute settlement mechanisms. On a regional basis, there are some regional groups to which Asian countries belong, such as the Asia-Pacific Economic Cooperation (APEC) forum, the Association of Southeast Asian Nations (ASEAN) plus three, and so on. Compared with the European Union, for example, these regional groups do not have such developed institutions, including with respect to dispute settlement, but they have already provided ample opportunities for regional consultations on various trade issues at all the levels, which could provide a meaningful step for the creation of a regional dispute settlement system in the future.

3. *Jurisprudence and compliance*

The continuous evolution of the WTO dispute settlement system will remain of special importance. From a user's perspective, one of the most relevant and significant achievements of the dispute settlement system is the accumulation of jurisprudence, which is frequently relied on by WTO Members, panels and the Appellate Body. The Appellate Body's reports are at the core of such jurisprudence and I believe that this should remain so in the coming decade as well. In other words, with regard to maintaining the quality of the case-law through appropriate rulings and recommendations, we can be rather optimistic about the future of the WTO dispute settlement mechanism.

One possible concern, which might cloud the prospects of the dispute settlement system, involves the issue of compliance. It is exaggerated to say that the overall record of compliance in the first ten years has been unsatisfactory. However, there have been a few symbolic cases, in which compliance was not sufficient or delayed. Every WTO Member has its own domestic agenda and difficulties, and it might be too simplistic to insist that 'a rule is a rule and one should obey it', and any Member can be tempted to excuse itself from complying with the rulings and recommendations of the DSB, particularly when there are strong domestic constituencies putting pressure on the administration not to comply with unfavourable decisions. This potential problem should be addressed before it becomes a real threat to the proper functioning of the dispute settlement system. It is crucial particularly because the next decade is likely to see more frequent users of the system. The DSU negotiation is one of the avenues to strengthen compliance, but perhaps more importantly, it seems that those WTO Members, which have utilized and thus most benefited from this precious system in the first decade since its inception, including Japan, have a moral responsibility to show the best possible compliance records. This should be the most effective way to enable the system to flourish in the years to come.

13

A review of some appellate decisions: law, policy, and economics in dispute settlement

MITSUO MATSUSHITA

Panels and the Appellate Body of the World Trade Organization (WTO) have sometimes been criticized as being too textual or literal in interpreting WTO agreements and, at the same time, as deviating too much from the texts of those agreements. These criticisms have been directed particularly at the Appellate Body because it has the power to make the final judgment on the issue in a case. Although such criticisms are not entirely unfounded, the Appellate Body has tried to be faithful to the wording of the WTO agreements and, at the same time, to accomplish the basic policy goal of those agreements. It is indeed difficult to reconcile textual or literal interpretations as mandated by the *Understanding on Rules and Procedures Governing the Settlement of Disputes* (DSU) and retain some flexibility in interpretation so that the dispute settlement system of the WTO can deal with the ever-evolving area of international trading relations and new issues arising thereunder.

Also, one may find that, in some cases, the holdings of the Appellate Body somehow lack economic rationale. Although the Appellate Body is not required to interpret WTO agreements according to economic principles, one might question the meaningfulness of a finding of the Appellate Body if it makes little sense economically because, after all, the WTO agreements were designed to promote good economic policy and performance in trading nations in one way or another.

In the following passages, a few important holdings of the Appellate Body will be taken up and analysed.[1]

[1] For detailed studies on the interpretive methodology applied to the WTO agreements, see Michael Lennard, 'Navigating by the Stars: Interpreting the WTO Agreements' (2002) 5(1) *Journal of International Economic Law*, 17–89; and Wolfgang Weiss, 'Security and Predictability under WTO Law' (2003) 2 *World Trade Review*, 183–219.

I. The Appellate Body and the *Vienna Convention*

Article 3.2 of the DSU states that the customary rules of interpretation of public international law reflected in the *Vienna Convention on the Law of Treaties*[2] (*Vienna Convention*) should be relied upon when interpreting WTO agreements. The Appellate Body always cites Article 31 (and sometimes Article 32) of the *Vienna Convention* when deciding cases. Article 31 requires that a treaty interpreter interpret a provision of a treaty in accordance with (i) the ordinary meaning, (ii) context, and (iii) the objectives of the treaty. Articles 3.2 and 19.2 of the DSU state that panels and the Appellate Body cannot add or reduce rights and obligations of Members. It is important for panels and the Appellate Body to follow the textual meaning of a provision of an agreement because the text of an agreement reflects the intentions of the drafters of the agreement. The Appellate Body is charged with the responsibility of interpreting provisions of WTO agreements but not of making new policy or a new law.

II. Policy considerations in the decision-making of the Appellate Body

Should policy considerations be taken into account?

There is continuity between law and policy. When a provision of an agreement is couched in general language and allows latitude for different interpretations, policy considerations can be taken into account to decide which interpretation should be adopted. Policy issues become more and more important as one progresses to higher stages of the judiciary process. The Appellate Body inevitably must consider the basic policy of a WTO agreement when interpreting the provisions of that agreement.

Article 31 of the *Vienna Convention* states that the objectives of a treaty should be taken into consideration when interpreting the treaty. Objectives in this sense are expressed in the texts of the treaty in question. Therefore, there may not be much difference between interpreting, on the one hand, a treaty on the basis of the wording in the ordinary sense of the term and the context used in the treaty, and interpreting, on the other hand, the treaty on the basis of the objectives of the treaty. The real issue is probably that the objectives of a treaty may not be clear and there may be more than one objective in one treaty. Also, the objectives in any one

[2] Done at Vienna, 23 May 1969, in force 27 January 1980, 1155 UNTS 331; 8 International Legal Materials 679, UKTS (1980) 58.

treaty may not be in perfect harmony with each other. For example, the Preamble of the *Agreement on the Application of Sanitary and Phytosanitary Measures* (*SPS Agreement*) states that (i) the right of Members to take necessary measures to protect the life and health of humans, animals, and plants within its domain should be respected, and (ii) national SPS standards should be harmonized with international standards. Both objectives are the policy goals envisaged by the drafters of the *SPS Agreement.* It takes creative thinking on the part of the Appellate Body to balance out these two requirements in interpreting the *SPS Agreement.* Sometimes it is necessary for the Appellate Body to look beyond the specific language of a WTO agreement in the entire WTO scheme to find the basic objective of an agreement. The Appellate Body has to take into consideration the underlying principles and policies of the WTO as a whole when interpreting a provision of an agreement.

In the following pages, some of the reports of the Appellate Body are examined to see if policy considerations have influenced the judicial decisions.

The EC – Tariff Preferences case (2004)

In *EC – Tariff Preferences*, the issue was whether the term 'non-discriminatory' in the Enabling Clause should mean identical treatment for *all* developing-country Members or whether different tariff treatment for *some* developing-country Members is allowed. The European Communities granted a preferential treatment in tariffs to some developing-country Members that had drug trafficking problems. India was excluded from this favoured group and so brought a claim against the European Communities. The Panel decided that the term 'non-discrimination' in the Enabling Clause means identical treatment of all developing-country Members and found the European Communities' measure to be inconsistent with Article I of the *General Agreement on Tariffs and Trade* (GATT) *1994* and not justified under the Enabling Clause. The Appellate Body reversed this finding and stated that the Enabling Clause allows for different treatment of some developing-country Members in special circumstances, with a view to meeting special needs, as long as such treatment is conditioned on the availability of the same treatment to all eligible beneficiaries of the Generalized System of Preferences (GSP).

The ruling of the Appellate Body allows for more flexibility to developed-country Members when granting tariff preferences according to the needs of some developing-country Members in similar situations, and to achieve some policy objectives such as the fight against drugs and mitigating environmental degradation. The Appellate Body arrived at this conclusion by combining textual analysis of the relevant provisions of the Enabling Clause with a review of the context of these provisions

An exclusively textual analysis of the term 'non-discrimination' can lead panels and the Appellate Body to conclude that either identical treatment must be accorded to all developing-country Members, or alternatively, they can conclude that some discretion is given to a developed-country Member when granting preferential tariff treatment to limit the beneficiaries to a certain group of developing-country Members. If a text can be interpreted in several ways, mere textual analysis would give little guidance to panels and the Appellate Body in arriving at the right conclusion. It is a sense of policy consideration incorporated in the agreement that should be taken into account in interpreting ambiguous terms. In the *EC – Tariff Preferences* case, the Appellate Body seems to have accomplished a policy goal that is one of the important objectives of the WTO, that is, the promotion of the interests of developing-country Members.

Of course, there may be contrary views as to the advantages and drawbacks of such an interpretation. One might argue that the interpretative approach adopted by the Appellate Body gives too much discretion to developed-country Members in deciding to which developing countries they would grant preferential tariff treatment under a GSP scheme, which would, in turn, lead to discriminatory treatment. This interpretation would subject developing countries to the caprice of developed-country Members. At worst, the Appellate Body's interpretation could be used by developed-country Members as a carrot to induce developing countries to adopt policies that the tariff-granting developed-country Member desires and that may not be in the interest of the developing country at hand.

Then again, there may be a view that this interpretation would give developed-country Members sufficient flexibility to use a GSP scheme as a tool for some policy goals that they regard desirable, and thereby increase the amount of preferential tariff treatment. This could prove to be beneficial to developing countries. After all, it is not a *right* on the part of developing countries to receive preferential tariff treatment from developed-country Members, and any interpretation that promotes granting preferential tariff treatment under a GSP scheme should be beneficial to both developed and developing-country Members.

This is an important question that needs to be addressed by WTO Members. However, the point that should be stressed here is that a literal interpretation cannot answer the question of which interpretation should be adopted. Interpretation belongs eminently to the realm of policy-making.

The US – Shrimp case (1997)

Another example is the *US – Shrimp* case, which is well known for its environmental implications. In this case, the United States prohibited imports of shrimp from India, Malaysia, Pakistan, and Thailand for the reason that these countries did not take measures to prevent the accidental capture and killing of sea turtles when harvesting shrimp. This US measure was challenged by the above-mentioned countries for the reason that it violated Article XI of the GATT, which prohibits import restriction. The United States invoked Article XX(g) of the GATT, which exempts measures to preserve exhaustible natural resources from GATT disciplines as long as these measures meet the requirements of the introductory clause (the chapeau) of Article XX. The panel found that this US measure was discriminatory and was in violation of the chapeau of Article XX. The Appellate Body modified this ruling of the panel. It examined whether the US measure fell under the Article XX(g) exception, decided that it was covered by this exception, and then held that the US measure was contrary to the requirements of the chapeau because it was a 'unilateral' measure.

The Appellate Body held that the United States should have consulted with India, Malaysia, Pakistan, and Thailand to see whether there was a possibility to resolve this conflict through international negotiations. The failure of the US government to do so constituted a violation of the chapeau of Article XX because it was arbitrary.[3]

The result of the Appellate Body's decision was the same as that of the panel – the United States was found to have acted inconsistently with its WTO obligations. However, there is an important difference between the two reports. The Appellate Body held that the US measure fell under Article XX(g) because it was a measure to preserve an endangered

[3] Subsequent to the adoption of the panel and Appellate Body reports, the United States consulted with shrimp-exporting countries on ways to protect sea turtles. Malaysia brought a claim against the United States that, although the United States had consulted with Malaysia about how to resolve this international dispute, an agreement had not been reached and the United States was therefore still in violation of its WTO obligations. However, the Appellate Body held that the obligation of the United States was to negotiate for the resolution of dispute and did not include an obligation to reach an international agreement. (See Appellate Body Report, *US – Shrimp (Article 21.5 – Malaysia)*, para. 119.)

species, and that the preservation of such species was an important part of environmental protection. In this sense, the Appellate Body's decision placed environmental policies firmly within the framework of WTO dispute settlement. In other words, the Appellate Body made clear that what was held to be WTO-inconsistent was not the US environmental measure as such, but the unilateral way in which it was enforced. It was clear that the US environmental policy itself was justified, and that only the unilateral aspects of its enforcement were held to be WTO inconsistent.

How to reconcile environmental protection and free trade has become an issue of paramount importance for the WTO. The Preamble to the *Marrakesh Agreement Establishing the World Trade Organization* (*WTO Agreement*) declares that 'to protect and preserve the environment' is one of the purposes of the WTO regime. The approach taken by the Appellate Body is more in line with this basic policy of the WTO compared to that taken by the panel. Also, this ruling of the Appellate Body is undoubtedly more acceptable to the US Congress, which otherwise would be required to change its domestic measure since the US environmental policy itself was justified within the framework of the WTO.

I do not intend to say that WTO law is what the Appellate Body Members say it is. However, at the level of the Appellate Body, law and policy seem to intersect, and the Appellate Body should not hesitate to take into account policy considerations as much as a textual analysis allows.

III. Economics and the Appellate Body

Is an economic rationale useful?

The Appellate Body decides cases not on the basis of economics, but in accordance with the customary rules of interpretation as developed in international law. However, WTO agreements deal with economic matters. The WTO regime is based on the principle of free trade in which the maximization of economic welfare, comparative advantage, optimum allocation of resources, and efficiency are, *inter alia*, key factors. Therefore, decisions of the Appellate Body should make some economic sense.[4] Decisions of the Appellate Body are read and relied

[4] A study has been undertaken by the American Law Institute in which lawyers and economists work together to analyze appellate decisions from both a legal and an economic viewpoint. Although still in its rudimentary stage, studies of this nature should be promoted. (For details, see Henrik Horn and Petros C. Mavroidis (eds), *The American Law Institute Reporters' Studies: The WTO Case Law of 2002* (Cambridge, 2005.)

upon not only by a handful of experts on the WTO, but also by governments, legal professionals, legislators, policy-makers, economists, and the general public. Decisions of the Appellate Body should be persuasive to all such people.

For example, there are people – such as some economists – who criticize anti-dumping legislation and argue that it should be done away with. It is not the responsibility of the Appellate Body to decide whether or not the *Agreement on Implementation of Article VI of the General Agreement on Tariffs and Trade 1994* (*Anti-Dumping Agreement*) should be abolished; this should be decided by trade negotiators of WTO Members. Nevertheless, when the Appellate Body deals with anti-dumping issues, it could explain why its rulings – based on the text, context, and legislative history of the *Anti-Dumping Agreement* – are economically rational and sound. If this sort of explanation were added to the textual analysis, this would increase the persuasiveness of appellate decisions.

The Chile – Price Band System case (2002)

In this case, Chile established a price band system that imposed a special levy on imports of agricultural products. Chile took the monthly average of international prices of an agricultural product for five years, lined up these monthly averages with the highest price at the top and the lowest price at the bottom, eliminated the top 25 per cent and the bottom 25 per cent and thereby established a price band. Chile also established a weekly reference price for the imported product. If the reference price was below the lower limit of the price band, a special tariff equal to the difference between the lowest price and the reference price was imposed in addition to the regular tariff. However, the total tariff rate could not exceed 31.5 per cent, which was the bound rate of Chile.

Argentina challenged this special levy system and argued that this amounted to import measures which had to be converted to regular tariffs in accordance with Article 4.2 of the *Agreement on Agriculture.* Chile argued that this special levy system was lawful under the GATT because the total of the levy and regular tariff together could not equal more than the Chilean bound rate, which was 31.5 per cent. The Appellate Body decided that the special levy system was similar to a variable levy and needed to be converted to a regular tariff. The Appellate Body arrived at this conclusion by a textual analysis of Article II.1 of the GATT and of the terms of the Chilean price band and the special levy system. The Appellate Body held that this special levy was similar to a variable levy – which was outlawed – and, therefore, inconsistent with the *Agreement of Agriculture* and the GATT. It also mentioned that, in this special levy system, transparency and predictability were lacking.

This interpretation by the Appellate Body is textually and grammatically correct. However, the question is whether or not this interpretation makes economic sense. An economic explanation as to why this textual interpretation was justifiable would have made this interpretation more persuasive.

Chile argued that the special levy plus the regular tariff could not exceed the bound rate. The total imposition by the Chilean government on imports of agricultural products was lower than the bound rate. The bound rate – 31.5 per cent on agricultural products – was the upper limit. If this price band and special levy system was held to be inconsistent with the GATT, Chile could have chosen to impose the maximum 31.5 per cent rate. Then the average tariff rate would have been higher. The question is: Why is the imposition of the special levy more harmful to international trade than the imposition of the 31.5 per cent tariff rate, which was Chile's right to impose? In other words, why would the decision of the Chilean government to impose the special levy cause more distortion than the imposition of the maximum tariffs on imports of agricultural products?

Perhaps the unpredictability surrounding the special levy was the problem. In some situations, stability of the terms of trade is more important than low costs. The question here is whether the special levy system was so unpredictable as to cause disturbance to imports of agricultural products. One may argue that the Chilean price band system was not based on arbitrary and capricious decisions of the government but, rather, that it was based on a certain published formula according to which the price band was calculated based on the past five year of international prices for agricultural products, and a degree of predictability was maintained.

Those are economic questions. The conclusion of the Appellate Body in the *Chile – Price Band System* case is probably correct as a matter of textual analysis, and it should be remembered that the Appellate Body cannot go beyond the power vested in it by the DSU. Nevertheless, the Appellate Body could have tried to provide some economic rationale that would have justified the interpretation it adopted.

The EC – Bed Linen case (2001)

Another case which presents the issue of whether economic considerations should be taken into account in interpreting the WTO agreements is the *EC – Bed Linen* case. In this case, there were three issues: (i) zeroing; (ii) constructed value; and (iii) normal course of trade. Perhaps the most important issue in this case is that of zeroing. However, there seems to be little problem with the panel's and the Appellate Body's rulings in this regard. Still, the rulings of the Appellate Body on constructed value and the normal course of trade are somewhat troublesome.

In the *Anti-Dumping Agreement*, an anti-dumping authority should determine the difference between the normal value (domestic price) of a product and its export price. However, the domestic price of the product may not be in question, which would be used as the basis for comparison between domestic and export prices. Even if the domestic price of a product is in question, this price may be below the cost of production and, therefore, not reliable. If so, Article 2.2.2 of the *Anti-Dumping Agreement* authorizes the anti-dumping authority to establish a constructed value and compare this with the export price.

The *Anti-Dumping Agreement* requires that, in establishing a constructed value, the anti-dumping authority needs to consider the cost of production, general and administrative expenses (SG&A), and reasonable profit. If the SG&A of the exporter in question are not available, then the anti-dumping authority can base its calculation on the weighted average of the SG&A of exporters of the product in the exporting country.

In this case, the European Communities imposed an anti-dumping duty on imports of bed linen from India. The SG&A of the exporter were not reliable and there was only one other exporter in India under investigation. Therefore, the European Communities established the constructed value by using the SG&A of that other exporter. India argued, *inter alia*, that the European Communities wrongly established the constructed value because the European Communities relied on the SG&A of only one exporter in India. The panel decided that, although Article 2.2.2 of the *Anti-Dumping Agreement* states that the 'weighted average' of the SG&A of 'exporters' in the exporting country should be relied upon, the plural ('exporters') includes the singular ('an exporter') and, therefore, the European Communities could have relied on the figures of a single exporter in India for such expenses. The Appellate Body reversed this finding and held that Article 2.2.2 of the *Anti-Dumping Agreement* clearly states that the 'weighted average' of the SG&A of 'exporters' should be used and that this excludes the SG&A of a single exporter.

In reversing the finding of the panel, the Appellate Body took a literal approach and held that the term 'exporters' cannot include 'an exporter' and that the term 'weighted average' is premised on the plurality of exporters. This is a correct grammatical analysis and the Appellate Body reached a textually right conclusion. However, it seems that a mere grammatical explanation may leave readers with the question of why the SG&A of a single exporter cannot be used as the basis for comparison. The mere statement that the term 'weighted average' cannot comprehend a single exporter is hardly satisfactory as an economic explanation.

A key question is: What would be an economic rationale for this holding? One possible explanation may be that the 'constructed value' in the *Anti-Dumping Agreement* is an artificial domestic price to deal with a situation in which the domestic value of the party under investigation is not available or not reliable. Although the constructed value is artificial, it is important to take into account real market data as much as possible when calculating the constructed value. Constructed value is an approximation of economic reality regarding the domestic price for the product in question. If there is only one other exporter selling this product domestically, this is not sufficient to constitute a market. That is the reason why Article 2.2.2 is couched in a plural such as the 'weighted average' of 'exporters'.

Another explanation may be that, by relying on the SG&A of only one exporter, the constructed value of the exporter in question would be based on the particular features of that other exporter with respect to its SG&A. This reflects neither the financial features of the exporter in question nor any reality in the market and would present a false picture of the SG&A of the exporter in question.

There is another issue in the holding of the Appellate Body that raises a question regarding the interpretation of the term 'normal course of trade' in Article 2.2.1 of the *Anti-Dumping Agreement.* Article 2.2.1 states that a sales price below the costs of production plus the SG&A can be regarded as being not in the normal course of trade, and can be disregarded in calculating the domestic value. In this situation, the anti-dumping authority can resort to the constructed value. Article 2.2.2 of the *Anti-Dumping Agreement* requires that the anti-dumping authority calculate the SG&A and the profits on the basis of actual data pertaining to the costs of production and the sale of a like product of the exporter under investigation. Article 2.2.2(ii) of the *Anti-Dumping Agreement* states that, if the above data are unavailable, the anti-dumping authority can resort to the weighted average of the SG&A of other producers and exporters.

The Panel held that, in applying Article 2.2.2(ii) of the *Anti-Dumping Agreement*, the SG&A and profits realized not in the normal course of trade can be included. The Appellate Body upheld this ruling and stated that, although there is language in the introductory part of Article 2.2.2 that the SG&A and profits realized in the normal course of trade shall be relied upon – implying that the SG&A and profits realized in trade that is not the normal course of trade should be excluded – there is no comparable language in Article 2.2.2(ii), and this should suggest that when calculating the SG&A and profits on the basis of those realized by exporters and producers subject to investigation of a like product, not only the figures in the normal course of trade but also those in trade which is not the normal course of trade can be included.

This interpretation simply makes no sense economically. Under this ruling of the Appellate Body, the SG&A of those transactions which are not in the normal course of trade can be included in the calculation under Article 2.2.2(ii). However, the purpose of the provision that transactions not in the normal course of trade can be excluded is to avoid distortion in calculation. The inclusion of figures in transactions not in the normal course of trade may cause distortion in calculation. The situation should be the same whether one is concerned with the introductory part of Article 2.2.2 or of Article 2.2.2(ii) because distortion may occur in the same way whether one is dealing with one situation or the other.

In this situation, the Appellate Body could have deviated from a mechanical interpretation, taken into consideration the purpose of the *Anti-Dumping Agreement* and drawn an analogy. It seems more reasonable to interpret that the provision in the introductory part of Article 2.2.2 regarding the SG&A in the normal course of trade should be applied *mutatis mutandi* to the situation that Article 2.2.2(ii) envisages given that the necessity of avoiding distortion is the same in both situations.

IV. Conclusion

One may question whether panels and the Appellate Body should regard the WTO agreements as perfect and infallible. The WTO agreements probably are not perfect; there are lacuna and loopholes in the WTO agreements. These may not have been intended by the drafters but may have been inadvertent omissions of necessary provisions. It seems that to fill in the gaps is an important part of interpretation when the structures and the texts of the WTO agreements are not perfect and a literal interpretation of these agreements results in unreasonable outcomes.

Criticisms have been made that the Appellate Body has interpreted the WTO agreements too literally and, conversely, that the Appellate Body has overstepped the boundary and 'made law' instead of 'interpreted law'.

However, the overall accomplishments of the Appellate Body have been remarkable. In spite of such criticisms, the Appellate Body has accomplished much in establishing WTO jurisprudence. The above discussions are nothing but a few suggestions for the Appellate Body in making future decisions.

14

Is the WTO dispute settlement mechanism important to business?

SOICHIRO SAKUMA

I have been working at a Japanese steel company for over 20 years on various investment and trade matters, including a number of trade disputes that have been brought before the dispute settlement system of the World Trade Organization (WTO). In the following chapter, I offer a personal perspective on the subject: 'Business and the WTO dispute settlement mechanism'.

My discussion addresses some basic questions.

I. Is the WTO dispute settlement mechanism important to business?

The first question is whether or not the WTO dispute settlement mechanism is important to business. Unquestionably, the answer is 'Yes'. The dispute settlement mechanism is very important to business. Every decision of the WTO dispute settlement system affects business.

Japanese taxes on alcoholic beverages

To demonstrate the importance of the WTO dispute settlement mechanism, consider a WTO case: *Japan – Alcoholic Beverages II.* The Japanese government lost this case. The rulings in this case had a tremendous impact on the Japanese alcoholic beverage business. The dispute concerned the Japanese Liquor Tax Law and *shochu. Shochu* is a traditional colourless distilled liquor ('white liquor'). The European Communities, together with the United States and Canada, claimed that: (i) *shochu* was directly competitive with whisky, brandy, and other 'brown' spirits; and (ii) *shochu* and these 'brown' spirits were substitutable products, but (iii) that higher tax rates were applied to 'brown' spirits, in violation of Article III (National Treatment) of the *General Agreement on Tariffs and*

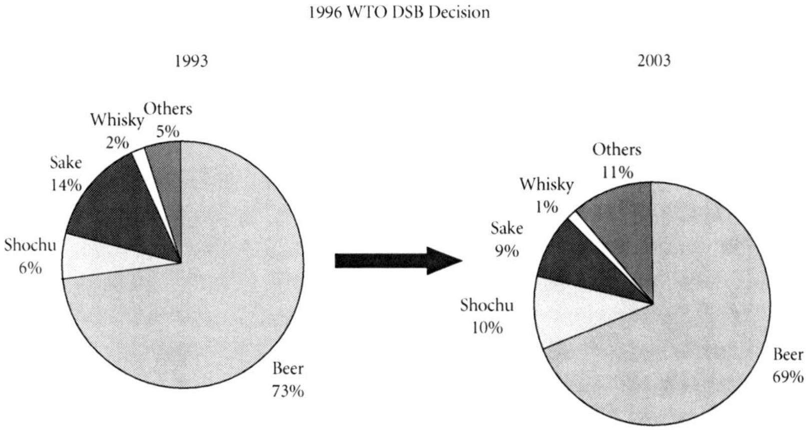

Source: National Tax Agency

Figure 14.1 Alcoholic beverage consumption in Japan (on a shipment volume basis)

Trade (GATT) *1994.*[1] In order to comply with the rulings and recommendations of the WTO's Dispute Settlement Body (DSB), the Japanese government raised the tax rates on *shochu* by 240 per cent while cutting tax rates on whisky/brandy by 60 per cent. Naturally, *shochu* became very expensive.

Then, what happened in Japan? As described in Figure 14.1, which shows alcoholic beverage consumption in Japan before and after the 1996 WTO decisions, *shochu* is now the second most popular alcoholic beverage in Japan. Prior to Japan's defeat in the WTO, *shochu* had long been the third most popular alcoholic beverage in Japan, after beer and sake. In contrast, sales of whisky/brandy remained sluggish.

When Japan lost, many thought that *shochu* would lose competitiveness in relation to whisky, and that its sales would fall significantly while Scottish distillers were expected to increase exports of whisky to Japan. But things turned out differently. Following the WTO rulings, *shochu* became more expensive. *Shochu* producers tried to adjust to the price increases by upgrading and changing marketing strategies. They have succeeded in shifting their market segment from low-priced, low-quality *shochu* to high-priced, high-quality *shochu*, attracting a large number of new consumers, including myself.

[1] See Panel Report, *Japan – Alcoholic Beverages II*, paras. 6.1–6.3.

Steel trade remedy cases: indirect effects of the WTO dispute settlement mechanism

Steel trade remedy cases are also good examples of how the WTO dispute settlement system affects business. First, one may see some indirect effect of the WTO dispute settlement mechanism in steel trade cases. The WTO dispute settlement mechanism ensures that WTO rules are complied with. In trade disputes, complainants may argue that domestic trade remedy laws and investigations do not conform to WTO rules, a set of fully binding international trade rules. Thailand, Indonesia and other Asian countries, are increasingly active users of trade remedies, such as anti-dumping measures, particularly in response to requests from their steel industries. Their domestic cases include an Indonesian anti-dumping case involving tin plate (1999) and a Thai anti-dumping investigation involving hot-rolled steel (2003). Both cases involved steel products from Japan. Anti-dumping orders were issued on these products. However, there are serious questions as to whether the investigations complied with WTO rules.

Thailand hot-rolled steel anti-dumping case (2003)

Let me be more specific about the Thai case. Thailand initiated an anti-dumping investigation on hot-rolled steel from Japan on 8 July 2002. The Thai government imposed, on 23 July 2002, a 30 per cent bank guarantee requirement for each entry of the subject product from Japan. The Thai government ordered the imposition of the guarantee before issuing a preliminary determination. This action was fully consistent with the domestic anti-dumping legislation of Thailand.[2] Despite being consistent with the domestic legislation, it was not consistent with the *Agreement on Implementation of Article VI of the General Agreement on Tariffs and Trade 1994* (*Anti-Dumping Agreement*). Article 7.1 of the *Anti-Dumping Agreement* provides that provisional measures shall be made only after a preliminary determination has been made. In addition, Article 7.3 states that provisional measures shall not be applied sooner than 60 days from the date of initiation of the investigation. The exception is the retroactive application of duties when the authorities find that the circumstances set out in Article 10.6 have been met.

In the Thai anti-dumping case, (i) the Thai authorities made no preliminary determination at all; (ii) the provisional measures were taken only 15 days after the date of initiation of the investigation; and (iii) the

[2] Antidumping and Countervailing Act, B.E. 2542 (1999), section 31.

Thai authorities made no determination whatsoever on whether or not critical circumstances existed. Japanese exporters urged the Thai authorities to comply with the WTO *Anti-Dumping Agreement* and revoke the bank guarantee requirement, suggesting that otherwise we might initiate discussions with the Japanese government on a possible WTO complaint. Simultaneously, we asked the Japanese government to warn the Thai government about the measures, which were potentially inconsistent with WTO rules. We believe that thanks to the existence of binding international trade rules, that is, the WTO agreements, our position was stronger. Otherwise, so long as the actions of the Thai investigating authority conformed to their domestic law, we would have no weapon of defence.

Steel trade remedy cases: direct effects of the WTO dispute settlement mechanism

The WTO dispute settlement mechanism ensures that WTO obligations are enforceable. We thus have double-layered defence. Even if we lose at the national level, there is another chance to win the case before a WTO panel. The Japanese steel industry has a positive view of the WTO's dispute settlement procedures. The cases initiated at the behest of the Japanese steel industry under the *Understanding on Rules and Procedures Governing the Settlement of Disputes* (DSU) include: *US – 1916 Act*; *US – Hot-Rolled Steel*; *US – Steel Safeguards*; and *US – Corrosion-Resistant Steel Sunset Review.*

Japan prevailed in most of these cases, leading to the abolishment or termination of the WTO-inconsistent measures by the United States. In contrast, we were less successful with respect to China's anti-dumping investigation on stainless steel from Japan. This case occurred before China's accession to the WTO. Not surprisingly, China's investigation was not consistent with several WTO rules, but the WTO rules were not applicable in that case. We lost this case, but had no forum in which to appeal against the decisions of China's investigating authority, domestically or internationally.

II. Is the WTO dispute settlement mechanism important to businessmen?

The second question is whether or not the WTO dispute settlement mechanism is important to businessmen. The answer should be 'Yes', but actually is 'No'. The WTO dispute settlement mechanism is not so important to or popular among businessmen in Japan.

Little knowledge about the WTO dispute settlement mechanism

It is no surprise that a typical Japanese businessman has very little knowledge about the WTO's dispute settlement mechanism. Experience with the system among businessmen is very limited.

In addition, the use of the WTO dispute settlement mechanism is not considered an activity of the private sector. That is a governmental activity, a battle between governments, rather than between businesses. All players are government officials. In particular, Japanese private parties may not formally petition the government to bring a case to the WTO, unlike their United States and European counterparts, who have such a right under the Section 301 statute and the Trade Barriers Regulation (TBR), respectively. Japanese businessmen show very little or no interest towards these types of activities. But, that does not mean that Japanese companies export their products without any problems. In fact, businessmen face a number of WTO-related problems everyday.

Steel cases: rather exceptional cases

Yet, despite the unfamiliarity with or unpopularity of the WTO dispute settlement mechanism among Japanese businessmen, why the positive attitude of the Japanese steel industry toward it? Are steel cases exceptions? Probably, yes, they are. We do not seek immediate direct benefits in most cases, as we are aware that the whole procedure of the WTO dispute settlement mechanism takes a rather long time, even if we prevail. It takes almost two years for the WTO DSB to adopt a final ruling, plus the additional time needed for its implementation. This rather long period would deter businessmen from thinking positively about using the WTO process. There is even less incentive when this period is compared to the duration of the targeted measures. In the *US – Steel Safeguards* case, for instance, the United States government proclaimed that the duration of the safeguard measure should be three years. This means that in many of the safeguard cases, a WTO victory would not bring any additional benefits in terms of timing, as compared with the results of a 'wait and see' approach. Another problem is that a WTO victory does not guarantee that the domestic measures will be changed, as discussed in the following section.

What is our motivation in the steel cases? First, even though there were no immediate direct benefits, we decided to pursue this course, aiming at, among other things, deterrence of similar measures that might otherwise be taken by the United States and other countries, such as Asian countries. This motivation may be justified given that many more steel cases will likely occur in the United States and other countries. I am not sure whether this is also the case with other industries.

Secondly, we had no, or very few, alternative solutions. The steel industry is a capital-intensive industry. A steel plant requires huge capital expenditures. This means that the steel industry would have difficulty shifting manufacturing facilities abroad and still staying viable. It is thus essential for the Japanese steel industry to keep on making substantial exports, and to that end the Japanese steel industry must pursue the revocation or termination of protectionist measures by importing nations. But, this might not be the case with other industries, either.

III. Why is the WTO dispute settlement mechanism not so important to businessmen?

We turn to our last question: 'Why is the WTO dispute settlement mechanism not so important to businessmen?' The previous section has partly addressed this question in discussing the steel cases. At the risk of being too simplistic, the answer to this question might be that, in most cases, businessmen do not need the WTO dispute settlement mechanism to solve certain problems. In other words, the WTO dispute settlement mechanism is not a good tool or is not worth pursuing to solve certain problems.

Alternative solutions

Why is the WTO dispute settlement system not a good tool or worth pursuing? The answer is that business has alternative solutions, which cover a broad spectrum of possibilities. To address a WTO-inconsistent trade protectionist measure, for example, we have the option of stopping exports and shifting the manufacturing base to the importing country or to another country. This solution might be at one end of the spectrum as representing a structural change. At the other end of the spectrum is just a 'wait and see' approach.

Obstacles relating to the use of the WTO dispute settlement mechanism

Even if we elect to bring the case before the WTO as the last resort, there still remain a number of obstacles or concerns over the use of the WTO dispute settlement mechanism.

Effectiveness

First, the WTO victory does not guarantee the implementation by the violating country of the WTO DSB's rulings and recommendations. This is a distinct disadvantage when we take this approach. It distinguishes the WTO dispute settlement process from judicial procedures. The *US – Offset Act (Byrd Amendment)* case is a good, but negative example. As the United States did not implement the DSB's recommendation within the prescribed time period, Japan and other countries imposed countermeasures by raising tariffs on some imports from the United States. But the companies that were hurt by the legislation, that is, exporting companies in Japan and other countries in this case, have not directly benefited from these countermeasures because the exported products were not the same as the products subject to the countermeasures. Or, in some cases, exporting companies might be criticized by consumers or users of the items subject to the countermeasures. If this concern applies to a large proportion of the exporting companies, these companies would naturally feel very reluctant to pursue the WTO solution or insist on its implementation. Typically, the users of the products on which the tariffs are raised are customers of the exporting companies, making the situation more difficult.

Timing

Secondly, the timing is crucial, but the timeline of the WTO dispute settlement procedures does not necessarily satisfy business needs. The entire WTO procedure takes almost two years, plus the additional time period for informal preliminary discussions between the government and affected businesses to convince the government to bring the case before the WTO panel. Moreover, additional time is required for implementation. A good example of what happens with implementation is the *US – 1916 Act* case. In February 1999, Japan made a request for consultation with the United States pursuant to the WTO's DSU, claiming that the 1916 Act did not conform with the *Anti-Dumping Agreement*.[3] A panel was established in July 1999. In September 2000,

[3] WT/DS162/1.

Japan prevailed in this case. The Panel circulated its report in May 2000 and, following the United States' appeal, the Appellate Body issued a report upholding the Panel's report in August 2000, which was duly adopted in September 2000.[4] After long consultations on the implementation issue between Japan and the United States, the United States finally repealed the 1916 Act in December 2004. We achieved a perfect victory, but nearly six years elapsed in the process. During the six-year period, some Japanese trading firms settled the civil suit filed by a United States steel producer under the 1916 Act, and a new suit was lodged against a Japanese printing machine producer in March 2000, which case is still pending.

Another good example to examine is the position of Japanese businesses toward China's foreign equity restrictions in the distribution services sector. In violation of China's commitments under the accession agreement, China does not allow foreign-owned joint ventures to engage in the wholesale business. This means that such joint ventures may sell products of their own manufacture, but may not sell any products produced by third parties, even by their parent companies and other affiliates. Despite this problem, I am not aware of any Japanese businesses requesting the Japanese government to resort to the WTO dispute procedure. In fact, the Japanese government did not challenge China's failure to eliminate foreign equity restrictions in the distribution services sector no later than certain dates (for example, 11 December 2004). From the viewpoint of Japanese business, it would not be a practical solution to use a lengthy procedure to demand conformity with the WTO rule. Rather, they chose to take a 'wait and see' approach and simply await China's implementation of that obligation without recourse to the WTO procedure.

Cost

Thirdly, some businesses hesitate to seek a WTO dispute settlement procedure because of its onerous cost. WTO dispute settlement cases are becoming increasingly complex, legally and factually. We would need reinforcements of experts and lawyers. Naturally we would have to bear these costs in no small amount. The question here is whether the costs of pursuing the WTO dispute settlement mechanism are economically justified.

[4] Appellate Body Report, *US – 1916 Act*; Panel Reports, *US – 1916 Act (EC)* and *US – 1916 Act (Japan)*.

Ability to control the procedure

Another matter of concern I wish to raise is the ability to control the procedure. Japanese businesses have no legal right to initiate the WTO dispute settlement procedure and, once started, no right to withdraw a complaint. Businesses might wish to withdraw the petition and be released from the time-consuming and costly procedures, if an alternative solution should begin to work. Only governments can make a 'go' or 'no go' decision and determine which countermeasures shall be taken. This would mean that, contrary to the wish of businesses, the procedure may not be stopped halfway or may result in such countermeasures as are dissatisfactory to consumers generally or users of subject products individually.

IV. Suggestions

To be a good business tool, the WTO dispute settlement mechanism should work more on the principle of 'the-shorter-the better', as suggested to some extent in the Geneva discussions. It is of critical importance to businesses for the WTO procedure to stick to the timeframe, without exception. That could also serve to increase the predictability of business activities, resulting in a more positive use of the WTO dispute settlement mechanism.

To ensure and expedite the implementation of the DSB rulings and recommendation, we need further improvements. Periodic penalty payments of a certain amount per day may be used, as employed in the EC Competition Law.[5] The penalty may be imposed until there is compliance with the DSB rulings and recommendation. The penalty would be paid to the WTO, rather than to the complaining WTO Member. In addition, to enhance the motivation and reduce an economic burden on the private sector, some mechanism would need to be devised. For example, duties raised and collected as countermeasures may be paid to claiming businesses to compensate them for costs such as legal fees incurred. It is high time to explore some new ideas for the improvement of the WTO dispute settlement mechanism.

[5] Article 24(1) of Commission Regulation (EC) No. 1/2003.

15

Japan's approach to the 'use' of the WTO: how can we achieve an effective link between business and the WTO?

SHIGEHIRO TANAKA

I. Importance of focusing on the 'use' of the WTO

The title of this chapter refers to the 'use' of the World Trade Organization (WTO).[1] The intention is to emphasize the dispute settlement aspect of the WTO, as opposed to the rule-making aspect, which has always attracted more attention. When the media writes about the WTO, it is mostly about the Doha Round. The importance of rule-making cannot be overemphasized. But the value of the WTO would be almost nil, if it did not have the dispute settlement mechanism to cope with the problems we face today. Indeed, compared to other international organizations, the WTO stands out for the effectiveness of its enforcement mechanism.

The effectiveness of this enforcement mechanism is essential to ensure business support for the WTO. Although trade measures that can be subject to dispute settlement concern a wide variety of stakeholders, the one sector that will have the greatest incentive to 'use' the WTO is the business sector. This is natural if we consider that trade is part of the conduct of business. Whether small or large, business operations will be the first affected by any WTO-inconsistent measure. Therefore, an effective dispute settlement system is key to maintaining support for the WTO among business. This is why it is important to focus on the 'use' of the WTO and the linkage between business and the WTO as a goal in itself.

[1] The views expressed in this chapter belong to the author and do not represent the official position of any organization.

II. Japan's experience with the GATT/WTO dispute settlement mechanism

How did Japan fare in past dispute settlement cases? If we look back to the days of the *General Agreement on Tariffs and Trade* (GATT), although we had many instances of trade friction with some trading partners, the use of the dispute settlement system by Japan was extremely limited. Table 15.1 provides a list of dispute settlement cases in which Japan was a complainant, and it shows that there were only two cases under the GATT. Managed trade was the more frequent route of solving problems, rather than having recourse to the 'toothless' GATT.

The establishment of the WTO and its dispute settlement mechanism changed the picture dramatically. It was rather symbolic that the first complaint filed by Japan under the WTO dispute settlement system was the United States' Section 301 case on automobiles.[2] Although the case ended at the consultations stage, it was widely perceived as a success of the rule-based WTO system with respect to a politically motivated WTO-inconsistent measure. In effect, this was the last case in which Japan became the target of a US Section 301 measure. This was a great lesson on what the WTO could do for business. The need for an impartial system to deal with trade problems became clear.

Since then, we have had on average one case per year as a complainant. The situation is almost the same on the respondents' side.[3] Overall, the results achieved in the cases in which Japan has been a complainant have been good.[4] This is a clear indication that we have been rather prudent in bringing cases to the dispute settlement system. This is not to suggest that every case had a positive outcome, as is clear from the implementation problems we are facing in some cases.[5]

The system helped de-politicize trade problems by applying an impartial rule in a fair and transparent manner. This is evident from the following. The country against which the most number of cases were brought was the United States. The fact that the overall United States-Japan economic relation have been good in recent years suggests that this did not affect the bilateral relationship, which is another tribute to the WTO.

[2] Request for Consultations by Japan, WT/DS6/1, 22 May 1995.

[3] See Table 15.2.

[4] See Table 15.1.

[5] The most famous one being the *US – Offset Act* (*Byrd Amendment*). Legislation repealing the Byrd amendment was pending in the United States Congress as of December 2005.

III. Selection of cases

How does Japan select the cases that are brought to the WTO's dispute settlement system? We do not have a fixed mechanism such as the US Section 301 legislation or the Trade Barriers Regulation (TBR) of the European Communities. Japan's selection of cases was made on a case-by-case basis, looking at the merits of each case and all other relevant factors.

Most of the cases are brought to the government's attention by the complaining industry. In the case of Japan, most of the cases were brought by the automobile or steel industries, which had strong export interests. Of course, every case will start with the question, '*do we have a reasonable chance of winning?*' But the process of selection will not stop there. Other questions that may have to be answered include: *How strong is the request to address the issue? Are there any alternatives for solving the issue? Are the complaining parties ready to cooperate in the dispute? Are there any conflicting interests that the government has to look into? Will the benefit from success outweigh the total cost?* These questions may change from case to case.

I do not think that this methodology stands in sharp contrast to the situation in the United States or the European Communities. Discretion is inevitable when governments decide whether or not to initiate a case. The most significant effect of having a formal system is not to put a strait jacket on the selection process, but to send a clear sign to business that the government is ready to take up a case. In this regard, the annual 'Report on the WTO Inconsistency of Trade Policies by Major Trading Partners' (hereinafter, 'Unfair Trade Policies Report'), published by the Japanese Ministry of Economy, Trade and Industry (METI), has played an important role, both in terms of providing transparency to the process and sending out a clear message to business on the government's resolve to tackle such issues.

IV. METI's 'Unfair Trade Policies Report'

The report has been published every year since 1992 and has taken up major trade problems that Japan faces *vis-à-vis* its major trading partners. What is important here is that, during the compilation process of the report, METI solicits views from business.[6] This effort has been

[6] The report is published by the Industrial Structure Council, which is an advisory body to the Minister of METI. METI functions as the secretariat to the Council.

ongoing for several years, and it has included industry associations,[7] individual firms and other interested parties. The views may be submitted in any form, either formally or informally, in writing or orally.[8] Electronic contact points have been established for the notification of WTO-inconsistent measures or problems relating to counterfeiting.[9] So there are various ways for business to make their views known to the government.

Although these things can never be perfect, in the long run, I believe this mechanism has been successful in receiving the views from as wide variety of businesses as possible. The issues that are presented will be examined, and basically those that are deemed to be in violation of WTO rules will be chosen for inclusion in the report. What should be pointed out, however, is that the criteria applied here is not the same as that for selecting a case to be brought to WTO dispute settlement. The criteria are much broader, reflecting the fact that the selection is not done exclusively for purposes of initiating a dispute at the WTO. The WTO is always regarded as the last resort, where cases will be taken only if there are no other effective means for solving the problem. This approach is consistent with business' preference for having as little intervention as possible from the government. The substantial cost and time accompanying a full fledged dispute settlement case is another reason.

The publication of the report by itself has served as a vehicle to convey the government's intention of dealing with a certain case vis-à-vis the foreign government concerned and the domestic interest. It could even help to facilitate the solution itself. This process has been strengthened recently by METI's decision to announce its priorities from among the measures contained in the report and to follow-up on the priorities of the previous year.

Table 15.3 shows the measures chosen as priority for fiscal year 2005. Since the report covers cases involving the top ten trading partners, the United States, China, the European Communities, and the countries of the Association of Southeast Asian Nations (ASEAN) are the natural source of priorities. Among them, China is on the rise in terms of the number of problems.

[7] For example, the Japan Business Council for Trade and Investment Facilitation has annually published its list of issues on the web, available at <http://www.jmcti.org/mondai/top_e.html>.

[8] It is not restricted to business interests, but complaints against foreign measures by non-business interests have been extremely rare.

[9] For example, <multitradesys@meti.go.jp>, or <seihumohoumadoguchi@meti.go.jp>.

It is also important to monitor the situation of these cases every year. Table 15.4 shows the follow-up result of the priorities for fiscal year 2004. This will help ensure that the cases are taken care of and will provide business with a sense of how things are going. The hope is that these efforts will help business understand that problems can be solved through these channels.

V. Key to better linkage between business and the WTO

The 'Unfair Trade Policies Report' is one of the efforts made by the government to bridge the gap between the WTO and business. But whether these efforts are bearing fruit is another problem, and will depend on the linkage between business and the government concerned. If there is a trade problem that arises involving a Japanese firm or a Japanese national, and if the involvement of the government could help solve the problem, the ideal situation would be for the private parties to draw the issue to the government's attention. The government then will make its decision on whether or not to take up the issue.

At present, some in Japan consider that the participation of business is less than should be expected. It is impossible to find out exactly how many potential cases there are, but compared to its trade volume, it may be argued that Japan has been less active in dispute settlement than the United States or the European Communities.[10] Certainly, the number of cases brought to the WTO's dispute settlement system cannot be regarded as a goal in itself. Nevertheless, it is important to bear in mind that such criticism exists, and to continue improving the environment for a better linkage between government and business.

What then would be the key to a better environment? Some say that because we lack a formal mechanism for bringing a WTO case, such as those that exist in the United States and the European Communities, it is not clear to business whether it can obtain the support of the government. But it is questionable whether this is the case. Even the United States and the European Communities do not use this formal process in all cases and it ignores the role played by the various routes that are available. Even if there were differences, the next question would be 'how much of a difference is there?' In any event, it seems that it is necessary to look carefully into the attitude of business.

[10] According to the WTO website, while the United States was a complainant in 83 cases, Japan was a complainant in 12. The difference in trade volume alone certainly cannot explain this discrepancy.

Then what exactly is hindering business from moving forward? There are several steps before business will decide to bring a case. Questions to be asked in each step include: *Is there a problem? Do you want to confront the problem? Do you want to use the WTO to deal with the problem ? How much do you want the government to be involved?* The answers to all these questions have to be positive, before the case can reach the government.

First and foremost, it is important to realize that business awareness of the WTO dispute settlement mechanism is not high. Small and medium-sized enterprises rarely know about its existence, not to mention its availability. This is most worrying.

Secondly, the attitude of business toward the use of legal instruments differs from country to country. Japan is clearly different from the United States and maybe even from the European Communities, although Japan's situation is much closer to that of the European Communities. If legal instruments are not frequently used domestically, it is even more difficult to expect companies to use them in an international context. This will require extra effort.

Thirdly, dispute settlement is time consuming and does not provide business with a clear timeframe. No business will embark on a project unless it knows when it can achieve a result. A timeframe of one year and a half may be already too long for many business people.

Fourthly, there is the cost incurred by the parties. This cannot be ignored especially for small and medium-sized enterprises.

Fifthly, the human resources necessary to advance a case may not be readily available. There are few domestic lawyers with enough understanding of the WTO in Japan. Japanese companies' legal staff often lack the necessary knowledge about the WTO. Even the government may not have sufficient people to deal with all of the demand. Foreign lawyers have often played an important role in filling such gap. But we must be reminded that for cost and other reasons, there is a genuine need for domestic professionals to provide such service. They will understand the value of the WTO and of its dispute settlement system, and they will be able to translate what they mean for the local business people. They can help small and medium-sized enterprises bring cases. This is essential if the WTO should be for the broader public and not only for a limited few.

Lastly, the situation is not the same across industries. Compared to the steel and automobiles sectors, there has been very little use of dispute settlement by the electronics sector, not only in Japan but also worldwide. This is probably due to the global nature of the electronics industry in procurement, sales, production and other areas, which makes it easy to evade the problem and/or difficult to use dispute settlement because it could hurt their own interests. This is not a problem, but a point that should be taken into account.

VI. Building a positive spiral

The above factors tend to reinforce each other and therefore their combined effect is more significant, resulting in a negative spiral. With the very low awareness of the WTO, business will not use dispute settlement as much as they should. This means less attention by the legal profession.[11] Even fewer professionals may become interested in the subject in the future. Cost will increase and there will be less opportunity for the relevant parties to be exposed to the WTO. This will again affect business attitude in a negative manner. And the spiral may go on.

Overcoming this trend and creating a positive spiral will require close cooperation among stakeholders. The challenge for the government, to begin with, is to make the value of dispute settlement better known to business by raising public awareness. Necessary resources within the government have to be maintained to cope with growing demand.

In terms of the WTO's dispute settlement procedures, shortening timeframes should be given higher priority. But it is unrealistic to believe that timeframes can conform to the extremely high expectations of business. The WTO's dispute settlement system, as it stands now, is doing its best. If we think of the possible consequence of forcing a change to a sovereign decision, it is of no surprise that it takes a couple of years to reach a conclusion in many cases. More effort may be required to narrow the gap, at least, between such reality and the expectation of business.

The challenge for the legal profession is to make efforts to develop the domestic market for WTO cases and prepare the necessary talent to deal with the potential demand. Business will be expected to listen carefully to such views and see if they can be applied to their business problems.

All this may sound paternalistic. But this is exactly the kind of effort that is most lacking. This can be key in gaining support for the WTO and to counter the numerous unfounded criticisms made about the WTO and its dispute settlement system. It is an investment worth making if we want to keep the WTO effective.

This is already a big challenge even for Japan. And if that is the case, I imagine that the situation is similar in most, if not all, developing countries.

[11] This includes academics.

The growing body of legal rulings coming out from WTO dispute settlement cases is making it increasingly difficult just to keep up with such developments.

Capacity building and global networking, facilitated by events such as the conferences celebrating the Tenth Anniversary of the WTO's dispute settlement system and the establishment of the Appellate Body, combined with efforts by individual WTO Members to strengthen and widen support among business for the WTO should continue to be one of the main goals of WTO's activities toward the future.

Table 15.1 *Disputes involving Japan as Complainant*

	Short title and document number	Agreement	Request for consultation	Panel establishment	Adoption of panel/AB reports	Result
1	*EEC – Parts and Components* (L/6657, BISD 37S/132)	GATT	July 1988	October 1988	May 1990 (Panel report)	Panel upheld Japan's claim
2	*EC – Audio Cassettes* (ADP/136)	AD	July 1991	October 1992	—	Panel report not adopted
3	*US – Autos* (DS6)	GATT DSU	May 1995	—	—	Parties reached mutual agreement
4	*Brazil – Autos* (DS51)	GATT SCM	July 1996	—	—	Brazil eliminated the measures concerned
5	*Indonesia – Autos* (DS55)	GATT TRIMS SCM	October 1996	July 1997	July 1998 (Panel report)	Panel upheld Japan's claim
6	*US – Procurement* (DS95)	GPA	July 1997	October 1998	—	Panel lapsed
7	*Canada – Autos* (DS139)	GATT TRIMS GATS	July 1998	February 1999	June 2000 (Panel and AB reports)	Panel upheld Japan's claim
8	*US – 191 6 Act* (DS162)	AD	February 1999	July 1999	September 2000 (Panel and AB reports)	Panel upheld Japan's claim

Table 15.1 (*continued*)

	Short title and document number	Agreement	Request for consultation	Panel establishment	Adoption of panel/AB reports	Result
9	*US – Hot-Rolled Steel* (DS184)	AD	November 1999	March 2000	August 2001 (Panel and AB reports)	Panel upheld Japan's claim
10	*US – Offset Act (Byrd Amendment)* (DS217)	AD SCM	December 2000	September 2001	January 2003 (Panel and AB reports)	Panel upheld Japan's claim
11	*US – Corrosion-Resistant Steel Sunset Review* (DS244)	AD	January 2002.1	May 2002	January 2004 (Panel and AB reports)	Panel dismissed Japan's claim
12	*US – Steel Safeguards* (DS249)	SG	March 2002	June 2002	December 2003 (Panel and AB reports)	Panel upheld Japan's claim
13	*US – Zeroing (Japan)* (DS322)	AD	November 2004	February 2005	—	Ongoing

Table 15.2 *Disputes involving Japan as Respondent*

	Short title and document number	Complainant	Agreement	Request for consultation	Panel establishment	Adoption of panel/ AB reports	Result
1	*Japan – Alcoholic Beverages II* (DS8/10/11)	EC US Canada	GATT	June 1995	September 1995	November 1996 (Panel and AB eports)	Panel dismissed Japan's defence
2	*Japan – Telecommunications Equipment* (DS15)	EC	GATT	August 1995	—	—	Parties reached mutual agreement
3	*Japan – Sound Recordings* (DS28)	US EC	TRIPS	February 1996	—	—	Parties reached mutual agreement
4	*Japan – Film* (DS44)	US	GATT	June 1996	October 1996	April 1998 (Panel report)	Panel upheld Japan's defence
5	*Japan – Distribution Services* (DS45)	US	GATS	June 1996	—	—	Consultations suspended
6	*Japan – Pork* (DS66)	EC	GATT	January 1997	—	—	Consultations suspended
7	*Japan – Satellite* (DS73)	EC	GPA	March 1997	—	—	Parties reached mutual agreement
8	*Japan – Agricultural Products II* (DS76)	US	SPS	April 1997	November 1997	March 1999 (Panel and AB reports)	Panel dismissed Japan's defence

Table 15.2 (*continued*)

	Short title and document number	Complainant	Agreement	Request for consultation	Panel establishment	Adoption of panel/ AB reports	Result
9	*Japan – Leather Quotas* (DS147)	EC	ILA SCM	October 1998	—	—	Consultations suspended
10	*Japan – Apples* (DS245)	US	SPS	March 2002	June 2002	December 2003 (Panel and AB reports)	Panel dismissed Japan's defence
11	*Japan – Quotas on Laver* (DS323)	Korea	GATT AA ILA	December 2004	March 2005	—	Ongoing

Table 15.3 *METI priorities for FY 2005*

Country / Territory	Priorities published on 18 April 2005	Remarks
United States	The Byrd Amendment (Amendment to the Tariff Act of 1930)	Ongoing
	Anti-dumping measures on certain hot-rolled steel products from Japan	Ongoing
	Calculation of dumping margins via the zeroing procedure	New item
China	Failure to fulfil tariff concessions for photographic film	Ongoing
	Implementation of anti-dumping measures	Ongoing
	Issues related to counterfeit, pirated, and other infringing products	Ongoing
	Problems related to the system for certifying finished vehicle characteristics	New item
European Union	Draft regulations on registration, evaluation, and authorization of chemicals (REACH)	Ongoing
	Directives on waste electrical and electronic equipment (WEEE)	Ongoing
	Directives on the restriction of the use of certain hazardous substances in electrical and electronic equipment (RoHS)	Ongoing
ASEAN countries	Malaysia: Problems related to imposition of internal taxes on automobiles	Ongoing
	Indonesia: Problems related to the imposition of tariffs on digital cameras	New item
East Asian countries	Issues related to counterfeit, pirated, and other infringing products	Ongoing

Table 15.4 *Follow up of METI priorities for FY 2004*

Country / Territory	Priorities published on March 29, 2004	Follow-up result
United States	Anti-dumping Act of 1916	⊙
	The Byrd Amendment (Amendment to the Tariff) Act of 1930	⊡
	Anti-dumping measures on certain hot-rolled steel products from Japan	⊡
China	Problems related to the refund of value-added taxes on semiconductors	⊙
	Problems related to the selling of both imported and domestic automobiles	⊙
	Enforcement of the quota system for imported automobiles and auto parts	⊙
	Failure to fulfil tariff concessions for photographic film	⊡
	Implementation of anti-dumping measures	⊡
	Delay in improving domestic legislations on the right to trade and distribution services	⊙
	Abundance of counterfeit, pirated and other infringing products	⊡
European Union	Draft regulations on registration, evaluation, and authorization of Chemicals (REACH)	⊡
	Directives on waste electrical and electronic equipment (WEEE)	⊡
	Directives on the restriction of the use of certain hazardous substances in electrical and electronic equipment (RoHS)	⊡
ASEAN countries	Malaysia: Problems related to imposition of internal taxes on automobiles	⊡
	Thailand: Problems related to imposition of tariffs on digital cameras	⊙
East Asian countries	The abundance of counterfeit, pirated and other illegal products	⊡

⊙ Problem has been mostly solved. Future developments may need to be watched.

⊡ Further action is required

PART IV

The Doha Development Agenda and Beyond

16

The central place of market access for the WTO's development round

ANDREW L. STOLER

The Uruguay Round agreements that established the World Trade Organization (WTO) and the rules-based system as a single undertaking represented a quantum leap forward in the history of the *General Agreement on Tariffs and Trade* (GATT) and the WTO. It was an immensely complicated undertaking to simultaneously negotiate and reach agreement in such complex areas as intellectual property protection, designing a workable approach to governing trade in services, developing an agreed approach to measuring support to agriculture and disciplining trade-distorting investment measures. It was also not a simple task to elaborate the structure of the WTO as an institution. Of course, the crowing jewel was the new understanding on dispute settlement which, over the past ten years, has proven to be the most effective system of international dispute settlement the world has ever seen. With all of that on the table, in additional to more traditional market access and trade regulation issues, no one was surprised that the Uruguay Round took an extra three years to conclude and that the subsequent implementation of the many different agreements has sometimes presented special problems to the Members of the WTO.

I begin my discussion of major issues in the Doha Development Agenda negotiations with this brief recollection of the Uruguay Round in order to drive home a very important point at the start of this chapter. The Doha negotiations are very different from the Uruguay Round. This is a market access round, not a round involving the introduction and elaboration of complex new rules like the last round. Because it is a market access round, and because market access is the oldest and most traditional of GATT-WTO topics, we have all the more reason to be deeply concerned about the current state of play in this negotiation. Whether we are talking about agriculture, industrial tariffs, services negotiations or trade facilitation, WTO Members are on solid, well-known, ground. If reaching agreement in a market access round is as difficult as it seems to be, we need to be very worried and we need to try to understand the reasons for the problems of the Doha Round. The complex Uruguay Round took an extra three years to conclude, but this more straightforward round is already nearly three years behind schedule. Results that were targeted for agreement in March 2003 were still on the table as objectives for the Hong Kong meeting at the end of 2005.

I. Market access

If this is the market access round, we need to know where we are starting from and where we want to go to in order to understand the major issues in the negotiations. The Uruguay Round produced some impressive results, but apart from the additional progress made in cutting industrial tariffs, it was only the first real multilateral access negotiation for trade in agricultural products and services. WTO Members are left with a substantial job ahead of them if our objective is to significantly improve market access opportunities through the Doha Round.

Industrial tariff negotiations

At the end of the implementation period for Uruguay Round tariff reduction commitments, the simple average level of bound tariffs for industrial goods in developed countries stands at around 6.5 per cent, but there are significant peak tariffs in sensitive sectors like textiles and clothing. One estimate of the simple average bound tariff level for industrial goods in Latin America is 35 per cent, although much of this is due to the use of 'ceiling bindings', with applied rates relatively lower. In Asia, average rates range from around 60 per cent for India to zero for Hong Kong, China, and Singapore. The WTO Secretariat estimates that average bound tariff levels in Africa are generally lower than in developing Asia, but there is evidence that the average rate is somewhere above 30 per cent. Given that the share of intra-developing country trade in manufactured goods increased from 29 to 34 per cent between 1990 and 1999, it is clear that enhanced market access for industrial goods in developing country markets is important to developing as well as to developed countries.[1]

[1] The information in this chapter about industrial and agricultural tariffs is taken from WTO Secretariat, 'Market Access: Unfinished Business: Post-Uruguay Round Inventory and Issues', Special Studies 6 (Geneva, 2001).

Overall, the Uruguay Round negotiations produced a 40 per cent cut in developed countries' average tariffs on imports from all sources, and a 37 per cent average cut on imports from developing countries. Developing countries cut industrial tariffs by an average of 21 per cent on imports from other developing countries and 25 per cent on imports from developed countries. The Uruguay Round also produced important forward movement in tariff bindings.

When the Doha Round was launched, WTO Members' stated objective for this Round was 'to reduce or as appropriate eliminate tariffs, including the reduction or elimination of tariff peaks, high tariffs and tariff escalation, as well as non-tariff barriers, in particular on products of export interest to developing countries'.[2] Product coverage in the negotiations was to be comprehensive and without *a priori* exclusions.

By the time of the August 2004 Framework document,[3] very little progress had been made on industrial tariff negotiations. Apart from reaching agreement on the desirability of a tariff cutting formula and eventual conversion of non-*ad valorem* tariffs to *ad valorem* equivalents, little progress toward agreed practical modalities was made by that point. At the same time, WTO Members recognized the 'challenges' faced by non-reciprocal preference beneficiaries and those Members highly dependent on tariff revenues. More than a year later, when the Chairman of the negotiating group reported to the September 2005 meeting of the Trade Negotiations Committee,[4] core elements remaining to be discussed included the formula, flexibilities and treatment of unbound tariffs – not a very different picture from two years earlier in Cancun.

Market access in agriculture

Notwithstanding all of the attention given to trade distorting export subsidies and high levels of domestic support to agricultural producers, it is the market access 'pillar' of the Doha Round negotiations that is proving the most difficult. This is no doubt due in large part to the very limited progress made in the Uruguay Round in providing real market access. In many ways, the Uruguay Round was focussed on setting rules and parameters for future negotiations in a way that the systemic architecture

[2] Doha Ministerial Declaration, WT/MIN(01)/DEC/1, para. 16.

[3] Doha Work Programme, Decision adopted by the General Council on 1 August 2004, WT/L/579.

[4] Trade Negotiations Committee, Minutes of the Meeting held 14 September 2005, TN/C/M/20.

would be more amenable to market access opening. For example, although 'tariffication' and the introduction of tariff rate quotas for many products led in the post Uruguay Round to some very high out-of-quota tariff levels, tariffs are inherently easier to liberalize than actual quantitative restrictions. The Doha Round is about what we are going to do with these opportunities.

The Uruguay Round succeeded in achieving the binding of all agricultural tariffs, but often at very high effective rates and in many circumstances with formulations which are far from transparent. The long argument about the technical difficulties associated with translating specific or mixed tariff rates into *ad valorem* equivalent rates was a direct result of the messy aftermath of the Uruguay Round talks. Even where they are already expressed as an *ad valorem* rate, the rates of protection for agriculture tend to be much higher than for industrial goods. On top of that, there is a good deal of evidence of large amounts of 'water' in the bound tariffs for agriculture trade. Even a cursory glance at some WTO Members' tariff rates for farm trade seems to support this charge.

If we look at the percentage of all agricultural tariff lines with bound duty rates over 100 per cent *ad valorem*, we can see some very protective regimes in Norway (45 per cent) and Switzerland (7 per cent). The degree of protectionism in Norway is equivalent to that for India on this scale (also 45 per cent), while Bangladesh has 69 per cent of its tariff rates for agriculture over 100 per cent. For the 15 nations of the European Communities at the end of the Uruguay Round, more than one-third of agricultural tariffs exceed 15 per cent, generally defined as 'peak' tariffs. Tariff rate quotas that were supposed to establish minimum access opportunities or maintain current access levels where high tariffs are applied to out-of-quota quantities of imports have had disappointing 'fill-rates' in the post Uruguay Round period, possibly in large part due to the fact that no harmonized system has ever been agreed by WTO Members to allocate in-quota trade and many systems operate to actively discourage full fill-rates. In the late 1990's the simple average fill rate for all tariff rate quotas for which information was available was only 62 per cent. Even where the in-quota amounts are fully filled, the chances of exporting to countries operating agricultural tariff rate quotas once the in-quota amount has been reached are pretty dismal: out of quota tariff rates for dairy products exceed 100 per cent *ad valorem* in the European Communities, 70 per cent *ad valorem* in the United States, 200 per cent *ad valorem* in Canada and 130 per cent *ad valorem* in Mexico.

Finally, WTO Members were forced by the result of the Uruguay Round to launch the Doha Round agricultural negotiations against the presence in many countries of additional protection in the form of the special agricultural safeguard mechanism – available to some 38 countries for certain products. How the special safeguard has come to be used as a tool to frustrate competitive exporters of agricultural products is evident in the switch from volume-based to price-based special safeguard actions.

If all of this appears to result in a very protectionist environment for agricultural trade, it does. Recent research by World Bank economists has made clear that in the Doha Round, we will need to see *very large* reductions in bound tariff rates before we will see *any* real improvement in market access for many products. These researchers have calculated that bound rates would need to be reduced by at least 45 per cent and up to 75 per cent (for the highest tariffs) under a tiered formula before the global average agricultural tariff could be brought down by one-third.

In the Doha Ministerial Declaration, WTO Members committed themselves to a negotiation that would lead to 'substantial improvements in market access' – and this objective was confirmed in the 2004 Framework text. However, the same Framework text opens the way for WTO Members to designate a negotiated number of tariff lines to be treated as 'sensitive' and presumably subject to smaller cuts. In addition, developing countries are to be offered special and differential treatment that would take the form of an appropriate number of agricultural products that could be designated as 'special products' subjected to more flexible treatment. All of this should be cause for considerable concern in the Doha market access round.

The researchers from the World Bank tell us why. Welfare gains from global agricultural reform in the Doha Round would be reduced by three-quarters if developing countries designated just four per cent of their agricultural tariff lines as either 'sensitive' or 'special' and developed countries classified two per cent of their tariff lines as 'sensitive'. Of course, one does not need to be an agriculture trade expert to imagine which products would be most likely to be so designated in the Doha Round. The case of sugar illustrates why we do not want to see 'sensitive products' excluded from meaningful results in the Round. Global protectionism in sugar and extremely high prices for sugar in protected developed country markets has created a situation where 10 million tons of sugar consumption annually have been displaced by sugar substitutes.

Trade in services

WTO Members addressed trade in services for the first time only in the Uruguay Round negotiations where a considerable percentage of the effort went into writing the rules to govern services trade. The complexity of that task is demonstrated by the fact that Members still have not been able to agree on how to write rules governing safeguards, subsidies and government procurement in a services context. In this context, it is not surprising that the degree of market access for services reflected in WTO Members' post Uruguay Round schedules of specific commitments is not very impressive. For the most part these schedules reflected the status quo of market access in the mid-1990s rather than real liberalization.

The very considerable scope for further sectoral coverage of services trade was highlighted in the WTO Secretariat's Special Study Number 6, published in 2001.[5] That study noted that of the 160 possible service subsectors on which WTO Members could choose to schedule specific commitments, about one-third of WTO Members have made commitments on 20 subsectors or less, one-third between 21 and 60 subsectors and the remaining third by more than 61 subsectors. On average, across all schedules, a 'typical' WTO Member has undertaken commitments on slightly more than 25 subsectors, thus covering only about 15 per cent of the total possible.

The Doha Round is the 'development' round. Today there is a very real relationship between services trade liberalization and economic development. The WTO negotiations are not addressed to investment, but they are very much concerned with trade in services and there is today a very strong connection between the two. This is due in part to the fact that most services are still not easily traded cross-border and require a local presence in the economy in which they will be provided. Today, more than two-thirds of all foreign direct investment (FDI) flows are services-related, with services industries accounting for more than 60 per cent of world FDI stock – compared to about 25 per cent in the 1970s.[6]

In developing Asia, two-fifths of total FDI inflows are from other developing Asian countries, some of which now invest more abroad than developed countries – measured as a share of gross fixed capital formation. We know for a fact that services-related FDI brings with it

[5] WTO Secretariat, 'Market Access'.

[6] Data on FDI is taken from United Nations Conference on Trade and Development (UNCTAD), *World Investment Report 2004: The Shift Towards Services* (Geneva/New York, 2004), p. 98.

important positive employment and technology transfer benefits and it can benefit the economy in other ways as well. Studies have shown that developing countries that liberalized telecommunications services and invited in FDI in the sector have grown by as much as 2 per cent more per year than those countries that have not liberalized the sector.

Countries need investment for development. If today most of this investment is services-related, then it is clear that open services trade regimes will attract more investment. It doesn't take rocket science to see that the current failure to enhance market access through the WTO services negotiations can only impact negatively on countries' ability to attract investment and stimulate growth.

In the services trade negotiations, now under way for more than five years, just 69 initial and 30 revised offers are on the table.[7] The WTO's 148 Members were all to have had their offers on the table prior to the September 2003 Cancun meeting. More than two years later, less than half of the WTO's Member governments are participating in the negotiations. As with agriculture and industrial tariffs, this is essentially a market access problem.

II. Reasons for the lack of progress

WTO Members' apparent inability to come to grips seriously with the core market access issues of the Doha Round is cause for serious concern. We need to try to understand the possible reasons for lack of progress to date.

I believe that the enormously expanded level of activity in the negotiation of preferential trade agreements (PTAs) could be part of the explanation for the lack of progress on market access issues in the Doha Round. Unless a PTA is comprehensive, covering substantially all trade and eliminating substantially all forms of discrimination, the agreement won't satisfy the WTO conditions for legal departure from the most-favoured nation (MFN) rule. This is, I think, a serious potential problem with PTAs, not because of non-compliance with a legal rule, but because the systemic exclusion of large sectors from trade liberalization in bilateral deals is very likely contributing materially to the Doha Round's problems with market access liberalization. Why would a government agree to open a sensitive sector to all potential WTO trading partners if it was able to exclude it from liberalization in a negotiation with just one partner?

[7] The list of WTO Members that have submitted offers is available at <www.wto.org/english/tratop_e/serv_e/s_negs_e.htm>.

Another issue arises out of many countries' evident commitment to preference maintenance and sectoral protectionism and their consequent unwillingness to participate in meaningful market access negotiations in the Doha Round. The wrong-headed nature of this approach was addressed in the 2004 World Bank publication *Global Economic Prospects and the Developing Countries – Realising the Development Promise of the Doha Round*.[8] That report noted that existing preference schemes are far from universal in their application and do not in fact benefit most of the world's poor. For example, a significant portion of the European Communities' low-tariff sugar quota benefits Mauritius, the richest country in sub-Saharan Africa, and half of the countries benefiting from American sugar quotas are net sugar importers. Trade under special preferences is made more problematic through complicated rules of origin. Seafood imports under the European Communities' 'Everything but Arms' preference scheme for least-developed countries (LDCs) have stricter rules of origin than do European Communities preferences under the Generalized System of Preferences (GSP) or the Cotonou Agreement. Many of these problems have been addressed in dozens of studies and are well known to economists and policy-makers; however, still we find WTO Members in the Framework documents willing to take into consideration the particular needs of preference beneficiary Members.

Finally, we have to admit that after more than fifty years of progressive liberalization in areas like industrial tariffs, most of the developed countries have probably reduced or eliminated all of the 'easy' tariffs and are now left with the task of dealing with politically sensitive sectors that were able to escape cuts in earlier GATT rounds. Where tariff peaks remain, they are there to attempt to protect sectors like textiles, clothing and footwear. With the end of the WTO-sanctioned quotas on textiles and clothing, these tariffs might be even more difficult to cut in the Doha Round.

III. The need for renewed commitment

If the Doha Round is to succeed, we need to see a renewed commitment from WTO Members to meaningful progress on the central issues of market access for agriculture, industrial products and trade in services.

In agriculture, we need an approach that minimizes the number of 'bands' in the tiered formula, broadens the upper bands as much as possible

[8] World Bank, *Global Economic Prospects and the Developing Countries – Realising the Development Promise of the Doha Round* (Washington, DC, 2004).

and uses a Swiss-type formula with the smallest possible coefficient. Because of the very significant amount of 'water' in many of the highest agricultural tariffs, the negotiating modalities should provide for a down payment initial across-the-board cut that would eliminate the excess protection in the 'overhang'. The modalities need to be especially restrictive on possible resort to sensitive and special products and severely restrict the flexibility to be shown to such products.

For industrial products, we need to agree on a non-linear formula that makes significant further progress in cutting higher tariffs, tariff peaks and attacks tariff escalation. This should be combined with an approach that permits WTO Members to go further on a sectoral basis and supplement formula cuts with a request/offer procedure.

In services, there should be agreement that all WTO Members, without exception, will table initial or improved offers and that these offers should demonstrably provide for actual improvements in market access.

If this Doha Round can be completed with substantial results in market access, global gains, in particular for developing countries are likely to be significant. A paper by Kym Anderson and Will Martin at the World Bank estimates that freeing all merchandise trade and eliminating agricultural subsidies could boost global welfare by US $300 billion per year by 2015.[9] A study by the University of Michigan estimates that cutting market access barriers in agriculture, manufacturing and services by one-third – not an impossible task – would boost the world economy by US $613 billion.[10] These numbers are too large to ignore.

Market access questions can seem tedious, with all the talk of linear formulae, tariff bands, *ad valorem* equivalents, etc. To many, this is not the 'sexy' part of trade policy. But market access means real money in the pockets of real exporters and importers and ever since the majority of this Round's rule-making negotiations were jettisoned in the August 2004 Framework package, market access has been the core of the Doha Round. Completing the Doha Development Agenda successfully should be a major priority for WTO Members.

[9] Kym Anderson and Will Martin (eds), *Agricultural Trade Reform and the Doha Development Agenda* (Washington, DC, 2005).

[10] Drusilla K. Brown, Alan V. Deardorff, and Robert M. Stern, 'Computational Analysis of Multilateral Trade Liberalization in the Uruguay Round and Doha Development Round', University of Michigan School of Public Policy, Discussion Paper No. 489 (Ann Arbor, 2002).

17

Agricultural issues in the Doha Development Agenda negotiations

MASAYOSHI HONMA

Agricultural negotiations in the World Trade Organization (WTO) began in 2000, before the launch of the Doha Development Agenda. Together with the negotiations in the services sector, the agricultural negotiations were part of the 'built-in agenda' agreed in the Uruguay Round. Agriculture is the key to making progress in the Doha Development Agenda, or it may lead to its unravelling. Without movement in the agricultural negotiations, movement in the other areas will be unlikely.

The agricultural negotiations are conducted on the basis of the following three pillars: market access, export competition, and domestic support. Among them, the export competition pillar has seen the most progress. At Hong Kong, Ministers agreed 'to ensure the parallel elimination of all forms of export subsidies and disciplines on all export measures with equivalent effect to be completed by the end of 2013'.[1]

The United States, the European Communities, and Japan are the major players with respect to domestic support, particularly in terms of reductions of subsidies in the amber box, under which the most trade-distorting support is classified. It is unlikely that tighter disciplines will be placed on the blue and the green boxes, even though a number of programmes eligible for green box status have been shown to encourage production and distort trade. At the same time, developing countries have insisted on introducing new provisions to take into account the realities of developing country agriculture. The most difficult issues are those in the market access pillar, which includes tariff reductions. Tariffs will be grouped according to the tariff levels and put into bands.

This chapter first describes the current stage of WTO negotiations on agriculture. This is followed by a discussion of the issues that are of particular interest to developed countries, particularly food importing

[1] Doha Work Programme Ministerial Declaration, WT/MIN(05)/DEC, para. 6.

countries like Japan. The issues discussed include multi-functionality of agriculture, food security and safety, and tariff peaks. Finally, the chapter offers some reflections on the potential for success in the agricultural negotiations and other areas of the Doha Development Agenda.

I. Review of the current WTO negotiations on agriculture

The agricultural negotiations originally were to result in an agreement on modalities by the end of March 2003. Establishment of a modality indicates the conclusion of actual negotiations for determining methods for tariff reductions, the figures that will form the basis for such reductions, and other matters. The Chairman of the Special Session of the WTO Committee on Agriculture, Stuart Harbinson, presented a first draft of the modalities document in February 2003 and a revised version in March 2003. The modalities could not be finalized because of objections by both exporting nations, which seek a major reduction in trade protection, and by importing nations, which are trying to keep such a reduction to a minimum.

As explained earlier, the agricultural negotiations are being conducted on the basis of the following three pillars: market access, export competition, and domestic support. All of the major trading nations have tabled proposals in each of these areas. As regards market access, the United States and the Cairns Group nations, such as Australia, have proposed a major opening of agricultural markets, insisting on applying the Swiss formula of tariff reductions in which the higher the tariff, the larger the reduction. Specifically, they proposed that tariffs be reduced over five years to the point where all tariffs would be less than 25 per cent. Thereafter, all tariffs would be reduced to zero by a certain deadline. The European Communities and Japan insist on maintaining a balance between trade and non-trade concerns, proposing reductions of no less than 15 per cent and averaging 36 per cent, similar to the previous Uruguay Round approach.

The tariff reduction methods in the Harbinson draft included a compromise proposal. Although it was not the Swiss formula, which would keep all tariffs below a certain level, it tried to achieve equality by applying higher rates of reduction to goods with high tariffs, instead of bundling all goods together as under the Uruguay Round approach. It also incorporates a reduction of tariff peaks (tariffs that are very high), one of the points of contention in these negotiations. The Harbinson draft was opposed by exporting nations such as the United States and the Cairns Group nations, who deemed it inadequate. It was also opposed by Japan and the European Communities, who deemed it too extreme and feared that it would lead to destruction of their domestic agricultural sectors.

Then, in August, the United States and the European Communities, which had formerly been on opposite sides of the debate, sought a new compromise draft and agreed on a joint draft. Based on this draft, the Chairman of the WTO General Council incorporated a proposal on agricultural modalities in the draft Cancun Ministerial Declaration. The draft Declaration called for adopting one of the following tariff reduction methods: the Uruguay Round approach, the Swiss formula, or the elimination of tariffs. In other words, tariffs would be classified into the following three groups and reduced accordingly: (i) tariffs to be reduced by setting minimum and average reduction rates; (ii) tariffs to be reduced to below a fixed uniform level; and (iii) tariffs to be eliminated. In addition, maximum tariff levels would be set, and tariffs exceeding these levels would be reduced to the maximum levels. If tariffs were not reduced, measures promoting increased imports (such as expansion of the tariff quota limits) would be adopted for the relevant goods or for other goods. This was a proposed framework only and did not include figures such as distribution ratios of goods among group and rates of tariff reduction.

However, many nations expressed dissatisfaction with this draft. Developing countries, such as India and Brazil, were particularly outspoken. They considered that special measures for developing nations were not as clearly reflected in the draft Ministerial Declaration as in the Harbinson draft, and that reductions in protection by developed nations, which would be likely to lead to expansion of exports from developing nations, were insufficient. At the same time, these countries were suspicious of the negotiations, which advanced under the guidance of the European Communities and the United States.

After the Cancun Ministerial Conference ended in deadlock in September 2003, WTO Members made efforts to put the negotiations and the rest of the work programme back on track. Work intensified in the first half of 2004, with the new target date of reaching a package of framework agreements by the end of July, in effect Friday, 30 July. The first draft of the 'July package' was circulated on 16 July 2004. Intense negotiations in various formats resulted in an agreement on 1 August 2004.

The July package includes agreement on the following issues relating to agricultural market access: tariff reductions will be made through a tiered formula that takes into account the different tariff structures of WTO Members; progressivity in tariff reductions will be achieved through deeper cuts in higher tariffs with flexibilities for sensitive products; the role of a tariff cap in a tiered formula with distinct treatment for sensitive products will be further evaluated; without undermining the overall objective of the tiered approach, Members may designate an appropriate number, to be negotiated, of tariff lines to be treated as sensitive, taking account of existing commitments for these products.

Subsequently, the negotiations moved to the stage at which specific numbers of tiers or bands and the tariff reduction rates are discussed. For example, the G-20 proposes five bands (four for developing countries) with each band assigned different rates of tariff liberalization. All products in every band would be subject to uniform rates of reduction, but products in the higher bands, meaning products with higher initial tariffs, would be subject to higher rates than those in the lower bands. In addition, tariffs would be capped at 150 per cent for developing countries and at 100 per cent for developed countries. The European Communities and the G-10 favour a more flexible formula, while the United States, Australia, and New Zealand favour a more radical formula.

II. Important issues for food importing developed countries

At the stage of submitting proposals for negotiations, Japan proposed taking into account the importance of non-trade concerns such as multifunctionality and food security, and insisted on flexibility in tariff reduction. The European Communities proposed, at an early stage of the negotiations, a gradual liberalization along the lines of the Uruguay Round linear reduction formula, which both Korea and Japan support. Importing economies prefer to maintain the current framework of amber, blue and green boxes, but agree on further reduction of the Aggregate Measurement of Support, but at a tolerable speed. Japan agrees on gradual reductions of export subsidies, but at the same time stresses the need for stronger disciplines on export prohibitions and restrictions and suggests converting them to export taxes.

As regards the other Asian countries, Korea proposed that it should be allowed to apply the developing country provisions for the next ten years during which time it will make a full-fledged effort at agricultural reform. China insisted on more special and differential treatment for developing economies with a view to ensuring food security and increasing income and work opportunities for low income people and resource-poor farmers in the rural areas. China also emphasizes that it has made substantive tariff reduction commitments in its accession negotiation and that the new WTO Members should be exempted from making further tariff reductions.

Both Thailand and China argue that, while developed economies utilize both border measures and domestic support to help domestic production, developing countries cannot afford to resort to domestic support due to budgetary constraints and still require special safeguards or other border restrictions. Thailand complains that 'unrealistically' stringent sanitary, phytosanitary, and zoosanitary standards by some developed countries tend to impede its export of agricultural products.

Multi-functionality of agriculture

The specific contents of the concept of multi-functionality, which Japan insists must be taken into account in the negotiations, vary according to the history and national conditions of each country. The following functions may be considered as major elements:

(i) Land conservation including preventing floods, preventing soil erosion, and preventing landslides;
(ii) Fostering of water resources;
(iii) Preservation of the natural environment, including management of organic waste, resolution and removal of polluted substances, air purification, and maintenance of bio-diversity and preservation of wildlife habitats;
(iv) Formation of scenic landscapes;
(v) Transmitting of culture;
(vi) Rural amenity; and
(vii) Maintaining and revitalizing the rural community.

Most of these are so-called externalities created by agricultural activities.

Recognition of the multi-functionality of agriculture itself is evidence that important progress has been made with respect to the evaluation of agricultural activities, especially from an environmental viewpoint.[2] But what needs to be asked is how to maximize the net benefits from the multiple functions of agriculture keeping in mind the cost of maintaining

[2] For a review of studies that attempt to estimate of the value of multi-functionality, see K. Demura, and K. Yoshida (eds), *Towards the Creation of Rural Amenities* (Tokyo, 1999) (in Japanese). There are criticisms of the methods, calculations and data used to evaluate the value of multi-functionality. See, for example, 'Multi-functionality: a pretext for protection?' Australian Bureau of Agricultural and Resource Economics (1999) *ABARE Current Issues*; and R. Trewin, 'Issues in Japanese Agricultural Policy', in Australian National University, 'A Way Forward for Japanese Agriculture?' (2000) *Pacific Economic Papers*, No. 300.

agricultural operations. We have to estimate the marginal loss (gain) of the social value resulting from multi-functionality as agricultural production shrinks (expands), if multi-functionality is to be placed at the centre of the proposal for the agricultural trade negotiations.

The relationship between multi-functionality and agricultural production is not straightforward. There are many alternative levels of production and many combinations of products to achieve a certain level of social value created by agricultural activities. WTO negotiations involve discussions of the levels of support and protection that affect trade and production. Thus, a quantitative assessment of multi-functionality in terms of agricultural production is necessary. However, the multiple functions of agriculture are not the targets that agricultural production directly aims to hit. They are not necessarily efficient in terms of fulfilling social needs. This complexity and the ambiguous relationship between multi-functionality and agricultural production make it difficult to conduct a quantitative assessment of multi-functionality based on scientific evidence. Instead, countries can directly subsidize, via the green box, activities relating to conservation, water resources, the environment, culture and other multi-functional values of rural areas.

Food security and safety

Food security, which is also an issue to be considered as a non-trade concern, is defined as a situation in which all households have both physical and economic access to adequate food for all members and where households are not at risk of losing such access.[3] There are two options on how to achieve food security at the national level. One is the pursuit of food self-sufficiency and the other is food self-reliance. Food self-sufficiency means meeting food needs as far as possible from domestic supplies and minimizing food imports. This involves the risk of relying predominantly on domestic production. In contrast, food self-reliance means maintaining a level of domestic production, but relying also on international trade to meet the food needs of the population. The strategy that a country should take will depend on the benefits and risks of relying on international trade.

Food security is an important issue in countries whose food self-sufficiency rates are very low. In Japan, the food self-sufficiency ratio has

[3] See Food and Agriculture Organization, 'Food and international trade', Technical Background Document 12 for World Food Summit (Rome, 1996).

dropped to 40 per cent on a calorie basis, which is the lowest among the developed countries. Some people are very concerned about this low level of self- sufficiency from the food security viewpoint. Ensuring food security is one of the basic roles that the government should play. The Ministry of Agriculture, Forestry and Fisheries of Japan has adopted as a guideline for public efforts to raise the food self-sufficiency ratio to 45 per cent by 2015.

Imports and stockpiling, as well as domestic production, are recognized as useful policy measures for achieving food security. However, excessive dependence on imports is considered to have the following problems: (i) the world food supply may become unstable in the short term and may become tighter in the medium to long term; (ii) agricultural trade has such unstable features because relatively lower shares of output are currently being exported and the major agricultural products are only being exported by some specific countries; and (iii) large purchases by an economically-dominant country at a time of food shortage may have a negative impact on the international market. Stockpiling is also questioned because it is only a short-term measure given the loss in quality and the cost of stockpiled food.

Policy measures for food security will differ depending on the type of crisis considered.[4] The predictions on future world market conditions depend on assumptions and forecasts of exogenous variables. It is important to prepare policy measures that respond to possible food security risks at a minimum social cost. In addition, the volatility of world food prices arises as a result of the intervention of governments endeavouring to insulate domestic markets from international trade, which makes the world market smaller than it would be without intervention. If all domestic markets are integrated to international trade, poor or rich harvests in some areas can be dealt with by the world market. Therefore, limiting trade for food security purposes is not the correct policy measure.

Full regard should be given to consumers' concern about food safety as well as prices and availability (security). Exporters should cooperate fully with importers to eliminate pesticide residues and causes of disease in foodstuff. However, standards and testing that are too strict, which is the trend in the name of safety, will impede food trade. The WTO *Agreement on the Application of Sanitary and Phytosanitary Measures* (*SPS Agreement*) sets out rules on the use of standards and recommends that SPS measures be well-founded in sound science and based on a risk

[4] For a classification of possible food crises and proposed appropriate policy measures, see Y. Hayami, *Japanese Agriculture Under Siege* (London, 1988).

assessment. Importing economies should also be encouraged to assist exporters, especially those of developing economies, to enhance their capacity to comply with SPS measures.

Tariff peaks

One of the important issues being discussed in the current negotiations is the reduction of tariff peaks. High tariffs for agricultural imports are not unique to Japan. Tariff peaks in agriculture are commonly observed in developed countries. Table 17.1 shows the number of tariff peaks in terms of tariff lines for the European Communities, Japan, and the United States. Tariff peaks, which are defined here as tariff rates of 20 per cent or more, are most common in dairy products, cereals (not in the United States), sugar, and the food industry (processed) products. For all agricultural and fisheries products taken together, the proportion of tariff lines for which duties exceed 20 per cent is about one-quarter of all tariff lines for both the European Communities and Japan and about one-tenth for the United States.

Problems relating to tariffication involve not only tariff peaks, but also tariff rate quotas. Tariff rate quotas apply to commodities for which border measures were converted from quantitative restrictions to tariffs. The quantities to which lower tariffs are applied are mostly the base period imports under the previous imports quotas. The over-the-quota tariffs were set at very high levels. If the these tariffs are prohibitively high, there are no imports beyond the tariff rate quotas. Thus, tariff rate quotas work the same way as previous import quotas.

Table 17.2 indicates the average difference between within-quota tariffs and over-the-quota tariffs for several countries. Japan, Canada, Norway, and Korea have extremely high over-the-quota tariffs that apply to newly tariffied products. Meanwhile, Norway has high tariffs even within the tariff rate quotas. These high over-the-quota tariffs suggest that tariffication has not fundamentally changed the nature of the previously existing non-tariff border measures. This is why exporting countries, particularly developing countries, demand reduction of tariff peaks in the negotiations.

New dimensions of agricultural negotiations

The Uruguay Round was concluded after the two-party, Blair House accord between the United States and the European Communities.

However, this was merely an arrangement composed of measures that would benefit the two parties. Other nations, particularly developing nations, felt strongly that they had been left out of the negotiations. In fact, many expressed dissatisfaction with the results of the Uruguay Round, claiming that developing nations derived no benefit from it. The European Communities and the United States are important players in the current negotiations, but with three of every four WTO Members being developing nations, it seems clear that the same method of reaching an agreement will not work.

In fact, the traditional alliances of agricultural producers were transformed in reaction to the United States–European Communities proposal of August 2003 and the counterproposal from a group of developing countries later known as G-20 countries. The emergence of the G-20 group, led by Brazil, China, and India, has complicated negotiations by turning the debate into a North-South discussion involving agriculture, which is one of the most sensitive issues in the Doha Development Agenda.

Among the major objectives, the G-20 group seeks: (i) further reduction in blue box domestic support, (ii) reduction of export subsidies, including export credit programmes, and (iii) to prevent the extension of the peace clause. The group intended to engage in serious negotiations and was disappointed by the collapse of the talks in Cancun before discussions on agriculture took place. A lesson learned at Cancun is the need for strong political will to negotiate, and for leadership.

Another important dimension that arose in Cancun is the so-called cotton subsidies initiative, in which four West African producing countries pleaded to reduce and eliminate cotton subsidies, particularly in the United States, the European Communities, and China, which are heavy subsidizers of cotton. The initiative itself was outside the context of agricultural negotiations, but drew attention to the plight of some of the poorest WTO Members. The Western African countries submitted a draft text to the WTO Director-General, who coordinated the negotiations on the cotton initiative.

The second draft of the Cancun Ministerial Declaration, however, reflected language proposed by the United States, which had resisted inclusion of the cotton initiative in the draft. The text suggested that the African countries stop growing cotton rather than compel the subsidizing countries to address the cause of the problem. This angered Western African countries, which were prodded on by anti-trade non-governmental organizations (NGOs). It then led the African–Caribbean–Pacific (ACP) group, who supported the cotton initiative, to refuse to negotiate on the Singapore issues. Here, again, it appears that the negotiations lack an appropriate coordinator to bridge the North and South countries.

III. Concluding remarks

The WTO is an international institution whose mission is to achieve economic prosperity through free trade. The preamble to the *Agreement on Agriculture* includes the following long-term objective: establishment of 'a fair and market-oriented agricultural trading system.' Article 20 of the *Agreement on Agriculture* states that the objective of agricultural negotiations is the continuation of 'fundamental reforms' through reductions in 'support and protection'. It is vital for all countries to link agricultural negotiations to structural reforms in agriculture.

Structural reforms in agriculture are also essential to achieve greater international cooperation. Agricultural products are now highly differentiated and one of the strategies to expand agricultural trade is to seek commodities that have comparative advantage and promote so-called intra-industry trade. For example, even rice is now highly differentiated in quality and it may be possible to trade different varieties of rice identified by the place of production.

Agricultural policy in developed countries has shifted toward decoupled policies like direct payments to protect farmers, if necessary. Governments should also promote seeking comparative advantage in the sector for intra-industry trade, assisting information gathering, and fostering investment for research and development.

In addition, it is becoming more important to harmonize SPS measures, particularly for agricultural trade between developing and developed countries. There is the WTO *SPS Agreement*, but the achievements in terms of enforcing effective disciplines are far behind expectations.[5] In particular, developing countries have not been able to participate in the implementation of the *SPS Agreement* as equal partners. It would be more effective if developed countries provide developing countries with technical and financial assistance for their participation in the SPS harmonization activities. This kind of mutual cooperation would promote sustainable development in agriculture.

[5] For a discussion of SPS issues and developing countries, see, for example, P. Athukorala and S. Jayasuriya, 'Food Safety Issues, Trade and WTO Rules: A Developing Country Perspective' (2003) 26 *World Economy*, 1395–1416; and J.M. Finger and P. Schuler, 'Implementation of WTO Commitments: The Development Challenge' in B. Hoekman, A. Mattoo and P. English (eds), *Development, Trade and the WTO: A Handbook* (Washington, DC, 2002), pp. 493–503.

Table 17.1 *Tariff peaks by agricultural product groups (EC, Japan, and the US)*[1]

Product group[2]	Number of tariff lines within a tariff range				No. of peaks	Share in total%
	Total	20–29 %	30–99 %	100 %		
European Community (EC)						
Meat, live animal (1–2)	351	68	79	14	161	46
Fish and crustaceans (3)	373	45	0	0	45	12
Dairy products (4)	197	21	77	9	107	54
Fruit and vegetables (7–8)	407	10	5	1	16	4
Cereals, flours etc. (10–11)	174	29	75	0	104	60
Veg. oils, fats, oilseeds (12, 15)	211	0	8	2	10	5
Canned & prep. meat, fish (16)	105	17	8	0	25	24
Sugar, cocoa & prep. (17, 18)	75	34	6	0	40	53
Prepared fruit, vegetables (20)	310	70	39	1	110	35
Other food ind. prod. (19, 21)	90	27	8	0	35	39
Beverages & tobacco (22, 24)	202	9	15	2	26	13
Other agr. prod. (5–6, 13–14, 23)	231	4	14	4	22	10
All agr. and fish prod. (1–24)	2,726	343	334	33	701	26
Japan						
Meat, live animal (1–2)	136	3	19	7	29	21
Fish and crustaceans (3)	189	0	0	0	0	0
Dairy products (4)	146	45	57	22	122	84
Fruit and vegetables (7–8)	209	1	2	7	10	5
Cereals, flours etc. (10–11)	132	37	24	10	71	54
Veg. oils, fats, oilseeds (12, 15)	161	1	1	3	5	3

Canned & prep. meat, fish (16)	101	21	3	3	27	27
Sugar, cocoa & prep. (17, 18)	80	26	19	6	51	64
Prepared fruit, vegetables (20)	231	52	5	2	59	26
Other food ind. prod. (19, 21)	232	113	2	15	130	56
Beverages & tobacco (22, 24)	65	8	0	0	8	12
Other agr. prod. (5–6, 13–14, 23)	208	0	0	0	0	0
All agr. and fish prod. (1–24)	1,890	307	132	75	514	27
United States						
Meat, live animals (1–2)	116	6	0	0	6	5
Fish and crustaceans (3)	114	0	0	0	0	0
Dairy products (4)	251	29	58	9	96	38
Fruit and vegetables (7–8)	269	13	0	0	13	5
Cereals, flours etc. (10–11)	59	0	0	0	0	0
Veg. oils, fats, oilseeds (12, 15)	124	0	2	2	4	3
Canned & prep. meat, fish (16)	90	1	1	0	2	2
Sugar, cocoa & prep. (17, 18)	144	6	13	2	21	15
Prepared fruit, vegetables (20)	169	3	2	3	8	5
Other food ind. prod. (19, 21)	156	11	18	2	31	20
Beverages & tobacco (22, 24)	126	1	3	8	12	10
Other agr. prod. (5–6, 13–14, 23)	161	0	2	0	2	1
All agr. and fish prod. (1–24)	1,779	70	99	26	195	11

[1] Tariff peaks are defined as tariff rates that are 20 per cent or more. All are MFN tariffs.
[2] The numbers within the parenthesis in the product are Standard International Trade Classification (SITC) numbers.

Source: Food and Agriculture Organization (FAO) compilation based on data provided in UNCTAD/WTO (1997), *The post-UR tariff environment for developing countries*, TD/B/COM.1/14, Tables 1–3.

Table 17.2 *Average tariff rates applied to agricultural imports for selected countries*

	All agricultural products	Products newly tariffied		
		Within TRQ	Secondary	All products
Japan	12 %	20 %	274 %	5 %
USA	6 %	10 %	29 %	4 %
EU	20 %	8 %	45 %	7 %
Canada	5 %	8 %	203 %	5 %
Australia	3 %	7 %	27 %	10 %
Switzerland	51 %	36 %	81 %	9 %
Norway	124 %	216 %	239 %	26 %
Korea	62 %	21 %	366 %	18 %
Thailand	35 %	31 %	91 %	29 %

Source: OECD, Review of Tariffs Synthesis Report, 1999.

18

Beyond Doha: reflections on the future of trade remedies

JAMES P. DURLING

We just commemorated the 100th anniversary of the first national anti-dumping law. For much of that history, anti-dumping laws and other trade remedies remained obscure and relative unimportant features of trade policy. That situation began to change in the 1980s. Over the past 25 years, however, trade remedies have grown in importance. As other forms of trade restrictions have been reduced or eliminated, trade remedies have taken their place.

As we now commemorate the 10th anniversary of the World Trade Organization (WTO), it is appropriate to review the experience of the past two decades and reflect on what might happen over the next two decades. In doing so, it is useful to consider the history of trade remedies before and after creation of the WTO in 1995. With that history as background, we can then discuss what trends seem likely in the future. We can also draw on the growing body of scholarly literature that has studied trade remedies, and tried to explain their trends and effects.

To borrow a phrase from the Princeton economist Jacob Viner, trade remedies have been a growing 'problem in international trade'.[1] We must now ask whether the problem will continue to grow beyond Doha. I fear the problem will continue to grow, as trade restrictions will continue to migrate from areas of tighter discipline to those areas – principally trade remedies – with weaker disciplines. This chapter offers some thoughts on this important question. As discussed below:

(i) Anti-dumping duties have been and will continue to be the trade remedy of choice. Although the trading system would be better off with more safeguard actions, that shift of focus is unlikely to occur.
(ii) The number of trade remedies is likely to continue to grow, but the magnitude of that growth probably will be limited unless there is a

[1] Jacob Viner, *Dumping: A Problem in International Trade* (Chicago, 1923).

sharp decline in the global economy. Ironically, when the economy declines, and when we most need *trade* to restart growth, we instead experience *trade restrictions* that retard growth.

(iii) The number of users of trade remedies has increased dramatically, although there have been more countries adopting trade remedy laws than countries using the new laws intensively.

(iv) Although the growing number of users and the tendency toward retaliatory cases will expand the number of trade remedies, there are offsetting economic and political considerations that may temper that growth.

(v) The shift to more frequent use of trade remedies by countries that have not traditionally been major users will continue. Most countries already have trade remedy laws, but there will be increased willingness to use those laws and bring more cases.

Although the problem will continue to grow, will the WTO be able to address this problem? The experience since 1995 does not inspire confidence that the WTO will effectively limit trade remedies:

(i) The effort to create more discipline through negotiations has had only a limited effect. The creation of new legal disciplines actually correlates with the increasing number of countries adopting national trade remedy legislation.

(ii) The new disciplines often prove to be very elusive, as the experience with sunset provisions and new rules on the use of 'facts available' have shown. We need new approaches to creating meaningful disciplines.

(iii) The pending negotiations during the Doha Round have not inspired much confidence that new and effective disciplines will be forthcoming.

(iv) WTO review of trade remedies has increased dramatically, and trade remedies now constitute a large portion of total WTO disputes, but still represent a tiny fraction of the total national trade remedies.

(v) The likelihood of a trade remedy being challenged is small. Certain countries and certain types of trade remedies are more likely to be challenged.

(vi) The trend toward WTO review will continue, but will shift increasingly to harder issues such as whether there is 'injury' or not. These future cases will continue to raise politically charged disputes about the proper standard of review.

(vii) Even when trade remedies are challenged, the implementation of those WTO decisions has been limited. Often trade restrictions tend to linger long after the WTO has condemned them.

(viii) The larger impact of trade remedies may be political and psychological, not economic. Trade remedies have become so politically sensitive that they are hard to discipline. Everyone could agree to cut tariffs over time. There seems to be no such consensus on trade remedies.

(ix) Trade remedies breed cynicism about the push toward trade liberalization. Many countries wonder if the other efforts at trade liberalization mean anything if the gains can be so easily taken away through arbitrary trade remedies.

(x) Trade remedies also breed cynicism about their use. When a country considers imposing a trade remedy, there really is no disincentive against wrongly imposing a trade remedy. The only consequence is that maybe at some point in the distant future the country might have to lift the wrongly imposed remedy.

(xi) Looking forward, although the number of cases may moderate, the impact may be greater. Those cases may be shutting off the early stages of new trading relationships, and thus causing damage far greater than just the elimination of small volumes of trade.

The first step to solving a problem is to understand that problem. This chapter offers some initial thoughts about past trends and future prospects. Initially, I discuss the trends in the use of trade remedies. I then turn to how the WTO has tried to discipline the use of trade remedies.

I. Trends in trade remedies

It is useful to consider three distinct aspects of how trade remedies have been used over time: the mix of trade remedies, the frequency of use, and the distribution of use. Although anti-dumping measures remain popular, the number of countries using safeguards measures has expanded considerably.

The mix of trade remedies

Past trends

Anti-dumping duties have been the consensus trade remedy of choice. Of the total 3,099 trade remedies cases filed over the 1995–2004 period, a remarkable 2,647 of those actions, or 85 per cent, have been anti-dumping cases. There have been some countervailing duty and safeguard actions, but these have been considerably fewer. Only 5 per cent of the total trade remedy cases were countervailing duty actions, and only 9 per cent were safeguard actions.[2]

There are natural reasons to prefer anti-dumping duties. First, anti-dumping duty cases apply somewhat more lax legal standards than safeguard actions. Second, anti-dumping duty cases involve only private companies, and not the government of the country targeted, which makes them somewhat less political. Third, the legal standards for 'dumping' are so lax that it is much easier to find evidence of 'dumping' than to find evidence of subsidies. Fourth, in many countries safeguards are discretionary, and require a political decision to impose them, while anti-dumping cases are automatic if the legal requirements have been met. Finally, once imposed anti-dumping duties can last for five years or beyond, while safeguard measures have a practical life span of only three years before the need to pay compensation for those restrictions makes them too expensive to maintain.

Notwithstanding the preference for anti-dumping measures, there was a burst of interest in safeguards in 2001 and 2002. There were 185 safeguard cases begun in those two years, compared to only 61 cases globally over the six-year period 1995 through 2000.[3] Many of these cases were retaliatory actions against the infamous United States safeguard investigation and trade restrictions on steel imports. As other countries feared diversion of steel into their own markets, they filed a large number of their own safeguard measures to prevent that diversion.

Future trends

The preference for anti-dumping duties is likely to continue. The reasons that have made anti-dumping measures so popular in the past all continue to exist and will apply for the indefinite future. Anti-dumping duties will continue to be the trade remedy of choice.

There may be some renewed interest in countervailing duties. Unlike anti-dumping investigations, which have averaged about 265 per year over the 1995–2004 period, countervailing duty investigations have aver-

[2] These figures come from the reporting by Members to the WTO, as reported at <http://www.wto.org>. Full year data for 2005 was not yet available as this chapter was being finalized.

[3] Safeguard data from Cliff Stevenson and Ilaria Filippi, *Global Trade Protection Report 2004*, January 2005, p. 4, available at <http://www.mayerbrownrowe.com/globaltrade/index.asp>.

aged about 18 per year, with a maximum of 41 investigations begun in 1999.[4] But countervailing duties share the key feature that makes anti-dumping investigations so attractive — the ability to label trade 'unfair' and to impose penalties to offset that perceived unfairness.

There will be even less interest in safeguards. Unlike anti-dumping and countervailing duties, safeguard measures attack only 'fair' trade, and so there is a harder political case for invoking such measures. The political case becomes even harder once those safeguard measures are challenged as inconsistent with WTO obligations. As discussed below, safeguard measures have been challenged more frequently and with greater success than other forms of trade remedies.

More importantly, however, countries imposing safeguards must be prepared to compensate the targets of those measures. Under Article 8.3 of the *Agreement on Safeguards* that obligation to compensate can be suspended for up to three years under certain circumstances. So far, that three-year rule has created a powerful incentive for countries to lift their safeguard measures within the three years, so that compensation is not due. Professor Davey summarizes the experience with seven recent safeguard actions challenged under the WTO. He shows that in six out of seven cases, the safeguards were removed within three years or less, and the seventh case ran only an extra few months.[5]

Although interest in safeguards will probably decline, this trend is unfortunate for the world trading system. There are several reasons why safeguards are a less problematic form of trade remedy, and should be preferred from a policy perspective. First, safeguards are harder to justify in the first instance, with higher legal standards and a greater willingness by national authorities to resist restrictions on so-called 'fair trade'. Second, safeguards have a true sunset mechanism, with a strong incentive for the countries imposing such restrictions to lift them before the three-year suspension of the obligation to compensation expires. Finally, safeguards generally require a country to make policy judgments about whether the measures are in their national interest and how their domestic industries should cope with international competition. 'Unfair' trade remedies have none of these features, and quickly become perceived as an entitlement by domestic industries.

[4] Information obtained from WTO reporting, available at: <http://www.wto.org/english/tratop_e/adp_e/adp_e.htm>; and at: <http://www.wto.org/english/tratop_e/scm_e/scm_e.htm>. [5] Davey, 'WTO: The First Ten Years', 49.

Frequency of trade remedies

Past trends

The long-term trend has been toward more frequent use of trade remedies. This trend can be seen by considering the number of anti-dumping cases filed in the ten years before and after the creation of the WTO in 1995. Over the 1985–1994 period, there were 1,844 anti-dumping cases. Over the 1995–2004 period, the number increased to 2,285 anti-dumping cases.[6] Note that since anti-dumping cases are such a large portion of the total trade remedy cases, this specific trend also describes the trend for trade remedies more generally.

The increase in anti-dumping cases actually dates back to the conclusion of the Tokyo Round in 1980. Even though the Contracting Parties of the *General Agreement on Tariffs and Trade* (GATT) added language that should have restrained the use of anti-dumping measures, the vagueness inherent in many of the new rules actually led to an increase in use. The United States, for example, used the new agreement as an opportunity to shift responsibility for its trade laws from the United States Department of Treasury to the United States Department of Commerce (USDOC). Congress felt that the Treasury was perceived as being too lax and that the USDOC would do a 'better job' by pursuing more cases. Numerous other changes to United States law at that time increased the incentives to file cases, and so the surge began. As the United States filed more cases, so did various other traditional users of anti-dumping laws.

After the creation of the WTO in 1995, the total number of trade remedy cases increased. Ironically, although United States cases fuelled the increase over the 1981–1994 period, the number of United States cases did not increase after 1995. The United States initiated 475 cases over the 1985–1994 period compared to just 328 cases over the 1995–2004 period.[7] But as United States cases declined, other new users began to replace the United States. These new users are discussed in more detail below.

It appears that retaliatory trade cases also explain part of this increase. Economists have long hypothesized that targeted countries would react to

[6] Data for 1985–2001 from Maurizio Zanardi, 'Anti-dumping: A Problem in International Trade' (June 2005), Working Paper available at <http://darkwing.uoregon.edu/~bruceb/adpage.html>. Unless otherwise indicated, all Working Papers cited here are available at this website. Data for 2002–2004 from WTO website, available at <http://www.wto.org>.

[7] Data from Zanardi, 'Anti-dumping: A Problem', and WTO website.

trade cases by filing trade cases against those that attack them.[8] A recent academic paper found strong statistical evidence of just this type of retaliation. Feinberg and Reynolds[9] considered the various anti-dumping cases filed by 41 different WTO Members over the 1995–2003 period. They found that filing an anti-dumping against one country increases the changes of being hit with an anti-dumping petitioner filed by that country by about 20 per cent. They also find that new users of anti-dumping measures are more like to file retaliatory cases than traditional users.

Most recently, however, there has been a noticeable drop off in new cases. Starting in 2002, the total number of anti-dumping cases initiated has fallen, as Table 18.1 shows.[10]

The drop off over the 2002–2004 period is an interesting phenomenon. Over the 1985–1994 period, there were about 184 cases per year. In the initial period after the establishment of the WTO, this frequency increased to about 270 cases per year over the 1995–2001 period. Then the frequency began to drop off.

This recent decline may reflect a drop in the number of cases files by steel industries around the world. Always prolific users of trade remedies, steel industries filed a number of cases over the 1999–2002 period. The decline may simply reflect the fact that once cases have been filed on a range of products, even the steel industries of the world begin to lose possible targets for future cases.

This decline is particularly noteworthy, given the increasing number of countries that could begin trade remedy cases, and have done so. Before the establishment of the WTO, only about 20 countries used anti-dumping laws. After 1995, the number of countries using anti-dumping laws began to grow. By 2004, more than 40 countries had enacted anti-dumping and other trade remedy laws, and had used them.

Future trends

There will be more opportunities for trade remedies cases on a global basis. Many new users are just beginning to develop the business culture

[8] Thomas J. Prusa and Susan Skeath, 'Modern Commercial Policy: Managed Trade or Retaliation?', in Eun Kwan Choi and James Hartigan (eds), *Handbook of International Trade, Vol. II: Economic and Legal Analysis of Trade Policy and Institutions* (Oxford, 2005).

[9] Robert Feinberg and Kara Reynolds, 'The Spread of Anti-dumping Regimes and the Role of Retaliation in Filings' (2004)(Working Paper).

[10] Data for 1985–1994 drawn from Stevenson and Filippi, *Global Trade Protection Report 2004*. Data for 1995–2004 drawn directly from WTO reporting, available at <http://www.wto.org/english/tratop_e/adp_e/adp_e.htm>.

Table 18.1 *Number of anti-dumping cases*

Year	Number
1985	195
1986	160
1987	125
1988	132
1989	101
1990	152
1991	222
1992	300
1993	242
1994	215
1995	157
1996	224
1997	243
1998	256
1999	354
2000	292
2001	364
2002	311
2003	233
2004	213

Source: Zanardi and WTO website: www.wto.org

of filing such cases. Indeed, in many new user countries, the authorities are actively encouraging industries to file petitions, so the officials will have something to do with their new laws. As the trade remedy mindset affects more countries, the number of cases will likely increase on a global basis.

Another key factor is the tendency toward 'tit for tat' retaliation. There is growing evidence that trade remedy cases themselves create yet more cases, as the victims seek to retaliate against those that have attacked them. In the recent work by Feinberg and Reynolds, discussed above, the authors find that new users are more likely to engage in retaliatory filings than traditional users. If this observation is correct, as more new users become more active, the number of cases could increase significantly.

But there are also other trends that may limit the frequency of trade remedies. One key factor is the shift away from manufacturing to services in many economies. As currently drafted, trade remedy laws only apply to goods, and not to services. This means that economies shifting increasingly to services will have fewer manufacturing industries that need protection through trade remedies laws.

Another key factor is the increasing globalization of production, and the political difficulty of bringing cases. In many cases, the domestic industry that wishes to bring a trade case discovers that there are producers with production facilities in both the country that wants to bring a case and the country that is being targeted. In such cases, reaching agreement that covers enough of the industry to have legal standing to bring the case can be difficult.

Even when production is not globalized, multinationals often face political challenges. For example, although China has become among the most popular targets of anti-dumping cases, many possible cases against China are never filed. Many possible petitioners have realized they have such extensive business dealings in China in other areas that they cannot risk antagonizing an important business partner. The potential threat to other areas of business if the Chinese retaliate in some way is too great a risk to take. Such anti-dumping cases are never filed.

In some countries, strict rules terminating orders after a certain period of time may mitigate the frequency of trade remedies. But in many other countries, orders are rarely terminated and tend to persist over time. Another factor is the stock of existing anti-dumping measures. Certain industries – like steel and chemicals – are more likely to file cases than other industries. But once these industries have filed trade remedies and obtained protection for key products, they cannot file again. So as more products are already burdened with anti-dumping orders or other trade remedies, there are fewer opportunities for new cases.

It is hard to say which set of influences will prevail. The most likely scenario is probably a gradual increase in the number of cases, but not a dramatic increase. The more stable the trends in the overall global economy, the more likely the trend in new trade remedies will remain stable.

The increase in trade remedies, however, could be much greater if the global economy weakens. Scholars have long found,[11] and practitioners concur, that trade remedies are more likely when the economy is

[11] Michael M. Knetter and Thomas J. Prusa, 'Macroeconomic Factors and Anti-dumping Filings: Evidence from Four Countries' (2003) 61 *Journal of International Economics*, 1–17.

experiencing a cycle downturn. Somewhat perversely, when the world economy needs the economic boost that free trade can provide, that is precisely when the incentives to file trade cases are at their maximum. When we need trade, we instead receive trade restrictions.

Distribution of who uses trade remedies

Past trends

Traditionally, a small handful of countries used trade remedies most extensively. Of the anti-dumping investigations initiated prior to 1981, the United States alone accounted for about 30 per cent of all cases. If we combine the United States, the European Communities, Australia, and Canada, these top four users accounted for about 74 per cent of all cases.[12]

That group of 'users' began to grow in the late 1980s, and expanded further with the establishment of the WTO. Mexico began to use its anti-dumping law in 1987, and soon became a major user. Brazil followed in 1988. India joined in 1992, and Argentina in 1993. Over the 1981–2001 period, these four new users all expanded the number of anti-dumping proceedings dramatically. Over the 1981–2001 period, the four traditional users initiated 2,947 investigations, or about 64 per cent of the total. The four new users initiated 716 cases, or about 16 per cent of the total.

If we focus on the 1995–2004 period, the shift is even more dramatic. The traditional top four initiated only 962 cases, or 36 per cent of the total. The four new users initiated 785 cases, or 30 per cent of the total.[13]

Looking at the total, however, masks the dramatic shift that has taken place over time. Consider Figure 18.1, which provides the new anti-dumping cases initiated by traditional users and new users over the 1981–2001 period.

New users now account for much more than half of the anti-dumping cases being filed. According to the most recent WTO figures, over the 2002–2004 period, the four traditional users (United States, European Communities, Canada, and Australia) accounted for 219 of 757 cases, only 29 per cent of the total. The remaining 71 per cent were new users.

The group of 'users' also began to expand as trade liberalization created a strong incentive to use trade remedies as an alternative form of protection. In another recent paper, Feinberg and Olson develop the first empirical evidence for this phenomenon. Although practitioners have

[12] These figures are drawn from Zanardi, 'Anti-dumping: A Problem'.

[13] These figures rely on information obtained from WTO reporting, available at <http://www.wto.org/english/tratop_e/adp_e/adp_e.htm>.

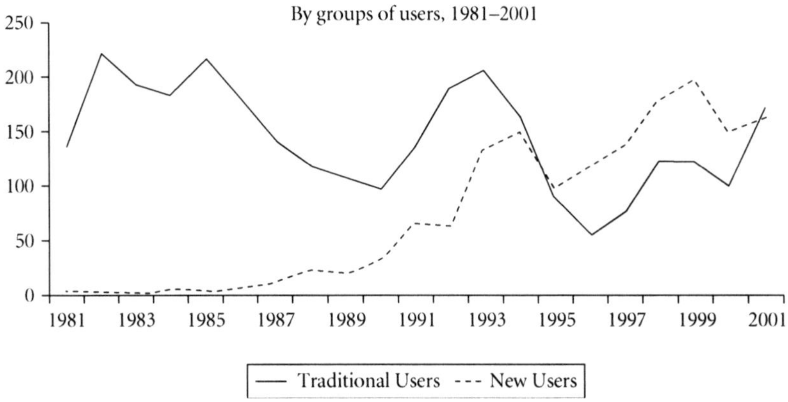

Figure 18.1 New cases initiated by type of user

Source: Zanardi, 'Anti-dumping: A Problem'

long had an intuition that trade remedies increased in the aftermath of trade liberalization – one restriction replacing another – Feinberg and Reynolds present a statistical analysis that shows the 'tariff reductions agreed to under the Uruguay Round not only increased the likelihood of a country using anti-dumping protection, but also the total number of anti-dumping petitions filed by countries.'[14] They also find that new users are more likely to respond to tariff liberalization by filing anti-dumping cases.

Future trends

The shift toward new users is likely to continue. One simple reason is that having enacted laws and regulations, these countries will create demand for the use of these legal tools. Anecdotal evidence suggests that government officials have been actively encouraging their domestic industries to file cases. With time, more industries will learn about these options to restrain foreign competition.

Another factor fuelling the proliferation of new users is the tendency toward 'tit-for-tat' retaliation. Scholars studying this phenomenon have found retaliatory trade remedies to be more common among new users than traditional users. So as more new users impose trade remedies, other new users are increasingly likely to file their own trade remedy cases in retaliation.

[14] Robert Feinberg and Kara Reynolds, 'Tariff Liberalization and Increased Administrative Protection: Is There a Quid Pro Quo?' (2005) (Working Paper), p. 13.

Yet another factor is the frequent lack of defence with respect to such trade remedies. When a large country like the United States or the European Communities begins a trade remedy proceeding, there is a better chance that the target countries will have a sufficient economic stake to defend themselves. But when a case begins in a smaller country, it is more likely that the trade flows are too small to justify the defence. Thus, the new cases emerging in the new user countries are more likely to result in easy trade restrictions – restrictions imposed without any serious defence effort having been mounted. This pattern will encourage yet more trade remedies.

II. What can the WTO do?

Trade remedies have continued to increase. The WTO has sought to impose discipline, but the experience to date has been mixed. Although a number of new legal provisions have been negotiated during successive rounds, many of those provisions are not having the effect intended. Despite the increase in WTO disputes about trade remedies, only a fraction of trade remedies ever end up in WTO dispute settlement. Abuses are proving hard to correct.

Negotiations about trade remedies

Past trends

We have completed three rounds of trade negotiations that addressed trade remedies. Over time, more and more language has been devoted to crafting – or at least attempting to craft – disciplines for trade remedies.

The amount of legal text devoted to crafting rules for trade remedies has grown significantly over the years as shown in Table 18.2. The Kennedy Round Anti-dumping Agreement set forth primarily procedural rules. The Tokyo Round and Uruguay Round *Anti-Dumping Agreements* sought to expand substantive disciplines as well.

What has been the effect of this increased volume of legal text? These prior agreements appear to have stimulated enactment of new national laws. Consider Figure 18.2, which shows enactment of national laws over time.

Although there are obviously other factors at play, the correlation between new international rules and new national trade remedy systems is quite remarkable. The increase over the period after the Tokyo Round in 1980 until the Uruguay Round was finalized in 1995 is particularly noteworthy. Many countries apparently saw the future, and realized that the future would be about trade remedies, not tariffs and other trade restrictions.

Table 18.2 *Pages of negotiated legal text*

	Kennedy Round	**Tokyo Round**	**Uruguay Round**
Anti-dumping	12	19	29
Countervailing Duties	0	30	51
Safeguards	0	0	10
Total	**12**	**49**	**90**

Tabulated by author

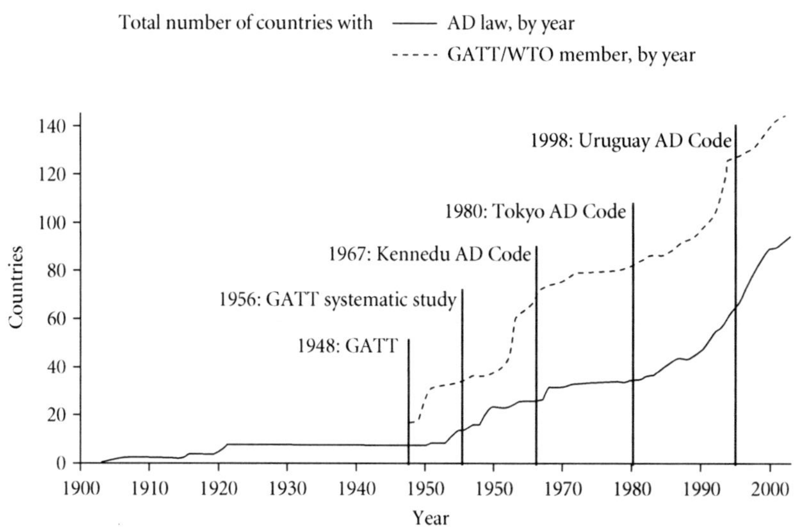

Figure 18.2 Enactment of national anti-dumping laws

Source: Zanardi, 'Anti-dumping: a problem'

Yet ironically, the degree of discipline has increased less than one would expect. Much of the drafting of new international rules over the years has served to codify the practices of the major users of the anti-dumping and other trade remedy laws. Indeed, from the perspective of an American specialist in trade remedy laws, one can review the history of the three WTO agreements dealing with trade remedies[15] and see the

[15] The three WTO agreements dealing with trade remedies are: the *Agreement on Implementation of Article VI of the General Agreement on Tariffs and Trade 1994* (*Anti-Dumping Agreement*), the *Agreement on Subsidies and Countervailing Measures* (*SCM Agreement*), and the *Agreement on Safeguards*.

clear imprint of United States law and practice on the international legal texts. As one of the earliest and most aggressive users of trade remedies, the United States negotiators have sought to leverage this comparative expertise in the technical details of how trade remedies work — or at least how the United States would like them to work.[16]

The impact of new disciplines

Even when there is a new discipline, making that discipline real has proven challenging. Specific and detailed procedural rules are usually easy. Everyone can agree that a deadline of 180 days means 180 days. But not all rules are so simple.

Consider one specific example: the enactment of new rules requiring the termination of anti-dumping duty measures after five years. Foreign exporters thought this was one of the major victories of the Uruguay Round negotiations. But the subsequent history has shown how hard it can be to change entrenched practice.

The first problem was textual. Instead of a simple rule on terminating anti-dumping orders after five years, Article 11.3 of the *Agreement on Implementation of Article VI of the General Agreement on Tariffs and Trade 1994* (*Anti-Dumping Agreement*) sets forth language allowing authorities to decide that continuing the order is necessary to prevent recurrence of dumping. The exception has tended to swallow the basic rule.

The United States' experience with sunset proceedings has been studied in depth by scholars, and provides the more dramatic evidence of this pattern. As Moore has summarized with respect to US Government determinations of dumping:

> For those cases in which the DOC undertook a review, only 2 of the 315 cases were decided in a way favorable to individual foreign respondents. In short, we will show that the Department of Commerce's sunset review decisions calls into question whether the US has lived up to its commitments under the Uruguay Round reforms.[17]

Scholars looking at decisions of the United States International Trade Commission (USITC) about injury find a similar tendency to continue

[16] Unlike anti-dumping disciplines, the new disciplines on safeguard measures, have been more significant. Prior the Uruguay Round, there was only the text of the GATT of 1947. With the new *Agreement on Safeguards*, there has been a substantial increase in concrete rules that have created meaningful discipline.

[17] Michael O. Moore, 'Commerce Department Anti-dumping Sunset Reviews: A Major Disappointment' (2001) (Working Paper), p. 3. See also Michael O. Moore, 'Anti-dumping Reform in the U.S.: A Faded Sunset' (1999) 33 *Journal of World Trade*, 1–88.

anti-dumping orders. Liebman studies USITC voting patterns in the initial round of decisions made about the so-called transition orders – those older orders in effect in 1995 when the WTO agreements went into effect. He reports that the USITC voted to continue these orders in 71 per cent of the cases.[18] In a more recent paper, Moore looks at the post-transition order sunset decisions of the USITC. Focusing on so-called 'contested orders' – ones in which the domestic industry even bothers to ask that the order be continued – he summarizes:

> Thirty out of 32 non-transition orders (94 percent) have been renewed for another five year period whereas 90 out of 102 contested orders (90 percent) in the post-1990 cases were not revoked. These results . . . raise grave doubts about whether the US is living up to the spirit of the its commitments to terminate anti-dumping orders after five years.[19]

These statistics present a rather grim situation for those foreign respondents who think that an anti-dumping order will terminate after five years.

The same pattern can be seen in other areas. Another Uruguay Round reform for which foreign respondents had high hopes was in the area of 'fact available'. Under prior practice, the administrators of national anti-dumping laws had a practice of punishing foreign respondents with what was euphemistically called 'best information available', which was usually punitive adverse inferences, whenever there was some gap in information. In the Uruguay Round, an entire new annex was added to the *Anti-Dumping Agreement* in an effort to moderate this use of adverse inferences.

Like the effort to terminate orders after five years, this reform floundered in actual implementation. In addition to his work on sunset reviews, Moore has studied recent patterns in the use of 'facts available' by the US authorities. He found that the frequency of the use of 'facts available' was 43 per cent before the Uruguay Round reforms and 45 per cent after the reforms. The average 'facts available' margin fell only slightly from 80 per cent before the Uruguay Round reform to only 74 per cent after.[20] Here again, the spirit of the reform effort largely died when the reform was implemented at the national level.

[18] Benjamin H. Liebman, 'ITC Voting Behavior on Sunset Reviews' (2001) (Working Paper). See also Moore, 'An Econometric Analysis of US Anti-dumping Sunset Review Decisions' (2001) (Working Paper).

[19] Michael O. Moore, 'Can the US Dump Anti-dumping?: Evidence from Past Reforms' (2004) (Working Paper available from author), p. 17.

[20] Moore, 'Can the US Dump Anti-dumping?', p. 10.

Future trends

Given the experience over the past twenty years, it is hard to be optimistic about the impact of the ongoing Doha Round on future disciplines on trade remedies. Creating new disciplines has proven very challenging. As more and more countries want to use trade remedies, there has been less and less interest in creating real discipline. Many countries that have traditionally supported limiting the use of trade remedies now have more complex interests to balance. These countries have to balance the demands of their exporters who are victims of trade remedies, but also their own domestic industries that want to use trade remedies.

The experience with national implementation of new disciplines has been mixed. When the rule is completely clear, the change takes place. But in those instances where the negotiations produced a rule with an exception – such as the new rules on terminating anti-dumping orders after five years – the exceptions often swallow up the basic rule, and the change does not take place.

But there are a few encouraging examples. One of the best examples of a new discipline having a positive effect came in the area of safeguards. Under Article 8.3 of the *Agreement on Safeguards*, WTO Members agree to withhold demanding compensation for safeguard measures for three years. This rule has had a very significant effect on the duration of safeguard measures. Most countries simply terminate their safeguard measures within three years, so as to avoid the need to pay the compensation for those measures.

This experience suggests a useful approach for the future. If it is difficult to create bright line rules that appear to encroach too much on national sovereignty, then perhaps we should have more rules based on clear incentives. Consider the experience with sunset reviews. The pattern of 'basic rule – limited exception' did not work. The exception proved not to be limited at all. Yet it probably is not politically feasible to eliminate the exception and have a fixed rule of terminating anti-dumping orders after five years. So perhaps a more politically practical approach would be to create an incentive to terminate orders after five years. An approach similar to Article 8.3 of the *Agreement on Safeguards* might be more productive – allowing countries to maintain the anti-dumping order beyond five years, but only if they are willing to pay some compensation (offsetting tariffs in some other area) as the price of continuing the order.

WTO review of trade remedies

WTO disciplines are generally not self-enforcing. They must be enforced through dispute settlement. WTO disputes about trade remedies have increased, both absolutely and relative to the total number of disputes. Even so, only a tiny fraction of national trade remedies are ever subjected to international scrutiny.

Past trends

Review of trade remedies under the GATT was extremely limited. Although there were more about 2,800 national anti-dumping cases initiated over the 1948–1994 period,[21] only ten of those cases made their way into the GATT dispute settlement system. Given the non-mandatory nature of GATT dispute settlement, it is not surprising that few targets of anti-dumping measures even bothered to try the system.

The review of trade remedies under the WTO system has increased dramatically. One measure is the number of dispute brought to the system. Over the 1995–2004 period, there have been 59 disputes involving anti-dumping measures, as shown in Table 18.3.

This pattern through the WTO dispute settlement system is roughly consistent with overall trends. Roughly one out of three requests for consultations produces a formal decision by a panel. The frequency with which panels about anti-dumping have been appealed – about 45 per cent – is less than the overall average of panel reports appealed, which is 70 per cent.

Over this same period, WTO disputes over other trade remedies also emerged. Another 12 disputes involved countervailing duty measures, as shown in Table 18.4.

Finally, another 32 disputes involved safeguard measures, as shown in Table 18.5. These disputes spiked over the 2001–2002 period, when US safeguard measures on a variety of steel products triggered a number of retaliatory safeguard measures by other countries. Those measures, as well as the measures threatened in response, then triggered a series of WTO disputes.

Relative to other types of WTO disputes, disputes about trade remedies have been growing in importance. Consider the trend in overall WTO disputes, and the trend in complaints under the *Anti-Dumping Agreement*, as shown in Table 18.6. Disputes about anti-dumping measures account for a growing percentage of the WTO case load. After an increase in WTO dispute settlement activity over the 1995–1997 period,

[21] Zanardi, 'Anti-dumping: A Problem'.

Table 18.3 *Trends in WTO challenges to anti-dumping measures 1995–2004*

Year	Requests for Consultations	Requests for Panels	Decisions by Panels	Decisions by AB
1995	1	0	0	0
1996	3	0	0	0
1997	3	3	0	0
1998	6	2	1	1
1999	8	4	1	0
2000	11	2	7	1
2001	6	6	3	2
2002	7	3	4	1
2003	6	5	3	3
2004	8	3	3	2
Total	59	28	22	10

Source: Figures drawn from www.worldtradelaw.net, as tabulated by author

Table 18.4 *Trends in WTO challenges to countervailing duty measures 1995–2004*

Year	Requests for Consultations	Requests for Panels	Decisions by Panels	Decisions by AB
1995	0	0	0	0
1996	0	0	0	0
1997	1	0	0	0
1998	1	0	0	0
1999	1	1	1	0
2000	2	0	0	1
2001	0	2	1	1
2002	2	1	1	1
2003	3	3	1	0
2004	2	2	0	1
Total	12	9	4	4

Source: Figures drawn from www.worldtradelaw.net, as tabulated by author

Table 18.5 *Trends in WTO challenges to safeguards measures 1995–2004*

Year	Requests for Consultations	Requests for Panels	Decisions by WTO Panels	Decisions by AB
1995	0	0	0	0
1996	0	0	0	0
1997	3	0	0	0
1998	2	2	0	0
1999	5	5	2	2
2000	3	1	2	1
2001	7	3	1	1
2002	11	9	2	2
2003	1	0	9	8
2004	0	0	0	0
Total	32	20	16	14

Source: Figures drawn from www.worldtradelaw.net, as tabulated by author. Based on number of complaints, not cases fully adjudicated

Table 18.6 *Number of WTO complaints about anti-dumping*

Year	Total complaints	AD complaints	Percentage AD complaints
1995	25	1	4.0%
1996	39	3	7.7%
1997	50	3	6.0%
1998	41	6	14.6%
1999	30	8	26.7%
2000	34	11	32.4%
2001	23	6	26.1%
2002	37	7	18.9%
2003	26	6	23.1%
2004	19	8	42.1%
2005	11	4	36.4%
Total	**335**	**63**	**18.8%**

Source: Figures drawn from www.worldtradelaw.net, as tabulated by author. See also Leitner and Simon, 'WTO Dispute Settlement 1995–2004: A Statistical Analysis', 8 *J. Intl Econ. Law* 231, 232 (2005)

the trend over the 1998–2003 period has been more stable, with a drop off in new disputes over the 2003–2005 period. The number of disputes about anti-dumping measures, however, has remained strong. By 2004, anti-dumping disputes were almost one half of the new disputes filed. The absolute number dropped in 2005, but the share of the case load had remained high. If we added disputes about countervailing duties and safeguard measures, the portion of the total would be even greater.

Likelihood of being challenged

Beyond shear numbers, these disputes about anti-dumping measures involve a growing range of countries. Under the GATT system, only five countries – the United States (4); the European Communities (3); Korea (1); New Zealand (1); and Sweden (1) – had their anti-dumping measures challenged. Under the WTO system, 18 countries have had their anti-dumping measures challenged. Not surprisingly, the United States was the largest target for WTO challenges, with 26 challenges – 43 per cent of the total number of challenges. But many other countries have been the target of more than one challenge, as shown in Table 18.7.

Indeed, the number of complaints against the United States is noteworthy, given the declining number of US anti-dumping cases. If we compare the number of WTO disputes to the number of anti-dumping cases, we can obtain a rough idea of how likely it is that each countries' anti-dumping measures would be challenged, as shown in Table 18.8. This table highlights a number of interesting points. Of the 41 different countries that began anti-dumping investigations over the 1995–2004 period, 18 of those countries had one or more of their measures challenged. Some countries – Ecuador and Guatemala – had their single anti-dumping measure challenged twice.[22] In both cases, the countries appear to have abandoned beginning more anti-dumping investigations!

Two countries – the United States and Mexico – stand out as having been heavy users of anti-dumping measures, but also having been heavily targeted by WTO complaints. Multiple complaints by different WTO partners signals a broader based dissatisfaction with how the United States and Mexico administer their anti-dumping laws.

Most of the heavy users of anti-dumping measures have had at least one measure challenged. These 18 countries began 2,142 out of 2,647

[22] Ecuador had its measure challenged at various procedural stages. Guatemala had its single measure on cement challenged early in the proceeding, at an early stage that the Appellate Body later determined was improper. So the measure was challenged again later.

Table 18.7 *Anti-dumping measures challenged 1995–2004*

Country	Number of WTO Challenges
United States	26
Mexico	6
EC	5
Argentina	3
India	3
Ecuador	2
Guatemala	2
South Africa	2
Trinidad and Tobago	2
Australia	1
Brazil	1
Egypt	1
Korea	1
Peru	1
Philippines	1
Thailand	1
Turkey	1
Venezuela	1
Total	**60**

Source: Figures from <http://www.worldtradelaw.net>, as tabulated by author.

cases, or about 81 per cent of the total. Only nine countries were frequent users (more than ten cases begun) but did not have any of their measures challenged at least once, as shown in Table 18.9.

To put the WTO dispute settlement into context, however, we need to compare this international activity against the underlying level of activity by national authorities. Table 18.10 provides a summary by type of trade remedy. This summary makes several interesting points. First, although there have been a lot of WTO disputes about anti-dumping, the number of disputes is small relative to the underlying level of activity by national authorities. Only about two per cent of the domestic cases initiated ever trigger a WTO dispute, and fewer than one per cent of those cases lead to a panel decision.

Second, although there are fewer cases, both countervailing duties and safeguard measures are much more likely to trigger a WTO complaint. Not surprisingly, countries targeted by accusations of subsidies are more likely to be indignant and inclined to bring the dispute to the WTO.

Table 18.8 *Likelihood of challenge to national anti-dumping measures 1995–2004*

Country	Cases Initiated	WTO Challenges	Per cent Challenged
United States	354	26	7.4%
Mexico	78	6	7.7%
EC	303	5	1.7%
Argentina	192	3	1.6%
India	399	3	0.8%
Ecuador	1	2	100%
Guatemala	1	2	100%
South Africa	174	2	0.1%
Trinidad and Tobago	12	2	16.7%
Australia	172	1	0.0%
Brazil	116	1	0.1%
Egypt	38	1	2.6%
Korea	77	1	1.3%
Peru	54	1	1.9%
Philippines	17	1	5.9%
Thailand	34	1	2.9%
Turkey	89	1	1.1%
Venezuela	31	1	3.2%
Total	**2,142**	**60**	**2.8%**

Source: Figures from <http://www.wto.org> and <http://www.worldtradelaw.net>, as tabulated by author

Similarly, countries seem more upset when affected by safeguard measures against 'fair' trade than anti-dumping measures against allegedly 'unfair' trade. Or perhaps it is simply that countries have become numb to the endless stream of anti-dumping cases.

Third, disputes about safeguards are more likely to lead to formal legal decisions. For both anti-dumping and countervailing duty measures, only about one third of the disputes ever make it to a final decision by a panel. The others settle out along the way. But for safeguard measures, about half of the dispute go to a formal legal decision.

Future trends

Looking forward, what will be the pattern of future WTO disputes settlement over trade remedies? We can make a few predictions.

Table 18.9 *Anti-dumping measures not challenged 1995–2004*

Country	Number of AD Cases
Canada	133
China	99
Indonesia	61
New Zealand	54
Malaysia	31
Israel	27
Colombia	24
Chile	14
Poland	12
Total	**455**

Source: Figures from <http://www.wto.org> and <http://www.worldtradelaw.net>, as tabulated by author

Table 18.10 *Frequency of WTO challenge to various trade remedies 1995–2004*

Type of Remedy	Number of Initiations	Requests for Consultations	Per cent	Panel Decision	Per cent
Anti-dumping	2,647	59	2.2%	22	0.8%
Countervailing	176	12	6.8%	4	2.3%
Safeguards	276	32	11.6%	16	5.8%

Source: Anti-dumping and countervailing duty initiations drawn from WTO website; safeguard initiation data from Stevenson and Filippi. WTO actions drawn from <http://www.worldtradelaw.net>.

First, there will be more WTO cases, but the frequency may begin to decline. One reason is that if the number of national trade remedy investigations moderate, the number of WTO disputes will decline. Moreover, a number of discrete legal issues have now been resolved, and do not need to re-litigated. Most national authorities are watching the emerging jurisprudence, and most will not knowingly take a position they know could be successfully challenged in the WTO. The drop in 2005 in both the total number of WTO disputes and the number of challenges to anti-dumping measures suggests such a trend.

Second, even though the number of WTO disputes might decline somewhat, they will probably continue to become a more important part of the overall dispute settlement landscape. Other types of WTO disputes are probably going to drop off even more sharply. Moreover, as other trade barriers fall, trade remedies will continue to represent a growing portion of remaining trade barriers.

Third, trade remedy disputes are likely to become more contentious over time. The easy cases tend to settle out along the way. For all trade remedies, fewer than half of the initial requests for consultations ever lead to a formal legal decision. Those that remain in the system, however, will present increasingly harder issues that can be quite contentious.

One of the most difficult areas will involve issues of 'injury', particularly the area of causation. There is a large amount of complex treaty text under Article 2 of the *Anti-Dumping Agreement* on the issue of 'dumping', but the emerging trend seems to be that unless the text explicitly prohibits some practice, the authorities have discretion. The rules are so detailed that the absence of a specific rule is being deemed to mean the absence of any rule. Injury issues are different. Article 3 of the *Anti-Dumping Agreement* explicitly requires a 'causal relationship' and explains that other causes 'must not be attributed to the dumped imports'. But the Appellate Body and panels have not had much luck in crafting jurisprudence to implement these clear legal obligations. So when national authorities make dubious judgment calls, WTO dispute settlement procedures struggle.

This issues of injury are particularly important because they go to legitimacy of the duty itself. If the dumping margin is wrong, the authorities can recalculate the margin. Few issues would drive the dumping margin completely to zero. But if the injury finding is defective, the only proper response is to terminate the duties completely. With the stakes so high, it not surprising that parties fight intensely over these issues.

Finally, the disputes over the proper standard of review are likely to continue. WTO dispute settlement will continue to confront decisions by a wide range of national authorities. Even within a single national authority, the various decisions could be of very mixed quality. So WTO panels and the Appellate Body will continue to struggle with a number of hard cases. Proponents of trade remedies insist that national authorities deserve considerable deference. But the victims of trade remedies based on dubious factual and legal grounds will continue to make compelling arguments.

III. Conclusions

This survey of past and future trends suggests that trade remedies are indeed a growing problem in international trade. As we look beyond the

Doha Round, it seems likely that there will be more trade remedy measures disrupting more trade and receiving only modest international discipline.

As we look forward, there will be several interesting trends to watch. First, scholars are developing much better data with which to measure the impact of trade remedies on a global basis. A young scholar at Brandeis University, Chad Bown, has been assembling a data base of global trade remedies, with the information on specific HTS (Harmonised Tariff System) codes that will enable scholars to measure trade impacts globally. This data will allow the prior work on trade remedies in developed countries that are the traditional users – such as the United States and the European Communities – to expand to include the various new users.[23]

Another important trend relates to tendency of cases to shut down trade flows before they have time to grow. Among cases in the United States, there has been a trend toward cases targeting smaller volumes of trade. Many United States cases now target annual trade flows of US $10 million or less. US industries have discovered that is sometimes better to 'take out the competition' before its even becomes established. This area needs further study.

These cases are particularly troubling for a few reasons. First, the trade is being shut off at an early stage. Second, these cases are usually not well defended. The economic stakes are not large enough for the affected foreign industries to invest the significant amount of time and money that it takes to defend the case. This practical reality means that the petition tends to lead to a trade remedy, whether the remedy is deserved at all, and the size of the margin is often quite high.

This problem is likely to be more severe as trade remedies expand to new users. On top of the difficulty of justifying the expense of the defence, targets of cases initiated by new users sometimes have trouble even finding experienced professionals to assist in the defence efforts. So as trade remedies expand around the globe, it is becoming harder to defend against them effectively.

Over time, the larger impact of trade remedies may be political and psychological, not economic. Trade remedies have become so politically sensitive that they are hard to discipline. The mantra about 'free but fair trade' has become all too popular around the world, as other countries join the United States and other traditional users as advocates of trade remedies. Everyone could agree to cut tariffs over time. Everyone agreed

[23] See <http://people.brandeis.edu/ncbown/global_ad/>.

tariffs were a problem that needed to be solved. There seems to be no such consensus on trade remedies. Trade remedies are often not perceived as a problem, but as a politically convenient answer to the dislocation that trade sometimes causes.

The other longer term effect may be psychological. Trade remedies also breed cynicism about the push toward trade liberalization. Many countries wonder if the other efforts at trade liberalization mean very much if the gains can be so easily taken away through arbitrary trade remedies. No one has yet systematically examined this issue, so the evidence is only anecdotal.

Another important trend to watch will be implementation of WTO decisions. Although beyond the scope of this chapter, implementation will become a more critical issue over time. Experience to date suggests that implementation has been a problem, particularly for trade remedies. Countries implement those changes that do not require major adjustments to their trade remedy practices and do not result in the trade restriction being lifted. There have been some exceptions, and developing countries have been better than developed countries in implementing the decisions of WTO panels. But in general, the reduction in the number of WTO complaints challenging anti-dumping measures may well reflect, at least in part, the realization that WTO disputes do not lead to prompt lifting of WTO impermissible trade restrictions.[24]

Although trade remedies are a growing problem in international trade, there is some reason to be cautiously optimistic. Our knowledge about trade remedies – including their direct and indirect effects – has been growing over time, as a small but dedicated group of scholars continue their work in the field. This work has the potential to expose more clearly and concretely the hidden cost and unintended consequences of trade remedies. It would be wonderful if the negotiators during the Doha Round could benefit from their research. There is still time.

But even if the Doha Round fails to make much progress in dealing with the problem of trade remedies, one must keep in mind the longer term perspective. After all, the problem of tariffs and quantitative restrictions has been resolved very slowly, starting with the GATT in 1948. More than 50 years later, we are still working on these issues. Trade remedies, in contrast, have been a significant problem for only 25 years. We still have time to work toward longer term progress, and more trade free of trade remedies.

[24] Professor William J. Davey has been doing interesting research in this area. His paper on WTO dispute settlement, which is included as Chapter 6 of this book, summarizes some of that work, and makes for very interesting reading.

19

Reflections on the relationship between WTO negotiations and dispute settlement: lessons from the GATS

HENRY S. GAO

The *General Agreement on Trade in Services* (GATS) includes many unique features. One of these unique features is the 'built-in agenda' for new negotiations, which is set out in Article XIX. Even though successive rounds of tariff negotiations were held under the auspices of the *General Agreement on Tariffs and Trade* (GATT) *1947*, the GATT Contracting Parties were never under any legal obligation to do so. In contrast, the GATS made it a legal obligation to conduct a new round of services negotiations. Specific mandates are given on the starting date of the negotiations (2000, or not later than five years from the date of entry into force of the *Marrakesh Agreement Establishing the World Trade Organization* (*WTO Agreement*); the aim of the negotiations (progressive liberalization 'directed to the reduction or elimination of the adverse effects on trade in services of measures as a means of providing effective market access'); as well as the negotiating guidelines and procedures which shall be established by the Council for Trade in Services.

Pursuant to the built-in agenda, the new services negotiations started in early 2000. They encompass both rules (domestic regulation, safeguard, subsidies, etc.) and market access issues. According to the Guidelines and Procedures for the Negotiations on Trade in Services,[1] the request-offer approach is the main method of negotiation of specific commitments. As of October 2005, the total number of initial offers submitted was 69 (representing 93 Members); with 54 initial offers remaining outstanding. The total number of revised offers submitted was 28 (representing 52 Members); with 63 revised offers outstanding if

[1] Guidelines and Procedures for the Negotiations on Trade in Services, S/L/93.

least-developed countries (LDCs) are excluded.[2] According to the data collected by the Secretariat of the World Trade Organization (WTO),[3] out of a total of 12 different services sectors, only five sectors (business services, communication services, financial services, tourism services, transport services) attracted more than ten offers. Moreover, even for those sectors, the majority of the offers are only improvements on existing commitments, rather than providing any new meaningful market access opportunities.[4] In summary, as noted by both the former and the current Directors-General of the WTO, 'the overall quality (of services offers) remains unsatisfactory' because '[f]ew, if any, provide new business opportunities to service suppliers'.[5] Thus, Members should try to achieve both 'an increased number' and 'an enhanced quality of the commitments'.[6]

While there could be many possible explanations for the *impasse* in the current services negotiations, this chapter argues that one of the reasons is the ruling of the panel in the *Mexico – Telecoms* case, which exacerbated the long-standing imbalance between the negotiation and dispute settlement functions of the WTO and discouraged Members from making commitments in services.

I. The *Mexico – Telecoms* case: how the panel reached its conclusion

In the *Mexico – Telecoms* case, the United States challenged several provisions of the telecommunication laws and regulations of Mexico, alleging that they violated Mexico's commitments under the GATS. Among other claims, the United States argued that Mexico failed to ensure that *Teléfonos de México, S.A. de C.V.* ('Telmex'), its dominant telecom service

[2] Council for Trade in Services, Special Session, 'Report by the Chairman to the Trade Negotiations Committee', TN/S/22, 13 October 2005. Unless otherwise noted, all WTO documents and dispute settlement reports are from the WTO website: <www.wto.org>.

[3] Presentation by Ruosi Zhang (WTO Secretariat, Trade in Services Division), 2nd Asia Pacific Regional Trade Policy Course held at the University of Hong Kong, 31 May 2005.

[4] Ibid. See also Rudolf Adlung and Martin Roy, 'Turning Hills into Mountains? Current Commitments Under the General Agreement on Trade in Services and Prospects for Change' (2005) 39 *Journal of World Trade*, 1161–1194, 1183–1187.

[5] Report by the Chairman of the Trade Negotiations Committee to the General Council, TN/C/5, 28 July 2005.

[6] Trade Negotiations Committee, 'Lamy opens 'new phase' in trade talks', 14 September 2005, available at <http://www.wto.org/english/news_e/news05_e/tnc_stat_lamy_14sep05_e.htm>.

provider, provided *interconnection* to United States basic telecom suppliers on a cross-border basis with cost-oriented, reasonable rates, terms and conditions, thus violating Mexico's obligations under Sections 2.1 and 2.2 of the Reference Paper, as inscribed in Mexico's GATS Schedule of Commitments.[7] As its first line of defence, Mexico argued that the Reference Paper only governs matters relating to domestic regulation and does not apply to the *accounting rates* set by bilateral agreements between US and Mexican basic telecommunications carriers.

The accounting rates are the rates per unit of traffic agreed upon between two countries for the joint provision of international telecommunications services.[8] International telecommunications services were traditionally provided jointly by monopolistic telecom operators in two countries.[9] Under this regime of joint provision, the telecom operator in the call-originating country carries the call over its own facilities to a certain point in the international gateway.[10] The telecom operator from the destination country then takes the call over from the mid-point and delivers it to the receiver using its own facilities.[11] If the traffic from both sides is the same, there will be no need to make adjustments. Obviously, this is rarely the case. In order to address the traffic imbalance, the carrier with more outbound traffic transfers funds to the carrier terminating those calls to compensate the terminating carrier for the service of delivering the call to its final destination.[12] The payment is called a 'settlement' payment, which usually represents half of the accounting rates.[13] Therefore, the accounting rates regime is determined on the basis of two important factors: the applicable rate per unit of traffic and the splitting formula according to which accounting rates are divided between operators.[14]

As countries liberalize their telecom industries, competition in the liberalized markets tends to lower the collection charge, that is, the amount charged to the customer by the telecommunication operator.[15] To the extent that international telephony typically faces an elastic demand, this increases the volume of outgoing calls in the liberalized market, *vis-à-vis*

7 Panel Report, *Mexico – Telecoms*, para. 4.1.

8 Boutheina Guermazi, *International Accounting Rates, Developing Countries and the World Trade Organization: The Dilemma and Possible Solution*, p. 4, available at <http://www.law.mcgill.ca/institutes/csri/paper-guermazi-accounting.php3?printversion=1>.

9 Ibid. 10 Ibid. 11 Ibid. 12 Ibid. 13 Ibid. 14 Ibid.

15 Bernard Hoekman and Carlos A. Primo Braga, 'Protection and Trade in Services', World Bank, Policy Research Working Paper No. 1747, pp. 8–9, available at <http://www.worldbank.org/research/trade/pdf/wp1747.pdf>.

incoming calls from monopolistic markets, which, in turn, leads to rent transfers from liberalized to monopolistic markets.[16]

According to Guermazi, the debate around accounting rates is mainly a North/South controversy.[17] On the one hand, developed countries with more liberalized telecom markets and wealthier customers suffer from deficit payments and thus are eager to reform the accounting rates regime and align it with costs.[18] The United States alone, for example, paid out US $5.6 billion more than it received in international settlement and this accounts for almost five per cent of its total trade deficit.[19] On the other hand, developing countries, many of which have started the liberalization process, but at a slower pace, largely benefit from the current regime and thus have resisted rapid changes to it.[20] In 1994, for example, 70 per cent of all net US payments went to developing countries.[21] In the same year, total settlement payments from developed countries amounted to US $10 billion.[22] According to the Secretary General of the International Telecom Union, the revenue generated by settlement payments in developing countries in one year exceeded by far the cumulative sum of the lending programmes involving telecommunications of all development banks around the world for the first half of the 1990s.[23]

Putting economic issues aside, the legal question is whether the term 'accounting rates' is a kind of 'interconnection rate' as is referred to in the Reference Paper. In the introduction to the Findings section of its report, the panel in *Mexico – Telecoms* claimed to be 'fully aware that the interpretation of the complex layers of GATS Articles, Annexes, Protocols, and Schedules with GATS market access commitments, national treatment commitments, and additional commitments poses many challenges to WTO Members and WTO dispute settlement bodies as this was the first WTO case to deal solely with trade in services under the GATS, as well as telecommunications services.[24] A careful reading of the panel's analysis reveals, however, that the panel either failed to fully appreciate or simply chose to ignore the fact that 'different approaches used by governments in the drafting of their respective GATS schedules may give rise to divergent understandings and expectations', especially 'in the early years of GATS jurisprudence'.[25] Indeed, rather than examining the terms in the light of 'the legal and technical complexity of the regulation of telecommunications

[16] Ibid.

[17] Guermazi, *International Accounting Rates, Developing Countries and the WTO*, p. 2.

[18] Ibid. [19] Ibid. [20] Ibid. [21] Ibid. [22] Ibid. [23] Ibid.

[24] Panel Report, *Mexico – Telecoms*, para. 7.2. [25] Ibid.

services, including their rapid technological evolution', as well as 'the drafting history of GATS provisions to which both parties to this dispute referred extensively', the panel simply opted for an interpretation based primarily on the plain meaning of the words.[26]

According to Section 2.1 of the Reference Paper, the Interconnection Section applies to 'linking with suppliers providing public telecommunications transport networks or services in order to allow the users of one supplier to communicate with users of another supplier and to access services provided by another supplier, where specific commitments are undertaken'.

This paragraph provides most of the basis for the panel's finding that the 'plain meaning' of the term 'interconnection' includes international or cross-border interconnection (as covered by the accounting rates regime). The detailed analysis of the panel seems quite complicated for the uninitiated. Boiling it down, however, the panel's reasoning is essentially as follows: Because the Interconnection Section applies to *linking*, and the ordinary meaning of linking does not preclude either *domestic* or *international linking*, and accounting rates are essentially payment for *international linking*, therefore, the Interconnection Section applies to accounting rates as a form of interconnection rate.

Even though the reasoning seems, on the face of it, quite logical, its fallacy can be easily exposed if we draw an analogy to the following story.

A person enters a *French* restaurant and is greeted by the waiter. Upon taking the order, the waiter asks if he wants any wine. The following is the exchange between them:

'What kinds of wine do you have?'

'We have all kinds of wine, Monsieur.'

'All right. A bottle of Shaoxing Rice Wine, please.'

'I am sorry, Monsieur, we don't have that wine.'

'But didn't you just say that you have "all kinds of wine"?' And, pulling out a well-used copy of the *Shorter Oxford English Dictionary* (5th edn) from his briefcase, the baffled customer shouted out, 'Right here! The "plain meaning" of the word "wine" includes "Alcoholic liquor . . . made from the fermented juice of . . . fruits, or from grain, flowers, the sap of various trees, etc."!'

Even though most people would agree with the waiter that wine normally does not include Shaoxing Rice Wine, the customer, strictly speaking, is correct. How could two conflicting positions be equally right? The

[26] Ibid.

answer to this paradox is that a term, which is capable of multiple meanings, may have a specific meaning in a particular context. In the context of a French restaurant, wine typically refers to varieties such as Cabernet Sauvignon, Chardonnay, Chianti, Merlot, or Pinot Noir. In the context of a traditional Chinese restaurant, however, wine is more likely synonymous with rice wine.

In its submissions, Mexico made several arguments concerning the specific meaning of the term 'interconnection' in the particular context of the Reference Paper and Mexico's domestic laws and regulations. Mexico's position was basically that 'interconnection', if interpreted correctly, is limited to domestic interconnection and does not include the accounting rates regime.[27] According to Mexico, during the negotiations on basic telecommunications, 'interconnection', 'accounting rates' and 'termination services' were all discussed, but agreement was reached only on interconnection.[28] In an earlier version of the Reference Paper there was a specific draft text on accounting rates, but the text was later deleted.[29] Furthermore, the issue of accounting rates is currently 'on the table' in the Doha Round of negotiations, suggesting it was not included in the Reference Paper.[30] Mexico also referred to the Understanding on Accounting Rates (the 'Understanding'), which was outlined in the 15 February 1997 Report of the Group on Basic Telecommunications.[31] The focus of the debate then was whether accounting rates negotiated between private entities could be considered 'measures' within the meaning of Article XXVII of the GATS.[32] Given this uncertainty, as well as the fact that the accounting rates regime was the subject of ongoing and active study in the International Telecom Union, the Members agreed that accounting rates would be treated as a subject for further negotiation, as part of the 'built-in' negotiations under the GATS.[33] In the meantime, the Understanding imposed a moratorium on dispute settlement actions relating to accounting rates in the WTO.[34] Mexico also referred to subsequent practice, and pointed out that all fifty-five WTO Members (including the United States) that inscribed interconnection commitments in Section 2.2(b) of the Model Reference Paper maintain the traditional joint service accounting rates regime.[35] Thus, they clearly do not want Section 2 to apply to accounting rates because otherwise they would all be in violation.[36] Mexico also set out, in detail, the differences between

[27] Ibid., para. 4.16. [28] Ibid., para. 4.22. [29] Ibid. [30] Ibid. [31] Ibid., para. 4.26.
[32] Ibid. [33] Ibid. [34] Ibid. [35] Ibid., paras. 4.28–4.29. [36] Ibid., para. 4.28.

domestic interconnection and the accounting rates regimes from commercial, contractual, technical and regulatory perspectives.[37]

Before starting its analysis on substantive issues, the panel devoted a whole section to discussing rules of interpretation and noted that 'the only rules which may be applied in interpreting the meaning of [Mexico's] commitment are the general rules of interpretation as set out in the [*Vienna Convention on the Law of Treaties*[38] (*Vienna Convention*)]'.[39] According to the Panel, such rules include the following. First, Article 31(1) of the *Vienna Convention* which requires a treaty interpreter to determine the meaning of a term in accordance with the 'ordinary meaning' to be given to the term 'in its context', and in light of the 'object and purpose' of the treaty.[40] Second, if, after applying the rule of interpretation set out in Article 31(1), it is desirable to confirm the meaning of the term, or the meaning of the treaty term remains ambiguous or obscure or leads to a result that is manifestly absurd or unreasonable, Article 32 allows the treaty interpreter to have recourse to 'supplementary means of interpretation, including the preparatory work on the treaty and the circumstances of its conclusion'.[41] Applying these rules, the panel discussed the meaning of 'interconnection' from several perspectives including its ordinary meaning, the context provided by the term itself, other contextual elements within Mexico's Reference Paper, subsequent practice, object and purpose of the GATS, and supplementary means of interpretation, which included both the 'Understanding' and legislative history of the Reference Paper.[42] Although the analysis, which runs to a dozen pages, looks very impressive on the face of it, in essence, the panel relied heavily on the 'ordinary meaning' argument made by the United States, while failing to provide much of its own analysis. The implication of the panel report is that a specific meaning for the term 'interconnection' will not be given unless explicit reference to that specific meaning is made in the WTO instruments.

II. The mismatch between the textualist approach and the GATS

When interpreting the law, the natural starting point is the text of the law itself. As explained earlier, however, the very same text might have

[37] Ibid., paras. 4.51–4.69.

[38] Done at Vienna, 23 May 1969, in force 27 January 1980, 1155 UNTS 331; 8 International Legal Materials 679, UKTS (1980) 58.

[39] Panel Report, *Mexico – Telecoms*, paras. 7.14–7.16. [40] Ibid., para. 7.16. [41] Ibid.

[42] Ibid., paras. 7.102–7.143.

entirely different meanings for different interpreters. Depending on the different interpretive approach, interpreters may be divided into two schools. One is the 'textualist' or 'literalist' school, which usually construes legal terms very strictly and narrowly based on their black-letter meaning. The other is the 'contextualist' or 'intentionalist' school which tends to draw on the context, or even the object and purpose, to ascertain the true intentions of the drafters. In modern democracies, built upon the principles of separation of powers and checks and balances, only the legislature can make the law because they are elected by, and thus presumed to be accountable to, the people; as to judges, because they are generally not elected, nor entrusted with the power to legislate, they can only interpret the law. In the early years of the GATT, when the disputes were decided by the Contracting Parties or Working Parties (which included representatives from the parties to the disputes), there was no clear line between making and interpreting the law as the parties were both legislators and adjudicators. Thus, they were more pragmatic and flexible in interpreting the GATT rules. This tradition continued even after the panel of independent experts became the prevailing model of adjudication in the GATT in the 1950's.

A shift to a more legalistic and textualist approach began to occur, however, during the 1970s and 1980s. It is interesting to note that this parallels the emergence of the Tokyo Round 'Codes', which were plurilateral agreements that not every contracting party was obliged to join. Many commentators criticized these Codes for causing the balkanization of the rights and obligations among GATT Contracting Parties as they only applied to some Contracting Parties, while the GATT 1947, with Articles corresponding to many of these Codes, applied to all Contracting Parties. In the author's view, it might well be the case that the textualist approach was adopted at this juncture because panelists realized that the provisions of the GATT 1947 and the Codes, with different wording, established different legal obligations. Thus, the pragmatic and flexible interpretative approach was no longer considered appropriate.

Another possible reason for the adoption of the textualist approach was the growing frequency of non-adoption of panel reports for political reasons during the Uruguay Round period. Obviously, a pragmatic and flexible interpretative approach was more vulnerable to allegations of political bias than one that relies on the strict 'black-letter' meaning of the law. With the establishment of the WTO, however, neither reason seems to be relevant any more. Thanks to the 'single-undertaking' approach in the Uruguay Round, the plurilateral Codes were converted into multilateral agreements. As such, they complement rather than compete with the GATT 1994. Even in case of conflict between provisions of the GATT 1994 and those of the specialized multilateral agreements on trade in goods, the *General Interpretive Note to Annex 1A of the WTO Agreement* explicitly provides that the provisions of the specialized agreements shall prevail to the extent of the conflict. The creation of the 'negative consensus' principle in adoption of panel and Appellate Body reports also removed the threat of non-adoption. Therefore, one might well expect the revival of the pragmatic and flexible interpretative approach. This optimism soon proved to be unjustified, however, with the release of the first Appellate Body report, in which the Appellate Body made the now famous statement that the general rule of interpretation in Article 31 of the *Vienna Convention* 'attained the status of a rule of customary or general international law'.[43] According to the Appellate Body, the terms of a treaty shall 'be given their ordinary meaning, in context, so as to effectuate its object and purpose',[44] which sometimes has meant looking at the entries under the *New Shorter Oxford English Dictionary*.

While one might suspect that this shows that old habits die hard, in the view of the author, there are some more important reasons behind the Appellate Body's insistence on the textualist approach. First, strictly speaking, under the WTO legal system, the panel and Appellate Body do not have the power to 'interpret' these agreements because Article IX.2 of the *WTO Agreement* grants the Ministerial Conference and the General Council the 'exclusive authority' to adopt interpretations on these agreements. At the same time, Article 3.2 of the *Understanding on Rules and Procedures Governing the Settlement of Disputes* (DSU) states that the panel and Appellate Body can only 'clarify' the provisions of these agreements. According to the *New Shorter Oxford English Dictionary*, 'clarify' means '[e]nlighten; make clear or *plain* to the understanding; remove complexity, ambiguity, or obscurity from (a subject, statement, etc.); remove ignorance, misconception, or error from (the mind etc.)' (emphasis added), while 'interpret' means '[b]ring out or represent stylistically the meaning of (a creative work, a dramatic role, etc.) *according to one's understanding of the creator's ideas*' (emphasis added). Thus, it is no surprise that the Appellate Body would be obsessed with the 'ordinary meaning' (or dictionary meaning) of the terms. Second, even though the principle of negative consensus confers legitimacy to the reports of the

[43] Appellate Body Report, *US – Gasoline*, p. 17, DSR 1996:I, 3, 16.
[44] Ibid., p. 19, DSR 1996:I, 3, 19.

panel and Appellate Body, it does not necessarily confer legitimacy to the panel and Appellate Body themselves. Indeed, the problem is even more acute with the Appellate Body. If a panel makes a mistake in its report, it can be expected that the mistake will be rectified by the Appellate Body. As to the Appellate Body, however, it cannot pass on the responsibility and blame to the next level as the negative consensus rule makes it impossible for the WTO Dispute Settlement Body (DSB) to veto or revise the Appellate Body reports. Unlike panels, which have built their reputation over 40 years, the Appellate Body is an entirely new institution. Therefore, to avoid risking the legitimacy of the Appellate Body, it is better for it to adopt a rather cautious interpretive approach.

While the use of the textualist approach might be justified for the interpretation of most WTO agreements, its utility in the context of the GATS is rather questionable for the following reasons. To start with, services are generally more complicated than goods: there are more categories;[45] each individual service could be supplied via many different ways;[46] they are generally subject to many sets of vastly different domestic regulations of WTO Members; and, even though national treatment and market access are basic obligations for all goods under the GATT 1994, in the services context, they only apply to service sectors on which Members have made specific commitments. Moreover, unlike goods, which have been subject to extensive multilateral negotiations for over 50 years, services have only been brought into the multilateral framework within the last ten years and Members are still trying to establish the common framework for classifying services and harmonizing the different terminologies. All of these differences could only be resolved by negotiations among the membership, rather than by blind incorporation of the dictionary meaning of the terms in the agreements. Of course, panels must contribute to the prompt settlement of disputes,[47] but this cannot be reached at the expense of adding to or diminishing the rights and obligations of the Members as provided in the covered agreements.[48]

Indeed, it is very unlikely that the Contracting Parties carried with them copies of the *New Shorter Oxford English Dictionary* during the Uruguay Round negotiations. Instead, it is more reasonable to assume

[45] Goods can be roughly divided into two categories – industrial products and agricultural products – while services include twelve sectors, which can be further divided into 160 subsectors (see Services Sectoral Classification List, MTN.GNS/W/120, 10 July 1991).

[46] The GATS recognizes four modes of supply: cross-border trade; consumption abroad; commercial presence; and presence of natural persons (see Article I.2 of the GATS).

[47] Article 3.3 of the DSU. [48] Article 3.2 of the DSU.

that they carried with them technical dictionaries. Thus, a strict textualist interpretation may be further from the true intentions of the negotiators than a contextualist approach. That is where the danger of the textualist approach lies: even though a Member never intended to make commitments on a certain sector when negotiating in technical terms, such terms might be later subject to a literal interpretation which can read new commitments into its schedule. As the saying goes, everyone has a skeleton in the closet. In the context of the GATS, however, such closet not only includes skeletons, but also many ghosts, whose existence is unknown until they come out to haunt you. Once Members realize that every commitment carries the risk of being misinterpreted, it is only natural for them to refrain from making any commitment at all. That explains why, six years after the services negotiations were launched, there are only few offers, and even fewer of them provide meaningful new market access opportunities.

III. Possible solutions to the problem

Even though the textualist approach is problematic, this does not necessarily mean that the contextualist approach should be adopted in its place. In addition to the potential political drawbacks discussed in the previous section, the contextualist approach is also difficult to manage from a technical perspective. The contextualist approach puts much emphasis on the object and purpose, which is typically ascertained by looking at the drafting history of the agreements. This creates several problems. First, there is usually no negotiating history available, or at least no official version of the negotiating history. Even in the rare instances where there is such history, it more often than not is couched in ambiguous terms, which could be used to support interpretations that are vastly different or the exact opposite of each other. For example, in the *Mexico – Telecoms* case, Mexico tried to argue that, the fact that earlier drafts of the Reference Paper included a transparency requirement on accounting rates, which was subsequently deleted, indicated that Members intended to exclude accounting rates from the scope of the Reference Paper.[49] The panel reasoned, however, that the deletion might simply have occurred because negotiators considered, based on the plain meaning of the word 'interconnection', that the matter was covered, and

[49] Panel Report, *Mexico – Telecoms*, para. 4.22.

that the special provision was no longer needed.[50] Also, once panels and the Appellate Body start to consider drafting history, WTO Members might all rush to place their diverse views on issues under negotiation into such history, thus destroying any value it might have.

In the view of the author, the solutions to this problem can only be found by looking beyond the choice of interpretative approaches. There are several possible solutions. The first and ideal solution is to have the Members themselves lay down clear definitions and detailed guidelines, which are acceptable to the whole membership. Given the slow pace of the negotiations, however, it might be unrealistic to expect that Members could reach agreement on such difficult issues. Indeed, as the panel in *Mexico – Telecoms* noted, WTO negotiators have to make frequent use of 'constructive ambiguity' as a diplomatic means of enabling consensus on WTO rules.[51] From the perspective of domestic politics, vague terminology may also have been used deliberately in some cases to safeguard sector-specific interests.[52] As observed by Adlung and Roy, 'trade ministries do not normally have a dominant influence on the domestic coordination process, they may have felt unable to resist' vague terminology proposed by other domestic sectors.[53] Thus, '[a]ccepting the language proposed (or imposed) by other ministries may have been a *sine qua non* for ensuring their cooperation in the whole exercise'.[54] Such technique, although useful in achieving agreement, only delays rather than solves difficult problems.

The second option is to borrow the political question doctrine. This is a doctrine in United States constitutional law which basically states that the court will not rule on issues that should be addressed by another branch of the government.[55] Even though the case of *Bush v Gore*[56] shows that even the United States Supreme Court can be subject to partisan politics from time to time,[57] this is still a useful option to ponder. Interestingly, in its

[50] Ibid., para. 7.140. [51] Ibid., para. 7.3.

[52] Adlung and Roy, 'Turning Hills into Mountains? Commitments under the GATT', 1178.

[53] Ibid. [54] Ibid.

[55] For a general review of the doctrine, see, for example, Fritz W. Scharpf, 'Judicial Review and the Political Question: A Functional Analysis' (1966) 75 *Yale Law Journal*, 517–598.

[56] *Bush v Gore*, 531 U.S. 98 (2000).

[57] For a critique of the judgment of the Supreme Court, see, for example, Laurence H. Tribe, 'The Unbearable Wrongness of *Bush v Gore*', George Mason Law & Economics Research Paper No. 03–33; Harvard Law School, Public Law Working Paper No. 72, available at <http://ssrn.com/abstract=431080>; 'Gore v Bush and Its Disguises: Freeing Bush v Gore from Its Hall of Mirrors' (2001) 115 *Harvard Law Review*, 170, available at <http://ssrn.com/abstract=433960>.

third party's submission, Japan also raised doubts as to whether it was appropriate for the United States to bring a case against the accounting rates regime and suggested that the panel should rule on this question first.[58] Unfortunately, the panel failed to address this issue in its report. Now, let us assume that the political question doctrine is applicable, what should the panel do once it determines that the case involves a 'political question'? In the view of the author, the panel can either suspend the case pending final results from negotiations on this issue, or refer the case to the General Council. As discussed above, however, this does not seem to be an attractive option either, because the WTO political organ is not functioning well.

The third option is to have a special arrangement for telecommunication along the lines of Article XV of the GATT 1994, which mandates the relevant WTO bodies to accept all findings of statistical and other facts presented by the International Monetary Fund (IMF) in matters relating to foreign exchange, monetary reserves and balance of payments. One might doubt whether this is really necessary, considering the fact that Article 27.1 of the DSU already states that the Secretariat shall provide panels with assistance on the legal, historical and procedural aspects of the matters dealt with, as well as technical support; the 1994 *Decision on Certain Dispute Settlement Procedures for the General Agreement on Trade in Services* (herein, the '1994 Decision') has explicitly provided that, in GATS disputes, panelists shall 'have experience in issues related to the General Agreement on Trade in Services and/or trade in services, including associated regulatory matters' and, in disputes regarding sectoral matters, the panelists 'shall have the necessary expertise relevant to the specific services sectors which the dispute concerns'; and Article 13 of the DSU specifically grants the panel 'the right to seek information and technical advice from any individual or body which it deems appropriate'. There are problems, however, with each of these provisions.

First of all, even though staff in the specialized divisions of the WTO Secretariat have considerable experience with some technical issues, their primary responsibility is dealing with trade agreements. As a consequence, their technical expertise might not be as extensive as those in specialized international organizations. Thus Article 27.1 of the DSU is of little use. Second, the language in the 1994 Decision is drafted in very general terms, which does not guarantee that the depth of expertise of the panelists will be sufficient. Third, even though Article 13 of the DSU

[58] Panel Report, *Mexico – Telecoms*, paras. 5.69–5.73.

grants panels the right to seek information, a panel is not legally bound to accept information presented by external sources. Thus, it is better to have an arrangement similar to Article XV of the GATT 1994, which would explicitly provide that the relevant WTO bodies shall accept all technical findings presented by the International Telecom Union in matters relating to telecommunications.

20

Trade in services and sustainable development in the context of the WTO: the case of higher education

CHOTIRAS CHAVANICH

The World Trade Organization (WTO) is the pre-eminent body governing international trade, including international trade in services. The WTO's *General Agreement on Trade in Services* (GATS) aims to liberalize trade in services. GATS is a multilateral, legally enforceable agreement. Education services, including higher education, are one of the 12 broad sectors included in the GATS. WTO Members of the WTO are currently pursuing the goal of further liberalization of trade in services as part of the Doha Development Agenda. Without the appropriate guidance, these negotiations may bring about practical and regulatory effects that negatively impact sustainable development.

The purpose of this chapter is to focus attention on trade in higher-education services and its possible impact on sustainable development. It examines the GATS and seeks to raise awareness about the importance of sustainable development. It also aims to stimulate debate and analysis of the role of governments and the WTO in promoting sustainable development through trade in higher-education services.

I. GATS and the education sector

The GATS has existed since 1995. The purpose of the GATS is to reduce or eliminate barriers to trade in services. It is a worldwide agreement covering all 149 WTO Members. GATS is the first multilateral agreement on trade in services.[1] Education is one of the 12 primary service sectors. There are five subsectors in education: primary, secondary, higher, adult, and other.

1 Organisation for Economic Co-Operation and Development, *The General Agreement on Trade in Services (GATS): An Analysis* (Paris, 1994); Julian Arkell, 'The General Agreement on Trade in Services (GATS): liberalisation concepts, structures and modalities', in Jacques H.J. Bourgeois, Frédérique Berrod, and Eric Gippini Fournier (eds), *The Uruguay Round Results: A European lawyers' perspective* (Brussels, 1995), pp. 373–393.

The GATS has three parts. The first part is the framework that contains the general principles and rules. The second part consists of the national schedules that list a WTO Member's specific commitments on access to its domestic market for foreign providers. The third part consists of annexes with rules for specific sectors.

The GATS uses four 'modes' to describe trade or supply of services. The four modes of trade in services are described as follows:

Mode 1: Cross-border supply focuses on the service crossing the border, which does not require the consumer or the service provider to physically move. Examples in higher education include distance education and e-learning.

Mode 2: Consumption abroad refers to the consumer moving to the country of the supplier, which in education means students taking all or part of their education in another country.

Mode 3: Commercial presence involves a service provider establishing a commercial facility in another country to provide a service. Examples in higher education include branch campuses or franchising arrangements.

Mode 4: Presence of natural persons means people travelling to another country on a temporary basis to provide a service, which in education would include professors or researchers teaching in a country other than their country of nationality.

II. Specific commitments in higher education

The GATS is described as a voluntary agreement because WTO Members can decide which sectors they will agree to bring under GATS rules. This is done through the preparation of their national schedules of commitments and through the 'request-offer' negotiation rounds.

The education sector is one of the sectors with the least commitments. The reason is not clear, but perhaps it can be attributed to the need for countries to strike a balance between pursuing domestic education priorities and exploring ways in which trade in education services can be further liberalized. Or it could be linked to the fact that, to date, education in general has taken a very low priority in the major bilateral agreements and rightly or wrongly, the same may be true for the GATS.

Only 44 of the 149 WTO Members have made commitments in education, and only 21 of these have included commitments in higher education. It is interesting to note that countries such as Congo, Lesotho, Jamaica, and Sierra Leone have made full, unconditional commitments in higher education, perhaps with the intent of encouraging

Table 20.1 *Mode of supply in higher-education services*

Mode of supply according to the GATS	Explanation	Examples in higher education	Size/potential of market
1. Cross-border supply	Provision of a service where the service crosses the border (does not require the physical movement of the consumer)	Distance education E-learning Virtual universities	Currently a relatively small market – seen to have great potential through the use of new internal cross-border supply and especially the Internet
2. Consumption abroad	Provision of the service involving the movement of the consumer to the country of the supplier	Students who go to another country to study	Currently represents the largest share of the global market for education services
3. Commercial presence	Service provider establishes or has presence of commercial facilities in another country in order to render service	Local branch or satellite campuses Twinning partnerships Franchising arrangements with local institutions	Growing interest and strong potential for future growth Most controversial as it appears to set international rules on foreign investment
4. Presence of natural persons	Persons travelling to another country on a temporary basis to provide service	Professors, teachers, researchers working abroad	Potentially a strong market given the emphasis on mobility of professionals

Source: Jane Knight, *Trade in Higher Education Services: The Implications of GATS*, Report of The Observatory on Borderless Higher Education (March 2002), p. 5

Table 20.2 *Highlights of negotiation proposals*

	Australia	New Zealand	United States
Role of Government	Government has a role in the financing, delivery and regulation of higher education – either alone or in partnership with individuals, non-governmental organizations (NGOs), and private education – governments must retain their sovereign right to determine own domestic funding and regulatory policies/measures	International trade in education services can supplement and support national education policy objectives (i.e. reduce the infrastructure commitments required of governments and so free resources for other aspects of education policy) The reduction of barriers does not equate to an erosion of core public education systems and standards	The principle that governments should retain the right to regulate to meet domestic policy objectives should be respected In education service sector, governments will continue to play important roles as suppliers of service 'Education to a large extent is a government function and it does not seek to displace public education systems. It seeks to supplement public education systems.'
Rationale/purpose of trade liberalization	Means of providing individuals in all countries with access to wide range of education options	Education as a role in economic and social development In New Zealand, education exports are the fourth largest service sector export earner and fifteenth largest foreign exchange earner overall	Help upgrade knowledge and skills through training and education, while respecting each country's role in prescribing and administering appropriate public education for its citizens

Benefits of trade liberalization	Increased access to education in qualitative and quantitative terms that would otherwise not be available in country of origin Competitive stimulus with flow-on benefits to all students Efficient encouragement of internationalization and flow of students	In addition to generating revenue for private and state sector education institutions and Member economies, there are benefits at individual, institutional and societal level through: Academic exchange Increased cross-cultural linkages Technological transfer Increased access for Members	These services constitute a growing, international business, supplementing the public education system and contributing to global spread of the modern 'knowledge economy' Benefits of this growth help to develop more efficient work force, leading countries to an improved competitive position in the world economy

Source: Jane Knight, *Trade in Higher Education Services: The Implications of GATS*, Report of The Observatory on Borderless Higher Education (March 2002), pp. 11–12

foreign providers to help develop their educational systems. Australia's commitment in higher education covers the provision of private tertiary education services, including at university level. Only three countries (United States, New Zealand, and Australia) of the 21 countries with higher-education commitments have submitted a negotiating proposal outlining their interests in this subsector.

III. The concept of 'sustainable development'

The concept of sustainable development was popularized by the International Union for the Conservation of Nature in its 'World Conservation Strategy,' and was refined in 1987 in the *Brundtland Report* of the World Commission on Environment and Development, which stated that: 'Sustainable development is development that meets the needs of the present, without compromising the ability of future generations to meet their own needs.'

While definitions and interpretations of the elements of sustainable development have varied, the concept is generally viewed as consisting of three primary aspects or 'pillars': economic (sustainable economic development); social (social development/equity); and environmental (environmental protection/conservation/preservation).

The objectives of sustainable development are recognized in the preamble to the *Marrakesh Agreement Establishing the World Trade Organization* (*WTO Agreement*). Liberalizing trade can help ensure that resources are used efficiently, to generate the wealth necessary for environmental improvement, development, the promotion of cleaner technology, and the improvement of social conditions.

The concept of '*sustainable development*' itself represents a form of development that seeks to integrate economic, environmental and social dimensions in a balanced way. Sustainable development is about finding more environmentally and socially responsible and sustainable ways of doing business.

According to Agenda 21 and the Johannesburg Plan of Implementation, the issue of sustainable development can be seen from various strategic perspectives:

> 3.1 Socio-cultural perspectives
>
> *Human rights*: a respect for human rights is a *sine qua non* of sustainable development. This approach leads to the adoption of a rights-based approach to development.

Peace and human security: enabling people to live in an environment of peace and security is fundamental to human dignity and development. Too often fragile processes of sustainable development are undermined by insecurities and conflicts. These result in significant human tragedies, overwhelming health systems, destroying homes, schools and often whole communities, and leading to increasing numbers of displaced people and refugees. Education for sustainable development therefore seeks to build skills and values for peace in the minds of humankind.

Gender equality: pursuit of gender equality is central to sustainable development where each member of society respects others and plays a role in which they can fulfill their potential. The broader goal of gender equality is a societal goal to which education, along with all other social institutions, must contribute. Women and girls suffer discrimination in many societies, both developing and industrialised. Such discrimination is often structurally embedded, where individual relationships between men and women follow the pattern of prevailing social norms or traditions.

Cultural diversity and intercultural understanding: Many opportunities for education and sustainable human development are undermined by the lack of tolerance and intercultural understanding, upon which peace is founded. This perspective must inform not only the content of educational programs, but also characterize teacher/learner and learner/learner relationships. Learning situations of all kinds are ideal opportunities for practising and deepening respect for and understanding of diversity.

Health: issues of development, environment and health are closely entwined – ill health hampers economic and social development, triggering a vicious cycle that contributes to unsustainable resource use and environmental degradation. A healthy population and safe environments are important pre-conditions for sustainable development. Hunger, malnutrition, malaria, water-borne diseases, drug and alcohol abuse, violence and injury, unplanned pregnancy, HIV/AIDS and other sexually transmitted infections are just some of the problems that have enormous implications for health. The school environment itself must be safe and healthy. Schools should act not only as centres for academic learning, but also as supportive venues for the provision of essential health education and services, in collaboration with parents and the community.

Research on the synergies between services liberalization and sustainable development is limited. The major reason for is the difficulty of assessing the exact nature of the linkages.[2] Looking at the education

[2] For a study of the linkage between trade and sustainable development, see Gary P. Sampson, *The WTO and Sustainable Development* (Tokyo, 2005).

sector, this chapter examines trade liberalization and deregulation within a sustainable development framework.

IV. Liberalization of higher education: a challenge for sustainable development

There are generally three terms commonly used by the education sector to describe the international nature of education, namely: 'internationalization', 'cross-border education', and more recently 'trade in education'. There is a hierarchy to these terms, with 'internationalization of education' being the most comprehensive, 'cross-border education' being one component of internationalization and then 'international trade in education' being used to characterize some cross-border activities.

A review of books, reports and articles by trade experts shows that often when talking about internationalization or liberalization of education, they actually are referring to international trade in education services. In contrast, when educators talk about internationalization, they are talking about a broad range of activities some of which have absolutely nothing to do with trade. More and more, internationalization is seen as consisting of two streams or components.

The first is 'internationalization at home' which refers to the international and intercultural dimension of curricula, the teaching/learning process, research, extra-curricular activities, and other activities that help students develop international understanding and intercultural skills without ever leaving the campus.

The second component is 'internationalization abroad', that is, cross-border education (often referred to as transnational education), which involves students, teachers, scholars, programmes, courses, curriculum, projects moving between countries and cultures, or across borders. 'Cross-border education' is a term that educators are using to capture a wide range of education activities that are part of international academic linkages and agreements, international development/aid projects, and international commercial trade initiatives. However, 'trade in education services' is usually understood by educators as being a subset of cross-border education, and for the most part it is described as including those activities that have a commercial or for-profit nature or purpose to them. This understanding is much narrower than the one used by economists or the trade sector. From their perspective, even if a cross-border education activity is seen to be non-commercial in purpose – for instance, the exchange of students or professors for a semester – there is still export value in a country's balance of payments from accommodation, living, travel expenses, and, therefore, there are commercial implications.

The demand for higher education is increasing in most countries. This is due to the growth of the knowledge economy, the movement to lifelong learning and changing demographics. While demand is growing, the capacity of the public sector to satisfy the demand is being questioned. This is due to budget limitations, the changing role of government, and increased emphasis on the market economy and privatization. At the same time, innovations in information and communication technologies are providing alternate and virtual ways to deliver higher education. New types of providers, such as corporate universities, for-profit institutions, and media companies, are emerging. This scenario is changing further as providers – public and private, new and traditional - deliver education services across national borders to meet the needs in other countries. Alternative types of cross-border programme delivery, such as branch campuses and franchise and twinning arrangements, are being developed. As a result, an exciting, but rather complex, picture of a higher-education provision is emerging. Today, in addition to more people moving, academic programmes and providers are moving across borders. Economic considerations are increasingly driving a large part of the international or cross-border supply of education. This commercial or profit motive is a reality today, and applies to both private providers and, in some cases, public institutions. It is therefore important that educators are cognizant of the impact of trade liberalization on higher education, and that they take steps to maximize the benefits and minimize the threats to a robust and high-quality higher-education system.

With regards to the role of education *vis-à-vis* the promotion of sustainable development, it is interesting to note that the United Nations Conference on Environment and Development in 1992, known as the 'Earth Summit', gave high priority in its Agenda 21 to the role of education in pursuing the kind of development that would respect and nurture the natural environment. It focused on the process of orienting education in order to foster values and attitudes of respect for the environment and envisaged ways and means of doing so. By the time of the Johannesburg Summit in 2002 the vision broadened to encompass social justice and the fight against poverty as key principles of development that is sustainable. The human and social aspects of sustainable development meant that solidarity, equity, partnership and cooperation were as crucial as scientific approaches to environmental protection. Besides re-affirming the educational objectives of the Millennium Development Goals and the

Education for All Dakar Framework for Action, the Summit proposed the Decade of Education for Sustainable Development as a way of signalling that education and learning lie at the heart of approaches to sustainable development. In its 57th Meeting in December 2002, the UN General Assembly proclaimed the Decade of Education for Sustainable Development for the period 2005–2014, emphasizing that education is an indispensable element for achieving sustainable development. It also designated the United Nations Educational, Scientific and Cultural Organization (UNESCO) as the lead agency to promote and implement the so-called Decade programme.[3]

In sum, by liberalizing trade in higher education, governments – Members of WTO – and the WTO itself must bear in mind the role of education as an integral part of a strategy of sustainable development. This means that they should focus on the relationship between education and the three areas of sustainable development which are society, environment, and economy. The underlying values which education for sustainable development must promote include at least the following:

respect for the dignity and human rights of all people throughout the world and a commitment to social and economic justice for all;
respect for the human rights of future generations and a commitment to intergenerational responsibility;
respect and care for the greater community of life in all its diversity which involves the protection and restoration of the earth's ecosystems; and
respect for cultural diversity and a commitment to build locally and globally a culture of tolerance, non-violence and peace.

Higher education has a special role to play in promoting sustainable development. Universities must function as places of research and learning for sustainable development, and as initiators and poles of activity in their communities and nationally. Educational theory and innovative practices frequently emerge from research programmes and academic investigation. Sustainable development needs to become a central preoccupation in determining areas of educational research and development. This sensitization is urgent because of the significant time lag between starting research programmes and putting useable results into practice.

The Global Higher Education for Sustainability Partnership (GHESP) initiated development of the Toolkit/Resource Centre Project for Higher

[3] UNESCO, 'United Nations Decade of Education for Sustainable Development 2005–2014' (Draft), International Implementation Scheme (January 2005).

Education for Sustainable Development, with the support of the UN University, to promote strategies for reorienting higher education toward sustainable development. It will provide high quality and regionally relevant resources and tools to individuals around the world who are striving to make education for sustainability a central focus of higher-education curricula, research, physical operations, student life and outreach to local, regional, and global communities. Cooperation and the twinning of universities across different regions of the world enables student exchange on innovative projects, for example, in environmental engineering, so that students begin to apply new knowledge and skills to problems of sustainable development. The GHESP provides a forum for cooperation and exchange of experiences.

Higher education should also provide leadership by practicing what it preaches through sustainable purchasing, investments and facilities that are integrated with teaching and learning. All college and university students should understand the importance of diversity and inclusion, be able to identify values, assumptions and ethical systems in order to make their own decisions, and understand geo-spatial and temporal frames of reference and the context of information. Higher education should emphasize experiential, inquiry-based, problem-solving, interdisciplinary approaches, and critical thinking. Curricula need to be developed, including content, materials, and tools such as case studies and identification of best practices.[4]

Higher education exists to serve the public interest and is not a 'commodity', a fact which WTO Members have recognized through UNESCO and other international or multilateral bodies, conventions, and declarations. The mission of higher education is to contribute to sustainable development and the improvement of society as a whole by mean of educating highly-qualified graduates able to meet the needs of all sectors of human activity; advancing, creating and disseminating knowledge through research; interpreting, preserving, and promoting cultures in the context of cultural pluralism and diversity; providing opportunities for higher learning throughout life; contributing to the development and improvement of education at all levels; and protecting and enhancing civil society by training young people in the values that form the basis of democratic citizenship, and by providing critical and detached perspectives in the discussion of strategic choices facing societies.

Higher education should be assessed in terms of the fit between what society expects of institutions and what they do. For this, institutions and

[4] Ibid.

systems should base their long-term orientations on societal aims and needs, including respect of cultures and environmental protection. Developing entrepreneurial skills and initiatives should become a priority for higher education. Special attention should be paid to higher education's role of service to society, especially to activities aimed at eliminating poverty, intolerance, violence, illiteracy, hunger, environmental degradation and disease, and to activities aiming at the development of peace, through an interdisciplinary and trans-disciplinary approach.

The internationalization of higher education is integral to the quality of the academic endeavour and its research mission. For most institutions, international trade in higher education is an important component for attaining the mission of higher education. For these institutions, education exports such as international student recruitment or the delivery of higher-education programmes across borders through distance education are part of a broader set of international activities, which include faculty and student exchanges, research cooperation and capacity-building initiatives in developing countries.

Quality in higher education is a multidimensional concept, which should embrace all its functions and activities: teaching and academic programmes, research and scholarship, staffing, students, infrastructure and the academic environment. Particular attention should be paid to the advancement of knowledge through research. Higher-education institutions in all regions should be committed to transparent internal and external evaluation, conducted openly by independent specialists.

V. Role of governments and WTO Members in promoting sustainable development within the framework of trade in education services

With respect to the higher-education sector, governments usually play a role in the funding, regulation, monitoring and delivery of higher education, or, at least, in designating bodies to do so. The advent of increased cross-border delivery by foreign education providers raises many issues all of which impact on the role of government, such as licensing and regulation procedures for foreign providers; quality assurance and accreditation for imported and exported education services; funding protocols, including operating grants, loans, subsidies and scholarships; and qualification, recognition and credit transfer systems.

In addition, governments play an importance role in the trade in services negotiations taking place within the framework of the WTO. It is crucial that the negotiations under the WTO to liberalize trade in services – especially in the higher-education sector – should not undermine the pursuit of sustainable development. Instead, the WTO obligations on higher-education services should support and complement governments' obligations and efforts to protect the environment and human rights and to promote social and economic progress. In this perspective, WTO Members must take urgent action. In particular, they should:

recognize that the liberalization of trade in services affects sustainable development, in both positive and negative ways;

honour their existing legal obligations to promote sustainable development and make sustainable development the key benchmark of any liberalization activities undertaken pursuant to current WTO services negotiations;

carry out thorough, comprehensive and fully transparent sustainability assessments before devising any new obligations in the WTO services negotiations; and

open their decision-making processes to guidance from relevant intergovernmental organizations and non-governmental organizations (NGOs).

VI. The WTO: a forum in which negotiations may pose challenges to sustainable development

In general, the WTO should play an active role in highlighting the issue of sustainable development and making sustainable development the key benchmark for the liberalization of trade in services in the current negotiations, particularly with respect to the education sector. The WTO should be made more transparent and accountable to the larger international framework of cooperation and promotion of sustainable development. This is crucial because the developments in the WTO have major ramifications for sustainable development and yet there is a lack of information and participation from the public, from many sections of national governments and parliaments, and from other international organizations. There should also be greater internal transparency within the WTO and developing-country Members must have full participation rights in discussions and decision-making.

To achieve these aims, the WTO should set up a work-programme and a body (such as Working Group on Trade in Services and Sustainable development!) that would deal specifically with the relationship between sustainable development and trade in services.

Moreover, the WTO should increase collaboration with other UN agencies and other international organizations, such as UNESCO, the International Labour Organization (ILO), the UN Commission on Sustainable Development, etc. This will give rise to synergies and contribute towards promoting sustainable development.

21

The WTO and sustainable development

MARK HALLE

The relationship between trade and sustainable development is complex and challenging. In this chapter, I shall focus on one component of that challenge: the relationship between trade and environment. I shall argue that, contrary to general opinion, the environment has made significant progress in the World Trade Organization (WTO). This arises not so much from the progress in environmentally-related negotiations nor from the regular work of the WTO Committee on Trade and Environment (CTE), but from the work of the Dispute Settlement Body (DSB) and, in particular, the Appellate Body. While this has led to charges of 'judicial activism' on the part of the Appellate Body, I argue that the Appellate Body is simply fulfilling its mandate to clarify and interpret WTO law and to fill gaps left by negotiators.

I. Environment: a fraught topic in the WTO

Environment is a sensitive topic in the trade context. Although the fear is receding somewhat, the environmental community is still concerned that trade rules will be used to challenge and roll back environmental achievement at both the international and domestic levels. At the domestic level, to the extent that environmental regulations, norms or standards impinge on the freedom to conduct business, they are vulnerable to challenge as unwarranted interference with open trade. At the international level, multilateral environmental agreements (MEAs) that use trade measures to encourage and enforce compliance appear especially open to challenge, even though the trade measures contained in these agreements have been agreed by consensus by all parties and many of these agreements have more members than the WTO itself.

Developing countries are also by and large circumspect about the environment in WTO. This is in part because they fear – with some justification – that it will be used for protectionist purposes by those countries with more stringent environmental requirements. They see environment as an area where the rich countries have a comparative advantage. It is also, however, because many of them already suffer from limited capacity in handling a complex and overloaded WTO agenda and are reluctant to see the agenda complicated further by what they regard as extraneous topics. Finally, many developing countries, while conscious of the importance of environmental management, do not see it as having a high priority in the trade context. They resist attempts to push environment higher on the trade agenda when so many issues of greater priority to them remain unresolved.

How, then, did environment make its way into the WTO?

In some ways, opening space for environment in the new WTO was inevitable. The WTO was set up soon after the Earth Summit in Rio, at a time when the environment was at the peak of its political momentum, a momentum that has since subsided. Politicians worldwide were scrambling to demonstrate their dedication to the environment, using every public platform available to show they were in tune with public sentiment. Many of them carried this opportunistic enthusiasm into the *General Agreement on Tariffs and Trade* (GATT), which at the time was concluding the Uruguay Round of multilateral trade negotiations.

At the same time, the message to the environmental community was that they had to think in terms of harnessing the market to achieve global environmental objectives, and not go on counting on heavy-handed and inefficient government action. Trade, not aid, would bring about an economy more concerned with the efficient use of resources, better able to value environmental services, and in which the general upgrading of technology and standards of production would lift the world onto a new environmental plateau. The environmental community, buying into this message, held out some not-unjustified hope that the soon-to-be-created WTO would be open to partnership with them in pursuit of their shared objectives.

Sure enough, the Preamble to the *Marrakesh Agreement Establishing the World Trade Organization* (*WTO Agreement*) – which concluded the Uruguay Round and established the WTO – includes a strong statement on the need for the trading system to be compatible with and supportive of the wider goal of sustainable development. While this was in no way intended to make trade liberalization subservient to sustainable development,[1] the

[1] The chief negotiator for Japan in the Uruguay Round, Ambassador Nobutoshi Akao, explained in a personal comment that the Preamble was used to park issues about which one or several delegations felt strongly, but around which there was no consensus.

formulation has been referred to with increasing frequency as one of the few statements that articulate the goal that trade liberalization is intended to serve. Indeed, the statement was repeated in even stronger form in paragraph 6 of the Doha Ministerial Declaration,[2] in which it is acknowledged that not only can open trade and sustainable development be compatible and mutually supportive, they *must* be.

Even if the Rio Summit had never taken place, or if sceptics had effectively blocked all mention of environment and sustainable development in the texts establishing the WTO, the new organization would have had no choice but to deal with environmental issues – whether domestic policies and regulations or relations with the complex and growing international regime on the environment. It is an inescapable fact that trade and environment can never be self-contained compartments. Inevitably, they overlap and, at a minimum, the WTO is obliged to deal with the issues that arise in this area of overlap.

II. Forms of progress in the WTO

It is now more than ten years since the WTO was established, and we have over a decade of experience in dealing with the trade/environment interface. What have we learned, and how has our vision of this relationship evolved?

Most observers of the WTO, and particularly those with an environmental bias, would say that the trade and environment debate has not advanced very much and that both the work of the CTE and the environmental negotiations in the Doha Round are going around in circles. While a superficial look at the record would tend to confirm this pessimistic judgment, I shall argue that this judgment is, at the least, incomplete. In many ways, I believe that it is outright inaccurate. I would like to suggest that there are other ways to look at the trade and environment issue in the WTO.

First, not only is environment accepted as a relevant topic for WTO deliberations, it was, at Doha, upgraded to become a topic for negotiation. For all of its tentative beginnings, environment is here to stay in the WTO. Nothing guaranteed this outcome. Indeed, several topics admitted to the WTO for clarification – such as trade, debt and finance – have failed so far to progress to the stage of negotiations. Others – for example, investment, competition policy, or transparency in government procurement – far

[2] WT/MIN(01)/DEC/1.

from having progressed to negotiation have, in fact, even been dropped as topics for discussion and clarification. Thus there is no guarantee that any topic will be 'upgraded' once it is on the WTO agenda. Yet environment was, a scant six years after it made its way onto the agenda as a topic in its own right. I submit that this is politically significant.

Second, it would be a mistake to regard negotiated outcomes as the only form of progress in the WTO system. Many issues cease to be issues because the presentation of positions of different Members and the debate on these reduce the contentious aspects to a point where no negotiated outcome is deemed necessary – the issue simply goes away. A number of issues on the CTE agenda, considered sensitive at the time, have lost their sensitivity, or at least their sense of urgency. Often, this is because a full airing of the views and preoccupations of the different Members leads to a better understanding of the point of view of each. The sense of threat disappears, and a sense of confidence grows in its place.

Other times, there is an issue, but the Members find another way to deal with it, outside the forum of the WTO, through domestic adjustments, improved information and notification, or in another international forum – for example, those provided by the MEAs. This process – that Professor Gregory Schaffer calls 'crystallization' – must be regarded as an important form of progress for which the WTO deserves some credit.[3]

III. Environmental progress – the role of the DSB

I would argue that the greatest progress for the environment in the WTO has come about as a result of the work of the DSB and more particularly by means of the Appellate Body carrying out its function of clarifying ambiguities in the WTO rules, filling gaps left by the negotiators, and interpreting the intent of negotiators in crafting the legal texts based on close examination of the negotiating history.

It is my contention that, through the DSB, environmental principles and perspectives have made an impressive advance in the WTO in its first ten years. I illustrate this below with three cases.[4]

[3] Gregory C. Shaffer, 'The World Trade Organization under Challenge: Democracy and the Law and Politics of the WTO's Treatment of Trade and Environment Matters' (2001) 25 *Harvard Environmental Law Review*, 1–93.

[4] In discussing these cases, I draw upon 'The State of Trade and Environment Law – Implications for Doha and Beyond', a 2003 publication of the International Institute for Sustainable Development (IISD) by Howard Mann (of the IISD) and Stephen Porter (of the Centre for International Environmental Law).

The WTO and MEAs

The first relates to the relationship between WTO rules and the MEAs, a subject that has made very little progress in ten years of review by the CTE and four years of specific negotiation under the Doha Round. Indeed, it can be convincingly argued that the negotiating mandate contained in paragraph 31.1 of the Doha Ministerial Declaration is so restrictive that any outcome is likely to represent a step backwards in establishing coherence and mutual supportiveness between the trade and environment regimes.

With one exception, the GATT deemed that international law from sources outside the GATT 1947 was not relevant for the deliberations of GATT panels. The exception (the *Canada – Herring and Salmon* case) referred to the UN Convention on the Law of the Sea to interpret and apply a trade law obligation.[5] Indeed, in the *US – Tuna (EEC)* and *US – Tuna (Mexico)* cases, the refusal of the panels to give much regard to applicable environmental legislation came as a shock to the environmental community and served as a wake-up call on the potential of the trade rules to interfere with the pursuit of legitimate international environmental objectives.[6]

It was therefore with some apprehension that the environmental community observed the establishment of the WTO DSB and the decision of the Members to give it considerable power to enforce compliance. And it came as an agreeable surprise when the WTO, in its very first case (the *US – Gasoline* case) stressed that the new *Understanding on Rules and Procedures Governing the Settlement of Disputes* (DSU) 'reflects a measure of recognition that the *General Agreement* is not to be interpreted in clinical isolation from public international law.'[7] It is unlikely many of them suspected just how far this new tendency would extend.

In the oft-cited *US – Shrimp* case the Appellate Body had to determine whether there was a case for Article XX exceptions to be applied. In seeking to define 'exhaustible natural resources' and the application of the chapeau of Article XX, they turned to a range of international agreements on the environment.[8] It is striking that they considered not only well-established treaties of global scope and reach, but also relevant

[5] GATT Panel Report, *Canada – Herring and Salmon*, para. 5.3.

[6] GATT Panel Report, *US – Tuna (EEC)*, para. 5.33; GATT Panel Report, *US – Tuna (Mexico)*, paras. 6.3–6.4.

[7] Appellate Body Report, *US – Gasoline*, p. 17, DSR 1996:1, 3, 16.

[8] Appellate Body Report, *US – Shrimp*, paras. 130–131.

regional agreements and, in one case, a convention that was not yet in force. They did so because they felt it was important to determine what had been the intention of the States party to these agreements in seeking to protect exhaustible natural resources. After all, these same States are the Members of the WTO.

It is interesting to contrast the negotiations under paragraph 31(i) of the Doha Ministerial Declaration and the decision of the Appellate Body in the *US – Shrimp* case. In the first, negotiations under a poorly crafted and confused mandate are making very little progress, leaving the threat of conflict between MEAs and WTO rules intact. In the decision of the Appellate Body, by contrast, the WTO-MEA relationship has been given specific and cogent direction in the dispute settlement process, that is, at the most critical point of potential conflict between the two bodies of law. In the absence of a negotiated agreement on how trade law relates to the environmental agreements relevant to the case, the decision of the Appellate Body in *US – Shrimp* and in other related cases remains the clearest statement of how the WTO rules are to be viewed in their relationship with the international obligations assumed by States under the agreements that make up the environmental regime.

The WTO and the precautionary principle

The second case deals with what is undoubtedly one of the most sensitive issues at the trade and environment interface: how to apply the precautionary principle. The precautionary principle is an established principle of international environmental law, but it is regarded with extreme circumspection in the WTO, even if the 'precautionary approach' is given a small space in the *Agreement on the Application of Sanitary and Phytosanitary Measures* (*SPS Agreement*).

The *EC – Hormones* case forced the Appellate Body to focus on this provision in the *SPS Agreement*. In considering how much scientific evidence is sufficient to justify a measure, it noted that responsible governments commonly act from a perspective of prudence and precaution where there is risk to human life.[9] It further ruled that measures taken by governments could be based on a minority scientific opinion.[10]

The *Australia – Salmon* case went on to lay down specific guidelines for what constitutes a proper risk assessment.[11] These do *not* include a

[9] Appellate Body Report, *EC – Hormones*, para. 124.
[10] Ibid., para. 194.
[11] Appellate Body Report, *Australia – Salmon*, para. 121.

minimum threshold of risk, leaving it to governments to decide what level of risk warrants a precautionary response.

Finally, the *Japan – Agricultural Products II* case sets out a rigorous set of conditions for the use of temporary measures in the absence of full scientific certainty, thus effectively defining (and limiting) the use of the one key embodiment of the precautionary principle in the *SPS Agreement.*[12]

Taking these three cases together, it can be said that the Appellate Body has set in place a set of daunting procedural requirements for use of the precautionary principle – some of which may effectively place use of the precautionary principle beyond the reach of some developing countries. However, a government that has fulfilled these criteria is free to choose its desired level of acceptable risk, and there is no minimum threshold of risk necessary to justify their decision to put these measures in place. Combined with the ability to base measures on minority scientific views this leaves significant scope for the application of the precautionary principle.

Had use of the precautionary principle been debated in the Committee on Sanitary and Phytosanitary Measures, or in the WTO General Council, it is inconceivable that a result anywhere close to the one effectively achieved by the Appellate Body could have been secured. Indeed, sensitivity on the introduction of the notion of precaution in the work of the WTO is such that the subject is virtually taboo. And yet the Appellate Body dealt with it sensibly, lucidly and unambiguously.

The WTO and process and production methods distinctions

Third and finally, probably the single most sensitive issue in the trade and environment is the issue of process and production methods (PPMs), or factors relating to how a product is made unrelated to the characteristics of the product itself. From the environmental perspective, how a good is made is of central importance. From a developing country perspective, dictating how a good is produced is an intrusion on sovereignty. It is generally agreed in trade circles that allowing such distinctions in the WTO would create a substantial avenue for protectionist measures dressed up in environmental clothing. Indeed, as noted above, the *US – Tuna* panels, consistent with GATT practice, ruled that only the characteristics of the final product are relevant under GATT law.

In the *US – Shrimp* case, however, the Appellate Body turned this approach on its head. While import bans are still clearly prohibited

[12] Appellate Body Report, *Japan – Agricultural Products II*, para. 89.

under GATT 1994 rules, PPM-based considerations at least have a chance to justify themselves under the General Exceptions (Article XX) of GATT 1994.

Of course, the Appellate Body does not offer a blank check to relax the basic rules of non-discrimination for either PPM or extra-territorial measures. In the *US – Shrimp* case, the Appellate Body sets out a number of criteria which would have to be met for such measures to be justified as Article XX exceptions.

The first is to ascertain whether the measure qualifies under the scope for exceptions intended by the drafters of GATT. This concerns principally the justification for extra-territorial measures, and establishes that there must be a 'sufficient nexus' between the country taking the measure and the cause (in this case, migratory and endangered sea turtles) for which the measure is taken.[13]

The second, which affects both PPM and extra-territorial considerations relates to the chapeau of Article XX, and considers whether the measure is being applied in an arbitrary or unjustifiably discriminatory way, or as a disguised restriction to trade. The tests used in *US – Shrimp* insist that:

the measure must be flexible – referring to the objective to be achieved but not to the way in which it is achieved;

the State employing the measure must demonstrate that it has made efforts in good faith to negotiate an agreement with the parties affected by the measure; and

it must allow a reasonable phase-in time to adopt the PPM measure.[14]

The *EC – Asbestos* case, which intervened between the first and second Appellate Body rulings in *US – Shrimp*, turned on exceptions for health, not environment, but the decision is significant in considering whether PPMs may be considered relevant to determining whether two products are 'like' in the sense of Article III of GATT 1994. The Appellate Body ruled that the carcinogenicity of a product (in this case asbestos) was relevant to whether or not it was a 'like' product when compared with alternatives available for the same purpose. It argued, among other things, that the carcinogenicity would affect the way in which consumers viewed the product.[15]

So, while it surely cannot be argued that the Appellate Body has thrown open the door for PPM distinctions in considering the 'likeness' of

[13] Appellate Body Report, *US – Shrimp*, para. 133.

[14] Ibid., paras. 158–186.

[15] Appellate Body Report, *EC – Asbestos*, para. 113.

products, it is equally clear that it does not regard such distinctions as taboo. Rather, the Appellate Body appears to feel that, at least in certain cases, Members should have the opportunity to argue for Article XX exceptions on grounds that include such distinctions, and that it is helpful to offer some guidance on how such arguments will be considered.

Lessons for trade and environment

What accounts for this fundamental change in approach between the GATT and the WTO? It is clear that, because the reach of trade policy now extends deep into the realm of domestic policy and affects so many sectors once the sovereign domain of national decision-making, the coherence between trade rules and rules in other areas has become increasingly important. Thus, in interpreting trade law, the Appellate Body must seek and consider statements – like the Preamble to the *WTO Agreement* – in which the purpose of trade policy and the intent of the negotiators are articulated. For the same reason, there is growing pressure to ensure that trade law is to the extent possible supportive of what governments have agreed to do in other fora.

What lessons can we draw from the three cases above? First, it is evident that the fortress walls that characterized the GATT have to a large extent broken down with the WTO. The trade policy community can no longer act as if the values, laws and practices agreed by States in other areas do not exist or apply inside the walls of trade policy. Just as the scope of trade policy has expanded well beyond the scope of border measures and manufactured goods to address key priorities of domestic policy, so the dispute settlement system must take account of the overlap between trade policy and regulation, and relevant policy and regulation in other areas. Indeed trade law, on its own, may be too narrow to deal with the complex relationships that affect trade policy, particularly in the domestic arena.

The second is that the lack of progress in discussions and negotiations is no guarantee that an issue will remain blocked in the trade regime as a whole. It may, as we have seen, move to the DSB for clarification. Or it may move to other trade fora outside the WTO, just as trade-related aspects of intellectual property rights (TRIPS) are under active discussion in the World Intellectual Property Organization, the Convention on Biological Diversity, and in the International Treaty on Plant Genetic Resources for Food and Agriculture. While, on balance, negotiated outcomes are preferable to Appellate Body decisions, in the absence of the former, we may end up with the latter. Perhaps this should serve as a stimulus for more active concession-seeking in the relevant negotiations.

Third and finally, there is a growing awareness that trade policy is no longer limited to border measures affecting traded goods. Instead, it now reaches deep into the domain of domestic policy, affecting the choices that governments have traditionally regarded as subject to their sovereign decisions. This means that trade policy must now find a peaceful coexistence with environment policy, a process which I have suggested is advancing well in the WTO. Indeed, the fact that it has progressed so far in respect of the trade and environment relationship (as compared to, say, trade and labour rights) reflects the strong public support for environmental values in most countries, and the reality that support for trade liberalization will be undermined if it continues to ignore this public sentiment.

What does this mean for the Doha negotiations?

What can we expect from the current negotiations on environment and sustainable development in the WTO? Most likely we will see no dramatic breakthroughs. We may well reach a limited agreement on accelerated liberalization of specific classes of environmental goods and services. And we may see some advance on disciplining the subsidies that currently encourage over-fishing.

I very much doubt that there will be much progress on the other environmental issues being discussed. For one thing, there is no significant negotiating group presently insisting on clear deliverables in the environmental area. The European Communities, the original *demandeur* of environmental negotiations, has clearly shifted its sights to the more commercially important areas of industrial tariffs and services, and appears to believe that it can achieve its environmental objectives better by other means.

Of course, this is no guarantee that the environment will remain a forgotten detail on the Doha Agenda. Indeed, the environment is and will always be an end-game issue in the WTO. Once the central structure of a new trade deal is clear, issues such as the environment will be brought forward if needed to give scope for the final trade-offs necessary to secure the central deal.

I would argue, however, that those interested in environment and sustainable development in the WTO should not focus on the Doha negotiations with a microscope, but instead step back and take both a longer and broader view of the multilateral trading system. They will be obliged to conclude that, contrary to first appearances, and somewhat counter-intuitively, the environment has secured for itself an established and honourable place in the multilateral trading system. Early resistance to the environment has reduced, shifted form, and is now focused not on whether environment should or should not be in the WTO, but on how to ensure that legitimate environmental aspects of trade are dealt with in a way that does not open scope for protectionist measures. This is an objective to which most environmentalists could subscribe.

As I have tried to indicate, while both the work of the CTE and the environmental negotiations under the Doha Agenda have yielded scant results to date, many aspects of the link between the trading system and the complex international environmental regime have been clarified and the level of apprehension at a possible clash between the two have receded. In some ways it is regrettable that the *Chile – Swordfish* case was settled 'out of court', because it would have shed light onto how the DSB approaches issues for which more than one juridical forum arguably had standing.[16] Nevertheless, the work of the Appellate Body to date has underlined strongly that it does not see itself as the sole, isolated arbiter of all law governing trade. The Appellate Body has made clear that trade law will be interpreted in light of the intentions that States have made manifest both in trade policy fora and in other fora relevant to trade policy.

The notion of sustainable development found its way into the *WTO Agreement*, and emerged strengthened in paragraph 6 of the Doha Ministerial Declaration. The Appellate Body has demonstrated that it considers sustainable development to be of central relevance in determining both the context in which the trade rules play out and the overall goal that the trade rules are intended to advance. In doing so, they may have pointed the way towards the path WTO must take in the future.

[16] WT/DS193/3.

PART V

Asian Regional Integration and the Multilateral Trading System

22

The adoption of the 'Best Practices' for regional and free trade agreements in APEC: a road towards more WTO-consistent regional trade agreements?

GABRIELLE MARCEAU[1]

I. States have a fundamental right to form regional trade agreements

Historically, States have always formed closer links with some other States for, *inter alia*, cultural, trade and security reasons. When they created the *General Agreement of Tariffs and Trade* (GATT) in 1947, States could not ignore this economic and political reality; hence the inclusion of Article XXIV, which recognizes the right (albeit conditional) of States to form preferential regional trade agreements (RTAs). The philosophy of the GATT/World Trade Organization (WTO) disciplines with respect to RTAs is to ensure that the formation and evolution of such preferential arrangements support the multilateral trading system. Since multilateral trade is about greater trade opening, RTAs have to be supportive of this principle: RTAs should facilitate trade between the constituent territories and not raise barriers to the trade of non-RTA States. This principle is reflected in paragraph 4 of Article XXIV:

> The contracting parties recognize the desirability of increasing freedom of trade by the development, through voluntary agreements, of *closer integration between the economies of the countries parties to such agreements.* They also recognize that the purpose of a customs union or of a free-trade area *should be to facilitate trade between the constituent territories and not to raise barriers to the trade of other contracting parties with such territories.* (Italics added)

[1] The views expressed in this chapter are personal to the author and do not bind the WTO Members or the WTO Secretariat. The author is grateful to Roberto Fiorentino, Pablo Furche, Arancha Gonzalez, and Alejandro Jara for comments on previous drafts. Mistakes are those of the author only.

As stated by the Appellate Body in the context of its discussion of the general exceptions in Article XX of the GATT 1994, WTO market access obligations must be balanced against the right of WTO Members to invoke exception provisions.[2] The Appellate Body repeated the same principle in *Turkey – Textiles* when dealing with a complaint by India that, as a result of the harmonization process that followed the formation of the European Communities–Turkey customs union, Turkey imposed a new import restriction on textiles that was contrary to the *Agreement on Textiles and Clothing* (*ATC*) and Article XI of the GATT of 1994. The Appellate Body stated:

> This objective demands that a balance be struck by the constituent members of a customs union. A customs union should facilitate trade within the customs union, but it should *not* do so in a way that raises barriers to trade with third countries. We note that the *Understanding on Article XXIV* explicitly reaffirms this purpose of a customs union, and states that in the formation or enlargement of a customs union, the constituent members should 'to the greatest possible extent avoid creating adverse affects on the trade of other Members'.[3] (Italics added; footnote omitted)

For RTAs, this balance has been articulated and made operational in the form of two conditions that must be respected whenever a WTO Member wants to justify a market access restriction or discrimination resulting from the formation of an RTA. In *Turkey – Textiles*, the Appellate Body made clear that RTAs must respect a series of conditions in order to be considered GATT/WTO-consistent:

> Accordingly, on the basis of this analysis of the text and the context of the chapeau of paragraph 5 of Article XXIV, we are of the view that *Article XXIV may justify a measure which is inconsistent* with certain other GATT provisions. However, in a case involving the formation of a customs union, this 'defence' is available *only when two conditions are fulfilled*. First, the party claiming the benefit of this defence must demonstrate that the measure at issue is introduced upon the formation of a *customs union that fully meets the requirements of sub-paragraphs 8(a) and 5(a) of Article XXIV*. And, second, that party must demonstrate that the formation of that customs union *would be prevented if it were not allowed to introduce the*

[2] Appellate Body Report, *US – Gasoline*, p. 22, DSR 1996:I, 3, 21; Appellate Body Report, *US – Shrimp*, para. 159; Appellate Body Report, *Korea – Various Measures on Beef*, para. 164. [3] Appellate Body Report, *Turkey – Textiles*, para. 57.

> *measure at issue. Again, both these conditions must be met to have the benefit of the defence under Article XXIV.*
>
> We would expect a panel, when examining such a measure, to require a party to establish that both of these conditions have been fulfilled. It may not always be possible to determine whether the second of the two conditions has been fulfilled without initially determining whether the first condition has been fulfilled. In other words, it may not always be possible to determine whether not applying a measure would prevent the formation of a customs union without first determining whether there *is* a customs union.[4] (Italics added)

Clearly, the formation of an RTA may justify measures that are inconsistent with any GATT rule, but only after having demonstrated compliance with a series of requirements relating to the RTA as a whole (Article XXIV:5) and to its internal and external (as far as customs unions are concerned), which must respect the provisions of Article XXIV:8. Finally, the inconsistent measure must be necessary to the formation of the RTA.[5] Note the onerous burden of proof imposed on the WTO Member invoking Article XXIV to justify an inconsistent measure.

It is in the context of the conditions that must be respected for an RTA to be WTO-consistent that the recent Guidelines of the Asia-Pacific Economic Cooperation (APEC) forum must be examined. Recall that in Bogor, Indonesia, the APEC economies committed to free and open trade and investment in Asia-Pacific by 2010 for developed countries and by 2020 for developing countries. Although APEC economies have achieved significant liberalization and facilitation of trade and investment since 1994, the target dates seem to have forced APEC Ministers to address the possibility of reaching these target dates through RTAs. Indeed, in order to accelerate progress towards the Bogor Goals, APEC Ministers emphasized the need for promotion of 'high quality' RTAs and free trade

[4] Ibid., paras. 58–59.

[5] In particular, (i) the overall effect of the RTA must be compatible with Article XXIV:(5), which provides that the situation of third countries after the RTA must not be worse than before the RTA; (ii) internally the RTA must respect the provisions of Article XXIV(8)(a)(i); (iii) externally the RTA must respect the provisions of Article XXIV(8)(a)(ii); and (iv) the inconsistent measure must have been necessary to the formation of the RTA. For further and expanded discussion on the conditions for WTO-consistent RTAs see Gabrielle Marceau and Cornelis Reiman, 'When and How is a Regional Trade Agreement Compatible with the WTO?' (2001) 28 *Legal Issues of Regional Integration*, 297–336; and Nicolas Lockart and Andrew Mitchell, 'Regional Trade Agreements under GATT: An exception and its Limits', in Andrew Mitchell (ed.), *Challenges and prospects for the WTO* (London, 2005), p. 217.

agreements (FTAs),[6] hence the adoption of the guidelines discussed hereafter. Will compliance with the APEC Guidelines facilitate or even ensure that WTO Members forming RTAs respect the requirements (conditions) for a WTO-consistent RTA? Hopefully, the APEC Best Practices for RTAs will have just this effect.

II. The 'Best Practices' for RTAs/FTAs in APEC

On the occasion of the 16th Ministerial meeting of APEC held in Santiago, Chile, on 17–18 November 2004, member economies endorsed the 'Best Practice for RTAs/FTAs in APEC' (herein, 'Best Practices'). On 6 September 2005, Chile and Korea jointly notified the APEC Best Practices to the WTO Secretariat and requested their circulation to WTO Members.[7] These APEC Best Practices are quite innovative and are discussed briefly below.

APEC's Best Practices are beneficial to all WTO Members to the extent that they either reinforce or clarify WTO disciplines applicable to RTAs; they also offer an improved monitoring and surveillance mechanism. By building upon the existing WTO provisions on RTAs, APEC countries indicated that they endorse the principles contained in these provisions, and therefore that they support the multilateral trading system. Notably, these principles are complementary to and aim at ensuring the effective operation of the principle mentioned in Article XXIV:4 that RTAs should facilitate trade between RTA parties and not raise barriers with non-RTA parties.

Let us look at some of the APEC principles.

> **Consistency with APEC principles and goals**
> Consistent with APEC goals, they promote structural reform among the parties through the implementation of transparent, open and non-discriminatory regulatory frameworks and decision-making processes.

The issue of decision-making is important, but has not been explored in the context of WTO law generally. What is the legal value of decisions taken by an RTA body in case of a dispute entertained by WTO adjudicating bodies? Can WTO Members, which are also members of an RTA,

[6] Statement of the Chair, Meeting of APEC Ministers Responsible for Trade, Jeju, Korea, 2–3 June 2005, available at <http://www.apec.org/apec/ministerial_statements/sectoral_ministerial/trade/2005_trade.html>.

[7] The APEC Best Practices were circulated as WTO document TN/RL/W/187, which is annexed to this chapter.

take a decision in an RTA that goes against other rules of the WTO? Does Article XXIV provide justification for any type of WTO- inconsistency?

A related issue is to what extent members of an RTA can have a dispute settlement mechanism that would complete (that is, add to) or override that of the WTO. For instance, if parties to an RTA impose countermeasures for a violation of an RTA obligation, in accordance with the RTA's specific dispute settlement procedures, is the imposition of those countermeasures inconsistent with Article 23 of the *Understanding on Rules and Procedures Governing the Settlement of Disputes* (DSU)? Or Article XI or II of the GATT 1994? Does Article XXIV of the GATT allow WTO Members to ignore Article 23 of the DSU, which prohibits a WTO Member from unilaterally determining that another WTO Member has violated the WTO agreements (including the application of countermeasures)? What is the reach of Article XXIV of the GATT 1994? Does it cover other multilateral trade agreements?

In addition, calling for transparency in decision-making is specially important when dealing with regulations of the members forming the RTA. Recall that the formation of an RTAs implies the evaluation of the impact of duties and other 'regulations of commerce' (Article XXIV:5 and XXIV:8). If, on the one hand, the elimination of duties in RTAs can be easily quantified, regulations, on the other hand, are hard to measure, though they are a central pillar of the requirements of XXIV, both in terms of internal liberalization and of not raising barriers to third parties. Transparency, as to the context for the adoption of such regulations together with their administration, would be crucial to ensure a decent assessment of their impact on international trade.

> **Consistency with the WTO**
> They are fully consistent with the disciplines of the WTO, especially those contained in Article XXIV of the GATT and Article V of the GATS. When they involve developing economies to whom the Enabling Clause applies, they are, whenever possible, consistent with Article XXIV of the GATT and Article V of the GATS.

This point is very interesting as it seems to imply that APEC would favour RTAs that would not use the flexibilities of the Enabling Clause,[8] whatever scope it offers (a full exemption of Article XXIV requirements or only an exemption from the internal requirements of RTAs provided in

[8] Decision on Differential and More Favourable Treatment, Reciprocity, and Fuller Participation of Developing Countries, GATT document L/4903, 28 November 1979, BISD 26S/203.

Article XXVIII:8). In other words, APEC developing countries would form RTAs that would (to the extent possible) respect the disciplines of Article XXIV of the GATT and Article V of the *General Agreement on Trade in Services* (GATS). Note that several developing countries have been notifying their RTAs under Article XXIV instead of the Enabling clause (or both).

> **Go beyond WTO commitments**
> In areas that are covered by the WTO, they build upon existing WTO obligations. They also explore commitments related to trade and investment in areas not covered, or only partly covered, by the WTO. By so doing, APEC economies are in a better position to provide leadership in any future WTO negotiations on these issues.

This principle raises the issue of the extent to which RTAs can cover matters not otherwise covered by the WTO law. Clearly, States have the right to sign treaties on any matter (that do not violate *jus cognens*), but in limiting the scope of the WTO's jurisdiction (by excluding labour norms, for instance), have WTO Members decided that such issues cannot be dealt with in an RTA? It is doubtful. The difficult issue is how to reconcile actions in RTAs that may have effects in sectors covered by the WTO. For instance, assume that an RTA member violates the labour provisions of that RTA and, in accordance with the RTA's dispute settlement procedures, countermeasures are imposed in the form of an import restriction on textile products from the other RTA member (also a WTO Member). Are these textile import restrictions consistent with the WTO agreements? Are they authorized by Article XXIV? Do they need to be?

> **Transparency**
> By making the texts of RTAs/FTAs, including any annexes or schedules, readily available, the Parties ensure that business is in the best position to understand and take advantage of liberalized trade conditions. Once they have been signed, agreements are made public, in English wherever possible, through official websites as well as through the APEC Secretariat website.
>
> Member economies notify and report their new and existing agreements in line with WTO obligations and procedures.

This is an important point calling for openness with respect to RTA information in line with the relevant WTO provisions. It also reflects the objectives being pursued by WTO Members in the Negotiating Group on Rules on RTAs in the area of transparency.[9]

[9] See Revised Informal Note by the Chairman, 'Elements for an RTA's Transparency Mechanism', JOB (06)/2. See also Decision TN/RL/18.

Transparency is a very difficult issue for all RTAs. Efforts have been made to encourage RTA parties to notify their proposed agreement as soon as possible so as to facilitate exchanges of views in the WTO Committee on Regional Trade Agreements (CRTA). The Decision of the WTO Council for Trade in Goods,[10] the procedures adopted by the Council for Trade in Services,[11] and the checklist prepared for the CRTA[12] also contain excellent wording requiring statistics and other technical information, but these decisions have not been adequately followed and respected by Members. Notification and review of RTAs covered by the Enabling Clause have also been problematic.[13] The APEC principle on transparency would mean that APEC developing countries will provide the information required pursuant to these decisions.

> **Simple Rules of Origin that facilitate trade**
> To avoid the possibility of high compliance costs for business, Rules of Origin (ROOs) are easy to understand and to comply with. Wherever possible, an economy's ROOs are consistent across all of its FTAs and RTAs.
>
> They recognize the increasingly globalized nature of production and the achievements of APEC in promoting regional economic integration by adopting ROOs that maximize trade creation and minimize trade distortion.

Simple rules of origin, which has become a very controversial issue in RTAs, deserve important attention. Indeed, rules of origin can nullify the benefits of any market access negotiation, including the increased market access possibilities offered by the RTAs.

One difficult issue is whether rules of origin are to be considered as 'other regulation of trade' and, if so, how to evaluate and calculate their impact under paragraphs (5) and (8)(a)(ii) of Article XXIV. Further research and proposals are needed in this area.

> **Mechanisms for consultation and dispute settlement**
> Recognizing that disputes over implementation of RTAs/FTAs can be costly and can raise uncertainty for business, they include proper mechanisms to prevent and resolve disagreements in an expeditious manner, such as through consultation, mediation or arbitration, avoiding duplication with the WTO dispute settlement mechanism where appropriate.

[10] Procedures on Reporting on Regional Trade Agreements, G/L/286.
[11] Procedures on Reporting on Regional Trade Agreements, S/C/W/92.
[12] Checklist of Points on the Operation of Regional Trade Agreements, WT/REG/W/3.
[13] See WT/COMTD/W/114.

The issue of the overlap of dispute settlement systems is complex. It is even more complicated in the area of trade because Article XXIV of the GATT 1994 explicitly authorizes States to form preferential groupings, which, by implication, would contain a specific RTA dispute settlement system. There are now a few examples of those situations where two parties initiated disputes involving the same issues both in the RTA forum and in the WTO forum.[14] We have had also an overlap of jurisdiction in the dispute between Chile and the European Communities over the landing of swordfish.[15] The recent *Mexico – Taxes on Soft Drinks* case examined whether non-compliance with the North American Free Trade Agreement (NAFTA) could be invoked as a defence/justification for non-compliance under Article XX of the GATT.[16]

Some FTAs contain a conflicts clause that gives priority, and sometimes exclusivity, to the FTA. However, it is difficult to see how these clauses could be enforced by WTO panels. This is because the WTO's DSU provides for an automatic process. Moreover, to the extent a simple allegation suffices to trigger the WTO dispute settlement mechanism, and because Article 23 of the DSU gives exclusive jurisdiction to WTO panels to determine WTO issues, the WTO adjudicating bodies will necessarily 'attract' jurisdiction. Often, States will prefer to initiate a dispute in the WTO, which is a faster and more efficient forum. In practice, because of its speed, the WTO dispute settlement mechanism will be able to provide adjudication – in the form of panel, Appellate Body, or arbitration reports – much faster than many other systems and will provide for automatic sanctions, while the other systems do not have such capabilities.

This means that, in the context of a dispute between two WTO Members involving situations covered by both an RTA and the WTO agreements, either WTO Member has the right to trigger the WTO dispute settlement mechanism and to request the establishment of a panel (even if there is a similar dispute in an RTA) if it considers that any of its WTO benefits have been nullified or impaired. Such WTO Member

[14] See Panel Report, *Argentina – Poultry Anti-Dumping Duties*, para. 7.38; and *Argentina – Cotton*, Request for Consultations by Brazil, WT/DS190/1. Aspects of these disputes were also brought before the dispute settlement mechanism of the Southern Common Market (MERCOSUR).

[15] See *Chile – Swordfish*, Request for Consultations by the European Communities, WT/DS193/1. The dispute was also brought to the International Tribunal for the Law of the Sea (See *Case on Conservation of Swordfish Stocks between Chile and the European Communits in the South-Eastern Pacific Ocean*).

[16] Appellate Body Report, *Mexico – Taxes on Soft Drinks*, paras. 66–80.

cannot be asked, and arguably cannot even agree under Article 23 of the DSU, to take its WTO dispute to another forum, even if that other forum appears to be more relevant or better equipped to deal with the sort of problems at issue. In initiating a parallel WTO dispute, the WTO Member may be in violation of an RTA (where it promised not to do so), but this is not a matter to be decided by WTO panels or the Appellate Body. If a different result were desirable, then Article 23 of the DSU, the reverse consensus rule and the entire WTO dispute mechanism would have to be adjusted. However, if the RTA treaty prohibits its signatories from taking RTA related disputes to the WTO in certain circumstances, a WTO Member that would ignore this RTA prescription may risk RTA retaliation if it triggers the WTO dispute settlement mechanism, and such RTA retaliation, in my view, could be WTO-consistent pursuant to Article XXIV of the GATT 1994, which allows for (effective) RTAs.

> **Sustainable development**
> Reflecting the inter-dependent and mutually supportive linkages between the three pillars of sustainable development – economic development, social development and environmental protection – of which trade is an integral component, they reinforce the objectives of sustainable development.

The APEC definition of sustainable development is remarkable, particularly its reference to the inter-linkages between its economic, social and environmental components. This principle is also reflected in the Preamble to the *Marrakesh Agreement Establishing the World Trade Organization* (*WTO Agreement*) and has had tremendous influence on WTO jurisprudence.[17] It would not be surprising to see the APEC definition quoted in future Appellate Body reports.

III. Conclusion

The issue of RTAs and their legal and economic compatibility with WTO disciplines and principles is complex. Although most WTO Members support multilateral liberalism, regional arrangements are often easier to negotiate and are often used as general foreign policy tools. They thus encompass policy considerations other than trade, although they are generally considered conducive to increased trade. If the WTO agreements provide that the formation of an RTA can justify inconsistencies with other WTO obligations, it also imposes conditions – relating to the RTA

[17] See, for example, Appellate Body Report, *US – Shrimp*, para. 153.

itself and its impact on non-RTA states – for such RTA to be WTO consistent. WTO Members and WTO jurisprudence have on occasion clarified the meaning of such conditions and have agreed on procedures to favour transparency and exchanges relating to the assessment and monitoring of RTAs. But WTO Members lack political will; as the number of RTAs increases, Members find themselves caught between difficult conflicting interests. In addition, given Members' limited human resources, WTO notification, reporting, reviewing and monitoring of RTAs are not handled seriously enough.

In this context, the fact that the APEC countries have decided unilaterally to set for themselves standards and principles that confirm, clarify and reinforce WTO disciplines and mechanisms set up to ensure that RTAs evolve so as to favour multilateral trade can only be received with praise. The APEC principles not only have the merit of pointing without any scruples to the difficult issues surrounding the co-habitation of regional and multilateral systems (Enabling Clause, RTAs, rules of origin, transparency of domestic regulations, reporting transparency and monitoring, dual dispute settlement systems, etc.), they also contain commitments that will strengthen the WTO multilateral system.

ANNEX

WORLD TRADE ORGANIZATION

TN/RL/W/187
12 September 2005
(05–3939)

Negotiating Group on Rules

Original: English

BEST PRACTICE FOR RTAS/FTAS IN APEC[1]

Communication from Chile and the Republic of Korea

The following communication, dated 6 September 2005, is being circulated at the request of the Delegations of Chile and the Republic of Korea, for information.

RTAs/FTAs involving APEC economies can best support the achievement of the APEC Bogor Goals by having the following characteristics:

Consistency with APEC Principles and Goals

- They address the relevant areas in Part I (Liberalization and Facilitation) of the Osaka Action Agenda (OAA) and they are consistent with its General Principles. In this way they help to ensure that APEC accomplishes the free trade and investment goals set out in the 1994 Bogor Leaders Declaration.
- They build upon work being undertaken by APEC.
- Consistent with APEC goals, they promote structural reform among the parties through the implementation of transparent, open and non-discriminatory regulatory frameworks and decision-making processes.

Consistency with the WTO

- They are fully consistent with the disciplines of the WTO, especially those contained in Article XXIV of the GATT and Article V of the GATS.

[1] Regional Trade Arrangements (RTAs), Free Trade Agreements (FTAs), and other Preferential Arrangements.

- When they involve developing economies to whom the Enabling Clause applies, they are, whenever possible, consistent with Article XXIV of the GATT and Article V of the GATS.

Go beyond WTO Commitments

- In areas that are covered by the WTO, they build upon existing WTO obligations. They also explore commitments related to trade and investment in areas not covered, or only partly covered, by the WTO. By so doing, APEC economies are in a better position to provide leadership in any future WTO negotiations on these issues.

Comprehensiveness

- They deliver the maximum economic benefits to the parties by being comprehensive in scope, and providing for liberalization in all sectors. They therefore eliminate barriers to trade and investment between the Parties, including tariffs and non-tariff measures, and barriers to trade in services.
- Phase-out periods for tariffs and quotas in sensitive sectors are kept to a minimum, and take into account the different levels of development among the parties. Thus, they are seen as an opportunity to undertake liberalization in all sectors as a first step towards multilateral liberalization at a later stage.

Transparency

- By making the texts of RTAs/FTAs, including any annexes or schedules, readily available, the Parties ensure that business is in the best position to understand and take advantage of liberalized trade conditions. Once they have been signed, agreements are made public, in English wherever possible, through official websites as well as through the APEC Secretariat website.
- Member economies notify and report their new and existing agreements in line with WTO obligations and procedures.

Trade Facilitation

- Recognizing that regulatory and administrative requirements and processes can constitute significant barriers to trade, they include practical measures and cooperative efforts to facilitate trade and reduce transaction costs for business consistent with relevant WTO provisions and APEC principles.

Mechanisms for Consultation and Dispute Settlement

- Recognizing that disputes over implementation of RTAs/FTAs can be costly and can raise uncertainty for business, they include proper mechanisms to prevent and resolve disagreements in an expeditious manner, such as through consultation, mediation or arbitration, avoiding duplication with the WTO dispute settlement mechanism where appropriate.

Simple Rules of Origin that facilitate Trade

- To avoid the possibility of high compliance costs for business, Rules of Origin (ROOs) are easy to understand and to comply with. Wherever possible, an economy's ROOs are consistent across all of its FTAs and RTAs.
- They recognize the increasingly globalized nature of production and the achievements of APEC in promoting regional economic integration by adopting ROOs that maximize trade creation and minimize trade distortion.

Cooperation

- They include commitments on economic and technical cooperation in the relevant areas reflected in Part II of the OAA by providing scope for the parties to exchange views and develop common understandings in which future interaction will help ensure these agreements have maximum utility and benefit to all parties.

Sustainable Development

- Reflecting the inter-dependent and mutually supportive linkages between the three pillars of sustainable development – economic development, social development and environmental protection – of which trade is an integral component, they reinforce the objectives of sustainable development.

Accession of Third Parties

- Consistent with APEC's philosophy of open regionalism and as a way to contribute to the momentum for liberalization throughout the

APEC region, they are open to the possibility for accession of third parties on negotiated terms and conditions.

Provision for Periodic Review

- They allow for periodic review to ensure full implementation of the terms of the agreement and to ensure the terms continue to provide the maximum possible economic benefit to the parties in the face of changing economic circumstances and trade and investment flows. Periodic review helps to maintain the momentum for domestic reform and further liberalization by addressing areas that may not have been considered during the original negotiations, promoting deeper liberalization and introducing more sophisticated mechanisms for cooperation as the economies of the Parties become more integrated.

Trade remedy systems for East Asian free trade agreements

DUKGEUN AHN

I. General observations

Trade remedy measures have always been a central issue for the trade policies of East Asian countries, not only because these countries have been primary targets for such measures, but also because East Asian countries have used trade remedy measures more actively in recent years. Accordingly, when East Asian countries joined the 'race' to free trade agreements (FTAs), trade remedy systems became a focal point in these FTA negotiations.

As illustrated in Figure 23.1 – and specified in more detail in Table 23.1 – most Asian countries have relied increasingly on anti-dumping actions to

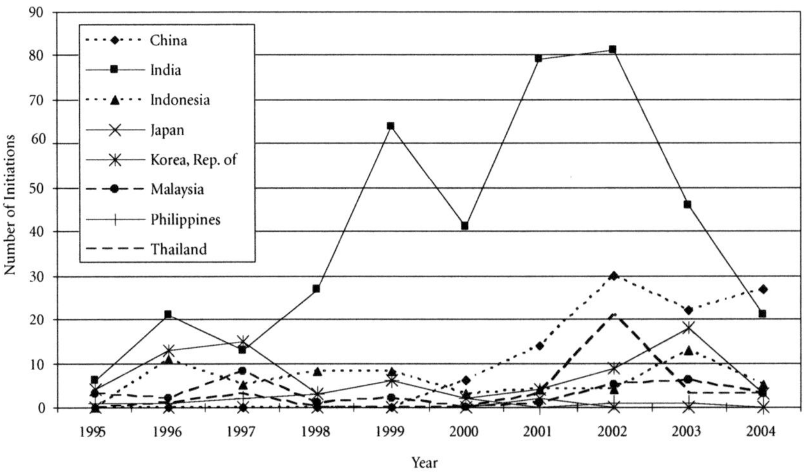

Figure 23.1 Anti-dumping actions by selected Asian countries 1995–2004

Table 23.1 *Anti-dumping initiations by selected countries 1995–2004*

Country	1995	1996	1997	1998	1999	2000	2001	2002	2003	2004
China	0	0	0	0	0	6	14	30	22	27
Chinese Taipei	0	0	0	0	0	3	3	0	2	0
India	6	21	13	27	64	41	79	81	46	21
Indonesia	0	11	5	8	8	3	4	4	13	5
Japan	0	0	0	0	0	0	2	0	0	0
Korea	4	13	15	3	6	2	4	9	18	3
Malaysia	3	2	8	1	2	0	1	5	6	3
Philippines	1	1	2	3	6	2	0	1	1	0
Thailand	0	1	3	0	0	0	3	21	3	3
United States	14	22	15	36	47	47	75	35	37	26

Source: WTO webpage, available at <http://www.wto.org/english/tratop_e/adp_e/adp_e.htm> (visited 1 May 2006)

protect their markets, especially after 2000. The notable exception to this trend is Japan, which is still very reluctant to utilize trade remedy measures. For example, Japan has initiated only two anti-dumping investigations since the inception of the World Trade Organization (WTO) (both in 2001), which led to two anti-dumping measures being imposed in 2002.

At the same time, taking into account all countries using trade remedy measures, East Asian countries have been the most frequent targets for anti-dumping actions, as summarized in Table 23.2. For example, four out of the top five anti-dumping targets are East Asian Members.

Considering the fact that China and Chinese Taipei have had relatively little experience in using trade remedy regimes, it is interesting to compare the vast difference between the Korean and Japanese systems. Despite various similarities in trade structures and export-oriented policy administration, Korea and Japan have maintained considerably different trade remedy systems and have thereby accumulated different experiences.

Firstly – and perhaps most importantly – Japan has no standing trade remedy institution and has historically scarcely applied trade remedy measures. In contrast, the Korean government established the Korea Trade Commission in 1987 which, since then, has played an important role in the administration of trade remedy actions when dealing with import competition. From the inception of the WTO to the end of 2004, the Korea Trade Commission initiated a total of 84 anti-dumping investigations and imposed 51 anti-dumping duties. Among them, 30 investigations were against imports from Japan. During the same period, however, Japan initi-

Table 23.2 *Top ten anti-dumping target countries 1995–2004*

Country	1995	1996	1997	1998	1999	2000	2001	2002	2003	2004	Total
China	20	43	33	28	40	43	53	51	52	49	**412**
Korea	14	11	15	24	34	22	23	23	17	24	**207**
United States	12	21	15	15	14	12	15	12	21	14	**151**
Chinese Taipei	4	9	16	10	22	16	19	16	13	21	**146**
Japan	5	6	12	13	22	9	13	13	16	9	**118**
India	3	11	8	12	13	10	12	16	15	8	**108**
Indonesia	7	7	9	5	20	13	18	12	8	8	**107**
Thailand	8	9	5	2	19	12	16	12	7	9	**99**
Russia	2	7	7	12	17	12	9	18	2	8	**94**
Brazil	8	10	5	6	13	9	13	4	3	9	**80**

Source: WTO webpage, available at <http://www.wto.org/english/tratop_e/adp_e/adp_e.htm> (visited 1 May 2006)

ated only two investigations and imposed three anti-dumping duties.[1] The two anti-dumping investigations were initiated on 23 April 2001 concerning certain polyester stable fibre from Chinese Taipei and Korea.

Whereas Korea has never used countervailing actions, Japan recently imposed the first countervailing measure concerning dynamic random access memory semiconductors (DRAMS) produced by Hynix from Korea that led to a WTO dispute.[2] Korea has frequently utilized safeguard actions as shown in Figure 23.2, especially in the early years of the Korea Trade Commission.[3] Japan has so far imposed a safeguard measure only once, namely against certain agricultural products from China.[4]

Due to its infrequent recourse to trade remedy actions, Japan has never been challenged in this policy area since its accession to the *General Agreement on Tariffs and Trade* (GATT). The Korean trade remedy

[1] One anti-dumping duty imposed in 1995 was based on an investigation initiated prior to 1995.

[2] The Japanese government imposed a 27.2 per cent countervailing duty in February 2006, the first countervailing measure ever imposed by Japan. Korea brought a complaint to the WTO (WT/DS336/1, 20 March 2006).

[3] Korea Trade Commission, *Report of Trade Remedy Actions*, 3 (KTC document 2005-2, January 2005 (*in Korean*)). In a sense, this experience of Korea is similar to those of many other developing country WTO Members that typically rely on safeguard actions to protect their markets when they have little experience or capacity to implement trade remedy systems. (See Dukgeun Ahn, 'Restructuring the WTO Safeguard System', in Mitsuo Matsushita, Dukgeun Ahn, and Tain-jy Chen (eds), *The WTO Trade Remedy System: East Asian Perspectives* (London, forthcoming).)

[4] G/SG/N/6/JPN/1, 5 January 2001.

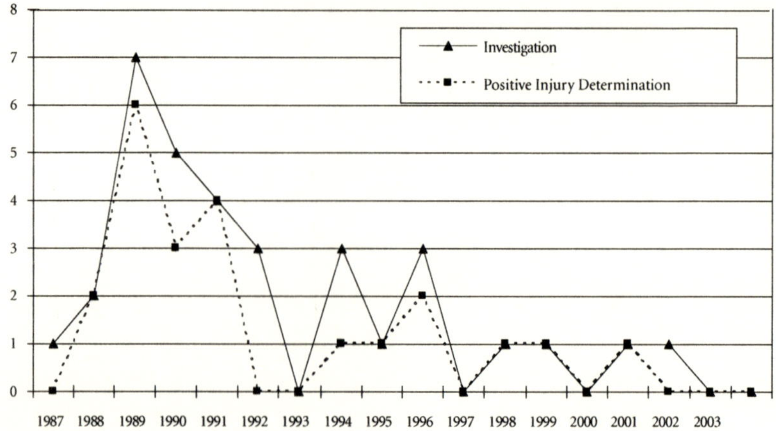

Figure 23.2 Safeguard actions by Korea

measures, however, have been challenged by other trading partners in the GATT/WTO dispute settlement system. The very first anti-dumping decision by the Korea Trade Commission was challenged under the Tokyo Round *Agreement on Implementation of Article VI of the General Agreement on Tariffs and Trade*[5] (the so-called '*Tokyo Round Anti-Dumping Code*').[6] The very first WTO panel decision under the WTO *Agreement on Safeguards* also dealt with a Korean safeguard action.[7] Moreover, in June 2004, Indonesia initiated consultations with Korea concerning anti-dumping duties by Korea on imports of business information paper and uncoated wood-free printing paper. The panel in that dispute basically dismissed almost all complaints raised by Indonesia except one minor argument, making this dispute practically the first anti-dumping case in which a respondent's measure was not found to be inconsistent with the WTO obligations.[8]

II. Anti-dumping and countervailing duty systems for FTAs

When Korea and Japan concluded their first FTAs with Chile and Singapore respectively, they adopted the same approach for anti-dumping and countervailing duty systems. In essence, they determined

[5] BISD26S/171.

[6] See GATT Panel Report, *Korea – Resins.* See more generally, Dukgeun Ahn, 'Korea in the GATT/WTO Dispute Settlement System: Legal Battle for Economic Development' (2003) 6 *Journal of International Economic Law*, 597–633.

[7] Panel Report, *Korea – Dairy.*

[8] Panel Report, *Korea – Certain Paper.*

that, instead of creating independent FTA disciplines, WTO rules and the WTO dispute settlement system would be used. The Korea–Chile FTA provides, in Chapter 7, that the parties maintain their rights and obligations under the WTO *Agreement on Implementation of Article VI of the General Agreement on Tariffs and Trade 1994* (*Anti-Dumping Agreement*), as well as the *Agreement on Subsidies and Countervailing Measures* (*SCM Agreement*), and that anti-dumping or countervailing actions taken pursuant to these agreements shall not be subject to the FTA dispute settlement system under Chapter 19. The Japan–Singapore Economic Partnership Agreement (EPA), for its part, does not include specific provisions concerning anti-dumping and countervailing duty measures, implying that those matters are governed solely by the WTO agreements.[9] This approach was also adopted for the Japan–Mexico FTA, signed in September 2004.[10]

Although many recent FTAs follow this approach of using WTO rights and obligations, some FTAs either completely exclude anti-dumping and countervailing duties or adopt the WTO disciplines with modifications. For example, Article M-01 of the Canada–Chile FTA provides for a reciprocal exemption of the application of anti-dumping laws, as well as the revocation of all existing duties and prohibition of new investigations. Article 9 of the Singapore–New Zealand FTA sets forth requirements that are additional to those of the WTO *Anti-Dumping Agreement* 'in order to bring greater discipline to anti-dumping investigations and to minimise the opportunities to use anti-dumping in an arbitrary or protectionist manner.' Under the Singapore–New Zealand FTA, the *de minimis* margin was increased to five per cent for both new investigations and review procedures, and the sunset period was shortened to three years.

Similarly, the Korea–Singapore FTA adopted additional commitments for the anti-dumping regime: prohibition of zeroing and the 'lesser duty' rule. Article 6.2.3 of the Korea–Singapore FTA stipulates:

> Notwithstanding paragraph 1, the Parties shall observe the following practices in anti-dumping cases between them in order to enhance transparency in the implementation of the WTO Anti-dumping Agreement:

[9] The Japan–Singapore EPA is available at <http://www.mofa.go.jp/region/asia-paci/singapore/jsepa.html> (visited 1 May 2006).

[10] Agreement between Japan and the United Mexican States for the Strengthening of the Economic Partnership, available at <http://www.mofa.go.jp/region/latin/mexico/agreement/index.html> (visited 1 May 2006).

(a) when anti-dumping margins are established on the weighted average basis, all individual margins, whether positive or negative, should be counted toward the average; and

(b) if a decision is taken to impose an anti-dumping duty pursuant to Article 9.1 of the WTO Agreement on Anti-dumping, the Party taking such a decision, should apply the 'lesser duty' rule, by imposing a duty which is less than the dumping margin where such lesser duty would be adequate to remove the injury to the domestic industry.

The above provisions are noteworthy in that they are the first instance of a FTA trade remedy system adopted in the East Asia that modifies or goes beyond the WTO anti-dumping and countervailing regime.

While the FTA between Korea and the European Free Trade Association (EFTA), signed on 15 December 2005, retains basically all the rights and obligations under the WTO *Anti-Dumping Agreement*, it also adopted the above mentioned 'lesser duty' rule. In addition, the Korea–EFTA FTA stipulates that the parties 'shall endeavour to refrain from initiating anti-dumping procedures against each other' and consult 'with the other with a view to finding a mutually acceptable solution', even if the Agreement does not mandate any specific legal requirements in addition to those provisions. Interestingly, the parties under the Korea–EFTA FTA are bound to review, after five years of application, whether there is a continued need to maintain specific anti-dumping measures. On the other hand, the Korea–EFTA FTA requires mutual consultations between governments during a period of at least 30 days before parties may initiate countervailing duty investigations.

Korea and Japan have been frequent targets of anti-dumping actions, indicating that their exports are generally vulnerable to anti-dumping mechanisms. Therefore, there is a considerable possibility that trade between these two countries may be subject to more anti-dumping actions in the future in the event that an FTA enhances bilateral trade. The potential risk of abusive anti-dumping actions in this context may be mitigated by incorporating into such an FTA disciplines additional to those contained in the current WTO *Anti-Dumping Agreement.*

Numerous proposals to amend the current *Anti-Dumping Agreement* have been submitted in the Doha round negotiations.[11] In fact, many of those proposals were prepared jointly by both countries. Moreover, Korea

[11] For a brief review of the proposals by WTO Members, see, for example, TN/RL/W/143, 22 August 2003.

has already begun to adopt a modified trade remedy system through its recent FTAs. Therefore, the Korea–Japan FTA may be a forum to actually implement some of elements discussed in the Doha negotiation and to show the effectiveness of amended disciplines.

Given the abundant inventory of proposals, it seems entirely left to the discretion of both countries how much they are willing to improve the anti-dumping or countervailing system by means of a bilateral agreement. For example, a more reasonable bilateral anti-dumping system to effectively ameliorate abusive manipulation may incorporate, *inter alia*, the explicit prohibition of zeroing, the same level of procedural rigor for review procedures, a higher *de minimis* margin, more disciplines on the initiation of investigations and consistent rules for review procedures. Since countervailing duty systems share many elements with anti-dumping systems, amended procedural and substantive elements for FTA anti-dumping systems may be equally adopted for FTA countervailing duty systems.[12]

III. FTA safeguard mechanisms

The Korea–Chile FTA refers to the WTO agreements for its safeguard mechanism. Chapter 6 stipulates that both parties are subject to WTO rights and obligations concerning safeguard matters. Challenges to safeguard measures would be brought exclusively in the WTO dispute settlement system.

Notwithstanding Chapter 6, Article 3.12 sets forth a special safeguard system for agricultural goods in the event that an import increase causes or threatens to cause serious injury or market disturbance.[13] This special agricultural safeguard provision, however, substantially differs from the special safeguard mechanism under the WTO *Agreement on Agriculture*, which employs an automatic triggering system. Moreover, although 'material injury' and 'threat of material injury' are defined in line with the WTO *Agreement on Safeguards*, the concept of 'market disturbance' is not specifically provided for and has not been used in any other previous agreement. The lack of a clear definition of this concept for safeguard actions in the Korean statutory system may lead to serious controversy in

[12] Subsidy disciplines currently provided under Parts II–IV of the *SCM Agreement* can be addressed in the context of a FTA only to a limited extent, since direct regulation of subsidy policies presupposes multilateral cooperation or enforcement of consistent rules. As a result, that part will typically be incorporated in a FTA as such.

[13] Article 22.3 of the Laws on Investigation of Unfair Trade and Safeguard, Public Law 7093, promulgated on 20 January 2004.

the actual application of the provisions in the future, unless more specific criteria are elaborated in order to define this legal concept.[14]

Unlike the Korea–Chile FTA, with its special sectoral safeguard system, the Japan–Singapore EPA has a customized transitional safeguard system that substantially differs from the WTO safeguard mechanism. In fact, the 'emergency measure' system under Article 18 of the EPA adopted a bilateral safeguard mechanism that is more typical for recent FTAs. This emergency measure system is to be applied only during the transition period. In other words, after transition arrangements have all been completed, both parties will apply the WTO safeguard system precisely as set out in the *Agreement on Safeguards.* In contrast to the WTO safeguard system – which allows broad trade restrictive measures, including quantity limitations as well as suspension of the obligation 'in whole or in part' or withdrawal or modification of the concession – Article 18 of the Japan–Singapore EPA permits only that the country taking the measure suspends the further reduction of customs duties or, alternatively, increases customs duties to a rate lower than the most-favoured nation (MFN) rate at the time when the measure is taken or the EPA entered into force. Transitional safeguard actions may be taken only after investigations have been conducted and concluded in accordance with the disciplines under the WTO *Agreement on Safeguards.* The duration of a safeguard measure taken under Article 18 shall not exceed one year, and, in very exceptional circumstances, three years. Furthermore, Article 18.7 mandates domestic judicial review systems.

The above bilateral safeguard system is different from the WTO *Agreement on Safeguards* in two important aspects. Firstly, bilateral safeguard action can be taken on the basis of a 'substantial' causation requirement.[15] This substantial causation requirement for safeguard actions features particular prominently in the North American Free Trade Agreement (NAFTA) and, since the coming into effect of that Agreement, has been adopted in many other FTAs, including the FTA concluded by Korea and Japan. In those countries, domestic safeguard regulations mandate mere 'causation' instead of 'substantial causation' requirement – in other words, increased imports must have been the 'cause' of serious injury to the domestic industry (or threat thereof), but need not

[14] Article 22.3 of the Law on Investigation of Unfair Trade and Safeguard was elaborated by Article 22.3 of the Implementing Regulation, Presidential Order 18565, promulgated and entered into force on 21 October 2004. However, the Implementing Regulation did not clarify the concept of 'market disturbance', either.

[15] Provisions concerning causation have raised many controversial problems in the WTO jurisprudence (See Ahn, 'Restructuring the WTO Safeguard System', forthcoming).

have been the 'substantial cause'. This is a noteworthy legal development because, unlike the United States and Canada whose domestic safeguard regulations set forth a 'substantial' and 'principal' causation criterion, Korea and Japan have no such regulation or jurisprudence in their domestic systems. Secondly, a bilateral safeguard system does not even include 'facilitation of structural adjustment' as a requirement for imposing or maintaining a safeguard measure. In contrast, the WTO *Agreement on Safeguards* specifically mandates the application of a safeguard measure 'only to the extent necessary . . . to facilitate adjustment', although in practice, this requirement has become almost dead language.[16]

The transitional safeguard system of the Japan–Singapore EPA was readopted essentially for the Japan–Mexico FTA, although some procedural and substantive elements were modified and defined in detail. This rather standardized bilateral safeguard mechanism was also adopted in the Korea–Singapore and the Korea–EFTA FTAs.

The safeguard system adopted by the Japanese government for its FTAs and also, for the first time, by the Korean government in the Korea–Singapore FTA, is a more typical kind of bilateral safeguard mechanism normally provided for in most of the recent FTAs. There are roughly three different approaches to safeguard systems for FTAs. Firstly, under the WTO approach, FTA parties maintain all their respective rights and obligations under the WTO system. In other words, FTA parties do not differentiate in terms of safeguard actions. If a country suffers serious injury or threat thereof, that country imposes safeguard actions regardless of a FTA membership.[17]

Secondly, under the NAFTA approach,[18] FTA parties may try to exempt other FTA parties from the application of global safeguard actions. Article 802 of the NAFTA stipulates that

> any Party taking an emergency action under Article XIX or any such agreement shall exclude imports of a good from each other Party from the action unless:
>
> (a) imports from a Party, considered individually, account for a substantial share of total imports; and
> (b) imports from a Party, considered individually, or in exceptional

[16] See Ahn, 'Restructuring the WTO Safeguard System', forthcoming.

[17] For critical review of the WTO safeguard jurisprudence, see Alan O. Sykes, 'The Safeguards Mess: A Critique of WTO Jurisprudence' (2003) *World Trade Review*, 261–295; and Ahn, 'Restructuring the WTO Safeguard System', forthcoming.

[18] Article 802 of the NAFTA.

> circumstances imports from Parties considered collectively, contribute importantly to the serious injury, or threat thereof, caused by imports.

An identical provision was adopted by Canada and Chile for their FTA.[19] A similar safeguard system that excludes FTA partners from the scope of application of safeguard measures was also adopted in the Singapore–United States FTA; that system authorizes a party taking a global safeguard measure to 'exclude imports of an originating good from the other party if such imports are not a substantial cause of serious injury or threat thereof'.[20] This approach, however, may not be consistent with WTO obligations if an investigating authority does not conform to the so-called 'parallelism' principle.[21]

Thirdly, FTA parties may adopt FTA-specific safeguard measures that can be applied either during a transition period or, alternatively, on a permanent basis. A transitional FTA safeguard typically suspends and subsequently restores a tariff reduction process and does not impose any additional trade barriers. As an alternative, however, a FTA safeguard action designed to address import surges from other FTA parties may be established as a safety net for complete trade liberalization; such a measure, when activated, does impose additional trade barriers on MFN partners. Bilateral safeguard systems adopted by Japan for its FTAs are examples of the former, while the special safeguard action for agriculture provided in Article 3.12 of the Korea–Chile FTA is an example of the latter.

What form of FTA safeguard systems should be adopted depends on fundamental views concerning trade relations between FTA parties. Where more trade liberalization through an FTA is sought, with a view to facilitating industry restructuring, safeguard actions will be aimed less at blocking imports and more at promoting structural adjustment. For example, in the case of the Korea–Japan FTA, the chronic problem of Korea's huge trade deficits with respect to Japan would inevitably have an impact on the overall framework of the FTA safeguard negotiations. Moreover, small-

19 Article F-02 of the Canada–Chile FTA, available at: <http://www.dfait-maeci.gc.ca/tna-nac/cda-chile/chap-f26-en.asp> (visited 1 May 2006).

20 Article 7.5 of the Singapore–United States FTA, available at: <http://www.fta.gov.sg/fta/pdf/FTA_USSFTA_Agreement_Final.pdf> (visited 1 May 2006).

21 See, for example, Appellate Body Report, *US – Line Pipe*, paras. 178–198; and Appellate Body Report, *US – Steel Safeguards*, paras. 433–456. In fact, a more difficult and fundamental question arises where an authority satisfies the 'parallelism' requirement, since the issue of an MFN exemption for FTA safeguard actions was not clearly resolved during the Uruguay Round negotiation.

and medium-size companies in Korea, particularly in the machinery sector, have been regarded as one of the most vulnerable economic segments in the context of the Korea–Japan FTA. On the other hand, it is the agricultural sector that Japan is most concerned about. These economic circumstances may lead the FTA safeguard negotiations in an overly protectionist direction. Although an FTA safeguard system plays a crucial role as a safety net in circumstances in which domestic industries may not be sufficiently prepared for injury arising from trade liberalization, a safeguard system should not become another systemic trade barrier or an element nullifying the mutual gains from trade that come from industry adjustment as well as from increased reciprocal trade.[22]

IV. Conclusion

Although most East Asian FTAs have primarily adopted the WTO trade remedy system, modified models have begun to emerge in recent FTA negotiations. It is indeed noteworthy that 'rule diversification' in terms of trade remedy systems has begun to seep into the systems of some of the key players of the world trading system, albeit those that are targets, not users. Such codification of differentiated rules at the international level may set important precedents for the future negotiation and development of the trade remedy regime of the WTO system.

In that regard, a trade remedy system to be included in the Korea–Japan FTA may be considered a litmus test for assessing how much East Asian countries are prepared and willing to restructure the WTO trade remedy mechanism. In fact, Korea and Japan are among the most active proponents and share most concerns arising in the negotiations on the WTO trade remedy rules under the current Doha Development Agenda. Both countries are probably the most 'like minded' WTO Members, at least in terms of trade remedy issues. Therefore, any new trade remedy system to be incorporated in the Korea–Japan FTA, whatever approach is ultimately adopted, may become a crucial precedent for the future development of the WTO trade remedy regime as well as the development of the world trading system at large.

[22] The import diversification programme maintained by Korea to address excessive bilateral trade imbalance problems considerably restricted the importation of Japanese products, especially final consumer products. That programme was repealed at the end of June 1999. For a more detailed explanation, see Dukgeun Ahn, 'WTO Disciplines under the IMF Program: Congruence or Conflict?', in Dukgeun Ahn and Mitsuo Matsushita (eds), *WTO and East Asia: New Perspectives* (London, 2004), 25–38.

24

Free trade agreements in Asia and some common legal problems

C. L. LIM

I. The Asian scene

The number of free trade agreements (FTAs) notified to the *General Agreement on Tariffs and Trade*/World Trade Organization (GATT/WTO) had grown to 285 as of February 2004. By 2005, the number of free trade agreements (FTAs) notified to the *General Agreement on Tariffs and Trade*/World Trade Organization (GATT/WTO) exceeded 300. East and Southeast Asia have been the most active in the last half decade or so, with individual countries like Singapore and Thailand being the most active in Southeast Asia and Japan being the most active in East Asia. On the East Asian front, China has also concluded its two Closer Economic Partnership Agreements with Hong Kong and Macao in June and October 2003, respectively, as well as the goods agreement with the Association of Southeast Asian Nations (ASEAN) in November 2004. Japan, in addition to its FTAs with Singapore, the Philippines, and Mexico, has further ongoing negotiations with Korea, Malaysia, Thailand and also ASEAN. Korea has, in turn, concluded its FTA with Chile in 2003, and is now negotiating with the European Free Trade Association (EFTA) while Taiwan had earlier concluded an FTA with Panama. ASEAN as a whole has also been pursuing FTAs,[1] particularly in East and South Asia and with the Closer Economic Relations (CER) nations of Australia and New Zealand; all this is in addition to the ASEAN Free Trade Area (AFTA) itself. Such activity in Southeast Asia is not, however, confined to intra-regional or intra-sub-regional trade. Singapore, for example, concluded the United States–Singapore FTA in May 2003 and has concluded or is negotiating FTAs with nations stretching from Latin America to the Middle-East,[2] while Thailand concluded a Framework

[1] See the ASEAN Secretariat website at <http://www.aseansec.org>.
[2] See the Singapore Government FTA website at <http://www.app.fta.gov.sg/asp/index.asp>.

Agreement on Economic Cooperation with Bahrain as early as December 2002,[3] as well as with Peru in September 2003. Likewise, in East Asia, mention has already been made of the Taiwan–Panama FTA concluded in August 2003, the Japan–Mexico FTA concluded in September 2004, the Korea–Chile FTA concluded in February 2003 as well as, for example, the negotiations between Korea and the EFTA which began in January 2005.

Outside East Asia and Southeast Asia, the South Asia Free Trade Area is currently being negotiated amongst the South Asian Association for Regional Co-operation Member States (India, Pakistan, Bangladesh, Sri Lanka, Nepal, Bhutan, and Maldives) following the conclusion of a framework agreement in January 2004. Other agreements currently being negotiated such as the proposed Bay of Bengal Initiative for Multi-Sectoral Technical and Economic Cooperation (BIMSTEC) Free Trade Area involve several South Asian and Southeast Asian Nations – Bangladesh, Bhutan, India, Myanmar, Nepal, Sri Lanka, and Thailand – negotiating between various 'sub-regions'. India, following its FTAs with Nepal in December 1991 and Sri Lanka in December 1999, has been especially active of late and concluded the Comprehensive Economic Cooperation Agreement with Singapore in November 2004, as well as framework agreements with both ASEAN and Thailand in October 2003 and the Southern Common Market (MERCOSUR) in June 2003. Pakistan, in turn, is currently engaged in active negotiations with Singapore, as well as with Nepal, Malaysia, Indonesia and China.[4] Pakistan is also negotiating a framework agreement with Sri Lanka. Lastly, Australia and New Zealand have also been active on the FTA front.[5]

II. The legal advisor's role

Legal creativity as much as policy imagination will both be required, and Asian legal advisors will have to look far and wide to craft what are some

[3] In addition to the ASEAN Free Trade Area (AFTA), Thailand has signed bilateral FTAs with China and Australia, and is negotiating with India, Japan, Bahrain, Peru, New Zealand, the United States of America and the BIMSTEC countries (Bangladesh, India, Myanmar, Sri Lanka, Thailand, Nepal, and Bhutan); Nataya Seetubtim, 'Thailand FTAs', June 2004, website of the ASEAN Secretariat at <http://www.aseansec.org>. The Thailand–Australia FTA entered into force on 1 January 2005; see the website of the Australian Department of Foreign Affairs and Trade at <http://www.dfat.gov.au>.

[4] See 'FTAs with Four Asian Countries', 12 February 2005, at <http://www.bilaterals.org>.

[5] Within the Asian region, Australia has concluded FTAs with Singapore (February 2003) and Thailand (July 2004) while New Zealand has concluded FTAs with Singapore (January 2000) and Thailand (November 2004). In addition to the ASEAN–CER Framework Agreement that was concluded in September 2002, New Zealand is now negotiating with China, both countries having issued a joint report in November 2004.

very diverse FTAs. These could range from FTAs resembling the comprehensive approach of the North American Free Trade Agreement (NAFTA) (with deep services, investment and intellectual property coverage, as in the case of Singapore's FTAs with the United States and Australia) to those which face the challenge of accommodating diverse economies and balancing resulting questions of individual economic interests and issues of sensitive imports. At the same time, virtually all of these countries are WTO Members as well, and complications are likely to arise in designing some of these FTAs in order to fit the requirements imposed by the rudimentary, but nevertheless real, multilateral disciplines currently in existence under the WTO. Moreover, many Asian countries are still on a steep learning curve when it comes to techniques of trade dispute settlement, and this too could raise questions of policy choice and treaty design.

The lesson ultimately may be that there are no uniquely 'Asian' FTA challenges on the legal front. In any case, this chapter proposes to adopt a slightly different tack from the usual treatment given to such questions. Our aim here is to seek to avoid both a general treatment of the policy issues, and a specific focus on such legal problems as might be raised by particular FTAs. Instead, we will focus on three categories of general legal issues that are likely to be faced by many Asian countries at the present time:

(i) Doctrinal issues arising under WTO multilateral disciplines;
(ii) 'Free standing' doctrinal problems in some typical FTA provisions, including the scope of most-favoured nation (MFN) clauses applicable to negotiations between unitary and federal entities; and
(iii) General international law problems relating to overlapping and interlocking dispute settlement mechanisms, as well as more specific dispute settlement problems in the investment and trade areas.

III. The framework of our discussion

As for doctrinal issues that arise under WTO multilateral disciplines, I shall further divide my treatment of the issue into two parts, involving (a) problems arising under the general 'gateway principles' imposed by WTO agreements,[6] and (b) those that have to do with more specific issues

6 Readers should turn to Gabrielle Marceau's chapter in this book. Won-mog Choi has also recently produced a fascinating study of the GATT 1947 records on the evolution of GATT Article XXIV and its application to FTAs comprising non-GATT members (unpublished manuscript, on file with the author).

concerning the relationship between the multilateral rules and certain questions that are likely to be raised by some relatively common FTA provisions. The analytical distinction here is neither neat nor watertight, and one way of thinking about the difference between (a) and (b) above is perhaps to say that there is a difference between approaching the issue of WTO multilateral disciplines from a multilateralist's viewpoint on the one hand, and from the viewpoint of an FTA legal advisor on the other (the latter perspective may also be described, loosely speaking as a 'bilateralist viewpoint').

Secondly, with respect to free-standing technical problems arising under typical FTA clauses, I would like to focus on one problem in particular, based on the example of a 'NAFTA' template of services and investment coverage. Due to the broad and diverse range of Asian countries and FTA partners that are involved, I shall also use this opportunity to mention a technical FTA design problem raised by the different kinds of domestic constitutional arrangements within countries entering into FTAs today. Unlike the GATT and the *General Agreement on Trade in Services* (GATS), which deal with the problem of federal states in a rather tepid fashion, countries seeking substantial gains from FTAs may wish to have deeper commitments from such sub-federal entities. However, the constitutionally enshrined distribution of powers within a federal system may present serious, sometimes even unique, obstacles both in international negotiations and in the process of drafting the FTAs themselves.

Finally, while acknowledging the contemporary debate surrounding resort to public international law rules and principles in the specialized trade law area, I should also say something about the problem of overlapping international dispute settlement regimes.

The aim of this chapter is therefore to focus on selected legal-doctrinal issues. But two caveats are in order. First, as mentioned previously, even if the problems analyzed here are problems faced or likely to be faced by the Asian FTAs, they are not specifically 'Asian'. Secondly, space does not permit an in-depth, systematic study of the FTAs that have been concluded. To my knowledge, no serious study of comparative FTA law has yet been published. The aim here is simply to sketch out the significance of some of the more general or illustrative problems that are likely to be faced today and in the future, in the belief that these problems have some salience or resonance, especially for practitioners who are responsible for developing legal strategies and drafting such FTAs. These are just some general, personal observations by a former FTA legal advisor for the purposes of encouraging further discussion with like-minded colleagues and others who may be interested in such matters.

IV. Doctrinal problems related to multilateral disciplines

As a threshold issue, any preferential trade agreement (PTA) – FTA or customs union – by Member countries of the WTO will have to observe the requirements imposed by GATT Article XXIV and GATS Article V.

1. The GATT

GATT Articles XXIV:4 to XXIV:10 (as clarified in the *Understanding on the Interpretation of Article XXIV of the GATT 1994*) govern the formation and operation of customs unions and free trade areas covering trade in goods. Under Article XXIV:4:

> The contracting parties *recognize the desirability of increasing freedom of trade* by the development, through voluntary agreements, of closer integration between the economies of the countries parties to such agreements. They also recognize that the purpose of a customs union or of a free-trade area should be to *facilitate trade between the constituent territories* [hereafter, 'the internal trade requirement'] and *not to raise barriers to the trade of other contracting parties with such territories* [hereafter, 'the external trade requirement']. (Emphasis added)

These internal and external trade requirements which Article XXIV:4 imposes set out the formal legal aims of customs unions and free trade areas. It is in the light of these aims then that Article XXIV:5 states:

> Accordingly, the provisions of this Agreement shall not prevent, as between the territories of contracting parties, the formation of a customs union or of a free-trade area or the adoption of an interim agreement necessary for the formation of a customs union or of a free-trade area.

Article XXIV:5 provides the legal basis for forming such customs unions and free trade areas, or to adopt interim agreements to that effect. Such agreements would otherwise be inconsistent with the GATT 1994, namely, with the MFN requirement under GATT Article 1.

GATT Article XXIV:8(b) then goes on to define the internal trade requirement; namely, the '*substantially all trade*' requirement that has been the source of so much doctrinal uncertainty. Article XXIV:8(b) states:

> A free-trade area shall be understood to mean a group of two or more customs territories in which the duties and other restrictive regulations of

> commerce (except, where necessary, those permitted under Articles XI, XII, XIII, XIV, XV and XX) [hereafter, the 'parenthetical list'] are eliminated on substantially all the trade between the constituent territories in products originating in such territories.

In addition to this internal trade requirement concerning the coverage of substantially all trade between the parties to the preferential trading agreement, an external requirement exists. This is to be found in GATT Article XXIV:5(b), which imposes the 'shall not be higher or more restrictive' standard:

> [W]ith respect to a free-trade area, or an interim agreement leading to the formation of a free-trade area, the duties and other regulations of commerce maintained in each of the constituent territories and applicable at the formation of such free-trade area or the adoption of such interim agreement to the trade of contracting parties not included in such area or not parties to such agreement shall not be higher or more restrictive than the corresponding duties and other regulations of commerce existing in the same constituent territories prior to the formation of the free-trade area, or interim agreement as the case may be.

In this regard, the WTO *Understanding on Interpretation of Article XXIV* states, in paragraph 2, that

> [t]he evaluation under paragraph 5(a) of Article XXIV of the general incidence of the duties and other regulations of commerce applicable before and after the formation of a customs union shall in respect of duties and charges be based upon an *overall assessment of weighted average tariff rates and of customs duties collected.* (Emphasis added)

Finally, with respect to these general formal constraints under the GATT, Article XXIV:7 also imposes a 'prompt notification' requirement. These notifications are submitted to the Committee on Regional Trade Agreements (CRTA).

None of these requirements has yet proven particularly difficult in practice and may even be viewed by trade lawyers as essentially 'political' questions that, in reality, involve Geneva representatives and delegations working on the CRTA process. Indeed, prior to the Appellate Body report in *Turkey – Textiles*, the view of Turkey and the European Communities, as well as of some other WTO Members, appeared to be that Article XXIV of the GATT 1994 was simply non-justiciable. Be that as it may, if the present trend towards more and more FTAs continues, the interpretation of these provisions can be expected to be driven by the mutual interest of

WTO Members in being party to one or more such agreements, in particular with respect to those agreement in which compliance with these internal and external trade questions may be questionable. Nonetheless, sharp doctrinal questions could still arise as in the *Turkey – Textiles* case. As such, it is somewhat problematic to simply assume that differences on these questions will likely be resolved through diplomatic efforts (as opposed to WTO litigation), because the reciprocal 'allowances' and flexibility between the Members in negotiations could be based on a mutually acceptable practice gradually evolving over time. While that approach may work in the context of surveillance or enforcement under the CRTA procedure (the so-called 'Track I' enforcement procedure) – excepting FTAs made under the Enabling Clause[7] – there would be less room for reciprocity and political accommodation under the 'Track II' enforcement procedure, namely that of submitting a dispute based on the interpretation of the above requirements to formal dispute settlement (for example, with respect to MFN violations). The disciplines imposed by the reverse consensus rule for the approval of panel and Appellate Body reports essentially allows any one Member State to trigger an Appellate Body ruling that could upset the whole doctrinal applecart in relation to the interpretation of the requirements under Article XXIV of the GATT 1994 or Article V of the GATS.

Against this possibility, there is only the soft, pragmatic 'assurance' that, if hard cases were indeed to arise in practice sufficiently widely amongst the Asian and other FTAs, the same set of incentives and disincentives that exist under Track I should, in principle, apply when a WTO Member decides whether to file, or not, a formal WTO claim to initiate formal dispute settlement proceedings. In other words, even if a disagreement arises, the aggrieved WTO Member would still have enough incentives to settle the issue amicably, rather than initiating a WTO dispute and taking the risk of having WTO adjudicatory bodies decide the disagreement – a matter that will typically also be of significant national importance for the complaining WTO Member, because that Member can also be expected to be a Member of one or more FTAs. However, this complacent way of looking at things most likely underestimates the potential difficulties in store for us. Those who, in principle, would have the most to gain and the least to lose in the event that the dispute settlement system

[7] For a recent argument that the CRTA should be reformed, see, for instance, Michael Ewing-Chow, 'South-East Asia and Free Trade Agreements: WTO Plus or Bust?' (2004) 8 *Singapore Year Book of International Law*, 193–206, 204.

would decide these issues would be the countries that have been left out of the spread of benefits under the various FTAs. This is said merely by way of a cautionary note. It is precisely because of the nebulous nature of these seemingly easy-to-satisfy formal requirements that GATT imposes that it becomes important that FTAs should be highly inclusive. FTAs should have broad memberships so as to avoid those who have not shared in the benefits of FTAs finding themselves in a position whereby they would be tempted to push for formal legal interpretations of Article XXIV of the GATT 1994.

It is also a roundabout way of saying that the external trade and 'substantially all trade' requirements may yet need to be reviewed in tandem with our growing experience in the coming years.

Nevertheless, these requirements serve the purpose of ensuring that at least a basic aim and justification for FTAs is met; namely, that FTAs should promote trade liberalization, despite the risk of trade diversion and a hike in transaction costs caused by complex FTA rules of origin. In other words, FTAs are best justified where an FTA is 'WTO-plus'. And that is not all there is to it. Asia's FTAs should also keep up with 'best FTA practices' globally and cannot be viewed in isolation only from the viewpoint of the GATT multilateral disciplines imposed by the provisions referred to above. FTA legal advisors generally should keep an eye on FTA legal designs and the different approaches that other countries have taken.

2. *The GATS*

In the case of the GATS, we find problems similar to those identified above in the context of the GATT 1994. Article V of the GATS governs the conclusion of PTAs in the area of trade in services. It states:

> 1. This Agreement shall not prevent any of its Members from being a party to or entering into an agreement liberalizing trade in services between or among the parties to such an agreement, provided that such an agreement:
>
> (a) has substantial sectoral coverage[[1]], and
>
> (b) provides for the absence or elimination of substantially all discrimination, in the sense of Article XVII, between or among the parties, in the sectors covered under subparagraph (a) . . .

Footnote 1 to Article V:1(a) in turn states that: 'This condition is understood in terms of number of sectors, volume of trade affected and modes of supply. In order to meet this condition, agreements should not provide for the *a priori* exclusion of any mode of supply'. What does the reference to an *a priori* exclusion of any mode of supply mean?

Take, for example, the Singapore–Australia Free Trade Agreement, which states in Article 2 of Chapter 8 (Investment):

> This Chapter shall apply to investments made, *in the process of being made, or sought to be made*, by an investor of a Party in the territory of the other Party.

This FTA provision extends MFN treatment and national treatment to the so-called 'pre-establishment phase', that is, in respect of investments that foreign investors are seeking to establish in Singapore or Australia. What if Singapore and Australia had sought to carve out pre-establishment? Would they have run up against the requirement of coverage of all four modes of supply due to an 'overlap' between mode-3 services and investment disciplines? Does an answer depend upon a clause such as Article 1112.1 of the NAFTA?[8] While these questions may appear abstract at first glance, they nonetheless demonstrate the need to exercise substantial care in both fulfilling the requirement imposed by Article V of the GATS and pursuing Singapore's and Australia's 'WTO-plus' FTA policies.

V. Relationship between multilateral disciplines and FTA commitments

Resolving the threshold issues above is not the end of the analysis. There are specific matters that FTA parties may wish to address, which are subject to multilateral disciplines whose precise requirements are, however, unclear. This reflects, to some extent, the fact that the current proliferation of FTAs was wholly unanticipated when the original GATT was drafted.

1. *A GATT illustration: the 'safeguards exemption' issue*

Would the FTA parties wish to permit the exemption of FTA partners from safeguard measures taken by other FTA partners? A general answer is practically impossible, because it depends on the specific individual policies and circumstances of each FTA. In this context, it may be noted

[8] Article 1112.1 of the NAFTA (Relationship to Other Chapters) provides:

> In the event of any inconsistency between a provision of this Chapter and a provision of another Chapter, the provision of the other Chapter shall prevail to the extent of the inconsistency.

that, for example, Asian WTO Members have generally not been high safeguards users – rather, the major users have been the United States, the European Communities, Argentina, and Chile. Instead, challenges have been brought by several Asian countries against the United States; China, Chinese Taipei, Japan, and Korea in the case of *US – Steel Safeguards*, and Korea in the *US – Line Pipe* case. As a result, the practical import of this question may, at least for the time being, not be high for FTAs between Asian countries. Nevertheless, we might pause to consider the issue further.

Let us assume that a WTO Member considers the exemption of FTA partners from safeguard action to be a policy worthy of being included in a particular FTA. Doctrinally, there has been much discussion about whether the 'parenthetical list' in GATT Article XXIV:8 (above) prohibits the imposition of safeguards (or any other trade remedy measures, for that matter) between FTA partners.[9] In the Uruguay Round, the following language was proposed to govern the relationship between Article XIX and Article XXIV, but was not adopted:

> When an action is taken by a member of a customs union or free-trade area . . . it [need not] [shall not] be applied to other members of the customs union or free trade area. However, when taking such action it should be demonstrated that the serious injury giving rise to the invocation of Article XIX is caused by imports from non-members; any injury deriving from imports from other members of the customs union or free-trade area shall not be taken into account in justifying the Article XIX action.[10]

The tension that arises here between the words 'need not' and 'shall not' in square brackets is that between (i) permitting the exclusion of intra-FTA safeguards and (ii) prohibiting intra-FTA safeguards outright. It may also be recalled that in the *Argentina – Footwear (EC)* dispute, the panel had rejected Argentina's contention that it was, in fact, required not to apply safeguards under MERCOSUR in respect of MERCOSUR members.[11] The panel's conclusions were driven by the narrower doctrine of parallelism – that the inclusion of an FTA or customs union Member in the analysis of imports in the safeguards investigation meant that that Member also had

9 See, for instance, Mitsuo Matsushita, Thomas J. Schoenbaum, and Petros C. Mavroidis, *The World Trade Organization: Law, Practice, and Policy* (Oxford, 2003), pp. 360–363.

10 Matsushita et al, *The World Trade Organization*, p. 362, referring to WTO, Committee on Regional Trade Agreements, '*Systemic Issues Related to "Other Regulations of Commerce"*', WT/REG/W/17, 31 October 1997, p. 4.

11 Panel Report, *Argentina – Footwear (EC)*, para. 8.93.

to be included in the application of the safeguard measure. The Appellate Body similarly considered that (i) when a WTO Member conducts an investigation on the basis of imports from all countries, that Member may not exclude from the safeguard its FTA partners.[12] However, the Appellate Body went on to add that (ii) it was not ruling on whether, assuming imports from another customs union member was excluded from the analysis, a member of a customs union can indeed exclude another member of that customs union from safeguard measures.[13] The problem arises because the Appellate Body avoided the general question about the relationship between Articles XIX and XXIV. It was not clear, at that point, that the doctrine of parallelism provided a comprehensive solution.[14] In other words, why not just exclude customs union and FTA members from the investigation?

Subsequent disputes raised the same question. The panel in the *US – Line Pipe* case held that the United States' exemption of Canada and Mexico from the application of safeguard measures was not a violation of Article XIX of the GATT 1994. Specifically, the panel concluded that Article XXIV of the GATT 1994 provided a justification for the United States' exclusion of Canada and Mexico from the application of the safeguard measures at issue.[15] Korea appealed and the Appellate Body in that case sought to maintain a neutral stance on the issue. The Appellate Body considered that the panel's reasoning above was 'moot' and had 'no legal effect' because the doctrine of parallelism had, in any case, not been met. As such, the question of the relationship between Article XIX and XXIV was irrelevant for the purposes of resolving that dispute. The Appellate Body's reasoning therefore did 'not prejudge whether Article 2.2 of the *Agreement on Safeguards* permits a Member to exclude imports originating in member states of a free-trade area from the scope of a safeguard measure.'[16]

Is a customs union or an FTA Member entitled to exclude imports from customs union or FTA Members from the application of a safeguard measure imposed on imports from other WTO Members, as long as these other customs union or FTA Members are excluded from the

[12] Appellate Body Report, *Argentina – Footwear (EC)* paras. 111–113.

[13] Ibid., para. 114.

[14] See also the *US – Wheat Gluten* case, which went on to uphold the doctrine of parallelism.

[15] Panel Report, *US – Line Pipe*, paras. 7.144–7.146. The panel rejected the claim by Korea that the United States had not fulfilled the parallelism requirement, because Korea had not made out a prima facie case in this respect (Panel Report, *US – Line Pipe*, para. 7.171).

[16] Appellate Body Report, *US – Line Pipe*, para. 198.

analysis of imports during the investigation? In the *US – Steel Safeguards* dispute, the panel ruled that account must be given to the 'fact that [the] excluded imports may have [had] some injurious impact on the domestic industry'.[17] This ruling was subsequently upheld by the Appellate Body.[18] But it raises the question, 'What then if such excluded imports really had no such impact?' The response of the panel and the Appellate Body in *US – Steel Safeguards* is for the safeguards user to show that this is the case. In particular, the Appellate Body upheld two key conclusions reached by the panel and which the United States had challenged. First, that the injurious effect of excluded imports should be accounted for (that is, the 'excluded sources accounting requirement'). Secondly, that the safeguards user should show explicitly that imports included in the application of safeguards measures satisfy the conditions for the application of safeguards – that is, where excluded imports had been included within the initial safeguards investigation, the included imports 'alone, and in and of themselves', satisfied the conditions for the application of safeguards. These requirements, which are based ultimately on the non-attribution principle under Article 4.2(b) of the *Agreement on Safeguards*, appear to suggest that imports from FTA partner countries will always have to be accounted for in any safeguards investigation.

2. *A GATS illustration: the investment/mode-3 services overlap*

It may be useful to consider another example in this context. The Asian FTAs concluded in the wake of the NAFTA would do well to limit innovation in their drafting language to what is necessary. Speaking only from experience of the FTAs concluded by Singapore (which have been the most numerous ones concluded by an Asian country), where well-understood and accepted language in the WTO agreements may be 'bilateralized', then such language should be adopted if what is prized is interpretative uniformity, consistency and predictability. Elsewhere, however, questions arise that have no WTO counterpart and one could turn, for example, to the most well-established and widely understood 'comprehensive' FTA, namely, the NAFTA. However, the NAFTA's answers may not necessarily reflect preferred policy choices in Asia and here we begin to encounter a different class of problem from those considered above.

[17] Panel Report, *US – Steel Safeguards*, para. 10.598.

[18] Appellate Body Report, *US – Steel Safeguards*, paras. 440–453.

Mention has been made of the potential overlap between 'mode-3' services supply (that is, supply through the establishment of a commercial presence) and investment disciplines. More specifically, for instance, the definitions of 'commercial presence' and 'service supplier' in the GATS resemble the definitions of 'investment' and 'investor' under the NAFTA. Assuming that a comprehensive FTA with chapters on goods, services, and investment is being sought, how does the legal advisor and treaty draftsman choose to account for the investment dimension when discussing mode-3 services supply, and vice-versa? Could the definition of an investor provide wider protection to the investor/supplier than the definition of a service supplier, for example? How should the services and investment chapters in the FTA relate to each other? Is it even always wise to try and imagine the possible sorts of scenarios in which the problem could arise in practice and to address them *ex ante* through a relation clause which governs that relationship *a priori*? The NAFTA's investment chapter states in Article 1112.1 that

> [i]n the event of any inconsistency between this Chapter and another Chapter, the other Chapter shall prevail to the extent of the inconsistency.

But it is hard to see why this approach should always govern our choices.

3. *A third illustration: the Government Procurement Agreement*

Aside from the WTO multilateral agreements, problems could also arise in respect of the inclusion of a subject-matter that falls under a WTO plurilateral agreement, such as the *Agreement on Government Procurement* (*GPA*).

When the GATT came into being in 1947, it was generally accepted that procurement was excluded from the application of the GATT's MFN clause (mainly due to the political sensitivity of the procurement issue).[19] Likewise, Article XIII:1 of the GATS excludes government procurement from the GATS MFN clause. GATS Article XIII:1 states that

> Articles II [most favoured nation treatment], XVI [market access] and XVII [national treatment] shall not apply to laws, regulations or requirements governing the procurement by governmental agencies of services purchased for governmental purposes and not with a view to commercial resale or with a view to use in the supply of services for commercial resale.

[19] For a contrary viewpoint, see Arie Reich, 'The New GATT Agreement on Government Procurement: The Pitfalls of Plurilateralism and Strict Reciprocity' (1997) 31 *Journal of World Trade* 2, 125–151, 142–143.

Therefore, leaving aside state-owned enterprises, procurement itself was left out of MFN treatment. The problem arises when we consider that, equally, the legal basis for establishing a customs union or an FTA as an exception to the MFN rule is only contained in the GATT and the GATS, but not in the *GPA*. There is no *GPA* equivalent of GATT Article XXIV and GATS Article V. At the same time, Article III.1(b) of the *GPA* states that

> [w]ith respect to all laws, regulations, procedures and practices regarding government procurement covered by this Agreement, each Party shall provide *immediately and unconditionally to the products, services and suppliers of other Parties offering products or services of the Parties, treatment no less favourable than ... (b) that accorded to products, services and suppliers of any other Party*'. (Emphasis added)

The better view, it might seem then, is that there is no MFN exemption under the *GPA* and that any more favourable treatment granted an FTA partner ought to be extended to all other *GPA* partners.

VI. Scope of MFN coverage for federal states

In addition to such categories of problems, FTA legal advisors would typically also wish to extend the coverage of concessions to the units of a federal state, an area in which GATT and GATS provisions are not as clear as would be desirable. In principle, any offensive negotiating strategy directed against a federal state would seek to include the most favourable treatment granted by a unit of a federal entity to any other unit of that federal entity or any other party, whichever is more advantageous. Indeed, the most robust, known version of such a clause combines both MFN and national treatment and requires the better of the two – in other words, the most advantageous treatment within the range of such forms of treatment given to any other country, any other unit within the federal entity, *or indeed to that unit itself.* Let us begin with a comparison of the GATT and the GATS. GATT Article XXIV:12 states that

> [e]ach contracting party shall take such reasonable measures as may be available to it to ensure observance of the provisions of this Agreement by the regional and local governments and authorities within its territories.

Its analogue is GATS Article I:3, which requires that

> [i]n fulfilling its obligations and commitments under the Agreement, each Member shall take such reasonable measures as may be available to it to

> ensure their observance by regional and local governments and authorities and non-governmental bodies within its territory . . .

What does the reference to 'reasonable measures' mean? Is this then only a 'good faith obligation'? The MFN provision under GATT Article I:1 is otherwise silent on the issue:

> [A]ny advantage, favour, privilege or immunity granted by any contracting party to any product originating in or destined for any other country shall be accorded immediately and unconditionally to the like product originating in or destined for the territories of all other contracting parties.

The MFN provision in GATS Article II:1 similarly provides only that,

> [w]ith respect to any measure covered by this Agreement, each Member shall accord immediately and unconditionally to services and service suppliers of any other Member treatment no less favourable than that it accords to like services and service suppliers of any other country.

Both these MFN provisions therefore refer only to the treatment given by a 'contracting party' or 'Member' to 'any other country'. This also holds true for the national treatment provisions under the GATT and the GATS. Thus, the (non-fiscal measures) national treatment provision under GATT Article III:4, for example, states that

> [t]he products of the territory of any contracting party imported into the territory of any other contracting party shall be accorded treatment no less favourable than that accorded to like products of national origin in respect of all laws, regulations and requirements affecting their internal sale, offering for sale, purchase, transportation, distribution or use.

Its analogue is GATS Article XVII, which also states only that

> each *Member* shall accord to services and service suppliers of any other Member, in respect of all measures affecting the supply of services, treatment no less favourable than that it accords to its own like services and service suppliers. (Emphasis added)

These national treatment clauses only speak of the 'territory of any other contracting party' and 'any other Member'.

These forms of language, with the exception of the oblique language of GATT Article XXIV:12 and GATS Article I:3 do not resolve the question whether *individual States* within a federal structure should *themselves* provide MFN and national treatment to an FTA partner or, indeed, whether the larger federal entities to which they belong should *ensure* (or be held legally responsible for) such treatment. In contrast, NAFTA Article 1202, in relation to the national treatment requirement in the services trade, states, for example:

> 1. Each Party shall accord to service providers of another Party treatment no less favorable than that it accords, in like circumstances, to its own service providers.
>
> 2. The treatment accorded by a Party under paragraph 1 means, with respect to a state or province, treatment no less favorable than the most favorable treatment accorded, in like circumstances, by that state or province to service providers of the Party of which it forms a part.

This is the NAFTA's 'Best-in-or-out-of-state' clause, which is also to be found in NAFTA Article 301 (goods trade) and Article 1102.3 (investment). Such a clause may also be linked with a clause adapted from that contained (in the NAFTA services example, above) in Article 1204:

> Each Party shall accord to service providers of another Party the better of the treatment required by Articles 1202 [national treatment] and 1203 [MFN].

This is a straightforward 'better-of-national-or-MFN-treatment' clause. When combined with the 'best-in-or-out-of-state' clause above, it is easy to imagine that the resulting obligation is quite powerful, provided that the FTA parties desire such an outcome. In effect, the outcome is a guarantee that the most advantageous treatment is granted within the range of such forms of treatment given to (i) any other country, (ii) any other unit within the federal entity (the import of the language 'of the Party of which it forms a part'), or indeed (iii) *to that unit itself* (should national treatment grant a better standard of treatment than MFN).

One reason, we might speculate, for the difference in approach towards federal entities under the WTO agreements and some of the FTAs we have today is that the WTO agreements and an FTA like the NAFTA lie at two extreme ends of a spectrum. The NAFTA was negotiated between three federal states, albeit with differing internal constitutional arrangements, whereas the WTO, with its more extensive membership, simply avoids the issue with the language we have seen. But this is not to suggest that the NAFTA-type approach above has only been applied between federal states–see, for example, the US–Singapore FTA. How FTA parties will choose to design legal solutions for themselves here would ultimately depend not only on the kind of membership each FTA contemplates, but also the individual negotiating dynamics and realms of negotiating possibilities which each FTA uniquely presents.

VII. Some thoughts on dispute settlement

Finally, there arises the opportunity here to raise a broad general problem having to do with FTA dispute settlement arrangements.[20] For the sake of analytical clarity, we could perhaps imagine three levels to the problem at varying degrees of generality. At the most abstract level, there is today (i) the problem of competing jurisdiction between international courts and tribunals (for example, between the WTO and some other dispute settlement forum). At a rather more concrete level, we have also seen how, (ii) in the investment disputes context, MFN clauses may serve to extend third-country FTA dispute procedure benefits to investor plaintiffs of the country in respect of which such MFN treatment has been granted (which I shall refer to below as the '*Maffezini* problem'). Finally, and at an even more concrete level, (iii) 'non-investment disputes' may be subsumed under the concept of an 'investment dispute', and thus the '*Maffezini* problem' just referred to might, in this way, be amplified because it will be imported into non-investment disputes as well. Much would of course depend upon the ingenuity of litigators in these contexts. I propose to deal with the latter two, relatively specific, kinds of problems above – that is, (ii) and (iii) above – before turning to the more general problem of competing jurisdiction.

1. The 'Maffezini' or 'Maffezini-type' problem

Let us start with the problem posed by the investment dispute in *Maffezini v Spain*.[21] Under an investment treaty, MFN treatment given by State A to investors of State B means that, if State A enters into a treaty with State C, and under that treaty grants investors of State C more favourable treatment than the treatment granted to investors of State B, investors from State B automatically become entitled to the more favourable treatment accorded to investors from State C. In *Maffezini*, there were two bilateral investment treaties (BITs) between Spain and Argentina, on the one hand, and Spain and Chile, on the other hand. A

[20] For a study of specific categories of FTA dispute settlement provisions, see Chang-Fa Lo's chapter in this book. See also Hsu Locknie, 'Dispute Settlement Systems in Recent Free Trade Agreements of Singapore: ANZSCEP, JSEPA and ESFTA' (2003) *Journal of World Investment*, 277–314. [21] ICSID Case No ARB/97/7.

dispute – not related to the MFN principle – arose in respect of the first treaty. Spain objected to the jurisdiction of the arbitral tribunal, on the grounds that the first treaty required the exhaustion of domestic remedies; in other words, the foreign investor (in this case the investor from Argentina) was required to pursue his claim in Spanish courts before resorting to arbitration. Hence, the issue was a procedural rule under the terms of the dispute settlement provisions of the bilateral investment treaty (BIT) between Spain and Argentina. The investor-claimant instead relied, however, on the second treaty to which Argentina was not a party – namely, the BIT between Spain and Chile – and which did not impose an equivalent domestic remedies rule; in other words, under the Spain–Chile BIT, a Chilean investor was not required to exhaust local remedies before resorting to arbitration. The Argentine investor claimed that MFN treatment covered also such procedural requirements and, consequently, that it (the Argentine investor) was entitled to the less onerous procedural arrangement. That argument in *Maffezini* was successful. Clearly, this *Maffezini* 'problem' that ensues could also apply outside the investment context. At the most basic level, one can envisage an FTA with an investment chapter resembling a typical bilateral investment treaty. But, as has been mentioned, one could also be faced with a services dispute, or some other dispute subsumed under the rubric of an investment dispute.

Treaty drafters and policy makers will, therefore, have to negotiate with an eye on the possible dynamics of future negotiations with other parties. This could prove a daunting task when we account for the fact that what drives a policy decision to include an MFN clause in an FTA chapter, say, the investment chapter, may not always account for the full ramifications of every procedural rule or device contained in the FTA investment dispute settlement provisions. Put simply, there is a potentially very wide scope of application of the MFN principle that may be impossible to predict *ex ante.*

Some might, however, hold the view that the *Maffezini* problem is not as serious as it appeared at the time *Maffezini* was decided. Indeed, critics of *Maffezini* could point to the importance of accounting for the specific intentions of treaty parties as opposed to some arbitral sleight of hand that results in using one treaty to interpret another. Thus, in two recent cases, *Salini v Jordan*,[22] which involved a dispute over the tribunal's jurisdiction over contractual claims under the MFN clause in the Italy–Jordan BIT, and *Plama*

[22] ICSID Case No. ARB/02/13.

v Bulgaria,[23] which concerned the MFN clause in the Bulgaria–Cyprus BIT, the two International Centre for Settlement of Investment Disputes tribunals appear to have departed from the *Maffezini* approach. In both cases, the tribunal ruled that it would not presume that the MFN clause in the BIT extends to commitments undertaken in relation to dispute settlement (that is, a blanket exclusion of dispute settlement provisions from MFN coverage), unless it could be shown that this was indeed what the parties had specifically intended. Hence, these investment cases provide some comfort to trade negotiators and their legal advisors. Having said that, it is another matter altogether to declare, quite simply, that we have therefore seen the last of *Maffezini.* That would be too much wishful thinking in place of prudence and pragmatism. Moreover, in July 2005, another tribunal went on seemingly to confirm *Maffezini*, and considered that an MFN clause can after all extend to procedural advantages. The tribunal ignored *Plama* altogether and took the view instead that the *absence* of an intention to extend MFN coverage to dispute settlement undertakings must be established.[24] Which line of cases will hold for the future? Calling it a matter of proof of treaty intent surely does not solve the practical problem that arises as a result.

2. *The larger 'international tribunals' problem*

Taking a larger imaginary step back from all this, just thinking about the *Maffezini* problem in the context of the further problem of extended coverage to non-investment disputes should lead us to consider its potential combination with a broader phenomenon in international dispute settlement; namely, the extent to which there are today numerous potentially overlapping and interlocking agreements that could trigger formal dispute resolution in an unpredictable manner. This is the problem of competing jurisdictions which I have already referred to.[25] Although it is a general international law problem, it nonetheless has some real salience in the trade context. We have seen this, for example, in *EU v Chile (Swordfish Stocks)*.[26] There, Spanish fishermen had wanted to dock in

[23] ICSID Case No. ARB/03/24, especially at para. 212.

[24] *Gas Natural SDG S.A. v Argentine Republic*, Decision of the Tribunal on Preliminary Questions of Jurisdiction, ICSID Case No. ARB/03/10. See the remarks by Mr Luis Paradell, representing Gas Natural, in Luke Eric Peterson, 'Tribunal OKs Treaty Shopping for Better Arbitration Options in Gas Natural Case', 13 July 2005, available at <www.bilaterals.org>. [25] See section VII above.

[26] 'Dispute Settlement: EU Chile-Swordfish; Asbestos Appellate Body: EU Requests WTO Panel to Rule on Swordfish Dispute' 43(4) *ICTSD Bridges Weekly Trade News Digest*, 14 November 2000.

Chilean ports and airfreight their catch to the European Communities but were refused. Chile alleged that they had been engaged in illegal fishing in the Chilean Exclusive Economic Zone. The European Communities however considered Chile's refusal a violation of WTO law and filed proceedings under the GATT and the GATS alleging that Chilean law breached MFN treatment as it discriminated against the European Communities. Chile argued that the dispute involved the UN Convention on the Law of the Sea[27] (Articles 64 and 116, amongst others), specifically, in respect of measures for the conservation of the swordfish population. As a result, two cases were initiated, turning on the same facts, but in different fora. One case was before the WTO, while the other was pending before the International Tribunal for the Law of the Sea. What are the rules of international law about what each tribunal should do in such a case? In the *Chile – Swordfish* case, Chile and the European Communities settled and, therefore, it is not known how that would have applied in the WTO dispute settlement context. Likewise, in the *Argentina – Poultry Anti-Dumping Duties* dispute, Argentina's objection to the filing of the WTO dispute by Brazil, in the light of an earlier action brought by Brazil under MERCOSUR's dispute settlement mechanism, signals the same sort of difficulty.[28]

The problem of competing jurisdictions as such is something familiar to public international lawyers, and other such examples exist. For instance, the dispute between Ireland and the United Kingdom in the *MOX Plant*[29] case involved the competing jurisdiction of the European Court of Justice (ECJ) and the tribunal under the UN Convention on the Law of the Sea.[30]

Here lies a lesson about what Asian countries that are members of FTAs, as well as FTA parties everywhere, should do when drafting dispute resolution arrangements in their FTAs. The basic problem is that FTAs create another layer of dispute settlement mechanisms, and the proliferation of FTAs could tend to multiply the number of available mechanisms, each happily going its own way in terms of individual drafting and design

27 Done 10 December 1982, 1833 UNTS 3, 397, 21 ILM 1261 (1982).

28 Panel Report, *Argentina – Poultry Anti-Dumping Duties*, paras. 7.34–7.42.

29 Arbitral Tribunal established pursuant to Article 287 and Article 1 of Annex VII, of the UN Convention on the Law of the Sea, *Ireland v United Kingdom*, available at <http://www.itlos.org/cgi-bin/cases/case_detail.pl?id=10&lang=en> (last visited 27 June 2006).

30 The tribunal suspended its proceedings in deference to the ECJ. For the arguments made before the International Tribunal of the Law of the Sea in seeking to have the case suspended, see Mr Plender, ITLOS/PV.01/08, 20 November 2001, 23–24, available at <http://www.itlos.org>.

idiosyncrasies with highly unpredictable results ensuing. One way of approaching the matter might be that proposed in respect of the Free Trade Area of the Americas; namely, that the MFN clause in the investment chapter should simply not apply to the international dispute settlement provisions.[31] My point, however, is broader than the one dealt with by this limited solution; namely, that what we are going to see is a very complex array of MFN clauses that extend *beyond* the investor-State dispute-type situation, which *Maffezini* and the line of International Centre for Settlement of Investment Disputes cases following *Maffezini* have dealt with (see section V.2 above).

We are facing not only a problem that non-investment disputes could become subsumed under the investment rubric under FTAs that contain deep and overlapping services and investment coverage. A broader problem also exists – namely the problem of competing jurisdictions between separate dispute settlement mechanisms. At present, international lawyers are only beginning to grapple with, for example, the kinds of problems posed by the *Chile – Swordfish* and *MOX Plant* arbitrations.[32] Addressing the matter in an express provision in the FTA, such as, for example, under either a provision akin to NAFTA Chapter Twenty's Article 2005.1 (choice of forum by a NAFTA party, which, once made, is final), or Article 2005.3 or Article 2005.4 (exclusive jurisdiction

[31] Footnote 13 to Article 5 (MFN) of Chapter XVII (Investment) of the 2003 'Third' Draft Agreement (Derestricted, FTAA.TNC/w/133/Rev.3, 21 November 2003) states:

> One delegation proposes the following footnote to be included in the negotiating history as a reflection of the Parties' shared understanding of the Most-Favored-Nation Article and the Maffezini case. This footnote would be deleted in the final text of the Agreement:
>
> The Parties note the recent decision of the arbitral tribunal in Maffezini (Arg.) v Kingdom of Spain, which found an unusually broad most favoured nation clause in an Argentina-Spain agreement to encompass international dispute resolution procedures. See Decision on Jurisdiction §§ 38–64 (January 25, 2000), reprinted in 16 ICSID Rev. – F.I.L.J. 212 (2002). By contrast, the Most-Favoured-Nation Article of this Agreement is expressly limited in its scope to matters 'with respect to the establishment, acquisition, expansion, management, conduct, operation, and sale or other disposition of investments.' The Parties share the understanding and intent that this clause does not encompass international dispute resolution mechanisms such as those contained in Section C.2.b. (Dispute Settlement between a Party and an Investor of Another Party) of this chapter, and therefore could not reasonably lead to a conclusion similar to that of the Maffezini case.

[32] The author is grateful to Philippe Sands QC for recently bringing these issues into sharper focus.

granted to a NAFTA panel at the insistence of a NAFTA party)[33] may, at the end of the day, be the best thing we can do at present. It may be argued that, if a FTA is a later treaty between two or more WTO Members, the FTA's dispute resolution should simply prevail over the WTO dispute settlement system, even if Article 23.2(a) of the *Understanding on Rules and Procedures Governing the Settlement of Disputes* (DSU) (exclusivity of the DSU procedure) seems to compel a different conclusion[34] Nonetheless, the matter *is* complex and would still require, in that case, the interpretation and application of principles of treaty law in relation to which, shall we just say here, there is still many a slip 'twixt the cup and the lip'. Other issues include the manner in which different dispute settlement mechanism for different policy areas (for instance, investment under NAFTA Chapter 11) dovetail into the general, overall policy preferences within a particular FTA. To return to our well-worn example, when is a dispute a services dispute, and when is it an investment dispute in the case of mode-3 services (that is, with respect to 'commercial presence')? Thus, there is this two-dimensional problem of 'internal' (that is, internal to the FTA) and 'external' relations with various forms and systems of dispute settlement. Things can get very complicated indeed and the challenge for negotiators trying to come up with bullet-proof drafting will always exist, given unanticipated subsequent litigator creativity.

VIII. Conclusion

What perhaps underlies some of the problems identified above is that we cannot assume that the '*Esperanto*' language of the GATT will necessarily suffice to fully comprehend the various kinds of FTA provisions that are emerging. For the most comprehensive kinds of FTAs today, which touch on antitrust regulatory cooperation and banking supervision, the 'trade model' of global regulation might also not prove a sufficient or even

[33] For a dispute relating to environment or conservation, or to a sanitary or phytosanitary (SPS) measure or standards-related measure.

[34] *Contra* the example of the NAFTA given in Michael J. Trebilcock and Robert Howse, *The Regulation of International Trade* (3rd edn, London/New York, 2005), p. 149. However, equally, in the case of an FTA dispute settlement provision that, unlike NAFTA, comes later in time than the DSU, and that specifies either a choice of procedure or exclusive recourse to the FTA's dispute settlement mechanism, it would be a highly implausible argument for a party to that FTA to then claim exclusive recourse to the WTO dispute settlement mechanism.

appropriate framework.[35] Equally, it seems unsatisfactory that we should engage in an exercise of perpetual invention and experimentation for each FTA. This chapter by necessity has had to be highly selective in terms of the issues discussed. It could have dealt with other areas of pressing importance, not least the design of rules of origin. But its aim has only been illustrative, and the intent is merely to suggest that it might be useful to focus more on the sorts of legal problems encountered in the very design of FTAs. A natural place to start would be under the auspices of the WTO. In the light of the proliferation of Asian FTAs, Asia, too, might be a natural place to start some serious scholarly discussion and work on these issues. Perhaps the time has also come to consider putting together a set of draft articles for a global model FTA.

[35] For a general theoretical exploration of the significance of differing models of international legal regulation and control in the era of 'disaggregated states', see Anne-Marie Slaughter, *A New World Order* (Princeton/Oxford, 2004).

25

Dispute settlement under free trade agreements: its interaction and relationship with WTO dispute settlement procedures

CHANG-FA LO

I. Dispute settlement is an essential element of free trade agreements

Free trade agreements (FTAs) are permitted by the covered agreements of the World Trade Organization (WTO). Pursuant to Article XXIV of the *General Agreement on Tariffs and Trade* (GATT) *1994*, the formation of free trade areas by means of voluntary agreements between WTO Members is permissible, as long as such integration meets the following main requirements: (i) the duties and other restrictive regulations of commerce are eliminated on substantially all the trade between the constituent territories in products originating in such territories;[1] (ii) the purpose of such integration is to facilitate trade between the constituent territories and not to raise barriers to the trade of other Members with such territories;[2] and (iii) the duties and other regulations of commerce maintained in each of the constituent territories are not higher or more restrictive than the corresponding duties and other regulations of commerce existing in the same constituent territories prior to the formation of the free trade area.[3]

Article V of the *General Agreement on Trade in Services* (GATS) has similar provisions, which state in part that the GATS is not to prevent any of its Members from being a party to or entering into an agreement liberalizing trade in services between or among the parties to such an agreement, provided that such an agreement (i) has substantial sectoral coverage, and (ii) provides for the absence or elimination of substantially all discrimination, in the sense of Article XVII of the GATS, between

[1] Article XXIV:8(a) of the GATT 1994.
[2] Article XXIV:4 of the GATT 1994.
[3] Article XXIV:5(b) of the GATT 1994.

or among the parties, in the sectors covered under subparagraph (a), through (i) elimination of existing discriminatory measures, and/or (ii) prohibition of new or more discriminatory measures.

There is no provision in these WTO provisions referring to FTAs that explicitly recognizes or refers to dispute settlement mechanisms under FTAs. As a result, neither is there a provision in the relevant WTO provisions governing FTAs that prohibits or otherwise refers to dispute settlement mechanisms that are part of individual FTAs. Since FTAs are admitted under WTO law, a mechanism designed to deal with disputes arising from the interpretation and application of an agreement should, as a matter of course, be part of the authorization of Article XXIV of the GATT 1994 and Article V of the GATS.

Similarly, since there is no specific provision under the WTO regulating the establishment of dispute settlement mechanisms under FTAs, and since different FTAs have their respective backgrounds and stipulated objectives, mechanisms aiming at solving disputes between members of different FTAs have also been different in their respective content and structure.

In this chapter, I list some examples of dispute settlement provisions in FTAs and elaborate to some extent on the differences among those mechanisms. I will also reflect on the interaction and relationship between the dispute settlement mechanisms in FTAs and the WTO dispute settlement system.

II. Reasons for dispute settlement provisions in FTAs

Dispute settlement mechanisms are important in all international agreements, not just in those concerning trade. However, such mechanisms are particularly important for trade agreements, given that trade agreements tend to have substantive impact on public and private economic activities and thus tend to give rise to more disputes. Thus, dispute settlement provisions are generally considered a principal element of FTAs.[4]

Furthermore, the purpose of dispute settlement mechanisms in an international agreement is to ensure the observance of obligations of the contracting parties under the agreement. One author commented on the previous Canada–United States Free Trade Agreement (CUSFTA) that: 'Effective and binding dispute settlement was seen as the most effective

[4] International Trade Canada, 'Dispute Settlement Under the NAFTA', available at <http://www.dfait-maeci.gc.ca/nafta-alena/settle-en.asp> (visited 8 May 2006).

means for dealing with security of access, hence dispute settlement became a political *sine qua non* for Canada in the negotiations for a [CUSFTA]'.[5]

III. Examples of dispute settlement mechanisms in FTAs

Example 1: less complex dispute settlement provisions

Most FTAs have detailed dispute settlement procedures. However, there are still some FTAs that have brief and less complex dispute settlement provisions. For example, the Turkey–Israel FTA,[6] signed in 1996, has a simple design in Article 30:

> 1. Each Party may refer to the Joint Committee any dispute relating to the application or interpretation of this Agreement.
>
> 2. The Joint Committee may settle the dispute by means of a decision.
>
> 3. Each Party shall be bound to take the measures involved in carrying out the decisions referred to in Paragraph 2.
>
> 4. If a dispute referred to the Joint Committee has not been resolved within a period of sixty days after the dispute was referred to it or within such longer period as the Joint Committee has agreed upon, each Party may notify the other of the appointment of an arbitrator within forty five days.
>
> 5. The two appointed arbitrators shall nominate by a common agreement within two months a third umpire arbitrator who shall not be a national of either Party and who will serve as chairman.
>
> 6. The arbitrators' decision shall be taken by a majority vote within ninety days.
>
> 7. Each Party shall be bound to take the steps required to implement the decision of the arbitrators.

One commentator considers this to be an insufficiently developed dispute settlement mechanism due to its rudimentary design, which would have to be elaborated in order to be operational:

> The dispute settlement mechanism in the Turkey–Israel FTA is lacking. Dispute settlement under the FTA is based on the assumption that a conciliatory and amicable atmosphere will govern any disagreement between the

[5] Gilbert R. Winham, 'Dispute Settlement in NAFTA and the FTA', available at <http://oldfraser.lexi.net/publications/books/assess_nafta/dispute.html> (visited 8 May 2006).

[6] The Agreement can be found at <http://www.dtm.gov.tr/ab/ingilizce/sta/israil/israel.htm> (visited 8 May 2006).

> parties. It does not deal with specific procedural rules or fundamental problems likely to arise during the proceeding. The inadequacy of the mechanism is further evident in the absence of any lists of arbitrators, or any reported decisions of panels under the Agreement. There is no official record as to the parties' experience with resolving disputes under the FTA. By conducting the process behind closed doors and under a tight veil of secrecy, government officials have kept the process within their complete control and have made it impossible for the public or other interested parties to apply pressure on the losing party to abide by the decision.[7]

In contrast to the Turkey–Israel example, some FTAs have featured rather detailed dispute settlement provisions from the beginning of their operation. A good example in this respect is the North America Free Trade Agreement (NAFTA). Yet other FTAs featured only brief dispute settlement provisions at the time of their entry into force, but later introduced a more comprehensive dispute settlement mechanism. The Association of Southeast Asian Nations (ASEAN) Free Trade Area (AFTA) belongs to this group of agreements.

Example 2: detailed dispute settlement provisions

One of the most detailed dispute settlement provision in FTAs is probably the NAFTA. There are several sets of dispute settlement provisions in the NAFTA. Chapter Nineteen deals with dispute settlement for countervailing duty and anti-dumping matters. Chapter Twenty provides for the avoidance or the settlement of all disputes between NAFTA governments regarding the interpretation or application of the NAFTA. Chapter Eleven (Investment) and Chapter Fourteen (Financial Services) contain rules dealing with disputes about investment and financial services. This chapter lists only some key elements in Chapters Nineteen and Twenty.

Chapter Nineteen provisions

Under paragraph 1 of Article 1902 of the NAFTA, '[e]ach Party reserves the right to apply its anti-dumping law and countervailing duty law to goods imported from the territory of any other Party.' As a general rule, an appeal against trade remedies adopted in a NAFTA country should be

[7] Tankut Aydin, 'A Critical View of the Dispute Settlement Mechanism Under the Turkey–Israel Free Trade Agreement' (August 2000) 11 *World Arbitration & Mediation Report*, 223–228, 225.

made within the legal framework of such country. Thus, prior to the entry into force of the CUSFTA and then the NAFTA, anti-dumping, countervailing duty, and injury final determinations of a government could only be appealed in the case of a US final determination, to the Court of International Trade; in the case of a Mexican final determination, to the *Tribunal Fiscal de la Federación*; or, in the case of certain Canadian final determinations, to the Federal Court of Appeal; or for some Revenue Canada decisions, to the Canadian International Trade Tribunal.[8]

Chapter Nineteen of the NAFTA provides for a system of binational panel review to replace final judicial review for domestic decisions regarding anti-dumping and countervailing duty matters. Article 1904 states that 'each Party shall replace judicial review of final anti-dumping and countervailing duty determinations with binational panel review.'

Article 1903 also requires amendments to trade remedy laws to be reviewed by a binational panel that may issue a declaratory opinion as to whether the amendment does or does not conform to the provisions of the agreement.

Finally, Chapter Nineteen sets forth an 'Extraordinary Challenge Procedure' in paragraph 13 of Article 1904 to deal with a situation where an involved party alleges that '(i) a member of the panel was guilty of gross misconduct, bias or a serious conflict of interest, or otherwise materially violated the rules of conduct, (ii) the panel seriously departed from a fundamental rule of procedure, or (iii) the panel manifestly exceeded its powers, authority, or jurisdiction.'

Chapter Twenty provisions

Chapter Twenty is considered a central element of the NAFTA. Its importance resides in its purpose to ensure that trade relations among NAFTA members are based on an established set of rules as opposed to economic or political power.[9] Article 2001 establishes the Free Trade Commission, comprising cabinet level representatives of the parties or their designees, to resolve intra-governmental disputes that may arise regarding the interpretation or application of the agreement.

In regard to dispute settlement procedures, Article 2003 requires parties at all times to 'endeavour to agree on the interpretation and application of

[8] International Trade Canada, 'Dispute Settlement Under the NAFTA', available at <http://www.dfait-maeci.gc.ca/nafta-alena/settle-en.asp> (visited 8 May 2006).

[9] Ibid.

this Agreement, and make every attempt through cooperation and consultations to arrive at a mutually satisfactory resolution of any matter that might affect its operation.'

Article 2005, paragraph 1, explicitly indicates that members of the NAFTA may decide to resort to dispute settlement procedures in the NAFTA or the GATT. It provides in part that 'disputes regarding any matter arising under both this Agreement and the *General Agreement on Tariffs and Trade*, any agreement negotiated thereunder, or any successor agreement (GATT), may be settled in either forum at the discretion of the complaining Party.' However, paragraphs 3 and 4 have exceptions to this discretion:

> In any dispute referred to in paragraph 1 where the responding Party claims that its action is subject to Article 104 (Relation to Environmental and Conservation Agreements) and requests in writing that the matter be considered under this Agreement, the complaining Party may, in respect of that matter, thereafter have recourse to dispute settlement procedures solely under this Agreement.' 'In any dispute referred to in paragraph 1 that arises under Section B of Chapter Seven (Sanitary and Phytosanitary Measures) or Chapter Nine (Standards-Related Measures): (a) concerning a measure adopted or maintained by a Party to protect its human, animal or plant life or health, or to protect its environment, and (b) that raises factual issues concerning the environment, health, safety or conservation, including directly related scientific matters, where the responding party requests in writing that the matter be considered under this Agreement, the complaining party may, in respect of that matter, thereafter have recourse to dispute settlement procedures solely under this Agreement.

There are three sets of dispute settlement procedures available in Chapter Twenty of the NAFTA, namely, consultations; good offices, conciliation, and mediation; and arbitration panel proceedings.

Regarding consultations, paragraphs 1 and 5 of Article 2006 specify that any Party may request, in writing, consultations with any other Party regarding any actual or proposed measure or any other matter that it considers might affect the operation of the NAFTA. Furthermore, the consulting Parties shall make every attempt to arrive at a mutually satisfactory resolution of any matter through consultations under Article 2006 or other consultative provisions of the NAFTA.

Regarding good offices, conciliation and mediation, Article 2007 provides that, if the consulting Parties fail to resolve a matter pursuant to Article 2006 within certain specified periods, any such Party may request in writing a meeting of the Commission and that a Party may also request in writing a meeting of the Commission.

Regarding arbitration panel proceedings, Article 2008 provides that, if the Commission has convened pursuant to Article 2007(4) and the matter has not been resolved within certain specified period, any consulting Party may request in writing the establishment of an arbitral panel; Article 2008 further provides that, on delivery of the request, the Commission shall establish an arbitral panel. Article 2009 requires the establishment of a roster of up to 30 individuals who are willing and able to serve as panelists.

Paragraph 3 of Article 2012 provides that, unless the disputing Parties otherwise agree within certain specified period, the terms of reference shall be: 'To examine, in the light of the relevant provisions of the Agreement, the matter referred to the Commission (as set out in the request for a Commission meeting) and to make findings, determinations and recommendations as provided in Article 2016(2).'

According to Article 2017, the final decision is made through the adoption of the final report of the panel transmitted to the Commission.

Example 3: from simple to more detailed dispute settlement provisions

In January 1992 at the ASEAN Summit in Singapore, the ASEAN heads of government formally agreed to establish an AFTA and signed the Singapore Declaration and the Framework Agreement on Enhancing ASEAN Economic Cooperation (the Framework Agreement). Later in January 1993, the AFTA was officially put into effect.[10]

The AFTA has loose dispute settlement provisions in the Framework Agreement, in particular Article 9, which stipulates:

> Any differences between the Member States concerning the interpretation or application of this Agreement or any arrangements arising therefrom shall, as far as possible, be settled amicably between the parties. Whenever necessary, an appropriate body shall be designated for the settlement of disputes.[11]

Subsequently, in 1992, ASEAN countries signed the Agreement on the Common Effective Preferential Tariff Scheme for the AFTA[12], Article 8

[10] Available at <http://www.itcilo.it/actrav/actrav-english/telearn/global/ilo/blokit/afta.htm> (visited 8 May 2006).

[11] The Framework Agreement can be found at <http://www.aseansec.org/12374.htm> (visited 8 May 2006).

[12] Available at <http://www.aseansec.org/12375.htm> (visited 8 May 2006).

(Consultation) of which has the following dispute settlement provisions:

> 1. Member States shall accord adequate opportunity for consultations regarding any representations made by other Member States with respect to any matter affecting the implementation of this Agreement. The Council referred to in Article 7 of this Agreement, may seek guidance from the AEM [the ASEAN Economic Ministers] in respect of any matter for which it has not been possible to find a satisfactory solution during previous consultations.
>
> 2. Member States, which consider that any other Member State has not carried out its obligations under this Agreement, resulting in the nullifications or impairment of any benefit accruing to them, may, with a view to achieving satisfactory adjustment of the matter, make representations or proposal to the other Member States concerned, which shall give due consideration to the representations or proposal made to it.
>
> 3. Any differences between the Member States concerning the interpretation or application of this Agreement shall, as far as possible, be settled amicably between the parties. If such differences cannot be settled amicably, it shall be submitted to the Council referred to in Article 7 of this Agreement, and if necessary, to the AEM.

Although, formally speaking, these are the applicable dispute settlement provisions, their practical usefulness for solving trade disputes is in doubt. A commentator observes that: 'This minimally defined approach to dispute settlement leaves open almost all procedures and mechanisms for conflict resolution. In comparison with its free trade counterparts in Europe and North America, the AFTA plan provides little guidance. This lack of a firm dispute resolution mechanism may prompt calls for an ASEAN legal framework to work in concert with the AFTA's goals.'[13]

Later in 1996, ASEAN countries signed a much more detailed dispute settlement document, namely, the Protocol on Dispute Settlement Mechanism.[14] This Protocol was further replaced by the ASEAN Protocol on Enhanced Dispute Settlement Mechanism in 2004.[15] The Protocol

[13] Deborah A. Haas, 'Note and Comment: Out of Others' Shadows: ASEAN Moves toward Greater Regional Cooperation in the Face of the EC and NAFTA' (Spring 1994) 9 *American University Journal of International Law and Policy*, 809–867, 839.

[14] The 1996 Protocol can be found at <http://www.aseansec.org/16654.htm> (visited 8 May 2006).

[15] The 2004 Protocol can be found at <http://www.aseansec.org/16754.htm> (visited 8 May 2006).

introduces consultation; good offices, conciliation and mediation; and panel procedures similar to the dispute settlement procedures in the WTO under the *Understanding on Rules and Procedures Governing the Settlement of Disputes* (DSU).

Article 3 of the 2004 Protocol requires member States to accord adequate opportunity for consultations regarding any representations made by other member States with respect to any matter affecting the implementation, interpretation, or application of the Agreement or any covered agreement and requires any differences to be settled amicably between the member States to the extent possible.

Under Article 4 of the Protocol, 'Member States which are parties to a dispute may at any time agree to good offices, conciliation or mediation. They may begin at any time and be terminated at any time. Once procedures for good offices, conciliation or mediation are terminated, a complaining party may then proceed with a request to the SEOM [Senior Economic Officials Meeting] for the establishment of a panel.' If the member State to which the request for consultations is made does not reply within certain specified periods or the consultations fail to settle a dispute within certain specified days, under Article 5, the matter shall be raised to the SEOM if the complaining party wishes to request the establishment of a panel.

Article 6 sets the terms of reference of panels by stating that 'Panels shall have the following terms of reference unless the parties to the dispute agree otherwise prior to the establishment of a panel: 'To examine in the light of the relevant provisions in (name of the covered agreement(s) cited by the parties to the dispute), the matter referred to the SEOM by (name of party) in (document) . . . and to make such findings as will assist the SEOM in the adoption of the panel report or in making its decision not to adopt the report.'

According to Article 7, the function of the panel is to make an objective assessment of the dispute before it (including an examination of the facts of the case and the applicability of and conformity with the sections of the Agreement or any covered agreements), and its findings and recommendations in relation to the case.

Under Article 9, the SEOM shall adopt the panel report within thirty days of its submission by the panel unless a party to the dispute formally notifies the SEOM of its decision to appeal or the SEOM decides by consensus not to adopt the report. If a party has notified its decision to appeal, the report by the panel shall not be considered for adoption by the SEOM until after the completion of the appeal.

IV. Relationship and interaction between dispute settlement provisions in FTAs and in the WTO

Forum selection

There is no provision in the DSU requiring that every conceivable trade dispute between two parties be resolved exclusively under the WTO. Generally speaking, neither do FTAs provide that disputes be resolved only under the dispute settlement procedures of FTAs. If there is no specific provision under FTAs in this regard, certainly contracting parties to the FTAs will have the right to decide whether to initiate a dispute settlement procedure under the WTO or under the relevant FTA.

However, sometimes FTAs set forth clearer principles to guide the selection of a forum. As indicated above, Chapter Twenty of the NAFTA permits a complaining Party to select, at its discretion, either the NAFTA or the WTO as the forum of choice to resolve its dispute with another Party. The exception to this rule is that, if a dispute involves environmental, sanitary and phytosanitary (SPS), or technical standards matters, the responding Party may demand that the matter be settled by a NAFTA panel.

What is the difference in having a dispute resolved under the WTO or under an FTA?

Although some dispute settlement procedures in many FTAs are increasingly similar to those of the WTO, there are a number of important differences when conducting dispute settlement procedures in the WTO and in FTAs. The most fundamental difference could be the law applicable in a given case. Basically, the applicable law for a WTO dispute should be the WTO agreements, while the applicable law for an FTA dispute resolved under dispute settlement procedures of such FTA should be the provisions of that FTA.

Paragraph 1 of Article 1 of the DSU provides:

> The rules and procedures of this Understanding shall apply to disputes brought pursuant to the consultation and dispute settlement provisions of the agreements listed in Appendix 1 to this Understanding (referred to in this Understanding as the 'covered agreements'). The rules and procedures of this Understanding shall also apply to consultations and the settlement of disputes between Members concerning their rights and obligations under the provisions of the Agreement Establishing the World Trade Organization (referred to in this Understanding as the 'WTO Agreement') . . .

In other words, if a dispute is resolved in the WTO, the dispute settlement procedure will have to be carried out in accordance with the substantive rules of the covered agreements, that is, the WTO agreements.[16]

If a dispute is decided under an FTA, the competent dispute settlement body would presumably also consider only the obligations of the relevant FTA. For instance, the above-mentioned Article 6 of the ASEAN Protocol of 2004 provides that dispute settlement panels will have to follow the relevant AFTA agreements to decide their cases. In other words, as a matter of general principle, WTO rules are not applied directly by a dispute settlement organ of an FTA, although sometimes WTO rules are incorporated in the relevant FTA provisions; in such circumstances, the WTO rules could be said to be applied indirectly through the provision of the FTA.

FTAs, generally speaking, are concluded to further liberalize trade between constituent members to the agreement. Thus, if a dispute is resolved in WTO, the complaining party will have to bring a complaint based on the WTO agreements as well as on the relevant commitments made by the responding party and will not be able to claim the higher level of liberalization stipulated by the FTA. Furthermore, most FTAs are 'WTO-plus' in nature and in their coverage.[17] The matters covered by FTAs are sometimes not covered by the WTO agreements. Thus, disputes under FTAs could be outside of the scope of the WTO agreements. Equally important, some FTA have provisions pursuant to which another international agreement prevails over provisions of the FTA.[18] Thus, a

[16] The Appellate Body Report in *Mexico – Taxes on Soft Drinks* provides some guidance on the issue of whether a dispute settlement body of an FTA or, instead, the WTO should be the proper forum to exercise the jurisdiction in a dispute relating to matters falling both under the WTO and an FTA. Before the panel, Mexico, as a preliminary matter, requested that the Panel decline to exercise jurisdiction in favour of an Arbitral Panel under Chapter Twenty of the NAFTA. The Panel rejected Mexico's request and found instead that, under the DSU, a panel had no discretion not to exercise its jurisdiction in a case properly before it. The Appellate Body upheld the Panel's conclusion on that point. However, the Appellate Body stated explicitly that it was not expressing a view on whether there may be other circumstances in which legal impediments could exist that would preclude a panel from ruling on the merits of the claims that are before it (Appellate Body Report, *Mexico – Taxes on Soft Drinks*, paras. 54–57).

[17] The term 'WTO-plus', as used in this article, refers to a situation in which an FTA includes disciplines or rights and obligations going beyond the provisions and requirements contained in the WTO agreements. In other words, 'WTO-plus' FTAs have commitments that are broader or deeper than those contained in the WTO agreements, or provide that commitments must be implemented in shorter periods of time than under the WTO.

[18] For instance, Article 104 of the NAFTA provides that: 'In the event of any inconsistency between this Agreement and the specific trade obligations set out in: (a) the *Convention on*

dispute concerning such other international agreements will lead to different results if they are resolved in the WTO or if they are resolved under a particular FTA.

However, in particular circumstances, there may be room to argue that in dispute settlement procedures under some FTAs, not only the provisions of that FTA, but also the provisions of relevant WTO agreements should be taken into account. It has been argued with respect to the NAFTA, although not very convincingly, that the NAFTA implicitly allows panelists to consider WTO rules in resolving NAFTA disputes:

> Just as there is ambiguity surrounding the question whether NAFTA or WTO rules prevail in the event of inconsistency, so there is ambiguity surrounding the question whether NAFTA panels may apply the law of the WTO in cases before them. On one hand, since the NAFTA expressly contemplates that claims arising under both agreements may be brought under NAFTA Chapter 20, it can be argued that the NAFTA implicitly allows the panelists to consider the law of the WTO. The NAFTA accepts that cases involving the Parties may involve overlapping rules and overlapping jurisdiction. If NAFTA panels are precluded from examining both sets of rules, then it cannot completely adjudicate a claim, and the Parties might be required to pursue a second proceeding in the WTO before a case is resolved. Since the NAFTA demands that the first selected forum be used to the exclusion of the other, it is clear that such dispute settlement procedures should – at the least – take place in sequence . . . . On the other hand, Article 2004, NAFTA, expressly provides that the Chapter 20 procedures shall apply with respect to interpretation or application of 'this Agreement'. Similarly, the NAFTA default terms of reference for panels refer to determinations under 'this Agreement'. On the basis of this language which identifies a specific legal instrument, it might be argued that only NAFTA rules may be applied in a proceeding, at least as to

Footnote 18 *(cont.)*
International Trade in Endangered Species of Wild Fauna and Flora, done at Washington, 3 March 1973, as amended 22 June 1979; (b) the *Montreal Protocol on Substances that Deplete the Ozone Layer*, done at Montreal, 16 September 1987, as amended 29 June 1990; (c) the *Basel Convention on the Control of Transboundary Movements of Hazardous Wastes and Their Disposal*, done at Basel, 22 March 1989, on its entry into force for Canada, Mexico and the United States; or (d) the agreements set out in Annex 104.1, such obligations shall prevail to the extent of the inconsistency, provided that where a Party has a choice among equally effective and reasonably available means of complying with such obligations, the Party chooses the alternative that is the least inconsistent with the other provisions of this Agreement.'

matters in which the Parties do not agree on alternative terms of reference incorporating WTO rules.[19]

Conflict between dispute settlement under FTAs and under the WTO?

There was discussion under the GATT of 1947 about the potential conflict between bilateral dispute settlement procedures under an FTA and the multilateral dispute settlement procedures under the GATT. A 1991 Report of the Working Party on the Free-Trade Agreement between Canada and the United States indicates that certain 'contracting parties feared this situation would result in either delays in the adoption of panel reports by Contracting Parties or the report never being adopted due to contradictory findings in the FTA bilateral dispute settlement process and the General Agreement multilateral process. In the view of one member "such obstruction of the proper functioning of the multilateral dispute settlement process was not in accordance with the obligations of parties under the GATT." The representative of the United States "emphasized that the rights and obligations of the FTA parties under the GATT remained unchanged."'[20]

This concern arose essentially as a result of the lack of effectiveness of the dispute settlement mechanism under the GATT 1947. Given that Articles 16.4 and 17.14 of the DSU now provide for so-called 'negative consensus' for the adoption of panel and Appellate Body reports, individual WTO Members cannot delay or veto the adoption of these reports. Therefore, there should be less concern about conflicts arising from the type of situations mentioned in the 1991 Working Party Report. The remaining question for FTA members is whether to initiate a dispute settlement procedure under the WTO or under the FTA procedures.

More resort to WTO dispute settlement procedures

It should be interesting to note that, in practice, rigid FTA dispute settlement procedures do not play an important role in resolving the

[19] Frederick M. Abbott, 'The North American Integration Regime and Its Implications for the World Trading System', available on the NYU School of Law Jean Monnet Center website at <http://www.jeanmonnetprogram.org/papers/99/990204.html#fnB43> (visited 8 May 2006).

[20] GATT Working Party Report, *Customs Unions and Free-trade Areas – The Canada–US FTA*, paras. 22 and 25. See also WTO Secretariat Analytical Index Guide to GATT Law and Practice (Geneva, 1995), p. 842.

disputes between the parties. For instance, there is very interesting statistical data calculated in a recent paper, examining to what extent NAFTA parties have used WTO dispute settlement procedures to settle their trade disputes rather than resorting to NAFTA procedures:

> The pattern of Canada's use of the WTO dispute settlement system is interesting. Initially, it brought cases against a variety of countries, but since mid-1997, it has brought cases only against the US and the EC. Indeed, of the 17 cases initiated since that time, 13 have been against the United States and four have been against the EC . . . . In terms of the subject matters of Canada's 26 complaints, 11 of them have involved trade remedy issues and have been brought against the United States . . . . Canada and the United States have made frequent use of the WTO dispute settlement system in managing their bilateral trade relationship. Canada has brought 13 cases against the US; the US has brought four cases against Canada. Although they are parties to the North American Free Trade Agreement (NAFTA), which has its own dispute settlement systems, they have only once used NAFTA Chapter 20's general dispute settlement system. Indeed, the NAFTA general dispute settlement system has been used only three times overall, and the roster of panelists that was to be established so as to make the operation of the system quasi-automatic has never been agreed.[21]

Although there are usually comprehensive rules and procedures set forth in FTAs for potential disputes arising from the interpretation and application of the agreements, their practical usefulness is sometimes questionable, as shown above. The practical importance of dispute settlement mechanisms under FTAs might not be as high as some might have thought initially. The advantage of resorting to multilateral dispute settlement should be to reduce the possibility of one party exploiting its power over the other party and to dilute the sensitivities of bilateral tensions arising from their dispute.

V. Some concluding remarks

Dispute settlement provisions could take on different forms in different FTAs. However, their purposes should be similar, that is, to ensure the observance of obligations of contracting parties and to secure market access under FTAs.

The author has not found an FTA that excludes completely the WTO as a forum to resolve the trade disputes between its parties. With the

[21] Davey, 'WTO: The First Ten Years', 34–35.

exception of the NAFTA, which excludes the WTO as the forum to decide certain specific kinds of disputes, other FTAs allow their parties to submit the trade disputes between their respective parties to the dispute settlement procedures under the WTO. Since the resolution of a dispute at the WTO and under an FTA could have different results, a complaining party certainly would make its decision based upon the type and the nature of the dispute at hand, taking into account also the credibility and effectiveness of the respective mechanism.

The continued use of the WTO as a dispute settlement forum by some countries that are also members of some FTAs has been positive for the WTO. The selection of the WTO as a forum indicates that this mechanism has earned the trust of the parties. It also demonstrates the effectiveness of resolving disputes under the DSU.

26

Regionalism under the WTO and the prospect of an East Asian free trade area

ZHANG YUQING

Regional trade agreements (RTAs) were permitted under Article XXIV of the *General Agreement on Tariffs and Trade* (GATT) *1947* and the Decision on Differential and More Favourable Treatment, Reciprocity and Fuller Participation of Developing Countries (Enabling Clause). RTAs are classified into customs unions, free trade areas and interim agreements leading to the formation of either, based on the criteria of 'substantially all the trade'[1] and 'not on the whole higher or more restrictive'.[2] RTAs formed by developing countries are afforded more favourable treatment.[3] Article XXIV of the GATT 1947 and the Enabling Clause were incorporated into the World Trade Organization (WTO) agreements, together with a new *Understanding on the Interpretation of Article XXIV of the General Agreement on Tariffs and Trade 1994.* The *General Agreement on Trade in Services* (GATS) adds another dimension to these exceptions from the most-favoured nation (MFN) principle, namely RTAs involving trade in services, with similar conditions applying as to RTAs on trade in goods.

Customs unions and free trade areas evolved from the frontier traffic between adjacent countries, which were 'grandfathered' by the GATT 1947 as a fact of life. Currently such agreements have to be notified to the Council for Trade in Goods (RTAs under Article XXIV), Committee on Trade and Development (RTAs under the Enabling Clause) or Council for Trade in Services (RTAs covering trade in services), and examined by a Working Party formed by the WTO Committee on Regional Trade Agreements (CRTA), which was established by the WTO General Council in February 1996. The CRTA has two principal duties: to examine individual RTAs and to consider the systemic implications of the RTAs for the

[1] Article XXIV:8(a) and (b) of the GATT 1994.

[2] Article XXIV:5(a) and (b) of the GATT 1994.

[3] Pursuant to the Enabling Clause.

multilateral trading system as well as the relationship between them.[4] The examination is conducted in accordance with Article XXIV of the GATT 1994, the Enabling Clause, or Article V of the GATS. Examination of RTAs covering trade in services is optional.[5] The work of the CRTA has turned out to be non-productive, as explained below.

At the very beginning, RTAs were formed only between neighbouring countries. Today geographical proximity is no longer a restriction. Indeed, the term, 'regional' has long lost its original geographical meaning and acquired the implication of 'plurilateral'. The bilateral free trade agreement (FTA) between Singapore and the United States is a good example.

In addition to their historical roots, there are also practical reasons for the emergence of RTAs: they are believed to be, on the whole, trade-creating, even though in some cases there are adverse effects on non-members. Different views exists on the implications of regionalism, ranging from debates between trade creation and trade diversion[6] to those of building blocks and stumbling blocks.[7] The general observations of empirical economists are favourable to RTAs because, according to those views, they tend to enhance total world welfare provided certain requirements under the WTO agreements are satisfied.[8] As of 8 July 2005, 162 RTAs have been notified to the GATT/WTO and the same number of RTAs was in force.[9]

China has begun participating in RTAs only recently. It has signed a Framework Agreement on Comprehensive Co-operation with the Association of Southeast Asian Nations (ASEAN), an Agreement on Accelerated Tariff Elimination under the Early Harvest Programme of the Framework Agreement with Thailand, two Closer Economic Partnership Arrangements with its two special administrative regions (Hong Kong and Macau, respectively), and a Memorandum of Understanding on the Free Trade Agreement and Other Issues as well as an Agreement on the Early Harvest Programme for the Free Trade Agreement with Pakistan; feasibility studies on FTAs with New Zealand and Australia have been

4 WT/L/127. 5 Article V:7(a) and (b) of the GATS.

6 Jackson, Davey, and Sykes, *Legal Problems of International Economic Relations*, p. 447.

7 Robert Z. Lawrence, 'Emerging Regional Arrangements: Building Blocks or Stumbling Blocks?', in Richard O'Brien (ed.), *Finance and the International Economy* (New York, 1991) Vol. 5, pp. 23–35.

8 Lawrence H. Summers, 'Regionalism and the World Trading System', in Lawrence Summers (ed.), *Policy Implications of Trade and Currency Zones* (Kansas, 1991), pp. 295–301.

9 See <http://www.wto.org/english/tratop_e/region_e/regfac_e.htm>.

completed and discussions on FTAs with the Gulf Cooperation Council, the Southern African Customs Union, and Chile are under way. In addition, a non-governmental joint study on the feasibility of an FTA between China and Korea was also initiated in March 2005.

I. Advantages and disadvantages of RTAs[10]

Regionalism began to proliferate in the later years of the GATT 1947, when various weaknesses of the GATT system came to light. Those weaknesses may have been one of the reasons for Lester Thurow to declare that 'the GATT is dead',[11] indicating that multilateralism was too cumbersome for a number of trade issues.

After the formation of the WTO, especially after trade ministers failed to reach agreements in Cancun when many people thought that the WTO was at a crossroads, the number of RTAs surged to a record level. There are voluminous articles analyzing the reasons for this proliferation of RTAs. The suggested arguments are: similar countries should be allowed to integrate at a faster pace or in different directions if they 'do not go it alone'; it is easier for fewer parties to reach consensus in forming RTAs because they share more similarities. In short, the weaknesses of WTO are exactly the strengths of RTAs.

The advantages of RTAs generally include trade liberalization, which is good for enhancing world welfare, even where liberalization is undertaken unilaterally. The practical advantage is that negotiation of RTAs is easier; protracted negotiations are not necessary as there are fewer parties concerned, and the parties have more common interests than those in the multilateral trade negotiations – after all, otherwise, these countries would not voluntarily sit at the same negotiating table. In addition, successful RTAs could set a precedent for multilateral negotiations; furthermore, there are benefits and disciplines that are not available under the WTO agreements, but can be negotiated under RTAs, of which a prominent example is the Common Agricultural Policy of the European Union.

However, there are also disadvantages: RTAs may well have trade diversionary effects. RTAs between partners with modest level of trade do not

[10] Some of the ideas are drawn from 'FTAs – Advantages and Disadvantages', in *An Australia–USA Free Trade Agreement: Issues and Implications*, Monash University APEC Study Centre (August 2001), chapter 3, available at <http://www.dfat.gov.au/publications/aus_us_fta_mon/Chapter3.pdf>.

[11] Lester Thurow, *Head to Head: The Coming Economic Battle Among Japan, Europe, and America*. (New York, 1992).

make much economic sense. Too many RTAs would also complicate the rules to be followed by business and hence increase transaction costs; by the same token, there is a breaking point beyond which countries cannot afford to participate in too many RTAs, as their resources are not unlimited, such that negotiations of RTAs and overlapping of memberships could strain the government resources as well (some countries have 20 RTAs or more[12]). All these factors may serve to diminish economic welfare, and hence frustrate the very purpose of RTAs.

Nevertheless, the Working Parties reviewing RTAs have been unable, for various reasons, to make findings that such agreements are incompatible with Article XXIV. One example is the European Communities, which threatened to withdraw from the GATT if its regional agreements were found to be WTO-incompatible. This illustrates that RTAs are, in a sense, a product of a power-based system. However, the questions surrounding RTAs are more complex and must be assessed in a more nuanced fashion, as evidenced by a report prepared by the WTO Negotiating Group on Rules, listing the various issues related to RTAs and their relationship to the multilateral trading system.[13] In addition, the laxity in regulating RTAs since the GATT years has not changed and no examination report has ever been adopted since 1995 by the CRTA, due to lack of consensus.

II. Trade diversionary effects revisited

It appears from numerous studies that RTAs are more likely to lead to trade creation than trade diversion.[14] The record indicates that there is little indication of trade diversion in terms of the existing trade; however, it goes without saying that, after an RTA is formed, the newly created trade volume is more or less diverted, non-members are placed at a disadvantage, since the creation effects are mostly felt within the RTA.

In addition, preferential treatments within RTAs will inevitably divert investments from non-members, as well as distort trade and resources allocation. This can be seen from the fact that some Chinese firms have made investments in the textiles industry in Mexico to

[12] See WorldTradeLaw.net, 'Bilateral and Regional Trade Agreements: Building Blocks or Stumbling Blocks?', pp. 32–34, available at <http://www.worldtradelaw.net/fta/ftadatabase/ftas.asp>. [13] TN/RL/W/8/Rev.1.

[14] See, for example, Franklin L. Lavin, 'Half a Loaf is Better Than None: The Case for Regional Free Trade Agreements' 00–02 *Economic Freedom Project Report*, The Heritage Foundation (2 June 2000), available at <http://www.heritage.org/Research/ TradeandForeignAid/loader.cfm?url=/commonspot/security/getfile.cfm&PageID= 10023>.

take advantage of the benefits under the North American Free Trade Agreement (NAFTA).

Moreover, given that the newly created trade volume mainly benefits the members of the RTA, the imbalance in the distribution of those trade may widen the long-existing gap of economic development between rich and poor countries. This is a problem that can only be dealt with under a multilateral system.

III. Dispute settlement

Under the GATT 1947, there was, in effect, no way that an RTA could be challenged given that a finding of incompatibility by a Working Party could easily be blocked. Moreover, it was not clear whether a GATT panel could make such a finding of incompatibility in the context of a dispute settlement proceeding. Under the WTO agreements, the same situation as under the GATT 1947 prevails in the CRTA. However, according to the Appellate Body in *Turkey – Textiles*, even where the CRTA has not determined whether a particular RTA satisfies the criteria in Article XXIV, a panel and/or the Appellate Body can make such a determination in a given dispute. In other words, a Member aggrieved by an RTA formed by other Members may bring the matter to a panel following the procedures under the *Understanding on Rules and Procedures Governing the Settlement of Disputes* (DSU). The aggrieved Member will typically allege a violation of Article I of the GATT 1994 (the MFN principle); the defending Member will invoke Article XXIV as a defence so as to justify the MFN violation; the panel will then examine whether the RTA at issue satisfies the criteria of Article XXIV and, hence, whether the defending Member may benefit from Article XXIV in its defence.

As mentioned above, no examinations of RTAs have been finalized since 1995; however, some draft reports have been presented to the CRTA.[15] The legal status of such reports is not yet clear. Although a draft report 'does not affect the rights and obligations provided for in the WTO agreements',[16] there is no denying that it may justify, as a matter of fact,

[15] No examination was completed or reports adopted under the old GATT, with the exception of the Czech Republic–Slovak Republic Customs Union, which became effective on 1 January 1993, and was examined in 1994. The Working Party concluded that the Agreement establishing the Customs Union was consistent with Article XXIV of the old GATT. (See GATT Working Party Report, *Customs Unions, Free-trade Areas, Regional Agreements – The Czech Republic-Slovak Republic Customs Union.*)

[16] For example, see Note by the Chairman, 'Draft Report on the Examination of the North American Free Trade Agreement', WT/REG4/W/1, 28 September 2000.

an RTA if that RTA is found, in the draft report, to be in conformity with Article XXIV of the GATT 1994 and Article V of the GATS. Assuming a finding of non-conformity, could the RTA at issue possibly be challenged on such ground until the draft report is rejected by the CRTA? Should the CRTA be required to 'treat like cases alike' in examining subsequent RTAs? As the legal status of the draft reports is unclear, it is difficult to answer these questions.

The notable case where Article XXIV was tested is the *Turkey – Textiles* dispute. The Appellate Body report in that dispute elaborated on the interpretation of this Article, however, it did not go far enough so as to address many issues that might arise under Article XXIV.

IV. Should the rules be changed?

The surge in the number of RTAs has given rise to worries that one of the very foundations of the WTO, the MFN principle, may become the exception rather than the rule. That may explain why years ago Lawrence, after exploring the various weaknesses and inadequacies of the GATT rules relating to RTAs and inquiring into the existing policy options, ranging from repealing Article XXIV completely to rules of origin to be adopted, asked whether the rules should be changed.[17] However, he fell short of dealing with another important issue, namely, the purpose of RTAs.

The purpose of the RTAs 'should be to facilitate trade between the constituent territories'.[18] Nevertheless, it can be seen from the existing hundreds of RTAs that the objective of 'facilitat[ing] trade' is not, in most cases, their ultimate purpose, or their only purpose; in some extreme cases, 'facilitat[ing] trade' is even not the purpose at all.

There are ample examples to illustrate this observation: the original purpose of the European Communities was to prevent a conflict between France and Germany, and this was also why the United States tolerated the existence of the European Communities.[19] The first bilateral FTA concluded by the United States, namely, the United States–Israel FTA, was no more than a disguised subsidization of Israel.[20] One of the reasons for Canada to sign the Canada–United States FTA was to avoid the United

[17] Robert Lawrence, 'Regionalism and the WTO: Should the Rules be Changed?', in Jeffrey Schott (ed.), *The World Trading System: Challenges Ahead* (Washington, DC, 1997), pp. 41–56, available at: <www.iie.com/publications/ chapters_preview/66/3iie2350.pdf>.

[18] Article XXIV:4 of the GATT 1994.

[19] Jackson, *Jurisprudence of GATT and the WTO*, p. 100.

[20] Jackson, Davey, and Sykes, *Legal Problems of International Economic Relations*, p. 465.

States' unfair trade laws.[21] As for the China–ASEAN FTA (CAFTA), through this arrangement, China reinforces its long-term friendly relationship with the ASEAN countries, while ASEAN countries probably attach great importance to China's large market.

Some Middle-Eastern countries clearly do not satisfy the 13 criteria[22] that the United States applies in choosing it potential FTA partners (these criteria have been elaborated by the former US Trade Representative Robert Zoellick); however, these countries may nevertheless be chosen as eligible for an RTA with the United States, presumably as a reward for their support to the United States in its war on terrorism.

Therefore, it is fair to say that the aim 'to facilitate trade' is only one of the purposes of RTAs, if at all. Could RTAs be challenged on this ground? Assuming the answer is positive, it would be a hard case to argue.

It would appear that the rules applying to RTAs are in need of changing. At the same time, however, the political circumstances in major trading nations – witness the repeated calls of some powerful vested interests in major trading nations to withdraw from the WTO, the conflict between support for international free trade rules and consideration of domestic policies in other countries, etc. – make such a move appear very controversial, if not outright impossible.

V. Prospect of an East Asian FTA

East Asia is the most dynamic area in the world today in terms of economic growth. According to the statistics of 2003, the total gross domestic product (GDP) of the countries and regions in East Asia, including China, Hong Kong, Japan, Korea, Chinese Taipei, and the ASEAN countries, reached US $7,700 billion. In 2004, Japan, Hong Kong, the ASEAN countries, Korea, and Chinese Taipei were among the top ten trading partners of China (occupying the third to the seventh ranks), the total trade volume between them and China reaching US $554.84 billion and accounting for 48.1 per cent of China's total foreign trade.[23] In fact, a feasibility study on an East Asian FTA has been started recently by China's Ministry of Commerce. Some authors have suggested that Japan and Korea may be included in an enlarged Greater China Economic Area, or

[21] Jackson, *Jurisprudence of GATT and the WTO*, p. 102.

[22] Available at <http://web.infoweb.ne.jp/fairtradec/new/w040213.pdf>.

[23] Customs statistics of the China, available at <http://gcs.mofcom.gov.cn/aarticle/Nocategory/200503/20050300021338.html>.

an East Asian FTA. In a recent visit to Japan, Chinese Vice-Premier Wu Yi stressed the importance of Sino–Japanese economic relations and called for the conclusion of a bilateral FTA.

However, given that political factors, as well as historical factors, can be obstacles to the creation of RTAs, in the short run the prospect of an East Asian FTA is not overly optimistic, especially in view of the historical feuds, territorial disputes and the rise of ultra-nationalism in some of these countries.

Historical grievances linked to World War II, the dispute between Korea and Japan over the Tokdo islets (Takeshima Island, as called by the Japanese) and the claims by both China and Japan on Diaoyu Dao (Senkaku Islands, as called by the Japanese) can all be threats to regional economic integration in East Asia. In addition, quite a number of countries, including China, Viet Nam, Malaysia, the Philippines, Indonesia, and Brunei have territorial claims over the South China Sea. These non-economic factors prevent these countries, despite their geographical proximity, from sitting at the negotiating table.

Political considerations also play a very important role in the conclusion of the CAFTA. As mentioned above, China aims at reinforcing its long-term friendly relationship with the ASEAN countries in forming the CAFTA after the cold war. During the cold war, the East Asian countries were members of one of the two alliances headed by the United States or the Soviet bloc, respectively. In fact, the ASEAN, officially launched in August 1967 as a result of the Bangkok Declaration, was a politico-security community rather than a trading bloc. It was not until the early 1990s that a formal attempt was made to form the ASEAN Free Trade Area (AFTA).

In addition, there are practical issues which hinder the conclusion of an East Asian FTA. As mentioned above, since the decision to form the CAFTA was largely motivated by political considerations, the difficulties and impediments were apparently underestimated at the outset. In fact, neither China nor the ASEAN countries are well-prepared to engage in free trade negotiations in a comprehensive manner. As the negotiations began, various problems emerged. China is a vast country, with significant differences in the level of economic development between the coastal areas in the east and the inland areas in the west; a similarly strong difference in economic development exists between the newly industrialized and the developing members of the ASEAN. Because of the huge differences, it is very difficult for the ASEAN countries to form a uniform position, which impedes the successful conclusion of the free trade negotiation.

Moreover, there is competition between China and some ASEAN countries (such as Malaysia, Thailand, and the Philippines) when it comes to export goods and to attracting foreign direct investment (FDI).

Furthermore, there are no major countries in the East Asian region that can take the lead, similarly to the role played by the Franco–German alliance in the European Communities. Sino–Japanese cooperation is unthinkable at present and even in the near future. Although the two economies are complementary in many economic sectors, the huge trade volume between the two countries is in stark contrast with the cold political relationship. Because of the attitude of the Japanese government to World War II and frequent visits to the Yasukuni Shrine by Japanese leaders, most East Asian countries harbour political suspicions of the Japanese government, which may also hold back the Chinese government in concluding trade agreements with Japan. China alone is not economically developed enough to lead the way. In the case of Japan, although it is the most developed country in the region, it does not command the respect of some countries or does not enjoy a good relationship with others.

The current situation calls for political leaders in those countries to defy ultra-nationalism, to set aside, at least for the time being, territorial disputes and to proceed with the negotiations for an East Asian FTA. If these potentially explosive issues are not properly addressed, an East Asian FTA is no more than wishful thinking, even though economically quite possibly viable. Could the political leaders in East Asia really depoliticize trade issues and use their political clout to press ahead with an East Asian FTA?

VI. The Chinese Taipei issue

Trade between China and Chinese Taipei is of great importance to both sides of the strait. In 2004, China was Chinese Taipei's largest trading partner, the trade volume between the two sides reaching US $78.3 billion, despite various restrictions and inconveniences.

However, China does not agree that Chinese Taipei should pursue FTA negotiations with other countries, simply due to political reasons. Nevertheless, it is possible that China and Chinese Taipei could conclude an economic and trade agreement in the context of a wider regional FTA, such as the CAFTA or an East Asian FTA; this would make economic sense for both sides, because closer economic relations are conducive to their stable economic growth and integration. The recent successful visits by Lien Chan and James Soong of Chinese Taipei to the mainland have paved way for an FTA between the two sides, even if a number of practical issues remain unresolved.

It goes without saying that, in terms of regional integration, the legal status of Chinese Taipei may be a major concern of China. In fact, a Chinese trade expert recently suggested that trade disputes between China and Chinese Taipei be resolved under the auspices of the WTO.[24] This is a sensitive political issue, an issue of particular interest to China, but it should be discussed, and further research should be done to explore the existing policy options.

VII. Concluding remarks

In the light of the historical, theoretical and empirical analyses of RTAs, it is readily apparent that RTAs are to be encouraged rather than worried about. If there can be a two-speed Europe, there may be a pluri-speed world as well. The inadequacies of the WTO, as exposed in Cancun, are alarming. The huge differences between various countries mean that the idea of 'one-size-fits-all' does not work. Competition between the WTO and regional trade blocs may also create pressure for improving the WTO system.

Nevertheless, from past experience, one can deduce that only the WTO can serve as the foundation and the central pillar for promoting world trade and maintaining the world trade order. The world trading system should not become one of fragmented markets. The expansion of regionalism should therefore not serve to undermine the WTO. Moreover, the WTO can also be a dispute settlement forum, should disputes arise between different trade blocs. Therefore, from the perspective of any WTO Member, the WTO cannot be replaced by any single RTA, even an enlarged RTA. A multilateral approach can best serve the world in liberalizing trade and safeguarding the trading interests of the poor and weak countries.

Even though the WTO, in a sense, is still a power-based system, the power of the developed countries has been restrained at a level where the developing countries can also benefit from it. Participation in the trading system is better for developing countries than staying outside of it. Moreover, a system based entirely on rules might not be attainable, even

[24] Interview with Zhou Shijian [*in Chinese*], available at: <http://news.xinhuanet.com/herald/2004–09/20/content_1997075.htm>.

if the GATT/WTO has been moving to such a rules-based system continuously over the past years and decades.

Before the political issues in East Asia are resolved amicably, the prospect of establishing an East Asian FTA, similar to the NAFTA or the European Union, is uncertain. The resources committed to the establishment of an East Asian FTA will probably be wasted. Therefore, East Asian countries should reconsider their strategies of regional integration before taking further steps. A practical alternative may be to put the limited resources on the multilateral negotiations and the strengthening of the WTO, given that the WTO is the only forum common to nearly all the countries and regions in East Asia.

The most practicable and economically meaningful RTAs for China would be one with Chinese Taipei, Hong Kong, and Macau, one with either Korea, or Korea and Japan, and one with India. It takes significant political courage and wisdom of the leaders in these countries to achieve those goals. These RTAs would rival the European Union and the NAFTA and could genuinely promote economic growth and benefit the people of East Asia.

INDEX

Printed in the United Kingdom
by Lightning Source UK Ltd.
131777UK00001B/156/P

9 780521 875691